KU-620-471

THE

INFLUENCE

OF

TROPICAL CLIMATES

ON

European Constitutions:

BEING A

TREATISE ON THE PRINCIPAL DISEASES INCIDENTAL TO
EUROPEANS IN THE

EAST AND WEST INDIES, MEDITERRANEAN, AND COAST OF AFRICA.

———

BY JAMES JOHNSON, M.D.

OF THE ROYAL COLLEGE OF PHYSICIANS, LONDON.

———

FROM THE THIRD LONDON EDITION.

GREATLY ENLARGED.

———

NEW-YORK:

W. E. Dean, Printer, No. 3 Wall-Street.

PUBLISHED BY EVERT DUYCKINCK, GEORGE LONG, COLLINS & CO.
COLLINS & HANNAY, O. A. ROORBACH, AND
JOHN GREGG, PHILADELPHIA.

———

1826.
[*Price Three Dollars.*]

TO

HEADS OF NAVAL AND MILITARY MEDICINE,

Dr. JOHN WEIR,

AND

SIR JAMES Mc. GREGOR, M. D., &c.

AND TO

HIS MEDICAL BRETHREN

IN FLEETS, ARMIES, AND COLONIES,

THIS

THIRD EDITION

IS RESPECTFULLY INSCRIBED,

BY THEIR SINCERE FRIEND,

The Author.

PREFACE

THE First Edition of the following Work was published in 1813, chiefly at the Author's own risk and expense, for he could find no Bookseller to undertake it. The Second, consisting, as the First, of 1000 copies, was published in 1818, and has been more than six months out of print. In the present Edition the Author has endeavoured to render the work more extensively useful than ever, by placing before the reader a series of Analytical Reviews of the best modern Works, embracing the Diseases of Tropical and other sultry Climates. Whoever has seen the diversified maladies produced by climate, season, constitution, and co-existing circumstances, will easily appreciate the utility of thus concentrating the experience, observations, and sentiments of many individuals, as multiplied resources in exigencies for ever varying.

The Author has the satisfaction of knowing that the former Editions of this Work have proved serviceable, not only to his junior Professional Brethren, serving in sultry climates; but also to a very considerable proportion of Naval, Military, and Civil Officers sojourning between the Tropics. In the Eastern Hemisphere a Work of this description was imperiously called for, where many of the Company's Officers, as Dr. Balfour has justly remarked—" being constantly employed during the first years of " their service, in the most unhealthy corners of country, remote " from medical assistance, their *success, reputation, health, and* " *lives,* and the lives of all around them, depend often on the " *medical skill* which they may have acquired."*

To the last and present editions of this Work, a new feature has been added—the consideration of Climates bordering on the Tropics, the diseases of which, at particular periods, resemble those of equatorial regions. The Author is convinced that this is an essential requisite in every Work on diseases of the Torrid Zone. These diseases acknowledge no cancer or capricorn boundaries. The *same class* sallies occasionally from La Plata to the Scheldt —sweeping the Banks of the Ganges, the Euphrates, the Nile, the Tiber, the Guadalquiver, the Chesapeake, the Mississippi, the Oronoco, and every sinuosity of the great Western Archipelago. He then who studies the influence of Tropical Climates on

---

* Preface to Treatise on Sol-Lunar Influence. p. xiii.

European Constitutions, by *parallels of latitude*, will do so inefficiently. It is like studying the physiology of the stomach or liver, without regarding the functions of the surrounding viscera. An appeal may be made to the *parallel* between the Valley of Egypt and the Coast of Coromandel, for the truth of this remark. It will there be seen that the climate and diseases of the one elucidate those of the other, and that this *comparison* has solved a problem in Etiology which has hitherto proved a stumbling block to Physicians—namely, the question of an indigenous poison existing in India, and occasioning the prevalence of Hepatitis there.

During the last few years, the Author has had extensive communication, personal and epistolary, with a very great number of his professional Brethren, on their return from various Climates of the Globe, and he can conscientiously aver that their reports have not given the slightest encouragement to change any of the sentiments or opinions broached in the former Editions of the Work. This is a source of great gratification to him—and on this fact he may reasonably ground a hope of the permanent utility of the publication to those for whom it is designed.

To the present Edition there is an addition of at least 250 pages of important matter, as will be readily seen on a comparison with the Second Edition. A few articles have been omitted, and others curtailed, in order that the new matter might not swell the Work beyond a single volume. And here the Author is in justice beyond to acknowledge the able and valuable assistance which he has received from Dr. Dickson and Mr. Sheppard, in the arrangment and composition of an important division of the Work.

The Author does not consider it necessary to make any further prefatory remarks, as the Work must rest on its own merits, whatever they may be, in its way through the World. He is very conscious, at the same time, that numerous imperfections and deficiencies may be readily detected in it by those who find it easier to judge than act—and whose trade is to point out the failings of others, without correcting their own. To the Criticisms of this class Author is perfectly callous—while to the judgment and opinions of the good and the wise, he acknowledges himself to be tremblingly sensible. On the liberality and indulgence of these he confides—convinced that the well-intentioned effort to be useful to his junior Brethren will be rewarded with the approbation of all those in whose esteem it is desirable to stand.

ANALYTICAL TABLE OF CONTENTS.

THE

INFLUENCE OF TROPICAL CLIMATES

ON

EUROPEAN CONSTITUTIONS.

———————

I BELIEVE it is a general opinion among philosophers, that the constitution of man is better adapted to bear those changes of temperature, &c. experienced in migrating from a northern to a tropical region, and vice versa, than that of any other animal. They proudly observe, that this power of accommodating itself to all climates, is a distinctive characteristic of the human species, since no other animal can endure transplantation with equal impunity. But I think it would not be difficult to show, that for this boasted prerogative, man is more indebted to the ingenuity of his mind, than to the pliability of his body.

To me, indeed, it appears, that he and other animals start on very unequal terms, in their emigrations. Man, by the exertion of his mental faculties, can raise up a thousand barriers round him, to obviate the deleterious effects of climate on his constitution ; while the poor animal, tied down by instinct to a few simple modes of life, is quite defenceless. Nature must do all for the latter ; and, in fact, it is evident that this indulgent mother does compensate, in some degree, for the want of reason, by producing such corporeal changes, as are necessary for the animal's subsistence under a foreign sky, in a *shorter* space of time than is necessary for effecting corrospondent changes in man. One example may suffice. The tender and innocent sheep, when transported from the inclemency of the north to pant under a vertical sun on the equator, will, in a few generations, exchange its warm fleece of *wool*, for a much more convenient coat of *hair*. " Can the Ethiopian change his hue," in the same period, by shifting his habitation from the interior of Africa to the shores of the Baltic ? Or will it be said, that the fair complexion of Europeans, may, in two or three generations, acquire the sable tinct of the inter-trophical natives, by exchanging situations ? Assuredly not. Where then is the superior pliancy of the human constitution ? The truth is, that the tender frame of man is incapable of sustaining that degree of exposure to the whole range of causes and affects incident to, or arising from vicissitude of climate, which so speedily operates a change in the structure, or at least, the exterior, of unprotected animals.

2

But it is observed, that of those animals translated from a temperate to a torrid zone, " many die suddenly, others droop, and all degenerate." This is not to be wondered at, considering the disadvantages under which they labour. Man would not fare better, if placed in similar circumstances. Even as it is, the parallel in not far from applying. Of those Europeans who arrive on the banks of the Ganges, many fall early victims to the climate, as will be shown hereafter. That others droop, and are forced, in a very few years, to seek their native air, is also well known. And that the successors of all would *gradually degenerate,* if they remained permanently in the country, cannot easily be disproved ; while a very striking instance, corroborative of the supposition, may be here adduced.

Whoever has attentively examined the posterity of De Gama, and Albuquerque, now scattered over the coast of Malabar, the plains of Bengal, and the Island of Macao, once the theatres of Lusitanian pre-eminence, will be tempted to exclaim :—

'Twas not the sires of such as these,
Who dared the elements and pathless seas ;
Who made proud Asian monarchs feel
How weak their gold was against Europe's steel.
But beings of *another mould,*—
Rough, hardy, vigorous, manly, bold !

In answer to this it will be alleged, " that they have married and blended with the natives until all shade of distinction is obliterated." But it is well known to those who have resided long in India, that the two great prevailing classes of society in that country, the Hindoos and Mahomedans, hold these descendants of the Portuguese in the most marked and sovereign contempt ; while the latter, still retaining a remnant of the religion, and all the prejudice of their progenitors, entertain an equal abhorrence to their idolatrous and infidel neighbours. This being the case, we may fairly presume, that the intermixture has been much less extensive than is generally supposed ; an inference strongly supported, if not confirmed, by the well known fact, that, while the people in question have forfeited all pretentions to the European *complexion,* their more stubborn *features* still evince a descent, and establish their claim to an ancestry, of which they are superlatively proud. Let those who deny *one common origin* of mankind, and that climate is the *sole* cause of complexion, explain this phenomenon if they can.

On the other hand, if we look at inter-tropical natives approaching our own latitudes, the picture is not more cheering. The African children brought over by the Sierra Leone Company for education, seldom survived the third year in this country. " They bear the first winter, (says Dr. Pearson,) tolerably well, but droop during the second, and the third generally proves fatal to them." ·

The object of these remarks, which, at first sight, might seem irrelevant, will now appear. Since it is evident that nature does not operate more powerfully in counteracting the ill effects of climate on man, than on other animals, it follows that we should not implicitly confide, as too many do, in the spontaneous efforts of the constitution, but on the contrary, call in to its aid, those artificial means of prevention and melioration, which reason may dictate and experience confirm. In short, that we should, as my motto expresses it :—

————————"Study well the clime,
Mould to its manners our obsequious frames,
And mitigate those ills we cannot shun."

That these salutary precautions are too often despised or neglected, a single quotation from a gentleman, who has resided more than twenty years in India, and whose talent for observation is, in my opinion, unequalled, will put beyond a doubt. "Nothing can be more preposterous, (says Capt. Williamson*,) than the significant sneers of gentlemen on their first arrival in India ; meaning thereby to ridicule, or to despise what they consider effeminacy or luxury. Thus several may be seen walking about without chattahs, (i. e. umbrellas,) during the greatest heats. They affect to be ashamed of requiring aid, and endeavour to uphold. by such a display of indifference, the great reliance placed on *strength of constitution.* This unhappy infatuation rarely exceeds a few days ; at the end of that time, we are too often called upon to attend the funeral of the self-deluded victim."†

I shall be my endeavour in this essay, after tracing the causes, and pourtraying the effects of tropical diseases, in such a manner as must impress the most heedless European with the necessity of circumspection.on approaching the scene of danger, to furnish a code of instructions deduced from principle and experience, that cannot fail to prove a useful companion to every one who regards health as the grand source of happiness, and the most invaluable blessing which heaven can bestow. Many a day's anxiety and personal suffering should I have escaped, had I been furnished with so friendly a monitor !

Without any very fastidious regard to arrangement, it will still be necessary, for the sake of perspicuity, to observe some order. I shall therefore divide the subject into three principal heads, viz :—

1.—The Primary or General Effects of a Tropical Climate on the European Constitution.

2.—The Specific or Actual Diseases.

3.—Prophylaxis; or the Means of Counteracting the Influence of Climate and Preserving Health.

* Author of "Oriental Field Sports," " East India Vade Mecum," &c.
† East India Vade Mecum, vol. 2. page ii.

PART I.

PRIMARY OR GENERAL EFFECTS.

———————

UNDER this head, I shall consider some of those gradual and progressive changes in the constitution, and deviations from previous health and habits, which, though predisposing, and verging, as it were, towards, yet fall short of actual disease.

These are consequences which all must expect, more or less, to feel, on leaving their native soil, and, of course, in which all are directly interested. For although a few individuals may occasionally return from even a long residence in hot climates, without having suffered any violent illness, or much deterioration of constitution, yet the great mass of Europeans will certainly experience the effects developed under this head, and many others of minor consequence, which will be taken notice of in different parts of the work.

It is, however, by the most scrupulous attention to these *incipient deviations from health*, by early arresting their growth, or at least retarding, as much as possible, their progress, that we can at all expect to evade those dangerous diseases, to which they inevitably, though often imperceptibly, tend.

Sect. 1.—The transition from a climate, whose medium heat is 52° of Fahrenheit, to one where the thermometer ranges from 80° to 100° and sometimes higher, might be supposed, a priori, to occasion the most serious consequences. Indeed, the celebrated Boerhaave, from some experiments on animals, concluded, that the *blood would coagulate in our veins*, at a temperature very little exceeding 100°. More modern trials, however, have proved that the human frame can bear, for a short time at least, more than double the above degree of atmospherical heat, and that too without greatly increasing the natural temperature of the body.

The benevolent Author of our existence has endowed man, as well as other animals, with the power not only of generating heat, and preserving their temperature, in the coldest regions of the earth; but has also provided an apparatus for carrying off any superabundance of it that might accumulate where the temperature of the atmosphere approaches to or exceeds that of the body. With the *former* process, which is supposed to be carried on in the lungs, we have, at present, nothing to do ; the *latter* is one which deserves great attention, and which will meet with ample consideration in various parts of this essay.

We are no sooner beneath a vertical sun, than we begin, as may naturally be supposed, to experience the disagreeable sensation of unaccustomed warmth ; and as the temperature of the atmosphere, even in the shade, now advances within ten or twelve degrees to that of the blood, and in the sun very generally exceeds it, the heat perpetually generated in the body, cannot be so rapidly abstracted, as hitherto, by the surrounding air, and would, of course, soon accumulate so as to destroy the functions of life itself, did not Nature immediately open the sluices of the skin, and by a flow of *perspiration*, reduce the temperature of the body to its original standard.

Whether the superabundant animal heat combines with the perspirable fluid, and thus escapes ; or whether the refrigeration takes place on the principle of evaporation, is more a matter of speculation than practical importance to ascertain. We know the fact, that perspiration is a cooling process. The modus operandi —

  " Let sages versed in Nature's lore explain."

When we contemplate this admirable provision of nature, against what might appear to us an unforeseen event ; when we survey the resources and expedients which she can command on all emergencies—her power of supplying every waste, and restraining every aberration of the constitution, we would be almost tempted to conclude, that man was calculated for immortality ! But, alas !

  ————————" There is a point,
 " By nature fixed, whence life must downward tend,"

'Till at length, this wonderful machine, exhausted by its own efforts at preservation, and deserted by its immaterial tenant, sinks, and is resolved into its constituent elements !

  Nascentes morimur, finisque ab origine pendet.

But, to return. We must not conclude that this refrigerating process, adopted by nature to prevent more serious mischief, is, in itself, unproductive of any detriment to the constitution—far otherwise. " If, (says Dr. Currie,) the orifices do *not* pour out a proportionate quantity of perspiration, disease must ensue from the direct stimulus of heat ; and if the *necessary* quantity of perspiration takes place, the system is *enfeebled* by the evacuation."*

Here, then, we have Scylla on one side, and Charybdis on the other : morbid accumulation of heat if we do not perspire enough —debility if we do. How are we to direct our course through this intricate and dangerous navigation ?

* Medical Reports, Philadelphia edition, p. 192.

Dr. Currie.

" Europeans who go to the West Indies are more healthy, in proportion, as they perspire freely, especially if they support the discharge by a moderate use of *gently stimulating liquids, stopping short of intoxication.*"—ib.

Dr. Moseley.

" I aver from my own knowledge and custom, as well as from the custom and observations of others, that those who drink *nothing but water*, are but little affected by the climate, and can undergo the greatest fatigue without inconvenience."—*Tropical Diseases, p.* 57.

Who shall decide when doctors disagree?

Without meaning to set up the judgment of a Moseley in competition with that of a Currie, on other subjects, candour obliges me to confirm, by personal observation and experience, the truth of Dr. Moseley's remark. Dr. Currie never was in a tropical climate, therefore had the above piece of information from others ; and it is one of the very few erroneous positions in his invaluable work. Nevertheless, these apparently opposite directions are not so contradictory in *fact* as in *terms.* The principle on which both act, is the same, though the means are different. Dr. Currie's plan of supplying the stomach with " gently stimulating liquids," will undoubtedly keep the morbid heat from accumulating, by driving out a copious perspiration ; but it will, at the same time, lead to debility, by carrying off much more of that fluid than is necessary ; by which means the thirst, instead of being allayed, will be increased ; and what is still worse, the body will be rendered more susceptible of the subsequent impressions of cold, the deleterious effects of which, at these times, are much more extensive than is generally believed, as will be shown in another part of the work.

Dr. Moseley's plan, on the other hand, far from preventing perspiration, will be found, in general, to promote it, but at the same time restrain its *excess.*— A familiar example or two will elucidate this subject.

We will suppose two gentlemen to be sitting in a room, at Madras or in Jamaica, just before the sea-breeze sets in, both complaining of thirst, their skin hot, and the temperature of their bodies 100°, or two degrees above the natural standard.

One of them, pursuant to Dr. Currie's instructions, applies to the sangaree bowl, or porter cup, and after a draught or two, brings out a copious perspiration, which soon reduces the temperature to 98°. It will not stop here, however, nor indeed will the gentleman, according to the plan proposed ; for instead of putting the bulb of the thermometer under his tongue, to see if the mercury is low enough, he, feeling his thirst increased by the perspiration, very naturally prefers a glass or two more of the sangaree—" to support the discharge"—still, however, "stopping short of intoxication." Now, by these means, the temperature is reduced to 97° or 96½°, in which state, even the slight and otherwise refreshing chill of the sea-breeze, checks more or less the cuticular discharge, and paves the way for future maladies.

Whether this is, or is not a true representation of the case, let Dr. Currie's own words decide.

"If," says he, ut supra, "the necessary quantity of perspiration takes place, (viz. by the use of gently stmulating liquids,) the system is enfeebled by the evacuation, and the extreme vessels losing tone *continue* to transmit the perspirable matter, *after* the heat is reduced to its natural standard, or, perhaps, *lower ;* in which situation, we can easily suppose that even a *slight degree* of external cold, may become dangerous."—Vol. I. p. 278.

Let us now turn to the other gentleman, who pursues a different line of conduct. Instead of the more palatable potation of sangaree, he takes a draught of plain cold water. This is hardly swallowed before the temperature of his body loses by abstraction alone, one degree, at least, of its heat. It is now we will suppose at 99°. But the external surface of the body immediately sympathizing with the internal surface of the stomach, relaxes, and a *mild* perspiration breaks out, which reduces the temperature to its natural standard, 98°. Further, this simultaneous relaxation of the two surfaces, completely removes the disagreeable sensation of thirst ; and, as the simple "antediluvian beverage" does not possess many Circean charms for modern palates, there will not be the slightest danger of its being abused in quantity, or the perspiratory process carried beyond its salutary limits. Nor need we, on the other hand, apprehend its being neglected ; since, from the moment that the skin begins to be constricted, or morbid heat to accumulate, the sympathizing stomach and fauces will not fail to warn us of our danger, by craving the proper remedy. Taken therefore as a general rule, the advantages of the *latter* plan are numerous—the objections few. It possesses all the requisites of the *former*, in procuring a reduction of temperature, (the only legitimate object which the admirers of sangaree and copious perspiration can have in view,) without any danger of bringing it below the proper level, or wasting the strength, by the profuseness of the discharge.

It is true, there is no general rule without exception ; and there may be instances, wherein the use of "gently stimulating liquids" is preferable to that of cold drink.

For example :—during or subsequent to violent exertion, under a powerful sun ; or in any other situation in a tropical climate, when profuse perspiration is rapidly carrying off the animal heat, and especially when fatigue or exhaustion has taken place, or is impending— then cold drink would be dangerous, on the same principle as external cold. But these cases rarely happen through *necessity* to Europeans, particularly in the east ; and they will be duly considered in the prophylactic part of this essay.

I have been more prolix on this point, than may have seemed necessary to the medical reader ; but considering that this is generally the first erroneous step which Europeans take, on entering the tropics, and that the function in question, (perspiration,) is more intimately connected with another very important one in the human frame, than is commonly supposed ; I thought it proper to set them right, *in limine.* The probability of *future suffering* will rarely deter the European from indulging in *present gratifications* ; but where these last, *i. e.* the stimulating liquids, are represented, from high authority, as not only innocent but salutary, it will require some strength or argument to persuade young men to relinquish their use, or to check the wide-spreading evil.

Sect. 2.—In attempting to delineate the influence of hot climates on the European constitution, although we may endeavour—

" To chain the events in regular array ;"

yet, it must be confessed, that nature spurns all such artificial arrangements ; since simultaneous impressions on several organs, must produce cotemporary and combined effects, which our limited faculties are scarcely capable of embracing in thought, much less of describing in the fetters of language.

Taking facts, however, and personal observation for land-marks, I shall pursue the investigation, as nearly as possible, in the order of nature and of events.

There exists between different, and often distant parts of the body, a certain connection or relation, which in medical language, is called " consent of parts :"—that is, when *one* is affected by particular impressions, the *other* sympathizes, as it were, and takes on a kind of analogous action.

This sympathy, or consent of parts, has never been *satisfactorily* accounted for, by the ablest of our physiologists, nor.—(mirabile dictu !) by the most ingenious of our theorists. As all, however, are agreed in respect to the *fact,* we may allow the *cause* to remain locked up in nature's strong box, in company with many other arcana, which she does not seem disposed to reveal.*

Of these sympathies, none is more universally remarked, or familiarly known, than that which subsists between the *external* surface of the body, and the *internal* surface of the alimentary canal This indeed, seems less incomprehensible than many others, since the *latter* appears to be a continuation of the *former*, with the exception of the cuticle. In the first section, I gave an instance of the skin sympathizing with the stomach, where the cold drink was applied to the latter organ. Had the water been applied to the external surface of the body, on the other hand, the stomach would have sympathized, and the thirst been assuaged.

The loss of tone, then, in the extreme vessels of the surface, in consequence of excessive, or long-continued perspiration is, on this principle, necessarily accompanied, or soon succeeded by, a consen-

* I do not see that Dr. Park's laboured discussion on this subject in the Journal of Science, has brought us a whit nearer the knowledge of sympathetic action.

taneous loss of tone in the stomach, and fully accounts for that anorexia, or diminution of appetite, which we seldom fail to experience
on entering the tropics, or, indeed, during hot weather in England.
Now this, although but a link in the chain of effects, seems to me a
most wise precaution of nature, to lower and adapt the irritable,
plethoric European constitution, to a burning climate, by guarding
very effectually against the dangerous consequences of repletion.
This view of the subject will set in a clear light, the pernicious effects of stimulating liquids, operating on an organ already debilitated,
(probably for salutary purposes,) and goading it thereby to exertions
beyond its natural power, producing a temporary plethora, with a
great increase of subsequent atony.

A remark, which every person of observation must have made,
even in this country, during the summer, but particularly in equatorial
regions, will further elucidate this subject.   If by walking, for instance, or any other bodily exercise, in the heat of the sun, during
the forenoon, especially near dinner hour, the perspiration be much
increased, and the extreme vessels relaxed, we find, on sitting down
to table, our appetites entirely gone, until we take a glass of wine,
or other stimulating fluid, to excite the energy of the stomach.   Under such circumstances of artificial or forced relish for food, it is not
to be wondered at, that the digestion should be incomplete, and that the
intestines should suffer from the passage of badly concocted aliment.
Observation and personal feeling have taught me this,—that in hot
climates, perhaps during hot weather in all climates, an hour's cool
repose before dinner is highly salutary ; and if on commencing our
repast, we find we cannot eat without *drinking*, we may be assured
that it is nature's caveat,—to beware of eating at all.   This will be
deemed hard doctrine by some, and visionary by others ; but I know
it is neither one nor the other : and those who shall neglect or de-
pise it, may feel the bad consequences when it is too late to repair
the error.

There are several other causes, however, which operate in conjunction with the above, to impair the appetite : —one of which is, the
want of rest at night.   After disturbed and unrefreshing sleep, (but too
common in tropical climates,) the whole frame languishes next day,
and the stomach participates in the general relaxation.   The means
of managing and obviating these effects, will be pointed out in the
prophylactic part of this essay.

Sect. 3.—We now take a wider range, and come to a subject more
intricate in its nature, extensive in its bearings, and important in its
consequences.   It will readily be understood, that I allude to the influence of a tropical climate on the liver and its functions.

This immense gland is the largest organ in the human frame ; for
neither the brain, heart, spleen, nor kidnies, can be at all compared
with it ; and the lungs, though occupying a larger extent when inflated, yet if condensed to equal solidity, would fall short in size and
weight.

Now, since nature, throughout her works, has seldom been accused of supererogation, we may safely conclude that the importance of

this organ's function, in the animal economy, is commensurate with its magnitude. The structure of the liver has been explored by the anatomist, and the bile secreted in it analysed. But, although the chymist has separated this fluid into its constituent parts ; yet physiologists are not exactly agreed in regard to the purposes which it answers in the system. It is proved to be antiputrescent, and in conjunction with the pancreatic juice, it probably assists in animalizing and eliminating the chyle from the chyme.

It is supposed not to enter the circulation naturally, at least in an unchanged state along with the chyle ; but, there can be little doubt of its preventing the putrefactive or fermentative process from taking place in the excrementitious part, which is, ultimately, to be expelled the body. Another, and a principal use of this important fluid, appears to consist in stimulating the intestines into their peculiar peristaltic motion, and thus propelling their contents continually forward, to give the lacteals an opportunity of drinking up and conveying to the blood the nourishment by which our frames are supported.

In this point of view, it is the natural tonic of the intestines, and also the purgative which frees them from all fecal matter, the retention of which is productive of so much inconvenience, not to say disease.

The first effect of a tropical climate on the function of the liver, is universally allowed to be an *increase* of the biliary secretion. This is so evident in our own country, where the summer and autumn are distinguished by diseases arising from superabundant secretion of bile, that it would be waste of time to adduce any arguments in proof of of the assertion. But why an increase of the atmospherical temperature should so invariably augment the hepatic secretion in all climates, and all classes of people, is totally unaccounted for. When Dr. Saunders conjectures that richness of blood, tenseness of fibre, grossness of diet, and rapidity of circulation, are the causes of Europeans being at first more afflicted with bilious redundancy in India than the native Hindoos, he gives us only a *comparative* view of things, and leaves us completely in the dark with respect to the *modus operandi* of heat, as a general and universal spur on the secretory vessels of the liver.

Were this a question of mere curiosity, or theoretical speculation, I should pass it by unnoticed : but from long and attentive observation, as well as mature reflection, I believe that I have discovered a connection between two important functions in the animal economy, which will let in some light on this subject, and lead to practical inferences of considerable importance.

The arguments and facts adduced in support of this connection will be found under the heads Hepatitis, Dysentery, and in other parts of this essay. In the meanwhile, I shall merely state in a few words the *result* of my observations, leaving the reader to give credit to it, or not as he may feel inclined.

There exists then between the extreme vessels of the vena portarum in the liver, and the extreme vessels on the surface of the body —in other words, between *biliary secretion and perspiration*, one of the strongest sympathies in the human frame ; although entirely unnoticed hitherto, as far as I am acquainted. That these two functions

are regularly, and to appearance, equally increased, or at least influenced by *one* particular agent, (atmospherical heat,) from the cradle to the grave—from the pole to the equator, will be readily granted by every observer : and that this *synchronous action* alone, independent of any other original connection, should soon grow up into
a powerful sympathy, manifesting itself when *either* of these functions came under the influence of *other agents*, is a legitimate conclusion in theory, and what I hope to prove by a fair appeal to facts.
This last consideration is the great practical one ; for it is of little
consequence whether this sympathy was originally implanted by the
hand of nature at our first formation, or sprung up gradually in the
manner alluded to, provided we know that it actually exists, and that
by directing our operations towards any *one* of the functions in question, we can decisively influence the *other*. This is what I maintain ;
but here I only offer assertions ; in a future part of the work I shall
bring forward facts and cogent arguments in proof of them. At present let this " consent of parts" between the skin and the liver, which
I shall beg leave to denominate the " *Cutaneo-hepatic Sympathy*," account for the augmented secretion of bile, which we observe on arriving in hot climates, corresponding to the increased cuticular discharge. I shall here offer one practical remark, resulting from this
view of the subject, and which will be found deserving of every
European's attention on his emigration to Southern regions. Namely,
that as the state of the perspiratory process is a visible and certain
index to that of the biliary, so every precautionary measure, which
keeps in check, or moderates the profusion of the *former* discharge,
will invariably have the same effect on the *latter*, and thus tend to
obviate the inconvenience, not to say the disorders, arising from redundancy of the hepatic secretion. To this rule I do not know a single exception ; consequently its universal application can never lead
astray in any instance. But this subject will be better elucidated,
and more clearly explained hereafter.

To proceed. It is well known, without having recourse to Brunonian doctrines, that if any organ be stimulated to *inordinate* action,
one of two things must in general ensue. If the cause applied, be
constant and sufficient to keep up, for any length of time, this *inordinate* action, serious injury is likely to accrue to the organ itself,
even so far as *structural* alteration. But if the cause be only temporary, or the force not in any great degree, then an occasional torpor,
or exhaustion, as it were, of the organ, takes place, during which
period its *function* falls short of the natural range. To give a familiar example, of which too many of us are quite competent to judge :
—thus, if the stomach be goaded to immoderate exertion to-day, by
a provocative variety of savoury dishes and stimulating liquors, we
all know the atony which will succeed to-morrow, and how incapable
it then will be of performing its accustomed office. It is the same
with respect to the liver. After great excitement, by excessive heat,
violent exercise in the sun, &c. a torpor succeeds, which will be more
or less, according to the degree of previous excitement, and the
length of time which the stimulating causes have been habitually applied. For instance, when Europeans first arrive between the tro-

pics, the degree of torpor bears so small a proportion to that of preceding excitement, in the liver, that it is scarcely noticed ; particularly as the debilitated vessels in this organ, *continue*, (similar to the
perspiratory vessels on the surface,) to secrete a depraved fluid for
some time *after* the exciting cause had ceased ; hence the *increase* of
the biliary secretion occupies our principal attention. But these torpid periods, however short at first, gradually and progressively increase, till at length they far exceed the periods of excitement ; and
then a *deficiency* of the biliary secretion becomes evident. This is
not only consonant to experience, but to analogy. Thus when a man
first betakes himself to inebriety, the excitement occasioned by spirits, or wine, on the stomach and nervous system, far exceeds the
subsequent atony, and we are astonished to see him go on for some
time without, apparently, suffering much detriment in his constitution. But the period of excitement is gradually curtailed, while that
of atony increases, which soon forces him not only to augment the
dose, but to repeat it oftener and oftener, till the organ and life are
destroyed !

Now it is somewhat singular, that this alteration of redundancy
and deficiency, or in other words *irregular* secretion in the biliary organs, should pass unnoticed by writers on hot climates. They, one
and all, represent the liver as a colossal apparatus, of the most Herculean power, that goes on for years, performing prodigies in the secreting way, without ever being exhausted for a moment, or. falling
below the range of ordinary action, till structural derangement, such
as scirrhosity, incapacitates it for its duty !

A very attentive observation of what passed in my own frame, and
those of others, has led me to form a very different conclusion, and
the foregoing statement will, I think, be found a true and natural representation of the case. I shall afterwards show that the secretion
in question is frequently below *par*, in quantity, at the very time
when it is considered to be redundant—all arising from irregularity
and vitiation.

Here then, we have two very opposite states of the liver and its
functions. ·1st, inordinate action, with increased secretion—the periods generally shortening. 2nd, Torpor of the vessels in the liver,
with deficient secretion—the periods progressively lengthening. In
both cases, the bile itself is *vitiated.*

We may readily enough conceive how this last comes to pass, by
an analogical comparison with what takes place in the stomach during,
and subsequent to, a debauch. In both instances, we may conclude,
that the chyme passes through the pylorus into the duodenum, in a
state less fit for chylification, than during a season of temperance and
regularity. So during the increased secretion, and subsequent inactivity in the liver, the bile passes out into the intestines deteriorated in
quality, as well as superabundant or deficient in quantity.

In what this vitiation consists, it is certainly not easy to say. In
high degrees of it, attendant on hurried secretion, both the colour
and taste are surprisingly altered ; since it occasionally assumes all
the shades between a deep bottle green and jet black ; ·possessing,

at one time, an acidity that sets the teeth on edge ; at other times, and indeed more frequently, an acrimony that seems absolutely to corrode the stomach and fauces, as it passes off by vomiting, and when directed downwards, can be compared to nothing more appropriate than the sensation which one would expect from boiling lead flowing through the intestines.   Many a time have I experienced this, and many a time have my patients expressed themselves in similar language.   But these are extremes that will be considered under Cholera Morbus, Bilious Fever, Dysentery, &c.   The slightly disordered state of the hepatic functions, which we are now considering as primary effects of climate, and within the range of health, may be known by the following symptoms :—Irregularity in the bowels ; general languor of body and mind ; slight nausea, especially in the morning, when we attempt to brush our teeth ; a yellowish fur about the back part of the tongue ; unpleasant taste in the mouth, on getting out of bed ; a tinge in the eyes and complexion, from absorption of bile ; the urine high coloured, and a slight irritation in passing it ; the appetite impaired, and easily turned against fat or oily victuals.   These are the first effects, then, of increased and irregular secretion of bile, and will appear in all degrees, according as we are less or more cautious in avoiding the numerous causes that give additional force to the influence of climate.   For example : if I use more than ordinary exercise—expose myself to the heat of the sun —or drink stimulating liquids to-day, an increased and vitiated flow of bile takes place, and to-morrow produces either nausea and sickness at the stomach, or a diarrhœa, with gripings and twitchings in my bowels.   But a slight degree of inaction or torpor succeeding, both in the liver and intestines, there will probably be no alvine evacuation at all the ensuing day, till a fresh flow of bile sets all in motion once more.   These irregularities, although they may continue a long time without producing much inconvenience, especially if they be not aggravated by excesses, yet they should never be despised, since they inevitably, though insensibly, pave the way for serious derangement in the biliary and digestive organs, unless counteracted by the most rigid temperance, and the prophylactic measures which I shall carefully detail in their place.   The reciprocal influence and effects which the hepatic and mental functions exercise on each other, will form an interesting inquiry, under the article Hepatitis.

Sect. 4.—Among the primary effects of a hot climate, (for it can hardly be called a disease,) we may notice the prickly heat, (Lichen tropicus,) a very troublesome visitor, which few Europeans escape.

This is one of the miseries of a tropical life, and a most unmanageable one it is.   From mosquitoes, cockroaches, ants, and the numerous other tribes of depredators on our *personal* property, we have some defence by night, and in general, a respite by day ; but this unwelcome guest assails us at all, and particularly the most unseasonable hours.   Many a time have I been forced to spring from table and abandon the repast which I had scarcely touched, to writhe about in the open air, for a quarter of an hour : and often have I returned to the charge, with no better success, against my ignoble opponent! The night affords no asylum. For some weeks after arriving in India, I seldom could obtain more than an hour's sleep at one time before I was compelled to quit my couch, with no small precipitation, and if there were any water at hand, to sluice it over me, for the purpose of allaying the inexpressible irritation! But this was productive of temporary relief only; and what was worse, a more violent paroxysm frequently succeeded.

The sensations arising from prickly heat are perfectly indescribable; being compounded of pricking, itching, tingling, and many other feelings, for which I have no appropiate appellation.

It is usually, but not invariably accompanied by an eruption of vivid, red pimples, not larger in general, than a pin's head, which spread over the breast, arms, thighs, neck, and occasionally along the forehead, close to the hair. This eruption often disappears, in a great measure, when we are sitting quiet, and the skin is cool; but no sooner do we use any exercise that brings out a perspiration, or swallow any warm, or stimulating fluid, such as tea, soup, or wine, than the pimples become elevated, so as to be very distinctly seen, and but too sensibly felt.

Prickly heat, being merely a symptom, not a cause of good health, its disappearance has been erroneously accused of producing much mischief; hence, the early writers on tropical diseases, harping on the old string of "humoral pathology," speak very seriously of the danger of *repelling*, and the advantage of "encouraging the eruption, by taking small warm liquors, as tea, coffee, wine whey, broth, and norishing meats."—*Hillary.*

Even Dr. Moseley retails the puerile and exaggerated dangers of his predecessor. "There is great danger," (says he,) "in repelling the prickly heat; therefore cold bathing, and washing the body with cold water, at the time it is out, is always to be avoided." Every naval surgeon, however, who has been a few months in a hot climate, must have seen hundreds, if not thousands, plunging into the water, for days and weeks in succession, covered with prickly heat, yet without bad consequences ensuing.

Indeed, I never saw it even repelled by the cold bath, and in my own case, as well as in many others, it rather seemed to aggravate the eruption and disagreeable sensations, especially during the glow which succeeded the immersion. It certainly disappears suddenly sometimes on the *accession* of other diseases, but I never had reason to suppose, that its disappearance *occasioned* them. I have tried lime juice, hair powder, and a variety of external applications, with little or no benefit. In short, the only means, which I ever saw productive of any good effect in mitigating its violence, till the constitution got assimilated to the climate, were—light clothing—temperance in eating and drinking—avoiding all exercises in the heat of the day—open bowels—and last, not least, a determined resolution to resist with stoical apathy its first attacks. To sit quiet and unmoved under its pressure is undoubtedly no easy task, but if we can only muster up fortitude enough to bear with patience the first few minutes of the assault, without being roused into motion, the enemy, like the foiled tiger, will generally sneak off, and leave us victorious for the time.

PART II.

SPECIFIC DISEASES.

EASTERN HEMISPHERE.

Sect 1.—*Fever in General.*—It is not my intention to include in this section what is called *Symptomatic* fevers. It is to the subject of FE-VER, strictly so called, that I shall confine my observations ;,and trite and exhausted as the theme may appear, I hope still to render it, in some measure interesting. If I have omited the adjective "*idiopathic*," it is not because I consider fever as in all cases dependent on topical inflammation or congestion ; but because I wish to avoid a " war of words" about an abstract term. Some late writings, and particularly Dr. Clutterbuck's Essay, have divided the medical world in opinion, a very considerable portion subscribing to the Doctor's theory. There is still, however, as far as I can learn, a majority in favour of the old doctrine that fever may originate, and even proceed some way in its course, without local inflammation—or those topical affections which may be considered analogous to, or synonymous with, local inflammation.

Contrary to the usual mode of proceeding, before entering on the nature of fever itself, I shall take a rapid survey of the *causes* of this wonderful disease. By systematic writers these have been divided into remote and proximate ; but the latter being the actual *state* of the disease, will not yet come under consideration. The remote causes are subdivided into predisponent and exciting. The predisponent, however, often become the exciting, and the exciting the predisponent causes, as the following example will illustrate. Two labourers set out from London, in the summer or autumn, to work in the fens in Lincolnshire. The one is a sober man, the other a drunkard. The latter is attacked with intermittent fever, while the former, thongh equally exposed, escapes. Here inebriety is evidently the predisposing, and marsh miasma the exciting cause of the disease. But the sober man having returned to London in the winter, commits a debauch, and immediately afterwads he is seized with ague. Here, on the other hand, the latent miasma becomes, the predisposing, and drunkenness the exciting cause of the fever. Let this be borne in mind, for it may help to explain more than at first sight might be expected.

Speaking generally, however, the two great exciting causes of fever are human and marsh effluvia ; while the predisposing causes are almost innumerable. The more prominent, however, are, plethora—

inanition from excessive evacuations—the depressing passions—excess, whether in eating, drinking, gratification of the sensual passions—mental or corporeal exertions—extremes of atmospheric heat and cold, especially alternations of these or of heat and moisture—sollunar influence.

Now experience has determined, that of the foregoing and many other predisponent causes, any *one*, (excepting the last.) will, when in a very high degree, induce fever without the assistance of any other. If this be the case, then, it is a natural and just inference that the operation of marsh and human effluvium on the human frame bears a very considerable analogy to the operation of those causes enumerated as generally *predisposing* to, but sometimes actually *exciting* fever. This may give us a clue to assist in unravelling the *ratio symptomatum* hereafter ; but before entering on the effects, we shall say something of the causes themselves.

Human Effluvium or Contagion.—The existence of this febrific miasm as the cause of fever does not appear to have been known to the ancients, since Hippocrates makes no mention of it, and the strict prohibitions against *contact* with unclean or diseased persons recorded in the Mosaic code, do not seem directed against febrile, but chronic or local infection—probably against cutaneous or genital defædations. It is curious, however, that Pliny, when describing the progress of an *endemic* fever, apparently solves a question which to this moment, gives rise to the most violent altercations— namely, whether endemic fevers ever become contagious ? " Et primo *temporis ac loci* vitio, et ægri rant, et moriebantur ; postea, *curatio ipsa et contactus* ægrorum vulgabat morbos." Lib. xxv. ch. 26. But more of this hereafter.

Notwithstanding the exertions of Dr. Bancroft and some others to invalidate certain testimonies respecting the generation of contagious effluvium, facts too stubborn to be swept away by the brush of sophistry, attest that the effluvium issuing from the bodies of a number of human beings confined too closely, whether in a state of health or disease, will occasionally produce a contagion whic h is capable not only of exciting fever among those so confined, but of propagating itself afterwards from them to others.

Setting aside the testimonies of Bacon, Lind, Pringle, and others, the transports which received and conveyed home the wretched remnant of Sir John Moore's army, after the battle of Corunna, afforded the most decisive and melancholy proofs that bodies of men confined close together between the decks of a ship in stormy weather, will soon become sickly, and that their diseases may be communicated to nurses and others, after they are landed, washed, and placed in the most clean and airy hospitals. It will hardly be contended that these men could have carried any infection on board, either in their persons or clothes, after a rapid retreat, during which, almost every stitch of garment was washed from their backs by the incessant rains. A dreadful and sanguinary battle at the water's edge, gave them no time to contract infection or even clothe themselves at Corunna. They precipitated themselves tumultuously, naked, exhausted, and wound-

ed, into the first vessels that came in their way, and were there crowded from choice or necessity during a cold, wet, and tempestuous passage
across the Bay of Biscay.   On this passage a most fatal typhoid fever
broke out, which spread far and wide among the nurses and medical
attendants of the hospitals in England where they were landed.
They embarked indeed with an unusual degree of predisposition to
disease, arising from excessive fatigue—chagrin—exposure to the
elements by day and night—nakedness—want—occasional inebriety—insubordination ; and last of all—exhaustion after a tremendous
conflict that closed this disastrous retreat.   It was utterly impossible, however, that a particle of fomites or the matter of contagion
could exist among them at the moment of their embarkation ; and it
was too fatally proved that every transport exhibited a most destructive focus of infectious fever before they reached England.   I have
dwelt the longer on this point, because it bears upon questions that
are now agitating the public mind ; and because Time's telescope
cannot be inverted here as it has been on other occasions, nor facts be
denied that are so recent in the memory of thousands now alive.
Within a few yards of the spot where I now write, the greater part of
a family fell sacrifices to the effects of fomites that lurked in a blanket
purchased from one of these soldiers after their return from Corunna !

It is not so well ascertained that the effluvia from *dead* animal matters *alone* will generate a contagious disease ; at least it has been fashionable to deny such an occurrence since Dr. Bancroft's publication.
But there are not wanting respectable testimonies in the affirmative;
and it does not seem very incredible that offensive exhalations from
large masses of putrifying animal matters should, under certain
circumstances, produce fever, as related by Forestus and Senac. The
late fatal fever at Cambridge appears to have been of local origin at
first, but propagated by infection afterwards.

Of what this contagious matter consists, we are totally ignorant, as
it is perfectly incognizable. by the senses, and incapable of being
submitted to chemical analysis. Many people have declared that they
felt an indescribable taste in their mouths, and sensation over their
frames, together with a peculiar odour impressed on their olfactories,
at the moment of imbibing the poison ; but it cannot be ascertained
whether these were produced by the contagion itself, or by any effluvium accompanying or conveying it.

With the laws which govern contagion, we are fortunately better
acquainted.   It does not appear to be much under the control of the
seasons, since a full *dose* of it will produce the specific effect at any
time of the year.   As warm air causes a greater exhalation from
bodies, it might, *a priori*, have been expected that this contagion
would spread most in the summer ; and the popular opinion to this day
is, that hot weather is prejudicial to patients labouring under typhoid
fevers.   We find, however, that it is in winter that these diseases are
most prevalent.   The reason appears to be simply this :—the freer
ventilation of summer dilutes and dissipates the exhalations from the
sick, rendering them innocuous ; while the confined air of small

apartments among the poor, in winter, tends to condense, as it were, the febrific effluvia, and embue the bedding, &c. of the sick with the same ; forming a fruitful source for the dissemination of the disease by means of *fomites*, a form in which the matter of contagion is eminently powerful. Experiments have proved that this contagion, when diluted with pure atmospheric air, becomes harmless at the distance of a few yards—perhaps of a few feet ; and hence the surest means of preventing its dissemination are, cleanliness and ventilation. Indeed it is only where these *cannot* be procured, that the *juggling* process of fumigation need ever be resorted to ; and I firmly believe that if the latter ever checked the spread of contagion, it was more by its effects on *mind* than on *matter*. The history of animal magnetism alone will teach us how far imagination may go in actually arresting the progress of disease in its full career ; and in no case have *mental* impressions more decided effects than in checking or facilitating the operation of contagion on the human body.

The next thing to be observed is, that from idiosyncrasy of constitution, some individuals are infinitely less susceptible of the contagion than others ; and also, that habitual exposure to it, renders us more capable of resisting it, as is exemplified among nurses and medical men. This circumstance appears explicable on the principle of *habit*, which renders us able to bear a larger dose of any other poison, as of arsenic, opium, &c. Dr. Haygarth affirms that he has been in the *habit* of breathing, *almost daily*, air strongly impregnated with the infectious miasms of fever, during a space of more than 50 years, and yet never but once caught a fever in all that time. Some periods of life, however, render the body more susceptible than others—the very young and very old are more exempt than those of intermediate ages. Ulcers and other chronic *diseases*, also, seem occasionally to confer an insusceptibility on the constitution. The *latent* period, or that which elapses between the reception and manifestation of the contagion differs exceedingly, according to the degree of concentration in the poison and the predisposition of the subject. There is no doubt but that many doses of the poison are received which produce the fever or not according as the various predisposing causes are applied. It is, however, seldom less than fourteen, or more than sixty days between the receipt of the infection and the unfolding of the fever.

Marsh Miasma.—The febrific effluvia of marshes, as well as human contagion, seem to have escaped the notice of Hippocrates. This is the more to be wondered at, as many of the fevers which he describes are clearly the bilious remittent fevers of the present day, [*see, for instance, Popularium* 1. *Ægrotus octavus*,] and produced, of course, by the same causes. Lancisius was the first who drew the attention of medical men to the subject, since which, march effluvium has been traced as the cause of some of the most destructive endemics that occur both within and without the tropics. The fevers of Cadiz, Carthagena, Gibraltar, and Zealand, may compete, in respect to virulence and fatality, with those of Batavia, Bengal, St. Domingo, and Philadelphia. The term *marsh*, is not so proper as *vegeto-animal* effluvium or miasma ; since experience and observation have proved that these febrific exhalations arise from the summits of mountains as well as from the surfaces of swamps. The mountains of Ceylon, covered with woods and jungle, and the vast ghauts themselves, give origin to miasmata that occasion precisely the same fever as we witness on the marshy plains of Bengal.—But the subject of Miasmata will again come under consideration, in the Section on Endemic of Bengal.

Ratio Symptomatum.—We now proceed to trace the *action* of these febrific causes on the human frame—or in other words, the *ratio symptomatum* of fever-itself ; for in nature and in truth, there is no such thing as a *proximate cause* of this disease, the whole train of symptoms being a series of causes and effects, extremely difficult to delineate or comprehend. If any thing could deserve the name of *proximate cause*, it would be some peculiar state or phenomenon *invariably present* at the beginning of fever, and without which, the disease could not be said to exist. But all writers agree that there is no *one* symptom, state, or phenomenon which is constantly observable in fever. Neither quickness of pulse—increased heat—thirst nor headache can be laid down as pathognomonic ; for although *some* of these are *always* present, no *one* of them is invariably so.

If an appeal, however, be made to accurate clinical observation, it will probably be found that from the first till the last moment of fever, *two phenomena* are constantly present—a derangement in the balance of the *circulation,* and of the *excitability.* If the calibre of the radial artery, or the strength and velocity of its pulsations show nothing preternatural, (which by the bye will be a rare occurrence,) yet, the experienced physician can instantly detect the unequal distribution of the vital fluid, as well by the torpid state of the *extreme* vessels on the surface, and throughout the glandular system, as by the turgidity of the *primary* trunks. The imperfect perspiration and secretions will point out the one ; the peculiar febrile anxiety—hurried respiration on attempting to sit up or move—fullness of the præcordia, and heaviness about the head, will clearly demonstrate the other. In no one instance, during a long acquaintance with fever, have I failed to notice these indications of a deranged balance of the *circulation.*

The proofs of broken balance in the *excitability* are equally manifest. It is now well known how much the functions of the glandular system are dependant on the nervous. In fever, the secretions are never perfectly natural. They are in general scanty—sometimes preternaturally copious ; but always depraved. While this torpor or irregularity is going on in the glandular system, the nerves of sense show plain marks of inequilibrium of excitability. The same degrees of light and sound that in health would be pleasing, will, in fever, be either distracting, or incapable of making any impression at all. The stomach will be in a state of morbid irritability, and the intestinal canal completely torpid. Speaking generally, however, the glandular or secreting system is irregularly torpid—the nervous or sentient system, irregularly irritable and debilitated.

Now if we find that the general operation of the various *predisposing* causes of fever, is to disturb more less, according to the force and condition of the subject, the balance of the circulation and excitability, we advance one step nearer to a knowledge of this *proximate cause* in fever, because we find in it the same *ratio symptomatum* as in all the phlegmasiæ; modified only by the exciting cause. For example : one man is exposed to a rapid atmospherical transition, or a current of cold air when the body is heated ; another man is exposed to the effluvium issuing from the body of a typhous patient ; a third commits a great and unaccustomed debauch in spirituous or fermented liquors :—a fourth is overhelmed with a series of losses and misfortunes ; a fifth is exposed to the exhalations arising from a fen ; while a sixth performs a rapid and toilsome march under an ardent sun. These six men, (and the list might be far extended,) will have six different kinds of fever—all agreeing, however, in the two points under discussion, [a derangement of balance in the circulation and in the excitability,] but each offering *peculiar* traits and phenomena, in consequence of the *peculiarity* of cause.

Thus the *first* patient will in all probability, have a fever remarkable for great vascular action, or derangement of the circulation, with a determination to some internal organ, most likely the lungs, in which determination or inflammation consists the chief danger.

The *second* man will have a fever at a much longer interval from the application of the cause, and which, contrary to the former case, will show greater marks of derangement in the balance of the excitability, than of the circulation. In this instance, the functions of all the organs will be more or less affected ; the fever sometimes running its whole course without producing morbid alteration of structure ; at other times, giving origin to congestion or inflammation in the brain, liver, stomach, &c. destroying the patient at various and uncertain stadia of the disease. To these peculiarities may be added the power of propagating itself by reproduction in other subjects.

The *third* man will have high vascular action, with considerable determination to the head, stomach, alimentary canal, &c. or probaly that peculiar affection denominated " delirium tremens."

The *fourth* will have what is called a slow nervous fever so admirably described by Pringle.

The *fifth* will have a fever differing from all the preceding, inasmuch as it will show great remissions, or even intermissions, on alternate days, with determinations, if long continued, to the liver and spleen.

The *sixth* man's fever will evince great violence at beginning, with little or no remission ; and end in a sudden determination to an internal organ—generally the liver ; or change into a long and dangerous typhoid type.

Now the only symptoms or circumstances that are *invariably* present in *all* these cases, are the *inequilibriæ* above-mentioned ; the other varieties appearing to depend on the difference of cause, and idiosyncrasy of constitution. Need we then seek further for a *proximate cause* of fever ?

All the causes then of fever, from the most remote and predisposing, to the most immediate and exciting, however varied may be their *mode of action*, tend constantly to one point, and directly or indirectly to induce derangement in the balance of the circulation and excitability. Some of these *appear* to produce their *first* effects on the vascular, others on the nervous system. Thus atmospherical vicissitudes evidently give rise to violent oscillations of the circulation; yet these transitions, and still more the oscillations must secondarily affect the nervous system. On the other hand, human and marsh effluvia seem to make their *first* impression on the nervous system, the circulation apparently becoming deranged consecutively. Of the two febrific causes, however, human contagion shows its effects most on the nervous—marsh miasma, on the circulation system. Debauches and excesses operate on both systems, hurrying the circulation, exhausting the excitability, and producing fever, with or without local inflammation. The depressing passions, like human and marsh poison, seem also to affect *primarily* the nervous system, which through every stage of the fever bears the onus of disease. Excessive muscular action and an ardent sun so much derange the circulation and the functions of certain internal organs, as to induce great fever, with determination to the biliary organs, in particular.

The manner *how*, and the reason *why* these various causes, pre ds - ponent and exciting, act on the human frame producing the phenomena of fever, are equally inscrutable as the manner *how*, and reason *why* tartrite of antimony should have a tendency to act on the *upper*, and aloes on the *lower* portion of the alimentary canal. Let any person demonstrate the *modus operandi* of these two simple substance, and then I shall engage to demonstrate the *modus operandi* of human and marsh effluvia. The nature or essence of many of these causes themselves, is also totally beyond our comprehension. Some of them are even *ideal*, as the various depressing passions, &c. Yet we must not cease to investigate the *effects*, though we are ignorant of the nature and mode of action of the *causes*.

We shall now select one cause, and trace its operations on the human frame, as a sufficient specimen and explanation of the ratio symptomatum in all. The varieties and peculiarities from this specimen being, as I have stated before, ascribable to variety of cause and peculiarity of constitution.

A man after exposure to the miasmata of marshes, begins to exhibit symptoms of diminished energy in the nervous system, evinced by the various feelings and phenomena which usher in the cold stage of fever.

The power of the heart and arteries appears evidently to be weakened, the consequence of which is an inability to propel the blood to the surface and throughout the secretory organs ; and from the diminished excitability of the system, we observe a quiescence of the capillaries, and a shrinking and coldness of all external parts, without the intervention or necessity of spasm. In this state it follows, of course, and is allowed by all, that the great volume of blood is confined to the heart, and large internal trunks of vessels. But this appears an inadequate explanation of the swelling, tension, oppression, and even pain about the hypochondria, as well as of many other of the symptoms attendant on the cold stage of fever in particular. If, during the latter, I place my hand on the radial artery and endeavour to estimate its calibre, and the quantum of blood transmitted through it in a given time, compared with what takes place in the hot stage, or even in health, I shall conclude that the artery is not then above one-third the size, nor the quantity of blood passing through it, more in proportion. Such being the case, it is difficult to conceive how the whole mass of blood can be in *actual* circulation at this time. Besides, therefore, the confinement of a large share of it to the heart and large vessels, where its motions must be slow, I venture to affirm that another considerable portion of it is *arrested*, as it were, and accumulated in certain situations, where it remains *pro tempore*, out of the course of *actual* circulation. This congestion or complete quiescence, takes place in the portal circle, where the blood is, at all times, languid in its current, there being only a slight *vis a tergo*, and but little muscular propulsion. The consequence of this must be, that not only the liver and the various branches of the vena portarum will become turgid, but also the spleen, (which returns its blood to the heart through this channel,) the stomach, pancreas, and intestines, will participate in this turgescence.

If it be asked why the blood should cease to circulate in these parts during the cold stage of fever sooner than in others; I answer that the portal is the only circle or set of vessels in the sanguiferous system, *originating and terminating* in capillary tubes, or inosculations with other vessels. They begin by the minutest threads from the stomach, spleen, pancreas, and intestines; these enlarge as they approach the liver; there they diverge, and finally dwindle again into the same diminution with which they commenced. All other veins dilate as they approximate to the heart, thereby affording more and more facility to the return of the blood, which is in most places assisted by the action of circumjacent muscles. The temporary quiescence or torpor, then, of the extreme branches of the vena portæ in the liver, from sympathy with the extreme vessels on the surface, (before elucidated, and I hope satisfactorily proved) must completely check and arrest the reflux of blood from the whole of the viscera above-mentioned. This state of things at once explains the tension, elevation, pain, weight, and anxiety about the præcordia. It shows why the biliary and pancreatic secretions are in common with, and still more particularly than others entirely checked for the time, while the gradual accumulation and temporary abstraction, as it were, of so great a proportion of the vital fluid from *actual* circulation, will readily account for most, if not all the phenomena of the *cold* stage, many of which were inexplicable on other principles. It appears to me, indeed, that this *temporary* arrest of so much blood in the liver and portal circle, (including the spleen,) is one of the most admirable of nature's expedients to obviate more dangerous effects. When the balance of the circulation is broken, and the blood is determined from the surface upon the internal parts, were it all to accumulate in the large vessels about the heart, and in the lungs, immediate death would be the consequence ; but the local abstraction of so large a proportion of it, from *actual circulation*, by its quiescence in the circle above-mentioned, (where plethora is not so immediately detrimental,)•preserves the heart and lungs from being over-powered and suffocated, till reaction restores the equilibrium between the surface and the interior. From this view of the affair the utility of the spleen, as an organ of preservation, is no longer doubtful.* But this accumulation of blood in the portal circle and viscera, must, of necessity, produce a corresponding plethora in the branches of the cæliac and mesenteric arteries leading to them ; and since such large and important exits for the blood from the descending aorta, are, as it were, blocked up, a greater share of the circulating mass will be thrown in consequence through the carotids and vertebrals on the brain, occasioning or increasing the headach and congestion in that organ. This, and the congestion in the lungs, however, will be principally caused by the difficulty, indeed the inability of the heart to propel the blood from the ventricles as fast as it returns to the auricles from the brain and lungs ; hence the *venous* turgescence in both these' organs. occasioning the headache, stupor, laborious respiration, and febrile anxiety attendant on the collapse or cold stage.

The effects of sympathy are likewise to be taken into consideration. I have mentioned that which exists between the extreme vessels on the surface, and those of the vena portæ. The lungs too will sympathize with the skin, while the stomach and liver will sympathize with the brain, and *vice versa*.

This state of things, however, lasts not long. Reaction at length takes place. Whether it be from " the stimulus of the blood itself"—from that of the " retained secretion"—from " accumulated excitability"—from the " vis medicatrix naturæ"—or from all combined, we need not stop to inquire, (because *final* causes can never be discovered, and because we are rather tracing the *quo* than the *quomodo* in fever,) but so it is, that the brain, the heart, and the arteries re-acquire vigour—the two last driving the blood to the surface, with great increase of heat, and a more rapid circulation of the vital fluid, all of which, nevertheless, does not appear to come into motion, till the sweating stage For this preternatural heat or febrile stricture, seems to have the same effect, for a time, as the previous coldness or collapse, in preventing perspiration externally, and secretion internally; since we find the load and uneasiness at the præcordia and epigastrium continue till the extreme vessels on the surface relax, and a sweat breaks out, when a *simultaneous* relaxation in the extreme vessels of the liver, lungs, &c. allows the blood to pass on freely to the heart, and the various secretions to flow, relieving the internal congestions. This last effect, so much accelerated by the cold affusion, in the hot stage of fever, seems to have escaped the notice of Currie and Clutterbuck.

As the headache of the cold stage, from *venous* plethora, is continued in the hot, from *arterial* distention, (with a corresponding difference in sensation, as noticed by Fordyce,) so the nausea and sickness at stomach,•arising apparently in the cold fit from sympathy with the brain and liver, perhaps the skin, in continued in the

---

* Vide Dr. Armstrong's query ; Essay on Typhus, p..78.

hot, from the same causes, (these organs being still affected, though in a somewhat different manner,) and the vomiting is often brought on and kept up, by the sudden augmentation of gastric, biliary, and other secretions of a depraved quality, which are poured out towards the commencement of the sweating stage, particularly in hot climates, and in the hot seasons of temperate climates. In general, however, the irritability of the stomach subsides *pari passu*, as perspiration and secretion commence, with relief to the brain, lungs, liver, &c.

If, as some suppose, the cold be the cause of the succeeding hot stage, so in the latter, the violence of the reaction, or rather overaction of the sanguiferous system, with the morbidly increased excitement of the nervous system, must predispose to a repetition of the fits, from the subsequent atony produced thereby. If there be sensorial energy enough to enable the heart and arteries to clear the viscera and brain of the load of blood with which they were oppressed, and to set the secreting organs in action, then an *intermission* takes place ; but if these circumstances be incomplete, a *remission* only. In what is called continued fever, it appears from the affection of the head, the load on the præcordia, the confined pulse, the dry, hot, and constricted skin, with a corresponding diminished biliary secretion, and costive bowels, that the constitution is called upon for almost constant, or at least frequently reiterated exertions to relieve the internal congestions, and restore the secretions and excretions, marked by more or less of diurnal remission and evening exacerbation, till it either becomes habituated to the original cause, and restores the balance of the circulation and excitability, or sinks, unequal to the task, most commonly with the destruction, (from inflammation or sanguineous determination,) of an organ essential to life. Dissection has so repeatedly detected the existence of these inflammations, congestions, and effusions, in all fevers of violence, that it is not necessary here to quote any passages from particular authors on the subject. But it may be remarked, *en passant*, that no *one organ*, not even the brain, is so invariably the seat of lesion as to enable us to build any theory on the subject, and hence Dr. Clutterbuck has overshot the mark by confining the cause of fever within the cranial parietes.

We now come to try the theory by a direct application of its principles to *practice*, the grand and only legitimate criterion of its truth. If we can show that it is consonant with, and elucidates the operation of those remedial measures which either ancient or modern experience has employed in fever, it is no trifling corroboration of its solid foundation. And, even if it points to the most successful plans of treatment which modern investigation has devised, in must be allowed to be a useful, though perhaps only a visionary theory.

It will not be necessary, however, to examine the whole farrago of remedies which ignorance, superstition, or prejudice had at various periods, introduced for the treatment of fever ; it will be sufficient to notice those which have stood the test of time.

1st.—VENÆSECTION.

Blood-letting is as ancient as the wars of Troy, and the practice of Podalirius. If Hippocrates neglected it, Areteus, Celsus, and Galen, made ample use of this important measure. It is true, that even in our own times, the dogmas of the schools had nearly proscribed for awhile, what nature and observation had pointed out from the earliest dawn of medicine to the present time, in every climate from the banks of the Scamander to the vales of Otaheite.

The bounding pulse, the fever-flushed cheek, the throbbing temples, and aching head, must indeed have vindicated the propriety of blood-letting in every æra, and in every mind not warped by the bias of some fashionable doctrine.

In these scrutenizing days of investigation and experiment, the lancet has dispelled the mists of prejudice, the phantoms of debility and putrescency, with the delusions of the Brunonian school ; and bleeding is justly regarded as the paramount remedy, not only in symptomatic, but in all the more violent and fatal idiopathic fevers.

The consonance of this measure with the principles I have laid down, is so evident as scarcely to need comment. When the balance of the circulation is broken, and determinations take place to one or more organs, the most effectual means of restoring the balance, and of relieving these organs or parts from their overplus of blood, will be found either in local or general abstraction of the vital fluid. It is not from there being *less* than usual of blood, in some parts, but from there being *too much* in others, that the danger consists, and that we are called upon to reduce the whole mass below par. Nature herself invariably points out this indication, and in perhaps a majority of instances, fulfils it in her own way. Thus we find that every paroxysm of fever is terminated by some evacuation from the system, whether by perspiration, urine, increased secretions, or some local hæmorrhage. In what is called *continued fever*, the nocturnal exacerbations are terminated in the morning by some slight modifications of the foregoing evacuations ; and in all fevers and all stages of fever, nature effects *depletion* by preventing *repletion ;* and hence that invariable attendant on fever *anorexia* is one of the wisest and most salutary measures which nature can put in force to finally overcome the disease ; though she is too frequently baffled in her attempts by the officious interference of the cook, the nurse, or perhaps the medical prescriber.

I shall now make a few remarks on the most judicious manner of employing this remedy in fever ; for on this, in a great measure, depends its success ; and to the contrary, I believe, may be attributed not only its failure, but its disgrace.

In the first place, the time for blood-letting in fever should be an object of great attention. It should not only be *early* in respect to the accession of the fever, but the acme of the paroxysm or the height of the exacerbation should be selected as the proper periods for making the abstraction. At these times the evacuation will produce an alleviation of symptoms, and often a solution of the paroxysm or exacerbation ; whereas if taken during the remission of the fever, when the system is, as it were, in a state of collapse, deliquium animi is often the consequence, followed by a train of nervous symptoms and debility that are charged on the *measure*, when they ought to be placed to the account of the ill-judged period of its application.

The manner in which blood is drawn ought not to be neglected. When any strong determination to the head, or other organs exists, the vascular system so accomodates itself to the loss of blood from a *thready* stream that little or no relief is obtained for the suffering viscus, while the general strength is unnecessarily reduced by the quantum lost.

Although we are to be much less guided by the appearance of the blood drawn, than by the order and violence of the symptoms ; yet as a certain coat or crust of fibrine very generally, though not invariably, covers the coagulum when there is any local inflammation going on, we should attend to those circumstances in the abstraction that are favourable to the development of this criterion. Thus the stream of blood should be free and of a good size ; and it should be received into the centre, not impinged against the side of, a narrow and rather deep basin, with a polished internal surface. If the reverse of these directions be observed, as is too often the case, the blood will not exhibit any inflammatory buff, though inflammation be actually present at the time.*

As in fevers as well as some inflammations, it is not so much the general plethora of the vascular system, as the broken balance of the circulation that is to be corrected, so local abstractions of blood from the vicinity of those parts where the congestion or determination exists, are often of more importance than general blood letting.

It is to be regretted that, whether from the prejudices of the patient or the inattention of the practitioner, the seat of the determinations in the fever is rarely ascertained and relieved by topical bleedings. The violent headache, indeed, and arterial pulsation at the temples, frequently draw the practitioner's attention to that part, and leeches are accordingly applied ; but the epigastric region, where there is always more or less fulness, and to which the vital fluid seems in most fevers to gravitate, is too much neglected. Leeches or scarifications should long precede the necessity for blisters in these parts.

2nd.—PURGATIVES.

The ancient physicians had a very limited range, and a very rough list of purgative medicines. They made, however, a considerable use of them. Of late they were almost neglected by Cullen, and proscribed by Brown, in the fevers of this country, unaccompanied with topical inflammation. Dr. Hamilton and the greater number of modern practitioners employ purgatives freely, without fear of that far-famed, and much dreaded debility. The principle on which .

* Vide the inestimable work of Dr. Armstrong on Typhus. Also Dr. Dickson's writings on Tropical Fever.

these act, in fever, are by no means generally understood ; and the practice itself is inefficient from this cause. Even Dr. Hamilton seems to attribute most of the good effects of purgatives in fever to the removal of irritating fecal remains. But if this were the case, the glysters of Cullen would have answered the same end, which, however, they did not. The removal of fecal accumulations, from the small intestines particularly, gives a more free descent to the blood through the abdominal aorta and its branches, and thus mechanically assists in the restoration of balance ; the increased secretion from the mucuous membrane of the alimentary canal, must also powerfully deplete the cæliac vascular system ; but a very salutary *modus operandi* of purgatives in fever, has, I believe, escaped the notice of physicians, although I conceive it to be an important one ; I mean the change from torpor of the intestines to a brisk peristaltic motion, whereby the blood which has been shown to accumulate, and as it were stagnate, in the portal circle, is propelled forward, and the biliary secretion increased. Another salutary effect is produced by the sympathetic influence which the internal surface of the alimentary canal exerts on the cutaneous surface of the body ; for although drastic purging will check profuse perspiration, yet where torpor pervades both the internal and external surfaces of the body, a restoration of the functions of the former contributes to the same event in the latter ; a fact, of which any one may convince himself at the bed-side of sickness by an attention to the circumstances under consideration.

When therefore the peristaltic motion, the gastric, and intestinal secretions are roused by purgatives, the head which, from the peculiarity of its circulation, must suffer sanguineous congestion, is almost immediately relieved by the *change of balance*, thereby induced. From these considerations it will not appear a matter of indifference, what purgative medicine we use. Experience has taught us that some, (for instance castor oil,) do little more than clear the intestinal canal of what already exists there ; that others, (for instance the neutral salts, jalap, &c.) produce copious *watery secretions* into the alimentary tube, during their operation ;—and that others still, (for instance the submuriate of quicksilver,) besides acting as a common purgative, increase particular secretions, as of the bile, and carry them off, whether in a healthy or morbid state.

From the importance of the hepatic function in the animal economy, and bad effects which result from any derangement or obstruction of it in febrile commotion, it is evident, and experience proves it, that into the combination of purgative medicines in fever, those of a cholagogue power should almost always enter. Hence it has been found both in this and other countries, that powdered jalap and submuriate of quicksilver formed a composition most admirably adapted to the purposes above mentioned, as may be seen by the writings of Rush, Jackson, Hamilton, Armstrong, Dickson, &c.

Hence also, we see how purging, by rousing the torpid circulation and excitability of the abdominal viscera, determining the blood through the various branches of the aorta which were before choaked up, and thereby removing the congestion in the head, restores strength, by relieving the sensorium, instead of adding to the pre-existent debility, as was dreaded by the Brunonians and Cullenians, and which dread still fetters the hands of numerous practitioners even in this country. The operation of purgatives then, is perfectly consonant with, and elucidates the fundamental principle, to be kept in view in fever—" *a restoration of equilibrium in . the balance of the circulation and excitability.*"*

3d.—COLD AND TEPID AFFUSION.

The operation of these *apparently* different measures, in mitigating or even arresting fever, is in perfect consonance with the principle laid down.

Leaving out the effect of *sensation* on the nervous system, during the affusion of cold water on the febrile surface of a patient, it is evident that the violence of reaction, (at which time alone it ought to be applied.) is mitigated by the cold, while the febrile irritation of a strictured surface is taken off.

That these objects tend to a restoration of balance in the circulation and excitability, need not be insisted on ; the other effect of cold affusion, namely, a subsequent perspiration, will also be found to have a similar tendency.

The effects of *tepid* affusion during reaction, or the hot stage of fever, is precisely analogous to that of the cold, only less forcible in degree ; for it must be remembered that the tepid bath is, or ought to be of a much *lower* temperature than the surface of the body, when applied in the *hot* stages of fever, and consequently acts in reality as a cold bath, only in a much more gentle manner.

When it is applied in the cold stage of fever, its operation in drawing the blood to the periphery, and thus restoring the balance of the *circulation*, is direct and obvious ; while in restoring sensibility to the torpid skin, the balance of excitability, is, of course, equipoised. The action of cool air in fevers is easily explicable on the same principles.

4th.—MERCURY.

Various have been the disputes respecting the operation of mercury on the human system. A stimulant property has been very generally attributed to this mineral, apparently from its quickening the vascular action, and " exciting an artificial fever."† " Hence," says the Enquirer [*loco citato*] " its efficacy in remittent and continued fevers is very equivocal. At the commencement of those diseases I believe that it does mischief, if exhibited in any form to exert its power on the salivary glands *alone*." It would be difficult to select

* Vide Dr. Dickson's admirable papers in various numbers of the Edinburgh Medical and Surgical Journal.
† Ed. Journal, vol. vi. p. 181.

a passage in any medical work which contains so much error and so much want of knowledge, in so small a space, as the above paragraph. In the first place, those who condemn the use of mercury most, condemn it on this principle, that in some very concentrated forms of inflammatory fever, as the endemic of the West Indies, it cannot be brought to exert its influence on the system in time, and therefore there is danger in trusting to its operation. Mr. Sheppard, of Witney, one of the ablest of the anti-mercurial party, expresses himself thus :—" The co-existence of febrile and mercurial action is generally admitted to be incompatible ; if, therefore, the action *could* be superinduced in violent fever, we should be possessed of an invaluable remedy."—*Ed. Journal, October,* 1817.

In the second place, who ever saw mercury affect the salivary glands *alone* ? Narrow indeed, is that view of the mercurial action which stops short at its quickening the pulse, "and exciting an artificial fever." The fact is, that ptyalism is merely a symptom that the salivary glands are affected, in common with every other gland, and every secreting and excreting vessel in the system. Thus floodgates are opened in all directions, and every part of the human fabric experiences a rapid diminution—in short, mercury is never more an *evacuant* than when it produces ptyalism. This general depletion is still further increased by the ptyalism preventing any supply of nutriment which the patient or friends might wish to introduce.

I am ready to grant, indeed, that in certain high grades of the western endemic, or yellow fever, we cannot bring on this much desired effect of mercury ; and why ? Let Mr. Sheppard himself answer the question. " From the experience of many years within the tropics," says this judicious observer, " I am disposed to coincide with those who believe that the disease, in the highest degree of concentration, is *irremediable* by any known means in medicine ; for I have remarked, in this extreme case, that whatever plan of cure may be adopted, the rate of mortality remained unaffected by variety of treatment." *Loco citato.* Now if mercury fails in these cases, so does depletion ; but I most solemnly protest against the inference that, because pyrexia ceases when ptyalism appears, the *latter* is merely an effect or consequence of the former.

In the inflammatory forms of West India fevers where hepatic congestions are comparatively rare, I conceive that depletion *alone* is the best mode of treatment ; but to draw a sweeping conclusion from this circumstance that mercury is totally useless, if not injurious, in all febrile states of the system, and in all climates, is most erroneous in principle, and injurious in practice. The ensuing pages of this essay will afford ample illustrations of the *febrifuge* powers of mercury ; while its *modus agendi*, as an equalizer of the circulation and excitability, will be found to be in exact consonance with the principles here laid down.

5th.—EMETICS.

The gastric irritability which accompanies most fevers might have led to the suspicion that nature aimed at relief by unloading the stomach, and hence the early use of emetics.—They are now much less frequently employed; though it is certain that they produce other salutary effects beyond the mere evacuation of the stomach. They determine to the surface, in common with diaphoretics, and produce a relaxation there, which generally ends in perspiration. Their utility therefore, in certain states and kinds of fever, is unquestionable, and consonant too with the principle which I have endeavoured to establish; but their violence, in certain fevers and climates where unusual irritability of stomach too often prevails, has brought them much into disuse, even in opposite circumstances. The debility also which they induce gave the Brunonians a dislike to their employment.

6th.—DIAPHORETICS.

These have a close affinity to the last mentioned remedies, but are of milder operation. In all fevers of a marked periodical type, there is such an evident remission, or solution of the paroxysm in the sweating stage, that physicians must have very early endeavoured to imitate this salutary process of nature by artificial means. This, however, has often led to disastrous results; for observing that heated rooms, multiplicity of clothing, warm liquors, &c. induced perspiration in health, the same means were resorted to in disease, and too often with the most pernicious consequences. They knew not till lately, that the strictured surface of a febrile patient will seldom relax into a perspirable state, till its temperature is *reduced* below the fever heat, and consequently when they failed in their object, they did much mischief, and when they succeeded in *forcing* out a perspiration, the temporary relief obtained, by no means counterbalanced the previous increase of febrile excitement.

Now that the principles which govern the perspiratory process are better understood, the long and endless farrago of sweating medicines is reduced to a few neutral salts, as the citrate of potash, or acetate of ammonia, accompanied occasionally with small doses of antimony. These, with *cool* diluent drinks, are the only safe or salutary diaphoretics in fever; and probably act on the surface from its sympathy with the stomach.

It is needless to state that the operation of this class of remedies is in perfect consonance with the principles I have endeavoured to maintain.

7th.—TONICS AND STIMULANTS, INCLUDING BARK, WINE, OPIUM, &C.

It may seem a little strange, that the most diametrically opposite plans have succeeded in fever, and been lauded to the skies by their supporters as infallible. Hence, many have supposed that were fevers left entirely in the hands of nature, as many would recover as under the most skilful treatment.

Whatever truth there may be in this, it is not equally correct that nearly the same proportion recover under all kinds of treatment.

There is very little doubt but that under *judicious* modern measures, not only a greater proportion recover from the graver types of fever, but a vast number of fevers are prevented from assuming the more dangerous forms.

Neither need it be wondered at, that both stimulants and sedatives should occasionally prove useful in fever. We have shown that when the excitability and vascular action are too great in one part of the system, they are deficient in others ; hence the diffusive stimuli' have the effect of rousing the torpid parts into action, but too often at the expense of the over-excited organs ; and this has been the distinguishing feature of the Brunonian practice. Tonics and stimulants were also frequently necessary in the ultimate stages of fever, where early evacuations were not premised ; because the system was exhausted by its own efforts, or by injudicious remedies, and nature required a stimulus at the close of the disease. But, now it is found, after fatal experience, that by lessening reaction at the beginning, we preserve the powers of the constitution for ulterior efforts, and thereby obviate the necessity of stimulation at almost any period of fever.*

To show how dangerous it was to draw conclusions respecting *debility* from the salutary operation of stimulants in fever, the following example may suffice. From deranged balance of excitability the heart and arteries become incapable of performing their office in a proper manner.—If their excitability be too great, they drive the blood with an impetus to the brain that may cause delirium : if their excitability be defective, the heart is incapable of unloading the venous system, and distention of the veins and sinuses of the head produce the same effect. Now, wine, if given *judiciously*, and to a certain extent, in the *latter* case, will impart such vigour to the heart as will enable it to unload the venous system of the brain, and thereby remove the delirium, without giving too much impetus to the arterial system ; but if the same medicine be exhibited in the former case, it will evidently increase the symptom it was intended to relieve ! — In other words, some parts of the system being in a state of *torpor*, and others in a state of *irritability*, if stimulants be applied to the *former*, they *may* do good, but if to the *latter*, they *must* do harm. Hence the value and the necessity of discrimination in the practitioner ; and the fatal effects of a *routine* practice.

In some of the more protracted fevers of this climate, assuming the typhoid and nervous type, the proper time for exhibiting the stimulating class of remedies requires the clearest judgment of the practitioner, and it is at these critical and decisive moments, that real ability unfolds its acuteness of discrimination, and snatches the patient from the jaws of death ; while the blundering routinist unconsciously signs his quietus !

Little need be said of the minor or subordinate remedies, as blisters, sinapisms, &c. as their operation is evidently to restore the

---

* Vide Dr. Armstrong's work on Typhus, where the subject is handled with infinite skill.

balance of the circulation and excitability by soliciting artificial determinations to superficial parts, with the view of relieving internal congestions or inflammations.

ENDEMIC FEVER OF BENGAL,
Commonly called the Marsh Remittent Fever.

SEC. II.—The importance of this disease will not be questioned, when it is considered, that in the small portion of the Hoogly, running between Calcutta and Kedgeree, full three hundred European sailors, (better than a fourth of the ships' crews,) fall annual victims to its ravages !* The subject therefore is highly interesting, and must receive a considerable share of our attention.

There is no unmixed good in this world. The inundations of the Nile and the Ganges, while they scatter fertility over the valley of Egypt, and the plains of Bengal, sow with a liberal hand, at the same time, the seeds of dreadful diseases ! Hence, Cairo and Calcutta have severely suffered from the overflowings of their respective rivers.

These consequences are not confined to tropical countries alone. Swamps and marshes, in all latitudes, give rise to intermittents and remittents, varying in degree and danger, according to the heat, rains, and other circumstances of the season. The deleterious influence of an atmosphere, impregnated with marsh effluvia, on the human frame, is in some places astonishing. In the lower districts of Georgia, life is curtailed to forty or fifty years.

I have myself, in rambling through the villages of Beveland and Walcheren, been struck with the conspicuous marks of premature old age, which all, beyond maturity, exhibited ; particularly among the peasantry. On inquiring the ages of decrepid wretches, withered, sallow, and apparently on the borders of fourscore, I was surprised to find that fifty-five or sixty years were all they had numbered in these noxious fens. Often have I been asked by inattentive observers, why so unhealthy a country should present so great a number of very old people ? But to return to the Ganges.

This immense river, originating in the mountains of Tibet, and winding in a south-eastern direction, collecting its tributary streams from all quarters as it proceeds, after a course of more than a thousand miles, bursts its boundaries, in the rainy season, and covers the plains of Bengal with an expansive sheet of turbid water. But the ground springing a little, as it approaches the coast, prevents the inundation from rushing at once into the ocean : it therefore disembogues itself slowly through a multiplicity of channels, that intersect the great Indian Delta, or Sunderbunds, in every possible direction.

. This check keeps the plains of Bengal overflowed from the latter end of July till the middle of October ; during which period, noted cities, populous villages, exalted mosques, and stupendous pagodas,

* Vide Captain Williamson's East India Vade Mecum.

are seen just above the level of this temporary ocean, surrounded by
innumerable boats, now the habitations of domesticated animals.

At this time, vessels even of an hundred tons are beheld traversing
the country in various routes, wafted by a breeze that seldom shifts
more than a point or two from south.—The depth of water during
the inundation, varies from ten to thirty feet, according to the undu-
lations of the ground. The original course of rivers is now known
only by their currents, which may have a velocity of four miles an
hour, on an average, while the great body of water, spread over the
plains, moves at the rate of half a mile or a mile, in the same space
of time.

A chemical analysis of the various impregnations and impurities
which the Ganges and its contributory streams sweep down to Bengal,
and which either subside in feculence on the soil, or are carried on to
the sea, would form an interesting memoir ;—It will be sufficient in
this place to glance at a few of them.

The Western bank of the Ganges itself, between Hurdwar and Benares, consists in general of lime, concreted in irregular masses ; and
all the rivers which issue from the Western bank are more or less
impregnated with the same substance ; while on the opposite bank the
waters partake of a strong solution of nitre, with which the plains of
Oude, Fyzabda, and Gazeepoor, abound. The country lying between the Ganges and the Goomty, on the Eastern bank, is replete
with fossil alkali, named " seedgy," giving rise to severe bowel complaints among the natives ; while the swamps of Sasseram are annually
in a state of partial corruption, sufficient to occasion the most malignant diseases in the month of November, when the sun's power promotes an astonishing evaporation, filling the air with miasmata, and
spreading destruction among all the living tribes.

The Mahana, the Mutwalla, and various other mountain rivers,
that rush into the Ganges between Patna and Boglepore, are frequently tinged with copper. The 12th Battalion of Native Infantry were
nearly poisoned by drinking at one of these streams.

But it would be endless to trace all the sources of pollution in the
vegetable and mineral kingdoms ; one or two only in the animal kingdom will be selected as specimens in that extensive department.

The Hindoo religion enacts, that as soon as the spirit has taken its
departure, the body shall be burnt on the banks of the Ganges, and
that the ashes, together with every fragment of the funeral pile, be
committed to the sacred stream. In a country where dissolution and
putrefaction are nearly simultaneous, the utility of such a measure is
self-evident ; but either from indolence or penury, the body is now generally placed on a small hurdle, and when little more than scorched, is
pushed off from the shore with a bamboo, there to float until it arrives at the ocean, unless it be previously picked up by a shark or
alligator ; or, which is frequently the case, dragged ashore by Pariar dogs and devoured by them, in company with a numerous train of
carrion birds of various descriptions. From one hundred to one hundred and fifty of these disgusting objects may be counted passing one
point in the course of a day ; and in some places where eddies prevail,

a whole vortex of putrid corses may be seen circling about for hours together ! It was very common for us to be obliged to " clear the cable" occasionally of a human body, speckled over by the partial separation of the cuticle and rete mucosum from putrefaction.

Each contributory stream brings down its full proportion of these ingredients to the general reservoir ; since the inland inhabitants have always recourse to that which is most contiguous to their village ; and strange as it may appear, where no stream is at hand, the nearest tank, or jeel, performs the vicarious office of the sacred Ganges, supplying drink for the living, and a final receptacle for the dead ! We may add, that the banks of this river present, particularly about the rising and setting of the sun, a motly group of all classes, and sometimes both sexes, sacrificing to the Goddess Cloacina, in colloquial association ; not indeed offering their gifts in temples, but committing them to the passing current.

> So born and fed mid Tauran's mountain snows,
> Pure as his source, awhile young Ganges flows ;
> Through flow'ry meads his loit'ring way pursues,
> And quaffs with gentle lip the nectar'd dews ;
> Then broad and rough, through wilds unknown to day,
> Through woods and swamps, where tigers prowl for prey,
> He roams along ; and rushing to main,
> Drinks deep pollution from each tainted plain.

I have remarked, that the ground springs a little near the sea, and by resisting the progress of the inundation, lays the more inland plains under water. This is an important circumstance in the medical topography of the country : since the more complete the inundation the more healthy are the inhabitants, till the fall of the waters in November and December exposes a number of miry and slimy marshes to the action of a still powerful sun, when those who are in their neighbourhood, are sure to come in for a share of remittents and intermittents.

It is worthy of remark here, that in those years, when the rains are late in setting in, many people are suddenly cut off by the intense heat of the sun in June and July. But this is nothing compared to the havoc produced by a sudden and premature *cessation* of the rains or *Bursautty*, as they are called. In this last case an immense surface of slime and feculence is all at once exposed to the rays of a vertical sun, that has lost nothing of his power by a Southern declination. The consequence is, that the profuse exhalation of miasmata spreads pestilence and death in every direction ; while famine, from the rice being left dry before it has attained maturity, completes the dreadful catastrophe !

But the sunderbunds, and the country for some way round Calcutta, being in most places rather above the level of high water mark, become, during the rainy season, an immense woody and jungly marsh, neither perfectly overflowed, nor yet quite dry—in a word, presenting a surface as well supplied with animal and vegetable matters in a state of decomposition, and combining all the other circumstances necessary for giving miasmata their full influence on the human body, viz. intense heat, moisture, calms, &c. as perhaps any spot of equal extent on the face of the globe.

These sunderbunds form a belt between the Hoogly and the Megna of about 180 miles in length, by 50 in depth, completely overrun with forests, underwood, and jungle ; and inhabited by animals of various species, who are left to the uninterrupted possession of this frightful territory !

The rainy season commences about the middle of June, and lasts till the middle or latter end of October, though the waters are not drained off low situations till December. During this period, the deluges of rain that appear to come down occasionally " en masse" from the heavens, would almost stagger the belief of any one who had not witnessed them.

The inhabitants and domestic animals of inundated districts are all this time cooped up in a state of ennui, or torpor, which to an active European would be dreadful, had he not a number of mental, as well as corporeal resources for beguiling the tedious hours. But at Calcutta and Diamond harbour it is far otherwise. There the Europeans are not confined, and business must be attended to, as much as during the dry, or the cool and healthy season. It will not, therefore, appear extraordinary, that under all circumstances related, the marsh remittent fever should make such ravages among all classes, but more particularly among those who are exposed to the sultry heat of the day—the rains, the dews, and intemperance.

Having sufficiently explored the sources from whence vegeto-animal miasmata take their rise, I shall defer the investigation of their nature, or operation on the human frame, till the fever which they occasion is considered.

There can scarcely be conceived a situation of greater anxiety and distress, than that in which a young medical man of any sensibility is placed, on arriving at an unhealthy spot in a foreign climate, unfortified by experience, unaided by advice, and, as is too frequently the case, but scantily supplied with books, containing local accounts of the country and its prevailing diseases.

In such cases, he is forced to explore his way in the dark, agitated and alarmed by the mortality around him ; a great share of which he attributes, perhaps with more remorse than justice, to his own misconduct, or ignorance of the proper treatment !

We arrived in the Hoogly in the month of September, after a short run of little more than three months from England ; which place we left without the least knowledge of our ultimate destination. The fever in question was then making prodigious havoc among the ships' crews at Diamond harbour, and other parts of the river ; nor were we long exempted from its visitation. All circumstances considered, I thought myself fortunate in having in my possession the works of two celebrated authors, (Clarke and Lind.) containing a full account of this fever, drawn from personal observation on the spot. I accordingly—

" Read them by day and studied them by night."

In short, I was quite anxious to grapple with this Hydra disease, and show the power of medicine over this scourge of Europeans.

Many days did not elapse before I had an opportunity of trying my strength against so formidable an opponent, and a very few trials convinced me I had calculated without my host, and that I must use other weapons than those furnished me by Drs. Lind and Clarke, if I meant to be victorious in the contest.

Dr. Clarke's *description* of this fever, however, is so singularly chaste and correct, that were I to draw the picture myself, I must either use his own words, or give a false portrait. I shall therefore only add a few observations of my own in a note, and recommend Dr. C's description to be carefully compared with that of the yellow fever in another part of the work.

" This fever attacked in various ways, but commonly began with rigors, *pain* and sickness at stomach ; vomiting, headache, *oppression on the præcordia*, and great dejection of spirits. Sometimes, without any previous indisposition, the patients fell down in a deliquium, during the continuance of which the countenance was very pale and gloomy ; as they began to recover from the fit, they expressed the *pain* they suffered by applying their hands to the *stomach and head ;* and after vomiting a considerable quantity of bile, they soon returned to their senses. Sometimes the attack was so sudden, and attended with such *excruciating pain at the stomach*, that I have been obliged to give an opiate immediately.*

" In whatever form the disease appeared at first, the pulse was small, feeble, and quick,—the pain at the stomach increased, and the vomiting continued. As the paroxysm advanced, the countenance became flushed—the pulse quick and full—the eyes red—tongue furred —thirst intense—headache violent, delirium succeeded, and the patient became unmanageable ; but a profuse sweat breaking out in twelve or fourteen hours, generally mitigated all the symptoms.

" In the remissions, the pulse, which before was frequently 130, fell to 90. The patient returned to his senses, but complained of great debility ; sickness at stomach, and bitter taste in the mouth. This interval,

* It is a little singular, that Dr. Lind, of Windsor, in his inaugural dissertation on this fever, never once mentions " oppression on the præcordia,"—" pain at the stomach,"—or " fullness and tenderness in the epigastric region." I can safely assert, that I seldom saw an instance in which all of these were wanting— seldom, indeed, an instance in which they were not all present. It is true, that this endemic is not always arrayed in the same colours; but the abovementioned symptoms are so constantly attendant on fevers, in all hot climates particularly, that the omission of them is rather remarkable.

Dr. Lind mentions a symptom not noticed by Dr. Clarke, and which I have often observed. After remarking that bile was frequently ejected both upwards and downwards, he says—" Vomitus et dejectiones tamen *plerumque albi coloris erant* calcis aquæ commistæ, vel lactis illius quod lactentes evomunt." Neither of them has mentioned delirium, as often the *first* indication of the fever. Many a time have I been called to see men, whom their messmates represented as " mad ;" not in the least suspecting that it was the fever which they were seized with. This symptom generally happened among young men who were employed in boats, and who were not only more exposed than others to marsh effluvia, but to the fervency of the sun by day, and often to the dews and night air. A few instances likewise occurred where the patient attempted to jump over-board. This symptom is not very rare in bilious and other fevers, where there is great congestion or determination to the brain.

which was very short, was succeeded by another paroxysm, in which all the former symptoms were aggravated, particularly the thirst, delirium, pain at the stomach, and vomiting of bile. If the disease was neglected in the beginning, the remissions totally disappeared, and the skin now became moist and clammy, the pulse was small and irregular, the tongue black and crusted, and the pain at the stomach and vomiting of bile become more violent." It is needless to say, that from this period till death closed the scene, the features of this fever were such as characterize the last moments of all violent and fatal fevers.

The unfavourable terminations were generally between the third and seventh day, though in some cases I have seen it go on to the fifteenth or twentieth day ; but visceral obstructions were almost always the consequence ; and hepatitis or dysentery completed what the fever failed to accomplish. I may add that several cases occurred under my own inspection where there was a yellowish suffusion on the skin, as in the endemic of the West, with vomiting of matter bearing a considerable similarity to the grounds of coffee. This suffusion of bile, or yellow colour on the skin, is by no means an uncommon symptom in the fevers of the East, as will be shown hereafter. The natives themselves frequently exhibit this appearance, when extensive epidemics prevail in the lower situations of Bengal, as appears by the following quotation from Captain Williamson. " Certainly, (say this intelligent officer,) it is common to see whole villages in a state of *jaundice ;* and in some years the ravages of the disease, (marsh remittent,) are truly formidable." A torpid, or, at least, irregular state of the bowels, almost invariably precedes this fever ; unless in cases where the effects of the paludal effluvia are suddenly brought out, by exposure to the intense heat of the sun by day, and the chilling dews and fogs of the nights, among boats' crews. In these, of course, there were few premonitory symptoms. In respect to the cure, Dr. Clarke asserts, that " nothing is more indispensably necessary in the beginning than to cleanse the intestinal tubes by gentle *vomits* and purges " * * * * " As soon as the intestinal tubes have been thoroughly cleansed, the cure must *entirely* depend upon giving the Peruvian bark, in as large doses as the patient's stomach will bear, without paying *any regard to the remissions, or exacerbations of the fever.*" Such are the plain and easy instructions which Drs. Clarke and Lind have left for our guidance in this fearful endemic. They certainly are not, apparently, difficult to follow ; and heaven knows I endeavoured, most religiously, to fulfil every iota of their injunctions ; but with what success a single case will show.

A young man, of a good constitution, in the prime of life and health, had been assisting with several others, to navigate an Indiaman through the Hoogly. The day after he returned, he was seized with the usual symptoms of this fever. I did not see him till the cold stage was past ; but the reaction was violent—the headache intense—skin burning hot—great oppression about the præcordia, with quick, hard pulse —thirst, and nausea. An emetic was prescribed, and towards the close of its operation discharged a quantity of ill-conditioned bile, both upwards and downwards ; soon after which, a perspiration broke out, the febrile symptoms subsided, and a remission, almost amounting to an intermission, followed. I now, with an air of confidence, began to "throw in" the bark ; quite sanguine in my expectations of soon checking this formidable disease. But, alas ! my triumph was of very short duration ; for in a few hours the fever returned with increased violence, and attended with such obstinate vomiting, that although I tried to push on the bark through the paroxysm, by the aid of opium, effervescing draughts, &c. it was all fruitless ; for every dose was rejected the moment it was swallowed, and I was forced to abandon the only means by which I had hoped to curb the fury of the disease.

The other methods which I tried need not to be enumerated ; they were temporizing shifts, calculated in medical language, " to obviate occasional symptoms."

The plain truth was, that I knew not what to do ; for the sudden and unexpected failure of that medicine on which I was taught to depend, completely embarrassed me ; and before I could make up my mind to any feasible plan of treatment, my patient died, on the third day of his illness, perfectly yellow — vomiting to the last, a dark fluid resembling vitiated bile, and exhibiting an awful specimen of the effects which a Bengal fever is capable of producing, in so short a period, on a European in the vigour of manhood !

With feelings more easily conceived than described, I had the body conveyed to a convenient place, in hopes that dissection might afford some clue to my future efforts. On laying open the abdomen I was surprised to find the liver so gorged, as it were, with blood, that it actually fell to pieces on handling it. Indeed, it appeared as if the greater number of the vessels had been broken down, and almost the whole of the interior structure converted into a mass of extravasation. The gall bladder contained a small quantity of bile, in colour and consistence resembling tar, and the ductus communis choledochus was so thickened in its coats, and contracted in its diameter, that a probe could scarcely be passed into it. Marks of incipient inflammation were visible in some parts of the small intestines, and the internal surface of the stomach exhibited similar appearances. The thorax was not examined, on account of the time taken up in getting at the brain. Marks of turgescence, in the venous system of vessels particularly, were there quite evident, and more than the usual quantity of lymph was found in the ventricles, but no appearance of actual inflammation.

This case requires little comment. It is pretty clear that it would have required some ingenuity to devise a more injudicious mode of treatment, than that which I pursued. But it taught me an important lesson—it opened my eyes to my own folly, and. pace tantorum, virorum, to the oversight of my teachers. It is but too true, that we are nearly as reluctant in acknowledging our failures, as we are forward in blazoning our successes. In so uncertain a science as that of medicine, this has always been a considerable obstacle to its progress and improvement ; since, while we read of the great good fortune of others, and the surprising cures they have performed, and then find our own so far deficient in that respect, even when we are carefully treading their steps, we despond, and become exceedingly sceptical in regard to the truth of those statements. These reflections are not meant to bear on the veracity or candour of Dr Clarke, both of which I highly respect :—but as he has only published two unsuccessful cases—" in the most malignant fever he had ever seen in any part of the East Indies,"—viz. the Bengal fever, it may justly be questioned whether he would not have done more good, by detailing a greater proportion of the fatal terminations, than by confining himself to two solitary instances, without a single dissection. A careful perusal of the first of these that occur on the list, (Henry Pope, case 6,) will probably convince the reader that I was not the only person who had mistaken the nature of the disease, and that—

, " Aliquando dormitat bonus Homerus."

In fact, the determination to the liver and the brain, is perfectly evident, from the beginning to the end of this case ; and although no dissection took place, we cannot for a moment, doubt the appearances which it would have exhibited.

The impression made on my mind, by the dissection on one hand, and the perusal of Dr. Clarke's case, (Henry Pope,) on the other, determined me to try venesection, notwithstanding the dreadful accounts which Dr. C. himself gives of its fatal effects. I had now several down with the fever ; and must confess it was with a trembling arm and palpitating heart, that I first opened a vein, expecting every instant to see my patient die under my hands.

He did not die, however ; nay, he seemed evidently relieved, but the bad symptoms soon returned, and the bleeding was repeated, with brisk evacuations. He recovered.

I now carried the evacuating plan with a high hand, and with much better success than I expected. Fortunately for my patients, a great majority of them were fresh from Europe, and high in health and strength ; these recovered wonderfully, after bleeding and evacuations, though not always.

But there was on board a class of men whom we had pressed out of ships on their return from India, who had experienced, not only the influence of the climate, but of depressing passions, arising from " hope deferred," and the galling disappointment they must have felt, while treading back their steps to a distant country, after they had been on the very point of mingling with their friends and relations at home !

These required a more discriminated mode of treatment. Evacuations at the very beginning were necessary ; but something more was requisite, to clear the congestions from the head and liver. The fluids here, to use a simile, were too stagnant to drain off, of their own accord, even when a sluice was opened—they required propulsion.

It would be humiliating to myself, and perhaps uninteresting to my readers, to enumerate the many glaring blunders which I committed, and the false conclusions which I drew, before I arrived at any thing

like a steady and successful method of checking this Herculean endemic. Let those whose eagle eye and towering intellect can penetrate,
at a single glance, the secrets of nature, and curb with ease the reins
of impetuous disease, place their hands on their breasts, (if something within does not prevent them,) and thank their God that " *they
are not* like other men."

But to return to our subject. The first symptom that claims our
most serious attention in this disease, is that irritability of the stomach, accompanied by a distressing vomiting. Till this is allayed,
nothing can be done towards the cure, by way of medicine. Now
venesection has considerable effect in procuring alleviation, even of
this symptom. But the trifling manner in which it is too often performed, when it is ventured on at all, does more harm than good.
*Bleed boldly and decisively till the head and præcordia are relieved, or
draw no blood whatever.*

While this is doing, a scruple of calomel, with half a grain or a
grain of opium, should be immediately given ; this will act like a
charm on the stomach. I shall prove, in the course of this essay,
what, indeed, is well known to many of my brother officers who
have served in India, that twenty grains of calomel will act as a *sedative*, and so far from griping and producing hypercatharsis, it will
sooth uneasiness, and rather constipate than purge. On this account,
in the course of a few hours, when the vomiting is assuaged, some
purgative must be given, as cathartic extract, with calomel, castor
oil, or even salts, which will seldom fail to bring away a most copious discharge of intolerably fœtid, bilious, and feculent matter, to
the unspeakable relief of the head and epigastrium. To facilitate
and accelerate this most desirable object, purgative glysters should
be thrown up. The more copious the catharsis, the less danger there
will be of the return of vomiting.

If there be now a return of any of those dangerous symptoms, intense headache, delirium, or pain in the epigastric region, no apprehension need be entertained of the lancet once more.* Those
bugbears, debility and putrescency, still paralize the arms of medical
men in hot climates, notwithstanding the clearest evidence in favour
of venesection, particularly where the subject is lately from Europe,
and not broken down by the climate.

Immediately after the operation of the cathartic, the main-spring
of the cure must be acted on. For this purpose, from five to ten
grains of calomel. according to the urgency of the symptoms, combined or not with half a grain of opium, should be exhibited every
four or six hours, till ptyalism is well raised ; when, in nineteen
cases out of twenty, (I might say forty-nine out of fifty,) there will
be a remission of all the febrile symptoms, and safety secured. This
is undoubtedly the *sine qua non*, in the medical treatment of this
fever, as well as many other fevers in the East.

It is hardly necessary to remark, that emetics are exceedingly
doubtful, if not prejudicial medicines in this endemic, since gastric
irritability is one of the most distressing and difficult symptoms with

---

* The jugular vein, where the head is oppressed, will be the best exit for the blood.

which we have to contend. Yet many judicious practitioners, in the navy especially, still employ them, as will be seen hereafter ; my own experience, however, and observations are decidedly against them.

But, on the other hand, cathartics are eminently useful. There is, in this fever, either an obstinate costiveness, or dysenteric purging ; no such thing as natural feces, tinged with healthy bile, will ever be seen : when such can be obtained by purgatives, a great and evident advantage is gained. It may seem strange that I should recommend calomel and opium anterior to the administration of laxatives ; but, independent of the necessity which there is of allaying the irritability of the stomach, whoever will compare the discharge procured by cathartics given *previously* to the calomel and opium, with that which follows the *subsequent* exhibition of them, will decide in favour of the latter plan.

Once every day then, the dose of calomel, usually given every four or six hours, should be conjoined with ten or fifteen grains of ex. colcynth. com. jalap, or an ounce of castor oil, omitting the opium for that time. These will be sure to bring down a copious alvine evacuation, composed of highly vitiated bile and fecal sordes, that had been lurking in the convolutions of the intestines and cells of the colon, during that torpid state of the bowels which generally precedes the attack of fever.

This will greatly relieve the oppression and tension of the epigastrium, as well as the headache ; indeed, so striking is the amelioration of symptoms, after these intestinal evacuations, that in two or three instances I was tempted to follow them up, and try if they might not supersede the necessity of impregnating the system with mercury. I trode here on tender ground ; I was forced to measure back my steps, and have recourse in the end to that powerful and invaluable medicine, but in one case it was too late ! Warned by this, whenever I combined a purgative, with the calomel afterwards, 1 directed a mercurial friction or two to be employed during their operation, to prevent a halt in the pursuit of my ulterior and principal object—ptyalism.

In the mean time, while things are in this train, there are several objects which, though of a secondary consideration, the prudent practitioner will do well to keep in view. In the first place, the patient should be removed to the most airy and cool part of the ship or house ; he should be made perfectly clean ; and as there is, in nine cases out of ten, a great determination to the brain, his feet may be immersed occasionally in warm water. His head should be elevated, shaved, and numerous folds of linen or cotton, moistened with vinegar and water artificially cooled, kept constantly applied to it.

Sir James Mc. Grigor remarks in his Medical Sketches, that the cold bath did not succeed in the fevers of India. " On my arrival there, (says he,) I tried it in several cases, but it failed. This fever is commonly of the remittent type, there is much reaction ; it seems in most cases *symptomatic of liver affection, and often terminates in hepatitis.*" There is some obscurity in the latter part of this passage ; but at all events, Sir James Mc. Grigor cannot allude to the fever under consideration; for although the liver, as I shall hereafter endeavour to prove, is in this, and perhaps in all other fevers, *affected;* yet it would be carrying a theory to extremes to assert, that the Bengal Marsh Remittent, confessedly produced by paludal effluvia, in conjunction with heat and moisture, was, " in most cases *symptomatic* of liver affection." It is probable that Sir James Mc. Grigor had not an opportunity of seeing *this* fever ; as his observation, in regard to " liver affection," applies more strictly to those fevers denominated " Bilious," which are prevalent at Bombay, the coast of Coromandel, and other elevated parts of India, in which Sir James Mc. Grigor served—Vide Sec. 7.

How far the cold affusion in these *last* fevers may be applicable, this is not the place to inquire ; but in the Bengal Remittent, it has been practiced, time immemorial, among the natives themselves, many a century before a Jackson, a Wright, or a Currie, ever thought or wrote on the subject, as the following quotation from a gentleman *out of the profession,* and who, of course, has no other object than truth in view, will prove.—" We must, however," says Capt. Williamson, author of Oriental Field Sports, &c. " do the natives the justice to allow, that the refrigerating principle, lately adopted by some of our leading physicians, owes its origin solely to the *ancient practice* of the Brahmans, or Hindoo priests, of whom the generality affect to be deeply skilled in pharmacy. I believe that, if taken in time, few fevers would be found to degenerate into typhus, and that very seldom any determination towards the liver, in acute cases, would occur, where the *refrigerating course to be adopted. Often have I known my servants, when attacked with fever, to *drink cold water* in abundance, and to apply *wetted cloths to their heads*; with great success. The *former* has generally lowered the pulse considerably, by throwing out a strong perspiration, while the *latter* has given immediate local relief."—Vol. 2. p. 308.

I can confirm the truth of this, by experience, acquired long before I knew any thing of this native practice, and to which I was led by the unconquerable headache, heat, and throbbing of the temples, which nothing but venesection and the cold ablutions above-mentioned, would completely allay.

Mr. Bruce describes a somewhat similar practice among the natives of Massuah, a very unhealthy island on the borders of Abyssinia.

" Violent fevers called the *Nedad*, make the principal figure in this fatal list, and generally terminate the third day in death. If the patient survives till the fifth day, he very often recovers, by drinking water only, and throwing a great quantity upon him, even in his bed, where he is permitted to lie without attempting to make him dry, or change his bed, till another deluge adds to the first." *Shaw's Abridgment, p.* 156. Cold water, cold cungee water, or either of these acidulated with tamarinds, chrystals of tartar, or nitrous acid, will be found the most grateful beverage. But it is necessary to remark, that, till the irritability of the stomach is allayed, however urgent may be the thirst, the patient should be restrained from drink, especially in any large quantities. The cold ablution over the surface of the body will help to mitigate the thirst, till the stomach is tranquilized.

Leeches succeeded by large and repeated blisters to the epigastric region, will be found a most valuable auxiliary to the above plan of treatment ; and where torpor in the lymphatic system of the abdomen is evinced by difficulty in affecting the mouth with mercury, the denuded surface should be dressed with mercurial ointment. With these means in use, I have generally awaited, with a kind of patient anxiety, the first symptoms of ptyalism ; and on the third morning I could frequently perceive a certain odour on the breath, prelusive of salivation. When this last came on *free*, I pronounced my patient to be secure.

But if no symptoms of saturation appeared, I have *then*, or indeed, if things wore an alarming aspect, I have sooner than this, either increased the doses of calomel, exhibited them at shorter intervals, or conjoined with them mercurial frictions. For if relief could not be procured on the third, fourth, or fifth day, the chance of recovery became smaller and smaller in proportion.

This relief sometimes preceded, sometimes succeeded ; but was generally synchronous with the visible or sensible effects of mercury on the constitution, as evinced by the gums or breath. A mild and uniform diaphoresis, a refreshing sleep, and the appearance of natural stools, were the usual indications of this happy change ; after which, as the ptyalism advanced, the train of morbid symptoms proportionally subsided, till at length the inability to eat, *in consequence of the soreness of the mouth*, became the principal complaint of the patient. Were I to go over the same ground again, I should be inclined to try a still more decisive system of depletion by blood-letting and purging, so as thereby to arrest the progress of the fever, even before the development of the mercurial action. But time and circumstances will so vary the features of this and other fevers, that different, and sometimes opposite modes of treatment must be adopted.

That there may be cases, wherein the use of wine, and even bark, is indispensable, I shall not attempt to deny. But the latter, in particular, I seldom had occasion to employ, except in cases of protracted convalescence ; or to prevent relapses at the full and change of the moon, when such accidents are very liable to happen.

I have only to remark further, that when this fever was combined with dysentery, an occurrence by no means unusual, the same treatment, with the exception of cold external applications, conducted equally to a happy termination.

As the object of this essay is unity, and its design, to convey as much information on each subject, in a small space as possible, it becomes a duty to notice in this place the opinions and practice of a very high medical authority in India—Dr. Balfour, whose abilities and experience entitle him to every respect. I shall endeavour to condense his doctrine and directions into as few pages as I can, referring to his *second* Treatise on Sol-lunar influence, (Edin. 1790,) where these are more explicitly developed than in any of his other publications.

Dr. B. considers the mild and regular intermittent, as well as the more violent and continued Bengal fevers, together with dysentery, as so many grades of the *" putrid intestinal remitting fever,"* all of which he pronounces to be *infectious.* He conceives that the contagion proceeds from putrefying or putrid bodies, and which, passing down with the saliva, corrupts the mucus of the stomach and intestines. That this putrid matter being absorbed, and carried into the circulation, gives rise to, and accounts for, the whole train of febrile symptoms. This is his theory, independent of " Sol-lunar Influence," which will be noticed hereafter.

With respect to the cure, he thinks that copious and continued purging would, in general, be sufficient to conduct mild cases to a successful issue ; but as we are liable to much deception, he advises that in these, as well as in the most violent fevers of Bengal, after *two days* purging with calomel and other cathartics, to begin, on the *third* morning, to "throw in" the bark in substance, so as to administer two ounces in the course of forty-eight hours. At the expiration of this period, the calomel is to be again repeated at night, and a laxative the next morning ; immediately after the operation of which, the bark is to be again reiterated for two days, and in the same manner as before. The purges and bark are thus to be alternated in exactly the above routine, till the disease is finally subdued. To give efficacy to this practice, a liberal use is to be made of opium, not only to keep the bark on the stomach, but to ease pain and procure rest.

With respect to those cases where there is *local affection,* Dr. B. only directs a superior degree of attention to be paid in guarding the body against cold, with occasional blisters and diaphoretics. In some rare cases, where the local affection is violent, he admits of bleeding, both general and local ; but all the other plans are to be pursued in the manner prescribed, without any regard to paroxysms, remissions, or exacerbations, whatever.—Fifteen years afterwards, however, Dr. B. appears to have remodelled his plan of treatment, as the following passage evinces—

" Considering." says he, " that obstructions of the liver very frequently show themselves, in the common fevers of this country, and may with great reason be suspected, in a certain degree, *in all,* we cannot hesitate to admit, as an essential and valuable principle, in the cure of fevers, *the introduction of mercury into the system, so as to affect the mouth in a moderate degree,* with the view of removing obstruction, or other morbid affections of the liver ; of obtaining natural secretions, and of its thus contributing, *with the other means* that have been described, to a speedy and permanent cure." *Preface to a collection of Treatises.*

I have thus given a fair view of two very different modes of treatment, (and likewise their combination,) in this dangerous disease. I have shown my own preference for one of them, and I think substantial reasons for such : but I do not wish to blindly condemn the others, because I did not find them successful,

He who treads over the same ground which I have done, will, in every probability, have ample opportunities of putting them all to the trial, and then he may decide on their merits. But I would recommend him not to be too sanguine, nor condemn a practice from a few failures. It has not been my lot to find intertropical fevers so very tractable as some medical officers have, or say they have, found them. Those indeed who are most conversant with disease at the bed-side of sickness are well aware that no fixed rules or general plan of treatment are applicable at all times in fever, or in almost any other disease. But although the *means* must vary, the *indications* may be always the same. Thus I conceive that in those times and places where bark and stimulants proved more successful than depletion in tropical fever, there was equally as great a *derangement in the balance of the circulation and excitability* as where venesection and purgatives were carried to the greatest extent. The great art indeed is to early ascertain the prevailing diathesis both of constitution and climate, and promptly apply the most appropriate Methodus Medendi.

I should be sorry to suspect, much less accuse, any of my professional brethren of *wilful* misrepresentation ; but when *young* medical men are setting forth their cures by a *new* remedy, we may at least be allowed to enter that remarkably significant, though apparently paradoxical caveat of Hippocrates, EXPERIENTIA FALLAX.

As the cold season approaches, the fever changes from an almost continued to a plainly remittent, and finally, in December, to an intermittent form. From this time, for two or three months, the climate of Bengal is cool and delightful ; the only diseases being visceral obstructions, the sequelæ of the preceding endemic.

It has already been remarked, that this fever, when epidemic among the natives, occasionally commits the most destructive ravages. But the assimilation of their constitutions to the climate, their singularly abstemious habits, and various other causes, concur to shield them, in general, from its violence, so that it appears, for the most part, among this class, as an intermittent, but often of great obstinacy.

I have alluded to the *refrigerating practice*, which they have employed time out of mind, in acute fevers : I shall now advert to some very efficacious native medicines, which they apply to the cure of this disease, especially when it manifests itself in the form of agues, which prove exceedingly troublesome to the inhabitants of villages scattered among the marshy, as well as hilly and jungly districts. Their first object is the complete evacuation of all bilious and sordid colluvies from the stomach and bowels. For this purpose they have recourse to a black purging salt—*Bit-Noben*, or *Cala Neemuck*, a solution of which in water is certainly one of the most nauseous potations that can well be conceived, having an abominable taste, and a flavour resembling rotten eggs, or sulphuretted hydrogen gas. This medicine proves eminently cathartic, and powerfully emulges the liver and its ducts, carrying off vast quantities of vitiated bile, and other offensive fecal matter from the intestinal canal. This being effected, the kernel of a seed, produced by a low, creeping kind of cow-itch, (Cœsalpina Bonducella,) called by the natives, *Kaut-Kullagee*, or *Catcaranja Nut*, is taken to complete the cure.

⹁The kernel is intensely bitter, and possesses the tonic or febrifuge powers of Peruvian bark, in a very high degree. But it has a manifest advantage over the latter ; for, instead of producing any constipating effects in the bowels, it, on the contrary, proves mildly laxative. It may be easily conceived that, in a tropical country, where the biliary system is so commonly deranged, such a qualification is of incalculable utility. One of the kernels pounded into a paste, with three or four corns of pepper, and taken three, four, or five times a day, in conjunction with the decoction of Cherettah, [Gentiana Cherayita,] is found so generally successful in curing intermittents, that it is adopted by many European practitioners ; and will probably, at no distant period, supersede entirely the bark, to which it seems infinitely preferable in a hot climate, on account of the aforesaid aperient quality.

The *Cherettah* is a species of gentian, indigenous in the mountainous [countries north of the Ganges, and is to be procured in every bazar throughout Bengal. It possesses all the properties ascribed to the gentiana lutea, and in a greater degree than are to be found in the latter root as it comes to us. The decoction of this herb forms a powerful auxiliary to the caranja nut, and their united efficacy in curing intermittents is undisputed.

CAUSES OF THE FEVER.

Drs. Lind and Clarke dwell much on the putrefying animal and vegetable substances left on the miry shores of the Hoogly by each retiring tide ; attributing a considerable share of malignity to the noxious exhalations arising from this source, during the intervals of high water, both by day and night. The argument is more specious than solid ; and perhaps it is not founded on accurate or discriminating observation.

During the months of August and September, for instance, when fevers rage with their greatest violence, the rivers are swelled to the summits of their banks by the inundation, and the volume of water disgorged into the ocean is so immense, that the stream is perfectly fresh, and the flood-tide scarcely felt at Calcutta ; consequently, the rise and fall are comparatively insignificant. But in May and the beginning of June, on the other hand, when the rivers are shrunk far within their autumnal boundaries ; when the heat is excessive ; and when the tides are so rapid, that the *bore*, as it is called, rushes up past Calcutta, sometimes with the amazing velocity of *twenty miles an hour*, not entirely stopping till it reaches Nia-serai, thirty five-miles above the capital ; then, indeed, at low water, each side of the river presents a broad shelving slope of mud and mire covered with vegeto-animal remains in all stages of putrefaction, and disengaging the most abominable stench,—yet no ill effects whatever are produced by such exhalations.

For the solution of this phenomenon, we must look to the tides themselves, which, sweeping along these shores, every flood and ebb, never allow sufficient time for the extrication of that noxious efflu-

vium which arises from the *stagnant surface* of marshes, either
partially covered, or just deserted by *annual* not *diurnal* inundations.
Such marshes, [and jungles which produce a similar effect,] spread
far and wide in every direction along the banks of this river, during,
and for some time subsequent to the rainy season ; to these, therefore,
and not to daily overflowed places, are we indebted for all the sickness
and mortality we so fatally experience.

Another circumstance may probably contribute its share in correcting these exhalations at the period alluded to.   During the inundation, the waters of this river are quite *fresh*, though turbid ; whereas,
in the dry season, when the tides are strong, a considerable proportion of *salt water* comes up every flood, and renders the stream, even
at Calcutta, so brackish, as to occasion smart bowel complaints among
those who drink of it at this time.   A mixture of salt water, with
fresh, therefore, does not, as was supposed by Sir John Pringle, *increase* the noxiousness of marshy exhalations ; on the contrary, we
find, in this instance, that they are quite harmless, while rising from
these extensive shores, when the water is considerably impregnated
with marine salt.   In respect to the marshes that run back from the
river, they cannot. *during the inundation*, be more subject to flux and
reflux than the river itself.   The shores of all inlets and minor
streams are under exactly similar circumstances to those I have stated of the Hoogly ; and finally, I may add, that it is the water of *inundations alone*, not tides, that ever bursts over the banks of the Ganges, to cover the adjoining plains ; consequently the *marshes* are not
subject to diurnal flux and reflux.   I have been the more particular
on this point, in order to set in a clear light the *validity* of these reasons which induced Dr. Lind, of Windsor, to read the recantation of
his medical faith in *lunar influence*, in favour of " *the increased effluvia
disengaged from the shores and neighbouring marshes at each retiring
spring tide*." Never was the fable of " dropping the substance to grasp
at the shadow" ' more completely exemplified than in this instance,
which shows that " second thoughts are *not always* best." I much wonder that the ingenious Dr. Balfour, while lamenting the defection of
of his quondam supporter, did not adduce this unanswerable refutation, among others, of Dr. Lind's hypothesis:

In so luxuriant a climate as that of Bengal, and on so fertile an al-
luvion as the Delta of the Ganges, we may well suppose, that every
spot, almost every particle of matter, teems with animal as well as
vegetable life.   As the scale of existence descends, in the animal
kingdoms, the amazing circle of reproduction and decay is perpetually trodden by myriads of animated beings, whose ephemeral vitality
has scarcely commenced, before it closes again in death ! No sooner
has the etherial spark — the " divinæ particula auræ," deserted its
tenement, than the *latter* is resolved, by the heat and moisture of the
climate, into its constituent materials, and formed without delay into
other compounds :—

" With ceaseless change the restless atoms pass
" From life to life, a transmigrating mass.

It is during this dissolution of animal and vegetable remains, preparatory to new combinations and successive reproduction, that a certain inexplicable something is extricated, which operates with such powerful and baleful influence on the functions of the human frame.

This exhalation is capable of concentration, or rather accumulation ; for when it is detained amid woods and jungles, as at this place, and especially during the rainy season, when there are no regular breezes to dissipate it, and when the beams of the sun are obscured, except at intervals, by dense clouds, it becomes exceedingly powerful, as the annual mortality too plainly proves.

That the exhalation of these miasmata, and their diffusion in the atmosphere should be greater during the heat of the day than at night, when the air is raw and cold, appears more than probable ; and yet an idea seems to prevail, that they arise from fens and marshes principally in the night. " The nature of an unhealthy, swampy soil," says Dr. Lind, " is such, that no sooner the sun-beams are withdrawn, than the *vapour emitted* from it renders the air raw, damp, and chilling in the most sultry climates.". It is difficult to imagine how dews *descend* and vapours *rise* at the same time.—Nevertheless, it is certainly true, that the stench emitted immediately after sunset, is much more perceptible to the senses than at any other period of the day. The reason of this is, that the shores and marshes *retain* their heat for some time *after* the rays of the sun are withdrawn, and consequently *continue* to emit vapours, which are not exhaled and diffused through the atmosphere, as by the sun and high temperature of the day ; they therefore meet the descending dews and cool air, condensing and forming a thick fog, which hovers over the swamps, accompained by a noxious and disagreeable odour. To this we must add, that the miasmata exhaled during the day, in all probability descend with the dews of the evening, and by meeting and combining with those that *continue* to be disengaged from their source, must form a concentration highly capable of affecting the constitution. We accordingly find, that four out of five of those who suffer, are attacked, or receive the deleterious principle, at the period above-mentioned.

Experience has shown that *marsh* effluvium, though by no means so limited as *human*, does not occupy a wide range ; at least, it becomes innoxious at a certain distance from its source, in consequence of dilution. The circumstance mentioned by Dr. J. Hunter, and confirmed by subsequent observations—namely, that " the difference of a few feet in *height* gives a comparative security to soldiers quartered in the same building," will be accounted for by the supposition which I have already stated, viz. *That as the miasms exhaled during the day descend in the evenings, they become more and more concentrated ; till, meeting the exhalations from the still reeking marshes, a dense stratum of highly impregnated atmosphere is formed close to the surface of the earth.* Hence the superior degree of salubrity in the *upper* ranges of buildings ; and, on the contrary, the extreme danger of sleeping on the ground in such places ; many instances of which are recorded in the writings of Lind, Bontius, &c.

I am the more inclined to believe that vegeto-animal miasmata des-

too destructive to human health and life ; and the system is *then*, too disposed to its reception, in consequence of the exhaustion produced by the heat and labours of the day, and the torpor induced by the coldness of the evenings.

This reasoning will be illustrated and confirmed by the following authentic particulars. In the month of November, 1804, two parties of men, belonging to his Majesty's ship Tremendous, were employed on shore, at the Island of Madagascar ; one party, during the night, filling water, the other cutting wood during the day. Four of the night party were attacked with the endemic fever of the country, and three of them died. The whole of the day party escaped the fever, though exposed to an intense sun, in the laborious occupation of wood-cutting.

About two years after this, his Majesty's ship Sceptre in the same place, and upon a similar occasion, experienced a still greater disaster among her watering or night party, to whom the mortality was confined. Some interesting particulars respecting this fatal occurrence, I shall give in the words of the surgeon, Mr. Neill.

"The fever which attacked our watering parties at the Island of Madagascar, bears a striking resemblance to the endemic fever of the west ;—like that too, it was not a contagious disease, of which we had the most cogent proofs, and corroborated' what we witnessed at a former period. I believe that the exciting cause of this disease was confined to the site of the watering place, as no person was affected upon the wooding party, though *constantly exposed through the day*. The deleterious effects of nocturnal exposure were particularly exemplified here, by the disease raging most violently among the marines, who were on shore at night for the protection of the casks, and to whom the mortality was confined. The fever made its appearance among some of the same party who did *not* pass the night on shore, but in them it was infinitely milder, though similar in type and general symptoms. The watering place was encompassed from the sea by an amphitheatre of hills ; and in nearly the centre of this ran the rivulet from which we filled, situated in a *marshy plain*, surrounded with some trees of the palm kind, and a thicket of *jungle*. The wooding place, on the other hand, was a *dry sandy soil*, though standing equally low, and covered with brush-wood, jungle, &c. in the same manner as the other. As the more minute features of the disease are described in the journal, I shall only remark, that it exhibited something of the remittent type, inasmuch as the paroxysms were more conspicuous and violent on alternate days; and on the intermediate, the system seemed less oppressed and more tranquil, with a different cast of features in the countenance ; but there never was any thing like an apyrexia. The general treatment adopted in these cases, and which the journey developes, consisted in blood-letting, purging, and exciting ptyalism ; the pre-eminence of which practice, several years experience in this country has amply confirmed. My sentiments have been so often expressed on venesection, that I need not repeat them. With respect to purgatives, I have always observed the greatest relief to follow, when they took full effect. That

they are beneficial in every stage of the disease, I infer from this ;—
that the pulse, from being depressed, weak, and void of energy, becomes open, energetic, and bounding to the surface with a corresponding animation in the countenance, after copious catharsis, even in the
last stage of debility.

The next and only remedy, where blood-letting and purging do not
check the disease at once, in its infancy, is mercury to excite ptyalism. I say ptyalism, for *soreness of the mouth* will not secure the patient in this endemic. In many of the *fatal* terminations, the mouth
was slightly affected ; but we never were able to excite ptyalism.
Wherever this last could be induced, a revolution, as it were, in the
whole train of morbid symptoms instantly succeeded, and a healthy
train supplied their place ! This revolution was most strikingly
evinced in the functions of the bowels, by the evacuations becoming,
all at once, copious and feculent : a circumstance, which previous to
ptyalism, no purgative, even of the most drastic nature, could effect.''

Although the latter part of this document is foreign to the subject
for which it was introduced, yet I trust it will be considered interesting. It is satisfactory to me, since it strongly corroborates what I
have advanced lately on the treatment of the Bengal endemic, both
in respect to bleeding and ptyalism ; the former being rather *heterodox* in India. I have only to remark, in reference to the striking
coincidence of our practical views, that the above document was never penned for my inspection, nor that of the public. The sensible
and well informed author of it, (Mr. Neill,) is alive, and can contradict any misrepresentation of his sentiments.

I shall here observe, once for all, that the foregoing remarks will
equally apply to all other documents and narratives introduced into
this essay, in addition to my own personal observations. They are
strictly authentic ; being the spontaneous records of facts, comme-
morated without preconceived theory or preconcerted design. I
need not say how much their value is enhanced by this consideration.

In the account of the Batavian endemic, some other striking instances, corroborative of the opinions here advanced, will be related.
In the mean time, the above examples will be sufficient to justify the
rules I have laid down, and put future navigators on their guard,
where disease and danger lurk in concealment.

And here I cannot help noticing the apathy or impolicy, which still
allows Diamond Harbour, the principal anchorage of our Indiamen,
to continue backed and flanked by woods, jungles, and marshes, to
the annual destruction of one-fourth of the crews of such ships as
load and unload at this place ! The objection to clearing the Sunderbunds, has been founded on the idea of their presenting an impenetrable barrier to the incursions of an enemy from that quarter ;
but the government does not seem to be aware, that to secure us from
a *domestic* foe, it is by no means necessary, *in this instance*, to throw
open the way to a *foreign*. A semicircle of cleared and drained
ground, even of six miles in radius, [not a thirtieth part of the Sunderbunds, and scooped as it were, out of their centre,] would sufficiently protect the anchorage and warehouses of Diamond Harbour,

from the baleful · influence of those exhalations we have been describing.

That the woods and jungles might be cleared, admits of no doubt ;
and that the country round Diamond Point might either be drained,
overflowed, or submitted to the flux and reflux of the tides, any one
of which measures would afford comparative security, can hardly be
denied. To add to this security, one or two narrow semicircular belts
of wood might be interposed between Diamond Harbour and the confines of the cleared space, to arrest any effluvium disengaged from
the surrounding wilds or marshes, and conveyed by the breezes towards the aforesaid anchorage. All writers agree, that marsh miasmata, although much less limited in their rage than the matter of contagion, would be perfectly harmless after traversing a much shorter
route than that proposed ; but where native labour can be so easily
procured ; indeed, where the convicts alone would be equal to the
undertaking in a very few years ; and finally, when it is considered,
that this salutary step opens not any facility to the irruption of an
enemy on the southern frontier of Bengal, we can hardly doubt that
the attention of the company will, ere long, be directed to so important a measure. Till then we can only remark, that the further
from shore, and the lower down the river ships lie, so much more
healthy will be the crews. On this account Saugur Road is more
eligible, in regard to salubrity, than Kedgeree ; and the latter much
less dangerous than Culpee or Diamnod Harbour. This was amply
proved by the comparative mortality in the Caroline, Howe, and
Medusa frigates. The two latter, by anchoring higher up than the
former, lost at least six times as many men, from fevers and fluxes.
Indeed, one was obliged to take a cruise to sea, and the other to retreat back to Saugur Roads, to avoid depopulation ! Some suggestions
will be given hereafter in regard to the means of obviating the
effects of marsh effluvium, even at Diamond Harbour, the focus of
this destructive principle.

In what manner, or through what channel it is conveyed to the
sensorium, so as to produce its effects on the constitution, we are
nearly ignorant. A general idea prevails, that the stomach is the
medium through which the matter of contagion acts ; and, by analogy, that marsh miasmata take the same course. But when we consider, that at each inspiration, the atmosphere impregnated with this
principle is largely applied to the delicate texture of the lungs, it is
not difficult to conceive, that it may pass into the blood, [if it is in
any case absorbed,] as readily as oxygen. There are, besides, the
schneiderian, and other membranes of the nares and fauces, to which
it must have constant access, while there is but one way for it to pass
into the stomach, viz. along with the saliva or food. Further, when
we see this principle, in a concentrated state, produce fever in a
very few hours, with high delirium, can we suppose that it enters
the system by the circuitous route of the alimentary canal and lacteals ? If it be said that it acts through the medium of the nerves of
the stomach, why not through that of the olfactory, which is a shorter
road ? Indeed, from a near view of its *effects*, there is every reason

to suppose that the brain and nervous system suffer the first impression and shock. To those *effects*, then, we are to direct our attention.

I believe it is nearly an unanimous opinion, at present, that both marsh and human effluvia are directly sedative or debilitating in their nature. Dr. Rush, indeed, uses the term "stimulus of contagion," in almost every page of his work on Yellow Fever ; but like the more celebrated "stimulus of necessity," it may be quietly laid in the "tomb of all the Capulets." By Dr. Jackson, the cause of fever is compared to electricity. "It seems to accumulate in the system by a regular but unknown process : in a certain state of accumulation, it seems to explode in a manner similar to the explosions of electricity."* The delirium and violent action early apparent in the jungle fever, might countenance the idea of a stimulus, and that the subsequent debility was of the *indirect* kind. I have heard this opinion maintained on the spot, by medical gentlemen ; but if we narrowly inspect the train of morbid symptoms, we find more of *irregular* than *increased* action ; more of apparent than real strength. If we carefully observe the delirious patient writhing and struggling under the first impression of this cause, we find the efforts not only momentary and less effective than healthy exertions, but accompanied even at the instant, and immediately succeeded by tremor and other marks of debility. The premonitory symptoms too, are all indicative of decreased sensorial energy. The mind is wavering and unsteady ; the appetite languid ; the secretions, particularly the biliary, diminished ; and the bowels torpid. Notwithstanding the determined phraseology of Dr. Rush, therefore, we may still adhere to the opinion of the venerable Cullen, that marsh, as well as human effluvium, is *sedative*. Dr. Jackson, indeed, will not allow it to be either stimulant or sedative, but a kind of *irritant ;* yet he gradually slides into the admission of its sedative nature : "It however appears, from the most general view of things, that the febrile cause is a cause of irritation, disturbing, but *not increasing* in a natural manner, the action of the moving fibre. On the contrary, interrupting, impeding, and as it were, *suspending* the operations essential to health and life ; by which means the expression of its effects principally consists in *debility and impaired* energy."†

The space of time which intervenes between the application of this poison to the system and its ostensible operation in the form of fever, depends on the degree of its concentration, and the predisposition of the patient. It will, for instance, be found in some places so powerful, that a man in perfect health, by remaining on shore during the night, in marshy situations, and wet or autumnal seasons, shall have the fever violently the next day, and die on the third or fourth. On the other hand, it may be applied in so dilute a state, as to require eighteen, twenty, or even thirty days,‡ to bring on fever ; and even then, perhaps, only in consequence of some of the nume-

---

* Outlines of Fever, p. 247.
† Outlines of Fever, p. 253.
‡ Dr. Jackson says two months, and Dr. Bancroft nine or ten.

rous predisposing or *auxiliary* causes concurring to enable the *original* to develope itself. If we take the medium of these two extremes, we shall have the ordinary period, viz. 'twelve or fourteen days, which elapses between the reception of vegeto-animal miasmata into the body, and their manifestation, in the shape of actual disease.

` We see, then, this important agent greatly varying in force ; and from standing occasionally the unaided *principal*,—the "instar omnium," in the production of fever, dwindle away till it can scarcely be distinguished, at least not prominently so, among the train of *auxiliaries*.

Such being the case, is it not probable that where the *latter* are numerous or powerful, they may, in some instances induce the aforesaid disease, without the assistance of marsh exhalation ?—See a valuable train of observations on this subject, in the Section on Yellow Fever of the West Indies, in a subsequent part of this work. , ʃ

PREDISPOSING CAUSES.

We now come to the predisposing causes, which are entitled to an equal degree of attention with that which has been bestowed on the remote, or exciting.

These may be divided into mental and corporeal. Of the former, none are so conspicuous as the *depressing passions ;* and of these Dr. Clarke informs us that FEAR produced the most striking and sudden effects, in aiding the remote cause of fever. This may, in some measure, account for the ravages which the yellow fever commits among those newly arrived Europeans, who are prepossessed with the idea and dread of this terrible scourge.

I have, indeed, remarked that most of those, who were of a timid disposition, and easily alarmed at the prevalence of the endemic diseases of the country, fell under their influence sooner than those of a contrary temperament. But grief, disappointment, and chagrin were the depressing passions which universally induced the most decided and unequivocal predisposition to disease. I saw many strong and melancholy instances of this among that part of our crew, which we impressed within sight of their own shores, and probably of their own habitations, when we were commencing our voyage to India. They were among the first and worst cases which I had under my care, and afforded ample proofs, that mental despondency can accelerate the attack, and render difficult the cure of intertropical fevers in particular. I have since seen the influence of this predisposing cause on a large scale ;—not on the banks of the Ganges, but much nearer home—on the banks of the Scheldt.

When our army lay entrenched under the walls of Flushing, without any other defence from the sun, the rains, and the dews, than some brushwood or straw ;—generally, indeed, with the humid earth for their beds and the canopy of heaven for their curtains ; still, with all these disadvantages, the animating prospect of success, the mental energy inspired by *hope*, united with corporeal activity, kept the whole army in health. When Flushing surrendered, however, and another object was not *instantly* held out for pursuit or attainment, a fatal pause took place, and a kind of torpor, or rather exhaustion ensued, during which, the remote cause of fever, viz. vegeto-animal miasmata, began to make some impression. But when from the ramparts of Batz, we clearly discover with our glasses a strong boom crossing the Scheldt from Fort Lillo,—the surrounding country in a state of inundation, and various other insuperable obstacles between us and the "*ulterior objects*" of the expedition;—then, indeed, the depressing passions, and some other predisposing or exciting causes communicated a fearful activity to marsh effluvium, which rivalled in its effects, any thing that has been seen in tropical climates !

It is an old complaint, that the medical topography, and healthy or unhealthy seasons of a country, are too often neglected in military and naval operations. Yet one would suppose that within sixteen or eighteen hours' communication of London, every medical and political expedient would have been speedily devised and applied, on such an emergency as this. But certain it is, that the army did not avail itself of some local advantages that presented themselves among these noxious islands. Walcheren, for instance, is bounded all the way round from Flushing by West Chapel, nearly to camp Vere—two-thirds of its circumference, by a chain of sand hills, from twenty to thirty feet in elevation above the level of the interjacent plains. These hills were not only dry, but open to the westerly winds which blew from the sea, and were then very prevalent. On these, therefore, had the soldiers, who *continued* in Walcheren after the fall of Flushing, been *tented*, the elevated site, combining with other local peculiarities, would in all probability, have kept them entirely out of the range of those exhalations which covered the country below.

On the other hand, although Beveland did not present such a favourable situation to the rest of the army, yet had they been provided with *tents*, the numerous mounds or embankments, which not only defend the island from the highest rise of the Scheldt, but intersect the country in every possible direction, frequently planted on each side with trees, and raised twelve or fourteen feet above the surface of the soil, would have afforded excellent encampments, where the men under the immediate inspection of their officers, would have been secured from intemperance and other irregularities, the inevitable consequences of being quartered in towns and villages, often in churches, barns, and other damp, unhealthy habitations throughout Walcheren and Beveland. But unfortunately, *tents* were not considered a necessary part of the baggage on this expedition. The French general, too, having opened the sluices, and *partially inundated* the country round Flushing, increased the force of the endemic. Indeed, the road leading from the last mentioned place to Middleburgh, might at this time vie, in respect to insalubrity, with any through the pontine fens of Italy. Lenity towards the *inhabitants* arrested the progress of the inundation before it was complete ; policy in guarding the health of *our own army*, would perhaps have suffered it to continue

9

till the cessation of the autumnal heats, and the commencement of cold weather and frost.

Nothing could more clearly prove the limited range of marsh effluvium, than the contrast between the health of the navy and that of the army. Although the ships were distributed all along the shores of Walcheren and Beveland, from Fushing to Batz, most of them within a cable's length of the banks, yet no sickness occurred, except among such parts of the crews as were much employed on shore, and remained there during the nights. Most officers of ships, and many of the men, were in the habit of making excursions through all parts of the islands by day, with complete immunity from fever. The night was here, as in sultry climates, the period of danger.

One more remark shall close this digression. We all remember the popular, or rather political outcry, that was made about the scarcity of bark : had the lancet, aided by calomel, and occasionally by jalap, been judiciously, but boldly· and decisively employed, the physicians of London and Edinburgh would not perhaps, since that period. have been so often consulted for infarctions and obstructions in the liver and spleen, with many other melancholy sequelæ of that destructive fever!

But to return. One would suppose that in a tropical climate, where nature is ever arrayed in her gayest livery, the cloudless skies above, and exuberant fertility around, would conspire to impart a degree of elasticity, (if I am allowed the term,) and exhilaration to the mind, similar to what we feel in Europe, at the approach of spring or summer. The reverse of this is the case. The animal spirits are in general, below par ; and the same cause of grief or disappointment, which in England would be borne with philosophical resignation, or perhaps indifference, will, in India, greatly predispose to all the diseases of the country, and very probably terminate the mortal career of the unhappy object.

The following melancholy facts are strikingly illustrative of this remark. His Majesty's ship Russel, (74,) sailed from Madras on the 22d October, 1806, and arrived at Batavia on the 27th November ; the crew healthy, and their minds highly elated with the sanguine expectations of surprising the Dutch squadron there. Such, however, was their sudden disappointment, and concomitant mental dejection, on missing the object of their hopes, that they began immediately to fall ill, ten, twelve, or fourteen, per day, till nearly 200 men were laid up with *scurvy*, scorbutic fluxes, and hepatic complaints ! Of these, upwards of 30 died before they got back to Bombay, and more than 50 were sent to the hospital there. The Albion did not fare better—the Powerful fared worse : so that, in these three ships only, in the short space of a few months, *full one hundred men died on board*, and double that number were sent to hospitals, many of whom afterwards fell victims to the diseases specified ; aggravated, and in a great measure engendered, by mental despondency.

Numerous are the instances of a similar nature, though on a smaller scale, which I could relate ; but the above specimen is sufficient.

The converse of this position is equally surprising : thus, success or good fortune will as forcibly counteract, as the contrary will predispose to, the malignant effects of climate. A familiar example will elucidate this.—Two ships, under equal circumstances, sail from Bombay, on a five months' cruise off the Isle of France, One of them takes a valuable prize, while the other, with every effort and, vigilance, is quite unsuccessful. The minds of the former crew are now perpetually employed in " building castles in the air," and forming the most extravagant anticipations of enjoyment on their return to port. The ship's company, without the aid of a single bottle of lime juice, or pot of spruce, will come back to Bombay at the end of the cruise in health. Not so the other : chagrin, envy, (for, after all the *poetical* portraits that are drawn of our noble tars, they are both envious and jealous at times, like other folks,) and various depressing passions, show themselves here, in the ugly shapes of scurvy, ulcers, and fluxes ; so that, in spite of all the artificial checks from lemon juice, sugar, porter, and even NOPAL itself, they are forced to Madagascar for refreshments, or else return with the other ship to Bombay, in a deplorable condition.

Here, however, the scene shifts again ; for Hygeia is as fickle as Fortuna. The crew of the successful ship having shared their prize-money,

" Balnea—Vina—Venus,"

become the order of the day ; and, for a short time, they are at the summit of human happiness ! But in a few weeks, on *leaving* port, this ship's company will exhibit as long a list of fevers, dysenteries, and venereals, as the other did of scurvies, ulcers, and fluxes, on *arriving*. Thus prize-money, or rather the hope of prize-money, is one of the most potent antidotes to disease among sailors at sea, but the most certain bane of their health on shore.

To return. This mental despondency may be attributed partly to physical, and partly to moral causes. I have already hinted that derangements in the *hepatic* and *digestive*, very soon affect the *mental* functions ; so, on the other hand, the depressing passions speedily derange the biliary secretion, digestion, and peristaltic motion of the intestines, consequently disposing the liver, stomach, and alimentary canal, to disease, as well as inducing general debility throughout the system. This sufficiently accounts for the phænomenon ; but it is also to be considered, that grief and disappointment must be, *cæteris paribus*, more poignant in India than in England ; since the loss of friends or relatives are more felt in proportion to the small number we possess ; and frustrated expectations will, of course, be more galling on account of the previous sanguine hopes which always accompany a foreign, and particularly an Indian speculation. We may therefore lay it down as an axiom, that in a tropical climate, the depressing passions above alluded to operate more immediately on those organs which, under all circumstances, are the principal sufferers in the diseases of the country ; viz. that they diminish the mental energies, or sensorial power, and impair the functions of the liver, stomach, and intestinal canal.

Within the torrid zone, philosophy seems to direct her influence, and reason its arguments, in vain, against these powerful disorders of the mind! Their frigid tenets are more efficacious beneath the gloomy skies of Europe. Religion, indeed, frequently asserts her superiority here, as well as elsewhere; and in conjunction with some pursuit or employment, mental or corporeal, will be found the best shield against the demon of despair, and, ultimately, the pangs of disease.

The destructive effects of intemperance, as a predisposing cause, are equally conspicuous, and I might say peculiar, in a tropical climate ; for the injuries it occasions in Europe, great as they are, bear no proportion to those which we witness in the East or West Indies. Whether spiritous and vinous potations act as stimulants or sedatives, or both in succession, we need not stop to inquire, since the final result is universally allowed to be debility. From the temporary increase of excitement in the system, and energy in the circulation, it is not impossible that the biliary secretion is for a short time augmented, and of course vitiated, by strong drink. This supposition is strengthened by the diarrhœa crapulosa which we frequently observe succeeding a debauch. But the great mischief seems to arise from the torpor communicated to the liver, through paralysis of its ducts, by which the secretion of healthy bile is not only greatly diminished in quantity, as well as obstructed, but deteriorated in quality ; and hence the way is paved for fever, dysentery, and hepatitis.

The debility of the stomach, too, occasioned by the climate, is further increased by inebriety ; and this atony is readily communicated to the liver, which bears the onus of disease in all hot climates.

The truth of these observations is amply exemplified among the crews of ships, when they have liberty to spend a few days at Calcutta, or go ashore, indeed, in any part of India, where intoxicating liquors are to be procured. During the indirect debility succeeding these debauches, the endemic of the country or port makes rapid strides among these deluded victims, converting what they erroneously conceived an indulgence, into the greatest evil that could have befallen them.

For obvious reasons, intemperance in eating is little less destructive than the other species ; since an overloaded stomach, which has previously been weakened, will of itself excite a temporary fever, and consequently predispose to that of the country.

That fatigue, especially during the heat of the day, becomes an exciting cause of this fever, is well known to those who have observed its effects among the seamen employed in stowing the saltpetre, or loading and unloading the company's ships at Diamond Harbour. Where those laborious occupations *must* be carried on by Europeans, they certainly should not take place between eleven o'clock and four in the afternoon ; the interval ought to be dedicated to dinner, rest, and light work under the awnings.

A very common, and powerfully predisposing cause of this fever, has seldom been adverted to, though highly deserving of attention —I mean those licentious indulgences which are but too easily procured, and too frequently practised on the banks of the Ganges, and in most other parts of India—I may say of all tropical climates ! 'I have seen many melancholy instances of their pernicious effects ; and therefore it is incumbent on commanding officers of ships, to keep as strict a curb as possible on the men, during the sickly season, and on no account whatever allow them to straggle through the villages, where inebriety, and that too from a very deleterious species of drink, is an inseparable accompaniment to the illicit amours abovementioned. In every region 'virtue is its own reward ; but within the torrid zone, its breach is more signally punished than in any other.

The last predisposing cause which I shall mention, is the influence of the sun and moon. However sceptical professional men in Europe may be, in regard to planetary influence in fevers, &c. it is too plainly perceptible between the tropics, to admit of a doubt. I have not only observed it in others, but felt it in my own person in India when labouring under the effects of obstructed liver.

It is a certain fact, that if we attend minutely to the state of our own frames and sensations, two, if not three slight febrile paroxysms, may be detected in the course of each diurnal revolution of the earth, independent of those which succeed full meals. In high health we may not be able to distinguish more than the nocturnal paroxysm, which commences about seven or eight o'clock in the evening, and is not over till two in the morning. This is the cause of that furred tongue, which all may observe on getting out of bed, more or less, according to the degree of the paroxysm ; and it likewise explains the evening exacerbation of fevers in general. But valetudinarians will feel, about mid-day, another slight febrile accession, similar to the preceding, except in degree ; and in some instances a third, but still slighter one, is felt between eight and ten o'clock in the morning. In India I have felt the two former very distinctly, and particularly at full and change,'when I used to be affected with tremor, a sense of weakness, and sometimes a dimness of vision about mid-day, succeeded by a certain quickness and irritability of pulse, which would continue for an hour or two. I was so well aware of this, that I made a point of keeping myself quiet, and as cool as possible, about the abovementioned period ; since any exertion at that time, in the heat of the sun especially, increased the symptoms which I have described, in a very considerable degree. I believe this is the case with most people, more or less, and accounts for the general complaint of faintness about twelve o'clock in the day, and which is relieved by a glass of wine or other refreshment. I found the cold bath, where I could conveniently apply it, almost entirely prevent this paroxysm, and hence the utility of bathing when the sun is at his greatest altitude. At those times too, my sleep was broken and disturbed with dreams, and a feverish heat towards midnight, all of which would go off about two o'clock in the morning. This accords with the general remark, that the morning repose is the soundest, and that if dreams do then occur, they are more distinct and better remembered than those which take place during the nocturnal paroxysm. It is very natural to attribute such regular and periodical changes or feelings in the human frame, to the revolutions of the planet we inhabit, and the influence' of the sun and moon. That this influence predisposes to, or exacerbates the paroxysms of fever, in India and other tropical climates, is incontestibly proved by daily observation, as the publications of the ingenious and respectable Dr. Balfour evince.

The difference between this and the yellow fever of the West has been always noticed, but, in my opinion, never adequately accounted for; and the investigation of this discordance is certainly interesting, since the same general causes, both remote and predisposing, are allowed to operate equally or nearly so, in both hemispheres. First, then, let me observe, that the average space which a ship traverses, between Spithead and the Ganges, is 14,000 miles. Secondly, that in this voyage we run twice through the tropics; first from Cancer to Capricorn, and afterwards from Capricorn back to Cancer again; besides a great deal of oblique sailing in the vicinity of the southern tropic. During the period of time neccessary for this performance, the human frame has the best possible means of accommodating itself to the change of climate : viz. a more steady range of temperature, and of a higher degree than that of the ultimate destination ; together with an atmosphere untainted by any noxious exhalation. In addition to these, the regular hours imposed on all classes, in ships proceeding eastward, the consequent habits of temperance acquired, and lastly, the paucity of luxuries which pretty generally attends a protracted voyage, especially the last weeks, sometimes months of it, all combine to lower the tone of the constitution, and impart to it a considerable degree of assimilation before the period of danger arrives. Thus the stomach and bowels will become somewhat accustomed to the increased secretion of bile, and even this last will be less profuse, as we are more inured to the high ranges of temperature, following the same laws and sympathizing with the perspiration.

Let us contrast this with a transatlantic voyage. The European, " full of flesh and blood," [to use a vulgar, but not inapplicable expression,] embarks for the West Indies, in a transport or other vessel, where regularity and order are by no means conspicuous.* As he is under little control, and generally supplies a great proportion of his own fare, he endeavours to guard against any deficiency in that important point ; in short, good English viands smoke daily on the festive board, while sufficient potation—" to keep the pores open," is steadily applied ; till after a few weeks run, he is launched at once into a tropical climate, and immediately landed, " with all his imperfections on his head." It is true that, when ashore, the facility of procuring the " *diffusible stimuli*" need not be much insisted on, since unfortunately, the *arrack* of the east is equally easy of access to the men, as the *rum* of the west. But unquestionably the bad effect will be greater in the latter case, for the reasons adduced above.

With respect to officers, and other genteel classes of society, on

* I allude principally to troops.

landing in the western world, they are destitute of many powerful shields which are pretty generally interposed between Europeans of the east and the burning climate. In the former case, we may look in vain for the palankeen, the budgerow, the punka, the tatty, and the light, elegant, and cool vestments of India, together with the numerous retinue of domestics, anticipating every wish, and performing every office, that may save the exertion of their employers. The untravelled cynic may designate these luxuries by the contemptuous epithet of " Asiatic effeminacy ;" but the medical philosopher will be disposed to regard them as rational enjoyments, or rather as salutary precautions, rendered necessary by the great difference between a temperate and torrid zone. Nor are these *dulcia vitæ* the exclusive property of the higher classes in India. The European soldier is permitted to intermarry with the native Hindostannee nymph ; and, whether married or not, he has generally a domiciliated *chere amie*, who cooks, washes, and performs every menial drudgery for *massa*, in health, besides becoming an invaluable nurse when he is overtaken by sickness.

Under the privation of these advantages, can we wonder at the effects, which exposure to all those causes, described as operating in Bengal, must produce on the full, plethoric habit of an Englishman, only four or five weeks from his native skies, before he debarks on the burning shores, or insalubrious swamps and vallies of our western colonies.

The more prominent distinctive features of the transatlantic fever, yellow skin and black vomit, [though by the bye they are frequently *absent* in this, and *present* in the eastern fever,] may I think be attributed to the more violent action in the hepatic system, and superabundant secretion of *vitiated* bile, which, by the ceaseless vomiting, is thrown out in deluges on the duodenum and stomach, deranging their structure, while regurgitation into the blood suffuses the skin. " On the first and second days of the disorder," says Dr. Rush, " many patients puked from half a pint to nearly a quart, of green or yellow bile. Four cases came under my notice, in which black bile was discharged on the *first* day. Three of these cases recovered. I ascribed their recovery to the bile not having yet acquired acrimony enough to *inflame or corrode the stomach.* There was frequently, on the fourth or fifth day, a discharge of matter from the stomach, like the grounds of coffee. I believed it first to be a modification of *vitiated bile*, but I was led afterwards to *suspect* that it was produced by a *morbid secretion in the liver*, and effused from it into the stomach."——" That the bile may become extremely acrid in this stage of the disorder, is evident from several observations and experiments. Dr. Physick's hand was *inflamed* in consequence of its being *wetted* by bile in this state, in dissecting a body." p. 54. " I am not certain that the black matter which was discharged in the *last stage* of the disorder was *always* vitiated or acrid bile. It was probably, in *some cases*, the matter which was formed in consequence of the mortification of the stomach." p. 55.

In respect to the yellow colour, Dr. Rush is fully convinced that it is attributable to bile. " From these facts it is evident," says he, " that the yellowness, *in all cases*, was the effect of an absorption and mixture of the bile with the blood." p. 70.—*Vide Hunter and Bancroft*.

It is not meant to infer from hence, that the febrific miasms are exactly the same in the east and in the west ; experience proves the contrary, as will be shown in the Section on Batavian endemic. I only mean to say, that the expression of their effects, on the biliary organs in particular, may be considerably modified by the circumstances above detailed. Neither do I suppose that in the last stages of black vomit, the matter ejected is bilious ; but I am confident that the gastric derangement is in a great measure occasioned by the deluges of acrid, vitiated bile, poured from the liver on the stomach, during the vomiting in the early stages of the disease.* Hence, to check the gastric irritability early, is a most desirable object.

The stomachs of newly arrived Europeans in the west will, for the reasons detailed above, be much more liable also to take on inflammatory action. This, and the more violent orgasm in the hepatic system, appear to be the principal distinctive features in which the fevers of the two hemispheres differ ; and are, I think, referrible to the aforesaid causes. These considerations also account for the more decisive system of depletion which is necessary in the western endemic ; and for the inutility of mercury till the inflammatory action is completely controlled. In the eastern hemisphere, on the other hand, where the biliary apparatus is very generally in a state of derangement, anterior to febrile attacks, the union of mercury with venesection is a rational measure.

In respect to the *yellow colour*, in the highly concentrated endemic fever of the western world, there is reason to doubt its cause being a simply *bilious* suffusion. It would almost appear to be a broken down state of the blood—or a stagnation in the capillary system, such as we see after contusions.

A practical point of much importance remains to be noticed ; namely, whether or not the fevers in question are contagious. It is lamentable to observe the discordance of medical opinions on a question that, at first sight, might seem so easily determined. Thus, Clarke, Lind, Balfour, Chisholm, Blane, and Pym, are positive in the affirmative ; while, on the other hand, Hunter, Jackson, Moseley, Miller, Bancroft, and Burnett, are as decided in the negative !

Yet here, as in most other instances, truth lies between the extremes. As far as my own observations and judgment could guide me, I have been led to conclude, that the endemic fevers alluded to, are *not* contagious, till a certain number of patients are confined together, under peculiar circumstances, when the effluvia *may* render

* The above observations are confirmed by the dissections of Dr. Ramsay, at Bellevue Hospital, in 1803. (Vide Edinb. Med. and Surg. Jour. No. xxxii, page 423.) He traced, in numerous instances, the *black vomit* to the gall-bladder and hepatic ducts ; and to this acrid discharge he attributes, in a great degree, the derangement in the stomach and bowels, which give rise to the *bloody vomit* subsequently.

them so. If, for instance, a man is seized with fever, from greater predisposition, or from greater exposure to the causes enumerated, than his companions, he will not communicate the disease to another, who may sleep even in the same chamber, where common cleanliness is observed. But on the other hand, if great numbers are attacked, nearly at the same time, and confined in the sick birth of a ship or ill ventilated apartments, in hammocks, cots, or filthy beds, it is possible that a contagious atmosphere may be formed, [without an attention to cleanliness and ventilation, scarcely compatible, or at least hardly to be expected, in such situations,] which spreads a disease *wearing the livery of the prevailing endemic*, but having a dangerous character superadded, namely, the power of reproducing itself in other subjects, both independent of, and in conjunction with, the original endemical causes.* This circumstance reconciles the jarring evidences which have long kept the public opinion in suspense. It has been urged, that we ought to err on the safe side, by considering it contagious, and guarding accordingly by early separation. But this plan is not without its disadvantages, and, if I am not greatly mistaken, I have seen it produce what it was meant to prevent ; viz. by confining all who had any symptoms of the fever in one place ; where, as on board a ship in a tropical, or any climate, it is exceedingly difficult, if not impossible, to prevent the generation of an infectious atmosphere, and the impregnation of bed-clothes, &c. with the effluvia from the diseased secretions and excretions of the patients. On the other hand, I have seen both sides of the main deck nearly filled with fevers of the country, where screens and other means of separation could not be obtained, or rather, were not insisted on, and yet no bad effects followed ; while under similar circumstances, where there were fewer sick, and all imaginable pains taken to insulate them, attendants have been seized, and other symptoms, indicative of contagion and virulence, have arisen, which, while they seem fully to justify the precautions used, were probably owing to them alone. These hints may not be entirely unworthy of attention, inasmuch as they show us how easily we may be deceived, and how positive we may be in our errors. They likewise show that free ventilation and cleanliness may in general be confided in, between the tropics, where seclusion is inconvenient or impracticable ; and that *separation of the sick from one another*, as far as possible, is a duty not less incumbent, than that of cutting off the communication between them and the healthy. There is this advantage attending the former, that alarm is in a great measure hushed, the depressing passion of fear so far obviated.

Before taking leave of this fever, it will be necessary to say a few words respecting—

INTERMITTENTS.

In those parts of India and China bordering on the Northern tropic, when the sun is in Capricorn, and the cool season sets in, viz. from the middle of November, till the middle or latter end of February, fe-

---

* Vide the Section on bilious fever, and also what has been said respecting the Corunna fever in the preceding Section.

vers change from the remittent to the intermittent form. Thus at Bombay, Calcutta, and Canton, particularly the last mentioned place, we have ample specimens during the above period of agues and fluxes. From the Bocca tigris up to Canton, the river is flanked with extensive paddy grounds, intersected and watered in all directions by the minor branches of the Taa and artificial canals. The surrounding country, however, is singularly mountainous; and at this season, has a dreary, wild, and bleak appearance. From these mountains the north-east monsoon comes down with a piercing coldness, which the Europeans, relaxed and debilitated by the previous heats, or their sojourn on the sultry coasts of Hindostan, are quite unable to resist. As the improvident mariner has seldom any European clothing in reserve, adapted to this unexpected exigency, especially if he has been any time in India, we need not wonder that in such circumstances, a great number should be afflicted with intermittents and dysenteries at this season. For many weeks, we had seldom fewer than thirty or forty, often more at one time laid up with these complaints: they were generally tertians with a few quartans. The apyrexia was tolerably clear, and the bark exhibited in the usual way recommended for similar fevers in Europe, was a certain and expeditious cure, where no visceral obstructions existed. In the latter case, which was but too frequent, mercury of course, was an essential auxiliary. It is proper to remark, that in two ships of war lying at the Bocca tigris, [the Grampus and Caroline,] the bark was entirely expended on the great number of intermittents. In this dilemma we had no other resource than mercury; and this medicine invariably stopt the paroxysms as soon as the system was saturated; but it must not be concealed, that three-fourths of our patients, treated on this plan, relapsed as soon as the effects of the mercury had worn off, and this after three, and in a few instances, four successive administrations, so as to excite ptyalism. I attributed these failures to the coldness and rawness of the air, together with the want of proper clothing and defence against this sudden transition from a hot to a comparatively cold climate; very unfavourable circumstances in the mercurial treatment. No ill effects, however, resulted.

. In the month of October the weather was so warm, and the night so cloudless and serene, with very little dew, that many of us slept in the open air at Lintin, an island about twenty-five miles above Macao, where we had tents ashore for the sick and convalescents, as well as the different working parties.

But in November the nights became exceedingly cold; and although there was hardly any thing that could be called a swamp or marsh on the island, yet intermittents and fluxes made their appearance, and continued to increase during our stay, without any very apparent cause, except this sudden vicissitude in the temperature of the air.

There was indeed a very high peak in the centre of the island, the sides of which were covered with thick grass jungle, and over this the winds blew towards the ship and tents. There can be no doubt that hills and mountains arrest the course of marsh miasmata through the air, and when a sufficient quantum of these is collected, they will produce their effects on the human frame, in a similar manner, as if issuing from their original source; especially when the predisposing causes are in great force. Hence we see how miasmal fevers may take place on the summit of *Morne fortunée*, or the rock of *Gibraltar*, without any necesssity for the supposition that the febrific exhalation arose from those places themselves. We next moved up to Bocca tigris, and got into the vicinity of extensive marshy and paddy grounds, which contributed greatly to the augmentation of the sick list.

It is somewhat curious, that a frigate, [the Dedaigneuse,] belonging to the squadron, which lay in the typa, near the city of Macao, remained perfectly healthy, while we were so afflicted with the diseases above-mentioned. As the crew of this ship, were exposed to all the causes, *predisposing and exciting*, which could exist further up the river, it follows that marsh exhalation must have been here, as elsewhere, the fundamental *remote cause*, that gave origin to the intermittents. At Wampoa, sickness was still more predominant among the Indiamen, than at the Bogue—not so much owing to any great difference in the medical topography of the two places, as to the vicinity of the former to Canton, to which city parties of the last-mentioned ships' crews were in the habit of repairing on leave, to the no small detriment of their health, from the course of intemperance pretty generally pursued. The great intercourse, likewise, between Wampoa and Canton afforded infinite facility to the introduction of inebriating materials among those who remained on board. The liquor retailed to seamen in China is certainly of a very destructive nature. Its effects have attracted so much attention, that when his Majesty's ships are leaving the coasts of India for China, there is generally an order received from the Admiral, enjoining the officers to guard as much as possible against the introduction of "SAMSOO" among the crews, which says the order, " is found to be poison to the human frame."—It were a consummation devoutly to be wished, could this injunction be extended to the arrack of India, from which the samsoo only differs in being more impregnated with certain stimulating materials prejudicial to the stomach and bowels.

The ordinary mode of preparing Samsoo is as follows :—" The rice is kept in hot water till the grains are swollen ; it is then mixed up with water, in which has been dissolved a preparation called ' Pe-ka,' consisting of rice-flour, liquorice-root, aniseed, and garlic. This hastens fermentation, and imparts to the liquor a peculiar flavour." It is probable, however, that other more active ingredients are added to that in use among the lower classes at Canton. Bontius, speaking of the dysentery at Batavia, alleges, as " the principal cause of this disease, the drinking an inflammatory liquor called *arrack*, which the *Chinese* make of rice, and the *holothuria*, or what is called quabbin in Holland. These holothuria have so *pungent* a heat, that the touch of them *ulcerates* the skin and raises vesicles." p. 16. He adds a pathetic remark. " Happy were it for our sailors, that they drank more moderately of this liquor ; the plains of India would not then be protuberant with the innumerable graves of the dead !" The same remark might be with strict propriety applied to the arrack of

India in general, where, as at Bombay for instance, its pernicious effects are equally conspicuous as at Batavia.

It may at first sight appear singular, that mountainous countries covered with lofty woods, or thick jungles, should give rise to fevers, similar in every respect to those of flat and marshy districts. But the reason is obvious, when we consider that in the first-mentioned situations the surface of the earth is constantly strewed, particularly in autumn, with vegeto-animal remains, and kept in a moist state by the rains or drippings of dews from the superincumbent foliage. The stratum of atmosphere, therefore, in contact with the ground, becomes highly impregnated with effluvia, which are seldom agitated by breezes, or rarefied by the rays of the sun; either of which would tend to dissipate the exhalations. Thus, among the lofty forests and impenetrable jungles of Ceylon, the most powerful miasmata are engendered, producing fevers of great violence and danger. " It is under the branches of these shrubs," [in Ceylon,] says Lord Valentia, " that the fatal jungle fever is probably generated. Not a breath of air can pass through; and the confined exhalations from the black vegetable mud, loaded with putrid effluvia of all kinds, must acquire a highly deleterious quality, affecting both the air and the water." *Travels, vol.* 2.

Generally speaking, however, these hill, or jungle fevers, as they are locally designated, appear in the form of intermittents, especially among the natives, and those Europeans, whose constitutions are assimilated to the climate. Unfortunately, among the latter class these fevers either soon produce, or are accompanied by, visceral obstructions, too frequently terminating in confirmed hepatitis; hence the necessity of checking them as soon as possible, and of using all imaginable precaution in guarding against the remote and predisposing causes. The treatment, of course, must vary, from a simple administration of bark, to its combination with mercury, or the exhibition of the latter alone, so as to keep up a gentle ptyalism for some considerable time. In these elevated situations, far from seas, or even rivers, and entirely out of the reach of tides, the influence of the moon is unequivocally evinced.

" It is by no means uncommon," says Captain Williamson, " to see persons, especially Europeans, who have to appearance been cured of jungle or hill fevers, as they are called, and which correspond exactly with our marsh fever, laid up at either the full or change of the moon, or possibly at both, for years after." This from a non-professional gentleman, is another proof of the sandy foundation on which Dr. Lind's hypothesis, before alluded to, rests; and of the truth of Dr. Balfour's observations.

Analytical Review of a Medical Report on the Epidemic Fever of Coimbatore, drawn up by Drs. Ainsly, Smith, and Christie.

Sec. III.—An epidemic, spreading its ravages from Cape Comorin to the banks of the Cavery—from the Ghauts to the coast of Coromandel, and sweeping to the grave 106,789 persons, presented a noble field for investigation—an unbounded theatre for the acquisition of medical knowledge ! But as the richness of the soil sometimes renders indolent the cultivator ; so a stunted harvest has been gathered from this most luxuriant field of medical science.

1. *Causes.*—Since the time of Hippocrates, *atmospheric vicissitudes* have been deemed insalutary ; and Hoffman set them down as the general remote causes of epidemic fever.—The committee believe that Sydenham's " *Secret Constitution of the Air,*" is as good an explanation as can be given. We shall not stop here to discuss the point. They justly remark, that an erroneous opinion has prevailed, that marsh miasmata can only be engendered in low swampy situations, " though it is well known that noxious vapours from woods, especially if thick and ill ventilated, are as certainly a source of the same mischief." This second source was very abundant in several of the ravaged provinces, many parts being so covered with wood, jungle, and rank vegetation, as to be nearly impervious. Another supposed origin of febrific miasmata was in the salt marshes found in the Tinnevelly and Ramnad districts, where the fever raged with uncommon severity. The committee are of opinion, that marshy situations are not sufficient to render fevers epidemic ; there is required the super-agency of a close, moist, and sultry heat, with imperfect ventilation. Such an offensive condition of the atmosphere was but too often experienced in several of the low tracts of these districts during the sickly season, and was pregnant with the most baleful consequences. Although great deviations from the natural order of climate are, fortunately, not very frequent in these regions, yet, as in the present instance, they do sometimes take place ; and are always followed by disastrous results. Major Orme informs us, that in the month of March the S. W. monsoon broke completely over the western Ghauts, and descended in vast floods over the Coromandel side of the Peninsula, destroying crops just ready to be cut, sweeping away many of the inhabitants, and ultimately, by creating a powerful evaporation during a sultry heat, producing an epidemic disease very fatal in its consequences.

The effects of those miasmata engendered amongst woods and jungles, have been too well authenticated to require additional testimony. As electricity has been said to promote putrefaction in animal bodies, the committee query how far this fluid, which was very abundant in the atmosphere during the sickly seasons, may not have assisted in producing a distempered state of the air. I think this is a very questionable cause of epidemia.

The predisposing causes of remittent and intermittent fevers are well known to be those which operate by producing debility, as bad diet, fatigue, exposure to cold and damp, grief, mental anxiety, &c. This is illustrated by a remarkable exemption from disease among the troops stationed at Madura, while the poor inhabitants of the garrison were swept off by sickness. The same was observed at Dindigul, where two deaths only occurred among three companies of troops, while the needy inhabitants of the town were dying by hundreds.

Of the *exciting* causes, the committee considered exposure to cold and damp, while the body had been relaxed by preceding heat, and the solar influence, as the most powerful.

" The heat of the early part of the nights, induced many of the natives to sleep in the open air, by which means they became exposed, while yet·perspiring, to the chill fogs and damps of the morning." p. 116.

2. *Nature and Types of the Endemic.*—This fatal fever did not differ essentially from the common endemic of the country. Its epidemic tendency on the present occasion, was altogether ascribable to the *causes* enumerated in the preceding section. It is either remittent or intermittent, according to the constitution, treatment, and season of the year. People by nature delicate and irritable, or rendered so by irregularities, or want of care, are sometimes attacked by the disease in the remittent form, proving bilious or nervous, as the constitution inclines. The same happens to the more robust, when improperly treated, as where bark is given early, and before proper evacuations have been premised. As the season becomes hotter, too, the remitting form prevails over the intermittent. Males suffered more than females, and young people and those of middle age, more than old people and children. The remittent form sometimes makes its approaches very insidiously. The patient feels himself out of sorts for a few days; his appetite fails him; he has squeamishness, especially at the sight of animal food; universal lassitude; alternate heats and chills; stupid heaviness, if not pain in the head. The eyes are clouded; the ears ring; the bowels are invariably costive. In other cases, the enemy approaches rapidly; and rigors, great prostration of strength, vertigo, nausea, or vomiting, usher in the disease.

The first paroxysm, which is often attended with delirium and epistaxis, after continuing an indefinite period, with varying symptoms, terminates in a sweat; not profuse and fluent, as after a regular hot fit of ague, but clammy and partial, with the effect, however, of lowering the pulse, and cooling the body, but not to the natural standard. The latter still feels dry and uncomfortable; the pulse continuing smaller and quicker than it ought. This remission will not be of long standing, without proper remedial measures. A more severe paroxysm soon ensues, ushered in by vomiting, (sometimes of bile,) and quickly followed by excessive heat; delirium; great thirst; difficult respiration; febrile anxiety; parched and brownish tongue. The next remission, (if it do take place,) is less perfect than the first, and brings still less relief. In this way, if medicine, or a spontaneous purging do not check the disease, it will run its fatal course, each succeeding attack proving worse than its predecessor, till exhausted nature begins to give way. The pulse declines; the countenance shrinks, and looks sallow; the eyes become dim; " *the abdomen swells from visceral congestion:*" the stomach loathes all food, when hiccup, stupor, and low delirium usher in death. Such severe cases, the committee think, were, in general owing to neglect or blunders at the beginning of the disease.

Intermittents were more intractable, as ·well as more common. The epidemic was void of any contagious character, except in cases that were allowed to run into the low continued form ; and even here, the contagion was circumscribed within very narrow limits. The types were, the simple tertian, the double tertian, the quotidian, the quartan, and the irregular. The following will give some idea of the relative numbers of these forms.—A native detachment at Dindigul, 255 strong, suffered in the following proportion : simp. tert. 30 ; doub. tert. 26 ; irreg. 24 ; quotid. 13 ; quart. 4. The quotidian form was well marked, returning at nearly equal periods, often attacking weak constitutions, and leaving but little time for taking the bark. It was more apt to occasion visceral obstructions and œdematus swellings than any other form of the disease. The quartan was rare, but obstinate, and frequently productive of splenic obstruction and dropsy. The irregular was very troublesome, and seemed to correspond with Hoffman's semi-tertian.

The Tamool, or native practitioners, ascribe the epidemic fever chiefly to two causes—a superabundance of moisture in the air and earth, and the bad quality of the water owing to unwholesome solutions. We think there is much truth in their opinions, and have had reason to believe ourselves, that the water, as well as the air, becomes impregnated with morbific miasmata.

Treatment.—On the first appearance of the epidemic, no time was lost in clearing out the bowels by brisk purgatives ; and soon after the medicine had ceased to operate, the cinchona was prescribed, observing this rule respecting it, that, the nearer the time of giving the last dose of bark for the day is brought to the period of attack of the cold stage, the more likely will it be to accomplish the purpose intended.—From six to eight drachms of the fresh powdered bark, taken in substance, were commonly sufficient to keep off a fit, especially if given in the four or five hours preceding the paroxysm. Some of the native stomachs could not bear the powder, unless mixed with ginger, or given in infusion or decoction, with tinct. cinchonæ, and conf. aromat. As the bark sometimes constipated, a few grains of rhubarb were added, or laxative glysters used. Thirty or forty drops of laudanum, with half an ounce of the acetate of ammonia, given at the commencement of the hot fit, often had the effect of shortening it, sustaining the strength, and rendering the stomach retentive. When the perspiration begins to flow, the drink ought to be tepid ; but when the body is hot and the skin dry, cold water is both grateful and salutary. The bark must be continued for some time after the fever disappears, to prevent recurrence. The committee, as was to be expected from the schools of debility and putrescency in which they were educated, declaimed against purgatives in this fever, " lest they be productive of mischief, by occasioning irritation, *debility,* and ultimately an obstinate disease—*mindful of the lesson that was taught them in early life,* by the writings of the judicious Hoffman," &c. I quote this passage, not to say that I think drastic purgatives necessary in the simple form of intermittent, for I know that they are *unnecessary,* and sometimes hurtful ; but to show that the committee were disciples of Hoffman and of Spasm.

When the fever, as too often happened, ran its course some days unchecked by medicine, then the case was altered, for abdominal

congestion and visceral obstruction soon took place, and a dangerous
state of the disease was induced. In these distressing circumstances,
change of climate was necessary, and a course of calomel. When
the mouth became affected, some of the most unpleasant symptoms
disappeared, and then the bark was administered with more safety.

The committee not unfrequently met with obstinate intermittents,
unaccompanied apparently by visceral obstruction, in which bark
was unavailing. They sometimes tried with success sulphuric
æther in doses of one drachm and a half, taken at the approach of
the cold fit ; and also full doses of laudanum. The sulphate of zinc
did not answer. The Hindoo practitioners have used arsenic in intermittent fevers time immemorial, and entertain a high opinion of
its virtues ; but the committee do not approve of it much, though it
sometimes succeeded when all other remedies had failed. The cold
affusion was useful in the hot fits ; nay, daily immersion in the sea
sometimes proved the happy means of checking agues which had
baffled every other exertion. A blister to the nape of the neck will
sometimes check the recurrence of the cold fit. A full dose of the
tinct. rhei et aloes, at bed-time, was found by Mr. Tait, of Trichino-
poly, to stop agues that resisted every other remedy. Notwithstanding all our endeavours, the disease will sometimes run on to coma
and death.

" In such cases calomel or the blue pill, continued till the mouth
is a little affected, *even when no obstruction has taken place*, is *often*
found to be of the greatest service." 145.

On this I shall make no comment ; the fact speaks for itself.
Alarming bowel complaints sometimes supervene on long protracted
intermittents ; not attended with much straining, but of an obstinate
and debilitating nature, requiring opiates, weak cretaceous mixtures,
and aromatics. They too often prove fatal, especially among the
natives.

Œdematous swellings and ascites not unfrequently supervene from
pure debility. These, where no visceral obstruction prevailed, were
best treated by tincture of squills, ginger, and tinct. cinchonæ, together with frequent friction with dry flannel, and proper attention
to the ingesta. But when the bowels were firm, and there was any
suspicion of organic derangement in the abdomen, calomel in small
doses was conjoined with the squills ; or what answered better, the
pilula hydrargyri.

This fever coming on patients who had previously suffered from
liver affections or dysentery, assumed an alarming and complex form,
requiring the nicest management. Bark was here to be used with
great caution. Even the infusion and decoction were dangerous,
where there was any pain or uneasiness in the right side. A blister,
without loss of time, was then applied, and mercury had recourse
to.—R. Pil. hydrargyri gr. vj ; pulv. ipecac. gr. iij. opii. gr. fs ; fiant
pilulæ tres. Sumatur una ter die ; resuming the use of the cinchona as the hepatic symptoms subside. Sometimes the two remedies were combined, where the hepatic affection was chronic and
not very obtrusive. An issue in the right side, with bitters and
tonics, often proved serviceable. Change of air was superior to all

other means, and diet of course required constant attention. Gentle exercise ; flannel next the skin, especially where hepatic affections existed ; and the most scrupulous attention to the state of the bowels.

When, from the appearance of the symptoms, a fever of the remittent kind is approaching, emetics are improper ; in this case, the committee recommended six grains of calomel and six of James's powder to be taken in the course of 12 hours, which will generally produce copious evacuations, and sometimes diaphoresis.

" On the second day, when the paroxysm will, in many cases, be found every way more severe than on the first, no time is to be lost in having recourse to mercury, *the remedy which, at such times, can best be relied on for producing a proper intermission.* Seven or eight grains of calomel, with three grains of camphor, are to be well rubbed together, and made into four pills, one of which is to be taken every three hours during the day. These will often have the desired effect, if continued for two or three days, by producing a desirable change in the habit, and so favourable a remission, that the bark may be given with safety." 154.

If this be not a decisive evidence in favour of the *anti-febrile* powers of mercury on the constitution, I know not what evidence would carry conviction to the minds of the declaimers against that medicine. It is the more satisfactory, as it comes from the anti-mercurial party themselves, surrounded with the prejudices of debility and putrescency.

The principal native remedies employed by the Tamool practitioners were, white arsenic, about the 15th part of a grain, twice a day ; the barks of the Swietenia febrifuga and melia Azadirachta ; the Catcaranja nut ; the Chukkoo, (Amom. Zingib.) ; the Sison Ammi ; bark of the Acacia Arabica, and Tellicherry bark.

We have lately heard it urged, that the causes of intermittent and remittent fevers must necessarily be sought in low and marshy situations ; whereas the testimony of unquestionable writers, and this document particularly, proves, that febrific miasmata may rise, under certain conditions, from almost any soil ; and what is still more extraordinary, that these febrific miasmata may be carried, by currents of air, to a distance far exceeding what has been laid down by some most respectable writers on the subject. This epidemic of India spread its poisonous breath from South to North, in the direction of the monsoon, and was confidently believed by the natives to have its sources in the Pylney mountains, whose overgrown woods, unventilated vallies, and stagnant marshes, could not fail to engender a more rapidly dangerous condition of the atmosphere, than that brought about by the same general causes on the drier and less woody plains of the eastern ranges of the Peninsula.

The observations of the committee are corroborated by the testimony of others, particularly Zimmerman and Jackson.

" Fevers of this sort, (says the latter,) arise in particular countries, or districts of a country. They travel in certain tracts : sometimes confined to narrow bounds ; at other times they are more wide-

ly diffused."—*Medical Dep. Brit. Army, p.* 212. ˙ *See also Zimmer-*
man's " Experience," vol. ii. p. 155.

It is greatly to be lamented, that some of the *energetic* modes of
treatment lately introduced into the *methodus medendi* of fever had
not been tried in the remittent forms of the eastern epidemic. It
does not appear that a lancet was wet in any part of the epidemic
range from Cape Comorin to the Cavery ; and therefore it is in vain
for our Oriental brethren to say that it would not have been useful,
when they never gave it a trial. The evidence, however, in favour
of MERCURY is most unequivocal, and will probably silence, if any
thing can, the clamour which has been raised against it in this country.

—————•————

Observations on the Fever prevalent in the province of Guzzerat, with
general remarks on the action of Mercury in the diseases of India.
By A. GIBSON, Bombay Medical Department.

SEC. IV.—It is now pretty generally known, that, in the fevers of
India, mercury alone is to be relied on in the early treatment, to
obviate immediate danger.—It may be supposed to have three modes
of action : 1*st*, On the hepatic system ; 2*dly*, On the intestinal canal ;
3*dly*, On the general constitution.—Probably all these modes of action are essential to a perfect cure ; and if either is deficient, the
certain consequence is death, or chronic obstructions, which only
yield, if ever, to a change of climate.   .

1*st*, If the liver is not acted on, it must, from the determination of
blood to it, during the increased febrile action, be in great danger of
being disorganized, or of its penicilli becoming consolidated, as a termination of the inflammatory state.

2*dly*, If the bowels are torpid and constipated, the liver will still
be in the same danger ; for though it may be pervious and active
enough to eliminate bile from the blood sent to it in the healthy state,
and in the moderate action of the system, yet during the continued
accessions of fever, it may be overpowered by the increased sanguineous afflux, which must either augment, or continue stationary, as
long as the alimentary canal refuses to be moved by such means as
would reduce or abate the volume of circulating fluid.

3*dly*, I have commonly observed the cure to be incomplete, unless
the general constitution was affected ; for such is the type which the
fever very frequently assumes, that, unless counteraction is excited
in the system, by the specific power of mercury, the healthy state both
of the liver and bowels is inadequate to a cure ; the paroxysms become
continued'; the febrile state is established, and in progress of time irremediable debility follows,   ‘   ’   .

The species of fever, which I have seen prevailing in the province
of Guzzerat, partakes chiefly of the typhoid character, though commonly denominated, I presume incorrectly, bilious. It differs from
the latter form of fever in requiring less evacuation ; and from the
former, in the remission being such as to admit of stimuli being administered. The effects of stimuli are what one would look for in

an inflammatory diathesis ; yet excessive evacuations of any kind seem only to hasten the fatal termination.

The affinity between the constitutional symptoms, at the period either preceding the attack of fever, when the patient has been long languishing and unwell, or consequent to it, when the mercury has acted imperfectly, and hectic fever commenced, cannot but strike every observant practitioner. Irregular accessions of slight rigors, sometimes quotidian, and sometimes not recurring for days, at uncertain intervals ; *burning heat of the palms and feet, extending up the legs ;* the feelings and actual heat of the body, always above natural ; a quick pulse readily increased by the most gentle exercises ; the easy excitement of the system to high febrile irritation, by the smallest meal of animal food and use of wine ; the flushed countenance : cold clammy sweatings at one period, and dry, hot, parched skin at another, with emaciations, seems to correspond with the phenomena of hectic. But as the phenomena in question occur without suppuration, we must seek for a cause in the general debilitated state of the system, unless an idiopathic origin is allowed ; and although I am not prepared to defend an opinion on this important point, the further investigation of the subject by others, may substantiate the hint at some furture period. A change to a cold climate, if timely adopted, or even to another with fewer natural disadvantages, and if by sea, so much the better, fortunately, in most instances, serves towards a recovery. In the pining state above described, are the majority of those composing the convalescent-list of an European regiment at sickly stations. Among the officers also who embark for England on sick-leave, will be found a very large proportion in a similar state. But the soldier, from his humble situation, has not this resource at command, but must patiently wait till a relief of his regiment takes place, when the only chance of a recovery is in his power ; but in this hope how many perish ! medicine being now exhausted on him in vain.

Absolute confinement during this unhealthy state of the body, is not often long endured, the person going about his usual occupation, unwilling to lay himself up in a country where the depressing passions are so predominant, and disease so fatal. But with a multiplicity of uneasy feelings, and a gradual decay of constitution, yet ignorant where to assign his chief complaint, in sleepless nights and restless days, he lingers on a life of extreme misery, till debility, or fever, or its relapse, compel him to his sick-chamber.

In better climates, the phlogistic state of the system is adverse to the introduction of mercury ; but the prudent abstraction of blood happily reduces it to that standard which is most favourable for its action. In India, however, in fever, the disease in which this is most speedily to be desired, the same mean would but in very few cases be admissible ; for the debility is so great and instantaneous, as well as the tendency to putridity, that only in the robust new-comer is it, if ever, to be hazarded.*

* The spontaneous hæmorrhages which are so distressing in the worst cases, from the nose, mouth, and ears, have always appeared to me to hasten death. Indeed I do not remember an instance of hæmorrhage which did not prove fatal, and without exhibiting the smallest remission, not even before the period when

I have only seen it used beneficially, where local pain indicated inflammation to be going on in the contiguous viscus. This, however,
is foreign to the fever which I am describing; for, most commonly,
no uneasiness is complained of, but the general feelings of pyrexia;
and the low delirium and stupor so soon follow, with the sinking pulse,
that no further information is to be accurately obtained from the patient; and dissection generally demonstrates nothing more than the
congestion in the brain, usually met with in the fatal cases of typhus.
In this low state of the system, no preparatory steps are required
by evacuation, further than the care and attention to the unloaded
and free state of the stomach and bowels, so necessary in all fevers.
On the contrary, in many instances, so great is the debility, that an
early tonic is indicated; for it would seem that debility, as well as a
plethoric system, is equally inimical to the specific mercurial action.
And if the patient is fortunately invigorated sufficiently in this way
to give the mercury influence, and before any organ essential to life is
injured, by the strictest nursing and attention afterwards, the recovery is almost certain, all morbid action yielding from the moment
ptyalism is brought on. But often during the long low period, when
every effort is making to mercurialize, the quantity introduced, but
as yet inactive, is so great, that when the effect is accomplished,
such is the profusion of the ptyalism, that the most disagreeable consequences succeed, and a long and precarious period of convalescence. It is therefore a desideratum, the greatest in the treatment
of this fever, to know a criterion by which to judge that you have
pushed the mercury to the necessary extent, and no further. In one
instance, where the patient was fast sinking and harassed with excessive diarrhœa, after long mercurial inunction, and the very large exhibition of calomel in commiseration of the last moments of one apparently moribund, all further medicine was desisted from, but such
as would give temporary vigour under causes so debilitating, while
the skin was yet hot and parched, tongue black and dry, thirst insatiable, and pulse rapid. The effects were marvellous. In twenty-
four hours after, the gums were inflamed, and in forty eight the salivation was begun, and with it all symptoms of previous disease vanished. This, I beg it to be observed, was accidental; and, since the
same cause did not once occur again, during a long period, among the
sick in a large and crowded hospital of one of his majesty's regiments, it may be inferred that a criterion cannot be derived from it.
This case, however, afforded a clear illustration of the inactivity of
mercury in certain states of the system, and also a useful caution
against persevering beyond a certain extent in its use.
No inquiry can be attended with a more beneficial result, if successful, than that which is now pointed out; for so universal is calomel
in use, and so sovereign is it in efficacy, above all medicines yet introduced into Indian practice, that unless administered by rule, and
watched strictly in its operation, there is much dread of its getting into
undeserved disrepute. Those of my professional friends in India,
who, with myself, have lamented, in so many instances, the futility

it might with certainty be considered an outward, and a truly alarming occurrence.

of medical science, in climates so deleterious, will, I trust, before the conclusion of their valuable services, by their researches into the arcana of disease, yet throw light on a subject so very obscure as the diseases of India still are. If, after the system is already saturated with mercury, and in a disease too of the greatest debility and tendency to putrescence, a medicine so very powerful as calomel be persisted in longer, in the vain expectation of effects which will never become apparent, it is not being too rash. perhaps, to pronounce every grain given above a certain quantity to be prejudicial, and when increased to a greater extent, an active poison.

It may seem empirical to European practitioners, that calomel should be given, apparently so indiscriminately, in the diseases of India ; but in all, either a counter-action to that existing in the system at the time, is supposed to demand its use, or it is rather to be presumed, perhaps, that the inflammation prevailing in many of them is of a peculiar and specific nature, as modified by climate, and will only yield to it. In fevers continued or remittent, and in dysentery and diseased liver, acute or chronic, it may be considered a palladium in medicine ; but in the unmixed enteritis, which is too often insiduous in its approach, and beyond the skill of the physician when first complained of, it is of very doubtful virtue. The preparations of mercury to be relied on are only the submuriate and the ointment. The blue pill is perfectly inadequate to any good purpose, and generally quite inert in India. To such as favour this essay with their perusal, it may meet their wishes to be informed of the tonic given in that stage of fever at which mercury was left off. A mineral acid, but above all, the nitric, is that which can with safety be ventured on, and it will be found to disappoint less than any other medicine. The cinchona, and all the class of bitters, only load the stomach, and increase the febrile irritation. Nitric acid is tonic without over stimulating. It is a grateful and cooling beverage to the parched mouth and burning body ; it is therefore febrifuge ; it is antiseptic, and in these combines the good qualities chiefly wanted at this period. The best test, perhaps, of its pleasant virtues, is the incessant call made by the sickly patient for the acid drink he got when last in hospital.—*Vide Ed. Journal, vol.* 11.

Observations on the nature of the climate, and the Fevers which prevail at Seringapatam. By A. NICOLL, M. D.

SECT. V.—Ever since the British took possession of Seringapatam, their forces, both European and native, have greatly suffered from the insalubrity of its climate. Any investigation, therefore, into the nature of the climate, and diseases which prevail there becomes peculiarly interesting and important.

The following observations made on the nature of the climate, and the fevers which appeared amongst 700 Europeans and some native corps stationed at Seringapatam for eighteen months, will, I hope, place this subject in a more clear and satisfactory light.

Intermittent fevers are prevalent in every part of the Mysoor country, but are much more common at Seringapatam than in any other; and they vary according to the changes of the season and conditions of the atmosphere. In the hot months of the year, the fever becomes remittent or typhoid; the latter usually of that species denominated by Cullen *Typhus icterodes*.* As the season cools, and the weather becomes more steady and pleasant the remissions of the fever become more distinct; and as the weather gets what may be called cold, the regular agues are formed. Dysentery is frequently combined, both with remittent and intermittent fevers; but is more common in the cold season than in any other. There is nothing peculiar in the approach of the remittent, much less in the ague. The yellow fever always presented itself in the beginning like a severe remittent, generally with great sickness at stomach, and vomiting of a greenish or bilious matter. A flushing of the face, and a degree of stupor and listlessness; a burning skin; full and quick pulse; frequent respirations, and excruciating pain in the head and loins, were the great pathognomonic symptoms of the disease. When at this stage of the disease a stop was not made to its further progress, still greater excitement and irritability of the functions of life came on, and incessant vomiting of a greenish or yellowish-coloured matter, delirium ferox, and sometimes dysentery, with great violence succeeded, and in the course of a few hours put an end to the sufferings of the patient. On or about the third day of the disease, the yellowness of the body generally appeared; the adnatæ, the neck, breast, and belly, showed at first the partial transfusion which became deeper in colour, the higher in violence the disease arose. Though the disease runs its fatal course in a few instances in 48 hours, yet it was generally on the sixth or seventh day that the patient died. This so often happened, that whenever I got my fever patients over these two critical days, I contemplated a speedy solution of the disease at hand.

The first four months of the year are excessively hot, close, and, sultry, until the Malabar monsoon sets in, in May. At 5 in the morning the thermometer is generally about 65°, and at 3 in the afternoon about 94° Fahrenheit. In May and June, by the refreshing showers and breezes wafted from the mountains, which separate the Mysoor from the Malabar country, the climate is rendered tolerably healthy and pleasant. Again it becomes hot and sultry in July, August, and September, but nothing like to the four first months of the year, until the Coromandel monsoon begins, in October, which, by its mild and salubrious influence, soon effects great and remarkable changes in the air and temperature of the place. At this season, especially in November, the thermometer at 5, P. M. has been so low as 48°, and in the middle of the same day, has risen to 88°. *I have also frequently observed a difference of 40 degrees between six o'clock in the morning and twelve of the day.* During the hot months of the year, the winds are generally southerly or easterly; in the cold season, they become westerly or northerly.

The *fort*, in which the troops chiefly reside, is in a very low situation, with lofty walls surrounding it, which, in a great measure, pre-

* Synopsis Nosolog. Meth. cl. I. Pyrexiæ, Ord. I. Feb. Gen. V. Typhus Sp. II.

vent the free circulation of air. Besides the barracks, hospitals, &c. for the forces being bad, and highly objectionable, there is an extensive bazar close to them, which, by its filth and situation, becomes no small nuisance to the Europeans.

Other sources of noxious exhalations are abundantly fruitful at Seringapatam. These, together with a moist sultry atmosphere, subject to great changes of temperature from intense heat to extreme cold, have in all ages, been viewed as the origin of pestilence and death.* In the ditches between the ramparts and in various parts of the fort, where all the Europeans and many thousand natives reside, are constantly deposited all the filth and corruption of the place. On the banks of the *Cauvery river*, and in several places of the island, pools, stagnant with offensive and putrid matter, are to be seen. All the mass of animal and vegetable corruption from a population, including Europeans and natives no less than 90,000, is collected on a small space of ground, the circumference of the island not exceeding three miles. These materials of putrefaction, for about eight months of the year, lie in those repositories which I have mentioned, until the periodical rains of Malabar begin, which, falling in the *ghauts*, run down, and fill the Cauvery river. The filling of this river is always very sudden, and it comes rushing along with great impetuosity; sweeps out all the filth from the ditches; clears away all the impurities, so long stagnant in the island; and leaves the place, for a while, tolerably healthy, and the air cool and refreshing.

With regard to the infectious nature of the yellow fever, some doubts are entertained, from never observing a single orderly attending those ill with the disease, or any of the other patients in hospital, who were oftentimes indiscriminately mixed together, for the want of room to put our sick and convalescents in, contracting the disease. However, the prevalence of this disease being regulated in its operation by a determined range of atmospheric heat, and, from numerous facts related, especially by that enlightened physician, Sir Gilbert Blane.† I have no doubt but that, under certain circumstances in regard to the constitution of the atmosphere, and the susceptibility of individuals. it may evince an infectious nature.

The persons who were most subject to yellow fever at Seringapatam, where the strong and robust, we had exposed themselves carelessly to the vicissitudes of the climate, and lived irregularly. Those who had been much exhausted by almost habitual drunkenness, and long residence in India, were the first who suffered, and fell victims to the disease. Three instances came under my notice, where, in characters corresponding to the above-mentioned, the powers of life were destroyed in the first paroxysm of fever. Irregularity, drunkenness, and exposure to the changes of the climate, when the body is in a state of perspiration or *indirect debility*, are powerful agents in rendering the functions of life susceptible of morbid associations, or liable to the impressions of the morbid *virus*; yet certain situations, in respect to dryness and ventilation, though

* Hippocrat. Op. om. De Epid. Lib. I. c. iii. p. 238.
† Blane, Diseases of Seamen, p. 605.

equally exposed to noxious blasts or exhalations, make no small change in the prevalence and nature of fever.

APPEARANCES ON DISSECTION.

The anatomical examination of the bodies of those who died of the yellow fever, was made with considerable attention and minuteness; but the appearances of the morbid structure of the most important organs, those connected with the functions of life, and seemingly with the disease, were by no means uniform or satisfactory, nor could they in any instance be applied to the full explanation of the morbid actions, which appeared in the rise, progress, and termination of the case.

Brain.—Always contained in its ventricles a large proportion of serum, and its vessels were generally turgid with watery blood.

Chest.—Seldom showed much signs of morbid alteration in any of its viscera. Sometimes the *heart* appeared enlarged, and the *pericardium* contained more water than natural. At times larger portions of lymph, or polypi were found in the venæ cavæ, right auricle, and left ventricle. The blood was always very dark, and watery, running soon into putrefaction.

Abdomen.—Presented various morbid appearances, slight marks of inflammation on the pyloric portion of the *Stomach*, but apparently proceeding from the acrid matters found in it, as the duodenum, which contained nearly similar matters, presented the same appearance. The *intestines* always held large quantities of fetid matter of various colours. The *liver* was rarely found any-wise diseased, but there was always a large secretion of bile. The *gall-bladder* was always turgid; frequently large quantities of bile were seen floating on the surface of the intestines.* When the bodies were inspected a few hours after death, the bile was *yellow*, but when kept more than twelve hours, it became black and putrid! The liquor found in the pericardium and ventricles of the brain, as also in the cavity of the abdomen at times, partook, but slightly, of some of the properties of bile; they were, however, sufficiently clear, as to put it beyond doubt, that the yellowness of the skin, and fluids of the body, in yellow fever, proceeds from the bile having entered into the circulation, and communicated to them its colour.†

From these facts and observations, I am sorry to say, I cannot derive that advantage and important results to the practice of medicine which might be wished. This branch of medical science, which has for its object the ascertaining the seat and causes of diseases in organic derangements, affords ample field for the investigation of physicians and anatomists, and can only be perfected by their unwearied exertions.‡

* How came the bile there? Is it not more likely to be an effusion of yellow serum. J. J.

† Blane, Observations on Fevers, Part III. chap. I. p. 411.

‡ Cabanis, Revolutions of Medical Science, translation by A. Henderson, M. D. p. 294.

The plan which was found most successful in curing the yellow fever at Seringapatam, was that which formed its indications : on 1st, removing the violence of reaction, and, 2ndly, preventing exhaustion of the system by a recurrence of the fever. When the violence of reaction and inflammatory diathesis were sufficiently manifest, blood-letting was employed, the quantity extracted being regulated by the strength. age, and plethoric state of the patient. The appearance of the blood, when drawn, was no criterion whatever. In no instance, where general bleeding was had timely recourse to, and the quantity judiciously taken away, did the reaction of the system, the morbid heat, and general irritability of the animal and natural functions, continue unabated in violence. When the disease has just commenced, in any constitution, whether robust or plethoric, or weak and emaciated, if there are symptoms of any inflammatory diathesis, bleeding must be employed.* Small doses of calomel and neutral salts must be exhibited every hour, until the bowels are unloaded of their morbid contents, and the capillaries of the skin opened, and the surface becomes moist. But, along with the exhibition of those medicines, and after bleeding, while the skin is dry, the respirations frequent, and the animal heat 103° or 108°, the cold effusion must be resolutely and judiciously applied, and repeated, until the reaction of the system, and progress of the disease, are arrested. The cold affusion is the most powerful remedy in subduing the fever : and the only preventive against the irritability of the stomach, was keeping the bowels open by small doses of calomel and jalap, or solutions of the neutral salts. As soon as a distinct remission was obtained, it was found absolutely necessary to throw in the bark and wine, and prescribe a very nourishing diet, in order to prevent a recurrence of the fever, which, though subdued, is apt to return again and again, as before. I found the bark thrown up by injection into the rectum, a valuable remedy in cases where the stomach was irritable and nauseated it. In intermittent fevers, I have often exhibited it in the quantity of an ounce, joined with a little tincture of opium, in this way, just before the expected return of the fit, and in no instance did it fail of moderating the violence of the fit, if it did not succeed in preventing its return altogether.†

When there was great irritability of the stomach, constant vomiting of greenish-coloured matter, great morbid heat of the skin, delirium, and much exhaustion of the powers of life, the cold affusion, constantly repeated, while the spasmodic constriction of the vessels of the skin continued, and the morbid associations remained, is the remedy to be depended on ; for, while it subdues the principle of fever, it invigorates the powers of life, and enables us to clear the stomach and intestines by gentle cathartics, and laxative glysters.—These remedies, when judiciously applied in the early stages of fever, will seldom fail indeed to stop its progress, or bring it to a speedier issue ; but they are not effectual in preventing its return where the body is

* Jackson's Treatise on Diseases of Jamaica, p. 31.
† Heberden, Commentarii de Morb. Hist. et Curatione, cap. xxxviii. p. 160.

again exposed to the cause which first produced it. Bark is the only remedy to be depended on, and when there is any morbid derangement in the *liver* or *spleen*, mercury must be employed. Blisters applied to the *head* and *stomach* were often of great service. When the paroxysm was subsiding, small doses of *opium* and *æther* were given with the most salutary effects. Under the above system of treatment, when the patient was brought to us on the first or second day of the disease, we generally succeeded in producing a final solution of the disease before the fourth or sixth day. When the fever continued beyond this period there was always great difficulty in putting a stop to its progress, if it did not kill the patient then. If the bowels were not kept open, and every slight exacerbation of fever checked by the cold-affusion, the disease generally terminated fatally, sooner or later. But when any slight accession or exacerbation of fever was carefully watched and stopped by the cold affusion, applied in one way or another, a considerable remission at last took place, which enabled us to give the bark, and support the powers of life by due stimuli. Carrying the effects of calomel so far as to produce salivation, was never found necessary or beneficial in the beginning of the disease, *but often found valuable, in conjunction with the bark, when the disease chanced to vary its type, or continued long, and gave us some reason to suspect the presence of some organic derangement, or dropsical diathesis.* It thus appears, that the treatment of fever, of whatever kind or form, unaccompanied with organic derangement, is, now-a-days, both as simple and successful in India as in Europe.— *Vide Ed. Med. Journal, July* 1815.

BILIOUS FEVER.

SECT. VI.—This is the grand endemic, or rather epidemic, (morbus regionalis,) of hot climates ; and although greatly allied in many of its symptoms, perhaps generally combined with the Marsh Remittent, already described, yet it occurs in various places, both at sea and on shore, where paludal effluvia cannot be suspected.

Notwithstanding that this fever is hardly ever mistaken, by the least experienced practitioner, yet so extremely diversified are its features, by peculiarity of constitution, climate, season, and modes of life, that it is very difficult to give even a general outline of it, without involving apparent contradictions. There are always, however, some prominent symptoms which sufficiently characterise bilious fever, for every practical purpose, which is the chief object in view. These are, gastric irritability — affection of the præcordia,*— and affection of the head. Rarely will all, or any of these be absent. The other items in the febrile train are by no means constant and regular. Thus the pulse is frequently regular, and sometimes up to 120 or 130 in the minute. It is the same with the temperature of the skin. Often, when mad delirium is present, the pulse will be 86, and the thermometer in the axilla at 96º of Fahrenheit. The bowels are

* In the term præcordia I always include those viscera and parts immediately below the diaphragm ;—the liver, stomach, and spleen, for instance, in the sense of Fernelius, lib. iv. De Febribus.

almost always constipated, or in a state of dysenteric irritation. No such thing as natural stools in this fever are ever to be seen, unless procured by art. Frequently, but not always, yellowness of the eyes, and even of the skin, takes place ; and the mental functions are very generally affected, which indeed is characteristic of all bilious diseases. This fever is not near so dangerous as the more concentrated marsh endemics, such as those of Bengal, Batavia, &c. Indeed I have long thought that these last are the bilious remittents of the country, modified and greatly aggravated by the peculiar nature of the local miasmata. However, that they occasionally exist independently of each other, I have likewise no doubt ; for we must not let the rage for generalising blind us to facts. My meaning is this, that the fever in question frequently arises from atmospheric heat, or rather atmospheric vicissitudes, deranging the functions or even structure of important organs ; and that it is, as Sir James M'Grigor supposes, symptomatic of local affection. Where marsh miasma is added, which is generally the case, then we have the endemic of the place, modified by the peculiar nature of the effluvia, and from which we are not secured but by local habituation to the cause. Residence, therefore, on the banks of the Ganges, is no protection from the miasma of St. Domingo, or Batavia, as will be proved in a subsequent section. See also what Mr. Boyle says on the Sicilian fever.

With respect to the treatment, I have never found it difficult, when the means which I have minutely detailed under the head of Bengal endemic, were early and steadily applied. Bleeding, I know, is seldom employed ; but I can state that three other surgeons on the station, besides myself, had recourse to venesection in the fevers of India, with the greatest benefit. These were, Mr. Dalziel, late of the Naval Hospital at Madras ; Mr. Cunningham of the Sceptre ; and Mr. Neill, formerly of the Victor, latterly of the Sceptre. This is a small band opposed to the host of antiphlebotomists ; but it must be remembered, that the evidence in favour of bleeding, is, from its very nature, more conclusive than that which is against it. In the first place, a great proportion of practitioners will be deterred from the use of the lancet entirely, by the current of prejudice. In the second place, a great many of those who do venture on it, will be easily discouraged by any reverse at the beginning, which is sure to be attributed to the heterodox remedy ; a striking instance of which will be given hereafter, in the section on " Endemic of Batavia." But on the other hand, those who persevere must be more than mad, if they continue a practice which is not beneficial ; and if it is, how must their proofs accumulate! and how solid and experimental must be their nature, compared with those on the opposite side of the question, where prejudice and timidity are so apt to mislead ?*

Finally, my opinion is this :—that when we wish to arrest the progress of bilious fever, " cito et jucunde," we should in all cases,

---

* Since the first edition of this work, the proofs of benefit from venesection in the bilious remittent fevers of all climates have so multiplied, that it is needless to insist further on the propriety of the measure, in this section.

where the constitution is not broken down by climate, and particularly where determinations to the brain or liver are conspicuous, as they
too often are, take one copious bleeding at the beginning,(the repetition must be guided by the judgment of the practitioner,) which will
effectually promote the operation of all the succeeding remedial
measures, and obviate in a great degree, those visceral obstructions
and derangements, which this fever so frequently entails on the patient.

The following condensed, but clear account of this fever, as it exhibited itself, in all its shapes and bearings, and with no small degree
of violence, on the great mass of a ship's company, will convey a
better idea of the disease, and in a more practical way, than any general description, however laboured, or however minute. I have
only to premise, that the symptoms were carefully noted, and the
practice detailed on the spot, by a gentleman of no mean talent for
observation ; and although I differ from him on the *exhibition* of emetics, and the *omission* of venesection, it is with regret, as I entertain the highest respect for his abilities and candour. It will be seen
that, in most other points, his practice is nearly similar to what I found
most successful in the endemic of Bengal.

" On the 2nd of March, 1804, His Majesty's ship Centurion dropped
anchor in Bombay Harbour, on her return from Surat : at which time
the ship's company were in good health. During the next week,
the weather was variable—hot and sultry, in general, through the
day, alternated with cold damp chills at night, when the dews were
heavy, and the land winds keen from the adjacent mountainous coast.

On the 9th of the same month, several men complained of slight
indisposition, which we did not consider of any importance, little
awareof the distressing scene to which this was an immediate pre-
lude.

Centurion, Bombay Harbour,
March 10*th*, 1804.

Eighteen man complained to me this morning, of having been taken
suddenly ill in the night. Their general symptoms were—severe
pain in the head, arms, loins, and lower extremities ; stricture across the
breast, with great pain under the scrobiculus cordis ; retching and
griping. In some, the pulse intermitted, and the temperature of the
skin was increased ; others had cold chills with partial clammy sweats ;
but all complained of pain under the frontal bone ; many of them
with white furred tongues and thirst. A solution of salts and emetic
tartar, designed to operate both ways, was prescribed, with plenty of
warm diluent drinks. P. M. The solution operated well, both upwards and downwards, in all the patients. Many complain now of
pain in the epigastric region and head, with burning hot skins. Gave
them Pulv. Antim. gr. vj. Tinct. Opii. gt. xx. Aq. Menth. un-
cias ij. hora somni sumend. with warm rice water, slightly acidulated, for drink during the night. The patients to be secured from the
land-winds, which at this season of the year are considered very
pernicious. Almost all these men had been exposed to the intense
heat of the sun by day, and to the influence of the night air, while ly-

ing about the decks in their watches. Mr. Brown, the carpenter, was on shore in the heat of the sun to-day, and attacked this afternoon with the fever.

Bombay, March 11th, 1804.

Nine patients added to the list this day. The bilious fever set in with nearly the same symptoms, as yesterday, and the same mode of treatment was pursued.

Many of yesterday's patients are very poorly this morning ; complaining of severe pain in the head, limbs, loins, and across the epigastric region ; with constant vomiting of viscid bile. Prescribed from five to ten grains of calomel, with small doses of antimonial powder, and tincture of opium, to be taken three or four times a day.

There is little intermission of pulse to-day. In some the skin is cold ; in others hot. with insatiable thirst. Tongue, in most cases, covered with a thick white crust. Great irritability of the stomach, aversion to food. Bowels rather constipated—some have a fœtid bilious purging. P. M. The calomel appears to allay the irritability of the stomach ; while the antimonial powder and tincture of opium keep up a warm moisture on the skin.

Bombay, 12th March.

Ten added to the list this morning, with bilious fever. The symptoms and treatment nearly as before. Some of the patients of the 10th are better to day, the irritability of the stomach being a good deal allayed by the calomel and opium ; but they still complain of pain in the head and limbs, with great debility. Eyes heavy, and tinged yellow—pulse full—bowels constipated. Prescribed a dose of Natron Vitriolat. after the operation of which, the calomel, &c. to be continued as before.

The emetic-cathartic solution operated well with the nine patients of yesterday, (11th,) most of them are very ill this morning. They have incessant vomiting of green thick bile, with pain in the epigastric region and head, thirst insatiable. Prescribed the calomel, opium, and antimonial powder, as in the other cases. No delirium has yet appeared in any of the patients ; nor much alteration from health in the pulse. In many, the temperature of the skin very little, if at all increased ; constipation of the bowels nearly a general symptom.

The decks are now crowded with sickness.

Bombay, 13th March.

Eight added to the list this morning, with the prevalent bilious fever. Scarce any heat of skin, or acceleration of pulse. *All appear to labour under some hepatic affection, which seems to be immediately communicated to the brain, causing great pain under the frontal bone.* Vomiting, I think, relieves them a good deal. The quanti-

---

* It was from observing this symptom, that I was long ago led to form the *ratio symptomatum* of fever, sketched out in the first section—namely, that independent of the sympathy existing between the brain and liver, the congestion, or as it were, stagnation of blood, in the portal circle, causes a greater determi-

ty of bile they discharge is enormous, and of a depraved or highly vitiated quality.

Most patients of the 10th and 11th appear very ill ; complaining of pains across the epigastric region, and in the head, with frequent vomiting of bile ; tongues swelled and furred—no great heat or acceleration of pulse. The constipation of bowels I relieve by doses of natron vitriol or calomel and jalap. The calomel, &c. taken from 15 to 30 grains a day, according to the urgency of the symptoms. No appearance yet of ptyalism in any of the patients. The thermometer placed in the axilla of several, did not show more than 96½° or 97°— the pulse not exceeding 88 in the minute.

Many of yesterday's patients (12th) are also very ill. All appear to labour under some morbid affection or secretion of the liver. Two of them much troubled with cough, and spasms in the muscles about the neck, impending deglutition and respiration. Blisters, with vitriolic æther and tinct. opii. relieved this symptom. The warm bath had no good effect. Pulse nearly natural.

Bombay, 14th March.

Nine added to the list this morning, with the prevalent bilious fever. Two of them were suddenly seized with violent mad delirium, and made a dart to get overboard, but were providentially secured in time. No heat of skin, or acceleration of pulse ; but all complain of pain in the head and epigastric region, which emetics and blisters frequently relieve.

Those patients who were first attacked (10th) are very ill, many of them highly tinged yellow ; their eyes swelled, and the blood vessels a good deal distended. Pain in the head still continues severe. At night many of them are delirious. The mercurial treatment continued. I tried the bark, with nitrous acid, in several cases to-day ; but it did much harm, greatly increasing the irritability of the stomach. The fever seems inclined to run through the whole of the ship's company.

The patients of yesterday (13th) are very ill. The calomel in general sits easy on the stomach, and appears to check the vomiting a good deal. I find doses of the natron vitriol. and emetic tartar cleanse the stomach and bowels better than calomel and jalap.

Bombay, 15th March.

Five men attacked last night ; one with violent phrensy, who was in good health a few minutes before. ' He was all at once seized with a mad delirium, and made a dart to get overboard, but was caught. Scarce any increased temperature of the skin, or acceleration of the pulse. The delirium was removed by an emetic. P. M. A few have

nation to the brain, whereby that important organ becomes oppressed, and keeps up the train of febrile symptoms. If this cerebral congestion is relieved by bleeding, or any other means, immediate energy is communicated to the heart and arteries—reaction and biliary secretion follow, and the balance of the circulation and excitability is once more restored. Vomiting, as determining to the surface, will produce this effect ; but the gastric irritability is dangerous. Lastly, mercury, as keeping up a steady action in the extreme vessels of the vena portarum, and in all the excretories, prevents the balance of the circulation and excitability from being again destroyed.

their mouths slightly affected, and are much better, but still complain of pain in the head and right hypochondrium. Our decks are now crowded with sick, and the effluvia intolerable. · The ship is daily fumigated. Sent twenty of the worst cases to Bombay Hospital, many of them very ill and changing yellow.

Bombay, 16th March. ·

Five men were suddenly seized during the night with violent mad delirium—great oppression at the epigastrium—abdomen distended—perfect loss of memory, and all recollection of their messmates and others around them, mistaking one person for another.—Great desire to destroy their own lives, and the lives of those who held them down.—The pupils of the eyes a good deal dilated, and not inclined to contract when exposed to a strong light.* All of these evidenced a great desire for lime juice, which I gave them, and which they frequently mistook for porter. But at times it was difficult to make them swallow any thing, as they would crash the vessel in which it was offered between their teeth. When full vomiting was excited, it generally relieved them, by bringing away immense quantities of viscid or vitiated bile. They all complained, at intervals, of pain in the head and epigastric region, but particularly in the right hypochondrium. I bled in one case, tried the cold affusion in another, and the warm bath with purgative enemas in a third, without success.†

Our decks now being crowded with sick, sent 21 men to Bombay Hospital, viz.

11 of those attacked on the 10 and 11th instant ; several of them changing yellow, and all of them labouring under hepatic affection, with great pain under the frontal bone.

5 of those attacked on the 12th ; not quite so bad as those who were first seized.

5 of those taken ill 13th and 14th.—Symptoms nearly the same.

Tot. 21 in number.

* The cerebral and abdominal plethora is here so strongly painted, that I should have considered myself authorised to bleed *usque ad deliquium*, or the relief of the symptoms

† The quantity of blood abstracted is not mentioned : but it is perfectly immaterial : for unless venesection be carried *usque ad deliquium, or the relief of the symptoms*, no possible good can accrue, but even harm. This is a practical fact, well known to those who have tried this remedy in the east. It may be accounted for thus : the portal congestion, from its peculiar position, (in a circle of vessels whose circumference is entirely composed of capillaries,) places a great portion of the vital fluid nearly at rest, and determines the remainder, more particularly to the brain, by which this organ becomes oppressed. Now, if venesection be not carried the length of relieving the cerebral congestion, and so letting loose the energy of the brain on the system at large, it is quite clear that we diminish the strength without gaining our object, and consequently retrograde from the proper path. This is not meant to censure the surgeon whose practice is detailed. Considering the general prejudice against bleeding in India at that time, it would have required no small degree of fortitude to employ so heterodox a remedy under the immediate eye of the presidency, where even success would hardly have supported the innovation.

The remaining patients on board are very ill. All complain of pain in the head and liver, with a diseased secretion of bile, and constipated state of the bowels—swelled furred tongues—restlessness and exacerbation at night, with slight heat of skin, thirst, and trifling acceleration of pulse—frequent giddiness and stupor, without the least relish for food. I continue to evacuate the bowels with natron vitriol. or calomel and jalap, and persevere in the mercurial treatment till ptyalism takes place.

Bombay, 17th March.

Eight men attacked with fever during the last twenty-four hours : four of them with violent mad delirium ; the others complained of pain in the head, loins, lower extremities, and epigastric region, with swelled tremulous tongues ; but no great heat of skin, or quickness of pulse. Some were slightly indisposed for a day or so before ; others had no premonitory sensations whatever. They were all well evacuated with the emetic-cathartic solution, or calomel and jalap : I prefer the former, as it acts both ways at once.

Several on board are very ill, without the least appearance of ptyalism ; others have their mouths affected, and the bad symptoms disappearing. In the former, I can perceive little or no alteration in the temperature or pulse from a state of health.*

Sent 17 to the hospital to-day ; many of them changing yellow, with *pain and fulness about the liver, and severe head-ache.*

Bombay, 18th March.

Six admitted this morning ; three with violent mad delirium, which lasted several hours ; in the others, the symptoms were milder. All our nurses are now dropping ill, and the fever seems to acquire a contagious character, as it is running through the whole of the ship's company.† One of the wardroom officers was attacked last night. We now send them on shore nearly as they are taken ill.—*All labour under some affection of the liver, which is immediately communicated to the brain.*

At noon sent 15 of the worst cases to the hospital ; several of them changing yellow. They are generally attacked first in the night, and always experience an exacerbation afterwards, as the evening closes in. No remissions on alternate days ; the only amelioration is in the mornings.‡

I this day visited all our patients at the hospital. Several of them are very ill—many quite yellow ; and all have great pain and fulness in the region of the liver, with constipated bowels. They are treated nearly in the same manner as on board ; the medical gentle-

* Is there not great torpor throughout the system here, from the state of the brain?

† Although it does not follow that the disease is contagious, because the nurses are taken ill ; yet it appears very probable that this fever *became* contagious *from accumulation.*

‡ Miasmal fevers, when not very concentrated, often show remissions on alternate days ; till at length, as the season changes, they slide into intermittents. When they are so virulent, however, as to occasion great and sudden derangement, whether of function or structure in important organs, it is needless to say, that such remissions cannot be looked for.

men there placing their whole confidence in a continuance of the mercury. They attach much importance, however, to friction with ung. hyd. fort. over the region of the liver ; giving three-grains of calomel four or five times a day, in conjunction with small doses of antimonial powder and opium, as occasion requires. Two patients at the hospital are delirious at night.

Bombay, 19th March.

Twelve taken ill with fever since yesterday ; most of them attacked during the night. In eight cases it set in with violent mad delirium. Several of them were in perfect health a few minutes before ; others had some slight previous indisposition.

Six cases on board have now shown symptoms of ptyalism, and are greatly relieved in all respects, with some return of appetite. As the spitting increases, the yellowness of the skin disappears proportionally. Prescribed the nitrous acid both to the convalescents, and those now under the mercurial course : a practice much recommended by Mr. George Kier, surgeon of this presidency.

Bombay, 20th March.

Five people attacked since yesterday ; two, without a moment's notice, were seized with violent mad delirium.* The other three with symptoms more moderate ; but all with pain in the head and epigastric region. They were treated as already detailed. Sent 18 of the worst cases to the hospital ; all labouring under hepatic affection, and many of them very ill. A few more have their mouths affected since yesterday, and are getting better.

Bombay, 21st March.

Ten cases of fever within the last 24 hours. Four of these were men who came on board from the Elphinstone East-Indiaman a few days ago, and were attacked with violent phrensy and convulsive exertions, craving for drink of various kinds. After the spasms were allayed, they complained of pain in the epigastric region and head—tongues swelled—pain in the liver—vomiting of acrid bile†—stricture across the forehead and sinciput—pulse natural. After vomiting, they found themselves much relieved. Prescribed calomel, opium, and antimonial powder, as already detailed. At ten o'clock this morning Lieut. P. was attacked with delirium—pain in his head and epigastric region—tongue swelled, and white—muttering between

* The nature and violence of the attack show that it could not proceed from *latent* miasmata received previously at Surat. Neither could the fever arise *entirely* from land-wind effluvia here, since the other vessels lying in harbour were not affected. Some people may suspect a local cause in the ship's hold, or elsewhere, but no such source is traced by the gentlemen composing the survey. The constitutions of the crew, coming in from the more equable temperature of the sea, were strongly affected by the abrupt atmospherical vicissitudes at Bombay ; and the effects resulting thence were aggravated by the miasmal impregnation of the land-wind by night.

† Did this violent mad delirium arise from the brain sympathising with the liver or stomach, where acrid bile might have been accumulated ? Or did it arise from exhalations conveyed by the land-winds, and acting on the brain ? I am inclined to think that it was owing to both.—Contagion !

13

his teeth—no heat of skin. He assisted last night in holding several men who had mad delirium, and probably inhaled the effluvia from their breath or bodies. Two patients, who were convalescing since the nineteenth, and taking nitrous acid, seem inclined to relapse as the soreness leaves their mouths ;—mercury again prescribed.

Bombay, 22d March.

Five added since yesterday, with the prevailing fever. All complain of pain in the head and right hypochondrium—eyes and tongue swelled ;* the latter covered with a bilious crust—small, hot bilious evacuations by stool, with great thirst.—*They cannot bear the slightest pressure on the region of the liver.*

I have applied for a medical survey on the state of the ship, to inquire whether or not the fever is contagious, and what is the best plan of arresting its progress.

Bombay, 23rd March.

A young man in perfect health, who has been ten years in India, while assisting his sick messmate into the hospital boat to-day, was all at once attacked with the fever. Severe pain in the head, epigastrium, and liver, was soon followed by the most violent mad delirium, and incoherent language : he fancying the people around him were going to murder him. No heat of skin, or acceleration of pulse. This state lasted four hours, and was relieved by a vomiting of foetid, green, acrid bile.

The fever not so prevalent now, and seems to have spent its force, as only one man was seized in the last twenty-four hours. The nights are becoming warmer, which I hope will soon check its progress.

Bombay, 24th March.

Five men attacked since yesterday ; one with the usual mad delirium. All labour under pain in the head, epigastrium, and liver ; with white swelled tongues ; pulse and temperature little increased. Prescribed gentle emetics of pulv. ipecacuan. with plenty of warm diluent drinks, on their first complaining.† After the operation, calomel, opium, and antimonial powder four times a day, with pediluvium.

Pursuant to my request, a medical survey was held on board to-day, by the following gentlemen, viz.

Dr. Moir, of the medical Board ;
Dr. Scott, ditto ditto ;
Dr. Sandwith, of the General Hospital ; and myself.

After an investigation and mature deliberation, it was agreed that

---

* This symptom is noticed by Mr. Tainsh, on the coast of Syria, (Medical and Physical Journal,) and by the Gentleman of Bussorah, who narrates his own case. (Transactions of a Society,) &c. &c.

† Some change in the administration of emetics is here evident, though no reason is assigned. I think the plan I have recommended, of allaying the gastric irritability by calomel, or calomel and opium, and then procuring copious intestinal evacuations, will be found the safest practice ; as it effectually emulges the liver and its ducts, and prevents, or lessens the abdominal and cerebral congestions ; especially when aided by early venesection.

the following would be the most effectual, means of checking this fever, *which appears to be contagious**—

" 1st. To land all the sick at the General Hospital.

" 2d. To remove the ship to Butcher's Island, and there dis-embark the remainder of the ship's crew, with their bedding, &c.

" 3d. To clean, whitewash, and paint the ship throughout,; to fumigate her, and likewise the people's bedding, with nitrous gas ; and to fire off all the lower deck guns."

Bombay, 25th March.

Nine cases of fever in the last twenty-four hours. Three, who were in perfect health a few minutes before, were seized at once with mad delirium. Several of those patients, whose fevers were checked at the commencement of the ptyalism, and where I trusted the remainder of their cure to nitrous acid, are now relapsing, their mouths being quite well.†

I cannot say much in favour of the acid, though so highly recommended by Dr. Scott and Dr. Kier of the presidency, who give it in all cases during and subsequent to the mercurial course. Those attacked yesterday were gently vomited with ipecac. and warm diluent drinks ; after which they took small doses of calomel, opium, and and pulv. ant. four times a day, with tepid bathing ; a practice much recommended by Dr. Moir of this presidency. Sent eight cases to the hospital—sixteen on board.

Butcher's Island, 26th March.

Pursuant to the decision of the Medical Survey, we this day landed on Butcher's Island our sick, sixteen in number, in various stages of the fever : some with their mouths getting sore, and the bad symptoms disappearing—some in a state of ptyalism and convalescence—and others with all the usual symptoms of the fever, particularly the hepatic affection, head-ache, and yellowness of the eyes and skin.

B. Island, 27th. March.

No addition to the list since landing. All those whose mouths are affected have no other complaint than debility.—The sick are comfortably situated in the castle, which is well aired and clean.

B. Island, 28th March.

Several patients now convalescent, with sore mouths. One patient

---

* " It has never been known,'' says Dr. Bancroft, " as I am informed, that a single case of this fever, (typhus,) had occurred on either side of the Indian peninsula." *Essay on Yellow Fever, page* 510. If this be the case, and if the respectable gentlemen above-mentioned, who had the best means of ascertainment *on the spot*, did not give an erroneous judgment, it follows, that *other fevers* may, under certain circumstances, *become* contagious.

† I have expressly remarked, in the second section, that *free and copious* ptyalism is necessary. Where this is brought on in a few days, and especially where bleeding or other evacuations have been early premised, there has seldom so much derangement taken place in the liver, or even its functions, as to require the continuance of mercury. But where no V. S. was employed, and the disease has gone on many days before ptyalism, as above, the action of mercury must be kept up for some time after the fever is checked, till the functions of the liver are completely restored.

very restless last night, with great heat of skin, and pain in 'the region of the liver, which was relieved by a blister, and calomel bolus,
wth opium and antimony.   Most of the others have hepatic affections, which subside as the system becomes impregnated with mercury.

.- *B. Island*, 29th *March*.

All in progress to recovery ; their mouths getting sore.

B. Island, 30th *March*.

Two men, who were yesterday employed in cleaning the ship,
have been seized with fever ; but the symptoms are milder than in
those formerly attacked on board.   Same treatment.

B. Island, 31st *March*.

Only twelve on the list.   Most of them convalescents with sore
mouths.

B. Island, 4th *April*.

The patients at Bombay Hospital recover very slowly.—Almost all
of them labour under affection of the liver, with severe head-ache,
debility, and want of appetite.   They have sent us over thirty cases
for change of air.   Two more were attacked yesterday with fever
and dysentery ; they had been employed in cleaning the ship.   After
evacuations, the calomel as in the others.

B. Island, 5th *April*.

Of the 30 patients received from Bombay Hospital none are worse.
They find themselves cooler and more comfortable here.   Several
have considerable affection of the liver, attended with night fever,
which is sometimes ushered in with rigors and cold chills, succeeded
by hot skin, thirst and head-ache.   Prescribed five grains of calomel,
one of opium, and two of antimonial powder, thrice a day ; blisters
to the part affected.   All my original patients are better, with sore
mouths and debility.   I *tried the decoction of bark in several cases, but
find they recover faster without it.*   I also tried the nitrous acid, but
cannot say much in its favour.   The two patients with dysenteric
symptoms have pain in the region of the liver.—The same treatment
as the others.

B. Island, 6th *April*.

The patients from Bombay Hospital recover surprisingly fast.
Three of them were highly tinged yellow, which goes off as their
mouths become sore.   Many have constipated bowels : decoction of
tamarinds, with natron vitr. an excellent laxative.   A few of the
convalescents, as they get stronger, have a return of pain in the liver,
for which the calomel is again prescribed.

The dysenteric patients are relieved by the calomel and opium—
the tenesmus not near so violent.   Mercury continued.

B. Island, 7th *April*.

The patients from the hospital daily gain strength and appetite ;
more particularly those whose mouths are well affected with mercury.

All the fevers experience a nocturnal exacerbation ; in some ushered in with rigors.

In Bombay Hospital this fever runs great lengths. Several patients are quite yellow, with debility—severe pain across the epigastrium, in the head, and in the loins. No great acceleration of pulse ; but all are much worse at night than during the day. Calomel, opium, and antimonial powder, internally, with frictions of the ung. hyd. and frequent purgatives, are the means employed by the physicians of the hospital. They also tried the bark and nitrous acid, with the worst success, it generally occasioned great sickness at stomach, stricture on the surface, and obstructed perspiration, with universal inquietude. Removed 32 cases more of fever to Butcher's Island from the hospital.

B. Island, 10th April.

The bilious fever not near so prevalent now, as when we were on board ; and in all attacks the symptoms are milder.

The patients from the hospital promise fair ; some have dysenteric complaints, which go off as the mouth becomes sorer. Two fresh attacks, with much pain in the region of the liver and bilious vomiting. The usual treatment pursued.

Many of those last received from the hospital complain of pain in the head and liver region. Their mouths had been affected at the hospital, but are not so now. The mercurial treatment to be renewed.

Butcher's Island, 14th April. Thermometer 90°.

In some of the last 32 patients from Bombay Hospital, the fever seems inclined to run great lengths. Sometimes they appear tolerably well ; at others, they labour under severe pain in the head, epigastrium, and liver, with great debility and aversion to food. I tried the bark in several of these cases, but think it did harm, by increasing the pain in the head, and general inquietude. In other cases, I gave small and frequently repeated doses of calomel, with the nitrous acid, which answered the purpose much better. The constipation was best obviated by decoction of tamarinds with natron vitriol.

The patients in the general hospital recover very slowly ; and several are extremely ill. The hospital is close, and badly aired ; and the men contrive to procure arrack, which they cannot so well do here. I therefore removed over sixteen patients to-day, all very ill ; two of them quite yellow, with severe affection of the liver.

B. Island, 16th April.

Most of those last from Bombay Hospital are under the influence of mercury, in which course I persevere. The others convalescing fast.

B. Island, 23d April.

Most of my patients are now in a fair way. We have removed all that are able to bear removal, from the hospital to this Island. They all labour under hepatic affection, and are under the influence of mercury, which I continue.

25th April.

We this day embarked all our sick, 84 in number, and dropped down to the middle ground. All our patients in rapid progress to recovery, and all under the influence of mercury.

At sea, 27th April.

Sailed yesterday for Goa. Our patients in a state of progressive convalescence ; thirty-two remained behind at Bombay Hospital.

(Signed) *Wade Shields*, Surgeon, Centurion.

The perusal of this narrative cannot fail to excite our interest, and strongly arrest our attention. We observe an unwearied assiduity and perseverance in the Surgeon, with a coolness of observation, and candour of recital, that greatly enhance the value of the document. It bears on its front intrinsic marks of fidelity. There is no finesse or disguise ; he tells a plain, unvarnished tale. Few medical men have gone through more trying scenes in India, than this gentleman, of which the above is but a trifling specimen.

The following reflections on this fever may here be allowed.

First, with respect to its contagious nature ; I believe that few, who have been much in hot climates, will hesitate to pronounce, that at its commencement, it did not exhibit a single trait of contagion. A ship comes in healthy from sea ; and after being a week in port, where no contagious disease prevails, has all at once eighteen of her crew knocked down in one night with fever, and every night afterwards a similar repetition, more or less, till in a few days—" the decks are crowded with sick, and the effluvia intolerable." From this period it certainly betrays some symptoms of a contagious nature, particularly in the check which it all at once experienced on their landing on Butcher's Island, and in the circumstance of the men who were cleaning the ship afterwards, being the principal sufferers. Add to this, the decision of the medical survey, judging it to be contagious. This corroborates my observation respecting the Endemic of Bengal, and which I believe will apply to most other endemics, as those of Batavia, Madagascar, Johanna, West Indies, &c. namely ; that they are never originally contagious in their own nature, but may under peculiar circumstances, acquire that character occasionally, from accumulation, confinement, and inattention to cleanliness and ventilation.

I myself could never see any just cause, why a number of sick men, crowded together, should not generate a contagious disease, as well as a crowd of people in health. That the latter circumstance has sometimes happened, will, I believe, be very generally admitted, notwithstanding the opinion of Dr. Bancroft. But be this as it may, the fever in question was a bilious fever, and one of very considerable violence too. Although the season of the year was not that of autumnal remittents, yet the land-winds, in all seasons, and in all tropical climates, are more or less impregnated with miasmata, and that these had a considerable share in the fever above described, I entertain no doubt.

2dly ; the determination to the liver and brain was here so conspicuous, that it became the prominent feature of the disease ; and although not always so unequivocally manifested as in this instance, is ever to be suspected in tropical fevers.

Many of the observations contained in the foregoing narrative, strongly corroborate my ideas on the nature of fevers in hot climates, as detailed in a preceding section.   The theory is perfectly applicable to the symptoms of this fever.

In miasmal fevers, the congestion in the head and abdominal viscera were the consequences of impaired energy in the brain and nervous system, as there explained.   The same congestion takes place here, partly from the same cause, (miasmata conveyed by the land-winds and acting on the brain,) but principally in the following manner :

The extreme vessels on the surface of the body, and by sympathy, of the vena portarum in the liver, having been excited into *inordinate* action during the intense heat of the day, are suddenly struck torpid by the raw, damp, chilling land-winds ; the consequence of which is, that perspiration and biliary secretion are checked ; the blood determined inwards, is impeded in its passage through the liver, and accumulation ensues in the portal circle, " which is immediately communicated to the brain," as observed in this gentleman's narrative more than once, and as I have already explained.*   During this period, the bile stagnating in the biliary ducts, becomes viscid ; and on the recommencement of a hurried secretion, from emetics or other medicines determining the blood to the surface, often so obstructs the natural passage into the intestines, that regurgitation into the circulation takes place and tinges the skin yellow.   A great deal, however, is forced up through the stomach in a viscid and vitiated state ; tending to keep up the gastric irritability, and sometimes to destroy the stomach altogether.   This view of the subject explains why the men were almost all seized in the night, and why a nocturnal exacerbation was ever afterwards observed.   With strict justice, therefore, and with more propriety, we might denominate the fever in question—" Hepatic," rather than Bilious Fever ; and with some slight modification, principally in degree of violence, I shall show, in a future section, that in reality it is *alter et idem*, hepatitis itself.

3dly, in regard to the treatment.   Although, as I have before hinted, I differ from this gentleman respecting the exhibition of emetics, and the omission of V. S. yet, it must be confessed that his success in the end was great, and sufficient to confirm him in opinion, that the practice was the best that could be devised.   Indeed, it was the general practice of the country.   It does not appear that any deaths occurred, either on board or at Butcher's Island ; and as eighty-two men were removed back to the latter place from the general hospital, and thirty-two left at Bombay, when the Centurion sailed, the whole number sent at different times on shore to the hospital is accounted for, viz. one hundred and fourteen.

Thus out of full 150 cases of this fever, (which it will readily be granted, was no very mild or tractable disease,) none died unless subsequently at the hospital, out of the 32 left behind.   But if we look to the sequelæ of the disease, resulting from the great hepatic

* " Is is evident," says Dr. Blane, speaking of fever, " from a number of facts,
" that the state of the *brain and viscera* depends on that of the external surface
" of the body ; for a free state of the pores of the skin, provided it is general,
" tends more than any other circumstance to relieve internal pain, and also to
" take off delirium." *3d edit. p.* 358.

derangement that accompanied the febrile state, there will be some drawback on the otherwise uncommon success of the practice pursued. The utility of early venesection and purgatives is no where more conspicuous than in obviating these disagreeable consequences, as will be fully shown in the next section, where they had a fair trial.

One thing, however, is certain ; and a very important consideration it is, namely, that as the *mercurial treatment, unassisted,* was here entirely followed, and implicitly confided in, both on board and at the hospital, so it will require some sophistry to explain away these stubborn proofs of its extraordinary power and success.

Had this fever, so strongly characterised by yellowness of the skin; bilious vomiting, head-ache, &c. happened in the West Indies, or at Gibraltar, or Cadiz, and in autumn instead of spring ; and had any new mode of practice just coming in vogue been strictly pursued, would it not have furnished a pompous communication to a medical board, announcing the agreeable intelligence, that *yellow fever* might now " hide its diminished head ;" for that 150 cases of it, in a very violent form, had been successfully treated, *on the new principle,* without the loss of a man !

Into how many delusions have the medical world been drawn in this manner ? And what jarring contradictions, and virulent controversies, have resulted from them !

ENDEMIC OF BATAVIA.

Drawn up by WADE SHIELDS, Esq. *Surgeon Royal Navy.*

SEC. VII.—" In the month of June, 1800, His Majesty's ships Centurion, Dædalus, La Sybille, and Braave, having on board a detachment of the 12th regiment, consisting of 127 men and officers, sailed from Madras, on a secret expedition ; and on the 23rd of August following, the squadron anchored in Batavia Roads. The Centurion and Dædalus were placed about four miles from the garrison, to blockade the port ; the Sybille kept constantly shifting about to interrupt the approach of small vessels to the city ; and the Braave lay at anchor under the small island of Onrust, about three miles from the main land of Java.

" During the first few weeks, the squadron continued tolerably healthy, and without any deaths ; although the crews were much harassed by night and by day, in chasing the enemy's vessels, rowing guard, and loading or unloading the prizes off the island of Onrust.* The weather was pretty temperate at this time ; the thermometer, in the shade generally ranging from 82° to 87°, with regular sea and land breezes. When the latter, however, came off from the low, swampy grounds about Batavia, early in the mornings, it

---

* Contrast this with what happened to the crews of the Russel, Albion, and Powerful, at the same place, in 1806, when their sanguine hopes of surprising the Dutch squadron were suddenly dissipated.

brought with it a thick mist, accompanied by a very fœtid smell ; all of which would gradually go off, as the sun rose, and the sea breeze set in. During the, prevalence of this fœtid mist in the morning, many people would complain of slight indisposition in the head and stomach, which likewise went off as the sun came out.

" About this time the Braave disembarked an officer and some men of the 12th regiment on duty at the island of Onrust, where a temporary hospital was established ; and here the first appearance of *endemic* fever was observed. It was not, however, in any alarming degree, but chiefly confined to those who lived intemperately ; as none of the officers of that ship were attacked, though they frequently slept on shore. Some of the people having broken open a spirit-store on the island, were in the habit of getting intoxicated, in which state they often exposed themselves to the intense heat of the sun, by day, and the damp, cold dews of the night. A few of the 12th regiment fell victims to fever, much aggravated, if not occasioned by irregularity ; in consequence of which, an idea was very generally propagated, that the island was peculiarly unhealthy.

" On the 14th September, the Centurion relieved the Braave, and took charge of the hospital, where twelve cases were left behind, most of them very ill, and some of whom died. Prepossessed against the island, the Surgeon of the Centurion declined landing any of his sick there, at first ; till, finding that some of the Braave's, who were exceedingly ill, recovered, and that none of the nurses were attacked at the hospital, he ventured to land six of his worst patients, (bilious remittents and fluxes,) who all did well. He therefore became convinced, that the reported insalubrity of the island was unfounded, in a great measure, at least.

" Unfortunately, however, the commanding officer of the expedition, conceiving that the vicinity of the island to the main land was the cause of sickness, (which supposition seemed corroborated by the fœtid mists that daily came off from thence to the island,) ordered the sick to be removed, on the 28th September, to the small island of Edam, situated nine miles out to sea ; a circumstance that he thought must insure its salubrity. Here the tragic tale commences ;—but first let us glance at the medical topography of the two islands. Onrust is a small island, three miles from the main, well cleared of trees, underwood, and jungle ; nearly flat, and free from swamps or marshes, except one very small spot, which, however, is daily covered twice by the tides. —On this island there were many excellent buildings, where the convalescents could be separated from the fever cases, and where all could have abundance of space and ventilation. From the fœtid exhalations which were conveyed by the land-winds from the neighbourhood of Batavia, the sick were easily secured, by closing certain apertures in their apartment, till the sun dispersed the vapours in the morning ; after which there did not appear to be any danger from the miasmata disengaged during the day. Edam, on the other hand, though further out of the reach of Batavian exhalations, is covered with trees, long grass, and jungle, having a part of the island itself in a stagnant, marshy state. The buildings here were indifferent, and only one long ward could be found, for the sick and convalescents ; in consequence of which the latter class of patients experienced ·all those dire effects produced by the depressing passions, forever nurtured by the melancholy scenes of death, which this fatal spot too constantly presented to their view ! Thus, in running from a doubtful danger, they precipitated themselves on certain destruction.   In leaving Onrust, (a cleared space,) to avoid the effluvium of Batavia, weakened and diluted by a three miles passage from its source, they settled on the jungly and marshy island of Edam, where pestilent miasmata, in a concentrated form, issued from every foot of ground around them !—The fatal effects which followed, were predicted by an eminent Surgeon on the spot, but his suggestions were disregarded or overruled ; *distance* from the main being held paramount to all other considerations.

Of sixty soldiers, (12th Regiment,) landed at different times, *in health*, to do duty at Edam hospital, and other buildings on the Island, between the 1st October and 12th November, thirty-one died, (besides five or six at Onrust, previously.)   Of the remaining twenty-nine, embarked on breaking up the blockade, (12th November,) twenty-two died at sea ; the other seven were sent to Malacca hospital, where all or nearly all of them, shared the same fate !—In short, only sixty-two returned out of the whole detachment ; the rest having fallen ingloriously without drawing a sword !

" All the soldiers getting ill on Edam, sixteen Marines were landed from the Centurion to do night duty, as they expected an attack from the Dutch gun-boats.   The whole of these were seized with the fever, and thirteen died ; two recovered, and one was sent to Malacca hospital. +   -

" The loss of seamen I have not been able* exactly to ascertain ; but it must have been considerable.   Almost the whole of the sick, [twenty-eight in number,] who were removed from Onrust to Edam, [28th September,] died.   And as nine Officers, including the Surgeon, Mr. Cornish, who were doing duty at this dreadful Island, perished, we may form some idea of the general mortality.

" It is worthy of remark, that the Dædalus, in which 25 of the detachment from the 12th Regiment, were embarked, did not land a man on any of the islands, nor did one of her men die, or suffer an attack of this endemic.   Such is the outline of its history ; the following are the features of this fever, principally as it appeared at Edam, its head-quarters :—

" The patient, without much previous notice, (of the first attack,) is suddenly seized with giddiness and cold chills—sense of debility, and vomiting, with pain over the orbits, and in the epigastric region. He frequently falls down, and is insensible during the paroxysm ; his body covered with cold clammy sweats, *Except at the pit of the stomach, which always feels hot to the palm of the hand*—the pulse is small and quick.   On recovering a little, this train of symptoms is succeeded by flushings of heat—increased pain over the orbits, and in the sinciput—pain and a sense of internal heat about the stomach and præcordia—oppressed breathing—the lower extremities, at this time, not unfrequently covered with cold sweats.   The eyes now be-

come, as it were, protruded, and the countenance flushed. Retching, and at length, vomiting of discoloured, bilious matter, comes on
—the tongue white and furred—the abdomen tense and full, with
pain in the loins and lower extremities. The length of this paroxysm varied from six to eighteen hours, and was generally succeeded
by cold rigors—very often low delirium, preparatory to the next
stage or paroxysm of the fever. The intellectual functions now become much impaired, the patient not being at all sensible of his
situation, or of any particular ailment.—If asked how he is? he
commonly answers, " Very well ;" and seems surprised at the question. This was a very dangerous symptom, few recovering in whom
it appeared. In this stage all the symptoms become gradually, often
rapidly aggravated ; particularly, the head-ache—pain and tension in
the epigastric region, and vomiting. Some patients, *on shore*, were
carried off in 18, 24, 30, or 40 hours, and others not till as many
days after the attack, especially when removed on board, from the
more noxious air of the island. A great proportion changed, in a
few days, to a bright yellow ; some to a leaden colour : other cases
terminated fatally, in a very rapid manner, too, without the slightest
alteration, in that respect. Generally, however, the change of colour, indicated great danger. Vomiting of black bilious stuff, resembling the grounds of coffee, frequently commenced early, and
continued a most distressing symptom ; too often baffling all our attempts to relieve it. In some, a purging of vitiated bile, or matter
resembling that which was vomited, occurred ; in a great many, a
torpor prevailed throughout the intestinal canal—rarely did any natural feces appear spontaneously.—The pupil of the eye was often
dilated, and would not contract, on exposure to a strong light—in
others there was great intolerance of light :—both indicated danger. Low delirium was a pretty constant attendant on this fever,
from first to last ; sometimes, though more rarely, raging high delirium. Mr. Carter's was an instance of the latter, which he had in a
very terrible degree, with red, inflamed, and protruded eyes—great
inquietude—hot, dry, skin—small, quick pulse ; his mind actively
employed about the stores and prizes on shore, of which he had
charge previous to his illness. During the violence of the paroxysms, he was quite insensible to every thing that was going on around
him, constantly grasping at, or wrenching those objects within his
reach. He made frequent attempts to get overboard. In the low
delirium, also, the mind is much occupied on avocational subjects ;
if a seaman, about the ship's duty ; if a soldier about his regiment,
marching, &c. Some patients were comatose from the first attack ;
in others, the fever was ushered in with convulsions, delirium, and
cold sweats, without any intervening heat of the surface, except at
the pit of the stomach, which, in most cases, was burning hot to the
touch, and accompanied internally by a similar sensation according to
the patient's own feelings.

" Hæmorrhage from the mouth or nose seldom occurred ; in two
cases, which terminated fatally, the blood did not coagulate, but tinged the linen yellow. Aphthæ appeared in a few cases, and indicated danger. Subsultus tendinum often attended both on the low and

high delirium. The pulse never could be depended on. In the very last stage it has been regular ; but in general it is small, quick, and either hard or stringy and tremulous; sometimes, during the reaction of the system, full and hard. Deafness was very common, and an unfavourable symptom. Two kinds of eruption appeared about the lips—one such as we often see at the decline of common fevers ; the other, consisted of small black or brown spots round the lips, and was likewise a dangerous, indeed a fatal symptom. With this eruption, the teeth, tongue, and fauces generally become covered with a brown or black crust, and the breath intolerably fœtid. Locked jaw took place in two cases at Onrust Hospital, but the patients were insensible of it :—both died. *The brain appeared the organ chiefly affected at first—the stomach and liver in succession**. In those cases which occurred on board, and where the patient had not *slept* on shore at Edam, the symptoms were much milder, and the fever resembled more the bilious remittent of other parts of the East. A great torpor prevails generally throughout the system, with the low delirium ; blisters, medicines, &c. having little effect on the patient, who appears as if intoxicated. When roused, he recollects the person who is speaking to him, for a moment, and answers in a hurried, incoherent manner ; then lies on his back, his mouth and eyes half open ; both feces and urine often passing involuntarily. I have seen them remain in this state for hours—nay, for days together, scarcely moving a single voluntary muscle all that time. In this melancholy situation, Lieut. Neville, of the 12th regiment, lay for some days previous to his death.—Never was there a disease so deceitful as this fever :- I have frequently seen instances where every symptom was so favourable, that I could almost have pronounced my patient out of danger : when all at once he would be seized with restlesness—black vomiting—delirium—and convulsions—which, in a few hours, would hurry him out of existence !

" This was the case with Mr. Broughton, Purser of the Dædalus, who died of the Batavian endemic at Edam Hospital. On the seventh day of his illness he took a change for the better ; and every thing was promising. The morning before he died, he expressed himself greatly relieved ; and called for some mutton broth and sago, both of which he ate with a good appetite ;† spoke rationally—and was in good spirits. Towards evening the delusion vanished—restlessness—black vomiting—delirium and convulsions supervened, and carried him off before morning ! I have seen many cases terminate in this manner. Two patients at Edam complained of a diminished size of the brain, and that they felt as if they could shake it about within the cranium : —both died. Mr. Cornish, Surgeon of the Dædalus, who had charge for a while of the hospital, was one ; he died on the seventh day of his illness.

" The fatal terminations generally happened on the third—fifth— seventh—ninth, and not unfrequently the eleventh and thirteenth day ; if they passed this period, they usually lingered out twenty or

---

* This accords with my observations on the Bengal Endemic, and with the mode in which I supposed miasmatâ to act on the human body.
† Hunger is a fatal symptom in the yellow fever.

thirty days. But very few indeed ever ultimately recovered, who had slept on shore, and were attacked at that dreadful island, Edam! No constitution was exempted from the assault of this fever. It seized with equal, or nearly equal violence, on those who had been many years in India, and on the most robust and plethoric, or newly-arrived European. Even the Dutch Officers and Malays, who had been drawn from different parts of Java, and whom we had prisoners at Edam, fell victims as fast, or nearly so, as the English. Several officers, seamen, and soldiers, were sent on board from this island in hopes that the change of air might mitigate the disease. Many of even the worst cases of these would promise fair for a few hours in the forenoon ; but night always dispelled our hopes, for then the patient relapsed as bad as ever :—they almost all died. But their fate was considerably procrastinated by the change ; many of them lingering out a great length of time on board, sinking at last from the consequences of the fever, rather than from the fever itself. Several of them changed into obstinate intermittents at sea, with great derangement of the liver, spleen, and bowels. Indeed the liver, in most cases, seemed affected from first to last in this fever ; but in all protracted states of it, this affection became the prominent symptom. In those that were cut off during the first 18, 24, or 30 hours, the brain appeared to be the organ oppressed. With respect to the question, whether or not this fever was contagious, I am decidedly of opinion that it was not so. For if all the nurses and medical attendants of the hospital at Edam died, it must be remembered, that they were equally exposed to the cause of fever, whatever it is, as the soldiers and seamen who did duty at the barracks and other buildings, or who were sent to the hospital for other complaints ; all, or nearly all of whom shared the same fate. Moreover, what I conceive decides the question is this ; that although on our raising the blockade of Batavia, great numbers of sick, in every stage of the fever, were brought on board from the hospital at Edam, yet not a single nurse, or medical attendant of any description, ever suffered the slightest attack of fever ; nor did any circumstances transpire, that could in the least favour the idea of contagion, notwithstanding that the great accumulation of sick on both decks rendered it a matter of impossibility to separate them completely from those who were well, nor at all times to prevent a considerable generation of effluvia.

"From our first arrival at Batavia, in August, until our return to Malacca, in January following, we only buried one man of fever, who had *not slept on shore at Edam, Cuypers, or Onrust islands; whereas almost every person who slept even a single night at Edam, died.* No ill effects were experienced from going on shore in the day time, or among the sick at the hospital. I myself regularly visited the hospital of Edam every day, with perfect impunity, till one night that I staid rather late, attending the unfortunate Surgeon of the Dædalus ; in consequence of which I was three days afterwards seized with the fever, but recovered by mercury carried to ptyalism. I think it highly probable, however, that had I slept on shore, no medicine would have saved my life.

"The night before we raised the blockade, parties of men and officers were sent on shore at Edam to blow up and destroy the works and buildings on the island, which operations detained them about half the night there. Most of these were shortly afterwards attacked with the fever, but all recovered except one, (Mr. Parry, midshipman ;) his fever too, was checked by mercury ; but being of a diseased habit, he relapsed when the soreness left his mouth, and died. The gunner, carpenter, and other officers, were all seized with the fever ; but the former, being principally employed among fires, in laying trains, blowing up, &c. had the disease in an infinitely milder degree than any of the others.

" One circumstance more is so singular in itself, and so much attracted our notice at the time, that I think it deserves commemoration. *Of all the people or patients who slept at the fatal island of Edam, four only, to the best of my knowledge, escaped the fever, entirely, and returned to Malacca.—These were two obstinate venereals, and two chronic dysenterics ; all under the influence of mercury, for some time before I sent them to the hospital. Their complaints did not get better in the least on shore, so that they continued to take mercury there. They slept in the same ward with the fever patients all the time, but never had the slightest symptom of fever themselves.* One other patient at the hospital did not catch the fever; but he was sent there in the last stage of phthisis, and died a few days after he landed.

" I have omitted to mention, that despondency, or anxious timidity, very frequently accompanied the access of this fever ; while a placid resignation to their fate, or rather, an insensibility to their situation, marked its fatal close.

Treatment.

" In this, as well as in the common fevers of India, where a redundancy of vitiated bile might be suspected lurking in the primæ viæ, I have always prescribed a solution of salts and emetic tartar, as the first medicine, which generally operated both upwards and downwards ; and subsequently, by perspiration, in a short space of time, to the great relief of the patient. On the same evening, an anodyne antimonial draught, (vin. ant. one drachm tinct. opii, gut. xv. vel xx. aq. menth. two ounces,) was exhibited, to allay the irritability of the stomach—promote the cuticular discharge, and dispose to sleep. Bleeding I was afraid to attempt, as in the *only case*, to my knowledge, where it was tried in this fever, the patient very soon afterwards died, in a state of putrescence. *From this circumstance, and from some accounts which I had read, of its bad effects in fevers of the West Indies, I gave up all idea of the lancet.* I therefore had recourse to evacuations from the bowels, and from the skin. For the latter purpose, I tried various medicines ; such as the saline draughts, with sp. æther. nitros. tepid bathing, with diluents, &c. ; but I found none equal to small doses of antimonial wine, and tincture of opium ; given frequently, with plenty of warm, diluent drinks, and occasional pediluvium. By perseverance in this plan, for a few days, *in the less violent cases*, the skin has become relaxed, with an equally diffused perspiration—the pulse soft and natural ;—the pains and delirium have disappeared ; and nothing but debility remained, which was soon removed by bitters, bark, wine, and nourishment.

" But alas ! in the more concentrated forms of the disease, by which we were now surrounded, this practice was far from successful. *For here the patient hourly lost ground ; and seemed to be hurried out of existence by the local effects of the fever ; chiefly confined to the brain and liver. What the nature of these local effects was, I am unable to say. They appeared to be either inflammation—an accumulation—or a greater determination of blood to those organs, or perhaps something compounded of all these ; and evinced by the red, inflamed state of the eyes—the delirium—the oppression, tension, and often pain, in the epigastric and hypochondriac regions.** Finding, then, that bleeding would be attended with fatal consequences, and that antiphlogistics and tonics were alike ineffectual, I was forced to have recourse to other means ; and knowing that mercury was a powerful specific against local inflammation, particularly of the liver, as well as a most valuable medicine in bilious remittents, where visceral obstructions were forming, or formed, I placed my last hopes in the employment of this active remedy. I generally prescribed calomel combined with opium, and antimonial powder, in some few cases with camphor, in the following manner :

Calomel, six or eight grains,

Antimonial powder, two grains,

Opium, one grain.

" These were made into a bolus, and taken every three, four, or six hours ; so that from twenty-four to thirty-six grains of calomel might be taken in the course of the day and night.—If a salivation could be excited in a few days, the patient experienced an immediate change. The fever entirely left him—the pains abated—the intellectual functions were restored—the stools became natural, and nothing but tonics, nourishing diet, and change of air were wanting to perfect the recovery. This last desideratum, (change of air,) the most important of all to convalescents, was least of all within our power, while we inhaled the noxious atmosphere of Batavia.

" Here, then, we had the mortification to see our patients, after being rescued from the jaws of death—every symptom of fever gone, and after being several days convalescent, with a relish for food—relapse one after the other, *as the soreness left their mouths,* and die almost to a man !.

" Many instances, however, occurred at Edam Hospital, where mercury was prescribed in large quantities, *after other medicines had failed in the beginning*, without affecting their mouths ; in which case, they all proved fatal. I have sometimes prescribed bark and wine, in conjunction with mercury, to support the system during its exhibition, and I think that in several instances it accelerated the ptyalism.† Blisters often gave temporary relief to local symptoms, such as pain —hepatic affection, and vomiting. They likewise served as stimuli, to rouse the patient from stupor and delirium.

---

* I need hardly remark, that these conclusions, the result of observations made at the bedside of fever, and in an extensive field, form a striking coincidence, and a corroboration of the theory of fever which I framed in the same school of experience.

† This is similar to Dr. Balfour's plan.

" In the early stage of this fever, the tepid bath was used with advantage ; but in advanced states of the disease, I think it did injury, by increasing debility. I have frequently, experienced the greatest benefit from sponging the body with cold vinegar and water, where there was low delirium—cold clammy sweats—and stupor. In such cases the pulse, from being 120 or 130, would fall to 90, and a refreshing sleep succeed ;—but night always brought on the usual exacerbation. Gentle emetics of ipecacuanha, I have often found to relieve the delirium, oppressed breathing, and load at the stomach or præcordia, even at an advanced period of the disease. *In cases where great determination to the brain appeared, I have often given brisk doses of calomel and jalap, with surprising good effect. Indeed, evacuating medicines of every kind, where they do not tend to debilitate the system, are extremely useful in the early stages of this fever.* Wine, porter, and nourishment, did more harm than good, except in the advanced periods of the disease, when porter was always beneficial in checking the vomiting, and allaying the irritability of the stomach. Bark, in many cases, did much harm, by bringing on or increasing the vomiting, and other dangerous symptoms—besides checking the perspiration, and rendering the patient hot and restless. In some cases, however, I think it produced good effects, especially when guarded with opium, to make it sit on the stomach.

" *But could the patient be removed from the noxious air of Batavia into a purer atmosphere during the mercurial course, I should not have a doubt in the efficacy of mercury ; for it was the only medicine that ever bade fair to check the ravages of this dreadful fever. Without this change of air, I believe that every human means will have but a temporary effect ; and excepting mercury, few of them will have even that.*

" It is necessary to say, that copious ptyalism must be brought on, otherwise it will prove ineffecient. I tried the nitrous- acid, as recommended by Dr. Scott of Bombay, but cannot say any thing in its favour. The Dutch medical practice at Batavia, consists in giving camphor in weak jalap ; making the patient drink quarts of it in the course of the day, till the perspiration teems from every pore of his body ; keeping him all this time in a close room well covered over with warm bed-clothes, and without paying the least attention to any urgent symptoms, or other means of arresting the fever. But this plan was very unsuccessful ; for the mortality in the garrison of Batavia, while we lay before it, was dreadful, particularly among the European soldiers.

" Previous to our appearance, the Dutch, in general, resided a few miles up the country, on elevated ground, and out of the reach of those pestilential vapours that issue from the low swamps in the vicinity of the city. There they enjoyed tolerable good health ; but our arrival forced them into the garrison, where they had hard duty, day and night, in keeping a lookout upon us, and throwing up works to defend the place. The fever therefore, swept them off in prodigious numbers, so that their loss far exceeded ours. In an action with some of their gun-boats, we had a few men wounded, who did well on board. But this seems to be a rare circumstance ; for one of our officers being on shore with a flag of truce, was asked by the

Governor, how our wounds succeeded ; and being informed that they were all nearly well, he seemed quite astonished, and would hardly give credit to the account ; declaring, upon his honour, that during fifty years which he had passed at Batavia, he never knew a single instance of a man surviving a wound received in the noxious air of the city and its neighbourhood.* He also expressed great surprise that our mortality in the squadron was not greater ; as he calculated on our losing at least half our men during our long stay there. The Dutch ships generally lost from half to three-fourths of their crews, between their arrival at Batavia and their departure for Europe..

" CASE I.—Jas. Barrett, Onrust Hospital.

" *September* 15th, 1800. Has been ill about forty-eight hours. At 5 P. M. to-day, a mad delirious fit ; with difficulty can be kept in bed ; tongue tremulous, white and furred ; eyes red ; complains frequently of his head, with pain in the epigastric region ; skin hot, with some perspiration on it ; has been taking bark three or four times to-day ; head to be shaved and blistered ; pediluvium ; an æther and anodyne draught at bed-time—the bark infusion to be given through the night.

" 16th. Had a very restless night ; pain in the head excessive, and not relieved by the blister ; calomel, gr. x. jalap one drachm, statim sumend ; at 1 P. M. it operated, and brought off numerous, copious, foetid green stools. At 6 P. M. head not relieved ; a profuse perspiration ; pulse 90 ; tongue brown ; talks incessantly, in the most incoherent language ; all the symptoms very unfavourable ; the anodyne antimonial at bed-time.

" 17th. He lay in a state of stupor all night ; this morning, skin warm, and a little moist ; decoction of bark every two hours, which he retains well on his stomach. At 1 P. M. lies in a state of stupor, and with difficulty can be roused ; mutters between his teeth incessantly ; eyes inflamed and prominent ; abdomen tense and full ; pulse frequent and hard ; tongue dry ; bowels opened by an enema ; continue the bark ; and to take calomel, gr. x. cpii. gr. j. at bed-time.

" 18th. First part of the night more composed ; restless in the latter ; this morning, stupor as before ; lies on his back, with mouth and eyes half open ; with difficulty can be roused ; body has an offensive smell ; cold, clammy sweats, skin changing yellow fast ; pulse small and quick ; when roused, will take whatever is offered ; the decoction of bark through the day ; repeat the calomel and opium at bed-time.

" 19th. Passed a tranquil night ; repeated the calomel this morning ; the decoction of bark to be continued ; at 1 P. M. omitted the bark, and exhibited a saline cathartic, which brought off three copious foetid stools ; at 8 P. M. he appears better ; he is perfectly sensible ; skin a bright yellow ; but is warm, and has an equally diffused moisture on it ; repeat the calomel and opium as in the morning.

* This corroborates the circumstance mentioned by Lind, of the slightest scratches turning into dreadful ulcers, on board the Panther and Medway, in 1764.

15

" 20th. Passed an easy night, but had no sleep ; at 8 this morning he seems better in every respect ; continues sensible ; repeat the calomel ; also decoction of bark ; at 1 P. M. uneasiness in his stomach and bowels ; fever increased ; great incoherence in language and ideas ; *omitted the bark ; prescribed a cathartic, which brought off many copious fœtid stools ; at eight in the evening a remission of the fever ; other symptoms more favourable ;* the calomel continued.

" 21st. Passed a good night, and is better this morning ; repeated the calomel twice to-day, with bark decoction ; at 8 P. M. an exacerbation of fever ; repeat the calomel.

" 22nd. Passed a tolerable night ; a mercurial odour on the breath ; skin becomes less yellow, with equally diffused perspiration ; the calomel and decoction as before.

" 23rd. Mouth sore, and all symptoms favourable ; yellowness goes off the skin ; perfectly sensible ; no head-ache ; stools more natural ; craves for food ; continue the calomel, with a pint of wine and nourishing diet."

" 27th. Ptyalism did not come on copious till to-day ; he is now free from every complaint, except debility ; appetite good—spirits free ; yellow tinge almost gone ; omit all medicine—convalescent list.

" 28th. He was this day sent, with other convalescents, &c. to Edam Hospital, where he afterwards caught the fever. He was removed immediately on board ; the same plan of treatment adopted, and as soon as ptyalism appeared he began to mend. He was one of the very few who ultimately recovered from the fever of Edam."*

" CASE II.—WM. WARD, Marine, *Onrust Hospital.*

" *September* 18th, 1800. At 1 P. M. to-day complained of pain in his head, back, and loins ; skin burning hot ; tongue foul ; pulse small and quick ; pain at the stomach ; nausea and retching ; an emetic, which operated well ; at night the anodyne antimonial draught.

" 19th Passed a restless night ; this morning complains much of his head ; severe purging and griping ; skin intensely hot ; tongue foul and dry ; the emetic-cathartic solution, which operated well both ways ; at 8 P. M. the anodyne antimonial draught.

" 20th. Passed a very bad night ; high fever this morning ; dysenteric purging ; skin burning hot and dry ; tongue foul ; pulse very quick ; fixed pain about the umbilicus ; tenesmus ; calomel, gr. viij ; pulv. ant. gr. ij ; opii, gr. j ; to be taken twice a-day.

" 21st. All the symptoms worse to-day ; skin clammy, with partial sweats ; stools green, thin, small, and frequent ; severe tenesmus ; burning heat and pain at the stomach ; omit the calomel ; saline draughts with camphor through the day ; anodyne antimonial at night.

" 22nd. Passed a very restless night ; severe purging of green, fœtid stuff ; pain in the head and epigastric region excessive ; skin in-

* I leave it to the candour and judgment of the reader, whether the cure is to be attributed here to the bark decoction, or to the intestinal evacuations and mercury. This is a very valuable case—for it was a very formidable one : on the 18th it appeared nearly hopeless.

tensely hot; pulse quick; thirst insatiable; great inquietude, never resting a minute in one position; had recourse again to the calomel, opium, and antimonial powder; but to be taken morning, noon, and night.—At eight P. M. a little more composed.

" 23rd. Passed a better night; this morning very restless and uneasy; all the symptoms as bad as yesterday morning, with the addition of frequent delirium, and pain in the right side.—The same treatment as yesterday.

"24th. Slept some last night; symptoms this morning rather more favourable; the internal burning heat in the epigastric region not so great; the extremities covered with cold, clammy sweats; the calomel bolus repeated three times as usual, with camphor mixture every four hours.

" 25th. The dysenteric symptoms not so violent to-day; heat and pain in the epigastrium diminished; the pain of the right side subsiding; at noon, a violent paroxysm of fever, ushered in with rigors, which has left him in a very debilitated state; added decoction of bark and port wine to the mercurial treatment.

" 26th. Mouth sore; fever gone; bowels easy; asks for food; medicines continued as yesterday;

" 27th. Ptyalism; recovering fast; omit the mercury, and to have nourishing diet.

" 28th. Ptyalism continues; free from all complaint; returned on board of his ship. *

" CASE III.—Jos. HUGHES, Marine, *off Edam.*

" *October 9th*, 1800. Complained this morning of the usual symptoms of the Batavian fever; his headache exceedingly intense. He had done duty on Onrust Island, where he slept and often got intoxicated with arrack; an emetic, and after its operation, the anodyne antimonial draught.

" 10th. A very restless night; great pain in the forehead this morning; internal heat and pain at the pit of the stomach; tongue foul; bowels uneasy; pulse full and quick; frequent small, green, fœtid stools; ordered the emetic-cathartic solution, which operated well both ways; the anodyne antimonial as last night.

" 11th. At one o'clock this morning he was seized with convulsive twitchings; difficult breathing; alternate flushes and rigors, rattling in his throat; insensibility; pulse small, quick, and irregular; sp. c. c. gt.xxx. aq. menthæ one ounce and a half, æther. vitriol. half a drachm; this paroxysm lasted three hours with momentary intermissions; at

---

* This is also a very valuable case. It shows us the fever accompanied with dysenteric symptoms—and where the determination to the liver was quite evident:

If these honest and plain narratives do not remove every shadow of doubt, in regard to the power of mercury in tropical fevers of the East, all human testimony is vain. These documents are more convincing than if they came from myself—for I might either be blinded by prejudice, or have some interest in distroying the truth. Neither of these can have operated here—for the practitioner evidently resorted to mercury with reluctance, and hardly ever, till other means were first tried.

eight this morning, more composed ; skin hot and dry ; tongue foul and furred ; abdomen full and tense : natron. vitr. one ounce ; two copious fœtid stools ; evening, something better ; perspires ; the night draught as before.

" 12th. Slept till midnight ; at one o'clock, stole out of bed, and leapt overboard ; but was instantly picked up by a boat that happened to be alongside. He was now perfectly sensible, and somewhat frightened ; could not account for his conduct ; returned to bed ; at nine this morning, tongue foul ; skin warm and clammy ; body has a disagreeable smell ; camphor julep every two hours ; at 1 P. M. became very restless ; made several attempts to get overboard, (to walk in the garden, as he expresses it ;) talks incoherently ; at 4 P. M. worse ; cold, profuse, clammy sweats ; complains of no pain ; when asked how he does, replies, " Very well ;" pulse small and fluttering ; lies on his back, in a state of stupor ; mouth and eyes half open : can hardly be roused ; the camphor julep continued, with an opiate at night. He drank a pint of Madeira wine in the course of the day.

" 13th. No sleep last night ; cold clammy sweats to-day ; made several attempts to get overboard ; pulse small and quick ; tongue covered with a brown crust ; still answer that he is " very well," (a dangerous symptom ;) decoction of bark and port wine ; his stomach retentive ; opium and camphor at bedtime.

" 14th. Very restless in the latter part of the night ; delirious ; made several attempts to get overboard. This morning, violent black vomiting, which was checked at 1 P. M. by opium, æther, and a blister to the epigastrium ; great restlessness ; constant desire to get overboard ; skin cold and clammy ; brain and mental functions still much disordered ; craves for wine, which is given to him ; at 4 P. M. more collected ; begs to be sent to the hospital ; his request complied with. At 5 P M he got up, in good spirits ; dressed himself ; went into the boat unassisted ; when landed, he insisted on carrying his own hammock and bed up to the hospital, which he actually did—he there drank a glass of port wine, and went to bed ; at eight in the evening he was in a sound sleep, with a fine warm moisture diffused over his skin, and every symptom favourable ; at five in the morning he was found dead in his bed : lying on his face, with nearly a gallon of red and yellow stuff, resembling blood and bile, under him; and which was still running from his mouth. On shifting him, to have him buried, his whole body emitted the most horrible effluvia. He must have died suddenly, and without a groan ; as three nurses sat up in the ward, and thought him asleep all night.*

* This is a singular, though I think, not inexplicable case. It furnishes at least one important reflection—namely, how easily we may be deceived by the phantom *debility*. Forty-eight hours *before* this man carried his hammock to the hospital,—" he lay on his back, his eyes and mouth half open—his pulse small and fluttering." Was not the debility here apparent, not real ? Were not his powers oppressed—not exhausted ? Else how could two short days of subsequent fever and delirium give him the almost miraculous strength—" to rise, take up bed, and walk ?" It is quite inconsistent with observation, that this could have been one of those fatal calms preceding death, from mortification of an important organ. In such cases, although the patient fancies himself relieved, or even that he is

"CASE IV. Robert Aldridge, Marine, *H. M. S. Centurion.* · *Off Edam.*

"13*th October,* 1800. Was seized last night with fever, ushered in by cold rigors. At eight this morning, skin clammy ; head giddy ; pulse small and quick ; tongue white and furred ; bowels uneasy, with pain about the umbilicus ; a saline cathartic ; after operation of the cathartic, camphor julep every two hours.

"·14*th.* Passed a tranquil night. At eight this morning, skin hot ; severe pain in his head ; stomach uneasy ; an emetic of ipecacuan, which brought off much green bile ; an anodyne antimonial at bedtime.

"15*th.* At ten o'clock last night, a great exacerbation of fever, with delirium, which remitted at four this morning. At 8 A. M. complains of debility and head-ache : skin soft and perspirable ; bark decoction every two hours ; at noon became delirious ; skin hot and dry ; at 6 P. M. high fever ; head much affected ; great incoherence ; pulse full ; tongue foul ; bowels costive ; omit the bark ; a saline purgative procured three stools ; the draught at bed-time as before.

"16*th.* Passed a restless night. At eight this morning, high fever ; severe pain in the head and stomach ; internal burning heat in the epigastrium ; calomel, gr. viij : pulv. ant. gr. ij ; opii. gr. j ; ft. bolus, ter in die.*—At 2 P. M. skin moist and warm ; pain in the head and stomach ; 6 P. M. became very hot and restless ; pain in the region of the stomach severe, with intense burning heat there, both internal and external ; calomel, &c. continued.

"17*th.* Was easy all night—passed too copious stools ; skin was warm, with equally diffused moisture ; at eight this morning, he is better ; the pain has left his head and stomach ; at 1 P. M. uneasiness

strong, there is little real force. The sound sleep, and warm moisture on the skin, are very incompatible with actual mortification. But if we advert to the state of the brain for several preceding days. we shall not hesitate to say, that effusion or rupture of vessels carried him off instantaneously.

The morning before, we see that he was seized with violent black vomiting which was checked by medicine. The return of this, when he was in bed, after the preceding exertion, and a great determination for some time past to the brain, has caused sudden rupture or effusion, which induced immediate death, or apoplexy ending in the same. Finally, was it not this *apparent debility* which prevented the exhibition of cathartics and mercury, so successfully employed in the preceding case?

* Too late. An active employment of mercury from the beginning without any other aid than venesection and copious intestinal evacuations, would have had the patient now on the verge of ptyalism.

Let those who are disposed to cavil at some points of practice pursued here, particularly the exhibition of bark, and omission of venesection, point out from what sources the Surgeon could have then drawn a better *methodus medendi.* Certainly not from books ; at least, not from the works of Bentius, Lind, Clarke, or Balfour. Nay, almost at this day, venesection is condemned and bark extolled! Dr. Bancroft, one of the latest writers on Yellow Fever, seems to rely principally on bark. Mr. Curtis, the last writer on the Diseases of India, boasts of having seldom " wet a lancet, except in specific inflammation."

If it be said, why did not *observation* point out the necessity of bleeding, and the injury occasioned by emetics and bark? I answer, by asking,—Why did not *observation* point these out long ago to those writers enumerated? Why did not Cullen find out the utility of purgatives in fever before Hamilton ?

in the region of the liver.; *cannot bear the least pressure over it ;* the calomel continued ter in die, as usual ; at 3 P. M. stomach uneasy ; black · vomit, (resembling coffee grounds, exactly ;) severe pain in the forehead ; the effervescing draughts every two hours ; added four grains of camphor to the evening dose of calomel.

" 18th. Restless night ; *delirium ; watery eyes;* skin changing yellow. This morning, complains of twitchings in the calves of his legs ; collected and sensible when spoken to ; calomel and camphor as before ; blisters to his legs ; at noon, skin cold and clammy ; profuse perspirations ; tried the bark in various forms ; but the very sight of it made him vomit ; the calomel and camphor continued ter in die ; at ten P. M. sensible to the pain of the blisters.

" 19th. Slept a little last night ; this morning, giddiness ; skin of a bright yellow colour ; took the bark with much persuasion : at 11 A. M. it made him sick, hot, and restless ; bowels uneasy ; abdomen tense and full ; glysters brought away several fœtid stools, and stuff like grounds of coffee ; took xxxiii grains of calomel to-day, but no appearance of its entering the system ; skin of a deep yellow colour.

" 20th. Restless and delirious in the night ; oozing of blood from nose and mouth, which tinged the linen yellow.* This morning, skin hot and dry ; tongue brown ; intolerance of light ; head much affected ; starts when spoken loudly to ; says he is " very well," and seems much surprized at being asked the question ; lies on his back, with mouth and eyes half open ; pulse small and stringy ; took xxxii grains of calomel to-day, with camphor julep.

" 21st. Symptoms as yesterday. In this state he continued for forty eight hours, when the black vomit, with convulsions, carried him off, on the 23d October, the 10th day of his illness. Not the least symptom of ptyalism could be seen, though he took calomel to the last hour.—He had done duty on shore, both at Cuypers and Onrust, where he lived very intemperately.†

" CASE V. Mr. THOS. F. CARTER, *from Edam.* .

" *October* 26th, 1800. Has been six days ill with the Batavian fever on Edam Island, and sent on board at six o'clock this evening, in hopes that change of air may mitigate the disease.

He now complains of coldness in the lower extremities ; bad taste in his mouth ; a troublesome purging ; great dejection of spirits ; pain in his head and epigastric region ; pulse small and quick ; frequently delirious before he came on board ; had taken bark in various forms at the hospital, without any benefit ; on the contrary he daily got worse. The emetic-cathartic solution was given him this morning on shore, which is still operating ; as he was much fatigued by coming on board, gave him a glass of port wine and the camphor julep.

" 27th. He was delirious and sleepless all night ; skin hot and dry ; the solution continued to operate in the night, both ways, and he passed several fœtid stools. At nine this morning, all the symptoms worse ; talks in the most incoherent language ; tongue very

* If this be not a case of " *Yellow Fever*," I know not what is.
† Was there not effusion in the brain here, as well as derangement in the liver?

foul ; *pulse full and quick ;* complains of great pain over the orbits and sinciput ; pain and burning internal heat at the stomach ; calomel, gr. viij ; camphor, gr. iv ; opii, gr. j. ter in die ;* a blister inter scapulas.

"28*th.* First part of the night restless ; latter part quiet, and sleep a few hours. At nine this morning, all the symptoms aggravated ; delirium ; *full quick pulse ;* pain over the orbits, and in the sinciput ; right eye much inflamed ; blisters rose well ; is sensible to the pain of it ; same treatment as yesterday.

"29*th.* Delirious all last night ; talks incessantly this morning, in very incoherent language ; says he feels as if he had two heads ; his eyes cannot bear exposure to the light ;† has frequent convulsive twitchings of the tendons ; repeated the calomel this morning ; he drank a little brandy and water, which he relished much ; at 8 P. M. very restless, skin hot and dry ; tongue foul ; twitchings of the tendons ; right eye much inflamed, and prominent ; had one fœtid, bilious stool ; when asked how he does, replies, " very well ;" and that nothing is the matter with him ; his mind constantly employed about the snip's duty and prize stores ; his countenance singularly wild and sallow : omit the calomel ; pediluvium ; diaphoretic powders of camphor and nitre ; diluents.

"30*th.* Very restless all last night ; with great difficulty could be kept in bed, preferring the cold deck ; was highly delirious ; right eye prominent, and much inflamed ; complains of pain in the calves of the legs ; blisters to his legs ; gave him a brisk dose of calomel and jalap, which operated, and brought off two copious fœtid stools ; at noon, he is much more composed ;‡ complains of strangury from the blisters. Semicupium and sp. æther. nitros. gave relief to this symptom ; great deafness ; clammy, profuse sweats ; small weak pulse ; bark and claret ; the calomel to be again renewed. At 6 P. M. his right eye still inflamed, red and prominent ; pulse full ; violent delirium subsided ; *half an ounce of bark, and a pint of claret, since morning,* which his stomach retains.§

* This is the seventeenth day of the disease—greatly too late !

† There are evident symptoms of congestion, if not inflammation in the brain here. This oppressed state of the sensorium renders the absorbent system so torpid, that there is no chance of the mercury being taken into the constitution. Evacuations, under these circumstances, by relieving the brain, invariably accelerate ptyalism.

‡ Although evacuations always give more or less relief in this fever, yet the idea of *debility*—that unlucky term—seems ever to have cramped their employment.

§ " The prejudices that formerly existed against the Peruvian bark, in fevers," says Dr. Hunter, " are no longer in being." " They were founded in *idle* " *speculations,* and originated with the learned, from whom they descended to the "great body of the people ; but even with the *vulgar* they are now extinct." *Diseases of Jamaica,* page 122. At page 98, we have this remark, " In almost "every case where the disease is *violent,* and the patient much reduced, it, " (wine,) is highly grateful and cordial. It is of the utmost consequence, in giv-" ing both nourishment and wine, that they be repeated often."

Dr. H. recommends about a pint a day, in small quantities at a time, and the same of food. Who can blame the surgeon for pursuing a plan recommended by such authority ? And, as I observed before, where has he any better instructions, in fevers of the East ?

"*31st.* Very restless all night, with *raging high delirium ;* great difficulty in confining him to his bed ; tongue and lips brown and crusted ; stomach tense, with burning internal heat in the epigastrium ; right eye red and prominent ; at one o'clock this morning, a blister renewed to the back of his head ; the calomel and jalap repeated ; at six this morning no better ; right eye inflamed, prominent, and seems *starting out of his head,* with other symptoms of a highly deranged state of the brain ; *neither the blister nor purgative has taken any effect,** two large yellow blotches have appeared on his neck ; I am forced to keep him lashed down in his bed, as he made several attempts to get overboard ; tore the blisters from his head ; constantly grasping at every object ; great deafness ; no recollection of any person ; his mind still employed about his accounts and the ship's duty ; strong convulsive spasms of the whole body ; so that it oft n requires two men, with all their strength, to keep him down ;† the raging high delirium sunk hourly, till, a few hours before his death, when we could hardly hear him articulate ; he was carried off with hiccup and convulsions next night, his body very little reduced, and without the least disagreeable smell.

" Previously to the attack of fever, he was constantly employed on shore at the island of Edam, where he had charge of the prize-stores, and where he frequently exposed himself to the intense heat of the sun by day, and the noxious influence of the air by night ; he used to sleep at the hospital ; he died on the 11th day of his illness, six days after he came on board.

"CASE VI. Mr. HAMMOND, Captain's Clerk. *Off Edam.*

" *October 23rd,* 1800. Was in the habit of being much on shore at Edam Island during the day ; but never passed a whole night there ; seized last evening with the usual symptoms of the Batavian fever ; head much affected ; great pain over the orbits ; took the emetic-cathartic solution, which operated well ; at night the anodyne antimonial.

" *24th.* Passed a restless night ; his bowels very uneasy ; this morning he is very ill ; all the symptoms violent ; small, hot, bilious stools ; the solution as yesterday, which operated both ways ; at night the draught repeated.

" *25th.* Passed a very bad night, with violent pain in the head and epigastric region ; hot, dry skin : quick pulse ; great inquietude of the system at large ; could not rest a moment in one position ; foul tongue. This morning all the symptoms the same as during the night ; calomel, gr. viij. ; pulv. ant. gr. ij ; opii. gr. j ; three times a day.‡ At 8 P. M. he appears a little more composed.

" *26th.* Had a violent paroxysm of fever in the night, ushered in

---

* The torpor alluded to is here manifest—and there can be little doubt of its dependence on oppressed sensorium.

† With the strength of two men the day before death—his body unreduced—and where mad delirium, and eyes starting from their sockets, declared the state of the brain I should have been tempted to bleed *usque ad deliquium,* or the relief of the symptoms, *coute qui coute.*

‡ This is the fourth day of the disease, counting the evening of the 22nd as one.

with cold rigors. This morning, he is very poorly indeed : distressing bilious purging ; countenance sallow and anxious ; all symptoms appear exceedingly unfavourable ; continue the same treatment.

" 27th. Passed a bad night ; no alteration for the better ; headache intense ; pain in the epigastric region ; hot, dry skin ; pulse quick ; dysenteric purging ; medicine continued.

" 28th. No alteration : had a violent exacerbation of fever to-day, ushered in, as before, with rigors ; continued the same treatment ; no appearance of ptyalism.

" 29th. Mouth sore. All the symptoms alleviated ; head-ache, and pain in the epigastric region, diminished ; bowels easier ; calomel bolus twice a day only.

" 30th. Mouth sorer ; all the bad symptoms disappearing ; complains only of debility ; decoction of bark and wine.

" 31st. Mouth very sore ; spits copiously ; keen appetite ; omit the calomel ; put him on the convalescent list, with wine, and nourishing diet ; from this time he recovered rapidly. This case was treated entirely with mercury.*

" CASE VII. Mr. POWEL, Master's-Mate. *At Edam.*

" *November* 13th, 1800. Was attacked with fever yesterday, on shore, at the island of Edam, where he had resided, in charge of the prize-stores, since the death of Mr. Carter. This morning, complains of the usual symptoms ; pain and giddiness of the head ; hot skin ; cold extremities ; quick pulse ; the emetic-cathartic solution ; after the operation of which, the anodyne antimonial.

" 14th. Restless night ; was much purged ; cold sweats, burning, acrid heat at the pylorus ; pain over the orbits ; six grains of calomel, and one of opium, thrice a day ; also the camphor julep every three hours ; port wine or porter, as much as he can take ; cold ablution ; at 6 P. M. symptoms nearly the same ; had many fœtid, bilious stools, during the day ; spirits greatly dejected ; cold sweats on the extremities ; pulse small, quick, and fluttering ; tongue brown and crusted ; great apprehension of death ; bark.

" 15th. No rest all night. This morning all the symptoms worse. At 10 A. M. the fatal black vomit has appeared ; cold sweats ; delirium ; omit the bark, which will not lie on his stomach ; repeat the calomel ; æther and laudanum draughts every two hours ; evening, the vomiting checked a little ; blisters to the head, and stomach ; skin begins to change yellow ; breath becomes fœtid ; every symptom unfavourable.

" 16th. No sleep last night ; worse in every respect this morning ; he sinks hourly ; low delirium ; muttering ; lips and teeth encrusted black ; breath fœtid ; insensible ; lies on his back, mouth and eyes half open ; skin intensely yellow ; pulse small and fluttering ; same treatment.

* It would be difficult to conceive how a more unequivocal proof of the efficacy of any medicine could be given, than is afforded in this case. I had set it down as lost, till I saw the words " *sore mouth*," on the 29th, which dispelled my fears ; for well do I know, from personal feeling, what *ease* this *soreness* brings.

" 17*th.* Black vomit all night ; cold sweats this morning ; tongue black ; pulse fluttering ; singultus ; eyes glassy ; breath very fœtid ; stools involuntary, and black, like coffee grounds ; lies on his back, eyes and mouth half open ; carried off in an attempt to vomit.*

" Wade Shields."

The foregoing cases, selected out of an immense number, will be sufficient to convey a very accurate idea of this endemic, and to support the remarks and general description which preceded them. I have exhibited more fatal than favourable terminations ; as the former must include the whole range of symptoms, from health to death, and ascertain the inefficacy of measures in which we might be apt to place too much confidence.

It certainly will not be denied that this is a very interesting and valuable document, as it gives us a much clearer view of the Batavian fever than any English work in circulation ; accompanied with numerous collateral incidents and observations, that excite reflection, while they strongly rivet our attention.

I shall glance hastily at some prominent traits in the character of this fever, with a few remarks on its cause, leaving the reader to form his own conclusions.

In the first place, the great similitude which it bears in most of its leading features, to the endemic of the West, cannot have passed unnoticed. Independently of the yellow skin and black vomit, they coincide in many minor, but characteristic symptoms ; for instance, the mental despondency, amounting to timidity at the beginning, veering round to nonchalance or apathy, in the progress of the disease.

The fatal lull, and occasional sensation of hunger too, which are so apt to deceive the inexperienced in the Western endemic, frequently appeared in that of the East. Neither would it seem very difficult to account for their discrepancies. For whether we allow that these endemics are solely caused by the local miasmata, or are the bilious remittents of hot climates, resulting from atmospherical influence, but aggravated by these invisible agents ; still, in either case, as the cause, or combination of causes must vary, according to the nature of the climate and soil, so we cannot expect to have their effects agreeing in every minute particular. Nevertheless, as the operation of these causes on the human frame appears to be nearly the same in all climates, we can clearly discern, (in the broad outline of their effects,) a strong family likeness through the whole ghastly tribe.

—————" facies non omnibus una
" Nec diversa tamen, qualis decet esse sororum."

The opinion that these grand endemics, (yellow fever for instance,) are only the bilious remittents of all tropical climates, in a more concentrated state or degree, is founded, I fear, on too great a rage for generalising. The bilious remittent may take place an hundred leagues at sea, in consequence of atmospherical vicissitudes acting

* Will any one assert, after reading this, and many other cases here, that the " *Yellow Fever*" never appears in the East ?

on particular organs, whose functions were previously disturbed by atmospherical heat. The endemic, on the other hand, is produced by a specific miasm, (witness that of the fatal island Edam,) which, independently of all those peculiar states of the air, or the body, requisite for the production of bilious remittent, will, when in a condensed form, kindle up at any season, and in any constitution, a fever of terrible malignity.

These diseases then, may be often, perhaps generally combined ; since their causes acquire force and subside, *pari passu*, and at the same period of the year. But assuredly they are sometimes totally distinct and quite unconnected with each other.

· This reasoning is corroborated by the fact, that time, (for instance, eighteen months or two years in the West Indies,) will accustom the human frame to the action of the febrific miasm, and thereby secure it, generally speaking, from the endemic, but no number of years is a protection from the bilious remittent.

The circumstance of the Dutch officers and Malays falling victims at Edam, might seem to militate against this doctrine ; but the objection vanishes, when we recollect, that by previously residing in the country, entirely out of the sphere of the local effluvium, they were in reality no more seasoned to it than the English ; and the mortality in the garrison proved it. They were in the same situation as the native or veteran West Indian, who, by spending a few years in Europe, or the interior of the country, loses his protection against a visitation of yellow fever on his return to the sickly towns.*

Neither will residence in one tropical climate, prove a security against the local endemic of another, as the above circumstances themselves render evident. Thus the crew of a ship, that has been two or three years on the Coast of Guinea, and sails direct from Sierra Leone to Barbadoes, which are nearly in the same parallel of latitude, will be as liable to yellow fever, as if they had sailed from England ; while a two year's station in the West Indies would have almost insured a subsequent exemption.

Indeed, the plan of seasoning troops against *yellow fever*, by stationing them for some time previously at Gibraltar, Madeira, or in the Mediterranean, has completely failed ; and how could it be otherwise, if the Coast of Guinea itself is no protection ? a melancholy proof of which was exhibited in H. M. S. Arab, in 1807 ; which ship came from the latter place, (where she had been nearly two years,) to the West Indies, and suffered dreadfully by the yellow fever. †

* Dr. Ferguson, in mentioning the fatal yellow fevers which ravaged the West India Islands in 1815, states—" In all it has been confined, for the most part, to the towns, and except at Bridgetown, to unseasoned Europeans. There it extended to unseasoned sojourners—even to *Creoles from the interior of the country*, who, in the time of the insurrection, were obliged to resort to the town on military duty." *Med. Chir. Trans. vol.* viii. *p.* 144. Again, Mr. Dickson, Surgeon to the Forces, states, in the 48th Number of the *Medical Repository*, that— " Dreadful were the numbers the writer saw under the mortal grasp of marsh fever at Prince Rupert's Dominico. *They were subjects assimilated to the climate, although strangers to that particular station.*

† " It is certain that if having had the West India yellow fever secures an ex- " emption from the Gibraltar one, this last gives no security in kind. Capt. John-

These facts, (particularly the last,) must go far to dissolve the theory of the ingenious Dr. Bancroft, who has laboured to prove, that " the security from the disease, (yellow fever,) is principally 'derived from the *ability to endure great heat.*" *Essay on Yellow Fever,* page 265. · The dangerous consequences which might obviously result from trusting to such a protection, as well as Dr. B.'s candour and humanity, will induce him to re-consider the subject. The officers and crew of the Arab, on their arrival in Carlisle Bay, considered themselves perfectly seasoned and secure : but on putting to sea, in the course of the month, the endemic broke out with such violence, that in one week they lost thirty-four men, and were forced to put into Antigua, in the greatest distress.

Dr. Bancroft, indeed, is not singular in his opinion, which appears to be copied from Dr. Trotter, [Medicina Nautica, vol. 1, page 336,] who has, *theorised* widely on a foundation which the foregoing *facts* completely overturn. Dr. T. probably took the doctrine from Dr. Moseley, who tells us, that a seasoning at *Bermudas* will secure us from the yellow fever of the *West Indies*, p. 65. Let no such plan be trusted.

The locality and range of this febrific miasma, are clearly decided by the Dædalus. Her ship's company breathed the same general atmosphere as the other crews, for months together ; but with the exception of the Purser and Surgeon, no man belonging to her came within the fatal circle, (in the night, at least,) though seldom more than two or three miles from its centre. The officers above-mentioned exclusively felt its influence, and like too many others, fell victims to its direful force. It is probable, however, that where a trade wind or monsoon sets over a large tract fraught with febrific miasmata, these invisible agents may be carried to a much greater extent tham where calms or gentle sea and land-breezes prevail. This is exemplified in the fever of Coimbatore, [Sec. 3.] and ought ever to be borne in mind by navigators in anchoring ships in the vicinity of swamps, or generals in pitching tents or stationing troops. The direction and prevalence of winds are ever to be coupled with the medical topography of a place. ·

This document furnishes decisive evidence on two points of great practical importance. One is, that even within the limited range of this poison, its power is nearly inert, comparatively speaking, during the day ; the other, that when nocturnal exposure has given rise to the disease, it is non-contagious. It is obvious what an influence the certain knowledge of these circumstances must have on our conduct, and to what useful purposes we may apply it.

In this, as in all other violent-endemics, the head and epigastric region were, as usual, the foci of the disease. The inutility, or rather the injury of every other medicine, than mercury and purgatives, was abundantly manifested. But with all due deference and respect for the Surgeon, and a proper allowance for the embarrassing situa-

" son, of the Queen's Regiment now here, had the Gibraltar fever in 1804, and " he has just now recovered with difficulty from a very alarming attack of the " prevailing Epidemic." *Ferguson on yellow fever, Med. Chir. Trans. vol.* viii. p. 124.

tion in which he was placed, I conceive that the first remedy was not applied early enough, or with sufficient boldness ; and that the purgatives, through a false fear of debility, were not so frequently administered as their evident utility warranted.

In the solitary instance where venesection had a trial, the hasty conclusion which was thence formed of its pernicious effects, in consequence of the sudden death and putrescency of the patient, deserves a remark. If the reader will revert to Joseph Hughes, (Case III.) who, after dressing himself in good spirits—going into the boat without assistance—carrying his hammock up to the hospital —retiring to bed, and falling into a sound sleep, was nevertheless found dead in the morning, " his body emitting the most intolerable effluvia ;" he will probably agree with me, that had this man been bled on entering the hospital, his death might have been attributed to venesection, with as much *apparent* justice, as any *single* incident could support.

This may serve as a lesson to us, how wary we should be in rejecting entirely a powerful remedy, from solitary or even several failures. For how difficult is it, in such cases, to say with certainty —such is the successful, and such the unsuccessful medicine ! The prejudice against bleeding, (seemingly justified by this event,) was engendered too, by " accounts which had been read of its bad effects in fevers of the West Indies ;"—fevers in which its preeminent service is now ascertained beyond the shadow of doubt.* From all these considerations, and from an attentive examination of the symptoms themselves, we may conclude, that venesection deserves a much further and fairer trial in this fever ; and I entertain little doubt, that it will be found a powerful auxiliary to the other means of cure.

Of the efficacy of mercury, under all its disadvantages, I need say little. There is the decision of the surgeon himself, who treated nearly 200 cases of the fever—there are specimens of these cases detailed—and there is a strong proof of the dependence placed on this remedy, where we find the surgeon himself confide his own life to its power, when attacked by the fatal fever of Edam. I would, however, recommend it to be used in the early and liberal manner pointed out in the Bengal endemic, with the same attention to venesection and intestinal evacuations. The constitutional effect of the mercury should be kept up till strength be completely restored. The cold affusion bids fair, during the reaction ; and, at all events, cold applications to the head, with warm pediluvia, will invariably prove serviceable.

The opinion of Dr. Cullen, that the influence of the remote cause ceases when the fever is once formed, is here proved to be not only erroneous, but dangerous. Removal from the sphere of its action, dur-

---

* What will the reader think of the following passage in a modern publication ?—" In such cases as seemed most to require it ; (blood-letting,) for example, where the patient was young, strong, of a full habit, and lately arrived from Europe ; where the pulse was quick and full, the face flushed, with great heat and headache ; and all these at the beginning of the fever, *bleeding did no good.*"— *Hunter on the Diseases of Jamaica,* 3rd edition, *page* 118.

ing fever, invariably protracted the fatal catastrophe ; and could the patients have been transported quickly into a pure air, while ptyalism went on, they would, in all human probability, have survived, as the surgeon himself believed. ,

One remarkable incident remains to be noticed, and cannot have eluded the observation of the reader. I mean the circumstance of the four *mercurial* patients, who resisted the baleful influence of Edam. Such an immunity cannot be attributed to chance. The proofs are both positive and negative. *They, and they only, escaped the fever.* It is rare that a person fairly under the influence of mercury, for the cure of any other complaint, is attacked either by endemic or contagious fever. I have seen several, who were reduced by long courses of mercury previously, and who had left it off, fall victims to fever and flux ; but seldom during the exhibition of the medicine. We know that a slight, or even a free ptyalism, may be kept up for weeks together, without any serious injury to health ; and if such a state proved an antidote, (as it did here,) against the most powerful cause of fever that ever, perhaps, had " a local habitation, or a name," the inconvenience of the prophylactic is very trifling, compared with the security it may afford. The rationale of the preservative is not very unreasonable. If it cure the disease, it *may* also have some power in preventing it. Bark was formerly considered capable of both—(witness the Peruvian drams that used to be served out to wood-cutters in hot climates ;) fatal experience, has proved it equal to neither ! Mercury, by keeping up the action of the extreme vessels on the surface, and in the hepatic system, prevents, what I conceive to be the paramount effects resulting from the application of febrific miasmata—INEQUILIBRIUM IN THE BALANCE OF THE CIRCULATION AND EXCITABILITY, AND CONGESTION OR INFLAMMATION IN ONE OR MORE OF THE INTERNAL ORGANS.

It is proper to observe, however, that many medical men of talents and observation, deny that mercury is possessed of any prophylactic power. I only state what has come to my own knowledge on the subject,

P. S.—Since the first and second editions of this work, the utility of venesection in even the Congestive Cholera of India, where the blood can scarcely be got to flow from the veins, has been proved beyond all cavil or doubt, and so has the auxiliary benefit of mercury, both as an evacuant and sialagogue. It is therefore gratifying to the author that twenty years' experience of others has confirmed all the leading points of his own.

DISORDERS OF THE HEPATIC SYSTEM.

Aspice quam tumeat magno Jecur Ansere Majus.—MARTIAL.

SEC. VIII.—"The exclusive efficacy of mercury," says Dr. Saunders, " in liver diseases of the continent of India, may perhaps be explain-" ed by supposing they arise from an *indigenous and local poison, or mi-*

" asma, peculiar to that country, unlike any thing known in any other
" part of the world, even under similar latitudes and temperatures."

Had this ingenious and deservedly eminent physician ever visited
the continent alluded to, his penetration would have discovered the
cause of this phenomenon, with out the aid of an " indigenous poison,"
which, like the introduction of an epic divinity, is a more poetical
than philosophical mode of extricating ourselves from difficulties, and
loosing the gordian knot.*

In order to clear the way for this investigation, it is necessary to
inquire, whether this " endemic of India" be equally prevalent in all
parts of that vast empire. Here universal evidence gives the negative, and every one, in the least acquainted with the medical topography of the country, knows, that genuine, or idiopathic hepatitis,
is ten times more prevalent on the Coast of Coromandel than on the
plains of Bengal ; while, on the other, hand, intermitting and remitting fevers are ten times more numerous in the latter than in the former
situation. Let us next see, if there be any particular difference in
the climates and temperatures of these two places. By exact thermometrical observations made at Calcutta, by Mr. Trail, during a
whole year, the following appears to be the monthly medium heat of
three different diurnal periods—morning, noon, and evening.

TABLE.—No. I.*

January........	66°	May	84°	September........	82½°
February........	74	June.............	83	October........	82½
March........:	79	July.............	83	November	76
April.............	86	August............	82	December........ .	68

Annual Average, 78½ Fahrenheit, 1785.

Let us compare this with the heat at the presidency on the coast.
—The following is copied from the Madras Gazette, showing the
state of the thermometer at the Male Asylum, during one week in
July, 1804, which was by no means remarkable for any extraordinary
range of temperature—

TABLE.—No. II.

State of the Thermometer at the Male Asylum, Madras.

1804.	7 A. M.	Noon.	3 P. M.	8 P. M.	Average.	Remarks.
July 11	81	88	89	85	86	" The thermo-
12	81	88	90	86	86¼	meter is plac'd in
13	81	91	92	86	87½	a room moderate-
14	82	90	93	84	87¼	ly exposed to the
15	83	91	94	88	89	weather and fac-
16	84	92	95	91	90½	ing the North-
17	85	94	96	91	91½	West."
Total Average, 88½.						

Now it is well known, that excepting for a few weeks at the change
of the monsoon, in October and November, the Coromandel coast is

* See the Section on Egypt in a subsequent part of this work, where Hepatitis is proved to be equally as prevalent on the Banks of the Nile as on the Coast of
Coromandel. Hepatitis is very prevalent also on the Coast of Africa, where the
heat is excessive.

† Vide 2d vol. Asiatic Researches.

remarkable for a cloudless sky and steady temperature, all the year round ; the heat, however, being often above the specimen exhibited, as the following table from Dr. Clarke will show ;—

TABLE.—No. III.

State of the Thermometer on board the TALBOT *Indiaman, in Madras Roads, from the 24th July to the 23d August,* 1771.

Month.	Day	Hour.	Ther.	Month.	Day	Hour.	Ther.
July . . .	24	12	90	August . .	8	7	96
		6	96		9	12	89
	25	12	88			4	87
	26	12	90		10	12	93
		3	93			4	88
	27	12	90		11	2	94
		3	93			4	89
	28	12	90		12	12	93
		3	92			4	90
	29	12	93		13	12	90
		4	96			4	87
	30	12	90		14	12	89
		4	94		15	12	89
	31	12	91			3	90
		4	93		16	12	90
August .	1	12	93			4	94
		4	94		17	12	94
	2	12	92		18	12	93
	3	12	90		19	12	90
		3	91			4	87
	4	12	90		20	8	90
		4	92			3	94
	5	12	92		21	8	92
		4	94			3	95
	6	12	89		22	11	94
	7	12	90			4	87
		5	92		23	10	86
	8	12	93			3	88

Total Average, 91°.

Dr. Clarke remarks that, " on account of the sandy soil of Madras, it was found moderate enough to allow a thermometer to rise six or seven degrees higher ashore." This would make the average, for a month in succession, 97 or 98°.—*Vide Clarke on Long Voyages, page* 56 *et seq.* Mr. Curtis, speaking of the Coromandel coast, where he remained on shore more than a year, observes—" Except for two or three weeks about the shifting of the monsoons, especially that which happens in the month of October, a shower of rain or a breeze, are (is) almost unknown ; scarce ever a haze or cloud appears upon the horizon, to mitigate the dazzling ardour of an almost vertical sun ; and the thermometer, through *the whole twenty-four hours,* seldom or never points under 80° of Fahrenheit, but generally *far above it.*" Introd. p. xvii. How far above 80° it generally points, the preceding tables will clearly evince.

The nature of the soil is such, that while the sun is above the horizon, it acquires a much superior degree of temperature to that which the plains of Bengal attain ; in consequence of which the nights are often hotter than the days, when the land-winds prevail in May, June, and July. I have seen the thermometer stand at 105⁹ of Fahrenheit, at *midnight*, and that too on board a ship riding at anchor in Masoolipatam Roads. Many causes combine to produce so much higher a range of atmospherical heat in the Carnatic than in Bengal. First, the coast in question trends away towards the equinoctial line, while a great part of Bengal lies *without* the tropics. Secondly, the soil of the former is gravelly or sandy, and vegetation stunted ; whereas that of the latter is clayey, and vegetation luxuriant. Thirdly, the periodical rains that fall, at the change of the monsoon, on the coast, are instantly absorbed by the parched and sandy surface, affording only a very temporary coolness to the air; while an actual and extensive inundation covers Bengal for months together. If therefore, the nocturnal temperatures of the two places were blended with the diurnal —if, for instance, the thermometer were marked every hour at Madras and Calcutta throughout the year, and the whole averaged, there would be full *ten degrees difference* in the annual mean temperatures of the two presidencies. Bombay is nearly on a par with Calcutta ; for although the country surrounding the former is neither flat nor inundated, as in Bengal, yet its northern parallel of latitude, its insular situation, and the montainous nature of the adjacent country, combine to render the average annual temperature of Bombay as low, if not lower, than that of Calcutta.*

An important, yet unnoticed circumstance, remains to be considered, in estimating the comparative influence and effects of the two climates.—Although *sudden* vicissitudes of temperature are highly injurious to the constitution, in general, and to the hepatic system in particular ; yet an *annual* change is eminently beneficial. Thus, the first table shows us, that at Calcutta, during four months of the year, viz. November, December, January, and February, the average heat of the day is only 71° Fahrenheit, five degrees *below* the common summer heat of England. As for the nights I can vouch for their being cooler than summer nights at home ; since a hoar frost is not an unusual sight on the plains of Bengal, in the mornings of this period ; and very gratifying have I found the heat of a blanket at Calcutta in the month of December.

Thus the Bengalese, and those in similar parallels of latitude, enjoy a kind of *tropical winter*, or exemption from high ranges of temperature, during *one-third* of the year ; the effects of which, in relieving the hepatic system from excessive action,—in bracing the whole frame, relaxed by the previous heats, and preparing it to sustain the subsequent ones, may be compared to a short return to our native skies.

This remark will be confirmed by the following analogical observations of Dr. Darwin. " Though all *excesses* of increase and decrease of stimulus should be avoided, yet a certain *variation* of stimulus seems to prolong the excitability of the system : thus, those who are *uniformly habituated to much artificial heat*, as in warm parlours in the winter months, lose their irritability, and become feeble, like hot-

* Vide Sir James M'Grigor's Memoir, Edin. Med. and Surg. Journal.

house plants; but by frequently going for a time into the cold air, the sensorial power of irritability is accumulated, and they become stronger. Whence it may be deduced, that the *variations* of the cold and heat of this climate (England,) contribute to strengthen its inhabitants who are more active and vigorous than those of either much warmer or much colder climates."—Zoonomia.

Knowing then, as we do, how uniformly a high temperature affects the biliary organs, and keeping the foregoing facts in view, can we be at a loss to account for the greater frequency of genuine hepatitis in the Carnatic, than in Bengal ?—I say genuine, or original hepatitis ; for most of those cases which we meet with at the latter place, are the consequences, or sequelæ of repeated intermittents and remittents, both marsh and jungle.

The same reasoning applies to Bombay, and all other parts of India, whose distance from the equator produces a *tropical winter*, when the sun is near Capricorn ; or where peculiarity of soil, elevated situation, or other locality, is incompatible with that high and almost unremitting range of temperature, so remarkable on the Coromandel coast, so fully adequate to the derangement of the hepatic functions.

Having thus explained, in I trust a satisfactory manner, the nature of this " local poison," and how it comes to operate more forcibly in one part than another of the Indian continent, it is necessary to show why, even in the less sultry parts of the latter—for instance, Bengal, the complaint is still more prevalent than under similar latitudes in the West.

Dr. Saunders quotes, in support of his hypothesis, the following observation from Hunter on the Diseases of Jamaica. " It is a re-" markable thing," says the latter, " that in the East Indies, under the " same latitude *nearly* as Jamaica, that is, at *Madras and Bombay*, the " disease known in those countries by the name of Liver, or Hepa-" titis, shall be the most prevailing disorder among Europeans, and " that the same should not be known in the Island of Jamaica." In the first place, there is a geographical error in classing Madras and Bombay in similar latitudes. In the second place, I assert, that there is a difference of ten degrees in the annual mean temperatures of the two places, taking the *hourly average height of the mercury by day and by night, throughout the year*. In the third place, hepatitis is by no means the most prevailing disease among Europeans at Bombay ; dysentery being infinitely more common.* But further, the Island of Jamaica, from its situation in the vicinity of Cancer, must have its " tropical winter," as well as Bengal, and at the same period ; while its insular nature, and distance from the American continent, insure it the advantage of sea and land-breezes, the *former* coming in cool and refreshing in every direction from the sea by day ; the latter descending *cold* from the blue mountains by night.

On the contrary, in Bengal, the land-winds are so distressing in April and May, as to oblige the Europeans to sit behind tattys, for weeks together, to avoid being stifled with heat and dust. It is far

---

* If I afterwards trace a connexion between dysentery and deranged hepatic function, it will not invalidate this position ; as the same observation will apply to the dysenteries of the West.

otherwise in the West. Indeed, it is computed by Dr. Mitchell, after thirty years observation, that it is as hot in the countries of the old continent, in latitude 29 or 30, as in the countries of the new continent which lie in 15 degrees of latitude. M. de Paw makes the difference between the old and new continents, in respect to temperature, amount to 12° of the thermometer.—*Recherches Philosophiques*.

" The vernal season in these parts," (West Indies,) says Mr. Edwards, ". may be said to commence with May.—The parched sa-
" vannahs now change their aspect, from a withered brown to a fresh
", and delightful green. Gentle southern showers presently set in,
" which, falling about noon, occasion bright and rapid vegetation.
" At this period, the medium height of the thermometer is 75°.—
" After these vernal showers have continued about a fortnight, the
" season advances to maturity, and the *tropical summer* burns in its
" full glory. During some hours in the morning, before the sea-
" breeze has set in, the blaze of the sun is fierce and intolerable.
" But as soon as this agreeable wind arises, the extreme warmth is
" abated, and the climate becomes even *pleasant* in the shade. The
" thermometer now stands generally 75° at sunrise, and 85° at noon.*

" But whatever inconvenience the inhabitants of these islands may
" sustain from diurnal heat, is amply recompensed by the beauty
" and serenity of the nights : the moon rises clear and refulgent in
" the cloudless horizon—the landscape is fair and beautiful—*the air*
" *cool and delicious.*

" In November or December the north winds commence ; at first
" attended with heavy *showers of hail*, till at last the atmosphere
" brightens, and the weather, till March, may be called *winter*. It
" is a winter, however, remote from the horrors of northern seve-
" rity :—*cool, wholesome, and delicious.*"—*History of the West Indies*.

Let this description be compared with that of the coast of Coromandel, and we shall see how easy it is to make a sweeping classification of climates on paper, where little similarity exists in nature.

To return. The average thermometrical range of heat ought to be, and really is, lower at Jamaica by three degrees than either at Bombay or Calcutta ; and if so, how much lower than at Madras ? In Jamaica, too, though the rainy season may leave swamps and marshes at the debouchures of rivers, yet there is nothing like the great annual inundation of Bengal, occasioning such numerous intermittents, that too frequently terminate in hepatitis.

Here then are the real causes why the last-mentioned complaint is more observed, and indeed more prevalent, in the East than the West ; viz. the great superiority of temperature on the Coromandel coast :—and the frequency of intermittents and remittents on the marshy plains of Bengal, or woody and jungly districts of other provinces, as well as of Bombay and Ceylon. To these may be added, the more sudden and extensive transitions of temperature, which take place on the continent of India, than in the islands of the West, owing to the greater degree of equilibrium preserved in the latter places by the surrounding ocean.

* Compare this with table No. II.—85° in the morning, 96° at noon.

" In Jamaica, (says Dr. Hunter,) the *coolest* month in the year is
" at least *twelve degrees* hotter than the *hottest* month in our sum-
" mers," page 174, 3rd ed.　Now the *common* summer heat of England is 76° ; consequently the thermometer must stand at 88° in the
" coolest *month*" at Jamaica ; and that too when there are even
" showers of hail," and when the weather is " cool, wholesome,
" and delicious !"　Let us compare this with Sir Gilbert Blane's
account of the West India temperature :—" The thermometer stands
" very commonly at 72°, at sunrise in the cool season ; rising to 78°
" or 79° in the middle of the day.　In the hot season, the common
" range is from 76° to 83°.　It seldom exceeds this in the shade at
" sea, and the *greatest* height at which I ever observed it in the
" shade, at land, was 87°."—*Diseases of Seamen*, page 12.

In a very interesting " Account of Jamaica," published in 1808,
by a gentleman twenty-one years resident at that island, it is distinctly stated that " the medium temperature of the air may be said to
" be 75° of Fahrenheit," *page* 21.

In the very same page, with some inconsistency, Dr. H. contra-
dicts his own statement.　" It was *hotter*," says he, " than common in
" the month of June, by *three or four degrees*, the thermometer ris-
" ing many days to 90°, an unusual heat in that climate."　If we take
" three or four degrees" from 90°, we shall have 86° or 87°, what
Dr. Blane states for the month of June in Jamaica, whereas, he just
before made the heat 88° in the " coolest month in the year," which
is nine or ten degrees too much.

I may here remark, that it must have been from *data* similar to the
above, that Dr. H. drew another conclusion—namely, that atmospherical heat has no effect in increasing or deranging the biliary secretion.　*Page* 277.　I shall merely place his opinion in juxta-position
with that of his friend who quotes him.

Dr. HUNTER.	Dr. SAUNDERS.
" A warm climate, it is alleg-ed, increases the secretion of bile, and renders it more acrid. There does not appear to be the slight-est foundation for this assertion." —*p.* 277.	" Such symptoms as I have now enumerated (viz. increased and vitiated secretion of bile,) are the spontaneous effects of a warm climate on healthy constitutions, independently of any intemper-ance."—*On the liver*, p. 159.

Every author with whom I am acquainted, excepting Dr. Bancroft,
and every one who has observed, or felt the effects of warm climates on his own constitution, will agree with Dr. Saunders.

Lastly, notwithstanding Dr. Hunter's assertion, that " Hepatitis is unknown in Jamaica," when we see so many sallow complexions—emaciated dysenterics—nay, obstructed livers, every day returning from
the West Indies ; when we hear Dr. Moseley, who practised twelve
years in Jamaica, assert, that in hot climates a sound liver is never
to be expected after death ; and Dr. Thomas, another West India
practitioner, make use of these expressions—" My own observations,
during a practice of *many years* in the West Indies, where Hepatitis
is a *frequent* occurrence," &c. &c. [Modern Practice of Physic,] we
may safely conclude, that in the endemic fevers, particularly the in-

termittents and remittents of both hemispheres, the hepatic system suffers proportionally in the Islands of the Caribean Sea, as well as on the Banks of the Ganges, or in the-forests of Ceylon. Indeed, Dr. H. himself admits, that enlarged and obstructed livers are frequently the sequelæ of intermittents in Jamaica.* Such, it is well known, would obtain the appellation of Hepatitis in Bengal ; but Dr. H. will not allow the term because, forsooth, these affections of the liver are not very apt to run into suppuration. Many people, indeed, cannot be persuaded that the hepatic functions are at all deranged, unless Hepatitis, *in propria forma,* be present.—Is the stomach never disordered except in *gastritis?*

Having ascertained the *quo,* we now proceed to the *quo-modo.* I have more than once in this essay alluded to a sympathy, or synchronous action, subsisting between the extreme vessels on the surface of the body, and those of the vena portarum in the liver ; a sympathy which, as far as I am acquainted, has not been noticed by any other ; and which, if proved, will account for the increased secretion of bile in hot climates, and lead to important practical conclusions. It is, however, in those climates alluded to, where the vessels in question are more violently stimulated than in Europe, that we can most easily and distinctly trace this sympathy. I have remarked, that when we first arrive between the tropics, the perspiration and biliary secretion are both *increased* ; and that, as we become habituated to the climate, they both *decrease, pari passu.*

It is very singular that the accurate Bichat should not only have overlooked this circumstance, which is evident to the meanest capacity, but advanced a doctrine quite the reverse. " A cold atmosphere," says he, " confines the functions of the skin, and occasions those of the mucous system to be proportionally extended. The internal secretions are more abundant, &c." And again. " In warm seasons and weather, on the contrary, the skin acts more powerfully, and the secretions, particularly the urine, are diminished." *Anatomie Generale.* This is all right, had he excepted the biliary secretion, which follows a law diametrically opposite to this ; viz. it is *increased* by a warm, and *diminished* by a cold atmosphere, in the same manner as perspiration.

I have likewise shown that in the cold, hot, and sweating stages of fever, the two processes are exactly simultaneous and proportionate. The *partial sweats* that break out towards the termination of the hot fit, are accompanied, as Dr. Fordyce remarks, with "*partial secretion,* and irradiations of heat arising from the præcordia." I shall now proceed to other examples illustrative of this sympathy. The Asiatic and African, though inured from their infancy to the high temperatures of their respective climates, guard, nevertheless, against

* It is remarked that the Creole children in Jamaica are subject to liver complaints. Since the 1st Edition of this Work appeared, the documents showing how much the liver suffers in West India climates and diseases, excepting perhaps in the Concentrated or Yellow Fever, where the brain and stomach bear the onus of disorganization, have so multiplied, that nothing more may be said on that score. Hepatitis is frequent in Egypt, Coast of Guinea, and Sicily, where the heat is occasionally excessive.

excessive perspiration, and its too frequent consequence, *suppression*, by keeping the skin soft and unctuous, whereby they maintain an *equable* flow both of perspirable matter and bile. The *former* is evident to the senses ; the *latter* is proved by the regularity of their bowels, and their general exemption from bilious or hepatic diseases. "The use of oil," says Dr. Currie, "instead of clogging the pores, keeps the skin moist ; and while it guards against *excessive*, promotes moderate and *necessary* perspiration,"—279. In our own climate, the gentle diapnoe, or insensible perspiration of *mild weather*, coincides with the regular biliary secretion ; while it is in August, when the perspiration is most in excess, that we see cholera morbus, and greatly increased secretion of bile.

Bichat ascertained, by direct experiments, that during the time of digestion in the *stomach*, the pylorus is closed, and the biliary secretion *diminished*. We know that a corresponding heat, dryness, and constriction on the surface of the body, are observable at this period. On the other hand, he found that, whenever the chyme began to pass into the duodenum, the biliary secretion was rapidly augmented. We know that, at this very time, the surface relaxes, and the perspiration is increased. Every one knows the effects of emetics and nauseating medicines on the skin and perspiration : the same effects are produced on the biliary secretion. "In all cases," says Dr. Saunders, "where bile is secreted in *too large* a quantity, the use of emetics is improper ; indeed, the actions of nausea and vomiting *increase* its secretion," p. 176. This sympathy is equally visible where the secretion is deficient.

If we observe those emaciated objects returning from the East and West Indies with indurated livers, sallow complexions, torpid bowels, and paucity of biliary secretion, we invariably find the skin dry, constricted, and harsh to the feel, without any thing like the softness and moisture of health.

In *diabetes*, where perspiration is notoriously defective, there is the most decisive evidence of diminution in the biliary secretion. "There are, perhaps, few cases of diabetes," says Dr. Watt, "without some affection of the abdomen, particularly in the epigastric region," p. 47. "Some morbid change," says the same accurate observer, "in the alvine excretion *always* accompanies the diabetic habit. *Costiveness* is perhaps the *most common* of these. In some instances the bowels have been so remarkably torpid, that even the most powerful medicines, in uncommonly large doses, produced but trifling effect." And, speaking of Stevenson's case, he says, "the quantity of alvine excretion was inconsiderable ; it had also an "*uncommonly white* appearance."–These facts speak for themselves.*

In chlorosis Dr. Hamilton observes, that—"the perspiration seems to be checked"—and "I am persuaded," says Dr. Saunders, "that "in chlorotic habits, the bile is more insipid—*is secreted in less* "*quantity*, and of a paler colour than in health," p. 232. "In ma- "niacal habits," continues the last-mentioned author, "there is gene-

---

* Are not the kidnies irritated by the non-secreted bile, (or rather the elements of bile floating in the circulation,) into inordinate action, in diabetes ?—Are not the effects of bleeding and mercury thus explained ?

rally a *defect* in the secretion of bile." I need not say how marked is the dry rigid skin, and deficient-perspiration in most maniacs. " Sea-sickness," says Dr. Saunders, " and a sea-voyage, contribute " very much to *restore the secretion of healthy bile.*" The well-known effect of these in determining to the surface, and promoting perspiration, especially that gentle diapnoe, corresponding with healthy secretion in the liver, need not be insisted on. The torpid state of the skin in melancholia, hypochondriasis, and most nervous disorders, exactly coincides with that of the liver and bowels in the same. " Hypochondriacal complaints," says Dr. Saunders, " are always at- " tended with dyspepsia and diminished secretion, with great torpor " of the alimentary canal,"—192. And again, " The symptoms of " dyspepsia and diminished secretion, which are now rendered more " conspicuous among females, from their sedentary life, are most ef- " fectually removed by the means suggested,"—viz. sea-sickness and a sea-voyage, the very surest means of keeping up a regular and healthy discharge from the pores of the skin.

The same may be said of exercise, which powerfully promotes the secretion of biles as well as perspiration.

There is a curious case related in the Edinburgh Medical and Surgical Journal, vol. 2, page 5, where an obstinate dyspepsia, [where bile is known to be deficient,] could not be cured till the exercises [broadsword] brought on a copious flow of perspiration. In cases of deranged structure and deficient secretion in the liver, Dr. Saunders recommends, what certainly will be found very useful—" the tepid bath, and small doses of mercury."

Here the bath must act first on the skin, and probably on the liver, from the sympathy in question—while, on the other hand, the mercury, which is known to increase the action in the liver, may produce its diaphoretic effect, from the same consent of parts above alluded to.

All the passions corroborate this doctrine. Fear, grief, and the other depressing passions, when moderate, lessen the secretion of bile—render the skin pale or sallow, and check the perspiration. On the other hand, anger and rage are well known to increase the biliary secretion ; and their corresponding effects on the surface are visible to every eye. Joy, hope, and what may be termed the elating passions, when in moderation, determine to the surface, and keep up a salutary flow of bile and insensible perspiration, so congenial to the healthy functions of the body. I shall adduce no more examples, till I come to speak of dysentery and cholera, which will, I think, afford undeniable proofs of the sympathy in question.

In the mean time, this connexion between two important processes in the animal economy, while it fully accounts for the increase of action in the hepatic system, from the influence of a hot climate on the surface, will be found to elucidate many of the phenomena attending those diseases we are considering ; and perhaps remove the stigma of *empiricism* so commonly attached to their cure.

It is allowed that perspiration and biliary secretion are increased by tropical heat, and that the latter is *vitiated.* Perhaps, even here the parallel holds between the two.—How different is the profuse and gross evacuation of sweat, from that insensible halitus, or gazeous fluid, which just keeps the skin soft and smooth in health!

We know that nature has recourse to the perspiratory process to obviate *greater* evils that would accrue from accumulated heat :—we have every reason to believe, from analogy, that the increase of the biliary secretion is also a wise mean employed by the same invisible agent, to guard against congestion, and derangement in the hepatic system.

I have shown, from Dr. Currie, that even " the *necessary* quantity " of perspiration in a hot climate enfeebles the system." So the increased and vitiated secretion of bile debilitates and renders irritable the whole tract of the alimentary canal. " The inhabitants of " warm climates," says Dr. Saunders, " are extremely subject to dis- " eases arising from the increased secretion of bile, and the excess " of its quantity in the primæ viæ, which either, by regurgitation " into the stomach, produces a general languor of the body, together " with nausea, foul tongue, loss of appetite and indigestion, or being " directed to the intestines, excites a painful diarrhœa, ultimately " tending to weaken their tone, and disturb their regular peristaltic " motion,"—*p.* 157.

As bile, especially when vitiated, is certainly apt to gripe and loosen the bowels, it might be supposed, that if it be increased with the cuticular discharge, those whose laborious exertions keep them every day bathed in sweat for hours, would be continually subject to diarrhœas. But Nature has admirably guarded against such an inconvenience by establishing what may be termed a *vicarious sympathy* between the skin and the internal surface of the intestines, by which the secretion of mucus, &c. on the latter is diminished, as the perspiration is increased. In temperate climates, therefore, and among the laborious classes of society, this increase of the biliary fluid is productive of little or no mischief, being all expended during the digestion of their food, which is generally composed of such materials as require strong organs and powerful fluids for that purpose.

But it is very different with Europeans in hot climates.—There the vicarious sympathy is not always able to keep in check the diarrhœa ; and when it *is*, the superabundant secretion of bile accumulates in the primæ viæ, producing all the symptoms above enumerated, till its quantity or quality raises a commotion in the bowels, in conse- quence of which it is expelled. Hence the impropriety of attempt- ing athletic exercises in the heat of the day between the tropics, which must greatly increase the ill effects described.

These then are the penalties, (aggravated, indeed, too often by our own misconduct,) which are incurred, more or less, by emigra- tion from a temperate to a torrid zone! They are the mild inflic- tions, however, of Nature, wisely calculated, and providentially de- signed, to ward off more serious evils.—They must be continued long before they induce actual and dangerous diseases ; and I am convinced we might, in general, escape the latter, by exercising our rational faculties in observing and rendering subservient to our use, the simple, but salutary operations of Nature. After having been severely taught to feel the ills I am going to pourtray, it is still a most pleasing task to trace the wisdom and benevolence of our Creator in what might *seem* the imperfection of his works.

We now proceed to the more serious injuries too frequently resulting from these spontaneous, but salutary efforts of the constitution, when counteracted or goaded on by our own injudicious management, or by unavoidable accidents.

I have shown, on the authority of Dr. Currie, that excessive perspiration occasions a loss of tone in the extreme vessels ; in consequence of which, the perspiratory fluid continues to be poured out *after* the cause or necessity has ceased to operate. It is precisely the same with respect to biliary secretion. He has likewise observed that, in the last-mentioned state, the application of even a slight degree of *cold* is pregnant with danger. It certainly is so ; and on more accounts than one. For not only is the animal heat too rapidly abstracted, but the extreme vessels on the surface, and likewise *those of the vena portarum*, are instantly struck torpid ; the perspiration and biliary secretion are arrested ; the passage of the blood through the liver is obstructed ; and a temporary *congestion* throughout the portal circle is the result.

This view illustrates, and is at the same time confirmed by, the observations of two physicians in very different and distant parts of the world. Sir James M'Grigor remarks, that during the march of the army over the sandy desert of Thebes, where the thermometer frequently stood at 118 in the soldiers' tents, the health of the troops was equal to what it had been at *any* former period in India. " Heat of itself then," says he, " does not appear to be the *principal* cause of the prevailing diseases." It certainly is not ; but when excessive and long-continued, it induces that state of the vessels on the surface, and of the liver, which is easily thrown into disease by the sudden application of slight degrees of cold . This accounts for Dr. Moseley's paradox, that " *cold* is the cause of almost all the diseases in *hot* climates, to which climate alone is accessary." He refers the mischief here entirely to checked perspiration ; but the connexion which I have traced between this and *internal* mischief, will more amply elucidate this affair. Thus, in the months of April, May, and beginning of June, at Calcutta the heat is considerably greater than during the subsequent rainy months ; but perspiration, though profuse enough, is steady and pretty uniform, and the only diseases are those from increased secretion of bile. From the middle of June, on the other hand, the close, humid, and sultry atmosphere, is attended with an absolute exudation from every pore of a European's body ; in which state the chilling application of rain—the raw, nocturnal vapours—or the atmospherical vicissitudes of autumn, will produce, as may easily be conceived, the effects I have described above ; the consequences of which will be fever, dysentery, or both.*
It is on this account that the Bengalese are observed to be more assiduous in using oily frictions at this period than at any other. They know, from experience, that by such precautions they are enabled to maintain a more *uniform* discharge from the pores, to check pro-

* Vide section on Bilious Fever.

fuse perspiration by day, and to obviate the effect of rain or cold by night.

On the Coromandel coast, however, where the range of temperature is higher and more permanent; where the duration of the rain is short; where the nights are either hot, as during the hot land-winds, or temperate, dry, and clear, as at other times, the deterioration of the hepatic organs is slow and gradual, *where temperance and regularity are observed.* But among heedless sailors, soldiers, and others, who, to the stimulating effects of the climate, add inebriety, too much food, or ill-timed exercise, then the biliary secretion and perspiration are so hurried and augmented, and the vessels so debilitated, that the smallest atmospherical vicissitude becomes dangerous.*

The effects resulting from the application of cold under these circumstances, will be in all degrees from a slight shiver to a fever, or even instant death. We will suppose them only in a low degree. During the temporary torpor of the extreme vessels on the surface, and of the vena portarum, the pori biliarii and excretory ducts will partake of the same atony, and the bile will stagnate, till the reaction succeeds and propels it forward in its accustomed course, with a degree of acceleration proportioned to the previous quiescence. It is plain, that by frequent repetitions of this, the vessels and ducts in question will lose tone; and as atony is the parent of spasm, constrictions of the ducts must at these times take place; the bile will become viscid, occasionally, from stagnation, and be with more difficulty brought forward into the intestines during the subsequent increased action of the vessels. Thus obstructions will form, and an inflammatory congestion be constantly impending, till time, or some accidental aggravation of the causes above-mentioned, kindles up HEPATITIS, which will run rapidly into suppuration, and perhaps in a few days destroy both the organ and the life of the patient, unless it be skilfully checked in its career.

If, during this catastrophe, we expect to find the pathognomonic symptoms of acute Hepatitis, as it appears or is described in Europe, we will be greatly deceived. In *comparatively* few instances have I seen the violent rigors, high fever, hard, quick, and full pulse, acute pain, &c. which we would naturally look for as preceding the destruction of such a large and important viscus.

Such cases, however, pretty frequently occur during the first twelve or eighteen months after arriving in the country. A young gentleman of great abilities, and a good constitution, but who despised all curbing rules of temperance or precaution, ran about in the sun for some days at Malacca, indulging in all sorts of licentiousness or inebriety; and was seized in a day or two afterwards, on our passage to China, with rigors and heat alternating; succeeded in a few hours by pain in the right side, extending across the pit of the stomach, accompanied with some difficulty in respiration. He did not send for me till twelve or fourteen hours after the attack. He had then high fever—hard, quick pulse—great dyspnœa—a short

* See the Section on climate of Egypt in the Mediterranean division of this Work, where the foregoing reason is still further elucidated, and confirmed.

cough, and the most excruciating pain in the region of the liver. Although I had then been accustomed to treat Hepatitis as it more usually appears in India, and this gentleman had been a voyage to Bengal in a Company's ship before he joined us, yet the disease had so decided a European character, that I determined on employing the European method of cure. Accordingly, blood was drawn "*pleno rivo*," from his arm, and repeated twice the next day. His bowels were kept open with saline cathartics; and antimonials, in nauseating doses, were prescribed, to relax the surface, which was dry and burning. By these means the febrile symptoms were greatly mitigated, and blisters to the side seemed to relieve the local affection. He still, however, had great tenderness on pressing the right hypochondre; and on the fourth day he complained of having a flux.

I knew but too well how sure an index this was of mischief going on in the liver. I therefore commenced the administration of mercury without delay. But while endeavouring to saturate the system with this medicine, we were overtaken by a most violent typhoon, or hurricane, in the Chinese seas, which kept the ship in the greatest agitation, and completely drenched with water, for many days together. I had reason to believe, that he neglected at this time, to take his medicines, and I was not able to pay minute attention to him myself. The flux was now the prominent symptom, and, though I used every exertion, I could never afterwards affect his mouth with mercury.

A fulness soon appeared in the right side; while the shiverings, cold sweats, and lastly, the colliquative diarrhœa, that terminated the scene, left no doubt that abscess had not only formed, but burst internally. He dragged out a miserable existence of more than three weeks from the commencement, and died at the island of Lintin, where I inspected the body.

Before his dissolution, the discharge *per anum* was purulent, and dreadfully fœtid. A few hours before his death he vomited a similar matter, and then sunk rapidly, retaining the possession of his mental faculties till the last moment; and regretting his inattention to the advice I had often given him, previous to his illness, warning him against the effects of intemperance and exposure to the heat of the sun.

On dissection, the liver was found one entire mass of suppuration and disease. I passed my hand from it into the stomach, to which it adhered, and through which an abscess had burst. Another adhesion had formed between the liver and the transverse arch of the colon, through which was an exit also for the matter. In short, scarce a trace of healthy organization was to be observed at any distance from the convex surface of this organ, which part alone preserved any thing like a natural appearance.

I met with few cases in India so exquisitely marked with acute European symptoms as this. But in all those which exhibited traits at all approximating to the above, I delayed not a moment in commencing the mercurial treatment, *in conjunction* with the anti-phlogistic; the *latter* being carried no further than the inflammatory symptoms appeared to require ; the *former* continued uninterruptedly till the full effect was produced, and till every shadow of danger was gone.

Such instances as these cannot be mistaken ; they can too often be traced to evident and adequate causes ; such as intemperance — vioent exercise in the sun—or sudden exposure to cold when the body has been some time in a state of perspiration. They will occur principally among those lately from Europe, or at least within a year or two after their arrival ; and such symptoms will be, in most cases, confined to the young, the robust, and plethoric habits.

But in general, the disease makes its approach in a much more questionable shape, though equally pregnant with danger as the foregoing, and not seldom more rapid in its course. A man comes to us, complaining of having a flux. He says, he is frequently going to stool —that he is griped ; but passes nothing but slime—that his stools are like water, or some such remark. It is ten to one if he mentions any other symptom at this time. But if we come to interrogate him more closely, he will confess that he has had some soreness at the *pit of the stomach*, or perhaps in the right side. If we examine the part, a fulness will sometimes appear—if we press upon it, he starts back, or shrinks at least from the pressure.

If we look into his countenance, besides a certain anxiety, we will observe a dark kind of sallowness in his cheeks, and a yellowish hue in his eyes. The latter is seldom absent in hepatic diseases, both in India and Europe.

The temperature of the surface will probably not be much increased ; but the skin will have a dry feel—his mouth will be clammy, and his tongue have a whitish or yellow fur towards the back part. His pulse, though neither hard nor very quick, will have an irritable throb, indicative of some internal affection. His urine, if inspected, which it always should be, will be found to tinge the bottom and sides of the pot with a pink sediment, or turn very turbid a few hours after it is voided ; and he will generally complain of some heat and scalding in making water.

These are all the external marks we can perceive ; and the few symptoms at the head of the list are all that the heedless soldier or sailor has noticed, or at least recorded. Happily for the patient, as well as his physician, the degree of violence in the bowel complaint, where other symptoms are not conspicuous, will be almost always a sure index to the rapidity or danger of that in the liver. Whereas in those cases where the symptoms are of the violent or European cast—particularly pain, fever, and dyspnœa, the bowels are very frequently costive for the first few days of the complaint.

If it is not early checked, it will frequently run on to suppuration, like the case described, and then the chance of its pointing, or of the matter finding its way through ducts or adhesions, with ultimate recovery, is faint indeed. Other symptoms will occasionally arise in this disease, or accompany it from the beginning. Thus the fever is sometimes smart ; the enlargement, hardness, or tenderness of the part, more violent ; the inability of lying on a particular side may be complained of a short cough may attend ; or that particular sensation in the acromion scapulæ may be noticed, though it is not very often that this last is present.

These symptoms and the duration of the complaint, will vary much. Indeed, the latter is very uncertain ; as its continuance may be protracted to several weeks, without suppuration or organic derangement of vital importance following.

This, then, is the hepatitis of India ; and certainly there is no small dissimilarity in symptoms, between it and the acute hepatitis of Europe. The flux, which may be termed the pathognomonic of the former, is almost always wanting in the latter. The one, (Indian,) partakes more of inflammatory congestion and obstruction ; the other of active inflammation, like that of the lungs, kidnies, &c.

Such are the marks that are to guide the practitioner when the disease is present. An attention to the following premonitory symptoms, described for the use of the more intelligent class of patients, into whose hands this essay may fall, will probably save them many a nauseous dose, and many a tedious day's illness.

In all bilious diseases, the *mind* is much affected. When hepatitis is impending, it loses a portion of its wonted firmness. Our spirits are unequal ; we are occasionally gloomy and irritable ; and apt to see things through a distorting medium. This too frequently drives patients to have recourse to those very means which hasten on the fatal catastrophe, but which give a temporary relief to disagreeable mental sensations, that are only symptomatic of the corporeal affection—I mean, an indulgence in the fugitive pleasures of the bottle.

The eye and countenance assume the appearance alluded to before, termed Bombycinous by Dr. Darwin ; and the urine becomes high-coloured, or tinged with bile ; and almost invariably produces considerable scalding in its passage through the urethra. Dyspeptic symptoms arise, and generally mislead the patient into a belief that his complaint is only indigestion. After any thing like a full meal, we feel a most uneasy load and sense of oppression about the pit of the stomach, which is relieved by yawning, stretching, or standing up, and aggravated by stooping, or the recumbent posture. The digestion is never equal to the appetite, though the latter is often deficient ;—and this leads to irregularity in the bowels. One day, there are dark, clayey stools, with costiveness ; another, they are fœtid and slimy, with flatulence and looseness. The skin has not the moist, soft feel of health ; but often a dryness, with partial clammy perspirations, and irregular flushes and chills.

We may not feel, at this time, any pain on pressing the region of the liver ; but a short and unexpected step on uneven ground, will frequently cause a most unpleasant sensation at the pit of the stomach, or in the right side, as if something dragged there. Indeed, if the patient be attentive to his own feelings, some internal uneasiness will always be found to precede the pain on external pressure ; at least I invariably found it so in my own person, and it has more than once admonished me of my danger.—The same remark has been made to me by intelligent patients. Disturbed sleep, and frightful dreams, precede and accompany this disease, in almost every case. Nothing harassed me more than this unpleasant symptom ; and on *inquiry*, I always found my patients make the same remark ; but they will seldom mention this, unless they are interrogated.

When all, or several of these symptoms, make their appearance, a few doses of calomel and cathartic extract, administered so as to keep up a regular increase of the alvine evacuations for some days, together with the strictest abstinence and caution in avoiding the extremes of heat, or sudden vicissitudes, will often anticipate the attack of this insidious disease, and entirely check it in embryo. If these means, however, do not remove the morbid train of premonitory sensations above described, mercury should be slowly introduced, so as to produce a brassy taste in the mouth, and kept at this point till the return of health and strength, which would haidily ever fail to result.

It will be readily understood, that the warning symptoms abovementioned, can only be expected where the disease is coming on gradually, from effects of climate, and the more moderate application of such causes as hasten these effects. Where the *excitantia* are strong and evident, such as great intemperance ; sudden exposure to considerable atmospherical vicissitudes, particularly to cold after perspiration ; violent exercise, &c. then the interval between them and actual disease, will not always afford many admonitory sensations.

Treatment.

The medical practice of India is more simple than that of Europe, evidently from the great connection which experience has traced between many *apparently* dissimilar diseases in the former country ; rendering it only necessary to vary, in some degree, the same methodus medendi.

During the first twelve months after arriving in the country, whenever the patient was at all robust, the pyrexia evident, or the pain considerable, I bled at the very *commencement*, and not with a sparing hand. I did so with a two-fold view. One was to relieve the febrile symptoms, by lessening the inflammatory congestion in the liver and portal circle ; the other to lower the tone of the constitution, which experience taught me, accelerated the effect of that medicine on which my principal reliance was placed. To further both these objects, one or two doses of calomel, or the pil. hydrarg. with opium, and antimonial powder, were given, after copious venesection, and followed by castor oil or jalap, which never failed to bring down a copious alvine discharge, consisting of any thing but natural fœces, or healthy bile. For in the flux attending hepatitis, the violent straining and griping are succeeded by nothing but mucus and blood, accompanied by a distressing tenesmus, *unless* when laxatives are taken, and *then* diseased secretions only, with occasionally a hardened scybala, or other fœcal accumulation, are passed

It appears, by Mr. Curtis, that the hospital practice at Madras in his time, [40 years ago,] was to give three grains of calomel, with some rhubarb and soap, night and morning, till ptyalism came on ; and if it was necessary to have the mouth sooner affected, a drachm of mercurial ointment was rubbed in on the affected side every night. No opium was then thought of; but the hypothetical prejudice against that valuable article is now, I believe, pretty well worn off ; and I know, from pretty ample experience, that in conjunction with antimonial powder, it forms a most admirable auxiliary to the mercury ; not only soothing many uneasy sensations of the patient, but determining to the surface, and promoting a diaphoresis, which is of infinite service in this, as in most other diseases.

In all *urgent* cases, I seldom gave less than twenty-four grains of calomel in the twenty-four hours ; and generally in the following manner :—

> R. Submur. Hydrarg. gr. vj.
> Pulv. Antimon. gr. iij ;
> Opii, gr. fs.
> M. ft. bolus — sexta quaque hora sumendus.

During the exhibition of these medicines, an occasional dose of castor oil or other laxative, and emollient injections, contributed to mitigate the griping and tenesmus ; while blisters and leeches often relieved the local pain of the side. But these were only secondary considerations : and the grand object was to get the mouth affected, when the flux and other symptoms were sure to give way.

The secretion of healthy bile—the flow of saliva from the mouth —and a gentle and uniform perspiration on the skin, were synchronous effects of the medicine, and certain indications of the approaching cure. But it was necessary to keep up these by smaller doses of the medicines alluded to, not only till every symptom of the disease had vanished, but till the clear countenance, keen appetite, and regularity of bowels had returned, and health and *strength* were completely restored.

Indeed, a degree of obesity generally succeeds the administration of the medicine, and the cure of the disease ; nor need we wonder at this, when we consider the previously deranged state of the digestive organs, to which a renewed energy is now communicated.

But in effecting these salutary objects, I have sometimes been obliged to push the mercurial treatment in a much bolder manner than above described. I have myself taken calomel in twenty grain doses, three times a day, without experiencing the slightest inconvenience from the quantity ; nay I often found large doses sit easier on the stomach, and occasion less irritation in the bowels than small ones. At this time, too, I was using every exertion, by inunction, to forward the ptyalism ; yet it was several days before I could produce any effect of this kind. These doses may astonish those who do not know the difficulty of affecting the mouth with mercury in a hot climate, when the liver is verging to suppuration. The idea of their purging and griping at these times is truly chimerical. Indeed, I never saw any of those terrible cases of hypercatharsis which people so much talk of, except where cold was applied, and perspiration checked during salivation, when certainly, as may naturally be supposed, a severe bowel complaint is the consequence.* But in that dangerous state of the liver which I have mentioned, when a few hours perhaps must determine, whether healthy secretion or de-

---

* " Granis viginti perfrequenter usus sum, duis autem, quotidiano, adhibitis aliquid incomodi, aut periculi, tali ab exhibitione pervenire nunquam observavi."—*Thesis on Hepatitis, by* T. B. Wilson, M. D. Surgeon, R. N. 1817.

structive suppuration is to result, a tardy, irresolute practice, is pregnant with mischief.   Unfortunately at this critical period, such is the
torpor throughout the lacteal and lymphatic vessels of the abdomen,
that the largest doses internally, and the most assiduous inunctions
externally, will sometimes fail in introducing a sufficient quantity of
mercury to saturate the system.   In the mild climate of Prince of
Wales's Island, where the temperature of the air might be supposed
to favour absorption, I have had a couple of Malays daily employed,
for hours at a time, in unsuccessful frictions, the lymphatic vessels refusing to take up the ointment in any considerable quantity.   At the
commencement of this disease, and of dysentery, I have often been
able to form a tolerably accurate prognosis of the difficulty that would
be experienced in raising ptyalism, by observing the aptitude of the
absorbents on the surface, while a drachm or two of mercurial ointment were rubbed in on the thigh or arm, under my own inspection.
This hint may be worth attending to.   Here the tepid bath, by determining to the surface, will sometimes so far restore the balance
of excitability and circulation as to promote the absorption of the
mercury, both from the external and internal surfaces of the body.
But great care is to be taken to avoid a subsequent chill, and a consequent recoil of the circulation. which will be sure to aggravate all
the symptoms instead of relieving them.—The nitro-muriatic acid
is also to be used in these cases.   The absorption of mercury into
the system is also accelerated by causing the patient to swallow a
considerable quantity of warm diluting drink, as thin water-gruel,
every night at bed time.

It might be expected that I should here point out the predisposing
and exciting causes of Hepatitis ; but these have been in a great measure anticipated by the preceding remarks.   I observed, that the application of cold to the body, during and subsequent to perspiration,
was by far the most frequent manner in which the disease was contracted ; but the European, and the casual visiter, may well wonder
how cold can be often applied on the burning coast of Coromandel,
where the temperature is high and steady by day—where the nights
are, for months together, hot—and seldom raw or damp, as at Bombay or Bengal.   A nearer inspection dispels the difficulty, and shows
us that nothing is more common than such an occurrence. The European soldier or sailor, exhausted by exercise in the heat of the
day and by profuse perspiration, strips himself the moment his duty
is over, and throws himself down opposite a window or port, to inhale
the refreshing sea-breeze ; his shirt, in all probability. dripping with
sweat.   The effect of this present gratification is well exemplified
every day before his eyes, by the officers of his ship or regiment,
who, when *hobdaars* and salt-petre are not at hand, refrigerate their
wine or water, by suspending the bottles in wetted cloths, (generally
worsted or woollen,) and exposed to a current of air, when the evaporation, in a few minutes, renders the contained fluid quite cold.

It requires more philosophy or self-command than generally falls
to the lot of the aforesaid classes, to resist the grateful refreshment
which this dangerous indulgence affords.   The dreadful sensations
arising from heat and thirst imperiously demand fresh air and cold

drink, which few have stoicism enough to forego, even where the bad consequences are previously known. I shall have occasion, hereafter, to relate some fatal instances of this kind, which happened under my own eye. The night, which nature designed as one of the grand restoratives of our energy, is the time when many imprudent exposures, of the species described, are made among sailors and soldiers ; particularly the former, on account of the close and sultry apartments in which they sleep, whereby they are forced to make frequent nocturnal visits, to the open air, while they are streaming with perspiration.

It is asserted by almost all writers on tropical climates, that atmospherical vicissitudes are comparatively trifling in those regions, and that the thermometrical range is seldom of greater extent, than from five to ten degrees daily, and fifteen or sixteen degrees annually. " In countries between the tropics," says Dr. Moseley, " the heat is nearly uniform, and seldom has been known to vary through the *year*, on any given spot, either by *day or night*, 16 degrees,"—p. 2. This is not correct ; the thermometer, at Bombay and Calcutta, in the month of January, is frequently as low as 55° in the night : and in the month of April up to 90°, or even higher, in the day ; making an annual vicissitude of thirty-five degrees. And notwithstanding Dr. Moseley's assertion to the contrary, a transition of eighty degrees *in one day*, has been witnessed between the tropics. Sir James M'Grigor, in his Report to the Medical Board at Bombay, for the month of November, 1800, observes, that, " the mercury had an extraordinary wide range, from 68°—50° to 130° in the open air."—*Edin. Med. and Surg. Jour. July*, 1805, *p.* 271. And he shortly afterwards adds—" More cases of *Hepatitis* appeared that in either of the two former months," —*ib*. But even on the Coromandel coast, the *actual* vicissitude to which the human frame is often exposed, far exceeds what is generally believed. Let a thermometer be suspended in the open air at Madras, and it will point for many hours in the day to 120° or 130°, but in the night it will fall to 80° or 82°. Here, then, is the range of 40 or 50 degrees in the day, to which hundreds of European soldiers and sailors are unequivocally exposed ; for, let it be remembered, that they are kept neither in glass cases, nor the cuddies of Indiamen, though the above consideration ought to intercede powerfully in their behalf, and induce their officers never to subject them to such dangerous vicissitudes in a climate of that kind, unless from inevitable necessity.

But this subject will meet with a very full consideration in the prophylactic part of this essay, where I hope to offer some important remarks on certain means of preserving health in hot climates, connected with the above topic, which have been hitherto passed over unnoticed or misunderstood by medical authors.

I need hardly remark, that intemperance in spirituous liquors strongly predisposes to and excites Hepatitis. But it is not generally known, or suspected, that the depressing passions, particularly grief, have the same effect. I have seen many instances, however, where no doubt could be entertained on the subject. I shall only relate one. In the month of December, 1803, while H. M. S. Centurion was lying at anchor in Mocha Roads, two men, when, in the act of loading a gun, had their arms blown away, and were otherwise dreadfully shattered, by the gun going off, in consequence of the neglect of a boatswain's mate, who was captain of the gun.   One of the men died, and the circumstance produced such a degree of remorse and grief in the careless boatswain's mate, that he was instantly seized with Hepatitis, [though in the prime of life and health,] and in a few days followed his unfortunate shipmate to the grave !——The close sympathy which subsists between the *brain and liver* is well known, and strongly illustrated in hot countries, where the latter organ, (like the lungs in Europe,) being predisposed to disease from the general effects of climate, suffers readily and obviously, in consequence of the sympathy in question.

I shall now make a few observations on those chronic derangements in the liver and its functions, which, in hot climates, succeed violent or repeated attacks, such as I have already described.   These derangements, however, (especially of function,) are but too often the consequence of long residence between the tropics, independent of any serious or acute inflammation in this organ.   Where induration, enlargement, or any particular structural alteration has taken place, the external accompaniments are evident to the most superficial glance. .

Sallow countenance—emaciation—irregular bowels—high-coloured urine—scalding in its discharge—low spirits—often a chronic flux, with pain, fulness, or hardness in the region of the liver—evening fever—dry cough, and swellings of the ancles, are the prominent features of this deplorable malady.   A degree of induration and enlargement continued nearly three months after a severe attack of Hepatitis which I experienced in my own person ; and a distressing bowel complaint succeeded, and harassed me for more than a year.

A return to Europe, brought me no relief ; on the contrary, by getting cold in my feet, while sitting in a dissecting room in London, a few weeks after my arrival, a violent Hepatitis was induced, accompanied by the usual dysenteric symptoms.   The flux that preceded, for so many months, this last relapse, may serve as a specimen of those connected with chronic hepatic obstruction.

Once, perhaps, in the twenty-four hours, generally in the morning, there would be an ill-conditioned fœcal evacuation, accompanied with mucus, slime, and apparently vitiated bile.   After this, I would have two, three, and sometimes four hours respite.   An uneasy sensation would then arise in my bowels, with rumbling and flatulence, which would proceed along the whole tract of the intestines, when I was forced suddenly to stool, nothing, however, coming away, but some slimy mucus, streaked occasionally with blood, or greenish, bilious sordes.   This discharge was always attended with more or less griping, straining, and some slight degree of tenesmus ; after which another interval of ease, two or three hours in duration, would take place, and then the same symptoms as before described, continuing with great punctuality, for weeks and months together. During this period, my apppetite was tolerably good, but my spirits exceedingly irregular—generally depressed.   The least excess in eating or drinking—the exposure to night air—or the slightest application of cold to my feet, aggravated my complaint. The cheering prospect of returning to my native home, and the hopes that climate alone would effect a cure, together with the want of accommodation for undergoing a course of medicine on a voyage, where I was only a passenger, induced me, most unwisely, to delay the only effectual means of curbing the disease ; till a nearly fatal relapse forced me to have recourse to that medicine which more than once before preserved my life. The flux, which all this time was symptomatic of liver obstruction and irregular secretion, was completely removed with the original cause.

Two circumstances appear to be almost always attendant on these chronic diseases of the liver—diminished secretion of bile, and low spirits. The former we may account for in two ways : either as resulting from that atony which takes place in an organ that has been long stimulated into inordinate, or at least irregula action, by hot climates, &c. or from structural derangement, generally induration, which but too often accompanies the preceding state. It is likewise certain, that the bile is vitiated in quality, as well as deficient in quantity. And the numerous complaints which we hear from people, with evidently torpid livers, of *excessive secretion*, which they conclude must be the case, from the nausea, vomiting of green bile, sick head-aches, yellowness of the eyes, gripes, &c. with which they are occasionally harassed, arise from irregular, but on the whole, diminished and disordered biliary secretion.

I do not think the ingenious Dr. Watt has been very happy in his pathological elucidation of bilious diseases.—" The liver," says he, " receiving its stimulus from venous blood, has more to do than in health ; hence the origin of bilious complaints, which, with low spirits, and prostration of strength, generally mark the first stage of disease,"—p. 207. The liver may have *more to do* in bilious diseases than in health ; but I am well convinced *it does less*. The torpor in that organ keeps a general plethora throughout the abdominal system of black blood ; consequently, when it happens to be occasionally excited into unusual action, a greater flow of vitiated biliary secretion ensues, from this very cause ; when, unless proper means are employed, the viscus falls back again into its previous state of inactivity. This view of the subject elucidates the effects of venesection, purgatives, and all the best remedial processes.

The torpid state of the bowels, dependent on that of the liver, admits of morbid bilious accumulations, (after those periods of excitement,) which lurk about the duodenum, or regurgitate into the stomach, by inverted peristaltic motion, producing all the phenomena alluded to. But, in a great proportion of patients, the torpidity of the alimentary canal is seldom roused by the acrimony of the bile ; costiveness and low spirits going hand in hand, with the most obstinate uniformity.

The increase and amelioration of the biliary secretion, then, must always be kept in view, when treating this chronic, obstructed, or torpid state of the liver.

The connection which I have traced between the biliary and per-

spiratory processes, will elucidate the operation of those means of
relief, which experience has determined ; it will also suggest the use
of some others.   Among the remedies for this complaint, mercury,
given in small doses, and slowly, so as to keep up a brassy taste in
the mouth for some time, holds a distinguished rank ; as it effectually
promotes the secretion of bile, and excites the extreme vessels on
the surface.

To increase the latter effect, however, it has been found useful
to combine with it a small proportion of opium, and antimonial powder, both to guard the bowels from irritation, and determine to the
skin.   It is quite evident, and ought ever to be kept in mind, that no
violent means should ever be used in stimulating an organ to action,
whose torpor or derangement has proceeded from this very stimulation.   The state of the liver here may be compared to that of the
stomach in a worn-out drunkard.   It requires stimulants ; but they
must be nicely managed, else they will be productive of mischief instead of utility.

The next most salutary remedial process, is to keep up a regular
perist.altic motion in the bowels, and excite the mouths of the excretory ducts of the liver, which will tend to eliminate the viscid and
depraved secretions from that organ itself.   I have found no medicine better adapted to this purpose than the following :

    R. Ex. Colocynth. Comp. drachmam.
        Subm. Hydrarg. gr. xx.
        Antim. Tartarisat gr. iv.
        Ol. Carui, gt. viii.
    M. Fiant pilulæ No. xxx.
                - Vel.
    R. Ex. Aloes spicat. scrupulum.
        Pulv. Antimonialis gr. x.
        Pil Hydrargyri scrupulos duos.
        Ol. Carui, gt. vj
    M. Fiant pilulæ No. xx.

One or two of these pills,. taken occasionally at bed-time, will
move the bowels gently next morning ; carry off disease, and promote healthy secretions of bile ; and will be found to obviate, in a
wonderful manner, that mental despondency, and long train of nervous symptoms, so constantly attendant on this complaint.

Our attention is next to be directed to the cuticular discharge.
This is never to be forced by heating or stimulating, but an insensible halitus promoted, by the most gentle means.   Moderate exercise,
particularly gestation, as determining to the surface without fatigue,
is highly useful.   A sea-voyage, combining these advantages with a
more equable temperature, and keeping up a slight nausea, as it were,
by which the cutaneo-hepatic secretions are increased, will be found
beneficial where it can be commanded.   The swing, an easy, and
perhaps no bad substitute for gestation, or a sea-voyage, I found very
useful in my own case.   I was led to try it for amusement only, and
to dispel the ennui of protracted convalescence.   It certainly has
considerable effect on the skin—powerfully determines to the surface—and relieves those internal congestions so connected with, and

dependent on, torpor or obstruction in the liver. The assiduous and daily application of the flesh-brush over the hypochondriac region will be found to excite the healthy action of the biliary organ in no mean degree. Blisters, or the more permanent drain of a seton in the side, where there is much local uneasiness, will likewise be had recourse to with advantage.

Flannels are essentially necessary, more particularly in the variable climate of this country, with the minutest attention to the warmth and dryness of the feet, especially where the bowels are tender. In torpid livers, where costiveness is a common symptom, flannels, by increasing the cuticular discharge, appear at first to constipate. But here, as in the costiveness arising from a sea-voyage, no ill effects whatever are induced ; on the contrary, the digestion improves, evidently from the biliary secretion being augmented in both cases.

On the other hand, where hepatic obstructions exist, with determination to the bowels, keeping them in an irritable state, as in my own case, the utility of flannels becomes both real and apparent.

In addition to the general use of flannel, the local application of a bandage of the same round the waist, in imitation of the Indian *cummerband*, is in these cases peculiarly advantageous. The native soldiery in India often contract bowel complaints from incautiously throwing off the *cummerband*, when heated on a march. I could state numerous instances, where the worst consequences resulted from negligence in this respect.

The tepid bath, using the utmost caution in avoiding a subsequent chill, will evidently be serviceable, on the same principle ; as well as the warm mineral waters taken internally, as recommended by Dr. Saunders. The night air and late hours, are to be most religiously avoided ; and a rigid temperance, amounting to abstinence enjoined. In short, he who labours under obstructed liver, and hopes to protract his existence with any kind of comfort to himself, must abandon what are called the " pleasures of the table ;" but which are, in reality, the bane of human health. Quantity is doubtless of more consequence than quality ; yet raw vegetables and pastry, from their increasing acidity and rancidity in the stomach, are very generally detrimental. Tender animal food, in small quantities, with well baked bread, or ship-biscuit, forms perhaps the most easily digested aliment in such cases In India, and I believe in Europe, rice and curry will be found a salutary dish. The stimulus of the spice is very different from that of spirits or wine ; and the rice is, without exception, the most unirritating, nutritious, and easily digested vegetable, which the bountiful bosom of the earth produces.

With respect to drink, although I certainly would recommend to my patient the laconic Greek prescription in the pump room at Bath ; yet I fear that most of those returning from the East and West Indies, afflicted with hepatic complaints, while they readily allow that " water is best,"—nevertheless, unanimously agree, that wine is most palatable. If the latter cannot be dispensed with, the acid and astringent kinds at least are to be rejected. Malt liquor will seldom agree, and spirits ought to be restricted as much as possible. I know well, that a dilute mixture of brandy and water has an indescribably soothing effect on the stomach and bowels, in these cases, and seems both to agree best, and prove most useful ; but I am fully convinced it ultimately injures the tone of these organs, and increases the mischief in the liver, unless it be taken in the most guarded manner. Water upon the whole is best.

All the preceding remarks presuppose that a change of climate has been effected ;—for such is the state of the biliary organ, after repeated attacks of Hepatitis, or a long residence between the tropics, that the most active of the above-mentioned remedial means will give but temporary relief, while the original cause continues to be applied.'

I shall elucidate this more fully hereafter, when treating on dysentery. And yet the removal from a tropical to a European climate, requires caution. Nature abhors extremes and sudden vicissitudes. It certainly is dangerous to return to this country in winter, as I myself experienced. I landed in January, and before the end of February, I had a complete relapse of Hepatitis, and its accompaniment, flux.

Those who cannot undertake the long and expensive voyage to Europe, should endeavour to change a continental for an insular situation in India. Pulo Penang, or Prince of Wales's Island, though within six degrees of the Equator, enjoys a milder air, and a lower range of temperature. than any of the presidencies. Here are neither the great vicissitudes of Bombay, the marsh effluvia of Bengal, nor the scorching heat of Madras. The climate is very salubrious. On the mountain. which occupies a great part of the island, and is of considerable elevation, bungalows are erected open to the sea and land-breezes, where the thermometer ranges between 70 and 80 degrees, and where the heat is never reflected or oppressive. From this mountain, too, the most romantic, extensive, and picturesque views, are presented to the delighted eye, contributing greatly to mental amusement and corporeal renovation.

' A temporary residence on that beautiful island, during a painful illness and tedious convalescence, has produced in my mind a strong local attachment towards it, and a vivid recollection of its enchanting scenery :—

> Illa terrarum mihi præter omnes
> Insula ridet, ubi non Hymetto
> Mella decedunt, viridique certat
>   Bacca venafro ;
> Ver ubi longum. tepidasque præbet
> Jupiter brumas : et amicus Aulon
> " Gracili palmæ,"* minimum falernis
>   Invidet Uvis.

The Malayan peninsula, from its being a narrow slip of land, washed on both sides, and nearly encompassed by the ocean—constantly covered with verdure. and open to the sea-breezes, is blessed with a milder and cooler air than any continental part of India between the tropics, and bordering on the coast.

Columbo, in the Island of Ceylon, has also many local advantages,

---

* The palma coccifera, or cocoa-nut tree, whose milk is equally delicious and salutary, flourishes here in the greatest perfection, and may vie with the falernian juice in every good quality, without any intoxicating effect.

that render it extremely salubrious to Europeans, and consequently a convenient and easy retreat from the opposite burning coast.

The Cape of Good Hope, however well adapted to the refreshment of a crew, after a long voyage, by its abundant supplies of animal and vegetable food, is by no means calculated, in regard to climate, for the recovery of hepatic or dysenteric individuals, returning from the East. The daily atmospherical vicissitudes, at this celebrated promontory, are very great indeed, [25 or 30 degrees,] and consequently injurious where the bowels were at all effected. I shall only mention one instance corroborative of this assertion.

His Majesty's ship Albion, on her late return from India, having touched at the Cape, sent a number of her people to the hospital, afflicted with chronic bowel and liver complaints. By the time of her departure for England, however, several of these had died, and all the others returned in a worse state than when they went on shore. This fact is worth attending to ; and deserves to be kept in mind by the valetudinarian.

The climate of St. Helena approximates more to that of Europe, than the climate of any other inter-tropical situation. A rock only, twenty-seven miles in circumference, surrounded by an immense equatorial ocean, above the level of which it projects 3000 feet ; whose summit is covered with perpetual verdure, and cooled by perennial breezes, must enjoy a serenity of air, and evenness of temperature, far beyond any part either of the Indies or Europe. The medium height of the thermometer is 64°, and atmospherical vicissitudes by no means great or sudden. At Plantation-House, the mercury does not rise higher than 72° in summer, nor fall lower than 55° in winter. A temporary stay at this island would probably be attended with a salutary seasoning, preparatory to exposing the debilitated frame to the rude inclemencies and transitions of northern regions. The scenery, too, of the *interior*, is as beautifully romantic, as that of the *exterior* is stupendously dreary and barren. The society, however, is confined ; and forms a striking contrast with the social ease and unbounded hospitality of the East. But alas ! it is a melancholy truth, that in the complaint I have been describing, a surprising mental despondency, or propensity to brood over misfortunes, pursues us through every climate !

> Scandit æratas vitiosa naves
> Cura !—Quid terras alio calentes
> Sole. mutamus ?—*Atrabiliosus*
> Se raro fugit !

Since the Second edition of this work was printed, it is well known that our squadron at St. Helena, suffered severely from dysentery and hepatitis at one time.—It is impossible to account for those visitations of sickliness which occasionally afflict the healthiest situations. At St. Helena, the mercurial treatment of dysentery, with general and local bleeding, was found upon the whole, the most successful, though many lives were lost by relapses, especially where suppuration took place in the liver, which frequently happened.

Sympathetic connection between the mental and hepatic Functions.

The manner in which this mental depression becomes connected with derangement in the hepatic function, is a subject of curious inquiry. It is not a little singular. that two of the most important organs in the human body—the lungs and the liver, when in a disordered state, should exhibit a striking contrast in their effects on the mind. Thus, even in the last stage of pthisis—·· Hope springs eternal in the *hectic* breast ;" and the final catastrophe stands a long time revealed to every eye but that of the patient.

In heptic diseases on the other hand, like Shakspeare's cowards, we " die many times before our death." It is a curious fact, that syphilis, a disease which can only be cured by that medicine, on which we placed our principal dependence in Hepatitis, is likewise attended with a similar despondency, but in a much less degree. There certainly is a greater connexion, or reciprocal influence, between the mental and hepatic functions than is generally known or suspected. Experience has shown, that both *excess* and *deficiency* in the biliary secretion affect the mental functions, though in a somewhat different manner. The former seems to exert its influence in two ways, viz. by its irritation in the primæ viæ. and by its absortion into the circulating system. That vitiated bile irritates the stomach and bowels, is admitted by all ; and that part of it is occasionally absorbed, or regurgitates into the circulation, is equally evident, from the appearance of the eyes and countenance. The mental effects in both these cases are characterized by irritability, and what is properly called a choleric disposition ; often, however, accompanied by the deepest dejection of spirits, amounting almost to despair, where no other adequate cause exists.

On the other hand, the defective secretion of bile seems to operate on body and mind in three ways, viz. by the insipid quality of the bile—by its absorption—and, simply, by its paucity : the mental effects characterized in such cases by melancholy or despondency. The insipidity of the bile in those diseases where the secretion is lessened, as in hypocondriasis, chlorosis, &c. has been noticed by Dr. Saunders and others. The consequence of this will be a torpor throughout the system at large, hence costiveness, imperfect digestion, chylification, sanguification, &c. ensue ; the influence of which on the mind is obvious.

The bile, however, is not always insipid in quality, where it is deficient in quantity. In those cases where it proceeds from structural alteration of the liver, or succeeds violent diseases of that organ, the bile is occasionally as vitiated and acrid, as where excessive secretion is going on. This takes place especially when those causes are applied which formerly produced great excitement in the extreme vessels of the vena portarum ; as, high temperature—exercise in the sun—debauches—violent gusts of passion, &c.

In hot climates, indeed, I have thought that an inflammatory state of the liver was sometimes induced, or at least increased, by the acrimony of its own secretions. It has frequently been remarked by others, and felt by myself, that after brisk doses of calomel and cathartic extract, the bilious evacuations have produced a sensation, as if boiling lead were passing through the intestines. The freedom of spirits, or sensorial energy, that succeeds, can only be appreciated by those who have experienced such disgorgements of vitiated bile ! Every one has observed how diseased secretions, from the internal surface of the urethra, occasionally inflame and ulcerate the preputium and glans penis, if the greatest care be not taken to defend them by cleanliness : can we doubt that something of the same nature may take place in the intestines, and even in the ducts of the liver itself, where the biliary secretion is extremely depraved and acrimonious ? The *remora* alone of viscid bile in the pori biliarii and excretory ducts of the liver, may often occasion such obstruction in its languid circulation as shall give rise to inflammatory congestion in the organ. As I have shown, therefore, that with irregular and diminished secretion, there is always a degree of vitiation, absorption, and irritation, I beg leave to designate their united effect on body and mind, by the term " *Morbid biliary irritation, or influence.*"

I conceive that this is quite equal to the task of originating those mental maladies, which in their turn *react* on the liver, stomach, and intestines, disturbing their functions still further, or increasing their torpor, as well as that of the whole system, by sympathy ; producing, at length, the extensive catalogue of dyspeptic, hypochondriacal, and perhaps hysterical complaints !

Is it not this " non-secreted bile"* which gives that peculiar sallow complexion to Europeans long resident in hot climates, so distinguishable from a jaundiced suffusion of absorbed or regurgitated bile ; and which is probably the first shade that Nature effects, in bending the colour to the climate ? Europeans do not begin to assume this *sallow* tint till the period of superabundant secretion is long past, and till atony and diminished action in the hepatic system have commenced. Indeed, it is very possible, that what at first produced such commotion and inconvenience in the animal economy, would, in the course of a few generations, effect those corporeal changes in the exterior, which ultimately counteract, in a considerable degree, the baleful influence of the climate itself. To be more explicit. The derangement in the hepatic functions, originating, indeed, through sympathy with the skin, affects in its turn the tincture of that skin, by means of absorbed and non-secreted bile ; and these yellow and sallow tints, acted on by the rays of a tropical sun, gradually verge, in the course of generations, to a sable hue. This change of colour, and in some degree, of texture also, [for the rete mucosum is *thicker* in Indians than in Europeans,] renders the exterior of man less sensible to atmospherical heat ; in consequence of which, a more mild and uniform action in the perspiratory vessels succeeds, and by sympathy, a correspondent equilibrium in the secreting vessels of the liver. Thus the skin, which was the first cause of disordered secretion in the liver, becomes ultimately the grand protection of that organ, and the derangement itself, in process of time, creates its own antidote ? This is quite conformable to the known wisdom of Provi-

* By " non-secreted bile," I mean the elements from whence bile is formed.

dence, and to the unceasing exertions of Nature, in remedying what she cannot entirely prevent.

This is a different doctrine from that of Dr. Smith : he attributes the black colour of Indians to the superabundant secretion of bile, and its suffusion on the surface ; but that will not stand the test of examination. He does not take *diminished secretion*, or the elements of bile, into the account ; nor does he trace any connexion between the hepatic and cutaneous functions. May not the disposition to ulcers in hot climates, and among drunken sailors in our own climate be accounted for by this *cutaneo-hepatic sympathy ?* In the first case, the *cutaneous* vessels are debilitated by the heat, and the *hepatic* by sympathy. In the second case, the vessels of the stomach and liver are debilitated by *drink*, and the *cutaneous* vessels by sympathy.

The effects of intemperance in spirituous liquors on the liver and its functions, are not only known to every Tyro in the profession, but are proverbial in the mouths of drunkards themselves ; little, therefore, need be said on this subject. But that the " depressing passions" should produce certain derangements in the hepatic functions, which, reacting on the mind, give rise to, or aggravate the whole protean host of hypochondriacal, hysterical, and nervous disorders, is by no means generally admitted ; though the doctrine will probably gain ground.

The first effect of these depressing passions in the female sex is felt in the organs concerned in digestion—atony in the stomach—torpor in the liver and intestines. The aliment passes into the duodenum imperfectly digested—it there meets a scanty supply of ill-conditioned or insipid bile, and pancreatic juice. Under these circumstances, the progress of the chyme through the convolutions of the intestines must be slow, and the chyle imperfectly eliminated. Fecal accumulations take place : and probably the fermentative process goes on, for want of bile, with an extrication of air, which gives rise to distressing colic and borborygmi. To procure relief from these, the spiritous tincture and cordial have often been the harbingers of more dangerous indulgences, and increased the malady which they were intended to alleviate !

By a careful course of cathartics, the bowels are cleared of that load of fecal and other matter, with which they were oppressed. Healthy bile is thus solicited into the intestines, instead of having its elements floating in the circulation.—This natural stimulus promotes chylification ; which, strengthening the whole material fabric, communicates energy to the mind, till at length, the bloom of health once more revisits the sallow cheek of despondency.

But the lords of the creation are not exempted from the widespreading effects of hepatic derangement. From our large manufacturing towns, the foci of sedentary habits, intemperance, and the depressing passions, its influence may be traced through every ramification of society. One or two examples will suffice. The whole of the literary world, from the poet in his garret to the learned president in his hall, feel more or less of its effects. This deficiency in the secretion of bile, the consequence of mental exertion and corporeal inactivity, is evidently the " morbus eruditorum," which sick-lies o'er, with the pale cast of thought, the countenances of the studious, who waste their hours and their health by the midnight lamp! To them I need not describe the malady ; they are too familiar with its various symptoms. But few of them are aware, how far material causes can influence intellectual ideas. If I wish, to exert, on any particular occasion, the whole force of my memory, imagination, perception, and judgment, I know, from repeated experience, that by previously emulging the liver and its ducts, and carrying off all bilious colluvies from the alimentary canal, by mercurial purgatives, which also excite a brisker secretion in the chylopoetic viscera, I am thereby enabled to avail myself of those faculties above-mentioned, to an infinitely greater extent than I otherwise could. This is no theoretical speculation ; it is a practical fact. It may help to explain the great inequality which we often observe in the brightest effusions of fancy ; and show us, why even the immortal Homer sometimes nods.*

DYSENTERY.

Sec. IX.—The disease in question is certainly one of great importance to be acquainted with in the practice of fleets and armies. No other complaint—not even excepting fever, so much puzzles the young beginner ; and for this plain reason, that in the hour of danger, both books and men distract his judgment, and paralyse his arm, by their diametrically opposite directions! Let any one, after reading Dr. Harty's volume on Dysentery, which gives a fair compendium of the principal modern opinions and practices in that disorder, be taken to the bedside of a patient, and he will be utterly unable to decide, in his own mind, upon the mode of treatment most eligible to adopt !

From this state of anxiety, is he relieved by applying for advice to men ? By no means. One tells him, he must consider dysentery as closely allied to *enteritis*, and depend principally on *venesection*.† Another comes round, and says, strictures in the colon, or small intestines, are the cause of dysentery, occasioning a retention of the fecal and other " *peccant matter ;*" therefore he must purge. A third assures him, he will purge his patient to death, and that nothing but *sudorifics* can effect a cure. A fourth informs him that *mercury* is a specific, and unless he raises a ptyalism, he will bury his patient. In this state of suspense, he vacillates from one direction to another, and his success is less than if he pertinaciously adhered to the worst plan proposed.

It is true that experience will *in general*, determine his choice ; but many an anxious hour will he spend, in exploring his way through this labyrinth of opinions, and many a blunder will he commit in the mean time!

* For an account of the effects of the Nitro-Muriatic acid bath in affections of the Liver, see my work on the Liver, p. 111, 3d edition. Indeed I have purposely avoided enlarging this section, since I conclude that the tropical visiter will place my work on the Liver on the same shelf with *this*.

† Vide Dr. Wright on the Walcheren fever, also Dr. Somers on extreme bleeding in dysentery of the Peninsula.

As there is hardly a disease in the whole range of nosology, more uniform in its nature and symptoms, than dysentery, this discrepancy among authors and practitioners must have originated, I conceive, in consequence of mistaking prominent *effects* for proximate *causes ;* and as the means of cure directed against the former have often removed the latter, each individual believed that he alone had found out the true cause and cure of the disease. Thus, one physician examining the body of a patient who died in a certain stage of dysentery, and finding many traces of inflammation, or even sphacelus, in different parts of the intestines, without any strictures, frames his inflammatory hypothesis ; and although he employs, as *auxiliaries*, some of the means recommended by others, he makes venesection the *principal* indication—has tolerable success, and becomes quite satisfied that he has hit on the proper plan. Another patient dies at a less advanced period of the disease, or where mortification had not relaxed and effaced all signs of stricture. He is examined by a different physician, who finds the inner coat of certain parts of the intestines corrugated, thickened, and the canal reduced to a very small diameter, with scybala, or rather fecal accumulations, [for those who talk about scybala, have not, I fear, examined the abdomens of many dysenterics,] lurking in the cells of the colon, or flexures of the small intestines, situated above these strictures. Establishing a doctrine on this, bleeding is only had recourse to occasionally ; and certain medicines, supposed to have the power of relaxing these spasms or strictures, are exhibited, with frequent laxatives, and success is often the result.

A third person, in examining the bodies of dysenteric patients after death, in hot climates, finds abscess, or other organic derangement of the liver, an appearance very common ; and concludes that Dysentery is Hepatitis in disguise. He prescribes mercury, and his success is still greater than that of others ; consequently he is *positive* that he alone pursues the true course, and entertains just ideas of the disease.

A fourth, observing that dysentery is always accompanied with defective perspiration, and taking up the idea of Sydenham, that it is a fever turned in on the intestines, has recourse to sudorifics, to turn it out again, and not without considerable success ; so that he pities the blindness of those who cannot see that the disease is merely " the perspiration thrown on the bowels." How are we to reconcile these jarring opinions and practices ? In adhering obstinately to any one of these plans we will be often right : but assuredly we will be not seldom wrong. On the other hand, by giving a discretional power to adopt one or other of them, as symptoms may indicate, we confer a license on the young beginner, for which he probably will not thank us in the hour of trial or responsibility. He who could lay down one fixed principle, which is uniformly to be kept in view, through every case and every climate,—a principle that would explain the phenomena and the cure ; who could give *plain and easy directions* when and where we are to lean towards one or other of the apparently opposite modes of treatment, without ever losing sight of the principle in question, or, for a moment, relaxing in the pursuit of that salutary object which this principle points to, would certainly deserve the thanks of the junior branches, at least, of the profession.

I have hinted what I suppose to be the origin of these clashing theories and practices ; to wit, the mistaking effects for causes. Thus, if we do find stricture in any part of the intestinal canal, what produced it? This must evidently be the effect of some cause. If we find inflammation there, it is proved to be a consequence, and not a cause of dysentery, from this plain fact, that in original and unequivocal inflammation of the bowels, or enteritis, constipation is almost always present. In hot climates, if we find dysentery, or, [as some will not allow it that name,] flux, a pretty constant attendant on Hepatitis, particularly the languid or chronic species of it, it does not follow that Hepatitis is a general concomitant, much less a cause of dysentery. In many cases of Hepatitis, especially when violent, there is obstinate costiveness ; and in numerous fatal cases of dysentery, no structural derangement in the liver can be observed.

Those who have attributed it to suppressed perspiration, have come nearer to, but stopped far, very far short of, the mark. The suppression of this discharge is, in itself, a trifling, though in its connexion with others, it becomes an important feature in the proximate cause of dysentery.

As causes can only be traced by their effects, we must endeavour to find out, among the latter, such as are *always* present in dysentery, and have a decided *priority* in occurrence. These, I conceive, constitute what is meant by proximate cause in this, as well as in every other disease. Are there any such, then, in dysentery ? I believe there are ; and this belief does not rest on speculative grounds. I have not learnt the knowledge of this disease from the ancients nor the moderns, but studied it in the book of Nature ; and every one of its symptoms has been deeply impressed on my memory, by painful personal experience, both within and without the tropics.

In every case of dysentery that has ever come within the range of my observation, [and the number has not been inconsiderable,] two functions were invariably disordered from the very onset, and soon drew other derangements in their train. These were, the functions of the skin and of the liver; or, perspiration and biliary secretion. I defy any one, who has minutely regarded this disease at the bedside, to produce a single instance in which these functions were carried on in a natural manner, at any period of the disease. The partial clammy sweats which are sometimes seen on the surface, with the occasional admixture of bilious sordes in the stools, so far from being objections, are proofs of this position ; for, excepting the above appearances, which are *unnatural*, the regular perspiration is suppressed, and the healthy secretion of bile entirely stopped. Dr. Balfour, who had some twenty years' experience in this complaint, and who treats of it under the name of " *putrid intestinal remittent fever*," states, at page 17 of his second Treatise on Sol-Lunar Influence, that,—" At the *very beginning* of putrid intestinal fevers, and also about the time of their *final crisis*, or termination, I have often observed copious discharges of recent bile ; but as the fever advanced, and remained at its height, such discharges have frequently *ceased to appear;* and I have been led to suspect, from these circumstances, that the passage of the bile into the duodenum, during this interval," [viz. from the very beginning to the crisis or termination,] " was al- together stopped." I beg the reader will keep this in mind.

These, then, are the two first links of that morbid chain which connects the remote cause with the ostensible form of the disease. Whoever can break these, by restoring those two functions to their natural state—I care not by what means or medicines—he will cure, or rather prevent, the disorder.—But we can seldom expect to be called in at this early period, for Dysentery is not yet manifested ; although an accurate observer might, in his own frame, often detect these nascent movements, and by prompt measures, extinguish the disease *in embryo.*

Some other invisible, at least, very obscure links, are now to be noticed :—for however confidently a *proximate cause* may be decided on in colleges and closets, it is, in nature, a series of causes. The equilibrium of the circulation and excitability becomes disturbed. In consequence of the torpor in the extreme vessels on the surface, the volume of blood is directed to the interior, and the balance is still further broken by the check which the portal current meets in the liver, from a corresponding torpor in the extreme or secreting vessels of that organ ; the effect of which is, that the plethora in the cœliac and mesenteric circles is now greatly augmented, and fe- brile symptoms commence. The perspiration being stopped, a vi- carious discharge of mucus and acrid serum is thrown from the ex- tremities of the turgid mesenteric vessels upon the internal surface, of the intestines, which by this time are in a state of irritability.* The disease now begins to exhibit itself unequivocally, by the un- easiness in the bowels, the frequent desire to stool, and the mucous discharges. We may now plainly perceive how all those consequen- ces, which have so often passed for causes, can arise. If the ple- thora be great, blood itself will be poured out from the mouths of the distended mesenteric and meseraic vessels ; hence inflammation and ulceration may ensue. If any hardened feces lurk in the cells of the colon, they will be grasped by the irritable circular fibres of the intestines, and rings or strictures will augment the tormina and griping in the bowels.

In this situation, Nature evidently attempts to restore, by reaction, the balance of the circulation and excitability with the cuticular and hepatic functions, but she rarely succeeds ; her abortive efforts too often aggravating, instead of relieving the symptoms. Thus we sometimes see a partial, ill-conditioned sweat on the surface, which is productive of no benefit ; while from the liver, an occasional gush of vitiated bile, like so much boiling lead, throws the irritable intes-

---

* It may be observed that the same phenomena take place in most tropical fevers, and also in severe cases of cholera morbus, mort de chien, &c. This I grant ; for the same causes that, applied to one person, produce bilious fever, will in a second give rise to hepatitis—in a third to mort de chien—and in a fourth to dysentery, according to the organ that happens to be most predisposed to dis- ease. Nay, a combination of all these diseases will often be found in the same case.

tines into painful contortions, and then the tormina and tenesmus are insufferable! Nature, to say the truth, is but a sorry physician in Dysentery. "In hoc enim corporis affectu," says Sir G. Baker, "aliquod certe in medicina opus est, haud multum in *Naturæ* beneficio." Where she ultimately gains her end, it is where the local plethora is reduced by the discharge from the mesenteric and meseraic vessels, without occasioning much organic derangement in the bowels. This being effected, she more easily restores the equilibrium of the circulation and excitability and the functions above-mentioned. But in a great majority of cases, where the disease is violent, her exertions either hasten the fatal catastrophe, or produce such lesion of structure and function in the chylopoetic viscera, as induces a tedious chronic state of the complaint, very difficult to manage.

The febrile symptoms will, at first, be in proportion to the *general* disturbance in the balance of the circulation and excitability; they will afterwards be kept up, or modified, by the extent of the organic derangement sustained. The discharge of blood by stool, on the other hand, appears to be proportionate to the *local* plethora in the portal and mesenteric circles, and to the permanence and degree of torpor in the liver, occasioning that plethora.

This doctrine, thus briefly sketched out, if impartially considered, and fairly applied, will, I think, clearly account for every phenomenon of the disease, from the derangement of the liver, the largest of all glands, to that of the mesenteric glands themselves, which have in their turn been considered as the seat, or even the cause of dysentery.

But it is not sufficient that it merely accounts for the phenomena. If founded in nature and truth, it should, like an arithmetical rule, prove itself in various ways. Above all, the practical application of it ought to involve no contradictions; however various the routes may appear, they must all be shown to tend ultimately to one point—the cure. It should explain how different means have attained the same end; and finally, it should chalk out the best and nearest path we are to pursue. To this task I consider the doctrine in question perfectly equal; though I shall not apply it further than to the leading phenomena of the disease, and the principal methods of cure.

Of the former I have spoken; I now come to the latter. The practitioner who has set down an inflammatory state of the intestines as the cause of dysentery, comes to patient, who is very ill with violent tormina and tenesmus; and passing blood, in alarming quantities with his stools, which consist of nothing but that and mucus. He bleeds copiously, as his principal indication, and prescribes laxatives or sudorifics as minor means, and in a trifling way, as auxiliaries. He soon finds that the flow of blood by stool, is much reduced—that the tormina are mitigated, and that something more than mere mucus comes away after the laxatives, with considerable relief to the patient. Nothing can be more plain than the way in which these means are beneficial, on the principle in question. Venesection lessens at once the plethora in the mesenteric vessels, and checks the effusion from their mouths. A general relaxation throughout the whole system follows—intestinal strictures are relaxed—scybala and fecal accumulations pass off; and Nature, thus, relieved, attempts a restoration of equilibrium in the circulation and excitability, evinced by some degree of action in the extreme vessels on the surface, and by sympathy, of the secreting vessels in the liver.

So far the physician has greatly assisted the spontaneous efforts of the constitution ; and if the latter be equal to the task of keeping things in this prosperous train, all will be well—If not, the morbid state returns, and with it a fearful debility, which paralyses his arm, and embarrasses his mind ! His patient may, or may not recover ; but I should not like to be in his situation, under a man who confines his principal aim to the obviating of inflammation.*

He who confides in purgatives, [and a great many do, who know little of the complaint,] from an idea, that stricture and a retention of the natural feces are the essence of dysentery, treads on exceedingly tender ground.   He certainly does assist Nature in her most ostensible, but dangerous method of cure.   If by a course of purgatives, he can lessen the local plethora, and excite the healthy action of the liver, [both which objects evacuating medicines, particularly of the mercurial kind, are without doubt calculated to effect,] before any material injury takes place in the intestinal canal, he will succeed; because the general balance of the circulation will soon be restored, when the portal and mesenteric plethora is removed ; and the sympathising function of the skin will participate in the healthy action of the liver.   But in a large proportion of cases, he will have the mortification to find, that such organic derangements occur, before he can attain his object, as will either hasten the fatal termination, or prove a fruitful source of misery in the chronic stage of the disease, which too often ensues.

The rationale of the emetic and sudorific plans, on the principle in view, is sufficiently obvious.   They not only determine generally to the surface, but, by exciting the healthy action of the liver, they locally relieve the meseraic and mesenteric plethora, [a circumstance which their employers did not calculate on,] and thus restore the balance of the circulation with the functions of perspiration and biliary secretion.

But however beautiful this plan may be in theory—however successful it may be in a few sporadic cases of dysentery in private life, or in a well-regulated hospital, a more *utopian* practice for fleets or armies, in a tropical climate, was never seriously recommended for general adoption ! Much do I suspect that those who praise or propose it, have never put it to the test of experience, except on a very confined scale, and with every convenience at hand.   " There would be this inconvenience," says the judicious Dr. Blane, " *in constantly*

* Since the first edition of this work was printed, Dr. Somers has drawn the attention of the medical world to *extreme* venesection in dysentery as it appeared on the Peninsula.   But I believe that experience, in tropical climates at least, will only assign venesection its proper rank as a powerful *auxiliary* in the treatment of this formidable disease.   Dr. Somers has not the honour of originality here. Dr. White used the same *venesectio ad deliquium*, in Egypt, in 1802. And Mr. White, a Navy Surgeon, published a work nearly a hundred years ago, in which he lays down a still more decisive system of blood-letting in dysentery.

encouraging a sweat, that if the tenesmus should return, it [perspiration] would either be *checked* by the patient getting frequently out of bed, or there would be danger of his catching cold."—*3d ed. p.* 457.

The mercurial plan is of a very different stamp, in regard to its applicability. Indeed, the *empirical* exhibition of mercury, as it is called. in hepatic and dysenteric complaints abroad, has quite shocked the feelings of some physicians at home. But the army or navy surgeon, who has a vast number of dysenteric patients coming every day under his care, smiles at these delicate scruples. He knows, by repeated observations, that if he can bring on free ptyalism, the patient is secure for that time ; and this begets a strong bias in favour, either of the *specific* power of mercury, or of the liver being the primary seat of the disease. With these prepossessions, he drives on for the object in view, regardless of particular symptoms, and disdaining to call in the aid of those means which I have been describing, and which are considered by others as the principal remedies. He is generally, however, successful ; and if he knew to what extent he might go with safety in this empirical manner, he would be still more so, as shall be shown in due time. But occasionally he is foiled, and cannot raise a ptyalism—then his resources are gone ! The patient wastes away – inflammation, ulceration—even gangrene may supervene ; or, some morning, he sees, with astonishment, several inches of the rectum, that have passed off by stool in the night ! This has happened under my own care, and *I know* that the same has occurred to several others.

Thus we see, that any one of the above methods, when set up as a principal to the exclusion of others is attended with inconvenience, and, [excepting perhaps the last,] with repeated failures, if not general want of sucess, particularly in hot climates. A heterogeneous combination of them all, on the other hand, without order or discipline, and guided only by the discretion or caprice of the young practitioner, would be little better, if not worse than a blind adherence to one. Nothing, in short, but a controlling principle, that is ever to be held in view, under whose superintendance the above-mentioned agents are to be employed in their proper spheres, can lead to a settled and rational practice in dysentery, or reconcile those jarring opinions and practices with which both books and men continue to puzzle the minds of all those whom personal and wide experience has not emancipated from the trammels of authority.

I have declared the *principle* that is to govern us, [the restoration, of *healthy* perspiration and biliary secretion, with an equilibrium of the circulation and excitability,] and enumerated, in a general way, the means which we are to use ;—the direct application of the whole to practice, will be illustrated presently, by an appeal to facts.

I have purposely avoided as much as possible, throughout this essay, to quote my own cases in support of my own doctrines. The following short narrative, however, may be allowed a place here ; and may not be uninteresting or uninstructive :—

A very few weeks after my first arrival in Bengal, I made one in a

party of officers who landed a few miles below Kedgeree, for the purpose of shooting and of seeing the country.—This day was excessively hot—the ground was half inundated, and we waded and rambled
about, through marshes, jungles, and paddyfields—often with one-half
of our bodies under water, and the other broiling in the sun, till we
were fairly exhausted.   As we had a sumpter-basket with us, we
spent the whole day in this manner ; and on returning in the evening
to the banks of the Ganges, at a place appointed, we found that the
boat could not approach the shore, the water was so shoally ; we
therefore dashed into the river, and waded off to where the boat lay
at a grapnel.   By this time it was sunset, and as we had a strong tide
against us, we sat in the boat nearly two hours, dripping wet, and
shivering with cold, before we got on board.   That night, my sleep
was disturbed, and I felt slight rigors or chills, alternated with flushes of heat ; but in the morning I got up as usual, and concluded that
all was well.   At dinner I had no appetite ; and soon afterwards I felt
uneasiness in my bowels.   As the evening advanced, I had frequent
calls to stool, with griping, and some tenesmus, nothing coming away
but mucus.   Fever now came on—my skin became hot, dry, and
parched—and by 11 o'clock at night, I could scarcely leave the commode.   The misery of that night will never be erased from my memory ! I was often delirious, especially when I lay down in bed ; but,
indeed, so dreadful were the tormina and tenesmus—so incessant
the calls to stool, that little respite could be procured.   I had taken
a dose of salts in the evening, but they afforded very trifling relief,
except by bringing off some feculencies, attended with a momentary
lull.   Early in the morning, a medical gentleman belonging to an
East Indiaman, visited me, and found me in a very bad way.   I was
now passing blood fast, and the fever ran high.   I was bled, and took
an ounce of castor oil immediately ; a few hours after which, six
grains of calomel, and one of opium, were taken, and repeated every
five hours afterwards, with occasional emollient injections.

  This day passed rather easier than the preceding night—the tormina was somewhat moderated by the medicine ; but I had considerable fever—thirst—restlessness, and continual calls to stool ; nothing,
however, coming away, but mucus and blood.   As night closed
in, the exacerbation was great.   The opium lulled me occasionally,
but I was again delirious ; and the phantoms that haunted my imagination were worse than all my corporeal sufferings, which were,
in themselves, indescribably tormenting.   The next day I was very
weak ; and so incessant were the griping and tenesmus, that I could
hardly leave the commode.   The tenesmus was what I could not
bear with any degree of fortitude ; and, to procure a momentary relief from this painful sensation, I was forced to sit frequently on
warm water.   The calomel and opium bolus was now taken every
four hours, with the addition of mercurial frictions.   An occasional
lavement was exhibited, which gave much pain in the exhibition, and
I each day took a dose of castor oil, which brought off a trifling feculence, with inconsiderable relief.   My fever ran higher this day
than yesterday, with hot, dry, constricted skin.   As night approached, my debility, and apprehension of the usual exacerbation brought

on an extreme degree of mental agitation. The surgeon endeavoured to cheer me with the hope of ptyalism, which, he assured me, would alleviate my sufferings—I had then no local experience in the complaint myself. As the night advanced, all the symptoms became aggravated, and I was convinced that a fatal termination must ensue, unless a speedy relief could be procured. I had no other hope but in ptyalism ; for my medical friend held out no other prospect. I sent for my assistant, and desired him to give me a scruple of calomel, which I instantly swallowed, and found that it produced no additional uneasiness—on the contrary, I fancied it rather lulled the tormina. But my sufferings were great— my debility was increasing rapidly, and I quite despaired of recovery ! Indeed, I looked forward with impatience to a final release ! At four o'clock in the morning, I repeated the dose of calomel, and at eight o'clock, [or between 60 and 70 hours from the attack,] I fell, for the first time, into a profound and refreshing sleep, which lasted till near midnight, when I awoke. It was some minutes before I could bring myself to a perfect recollection of my situation prior to this repose ; but I feared it was still a dream, for I felt no pain whatever ! My skin was covered with a warm moisture, and I lay for some considerable time, without moving a voluntary muscle, doubtful whether my feelings and senses did not deceive me. I now felt an uneasiness in my bowels, and a call to stool. Alas, thought I, my miseries are not yet over ! I wrapped myself up, to prevent a chill, and was most agreeably surprised to find that, with little or no griping, I passed a copious, feculent, bilious stool, succeeded by such agreeable sensations—acquisition of strength, and elevation of spirits, that I ejaculated aloud the most sincere and heartfelt tribute of gratitude to Heaven for my deliverance. On getting into bed, I perceived that my gums were much swollen, and that the saliva was flowing from my mouth. I took no more medicine, recovered rapidly, and enjoyed the best state of health for some time afterwards.

Mr. Curtis may denominate this disease, " Bilious fever and flux," or " Hepatic flux," but as its answers to every part of Dr. Cullen's definition, except the *erroneous* part, I must say, that it is a very fastidious multiplication of distinctions without any real difference.* The " nature of the discharge" has led Mr. Curtis, and many others astray. Often have I been told by gentlemen that their patients were passing great quantities of bilious redundancies, when, upon examining the stools, four-fifths of these were composed of mucus, *tinged* of various hues, with vitiated bile and blood. It is astonishing how small a quantity of the former will communicate even a deep colour to any other fluid. Mr. Curtis's practice, too, consisted almost entirely in purgatives ; consequently, what with this and the previously disordered state of the liver and its functions, we need not wonder that considerable quantities of depraved bilious secretions were brought off during the treatment. But these accidental varieties in the appearance of the discharge, arising from local causes, and greatly modified by the means employed for cure, do not authorize us to change the name of the disease. Such appearances have been

* Vide Curtis on the Diseases of India.

observed in all countries, especially in autumnal seasons, and where purgatives formed a prominent feature in the *methodus medendi*. They have even led to the idea, that bile was the cause of dysentery.

Of the *remote* causes I need say little. They are the same in all parts of the world—atmospherical vicissitudes. Perspiration and biliary secretion being in excess during the intense heat of the day, are so much the more easily checked by the damp chills of the night; and the consequences which ensue are clearly deducible from the principle I have stated. In short, the same general causes produce bilious fever, hepatitis, and dysentery. They are three branches from the same stem, the organs *principally* affected occasioning the variety of aspect.

Dysentery, *ceteris paribus*, will be the most frequent form; first, on account of the injury which the intestines are in the habit of previously sustaining, from the irregular or disordered function of the liver, whereby they become weakened and irritable; secondly, because they are destined, by Nature, to sustain the vicarious afflux of suppressed perspiration. They are all cured on the same principle, and with some slight variety, arising from local circumstances, by the same remedies—a strong proof of the connexion which I have traced.

We now see how a few year's residence in hot climates predisposes heedless soldiers and sailors to Dysentery, as remarked in the section on Yellow fever, by the experienced author of that article, and as is well known to those who have practised between the tropics. The same principle explains the reason why we so frequently find dysentery a concomitant on hepatitis, especially that languid species of it, arising from obstruction and congestion, with previous derangement of function in the liver, rather than acute European inflammation. In the latter as in enteritis, the bowels are, for the most part, costive. We next proceed to the cure, and various practical remarks connected with it.

There are two safe and comparatively effectual modes of curing dysentery. I shall point out the principal remedy in each method first, and notice the subordinate auxiliary ones afterwards. One method is, to give mercury, in comparatively small doses, either alone or combined with an anodyne, or with an anodyne and diaphoretic, [which I prefer,] in such a manner, that from 24 to 36 or 48 grains of calomel, according to the urgency of the symptoms, may be exhibited, in divided portions, at three, four, or six-hour intervals, during the course of the day and night. In the same space of time, from two to four grains of opium, and from ten to fifteen grains of antimonial powder or ipecacuan, may with advantage be administered, in combination with the calomel. One or two doses, at least, should be given before a laxative is prescribed; and an ounce of castor oil is the best medicine I can recommend for the latter purpose. It will often bring away hardened fecal, or vitiated bilious accumulations, when the irritability of the intestines is previously allayed by the calomel and opium; and it will, in that manner, soothe the tormina and tenesmus. But although it may be repeated every day, it is never to interrupt the progress of the main remedy.

When blood appears alarmingly in the stools, whether the fever runs high or not, venesection may be employed without the smallest apprehension of that bugbear—DEBILITY.—Emollient oily glysters may also be occasionally thrown up, to lull the tenesmus ; but as the rectum is generally in a very irritable state, glysters are often unmanageable remedies. A flannel shirt is to be put on, and a bandage of the same with a double or treble fold of flannel round the abdomen, which is to be rubbed, once or twice a-day, with a liniment, composed of mercurial ointment and tincture of opium, well incorporated. By a steady perseverance in this simple plan, for a few days, the mouth will become sore, and every bad symptoms vanish.

Thus, in less than a page, is stated a practice, which being founded on principle, is generally applicable to almost every stage and degree of Dysentery, and contains within itself resources against most emergencies. While we proceed directly forward to our final object—the restoration of the cuticular and hepatic secretions; with an equilibrium in the circulation and excitability, by a combination of mercury and diaphoretics, we lull pain, and relax strictures, at the same time, by the opium. To guard against inflammation of the intestines, we have the lancet on one side—and to carry off diseased, or irritating accumulations, we have laxatives on the other ; the fever being principally symptomatic, will, of course, cease with the cause. For the successful issue of this treatment, in general, I appeal to the rigid test of future experience with others, perfectly conscious from my own, of its superior efficacy.

This was the usual method I pursued, and with results far exceeding my most sanguine expectations. In some cases, of more than common violence, I was occasionally led into a practice somewhat different, which will be noticed presently.

It is a little singular, that no two medical gentlemen on the station agreed exactly in the mode of administering mercury—each was probably attached by habit to his own formula : but in one thing they were all unanimous—its astonishing power over the disease. This speaks for itself. I shall here exhibit a few specimens of the practice adopted by some of the most intelligent surgeons, and who had the longest and most extensive experience it the Eastern hemisphere.

Mr. Rowlands, surgeon of H. M. S. Tremendous, [now surgeon of Halifax Hospital,] when called to a dysenteric patient, prescribed, first of all, a dose of sulphate of magnesia or soda ; immediately after the operation of which, one grain of calomel was given every half hour, with interruption, till ptyalism took place, which was generally on the third day.—Scarce any other medicine was employed, except bladders of warm water to the abdomen, and the anodyne mercurial ointment, which I have already noticed.

Mr. Henry, surgeon of the Trident, a gentleman who passed a great number of years in India, and had ample experience, proceeded on the following plan : ten grains of colomel where given three times a-day, till ptyalism ensued ; interposing occasional laxatives

—generally castor oil, or salts ; and in the more advanced stages of the disease, combining small doses of opium with the calomel.

Mr. Shields, of the Centurion, a very experienced surgeon, commenced with a dose of castor oil in mint water, and after it had taken effect, prescribed an anodyne antimonial draught in the evening. Mercury was then administered in the following. formula :—calomel, a drachm, ipecacuanha, half a drachm, opium, gr. xii. These were made into twenty-four pills, two of which were taken two or three times a-day according to the urgency of the symptoms, till salivation came on, with an occasional laxative of castor oil.

Mr. Scott, surgeon of the Caroline, a judicious practitioner, and who, like myself, had been—" severely taught to feel" the violence of this disease, as well as of hepatitis, pursued the following method : — A saline cathartic, [magnes. sulphat. an ounce,] was first ordered, and, after its operation, an anodyne diaphoretic draught in the evening. From this time mercury was given as follows : calomel, a drachm, opii gr. iv. saponis q. s. ft. pil. xx. One of these to be taken every two hours, till ptyalism ensued, interposing a laxative when griping was troublesome, and giving an anodyne draught every night.

It would be useless to multiply examples—the above are sufficient to give an idea of the general practice pursued in the East, and form so many living testimonies of its efficacy, of which not a shadow of doubt can be reasonably entertained.

I have now to notice a still bolder tract which was followed by a few surgeons in that quarter, without the least communication of sentiments on the subject—each conceiving his own plan to be perfectly unique. I have mentioned that, in my own case, when despairing of recovery, I took, in one night, two scruple doses of calomel, without experiencing any increase of the tormina, or urgency to stool ; but on the contrary, with an apparent alleviation of those distressing symptoms. Although this circumstance did not make much impression on my mind at the time, as I considered it merely accidental, yet, when some of my patients afterwards appeared in similar situations, and I was in great anxiety about the event, I ventured to have recourse to the same measures, and never in any one instance, with injurious effects, but very generally with an amelioration of symptoms, and an aceleration of the object in view—ptyalism. Emboldened by this, I afterwards tried calomel in scruple doses, two, three, or even four times a day, without any other medicine whatever ; and found that it almost invariably eased the tormina, and lessened the propensity to stool ; and, upon the whole, brought on ptyalism sooner than any other plan of smaller and more frequent doses. In one or two instances, however, it produced great nausea and sickness at stomach, with spasmodic affections of different parts of the body, which were soon removed by an opiate, combined with a diaphoretic, to determine to the surface. I did not, indeed, adopt this practice generally, being quite satisfied, in ordinary circumstances, with the plan which I have above detailed. But whenever, in doubtful cases, I had occasion to push boldly on for ptyalism, I gave the calomel in scruple doses ;which I found by repeated experience, to sit easier than either a smaller or a larger quantity of that medicine—a curious, but a certain fact.

I was surprised, long after this, to find that a German assistant-surgeon, who had charge of my patients for some time, while I was at sick quarters on shore, made it a very common practice to cure dysenteries in this way. But the following table will show, that experience had pointed out the knowledge of this fact to others also.

Tabular View of Thirty Cases of genuine idiopathic Dysentery, treated with Calomel, in scruple doses, on board H. M. S. Sceptre, in the East Indies, by Mr. JOHN CUNNINGHAM, Surgeon of that Ship. 1805.

Men's Names.	No. of days under cure before the purging stopped.	No. of days on the list afterwards, before fit for duty.	Total number of days on the list.	Scruples of calomel, taken in scruple doses twice or thrice a-day.	Remarks.
Henry - -	3	10	13	Scr. VI	Average number of days before the disease was checked, 4. Average convalescence afterwards, 7. Average number of days on the list; in toto, 11. Average number of scruples of calomel taken, 7 and half by each man. Of 231 cases of dysentery, treated with calomel in different ways, 6 died. Of the last 80 treated in the annexed manner, none died.
Davis - -	4	3	7	X	
Kenan - -	4	3	7	V	
Jackson -	4	5	9	IV	
Humphries	6	14	20	VIII	
Cradock -	8	5	13	XII	
Paterson -	2	3	5	IV	
Vinton - -	6	7	13	IX	
Connor - -	3	10	13	V	
Richardson	4	9	13	V	
Mabley -	9	3	12	XII	
Smith - -	4	6	10	V	
Dixon - -	4	3	7	VI	
Noble - -	6	12	18	XIII	
Smith (2) -	3	11	14	VI	
Williams -	4	6	10	IV	
Murray -	3	6	9	V	
Stendon -	2	7	9	IV	
Palmer - -	4	7	11	VII	
Lum - - -	3	11	14	V	
Salter - -	8	5	13	XVIII	
Stoner - -	5	3	8	IX	
M'Cormick	4	6	10	V	
Stoneham -	8	13	21	XV	
Kinch - -	2	5	7	IV	
Smith (3)	4	16	20	IX	
Bell - -	2	3	5	III	
Whitehurst	4	13	17	X	
Kenan (re-lapsed)	3	7	10	VI	
Wilmot -	4	6	10	XII	

If this document, confirming what I have related before, does not remove every doubt or prejudice from the minds of European practitioners, they must be proof against the impressions of truth. It is accompanied by the following remarks :—

" I am perfectly convinced," says Mr. Cunningham, " that this is the most successful method of speedily impregnating the system with mercury, because it does not excite the alvine discharge, so as to carry off the medicine by stool, as I have too often found smaller doses do.* As far as I could observe, larger doses than a scruple had the same effect as smaller, in aggravating the griping and purging. The whole amount of my experience, then, in the treatment of more than 200 cases of genuine idiopathic dysentery, is this :—that calomel, administered in scruple doses twice or thrice a-day, is an almost certain remedy for dysentery—in hot climates, at least. There is no occasion to continue its use longer than till the symptoms fairly give way. But in obstinate cases, the system must be well impregnated before a permanent cure can be expected. When the griping or fixed pain in the bowels ceases after the administration of a few scruples, and especially if the ptyalism be appearing, although the stools may continue frequent, it will be prudent to omit the medicine for a period or two, to ascertain the consequence ; for it generally happens that under such circumstances, the purging also subsides, as the ptyalism rises, and entirely disappears with the cessation of the mercurial action, which ought always to be allowed to abate gradually of itself, without purgatives or diaphoretics, otherwise a disagreeable return of the purging may be the result.

" I ought to notice, that although dysentery prevailed in the Sceptre to a greater extent than in any ship of her class in India, during the time I belonged to her, yet not a single instance of hepatitis, supervening on the former disease, occurred. This was attributed by others, as well as by myself, to the liberal manner in which I prescribed mercury for the cure of dysentery, which I am convinced has some intimate connexion with hepatitis. In the Albion and Russel, where much less calomel was used, liver complaints were very prevalent The foregoing table exhibits the quantity of calomel taken, and the time required for the cure of the last thirty cases of dysentery, without any selection, that came under my care." I may here add, that Mr. Cunningham, by way of experiment, took, when in perfect health, three scruple doses of calomel in one day ; the only effect of which was an indescribably pleasant sensation along the line of the alimentary canal, with one natural stool in the evening. Mr. Neill, of the Victor, was also in the habit of giving calomel in scruple doses, for the cure of dysentery and bilious fever, with great success, and without ever experiencing any inconvenience from the largeness of the quantity.

Since the first edition of this work appeared, numerous testimonies in favour of *scruple* doses of calomel in dysentery have been published by able practitioners. But, as I stated before, it is only in cases of great urgency, where such large doses of calomel need be exhibited.

If it be still urged, that there is something peculiar in the nature of India fluxes, which renders them tractable under mercury, and that the same treatment will not succeed in the West, I happen to have before me a document, which will go far to settle that point. In the years 1809 and 1810, fever and dysentery prevailed to a

* Mr. Cunningham had a great prejudice against opium in this complaint, which accounts for the remark on small doses of calomel. A small proportion of the former medicine will completely obviate this effect, without any injury, especially if determined to the skin by diaphoretics.

great extent on board H. M. S. Sceptre, in the West Indies. Mr. Neill was surgeon of the ship ; and adopting the Eastern practice, with which he was well acquainted, his success was equal to his hopes or wishes. I shall quote his own words, and he is now in England to vouch for their correctness.

" Dysentery is certainly a disease of the utmost importance in this climate, (West Indies,) and may perhaps be connected with other complaints, which we might not have the most distant suspicion of.* Out of eighty well-marked cases, three have died. The first was an old man, who had two violent attacks previous to the last, or fatal one. The second was a very fine young man, who had scarcely ever been free from the complaint since we left England. The third died of the primary attack, which was accompanied with a much greater degree of fever than usual. In this *last* case, I deviated in some measure from my usual plan of cure, in consequence of calomel not standing high in the estimation of some medical gentlemen on this station. Confiding, therefore, more in the use of occasional purgatives and opiates, with diaphoretics, my patient died. From much experience in this disease, I may with confidence assert, that I scarcely remember to have lost a patient in primary attacks, or where the constitution was not cut down by climate and repeated attacks, when mercury [calomel] was given freely, so as to open the bowels, and bring on ptyalism."

I have only to add, that since my return to Europe, I have never met with a case of dysentery, where I had the treatment from the beginning, in my own hands, that did not give way to mercury and its auxiliaries as before directed, and generally with more facility than between the tropics.—In many cases of chronic dysentery, too, which I have met with among French prisoners and others, the practice, with some slight modification, principally in the *quantity* of the chief remedy, has succeeded beyond my expectation, where the degree of emaciation, and the extent of local derangement, had rendered the prospect of a cure almost hopeless. A reference to numerous communications in the periodical journals of late, and particularly to the valuable work of Dr. Armstrong on Typhus, will show how much the mercurial practice is preferred to others in dysentery.

Hitherto, I have only presented the favourable side of the picture to view ; it now becomes a duty to exhibit its sad reverse ! In doing this, however, I have the consolation of hoping that, sooner or later, it may induce those in whose hands alone the remedy is placed, to apply it efficaciously. I may add, that the *rationale* which I have attempted of the disease, is equally elucidatory of the failure as of the success in the *methodus medendi* recommended.

Those, then, who have had most experience in hot climates, best know the melancholy fact, that in every repetition of dysentery, and after every successive year of our residence between the tropics, we find the remedy has greater and greater difficulty in conquering the disease. In process of time, as the intervals between attacks become

* From conversations with him on this subject many years ago in India, I know he alludes to the functions of the liver.

22

curtailed, we find it a very tedious process to bring the mouth affected with mercury ; and, what is still worse, the check thus given to the complaint is only temporary ; for soon after the influence of the medicine wears off, our patient returns upon our hands as bad as ever. At length the system absolutely refuses all impregnation from mercury : and we have the mortification to see our patient waste away, and die, for want of the only remedy that possibly could arrest the hand of death—CHANGE OF CLIMATE !

And how can it be otherwise, upon the principle which I have stated ? The perspiratory and biliary vessels become gradually weakened, by their inordinate and irregular action, from the stimulus of atmospherical heat : they are consequently more and more easily struck torpid by the least atmospherical vicissitudes, and require the additional stimulus—or rather, the change of stimulus from medicine, to excite their healthy action. Hence, the longer we ring those changes, the nearer we approach that state when the vessels, at last, cease to obey all stimuli—the functions alluded to cannot be restored, and the unhappy victim dies ! Add to this, that the intestines themselves become more irritable by every subsequent attack, and even without any attack, by the impaired state of the functions in question, which annually increases.

This view of the subject leads me to deplore the great waste of human life occasioned, in ships of war, by protracted stations in the East and West Indies ! The notion that *time* seasons us against all other diseases, as well as yellow fever, cannot now be urged, for its fallacy is detected. From the great endemic scourge we might, in general, protect our seamen, by proper care ; but over the disposition to dysentery and ulcers, in that class of Europeans, we have little control, since time itself is our adversary—*omnia metit tempus !*

I shall now advert to some more minute particulars in the treatment of this complaint, which, from the documents I have produced and my own testimony, will, I trust, no longer be viewed in the terrific habiliments wherewith it is clothed by Dr. Moseley.

The use of opium in dysentery has been loudly applauded, and as unconditionally condemned. Yet here, as in many other instances, it is the *abuse* only which has brought odium on a valuable medicine. Opium will do harm, if given alone ; particularly in primary attacks, and in young or plethoric habits. If alternated with purgatives, it will do little good—perhaps even harm. But if combined with calomel and antimonial powder, it will be found a most important auxiliary to these medicines, both by preventing any intestinal irritation from the one, and by increasing the diaphoretic effect of the other. All its injurious consequences, (if any such result in this way,) may be easily obviated by the lancet and laxatives, when symptoms require them.

The nitrous acid I have often found a useful adjuvant, particularly in secondary attacks, where the relaxed and weakened state of the bowels seemed to keep up the disease. A couple of drachms per diem, in barley or cungee water, will diffuse an agreeable sensation of warmth through the alimentary canal, and increase the tone of the intestines.

An infusion of quassia, or other light bitter, should be immediately commenced on leaving off the mercury, and continued till the stomach and bowels have recovered their vigour. This should never be omitted.

It is hardly necessary to remark, after the principles I have laid down, that flannel next the skin is indispensable, and that the most scrupulous attention in avoiding dews, damp night air, or sudden atmospherical vicissitudes, is necessary during convalescence, to prevent a relapse.

In no disease is patience, on the part of the sick, a greater virtue, or more calculated to forward the good effects of medicine, than in dysentery. If obedience be paid to every call of nature, the straining which ensues is highly detrimental, and I am convinced, augments, in many cases, the discharge of blood—every motion of the body, indeed, increases the desire to evacuate. As little or nothing, except mucus and blood, comes away in four efforts out of five, we should endeavour to stifle the inclination to stool; and, (as I know by personal experience,) we shall often succeed; for the tormina go off in a few minutes, and by those means we elude not only the straining, but the painful tenesmus which continues so long after every fruitless attempt at evacuation. This circumstance, though apparently of a trifling nature, is of considerable importance; and yet it has seldom been attended to, either by authors or practitioners. It has the sanction of antiquity, however, as may be seen in the following precept of Celsus—" Et cum *in omni fluore ventris*, tum in hoc precipue necessarium est, non quoties libet desidere, sed quoties necesse est; ut *hæc ipsa mora* in consuetudinem ferendi oneris intestina deducat."—*lib. iv. xvi.*

In the *chronic dysenteries*, which so perplex us after returning from tropical climates, all those precautions and directions detailed under the head of *Chronic Hepatitis*, (with which the complaint in question is generally associated,) will be found well worthy of attention—particularly flannels and occasional opiates.

The diet in dysentery must of course be of the most unirritating and farinaceous nature; such as sago, arrow root, rice, &c. A very excellent dish for chronic dysenterics, is flour and milk, well boiled together, which with a very little sugar and spice, is highly relished by the debilitated patient.

But there is one remark applicable to this, and every febrile complaint, whatever may be the organ most affected; namely, that, when convalescence takes place, the appetite too often outstrips the digestion, and so do chylification and sanguification exceed the various excretions, so as to occasion a dangerous inequilibrium between assimilation and secretion; the consequence of which is, that the weakest viscus, or that which has suffered most during the previous illness, becomes overpowered, and relapse ensues! This is the great error of inexperience, and it is generally seen too late!—I appeal to clinical observation for the truth and the importance of these remarks.

In order to render this work as complete as possible for the Tropical sojourner, I shall add to this section two Analytical reviews,—

one of Mr. BAMPFIELD's work on Dysentery ; the other of Dr. Ballingal's Treatise.

A Practical Treatise on Tropical Dysentery, more particularly as it occurs in the East Indies; illustrated by Cases and Appearances on Dissection : to which is added, a Practical Treatise on Scorbutic Dysentery, with some Facts and Observations relative to Scurvy. By R. W. BAMPFIELD, Esq. Surgeon, Author of an Essay on Hemeralopia, or Night-blindness ; and formerly Surgeon of the Belliqueux and Warrior, His Majesty's Ships of the Line, serving in the East and West Indies. Octavo, pp. 352. London, 1819.

The work, though there is no formal division of chapters to that effect, may be said to consist of three parts. The 1st treats of *acute*, the 2d of *chronic dysentery* : and the 3d describes another species which the author chooses, (whether rightly or not will appear in the sequel,) to denominate *scorbutic dysentery*. I shall briefly review each of these in the order here mentioned.

I shall begin by extracting the author's description of the species and varieties he has observed in tropical dysentery, whether acute or chronic.

" Species 1 ma. *Dysenteria acuta. Character;* while the fæces are commonly retained, frequent evacuations from the intestines, consisting of mucus, serum, or blood, or a mixture of these, take place ; and are preceded and attended by pain in some part of the abdomen, and accompanied and followed by tenesmus ; pyrexia is not often evident, but is sometimes urgent.

" It varies in degree. (A.) *Dysenteria mitis.* In which the stools are not frequent ; the quantity of mucus or serum evacuated is small, and rarely tinged with blood ; there is not any fever present ; and the pain of the abdomen is never constant, and is only felt together with tenesmus, about the periods of evacuation.

" (B.) *Dysenteria severa.* In which the stools are frequent, and recur from twelve to forty-eight times, or even oftener, in twenty-four hours ; the excretions of mucus, or serum, and the discharges of blood, or a mixture of these three, are copious. The tenesmus and tormina about the periods of evacuation are severely felt ; but there is no *constant*, fixed, and acute pain in any part of the abdomen, or unequivocal synocha.

" (C.) *Dysenteria inflammatoria.* In which there is a constant, fixed, acute pain of some part of the abdomen or intestinal canal, including the parts contained in the pelvis ; unequivocal inflammatory fever, (or synocha ;) obstinate retention of fæces, while there are very frequent and copious dejections of mucus, serum, or blood, or a mixture of these, together with severe tormina and tenesmus. The blood drawn and concreted exhibits the inflammatory buff.

" Species 2da. `Dysenteria chronica.* The acute is frequently succeeded by chronic dysentery, as a sequela of the varieties B and C. In chronic dysentery, the fæces are not retained ; but frequent, loose fæcal stools, (a state which, for brevity, I shall term diarrhœa,) ensue, mixed with dysenteric excretions, and accompanied with tenesmus and tormina.

" Acute dysentery is sometimes followed by diarrhœa, uncombined with dysenteric excretions, that will be noticed when we come to
the treatment."

" Variety, (A.) In which diarrhœa is accompanied with an uniform continuance or a frequent recurrence of dysenteric excretions,
and of intestinal pains at the periods of evacuation."

" (B.) In which the dysenteric excretions of the intestines are
continued and often evacuated, while the bowels observe regular periods of discharging fæces of natural consistence and colour, the same
as in health.

" (C.) In which the chronic stage of dysentery is protracted by
an ulceration or excoriation of the intestines : the diarrhœa and morbid secretions are maintained ; and pus is observed in the evacuations."

" (D.) In which the chronic stage is protracted by a diseased enlargement of the mesenteric glands, and, with the following variety,
may be considered symptomatic.

" (E.) In which it is maintained by an abscess formed in one of
the abdominal viscera or their membranes, and is generally accompanied by hectic fever," p. 2, 3.

This arrangement is certainly logical and luminous, but I scarcely
see any advantage in thus splitting down diseases into so many minute
varieties. It was the celebrated Cullen who gave currency to this
custom ; swayed, perhaps, more by the example of preceding noso-
logists, than by his own excellent judgment. Of some diseases this
famous physician has enumerated as many varieties as there are exciting causes ! Upon the whole, I greatly doubt whether such minuteness of diagnosis is often possible, or if it be, whether it is of any
avail in actual practice.

I shall now follow the author into his account of the first or acute
species. He has never seen any thing that could lead him to suspect
dysentery to be contagious. This entirely coincides with my own
observations, and not with mine, merely, but with that of every modern practitioner with whom I am acquainted. The opinion of Cullen, Pringle, Hunter, Harty, and others, upon this point must therefore be set aside. Either the dysenteries of their day was a different disease from what it now is ; or these eminent individuals were
betrayed by their preconceived ideas, into a mistake.—It is surely
of very little present importance which of these alternatives may be
the truth ; for opinions must now-a-days be decided not by authority,
but by the touchstone of facts carefully observed and faithfully recorded.

Mr. Bampfield very candidly admits that he has seldom or never
found scybalæ in the stools of dysenteric patients. This is another
particular in which his observation coincides with mine.

The author goes on to describe the symptoms that affect the tongue
and fauces, the stomach, intestines and liver, the urinary organs, the
vascular and nervous systems, together with the appearances on dissection in dysentery. What he has advanced on these subjects is exceedingly accurate and methodical, but not particularly new. I shall

therefore pass this part altogether, as I shall also the chapters on diagnosis and prognosis, and proceed at once to his observations on the
predisposition to this *disease*. He is of opinion that the predisposition to
an increased secretion from the lining membrane of the organs of smell
and respiration in Europe, becomes in India a predisposition to an increased secretion from the villous coat of the intestines. Hence fluxes
are as common in the latter climate as coughs and colds are in the former.
This conversion or change in the *locale* of increased action, he thinks
chiefly attributable to the indulgences in heavy and stimulating diet,
and the imprudent exposures to the night air, of which the unwary
European newly arrived from his native climate, is wont to be guilty.
Atmospheric vicissitudes, by checking perspiration, produce a similar
detrimental effect. I do not recollect that the following circumstance has ever been noticed heretofore as a predisposing cause of
dysentery :

" The copious perspiration of the newly arrived European becomes accumulated, when he is sitting or walking, on the lower part
of the shirt, more especially about that part of the abdomen where
the waistband of the small clothes or pantaloons presses against it,
the tight or close application of which occasions an increase of heat
and of perspiration at this particular part, during the day, and intercepts the exhalation as it flows down the body ; hence if he should lie
down in this state, cold will be induced on a particular part of the
abdomen, by the evaporation of the exhaled fluid from the wet linen
in contact with it ; perspiration, before profuse, will be now effectually suppressed, and its injurious consequences be felt by the chylopoetic viscera," p. 69.

According to our author's observations, the stools in dysentery are
more frequent during the night, and especially towards morning than
at any other period of the twenty-four hours. This he seems inclined to ascribe to " solar influence."

" The periods of dysenteric attacks and relapses I have observed
to be more common at the plenilunar and novilunar periods, than at
the interlunar intervals. But whether the increased attraction of
the moon, at the change and full, has any *direct* power in producing
diseases, I believe will never be satisfactorily determined ; and notwithstanding the ingenious hypothetical explanations of Dr. Balfour,
Dr. Darwin, and others, I am induced to conclude that it has only an
indirect influence or power by the changes which it occasions at
those periods on the atmosphere and winds; for the prevalence of
fresh winds, strong gales, and showers of rain, has been observed to
be much greater at these periods of the moon, than at the interlunar
intervals ; and these by checking perspiration, produce effects on
the constitution excitive of many acute diseases, which have been in
part ascribed to the direct agency of lunar attraction on the fluids of
the body, by supposing that it decreases the gravity, and diminishes
the stimulus, of the particles of the blood," p. 84.

With regard to the proximate cause, our author seems to be of
opinion that dysentery is to all intents and purposes inflammation : or
if these two diseases are not exactly identical, that, at least the former
is attended with analogous symptoms and actions of vessels, and is

followed by similar consequences as inflammatory action of other organs of the body. What tends to confirm him in this theory is the disclosure so often made by dissection. On examining the body after death we find visceral enlargements and adhesions, a blood-shot appearance of the intestines, ulcers, abscesses, and sometimes mortification, similar to what are observed after inflammation of other parts external or internal. These appearances are very striking, yet we hold them to be equivocal. Mr. B. like many others, has been deceived by confounding the ultimate changes with the primary diseased movements. I am, in every case, inclined to regard inflammation rather as a sequence than a cause of dysentery, as a contingent effect, and not as a uniform result. Indeed the author goes nigh to admit this ; for in order to make good his theory he is obliged to extend the term inflammation to *every increased action* of the capillary vessels of secreting membranes. He says,

" Those who do not choose to admit inflammatory action to be, in all cases, the proximate cause of dysentery, in mild and less severe cases, still call it an increased and morbid excretion of the capillary vessels of the intestines, although it is assuredly, equally philosophical to denominate this action in dysentery inflammatory, as it is the action of the minute secreting vessels of the urethral membrane in gonorrhœa, or of the membranes of the bronchia and nose in catarrh ; for in mild cases of those diseases, the pain accompanying them is not constant and acute, nor accompanied with fever, or hard pulse ; nor are recoveries often doubtful," p. 90.

But although it may be incorrect in speculation to view dysentery and inflammation as one, it will generally be safe in practice to apply to the former the same *principles* of treatment as to the latter. We should never forget that a disease, though not primarily inflammatory, may often have a strong tendency to run into that state. This I believe to be the case in dysentery ; consequently we should use the lancet as boldly in the early stage of that disease, as we do in severe cases of spasmodic colic, and with the same views, namely, to remove pain ; and, (above all,) to *prevent inflammation*. Whenever the pulse and heat are high, and the abdomen painful on pressure, that is to say *permanently* painful on pressure, and the pain is confined to any given point, there is reason to fear that local inflammation is begun there ; and thenceforward it behoves us to subdue it by vigorous depletion. The mere intensity of the febrile symptoms, considered *per se*, is by no means to be neglected ; for, as the author judiciously observes, " fever rarely exists in the tropics without being occasioned by local inflammation or determination."

This leads me to speak more in detail of the mode of cure laid down by Mr. Bampfield. The remedies he trusts to are, 1st. bleeding ; 2d. cathartics ; 3d. diaphoretics ; and 4th. mercurials. He discusses these under separate heads, and each of them at considerable length. His remarks on blood-letting are singularly valuable, and have my cordial approbation. I think he has deserved well of the profession for the pains he has taken to introduce this remedy to more general attention. It is gratifying to think that experience, on matters of great importance, is always uniform ; and that where it finds men

willing to obey its dictates, it always conducts them to the same mode
of practice. For instance, it was not by any preconcerted opinions
that Mr. Bampfield was induced to employ the lancet in dysentery ;
but by the careful observation of actual cases. I can say the same
thing of myself, for experience led me to the same conclusions with
those here stated by the author. I well recollect the reluctance and
trepidation with which I first " wetted a lancet" in a disease where it
had been totally proscribed by the concurrent authority of all those
authors whose works on the subject were most esteemed. " We
watched the patient, (says the Reviewer in the Medico-Chirurgical
Journal,*) in anxious dread of those formidable consequences which
has been alleged to follow venesection. But the result was quite
contrary to what we had been taught to expect ; for all the severe
symptoms were greatly mitigated by the evacuation. Emboldened a
little by success, we began cautiously, but regularly, to employ blood-
letting whenever the state of the pulse and the heat of skin seemed, on
general principles, to warrant it ; and ere long we found that dysentery,
from being an unmanageable and baffling disease, was converted into a
form much more responsible to the ordinary medical treatment. Even
when the quantity of blood evacuated by stool was so considerable as
to cause debility or prostration of strength, we did not refrain from the
lancet ; nay, we considered the use of it to be rendered if possible,
more imperative on that account ; for we viewed the hæmorrhage
from the intestines to be *active* in its nature,-and thought it as incumbent upon us to check it by venesection, as it is to check, (by bleeding at the arm,) hæmoptysis, or any other internal hæmorrhage. We
are convinced that four ounces of blood lost by the anus causes more
debility than four and twenty lost by the arm. We look upon blood-
letting to be a very great improvement in the modern treatment of
dysentery. We give the praise of it to modern times, because, although it was practised and recommended by Sydenham, we greatly
doubt whether the limited quantities he was in the habit of taking
away, could have exerted any very marked benefit on the disease. It
is, we believe, to Dr. Whyte that the profession are indebted for having shown the perfect safety of this remedy ; and had this gentleman
lived to publish more extensively upon his experience, we have little
doubt that venesection would have been earlier and more effectively
adopted in military and naval practice than it has been. But the
premature death of this lamented individual, from inoculating himself
with the matter of a plague bubo, cut him short in the middle of his
honourble career ; and the air of rashness which attended the circumstances of his decease, induced many to discountenance the practice,
(stated in his letter to H. R. H. the Duke of York ; see Med. and
Phys. Journal, vol. ii.) of bleeding to syncope in dysentery, as the
hazardous experiment of a well-meaning, but hot-headed medical
enthusiast. In consequence of this prejudice, blood-letting never
became fully established as a remedy in this disease until the late
Peninsular campaigns. Experience there pointed out to military
medical gentlemen a similar mode of treatment to what had suggest-

* I may here state the Reviewer's name—Dr. Archibald Robertson of Northampton.

ed itself to Mr. Bampfield and others of his naval brethren employed within the tropics. The whole of our author's section on this subject is so excellent, that we are at a loss what paragraph to extract in preference to another. We take the following passages almost at random."

" In dysentery it happens that a certain degree of debility must be induced either by the antiphlogistic regimen, or by the protracted disease gradually exhausting the animal and vital powers; hence it is thought preferable to induce a certain degree of it at once, (by bleeding, to wit,) and thus put a speedy termination to the disorder, and prevent the distressing and sometimes fatal effects of the chronic stage."

" In this disease, venesection is said to be injurious by Dr. J. Clarke, (p. 324, 325,) and probably his authority has given rise to the neglect and omission of the practice. He admits that " no evacuation is better calculated for the relief of the patient, when the disease is accompanied with a fever of the inflammatory kind. But, in hot climates, fluxes being either of a chronic nature, or accompanied with a low fever, the strength of the patient sinks from the beginning."

It is granted that there is a peculiar sensation of debility, the companion of the very severe and inflammatory varieties of dysentery, resembling what occurs in enteritis, and this sensation is maintained and increased by the constant dysenteric evacuations, the severe pains, the want of sleep, and the exhaustion of the sensorial power in the sensitive and irritative motions : but, as no judicious practitioner is deterred from bleeding by the peculiar sensation of debility attending gastritis and enteritis, so let no one be deterred from employing it in the inflammatory forms of dysentery. It has been already remarked, that the chronic stage is generally a sequela to the severe and inflammatory varieties, if their acute stage be not arrested and cured. If bleeding be not employed in the inflammatory variety, either death, or a very long chronic stage, almost invariably ensues. Hence bleeding often does away with the " chronic nature of fluxes." I have not observed that the " fever" which accompanies dysentery is particularly " low :" however, Dr. Cullen, in his *Nosology* has enumerated " typhus fever" as a characteristic symptom of enteritis, but he nevertheless recommends bleeding for its cure. The author adds—

" Venesection can be dispensed with in the milder and safer forms of dysentery, where the symptoms of inflammation are not present, where the pain is only occasional, and the evacuations are not copious nor frequent : these varieties will, in general, yield to the other remedies employed for the cure of dysentery," p. 110, 111, 113.

I cannot bestow so much commendation upon our author's chapter on cathartics as upon that on bleeding. I conceive the purgatives recommended by him to be far too drastic and stimulating ; and I entertain very serious doubts whether jalap, extract of colocynth, or infusion of senna, can be with propriety employed in any stage of dysentery. Surely, on his own notions as to the strictly inflammatory nature of the disease, these medicines must be highly unsuitable ;

for would it not follow, from his doctrine, that they should aggravate the symptoms ? What practitioner will venture to prescribe drastic purgatives in enteritis, or to excite vehement action in an intestine whose calibre is already inflamed ? If it is necessary to give rest to an inflamed muscle, or to withhold the stimulus of light from an irritable eye, it is no less necessary to tranquillize and soothe the bowels by all the means in our power. In dysentery, when purgatives are necessary, (and generally they are indispensable,) I never employ any other than those of a mild and lubricating nature. Castor oil is almost the only one that is proper ; and when it is necessary to increase its activity, that can be readily accomplished by adding to it a few grains of calomel. Indeed Mr. B. himself is fully aware of the virtues of this medicine.—The following passage is an excellent one, though rather at variance with his recommendation of the dry and more acrid purgatives.

" The oleum ricini is perhaps better calculated to afford relief in dysentery, than any other aperient or cathartic ; for its action is not only mild and generally effectual, but I have observed that some of it passes undecomposed, in its oily form, through the intestines, and appears on the surface of the excrement, and hence may serve as a sort of sheather or defence to the diseased intestines, from the stimulus of fæces and morbid secretions," p. 124.

The observations on diaphoretics contain nothing new ; we shall therefore pass on to the subject of mercurials.

The author has been in the habit of prescribing calomel, but he seldom gives it alone. He thinks it greatly better to combine it with other purgatives, or with ipecacuanha. This remedy is generally given with the view of correcting the condition of the liver ; for all practitioners concur in thinking that the function of this mighty gland is greatly depraved in dysentery, though they may differ in opinion as to the relative importance of this depraved state—some regarding it as the primary cause of the symptoms ; and others viewing it merely as one link in the chain of effects. It would probably be alike tiresome and unprofitable to the readers were I, in this place, to enter into minute discussions on the subject. I shall therefore wave the matter altogether, only remarking that I suspect the liver has not, till lately, been allowed its due share of importance among the phenomena of this disease. I am persuaded that much of the exquisite pain and tormina is assignable to vitiated bile passing over the irritable, excoriated, or ulcerated surface of the intestines ; for I do not see how otherwise the pain, which succeeds the fullest operation of a cathartic, is to be accounted for. The renal discharges also afford an additional presumption that unhealthy bile performs an important part in the malady. When the urine is collected, it is generally of a green or yellowish colour, and tinges linen, evidently from the admixture of bile ; and it is generally passed with considerable heat and smarting. The latter uncomfortable sensation is always ascribed to *sympathy* betwixt the rectum and bladder ; but instead of taking for granted that tenesmus is the cause of the difficult micturition, it is more reasonable to believe that the bile, mixed with urine, is the occasion of that teasing phenomenon.

The mercurial preparations prescribed in dysentery are found to produce a solution of the disease ; but whether they do so by rectifying the hepatic secretion, or by producing some more secret and inexplicable change in the system at large, is, at present, quite unknown. One thing, however, is certain :—as soon as ptyalism takes place, the disease generally disappears as a matter of course.

In consequence of this last fact being so universally noticed, some practitioners have directed their views to salivation as the sole indication of cure, and have boldly prescribed calomel alone in doses of one scruple twice or thrice a day.

" I myself," says Dr. Robertson, " have employed the scruple doses in the dysentery of the western hemisphere, and have seen it, in the great majority of instances, produce all the benefit which Dr. Johnson taught us to expect. It deserves to be remarked, however, that it is a practice only adapted to tropical climates, for *there* the human frame is much less susceptible of the action of mercury, and consequently will bear much larger doses of that metal than it would be prudent to prescribe in the climate of this country."

I frankly admit, indeed, that the first stage of dysentery cannot be treated on principles too strictly antiphlogistic ; but I contend, that when the second stage has commenced, or in other words, when the previous increased action has ended in congestion, nothing can be more useful than to saturate the system with mercury. This mineral does more to resolve irritative fever, to equalize the circulation, disgorge the capillary vessels, restore the balance of the nervous power, and open the sluices of the various healthy secretions and excretions, than any other remedy with which I am acquainted. Besides, it should be remembered, that calomel is a restringent as well as a cholagogue, and that its efficacy consists as much in restraining and rectifying the biliary and intestinal secretions, when they are excessive or morbid, as in exciting and augmenting them when they happen to be torpid or too scanty.

" The propriety of impregnating the constitution," says Dr. Robertson, " then being admitted, the only question of importance is, how it is to be done most speedily ?" I answer with confidence, says he, " By means of calomel in scruple doses, night and morning." " We should recollect that the cases to which alone this practice is applicable, are pregnant with great distress and danger, and that, consequently, delays are dangerous. Nothing but the most energetic practice will prove available to save life, and *that* even, in too many instances, fails. Upon the whole, deferring to Mr. Bampfield's judgment and experience, but at the same time abiding by my own, I must take the liberty to declare, that I consider all his fears about excessive salivation, hypercatharsis, and so forth, as the results of this new practice, to be entirely illusory. His opinion that, " the induction of salivation is incompatible with a high degree of inflammation," not only takes for granted the correctness of his own theory of dysentery, but is in itself perhaps little better than a hypothesis. Besides, it carries no weight with it as an objection ; because, where is the practitioner that would proceed to mercurialize the system until he has reduced the existing febrile excitement ? Neither myself, nor

Dr. Johnson, have ever administered scruple doses or any other doses of calomel, with an attempt to salivate, without premising active depletion both by blood-letting and purgatives."

His chapter on chronic dysentery, is chiefly valuable on account of the clearness and earnestness with which he points out the necessity of dietetic restrictions as auxiliary to the medicines employed. He details several very illustrative cases, where irregularities, whether in eating or drinking brought on fatal relapses.

" The evil and mortal consequences resulting from intemperance, imprudent indulgences of the appetite, and of the social disposition, have been depicted in treating of the variety A : these errors are more pernicious in this, and the necessity of a most regular and temperate life, and of a strict dietetic regimen is consequently greater. Obstinate or ill-fated patients are sometimes met with, who cannot be persuaded, or induced by sufferings, to a proper diet. I have sometimes eluded the bad effects of their folly and obstinacy, by keeping up a slight mercurial soreness of mouth, which has compelled them to relinquish solid food, and to live on broths and farinaceous preparations of diet, so long as to allow of a favourable state of quiescence to the bowels, and to admit of the establishment of a healty action of the ulcer in the intestines. We have no indirect means of adroitly warding off the fate of the determined inebriate, and can only succeed by resolute compulsion," p. 242.

Perhaps the most original portion of the volume is the part that treats of scorbutic dysentery. I read it with very great pleasure, and give Mr. Bampfield the highest praise for the number of curious, instructive, and interesting facts which he has collected on the subject of scurvy. Yet I have doubts as to the correctness of his nomenclature, when he speaks of *scorbutic dysentery :* I indeed suspect that it ought rather to be considered an accidental co-existence of the two diseases in the same subject, than a distinct and specific variety of dysentery. This, however, is in a great measure, matter of opinion.

He relates some singular cases, where scurvy appeared in the men in a week, or less, after putting to sea ; and others, where the sea air was the only obvious cause. The pathology of scurvy is still very obscure, notwithstanding all the experience of the late war; that neither salt meat, sea air, nor atmospheric heat is indispensably necessary to the production of the disease, is proved by what Dr. Gregory relates of a family that came under his observation, who suffered severely from scurvy, during a season of dearth, in consequence of their chief diet having been tea. They had used it three times a-day.

Notwithstanding my objections to some of Mr. B.'s doctrines, I entertain a high opinion of his work. The talent, learning, and sagacity it displays, will render it a rich treat to those who are fond of a well-written and well-digested treatise on this fatal disease. To them I conclude by recommending it."--*Med. Chir. Journal, Vol.* 1.

Analytical Review of Dr. BALLINGAL's *Observations on* DYSENTERY.

Dr. Ballingal objects, in limine, and well he may, to Dr. Cullen's definition of dysentery, at least as it appears in India, and we may add, in Europe. In our eastern colonies, he observes, this disease often makes considerable devastation on the intestinal canal before pyrexia becomes evident ; and as to its contagious nature, it is totally unnecessary to mention the absurdity of the opinion, once so curⁿ rently adopted, and even yet pertinaciously retained by a few individuals. " The appearance of scybalæ, another striking feature of the disease, as characterized in Europe, is comparatively a rare occurrence in India." I would ask Mr. Ballingal, if his own *post mortem* examinations, or personal observations, confirm this story of scybalæ in European dysentery ? I can only say, that during the late war, chance threw me in the way of opening, and seeing opened, some hundred bodies who died of dysentery in Europe ; and I can safely assert, that scybalæ are as infrequent here as in India. We thus see how error may be propagated. The above distinction, which exists only in books, and in Mr. Ballingal's imagination, is brought forward as a proof that tropical and Hyperborean dysentery are different diseases !

Dysentery then, in our Indian territories, is divided into two varieties ; colonitis, (not necessarily implying the existence of any discharge from the bowels;) and hepatic flux.

It is colonitis, which, according to our author, makes the greatest ravages, *at first*, among the European troops. The causes are conceived to be " Heat, particularly when combined with moisture ; the immoderate and indiscriminate use of fruits ; the abuse of spirituous liquors ; exposure to currents of wind and noxious high dews." But without attempting to account satisfactorily for colonitis, our author proceeds to a description of the disease, taken from the Critical Review for 1802, as given in the extract of a letter to Sir Walter Farquhar. The writer of this letter states, that the disease is attended from the beginning with a severe fixed pain above the pubes, attended with extreme difficulty of making water, and frequently an entire suppression of urine. There is, at the same time, a violent and almost unceasing evacuation from the bowels, of a matter peculiar to the disease, and which exactly resembles the washings of raw flesh. High fever, unquenchable thirst, and perpetual watching, attend the complaint. The pulse is hard and strong, resembling that in the highest degree of pleurisy, or acute rheumatism. The fixed pain above the pubes ; the peculiar evacuation ; and the suppression of urine, may, it is thought, be considered pathognomonic of this disease. From dissection, the colon seems to be primarily affected ; and the bladder suffers only from communication, as the lower part of the large intestine is generally inflamed. " Bleeding seems useful ; but opium given in the commencement is the most effectual remedy." If omitted till the fever supervenes it is injurious, and can only be administered towards the decline of the disease. The remedies then are emollient glysters and drinks, with fomentations above the pubes, which are more useful than blisters.

It has only happened to Mr. Ballingal to meet the disease with these highly inflammatory symptoms, where it occurred as a consequence of hard drinking, and where it had made considerable progress before medical assistance was called in.

" The form of flux, now under consideration, commences in general with much of the appearance of a common diarrhœa ; frequent and unseasonable calls to stool, with an irresistible inclination to strain over it. The evacuations are generally copious, of a fluid consistence, without any peculiar fœtor ; sometimes streaked with blood, and at other times a small quantity of blood is voided in a separate form, unmixed with the fæcal matter. The pulse in this stage of the disease, is seldom altered ; the heat of the skin not perceptibly increased, and the tongue is frequently but little changed in its appearance. There is always a great prostration of strength and depression of spirits ; the former symptom being always strongly dwelt upon by the patient ; the appetite is indifferent, and thirst urgent. To these symptoms succeed a fixed pain in the hypogastrium, more or less acute ; the pain sometimes extending to, and peculiarly urgent in one or both the iliac regions ; and sometimes to be traced along the whole course of the colon, with a sense of fulness, tension, and tenderness upon pressure ; and on applying the hand to the surface of the abdomen, a preternatural degree of heat is frequently perceptible in the integuments ; the evacuations now become more frequent, and less copious ; they consist chiefly of blood and mucus,' or are composed of a peculiar bloody serum, which has very aptly been compared to water in which beef has been washed or macerated. A suppression of urine and distressing tenesmus now become urgent symptoms ; the indifference to solid food increases, while there is an uncontrollable desire for liquids, particularly cold water, which the patient prefers to any drink that may be offered to him, and from which he expresses his inability to refrain, although prepossessed with the idea of its being injurious. The tongue is now generally white, and furred ; sometimes, however, exhibiting a florid, smooth, and glassy appearance, with a tremulous motion when thrust out ; the skin is either parching hot, so as to render it even painful to retain the hand in contact with it, or covered with profuse perspiration, insomuch that it may often be observed standing in large drops on the surface ; the pulse is still frequently but little affected ; sometimes, however, it assumes a febrile quickness, without any other remarkable feature ; at other times it will be found without any increase of velocity, but full, and bounding with a peculiar thrilling sensation under the fingers. This state of the pulse, whenever it takes place, always denotes extreme danger, and shows that the disease is rapidly hurrying on to the final stage, in which the lassitude and dejection, so conspicuous throughout its course, are now converted into the utmost degree of anxiety, depression, and fear of death. The patient generally shows an inclination to dwell upon symptoms, which to a spectator would appear of minor importance. He evinces the greatest reluctance to part with his medical attendant, though fully sensible how unavailing the efforts of medicine are likely to prove. The discharges by stool, which are frequently involuntary, are now accompanied with the most intolerable fœtor ; they are frequently mixed with shreds of membrane, and quantities of purulent matter ; a protusion of the gut, forming a complete procidentia ani often takes place ; and cases are not wanting, where a portion of the inner coat of the intestines, amounting to some inches, has been thrown off in a state of mortification," p. 49.

When things come to this pass, death soon closes the scene. The periods occupied in passing through the different stages are very various, the disease often proving fatal within a week — and at other times being protracted to two or three weeks, but seldom longer, where the inflammation is solely confined to the colon.

Our author next proceeds to the symptomatology of the more chronic form of disease, denominated " Hepatic Flux." This is more incident to men after some residence in India, and particularly those who are prone to irregular and disordered secretions of bile. It often, like the other, assumes the form of diarrhœa at first, and becomes afterwards characterized by frequent and severe fits of griping, resembling cholic pains, particularly urgent about the umbilical region. The evacuations at the beginning always exhibit something unnatural in their colour, varying from the darkest inky hue to the different degrees of green and yellow ; all these colours often alternating. The stools are accompanied with much flatus, and generally exhibit a frothy appearance, attended with a sense of scalding about the anus, the patient enjoying an interval of ease after each evacuation. The intervals, however, are generally so short, that the soldier often prefers carrying a mat with him to the necessary, in order to pass the night there, rather than have to run backwards and forwards to the barrack-room.

" From the commencement the patient complains of nausea, inappetency ; preternatural thirst ; bad taste in the mouth, the tongue being furred, and loaded with a bilious crust ; the pulse quickened and the skin parched. After a few days, the stools become white, passed with straining, and mixed with half-digested aliment. The complaint, is now denominated by the soldiers " the white flux," and its obstinacy is well known among them. The griping pains continue, and sometimes the patient feels a permanent degree of oppression about the epigastric region. Nausea, hiccup, and bilious vomiting now become highly distressing ; the thirst becomes urgent, with lassitude, debility, and increasing emaciation. The skin often communicates a greasy sensation to the touch. In this way the patient goes on for weeks, or even months, the complaint terminating in recovery, or the patient is carried off by an abscess in the liver, or by the accession of ulceration and mortification in the course of the colon ; the accession of the latter is to be apprehended from the appearance of blood in the stools, and the other symptoms of colonitis formerly detailed," p. 53.

Post-mortem Appearances in Colonitis. Inflammation of that part of the tube situated below the valve of the colon. No disease of the structure of the liver.

" Yet I am by no means disposed to infer, from the want of morbid appearances in the liver, that this viscus may not have been, in many cases, the seat of *diseased action*, during the life of the patient," p. 53.

When the abdomen is laid open, an effusion of serum, sometimes mixed with coagulable lymph, is found accumulated in this cavity ; the omentum generally shrunk firmer than usual, and of a doughy feel, with slight adhesions, to the convolutions of the intestines ; at other times shrivelled and destitute of fat. The stomach seldom altered in its appearance. The small intestines sound, sometimes exhibiting slight inflammatory patches adhering to the omentum. No peculiar appearance on the inner coat of the small intestines.

" The great intestines again, the principal seats of disease, show the strongest marks of inflammation in all its stages ; some portions exhibiting externally a slight inflammatory redness, while others are marked by the highest degree of lividity ; and in some cases, parts of the gut will be found to have given way, so as to permit the escape of air, and even of fæces, into the cavity of the abdomen ; and in these destructive effects of inflammatory action, the cæcum, with its appendix vermiformis, and the sigmoid flexure of the colon, will, in most cases, be found to participate largely." p. 55.

The appearance of cells in the colon is, in a great measure, obliterated, and the coats of the intestine often so thickened throughout, as to suggest the idea of a solid rope ; and so much altered in tenacity—so brittle in texture, as not to admit of being handled without the risk of rupturing them. The calibre of the gut is found much diminished by the thickening of the coats ; the villous coat in some places abraded simply, in others ulcerated, and besmeared with bloody mucus, mixed with specks of pus. In some places, this coat of the colon exhibited a tuberculous appearance, not inaptly compared to small-pox. Extravasated grumous blood is not unfrequently found in the colon. Scybalæ very seldom met with. The liver sometimes free from apparent disease, at other times preternaturally small and indurated, or enlarged and hardened ; the bile unhealthy looking. The other viscera not often or materially affected, excepting the mesenteric glands, which are frequently found enlarged and obstructed.

Dr. Ballingal having endeavoured to establish the existence of two distinct modifications or varieties of India flux, proceeds to the treatment, which is very briefly detailed. He considers the colonitis, or acute form of flux, as a local disease, unconnected with the liver or the constitution—an inflammation, in short, of the large intestine, tending rapidly to mortification.

" But even allowing that a diseased action of the liver, and a vitiated state of the biliary secretion, have always preceded the attack of colonitis, and have been, in some measure, the cause of the latter affection, still, in the state we meet the disease, the effect appears to have greatly outrun the cause ; they bear no adequate proportion to each other ; and it is too much to expect that, by taking away the one, the other will cease," p. 66.

I do not conceive that this is very good reasoning. The disordered function of one organ will sometimes produce diseased structure in another, which is infinitely worse ; yet the latter might have been prevented, (not indeed cured,) by removing the former. I have no objection, indeed, to our author's mode of obviating the local affection of the intestine, whether it be primary or secondary ; but if the *latter*, the original source of the mischief ought also to be sought after. and. if possible, removed.

Dr. B. then recommends the vigorous use of topical remedies, as leeches, blisters to the surface of the abdomen, fomentations, anodyne, and astringent injections. But our author does not reject the use of general remedies, and particularly of *blood-letting*. Of this measure he entertains a very favourable opinion. He candidly owns, however, that this opinion is grounded more on the ravages of inflammation, so universally apparent in the dead. than on any repeated or extensive experience of its beneficial effects on the living." In the regiment where our author served, there was a general dislike to the use of the lancet ; as indeed, there was, and we fear still is, among the old practitioners in India." Moreover, a long voyage of full five months, without having touched any where for refreshments, had lowered the tone of the European constitution, so that by the time they got over the first objection, from repeated experience of the safety and utility of bleeding in other diseases, the period for its employment in dysentery was past, or at least rendered extremely questionable, while the complicated nature of the cases latterly occurring lessened its necessity.

" In short, (says Dr. B.) of the few cases of dysentery in which I have employed bleeding, the majority have, I think, terminated favourably ; and of those in which the result has been fatal, the appearances on dissection have been such as to excite a sentiment of regret at not having carried the evacuation further." p. 68.

Purgatives, Dr. B. exhibits at the very beginning, in order to clear the alimentary canal, and ascertain the state of the fæcal matters. If the *latter* are not unhealthy. while at the same time the purgatives produce an increase of pain and tenesmus, with more copious discharges of blood and mucus, then they become, to say the least, unnecessary, perhaps detrimental, by increasing the irritability of the intestines, and determining a greater flow of blood to those parts. When purgatives are deemed necessary, our author has been in the habit of administering the neutral salts, with or without the infusion of senna.

Emetics our author has no experience of in dysentery, and does not approve of them.

Sudorifics. " Of all the general and constitutional remedies employed in the form of flux, now under consideration, this is the class of articles of which I have the most extensive experience, and to which I am disposed to assign the most powerful and salutary effects."

In this light he considers the employment of opium and ipecacuan. introduced into India by Mr. Abercrombie, of the 34th Regt. The practice was to give several grains of solid opium, following it by the exhibition of two or more ounces of infusion of ipecacuan. The other forms of sudorifics which our author chiefly employed were Dover's powder, and a combination of laudanum and antimonial wine ; from all of which he observed beneficial effects. I would just here ask our author, if he

24

conceives the form of dysentery now under consideration to be simply
and purely inflammation of the colon, why opium and ipecacuan, should
not be equally beneficial in simple enteritis, of every-day occurrence ? But here is the rock on which most writers on dysentery
split.   They find, when the disease proves mortal, inflammation and
ulceration in the bowels, and they immediately conclude that the very
last link in the chain of *effects*, was the first in the chain of causes.
In almost every case of fatal phrenitis, we find effusion of water at
the base of the brain ; but who, in his right senses, would set down
hydrocephalus as the cause of phrenitis ? So it is in dysentery.   Inflammation and ulceration are secondary or ternary links in the morbid chain ; and many a case of real dysentery is checked and cured,
before either of these takes place—that is, when there is merely an
increased afflux of blood to the mesenteric and portal vessels, a
super-irritation in the mucous membrane of the bowels, and an increased discharge of acrid secretions from the intestinal glands. But
to return.

Warm Bath. This remedy was found particularly useful in allaying
pain, inducing sleep, diminishing the frequency of the stools, and
promoting the discharge of urine.   Fomentions to the abdomen, on
the same principle, are serviceable.

Mercury. When the regiment was first disembarked at Prince of
Wales's Island, in full European health and vigour, mercury *alone*,
carried to ptyalism, was not very successful ; and truly we wonder,
how men can be blind to the obvious inflammatory condition of the
system at these times, and withhold the lancet, as auxiliary to the
other means.

" I can readily conceive, and indeed know, that, in cases of a protracted disease, where the discharges from the intestines degenerate
from pure blood and mucus, and become of a more diseased nature ;
that there is no remedy so much to be depended upon for the restoration of healthy secretions ; but in the pure inflammatory complaint
I am now speaking of, mercury can seldom be useful," p. 74.

Tropical Bleeding, by leeches especially, is much recommended
by Mr. B. on the authority of a letter from Dr. Annesley, surgeon
of the Madras European Regiment.   Dr. Aitkin also suggested to our
author the application of leeches to the anus in dysentery.

Blisters are spoken of as useful auxiliaries, whenever there is any
fixed pain in any part of the colon.

Injections. These, of all remedies employed in dysentery, have appeared to our author, and to his patients, the most instrumental in alleviating the distressing tenesmus, diminishing the calls to stool, and
lessening the profuse discharge of blood and mucus.—We can truly
say that we have not found them so.

" In the composition of injections, decoctions of bark, solutions of
the acetate of lead, and of the sulphate of zinc, were at first, pretty
extensively employed, and with a view of increasing their efficacy,
were occasionally thrown up cold."

Chronic or Hepatic Flux. This our author looks upon, and jutly too,
as much more of a constitutional than a local disease.   The circumstance of its prevailing among those who have been some time in
the country ; the degree of fever attending it ; the diseased secre-

tions in the stools, all evince functional derangement of the glandular viscera of the abdomen, as well as of the intestinal tube.

" That the functions of this organ, [the liver,] are, in most cases, materially, and perhaps primarily deranged, and that without a healthy action of this viscus, all our curative efforts will prove nugatory, are facts very generally, and as far as I know, most justly believed," p. 80.

Mercury. " If, in treating of the acute form of flux, I have refrained from an indiscriminate, and, as I conceive, unmerited commendation of this powerful medicine, it is only in hopes of being able to urge its employment with double force in the *form of* disease now under consideration ; to recommend an implicit reliance on it in the chronic form of flux ; to ascribe to it an almost unlimited power in this disease ; and to express an opinion, that it will seldom disappoint our most sanguine hopes. A partiality for the use of mercury is as conspicuous in India, as the aversion to blood-letting, formerly noticed— that partiality is, however, much better founded," p. 81.

Almost every practitioner in India gives a preference to some particular preparation or form of the remedy ; no weak proof, by the bye, how much depends on the medicine itself, and how little on the form of administration. If our author has formed a prepossession on this subject, it is in favour of the common blue pill. Before irritability of the stomach came on, Dr. B. thought that he could affect the system more speedily, and produce a change in the nature of the evacuations sooner, " by the daily exhibition of from twelve to twenty grains of the blue pill," than by any other preparation. Where gastric irritability prevails, or where mercury appears to affect the bowels, then he thinks mercurial frictions are preferable, as the system should be impregnated by rubbing in daily from one to two or three drachms of the blue ointment, according to the urgency of the symptoms, the rapidity with which the disease is proceeding, and the constitution of the patient.

" The exhibition of calomel, with opium, is a very favourite practice with many, and I have entered into this to a very considerable extent ; three or four grains of calomel, and a grain of opium, made into a pill, and exhibited every three or four hours, I have soon found to produce all the beneficial effects resulting from the employing of mercury," p. 82.

The quantity will vary greatly in different individuals—

" But it is always to be carried the length of producing considerable ptyalism ; and this, wherever the exhaustion of the patient does not forbid it, is to be kept up without intermission, until natural secretions return, and the stools resume a healthy appearance," p. 83.

But Dr. B. wisely avails himself of other auxiliaries in this form of dysentery. Purgatives, he thinks, are essentially necessary.

" The castor oil is a purgative in very extensive use amongst the natives of India, and many of the practitioners there give it a preference to every other."

This is the purgative, indeed, which I have always found to answer best in India. The warm bath and sudorifics are often useful to obviate the heat of the skin, and relieve the febrile symptoms in general, when they become urgent.—Opiates, blisters, effervescing draughts, &c. are occasionally necessary ; and tenesmus, he thinks, is best relieved by the anodyne glysters.   The cummerband or belly band of flannel, is deservedly praised by our author.

" I have thus far endeavoured, both in the history and treatment, to show, that under the general denomination of dysentery or flux, we have two distinct forms of disease prevalent in India ; and I now proceed to observe, that although, during the first years of my service in that country, these two diseases were often to be met with in practice as distinct as I have studied to keep them in description ; they became latterly more and more blended together, and were to be found in all possible varieties of combination.   This is what we should naturally expect from reasoning, and what is amply confirmed by my experience, so far as it goes.   The well-known effects of warm climates, independent of the habitual use of spirits, will account for the existence of a liver affection in most of the cases of colonitis, which latterly occurred : while the well-known tendency of the country or pariar arrack, (often rendered more deleterious by the mixture of acrid ingredients,) to induce the acute or inflammatory flux, will account for the disposition latterly evinced by the hepatic fluxes, to terminate in inflammation of the colon.   While the two forms of disease were thus frequently found co-existent and running insensibly into each other, it was by no means uncommon to find them existing alternately for weeks or months, and destroying the patient by a form of flux, the symptoms of which alternately bore a nearer relation to one or other of the diseases I have described. These form a description of cases by far the most perplexing and troublesome we meet with ; and with respect to their treatment, the only general rule that can be laid down is, to urge the one or other mode of cure, in proportion as the one or other set of symptoms become more pressing.   And where the co-existence of both forms of flux renders it necessary to adopt a means of cure suited to this form of disease, we can only meet it by the simultaneous adoption of both modes of treatment.   These, it will be observed, are by no means incompatible with each other ; the one consisting chiefly in the exhibition of local remedies, directed to the lower part of the intestinal canal, while the other consists chiefly in the exhibition of mercury to affect the system.   Had the appearance of one form of flux uniformly, or even generally, preceded the other, I should have been most ready to take the opportunity of considering them as different stages, rather than different forms of disease ; but the want of uniformity in this respect leaves, in my opinion, no room for such a description," p. 89.

From the foregoing extract, the reader will be ready to suspect that the division of dysentery into colonitis and hepatic flux is rather fanciful than solid ; and that the practical indications are full as well founded on the theory that dysentery is an increased irritation and afflux of blood to the mucous membrane of the intestines, with *functional* derangement in the liver, *ending* often in inflammation of the said membrane.   On this account I have always considered the lancet as a material instrument in the treatment of dysentery ; more, however, to prevent the *effects* than to remove the *causes* of this disease. Whoever encounters dysentery successfully, will aim at the restoration of the balance of the circulation and excitement, with the healthy *functions* of the skin and liver. He will do this, and guard at the same time against inflammation of the intestines by blood-letting, whenever pain on pressure of the abdomen, sanguineous discharge in the stools, and febrile movements in the system, indicate the necessity of this measure. The functions of the skin and liver will be best restored by calomel, opium, and ipecacuan, or antimony, assisted by the warm bath, quietude, and a regulated temperature.

Cholera Morbus, Mort de Chien, and Spasmodic Cholera of India.

Sec. X.—In no disease has a *symptom* passed for a *cause*, with more currency and less doubt, than in cholera. From Hippocrates to Celsus, and from Celsus to Saunders, *bile* has been condemned, without a hearing, as the original perpetrator of all the mischief. " Bilis sursum ac deorsum effusiones," says the first ; ` Bilis supra, infraque erumpit," says the second ; and, " Cholera Morbus," says the last of these authors, " may very properly be considered under the head of those diseases which *depend* on the *increased secretion* of bile." *On the liver, p.* 179. Yet I venture to affirm, that the Cholera does *not* `` depend" on an increase, but on a diminution, and, in many cases, a total suppression of the biliary secretion.

A very excellent description of the disease in question, as it appears in this country, will be found under its proper head, in Rees's new Cyclopedia, written, I believe, by Dr. Bateman, and taken principally from Sydenham. I shall extract the following passage for my text : " The attack of this complaint is generally sudden. The bowels are seized with griping pains, and the stools, which are at first *thin and watery*, as in common diarrhœa, are passed frequently. The stomach is seized with sickness, discharges its contents, and rejects what is swallowed. In the *course of a few hours*, the matter vomited, as well as that which is discharged by stool, appears to be *pure bile*, and passes off both ways, in considerable quantities. The griping pains of the intestines now become more severe, in consequence of the extraordinary irritation of the passing bile, which excites them to partial and irregular spasmodic contractions. These spasms are often communicated to the abdominal muscles, and to the muscles of the lower extremities. The stomach is also affected with considerable pain, and a sense of great heat, in consequence of the same irritation. There is usually great thirst, and sometimes a severe head-ache, from the sympathy of the head with the stomach. The pulse becomes *small and frequent*, and the heat of the skin is increased. A great degree of debility, languor, and faintness, amounting even to syncope, speedily comes on ; sometimes attended with colliquative sweats, coldness of the extremities, ' and such like symptoms,' says Sydenham, ' as frighten the bye-standers, and kill the patient in twenty-four hours.' "

Now it does appear somewhat curious to me, that if an increased secretion of bile were the *cause* of the disease, we should see nothing of it till—"a few hours" after the *effects* become obvious! Where is the increased secretion all the time ?   Not in the stomach, for it "discharges its contents, and rejects what is swallowed" long before.   It is not in the intestines, for the stools are at first "thin and watery."   At length, however, "*pure bile*" makes its appearance ; and lo! it is accused of being the *cause* of all !

At what season does this commonly take place ?   In August and September.   Certainly that is the time for great heat and increased action in the hepatic system.   But are there no particular attendant circumstances ?   Yes, says the author of the foregoing passage.   "It has been remarked, that both in hot climates and in the hot seasons of mild climates, *occasional falls of rain* have been particularly *followed* by an epidemic cholera,"—*ib*.   Indeed ! a fall of rain is wonderfully well adapted to *increase* the secretion of bile !   But again : "In some places it is probable, that the heat of the season may give only a *predisposition*, and that certain *ingesta, sudden changes of temperature*, or other causes, in this state readily excite the disease," —*ib*. All these are admirably adapted, no doubt, to produce a great flow of bile !   But let us return to Dr. Saunders, who has already informed us, that Cholera "depends on the increased secretion of bile."   He says, "it frequently takes place spontaneously, and independently of any *sensible* occasional cause.   At other times it is *evidently* connected with a *sudden change of temperature* in the atmosphere during those months, (August and September,) or brought on by drinking *cold* liquors, or by any thing else that *suddenly chills the body*, especially when *overheated* by exercise or labour,"—*p*. 181. Now, in what manner we are to connect these "evident" causes with an "increased secretion of bile," Dr. Saunders leaves us to find out as we can, for he has not even attempted an explanation.   But, in truth, to set about proving that *cold* increased the hepatic action, would have been inconsistent, after what he previously advanced respecting the operation of *heat* on the biliary system.

Having shown, I think satisfactorily, the inadequacy of these doctrines to an elucidation of the phenomena, I shall proceed to prove, that an "increased secretion of bile," so far from being the *cause* of Cholera Morbus, is, upon the whole, *a favorable symptom ;* and that, in the very worst forms of the disease, it is *entirely absent*.

In no part of the globe does this terrific disorder assume a more concentrated state than on the coasts of Ceylon, especially its eastern side.   The mountains tower to a great height, in fantastic shapes, or conical peaks, clothed from base to summit with almost impenetrable forests of lofty trees, underwood, and jungle.   Deep vallies and ravines, still more thickly covered with similar materials, and choaked up, as it were, with all the wild exuberance of tropical vegetation, separate the mountains from each other, and swarm with myriads of animals and reptiles.   From these vallies, in the months of May, June, and July, when the S. W. monsoon is in force, the gusts of land-wind come down, hot and sultry by day, but chilling cold and damp by night.   Where mountainous and woody, or flat, marshy, and jungly tracts, border on the sea, atmospherical vicissitudes will, *ceteris pari-bus*, be greater, than where the coast is flat and gravelly, or dry and cultivated. The reason is obvious. Thus, the vicinity of Madras, for instance, being a sandy or gravelly soil, which, during the intense heat of the day, acquires a temperature, perhaps 60 or 70 degrees above that of the contiguous ocean, a considerable share of the night elapses before the heat of the earth sinks to an equilibrium with that of the water ; and consequently, we seldom have the land-wind cold there, except after falls of rain ; and on the contrary, in May and June, it is hot throughout the night. At Ceylon, on the other hand, the surface of the ground being so defended from the sun's rays by woods and jungles, it never acquires any thing like the temperature of the opposite Coromandel coast ; and although during the months alluded to, when the south-west monsoon passes with great strength over Ceylon, the wind by day be hot and sultry, as soon as the dews have fallen in the evening, and evaporation commences from a very extended surface, the land-breeze is instantly rendered cold and raw ; and being then loaded with vapour, together with all kinds of terrestrial and vegetable exhalations, communicates to our feelings and frames a chill, far exceeding what the thermometer would actually indicate. The same remark applies to Bombay ; but in Bengal there are no regular sea and land-breezes ; consequently the changes of temperature are not so abrupt and extensive as in the fore-mentioned places.

Numerous cases, exhibiting the dire effects of these atmospherical vicissitudes, aggravated, no doubt, by the land-wind effluvia, now lie before me—effects, indeed, that might well " frighten the bye-standers," or even Sydenham himself; for the patient is often cut off in a much shorter space of time than twenty-four hours !"

A seaman on board a ship, lying in Back-Bay, Trincomallee, in the month of June, went to bed rather intoxicated. About midnight however, he turned out, in a state of perspiration, and got upon deck, as is very usual, where he lay down in the cold land-wind, and fell fast asleep. During the preceding day, the land-wind had been hot and sultry, the thermometer ranging from 86 to 88 degrees. In the night, the mercury fell to 74°, with raw, damp gusts from the shore. About four o'clock in the morning, he awoke with a shiver, and left the deck ; but was soon seized with frequent purging and griping, his stools consisting of mucus and slime. Nausea and retching succeeded ; nothing being ejected but phlegm, and the contents of the stomach. His pulse was now small, quick, and contracted—his skin dry, but not hot. About eight o'clock in the morning, he began to feel spasms in different parts of his body, which soon attacked the abdominal muscles, and threw him into great pain. During these paroxysms, a cold, clammy sweat, would be occasionally forced out, especially on the face and breast. The extremities now became cold, his features shrunk—the stomach rejecting every thing that was offered, either as medicine or drink. The abdomen and epigastrium, all this time, was distended and tense, with incessant watery purging and painful tenesmus. By ten o'clock, his pulse could scarcely be felt—his breathing was oppressed and laborious—

his eyes sunk, and the whole countenance singularly expressive of internal agony and distress! The extremities were cold, shrivelled, and covered with clammy sweats. The violence of the spasms now began to relax; and by eleven o'clock, or seven hours from the attack, death released him from his sufferings! The warm bath, opium, æther, and various medicines had been tried, without affording any relief.

This may serve as a specimen of the worst form of that dreadful disease, which has obtained the appellation of—" *Mort de Chien,*" or Spasmodic Cholera. No bilious accumulations are to be seen, either in the stools, or what is ejected by vomiting, from the beginning to the end of the disease. Neither is there ever the slightest appearance of ' *natural and healthy perspiration.*' A watery fluid is occasionally forced out by the spasms and pain, while the skin is shrivelled and tense, and the sub-cutaneous, or perspiratory vessels, perfectly torpid.

From such an awful state of concentration, the disease assumes all degrees of violence, down to a common Cholera. In exact proportion as bile appears, and the nearer it approaches to a natural quality, so much the less is the danger.

. A seaman, from like imprudent exposure to the cold land-winds, after great fatigue during the heat of the preceding day, was attacked with symptoms nearly similar to the former. After the spasms came on, however, he had cold and hot fits alternately, with corresponding sweats, and bile appeared occasionally, both by vomit and stool. He had swallowed a scruple of calomel, and in this case, blood was taken from the arm, which instantly alleviated the spasms. In an hour after the calomel was taken, a purgative enema brought off several copious alvine evacuations, followed by large quantities of bile, some of which was highly fetid and depraved. He now felt greatly relieved—fell into a fine perspiration and sleep, and by the next day was perfectly well.

. I could here adduce numerous cases, both favourable and fatal, and little differing, in essential symptoms, from the two related above. But as the point which I have pledged myself to prove, must be decided by unequivocal and disinterested evidence, I shall bring forward the testimony of Mr. Curtis, a most faithful and candid reciter of facts, as every page in his volume evinces.

It is necessary to recollect, that the disease which Mr. Curtis describes, and the place where it happened, [Trincomallee,] are those alluded to in Dr. Paisley's letter, where the latter affirms, and I think with justice, that *Mort de Chien* is nothing more than the highest degree of Cholera Morbus.

- " Early in the morning of the 21st June," says Mr. Curtis, " we had two men seized with the *Mort de Chien*, both of whom we lost in a few hours; and in the course of the two following days, three more in the same complaint, without meeting with one fortunate case. To the 25th, when we sailed for Negapatam, we had three new cases of the same kind, all of whom were saved, but two of them with great difficulty. Besides these, we had several others, which were of a nature considerably different; *being evidently combined with bi-*

lious colluvies in the first passages, a circumstance *not at all discovera-*
ble in the five cases that ended fatally. All these, [viz. where bile
appeared,] were found to be much more tractable—easily removed,
and attended with little danger,"—p. 48. " In all of them, [the
eight cases alluded to,] the disease began with a *watery purging*, attended with some tenesmus, but little or no griping. This *always*
came on some time in the night, or early towards morning, and continued some time before any spasms were felt."***** " This purging soon brought on great weakness, coldness of the extremities, and
a remarkable paleness, sinking, and lividness of the whole countenance. Some at this period had nausea, and retching to vomit, but
brought up *nothing bilious*. In a short time, the spasms began to affect the muscles of the thighs, abdomen and thorax ; and lastly, they
passed to those of the arms, hands, and fingers,"—p. 49. " The
patients complained much of the pain of these cramps.——As the
disease proceeded, the countenance became more pale, wan, and dejected. The eyes became sunk——The pulse became more feeble
and sometimes sank as much, as not to be felt at the wrist,"—p. 50.
" The tongue was generally white, and more or less furred towards
the root, with thirst, and desire for cold drink.". . . . . . . " The coldness of the extremities, which was perceptible from the first, continued to increase, and spread over the whole body, but with *no moisture on the skin*, till the severity of the pain and spasms *forced out* a
clammy sweat, which soon became profuse,"—p. 51. " All this
time, the purging continued frequent, and exhibited nothing but a
thin watery matter, or mucus. In many, the stomach became at last
so irritable, that nothing could be got to rest upon it, every thing
that was drank was spouted up immediately. The countenance and
extremities became livid—the pulsations of the heart more quick and
feeble—the breathing laborious. In fine, the whole powers of life
fell under such a great and speedy collapse, as to be soon beyond the
reach of recovery. In this progression, the patient remained from
three to five or six hours, from the accession of the spasms, seldom
longer,"—p. 52. " In the Sea-horse, it attacked some remarkably
robust, powerful, and muscular men, who had been in *perfect health
immediately before*. Neither, in all our class of *bad and fatal cases*,
did there appear any marks of *bilious* colluvies, either in the colour
of the *ejected matter*—the state of the abdomen, or the appearance
of the tongue, eyes, and urine,"—p. 56. . . . . " We had, indeed, another set of cases, where the presence of this, [bile,] was
distinguishable by *all these characters*, but *these* were of a far *slighter*
nature, and *none* of them turned out any way untractable or fatal."
And again, at Madras, Mr. Curtis observes—" Out of about twenty
under my care, a *third* were evidently connected with *bilious* colluvies ; and in *these* there was no great sinking of the pulse, or diminution of the heat, and the spasms were confined to the legs and
feet,"—p. 69. These all recovered. Lastly, in two cases of dissection which took place immediately after death in this disease,
Mr. Curtis affirms that—" there were *no bilious accumulations* found
any where, and the internal organs were all in a sound state ; only

there was more water than natural in the pericardium, and the vessels of the lungs, liver, and mesentery, appeared to be very *turgid, and full of blood,*"—p. 72.

I appeal to every unbiassed mind—nay, to prejudice itself, whether I have not now proved, (I had almost said to a demonstration,) the truth of that heterodox position with which I set out —namely, that " an *increased secretion of bile,*" so far from being the *cause* of Cholera Morbus, is upon the whole, a *favourable symptom ;* and that in the very worst cases of the disease, (Mort de Chien, for instance,) it is *entirely absent.*

This point being settled, the application of that principle, to which I have so often adverted—*the connexion or sympathy between the functions of the skin and liver,* will afford a more rational explanation of the phenomena, than either " an increased secretion," or a lurking, putrid accumulation of that far famed mischief maker—BILE.

The sudden and powerful check to perspiration—the unparalleled atony of the extreme vessels, debilitated by previous excess of action, and now struck utterly torpid, by the cold, raw, damp, nocturnal land-winds, loaded with vegeto-aqueous vapour, and abounding with terrestrial and jungly exhalations—break at once, and with violence, the balance of the circulation. The extreme vessels of the hepatic system, sympathising with those on the surface, completely arrest the reflux of blood from the portal, cœliac, and mesenteric circles ; hence, in the worst cases, a *total* suppression of biliary secretion, with distension of the abdomen, and shrinking of all external parts. If this continue any time, as in *Mort de Chien,* death must be the inevitable consequence, notwithstanding the unavailing efforts which nature makes, by vomiting to determine to the surface—restore the equilibrium of the blood and of excitability, and, with them, the functions of perspiration and biliary secretion. In proportion, then, as the two latter appear, will the danger be lessened—our most salutary objects attained, and the disease become " less untractable and fatal."

The deluges of bile which occasionally burst forth on the *recommencement* of secretion in cholera, are the natural *consequences* of the great plethora in the portal and other abdominal circles of vessels, which took place during the previous check to biliary secretion, and free passage of blood through the liver. And thus we see, that the very *last* link in the chain of *effects,* and that too, a *salutary* one, has, for ages, been set down as the *cause* of Cholera—" increased secretion of bile ! !"

With respect to the spasms, as they are totally unaccounted for by my predecessors, neither am I bound to dive into the mysteries of the nervous system, for a solution of the phenomenon. I think I have pretty clearly proved, that they are not attributable to bile ; since, in the most dangerous and fatal cases, no bile is to be found. I can easily conceive that the brain must suffer, from the broken balance of circulation, as well as from its known sympathies with the stomach and liver, and thus, in some measure, account for the unequal distribution of nervous energy, which may excite cramps, and throw various classes of muscles into convulsive agitations. I am the more disposed to this opinion, from the circumstance, that in three desperate cases of *Mort de Chien*, the spasms were instantaneously relieved by venesection. In one of them which happened on board the Centurion, *trismus*, (an unusual symptom,) had taken place—the eyes were fixed, and the pupils dilated. Bleeding was attended with immediate good effects, and the patient was well next day.

Having mentioned trismus, I may here remark, that *Mort de Chien* must not be confounded with that or tetanus. For although the latter have arisen from checked perspiration in many instances, they are totally different from the disease under consideration. The gastric irritability, and dysenteric purging, might be a sufficient diagnosis; but the spasms themselves are dissimilar. In *Mort de Chien*, the affection is not confined to a particular class of muscles; it passes from one to another, and those of the neck, face, and back, are almost always exempted. Neither is it a *rigidity*, but a fixed *cramp* in the belly of the muscle, which, as Mr. Curtis justly observes, " is gathered up into a hard knot with excruciating pain." Lastly, the vascular system is infinitely more affected in *Mort de Chien* than in tetanus, and the fatal termination, beyond all comparison, more rapid.

Nor is this investigation of the *proximate cause* of Cholera, a subject of mere curiosity; it is highly useful; inasmuch as it strongly confirms and elucidates the principle which I have kept in view through various diseases in this essay; and what is of more consequence, it points directly to the most indispensable part of the cure, in the awful and terrific forms which the disease assumes in these parts of the world—namely, *the early restoration of balance in the circulation and excitability;* an indication but little dreamt of in the old *bilious theory*, where every eye was kept fixed on the lurking demon—BILE !

" In strong habits," says Dr. Paisley, " when the pulse keeps up, evacuations should be promoted both ways, by a vomit of two or three grains of *emetic tartar*."—*Curtis, p.* 86. But soon after, he observes, " In relaxed habits, where the pulse sinks suddenly, and brings on immediate danger, the *same method must be pursued*, but with greater caution. The emetics and purges must be gentle, and made cordial with wine, and sp. lavend. Laudanum must be at hand, *to gain time;* and though it is a *dangerous* expedient to *suspend evacuations where putrid bile lurks*, yet, of two evils, the least is to be chosen; for the patient must sink to death, if a respite from evacuations, pain, and spasm, is not procured." Nothing so true as this last. Nature is here, as it were, stunned with the blow; and the struggling efforts which she makes to relieve herself, by vomiting, &c. only exhaust her the sooner, if not effectually assisted by art. We must therefore have recourse to more powerful means than wine, laudanum, or lavender. The warm bath—cordials of the most stimulating kind, such as warm punch, or toddy, must be added to opium and calomel, together with friction, hot flannels, &c. In short, every means must be tried to determine to the surface, restore the equilibrium of the circulation and excitability, and with them natural perspiration, (not the clammy fluid forced out by pain and spasm, but a mild, warm sweat,) and biliary secretion. Calomel must never be omitted, because it answers a tripple purpose :—it allays the inordinate gastric irritability—it excites the action of the liver—and it corrects the constipating effects of the opium ; so that, when the orgasm is over, some gentle laxative medicine may, with it, carry off the diseased secretions, which must sooner or later take place, if reaction can be brought on, or recovery effected. When all medicines by the mouth have been ineffectual, in allaying the orgasm of the stomach and bowels, laudanum, by way of injection, has succeeded, and should be had recourse to, though it is generally neglected. I have only slightly mentioned venesection, though, from its instantaneous good effects in three desperate cases, I am inclined to think it might prove a powerful auxiliary in relieving the brain, and other internal organs, when overwhelmed with blood, even anterior to reaction ; and also by moderating the violence of the reaction itself. This idea is strengthened by the success which has lately attended depletion in various forms of *spasmodic diseases*, and by the following communication from my able friend Mr. Sheppard : —" Your account of Dr. Moulson's paper brings to my recollection a practice somewhat analogous, (though with a different intention,) which I pursued during a short service in the Brazils, a few years since, in the violent form of cholera which seems to be endemic there. You have, I believe, described a similar disease, in India, under the name of *Mort de Chien*, in which you recommend bleeding with other remedies ; but I have now reference only to the notes which I made of your book, and therefore am not positive. In more than forty cases which came under my care, during the four months we were in the harbour of Rio Janeiro, and on the coast, I found bleeding to *syncope* instantly and uniformly successful *alone*. There was no critical biliary discharge, but the disease was removed before the arm was secured, and no subsequent medicine was required. The intestinal spasm was far more violent than any I had ever witnessed in the West Indies, (where the disease is pretty severe,) and bore a strong resemblance to the convulsive paroxysm ; so much so, that I was generally called to patients said to be in fits ; and the powers of several men were required to restrain them. The first cases I treated by warmth, frictions, volatiles, and opium, but did no good until I adopted the plan I have mentioned, which in no instance disappointed me ; the variations of temperature in that climate are extraordinarily great, frequent, and sudden : and to such mutations the prevalence of intestinal spasms may be ascribed."*

" I had heard much," says Mr. Curtis, " of latent and lurking bile, as the general source of India diseases, and resolved to seek for and hunt it out, by the means employed by others—viz. repeated small doses of sal. glaub. in aq. menthæ piper. sharpened with a very small proportion of emetic tartar. This plan was accordingly tried

---

Mr. Sheppard will see a striking elucidation of this subject in a case of hydrophobia, by Mr. Webster, related in the Medico-Chirurgical Journal. Dr. Saunders of Edinburgh has long been investigating these points of pathology, and will, we hope, soon lay the results of his labours before the public. The next article on the great Epidemic Cholera of India will show how far my suggestion of venesection has since been acted on.

with our next patient. He threw up a *very small quantity* of greenish-coloured bile, and the solution operated much downwards, without any relief or discharge of bilious matter."—p. 59. After the warm bath, opium, and mulled wine, had been tried without success, Mr. Curtis continues—" A warm, purgative glyster was given him, but was followed by *no bilious discharge*. No vomiting continued after the first exhibition of the purgative, but a repetition of it, to see if *any bile lurked still in the stomach*, and could be solicited downwards, brought on continued retching, and he threw up every thing after this till his death."—*ib*. Mr. Curtis now gave up the pursuit of "lurking bile," and saved his next two patients by the warm bath—frictions with hot arrack—wrapping them up in blankets, and supplying them with warm tea and arrack, till perspiration broke out, when they were relieved, and soon recovered.

It is only necessary to remark, in conclusion, that in the milder cases of *Mort de Chien*, corresponding to common *Cholera Morbus*, when the bilious vomiting and purging appear, Nature has then repelled the original cause of the disease, and is fast advancing with the cure. We have only now to moderate and regulate her hurried, and, as it were, frightened movements by opium and calomel, in pretty large doses ; the former, as I have before hinted, in glyster ; and when all is quiet, to carry downwards, by mild laxatives, the *effects* of the disorder, and its cure—DISEASED SECRETIONS OF BILE.

———◆———

Reports on the Epidemic Cholera which has raged throughout Hindostan and the Peninsula of India, since August, 1817. *Published under the Authority of the Bombay Government.* One Vol. 4to, 228 Pages. Bombay, 1819.

———

————————seu dira per omnes
Manarent populos sævi contagia morbi.

———

This important series of documents, drawn up by the Medical Board of Bombay, was presented to me through the medium of Dr. Scott, by the desire of the head of that board, lately returned to Europe.* The work is circulating widely in India, but cannot of course, be known here, except through such vehicle as the present. I deem it a duty, therefore, to the profession at large, to make them more intimately acquainted than they have hitherto been, with one of the most awful and fatal epidemics that ever ravaged our widely extended Indian empire. The event itself is extremely interesting to the profession in general, in a pathological and therapeutical point of view, independently of those numerous ties and associations, by which we are linked to the fate of our Asiatic possessions. On all these accounts I shall be pardoned for the length to which this analysis may extend, especially as I shall strain every nerve to make it as concentrated as literary labour and typographical closeness can render it.

*Dr. Steuart, since deceased.

There are some curious particulars attending the history of this epidemic, which are worthy of record. It first appeared in August 1817,
in Zilla Jessore, about 100 miles North East of Calcutta, but without
any previous peculiarity of weather ; being considered by the authorities on the spot, as of a local nature, and attributable to the intempe-
rate use or rank fish and bad rice ; but it rapidly spread through the
adjoining villages, running from district to district, until it had brought
the whole province of Bengal under its influence. It next extended
to Behar ; and, having visited the principal cities West and East of the
Ganges, reached the upper provinces. Through the large cities here
it made a regular progress ; but it was otherwise in the more thinly
peopled portions of country. " The disease would sometimes take a
complete circle round a village, and leaving it untouched, pass on as
if it were wholly to depart from the district. Then, after a lapse of
weeks, or even months, it would suddenly return, and scarcely reap-
pearing in the parts which had already undergone its ravages, would
nearly depopulate the spot that had so lately congratulated itself on
its escape. Sometimes, after running a long course on one side of the
Ganges, it would, as if arrested by some unknown agent, at once stop ;
and taking a rapid sweep across the river, lay all waste on the opposite bank." *Report of the Calcutta Medical Board.*

In Calcutta it showed itself in the first week of September, and each
succeeding week added strength to the malady, and more extended
influence to its operation. From January till the end of May it was
at its acmé, during which period, the mortality in the city was seldom
under 200 a week !

The centre division of the army, under the Commander-in-Chief,
exhibited an awful specimen of the fatality of the disease. It consisted of less than ten thousand fighting men, and the deaths, within
twelve days, amounted, at the very lowest estimate, to three thousand ;
according to others, to five and even eight thousand !

On the 6th of August, 1818, it reached Bombay, taking about a
year to cross the base of the Great Indian Delta. It appeared to Drs.
Steuart and Phillips, the enlightened members of the medical board
at Bombay, that the disease was capable of being " transported from
place to place as in cases of ordinary contagion or infection, and also
to possess the power of propagating itself by the same means that acknowledged contagions do." *Preface,* xii.

The partial and irregular manner in which the disease spread and
operated in the neighbourhood of Bombay, as the cold season advanced, could not be accounted for by the medical board, " unless by supposing that a diminution of temperature, together with exposure, may
have called into action some latent remains of an active poison." The
board next proceeds to a description of the disease, as drawn up by
the Medical Board of Bengal, which I shall here introduce verbatim.

" Having thus given a rapid and imperfect sketch of the history of
the epidemic, the board should now proceed to detail the symptoms
which attended its attack. This part of their task they will not find
it difficult to accomplish. The leading appearances of this most fatal malady were but too well marked on their approach and subse-

quent progress ; and amongst the myriads who were attacked, exhibited perhaps less variety and fewer discrepancies than characterize the operation of almost any other disease to which the human body is subject. The healthy and unhealthy ; the strong and feeble ; Europeans and Natives ; the Mussulman and Hindoo ; the old and young of both sexes, and of every temperament and condition, were alike within its influence.

" The attack was generally ushered in by a sense of weakness, trembling, giddiness, nausea, violent retching, vomiting and purging, of a watery, starchy, whey-coloured, or greenish fluid. These symptoms were accompanied, or quickly followed by severe cramps, generally beginning in the fingers and toes, and thence extending to the wrists and fore-arms, calves of the legs, thighs, abdomen, and lower part of the thorax. These were soon succeeded by pain. constriction. and oppression of stomach and pericardium ; great sense of internal heat ; inordinate thirst, and incessant calls for cold water, which was no sooner swallowed than rejected, together with a quantity of phlegm or whitish fluid, like seethings of oatmeal. The action of the heart and arteries now nearly ceased ; the pulse either became altogether imperceptible at the wrists and temples, or so weak as to give to the finger only an indistinct feeling of fluttering. The respiration was laborious and hurried, sometimes with long and frequently broken inspirations. The skin grew cold, clammy, covered with large drops of sweat ; dank and disagreeable to the feel, and discoloured of a bluish, purple, or livid hue. There was great and sudden prostration of strength ; anguish, and agitation. The countenance became collapsed ; the eyes suffused, fixed, and glassy,' or heavy, and dull ; sunk in their sockets, and surrounded by dark circles ; the cheeks and lips livid and bloodless ; and the whole surface of the body nearly devoid of feeling. In feeble habits, where the attack was exceedingly violent, and unresisted by medicine, the scene was soon closed. The circulation and animal heat never returned ; the vomiting and purging continued, with thirst and restlessness ; the patient became delirious or insensible, with his eyes fixed in a vacant stare, and sunk down in the bed ; the spasms increased, generally within four or five hours.

" The disease sometimes at once, and as if it were momentarily, seized persons in perfect health ; at other times those who had been debilitated by previous bodily ailment ; and individuals in the latter predicament, generally sunk under the attack. Sometimes, the stomach and bowels were disordered for some days before the attack, which would then, in a moment, come on in full force, and speedily reduce the patients to extremities.

" Such was the general appearance of the disease where it cut off the patient in its earlier stages. The primary symptoms, however, in many cases, admitted of considerable variety. Sometimes the sickness and looseness were preceded by spasms ; sometimes the patient sunk at once, after passing off a small quantity of colourless fluid, by vomiting and stool. The matter vomited in the early stages was, in most cases, colourless or milky ; sometimes it was green. In like manner, the dejections were usually watery and muddy ;

sometimes red and bloody ; and in a few cases, they consisted of a greenish pulp, like half-digested vegetables. In no instance was feculent matter passed in the commencement of the disease. The cramps usually began in the extremities, and thence gradually crept to the trunk ; sometimes they were simultaneous in both ; and sometimes the order of succession was reversed ; the abdomen being first affected, and then the hands and feet. These spasms hardly amounted to general convulsion. They seemed rather affections of individual muscles, and of particular sets of fibres of those muscles, causing thrilling and quivering in the affected parts, like the flesh of crimped salmon ; and firmly stiffening and contorting the toes and fingers. The patient always complained of pain across the belly, which was generally painful to the touch, and sometimes hard and drawn back towards the spine. The burning sensation in the stomach and bowels was always present ; and at times extended along the cardia and œsophagus to the throat. The powers of voluntary motion were, in every instance, impaired ; and the mind obscured. The patient staggered like a drunken man, or fell down like a helpless child. Head-ache over one or both eyes, sometimes, but rarely occurred. The pulse, when to be felt, was generally regular, and extremely feeble, sometimes soft ; not very quick ; usually ranging from 80 to 100. In a few instances it rose to 140 or 150, shortly before death. Then it was indistinct, small, feeble, and irregular. Sometimes very rapid, then slow for one or two beats. The mouth was hot and dry ; the tongue parched, and deeply furred, white, yellow, red, or brown. The urine at first generally limpid and freely passed ; sometimes scanty, with such difficulty as almost to amount to strangury ; and sometimes hardly secreted in any quantity, as if the kidnies had ceased to perform their office. In a few cases, the hands were tremulous ; in others, the patient declared himself free from pain and uneasiness, when want of pulse, cold skin, and anxiety of features, portended speedy death. The cramp was invariably increased upon moving.

" Where the strength of the patient's constitution, or of the curative means administered, were, although inadequate wholly to subdue the disease, sufficient to resist the violence of its onset, nature made various efforts to rally ; and held out strong, but fallacious promises of returning health. In such cases, the heat was sometimes wholly, at others partially restored ; the chest and abdomen in the latter case becoming warm, whilst the limbs kept deadly cold. The pulse would return ; grow moderate and full ; the vomiting and cramps disappear ; the nausea diminish, and the stools become green, pitchy, and even feculent ; and with all these favourable appearances the patient would suddenly relapse ; chills, hiccup, want of sleep and anxiety would arise ; the vomiting, oppression, and insensibility, return ; and in a few hours terminate in death.

" When the disorder ran its full course, the following appearances presented themselves. What may be termed the cold stage, or the state of collapse, usually lasted from twenty-four to forty-eight hours, and was seldom of more than three complete days' duration. Throughout the first twenty-four hours, nearly all the symptoms of deadly oppression, the cold skin, feeble pulse, vomiting and purging, cramps, thirst and anguish continued undiminished. When the system showed symptoms of revival, the vital powers began to rally, the circulation and heat to be restored ; and the spasms and sickness to be considerably diminished. The warmth gradually returned ; the pulse rose in strength and fulness, and then became sharp and sometimes hard. The tongue grew more deeply furred ; the thirst continued, with less nausea. The stools were no longer like water ; they became first brown and watery ; then dark, black, and pitchy ; and the bowels, during many days, continued to discharge immense loads of vitiated bile, until, with returning health, the secretions of the liver and other viscera gradually put on a natural appearance. The fever, which invariably attended this second stage of the disease, may be considered to have been rather the result of Nature's effort to recover herself from the rude shock which she had sustained, than as forming any integrant and necessary part of the disorder itself. It partook much of the nature of the common bilious attacks prevalent in these latitudes. There was the hot dry skin ; foul, deeply furred, dry tongue ; parched mouth ; sick stomach ; depraved secretions ; and quick variable pulse ; sometimes with stupor, delirium, and other marked affections of the brain. When the disorder proved fatal after reaching this stage, the tongue, from being cream-coloured, grew brown, and sometimes dark, hard, and more deeple furred ; the teeth and lips were covered with sordes ; the state of the skin varied ; chills, alternating with flushes of heat ; the pulse became weak and tremulous ; catching of the breath ; great restlessness, and deep moaning succeeded ; and the patient soon sunk, insensible, under the debilitating effects of frequent dark, pitchy, alvine discharges.

" Of those who died, it was believed, perhaps rather fancifully, that the bodies sooner underwent putrefaction, than those of persons dying under the ordinary circumstances of mortality. The bodies of those who had sunk in the earlier stages of the malady, exhibited hardly any unhealthy appearance. Even in them, however, it was observed, that the intestines were paler and more distended with air, than usual ; and that the abdomen, upon being laid open, emitted a a peculiar offensive odour, wholly different from the usual smell of dead subjects. In the bodies of those who had lived some time after the commencement of the attack, the stomach was generally of natural appearance externally. The colour of the intestines varied from deep rose to a dark hue, according as the increased vascular action had been arterial or venous. The stomach, on being cut into, was found filled, sometimes with a transparent, a green, or dark flaky fluid. On removing this, its internal coats, in some cases, were perfectly healthy ; in others, and more generally, they were crossed by streaks of a deep-red, interspersed with spots of inflammation, made up of tissues of enlarged vessels. This appearance was frequently continued to the duodenum. In a very few cases, the whole internal surface of the stomach was covered with coagulable lymph ; on removing which, a bloody gelatine was found laid on the interior coat, in ridges or elevated streaks. The large intestine was sometimes filled with muddy fluid, sometimes lived, with dark bile, like tar ; just as the individual had died in the earlier or later periods of the attack. In most cases, the liver was enlarged, and gorged with blood. In a few, it was large, soft, light-coloured, with greyish spots, and not very turgid. In others again, it was collapsed and flaccid. The gall-bladder, was without exception, full of dark green or black bile. The spleen and thoracic viscera were, in general, healthy. The great venous vessels were usually gorged ; and in one case, the left ventricle of the heart was extremely turgid. The brain was generally of natural appearance. In one or two instances, lymph was effused between its membranes, near the coronal suture, so as to cause extensive adhesions ; in other cases, the sinuses, and the veins leading to them, were stuffed with very dark blood." xv.—xxi.

The following extracts will show that the disease was known to Sydenham, and accurately described by that observant physician. He no where mentions bile as forming any part of the discharges from the stomach or bowels ; and hence it may be fairly inferred, that such discharges were not present.*

" Qui ab ingluvie ac crapula nullo temporis discrimine passim excitatur affectus, ratione symptomatum non absimilis, nec eamdem curationis methodum respuens, tamen alterius est subsellii. Malum ipsum facile cognoscitur, adsunt enim vomitus enormes, ac pravorum humorum cum maxima difficultate et angustia per alvum dejectio ; cardialgia, sitis. Pulsus celer ac frequens, cum æstu et anxietate, non raro etiam parvus et inæqualis, insuper et nausea molestissima, sudor interdum diaphoreticus, crurum et brachiorum contractura, animi deliquium, partium extremarum frigiditas, cum aliis notæ symptomatibus, quæ adtantes magnopere perterrefaciunt, atque etiam angusto viginti quatuor horarum spatio ægrum interimant."

And again, in his letter to Dr. Brady, describing the epidemics of 1674, 5, and 6, he says,

" Exeunte æstate Cholera Morbus epidemice jam sæviebat, et insueto tempestatis calore evectus, atrociora convulsionum symptomata, eaque diuturniora secum trahebat, quam mihi prius unquam videre contigerat. Neque enim solum abdomen, uti alias in hoc malo, sed universi jam corporis musculi, brachiorum crurumque præ reliquis, spasmis tentabantur dirissimis, ita ut æger e lecto subinde exiliret, si forte extenso quaquaversum corpore eorum vim posset eludere," xxiii.

---

* I have diligently searched the writings of Sydenham, and I assert, that in no one instance, when treating of Cholera Morbus, whether epidemic or sporadic, has he mentioned a discharge of *bile* as forming any part, much less as being the *cause* of cholera. And as Sydenham is allowed to be one of the most accurate observers of nature, we see on what foundation Dr. Saunders and others have built their *bilious* theory of the disease. The fact is, as I have long ago stated, that the discharge of bile in cholera, is a secondary or ternary link in the chain of cause and effect—and always a sanative effort of the system, as well as a favourable symptom of the disease.

I observe too, that Areteus describes the discharge of *bile* as only an ulterior effect. " In primis," says he, " quæ evomuntur, *aquæ similia sunt ;* quæ anus effundit, stercorea, liquida, tetrique odoris sentiuntur. Siquidem longa cruditas id malum excitavit, quo si per clysterem eluanter, *primo pituitosa, mox biliosa feruntur.*"—*De Cholera*, Chap. 5.

The first of the foregoing extracts describes the disease with great accuracy, as it very generally affected the natives ; the second is well exemplified in Dr. Burrel's Report, as it attacked the Europeans of the 65th Regiment, at Seroor. The disease is also accurately described by Girdleston, and by Mr. Curtis of Madras, in 1782, when it raged in the Southern Provinces of the Peninsula. Dr. Taylor also furnished the Medical Board with the account of a disease from a Sanscrit medical work, the MADHOW NIDAN, which clearly proves that the complaint has been long known to the natives.

" It is obviously unnecessary to prosecute this inquiry further ; and we shall only add, that Dr. James Johnson is the latest author, so far as we know, who has treated this subject, and who has also the merit of having been the first who has generally pointed out the best method of cure, from a few cases he met with on the eastern coast of Ceylon, where the disease seems to be more prevalent than in any other part of India," xxviii.

The exciting and proximate causes of this interesting epidemic are, like those of most others, concealed in utter darkness—" atra caligine mersæ;" great discrepancy of opinion obtains in India respecting its contagious or non-contagious influence, arising naturally out of the difficulty of the subject.

" Several irresistible facts already noticed or related in the following Reports, and its marked anomaly from all hitherto known simple epidemics, would seem to favour the doctrine of contagion, while the contrary supposition is only supported by a species of negative evidence," xxix.

The Board, however, very properly observe, that this is a question of such importance, that it ought not to be too hastily entertained as proved, nor rejected as unfounded ; but prosecuted with that diligent inquiry and cautious induction, which on every subject of science, are so necessary to the attainment of truth.

In respect to the predisposing, [or rather the *exciting*,] causes, practitioners are unanimous.

" Rapid atmospherical vicissitudes, in regard either to temperature or moisture : exposure of the body to currents of cold air, particularly the chill of the evening, after being heated by violent exercise of any kind, inducing debility or exhaustion ; low marshy situations, flatulent or indigestible food, especially crude and watery vegetables, which compose a large proportion of the diet of the natives ; and particularly that gradual undermining of the constitution which arises in a condensed, dirty, and ill-fed mass of population, are all unquestionably powerful predisposing causes."

Sad experience, however, has shown that the absence of all these afforded no security against the attack. Whether the invisible cause, (whatever that may be,) acts more immediately on the vascular or nervous system, the Board cannot take upon them to determine ; but from the various modes of attack which gave rise to the division of the disease into two species and varieties, they are led to the supposition that sometimes the one system, sometimes the other, bears the onus of the first onset of the malady.'

" The most general attack seems to consist in a spasmodic affection of the stomach, duodenum, and more especially the biliary ducts, (the total absence of bile in the matter voided upwards and downwards being, perhaps, the most uniform characteristic of the disease,) which quickly extending through the whole intestinal canal, discharges its contents. It is more than probable, however, that these are merely the first perceptible symptoms ; for it would appear that a great change has already taken place in the circulating system, and that the action of the heart itself has been greatly diminished before they occur. This seems evident from the numerous cases in which neither vomiting or purging is present, and in which the first appearance of the disease is the almost total suspension of the vital functions, immediately followed by severe spasmodic affections of the muscles and coldness of the extremities," xxxiii.

Here the Board have copied Dr. Armstrong's description of the attack of *congestive* typhus, remarking that

" Those who are most intimate with the disease in question, will be struck with the great similarity between this and typhus, at their first appearance."

Dissections, they state, abundantly prove that venous congestion constitutes the principal change that takes place during life.

The following passage, though long, cannot be abridged without greatly lessening its value.

" On the subject of the cure of the disease, we need say but little. The practice so judiciously and speedily adopted by Dr. Burrell in the 65th Regiment, clearly proves, that at the commencement of the disease in Europeans, blood-letting is the sheet anchor of successful practice ; and perhaps also with natives, provided it be had recourse to sufficiently early in the disease ; and as long as the vital powers remain, so as to be able to produce a full stream, it ought perhaps never to be neglected, it having been sufficiently proved, that the great debility so much complained of is merely apparent. Calomel, as a remedy, certainly comes next in order, and when employed in proper doses, with the assistance of opium, and more particularly in the early stage of the disease, seems to be equally effectual among natives, as venesection among Europeans, in arresting its progress. In all the cases formerly alluded to, when we met the disease on its first attack, a single scruple dose of calomel, with sixty minims of laudanum, and an ounce of castor oil seven or eight hours afterwards, was sufficient to complete the cure. The practice of this place, as sufficiently appears by Dr. Taylor's report, bears ample testimony to the control which calomel possesses over the disease, in as much as it has often preserved life, when blood-letting could not be put in practice.

" All other remedies must, in our opinion, be considered as mere auxiliaries, no doubt extremely useful as such, and ought never to be neglected ; but particularly the warm bath and stimulating frictions. Even where the disease appears to have given way to bleeding, we think it highly necessary constantly to administer calomel. The powerful effect of this remedy in allaying irritability of the stomach and intestines, when given in large doses, is generally acknowledged by practitioners, in the severer attacks of dysentery : as a great and permanent stimulus to the vascular system, it will be readily acknowledged by every one who has suffered for any length of time under its effects in ptyalism, where the bounding pulsations of the arteries of the temples and neck produce very disagreeable sensations, and even preclude sleep. Its powers over inflammation of the abdominal viscera, the liver in particular, and indeed in membranous and glandular inflammation generally, are now universally acknowledged.

" In a disease, therefore, in which we have every reason to believe that venous congestion has taken place to a great extent, and where we conclude that the liver, from its peculiar circulation and structure, is more immediately liable to become seriously and permanently injured, it should not be admitted. We have before mentioned, that Dr. James Johnson seems to have been the first who pointed out the best method of cure. Since most of the foregoing remarks were written, we have seen the second edition of that gentleman's valuable work, in which we find a strong corroborative testimony to the utility of blood-letting in this disease, or one somewhat similar to it, on the coast of Brazil, by Mr. Sheppard, of Witney, without the assistance of any other remedy. The public are greatly indebted to Mr. Corbyn, of the Bengal Establishment, for his clear and comprehensive letter on this subject, at a time when the disease was producing the most dreadful ravages : the early communication of his practice has been the means of saving thousands of lives in situations where Dr. Johnson's work might not be known," xlii.

About forty official reports from various medical officers, compose the great body of the work before us, and form the materials from which Drs. Steuart and Phillips have drawn up the foregoing luminous and interesting digest. It is not necessary to go into these reports individually. There never perhaps existed so unanimous a consent respecting the treatment of such a wide-spreading epidemic as these documents disclose.

FURTHER DOCUMENTS RESPECTING CHOLERA.

1. *Report on the Epidemic Cholera Morbus, as it visited the Territories subject to the Presidency of Bengal, in the Years* 1817, 1818, *and* 1819. *Drawn up by order of the Government, under the superintendence of the Medical Board.* By JAMES JAMESON, Assistant Surgeon and Secretary to the Board. One vol. 8vo. pp. 325. Calcutta, 1820.

2. *Account of the Spasmodic Cholera, which has lately prevailed in India and other adjacent Countries and Islands, &c. in a Letter from Mr. Corbyn to Sir Gilbert Blane.* Medico-Chirurgical Transacactions. Vol. xi. part i. 1820.

" Noxia si penitus CHOLERAM sævire venena." SER.

Having given so full an account of this tremendous epidemic in my Review of the excellent report drawn up by the Bombay Medical

Board, I dare not trespass on the patience of my readers, by entering into an extended analysis of the present documents. Mr. Jameson appears to me to have drawn up a very impartial digest of the various returns made by full 100 medical officers. It could hardly be expected that no discrepancy of opinion should prevail respecting the cause and treatment of such a wide-spreading epidemic.—There was, in fact, considerable clash of sentiment, but as far as therapeutics were concerned, a very large and preponderating majority of evidence furnished ample grounds for the following conclusions, which I shall give in the words of the author.

1. " The disease sometimes attacked with such extreme violence, as, from the commencement, apparently to place the sufferer beyond the reach of medical aid, and to render every curative means employed equally unavailing.

2. " The difference in the degree of mortality amongst those who did, and those who did not, take medicine, was such as to leave no doubt, that, when administered in time, and with discrimination, it frequently saved the patient from death.

3. " The chances of a patient's receiving benefit from medicine, diminished in proportion with the increased duration of the attack.

4. " In Europeans generally, and in robust natives, bleeding could be uniformly practised, where the patient was seen within one, two, or perhaps three hours, from the beginning of the attack ; and in all cases, in which it is resorted to, under such favourable circumstances, it was more successful than any other remedy in cutting short the disease ; usually resolving spasms ; allaying the irritability of the stomach and bowels ; and removing the universal depression under which the system laboured.

5. " Amongst the generality of natives, the depressing influence of the disease was so powerful and rapid in its operation, as almost immediately to produce a complete collapse, and nearly destroy arterial action ; and therefore to render venesection for the most part, from the beginning, impracticable.

6. " Although it cannot be affirmed that calomel possessed any specific power in checking the disorder, it was undoubtedly frequently useful in soothing irritability ; and was, perhaps of more certain sedative operation than any other medicine," 247.

Whether it was that the epidemic, in a few places, totally changed its nature, or that the mental telescopes of a few individuals had one lens more, or one lens less than those of the generality of mankind, (of which we see occasional examples in this country,) but so it was, that the above-mentioned remedial measures found useful by nine-tenths of the community, not only failed, but proved *highly prejudicial* in the hands of some.

In a supplement to the work, it appears that subsequent to the month of June, 1819, the disease re-appeared in the upper provinces, and, it would seem, with some modification, as bile was frequently seen in the stools ; and reaction was more violent. It is not difficult to conceive that, under such circumstances, " large and repeated bleedings proved the only efficacious means of opposing the disorder."

Of the *remote* causes of this epidemic, Mr. Jameson, and conse-quently the Calcutta Board, can offer nothing satisfactory. They conceive that it could not be owing solely to atmospherical vicissitudes —though they were great—nor to contagion—nor to any thing con-nected with food. They conjecture that a morbific poison or miasm, however produced, was carried along by the easterly winds, and gave origin to the epidemic. This is all the explanation we can expect in the present state of our knowledge, and on which we shall make a few remarks further on.

Mr. Jameson, in labouring to subvert the hypothesis of others, re-specting the proximate cause, or rather the immediate seat of the disease, has fallen, as usual, into an hypothesis himself. He endea-vours to show that the impression of the morbific cause is not exclu-sively made on the skin, nor on the liver ; but as far as I can gather from him, it is on the *stomach*. Now this I think is only substituting one *exclusive* doctrine for another. I believe that all the great or-gans of the body, are so intimately linked together, not only by blood-vessels and nerves, but by sympathetic association of function, that no one can bear the onus of disease without drawing in the others to a participation. Moreover, I cannot but conclude that a cause, so generally diffused in the atmosphere as that of an epidemic must al-ways be, will affect a number of organs and parts simultaneously—particularly the whole of the nervous or sentient system distributed over the surface of the body, the mucous membrane of the lungs, and the lining membrane of the digestive organs.

It is hypothetical then to limit the primary morbid impression to a single organ or tissue, however that part may appear to suffer in the course of the disease. That the nervous system in this, as indeed in almost all other epidemics, suffered the first shock, we can prove from Mr. Jameson's own symtomatology of the disease.

" The irritability of stomach, and vomiting formed a very distress-ing part of the disorder. They were generally *preceded* by a feel-ing of giddiness, and inclination to faint." And in another place, " In some rare instances, the virulence of the disease was so powerful as to prove immediately destructive of life ; *as if the circulation were at once arrested*, and the vital powers wholly overwhelmed. In these cases the patient fell down as if struck by lightning, and instantly ex-pired," 42.

Still less will the *post mortem* researches bear out our author.

" In many, especially those who died early, the stomach and in-testinal canal were found full of muddy fluid, without the slightest mark of inflammation. In others, the vessels of their inner coats were turgid, sometimes highly inflamed, ulcerated, and gangrened. The liver was congested, inflamed, and darker than usual, &c." 72.

The Bengal Board corroborate the statement of the Bombay Board respecting the non-appearance of bile in the stools or in the bowels after death. " Neither in Europeans nor in natives, was any tinge of that secretion discovered in the intestinal canal."

Mr. Corbyn's communication to Sir Gilbert Blane, in the Medico-Chirurgical transactions, is now more than a thrice told tale—having been published substantially in the Edinburgh Medical Journal, in the Bombay reports, and in the Medico-Chirurgical Journal for April, 1820. A further experience of better than a year, (being brought up to Sept. 1819, nearly as far as the Calcutta reports,) has confirmed Mr. Corbyn's former statements relative to the treatment of this formidable epidemic.

" The outline of the treatment alluded to, is, to administer twenty grains of calomel, (in powder, not in pills,) and to wash it down with sixty drops of laudanum and twenty drops of oil of peppermint in two ounces of water—to bleed freely in the early stage—and to support the warmth by external heat, the hot bath and hot friction, and internally by cordials," 122.

Sir Gilbert Blane, in a commentary on the different communications, has laboured to render it at least probable that this epidemic was *contagious*. It is sufficient to say that the Calcutta Medical Board, who had better opportunities of ascertaining this point than Sir Gilbert Blane, gave a decided negative to the supposition.

Sir Gilbert Blane has been favoured by the Army Medical Board, with a document from the principal medical officer in the Isle of France, showing that the epidemic appeared there on the 20th November, 1818. It has since raged with great violence.

Here, as in India, the laborious classes of the population suffered most. " With regard to the practice, opium and calomel were administered to the cases in the army, but in smaller doses than in India." The principal medical officer denies contagion, attributing the epidemic to atmospheric influence. The inhabitants, however, believed the infection was imported by the Topaze frigate ! Such popular *beliefs*, like some popular *disbeliefs* here, are little worthy of notice.

" Non ego ventosæ *plebis* suffragia venor."

The inhabitants of Bourbon acting on the contagious creed, instituted a strict quarantine. But the epidemic laughed to scorn these little hypothetical barriers, and marched into the place without ceremony.

One of the medical officers having stated his opinion that the cause of this epidemic was owing to the issue of a morbific effluvium from the earth, as was long ago maintained by Sydenham, Sir Gilbert Blane characterizes this opinion as " an assumption purely gratuitous, and neither supported by fact nor countenanced by analogy." Now I would ask Sir Gilbert Blane if the matter of contagion, or the febrific miasm from marshy soils, has ever been rendered cognizable to the senses ?—and what proof have we of their existence but by their effects ? The epidemic in question, as well as many other epidemics, could not be traced to contagion, for even, according to Sir Gilbert's own confession—" it has been found occasionally, like the small-pox, to break out in spots a few (he might have said a few hundred,) miles distant from the known seat of contagion, *without its being possible to trace it*." The idea of contagion then being almost universally given up, we have but two other probable sources—the earth and the air. The longer I have reflected on this subject, the more I am convinced of the truth of Sydenham's conjecture. We know that certain states of the earth's *surface* will disengage morbific agents. But it will be triumphantly asked, " have these agents or effluvia been ever seen issuing from the *bowels* of the earth ?" I answer, by asking if they have ever been seen descending from the regions of the air, or passing from one person to another ?—And are there no subterraneous agents at work ? Do we never feel the earth itself tremble under our feet from one extremity of Europe to the other, from the agency of subterraneous and unseen causes ? Have we not seen pestilences quickly succeed these intestinal commotions of nature ? Do we not actually see the electric fluid itself, at one moment forsake the air and plunge into the bowels of the earth ; while the next instant, it springs from thence to the clouds over our heads ? And is morbific effluvium a *less* subtle fluid than the electric ? Oh! but, says Sir Gilbert Blane, " how is it conceivable that these effluvia could exhale from the earth in the progressive manner in which this disease extended itself, and how will it account for its appearing *on board of ships at sea ?*" In answer to this I must first state, that the great Eastern epidemic spread from one extremity of India to the other, often *directly against monsoon.* Now, how is this reconcileable with atmospheric influence ? It would be very curious, too, if human *contagion* had the power of selecting a single point out of the thirty-two in the compass, and of refusing to travel for a time on any other parallel ! . It would be equally curious if *atmospheric* influence could propagate itself directly against a trade wind, which blew in one direction for six months together !

Indeed, the capricious as well as obstinate courses which this epidemic occasionally pursued, are much more explicable on the principle of a terrestrial, than of an atmospheric or contagious influence. We see the causes which produce earthquakes take the most irregular and unaccountable routes ; and as for this morbific agent appearing at sea, we can have no great difficulty in conceiving the possibility of such an occurrence, after seeing in our own days, volcanic islands boiling up from the bottom of the ocean.

Upon the whole, I think that we have been much too precipitate in rejecting the opinion of Sydenham, and that no other hypothesis, if such it be, is half so plausible as the terrestrial origin of epidemic influence, however that influence may be subsequently transported about, or modified by atmospheric constitutions.

And here I cannot help stating it as my decided conviction, that the ever-varying *causes* of epidemic diseases will produce an ever-varying character of them, and consequently an ever-varying pathology and treatment. This may be mortifying to the pride of man, who often builds an ingenious theory on the symptoms and treatment of a single epidemic, the whole foundation of which is shaken to the centre by the next visitation of disease. It is in vain to say that epidemics differ only in the organs principally affected. What produces this difference of seat ? Here we must recur to an *occult* cause, however we may be inclined to account for things without it. The fact is, what all unbiassed observers have long ago acknowledged, that not only do the causes and seats of epidemic diseases materially differ at different epochs ; but their whole nature is modified, and requires an ever-varying modification of management.   Nor do I think that this impassible bar to perfection is at all injurious to medical science. If pathology and therapeutics could be reduced to certain fixed and invariable rules, inquiry would languish, and the human mind would soon lose its most powerful stimulus to exertion.   Medicine might then be administered by the mere routinist with as much success as by the most intelligent physician.   But there is no fear of this consummation in the practice of physic ! Our descendants will have to go all over the same ground that we are treading, and probably not a single tenet of the present time will hold good fifty or even thirty years hence.   But if we roll the stone of Sisyphus, it is not in vain. The exertion, though it may be useless to futurity, is salutary, nay absolutely necessary for us.   If our utmost efforts are incapable of placing us one step in advance, still a moment's cessation from labour would inevitably cause us to retrograde.   But to return.

The Army Medical Board have recently received intelligence from Ceylon, and with their accustomed liberality have communicated the same to the profession.

Dr. Davy, who is already known to the profession, considers that the epidemic was unconnected with the direction of the winds, the topography of the places visited, or any sensible changes in the state of the atmosphere.   In some cases, the flaccidity of the muscular parts after death, resembled that produced in animals by electricity, or when hunted to death.   The colour of the venous and arterial blood was the same—both being of the dark venous hue.   The blood drawn never presented a buffy coat.   The air expired from the lungs of the sick, did not contain more than one-third of the carbonic acid contained in the breath of healthy people.   Mr. Finlayson observed in some cases, what happened often in Bengal, that the operation of the morbific cause was so violent as to destroy life in a few hours, without any of the characteristic tokens of the disease, except the extreme prostration of strength.   The warm bath and all other medicines seemed rather hurtful than beneficial.

"Non vota, non ars ulla correptos levant !"

In these particular cases there was such great congestion of blood in the brain " that it had the appearance of being enveloped in a layer of dark coagulated blood, or by a diffuse and general ecchymosis, and in some cases, when it was cut into, large quantities of dark coagulated blood gushed from it and from the theca of the spine." In the ordinary form of the disease, this appearance was wanting, the blood being principally collected in the abdominal viscera.   The blood was so fluid that any opening of the larger vessels produced an inconvenient effusion.   In several cases, the surface of the heart and pericardium was lined with a green-coloured gelatinous fluid.   There was found a dark-coloured fluid in the stomach and a colourless fluid in the rest of the intestines, which were blanched like tripe.   These appearances were peculiar to cases of early death.   In the more advanced stages, the morbid appearances did not differ materially from what has already been described in another part of this work. The deaths, in several of the stations, equalled the recoveries, or even exceeded that proportion. In two cases, the spasmodic contractions continued for some time after death! "The stress of the cure was laid on twenty or thirty grains of calomel given at first, and repeated in doses of eight or ten grains every second, third, or fourth hour. Blood-letting was practised with the same relief as in other parts of India." I fully coincide with Sir Gilbert Blane in the following passage.

"We cannot conclude this article without remarking that the medical officers of the British empire in India have done themselves much honour, by the great ability, zeal, and humanity displayed in the preceding communications."

Our brethren in the Eastern hemisphere have had most arduous duties to fulfil during the last few years, and I have reason to believe that the manner in which they performed them has reflected credit on the profession, and on humanity.

"Vir bonus, quod honeste se facturum putaverit, faciet, etiamsi laboriosum erit :—faciet, etiamsi damnosum erit :—faciet, etiamsi periculosum erit."

BERIBERI.

Sec. XI.—The *Beriberi* is a disease of a peculiar nature, which has been extremely frequent, and fatal amongst all the troops, both *Europeans* and natives, in Ceylon. In the milder cases of this disease, the patients are first attacked with some stiffness of the legs and thighs, and this is succeeded by numbness and œdema, sometimes paralysis of the lower extremities.

In a course of a few days, if not prevented by medicine, these symptoms are succeeded by swelling of the whole body, attended with a sense of fulness of the belly, and more particularly with weight and oppression at the præcordia ; dyspnœa, starting in the sleep, and all the usual symptoms of hydrothorax. In the latter stage, the dyspnœa and anxiety become extreme, the uneasiness at the epigastrium increases, attended with almost constant vomiting, and occasionally spasms of different muscles : the pulse becomes very feeble, the lips and countenance livid, and the extremities cold.

Some fever, with delirium, often now accede, and terminate the life of the unfortunate sufferer. In the more sudden and severe instances, the patients, from the first, complain of universal debility and extreme oppression, anxiety and dyspnœa. In some of these instances, the progress of the disease is so rapid, that it carries off the patient in six, twelve, twenty-four, or thirty-six hours after its first attack : more frequently, however, its duration is for several weeks.

In a few cases, where the disease was no less fatal, there was not any swelling observable externally ; but the patient with the other symptoms, had evidently the bloated leucophlegmatic face of a dropsical person.

Upon dissection of different subjects, who had died of this disease, more or less water was found in one or all the cavities of the chest ; most commonly in the pericardium, but in general, more inconsiderable than might have been expected from the violence of the symptoms. The cellular substance surrounding the heart was, in some instances, loaded with water ; and the heart seemed, in two or three cases of an uncommon size. In one instance, in which the progress of the disease had been very rapid, I found a large coagulum of lymph in the right auricle. The cellular substance of the lungs was, in many cases, loaded with water. In a few cases, also, there was water effused in the cellular substance on the surface of the brain ; and, in one instance, more than an ounce of water was collected in the ventricles. In most cases, water was found in the abdomen, and cellular membrane throughout the body ; and, in many subjects, there was a remarkable obesity, even after a long continuance of the disease, and of the use of mercury, antimony, and other powerful medicines. Men of every constitution are occasionally attacked with the *Beriberi*, but the aged and debauched seem to be most liable to it ; and men who have once had the complaint, are the most subject to it in future. 'I have remarked that a very great proportion of the patients, seized with this disease, were men who were accustomed to lead a sedentary and debauched life, such as taylors, shoemakers, &c. who, when working at their trade, are often excused the duty of the field, and, by their double earnings are enabled to procure a larger quantity of spirits than the other men.

I have never met with an instance of this complaint in a woman, an officer, or a boy, under 20 ; although persons of every description seem equally liable to the other diseases of the place, such as fever, flux, or liver complaint.

It would appear that a stay for some months on the station, is almost essential for the production of the disease ; and that the greatest predisposition to it exists, when troops have been about eight or twelve months in the settlement.

The 72d regiment and Coast artillery landed here in July, 1795. The *Beriberi* was with them most prevalent in the autumn of 1796 ; but they had little of it in March, 1797, when it was extremely frequent with the 1st battalion *European* infantry, who had arrived here in August, 1796.

The 80th regiment relieved the 72d in March, 1797, but suffered little from the disease till the November following. The Honourable Company's *Malay* corps arrived here, from *Jaffnapatnam*, in June, 1797 ; but the complaint did not appear amongst them till the January following, when it became very frequent and fatal. Two hundred drafts joined the 80th at *Trincomalee*, on the 3d of January, 1798 ; but none of these men had the disease in January, February, or March, although it was then very frequent with the other men of the regiment : since that time, however, these drafts have been at least as subject to it as the other men.

Various modes of cure have been attempted in this disease : but I have of late uniformly pursued the following plan with uncommon success.

In the more mild cases, the patients are immediately put upon a course of calomel and squills. The perspiration and other evacuations are promoted by saline drinks, or small doses of antimonial, or James's powder; and the strength supported by cordial liquors, most generally gin punch, which assists much the effect of the squills.

By these medicines, the symptoms are very often removed in the course of a few days; except the numbness of the extremities, which generally remains longer than the rest. Pediluvium and stimulant liniments are then ordered to the extremities, and the patients are put upon a tonic plan, of bark and wine, or porter, which is continued for some time after all the symptoms have disappeared. In the more severe cases, where the dyspnœa, vomiting, spasms, or other symptoms are violent, it is necessary to apply blisters to the breast, to make use of fomentations, and the hot bath, and to exhibit the strongest cordials, and anti-spasmodics, as brandy, and particularly laudanum and vitriolic æther. By these means I have, in most instances, been enabled to relieve the dyspnœa, and other urgent symptoms; and procure time for the exhibition of the medicines mentioned above, which it is sometimes necessary to use for several weeks. —*Christie's Report, &c.*

THE DRACUNCULUS, OR GUINEA WORM.

Sec. XII.—Although this worm attacks most parts of the body, it shows a preference to the lower extremities, particularly the feet and ankles, where it is painful and dangerous in proportion as the parts are thinly covered with flesh. It is difficult to extract it from the tarsus and metatarsus—sometimes impossible from the toes. The consequences are often, tedious suppurations—contraction of the tendons—diseases of the joints—gangrene. When the worm is pulled, the pain is sometimes excruciating, as the animal would appear to attach itself to the nerves, ligaments, and tendons. The track of the worm seems to be in the cellular membrane, rarely deeper. There are seldom any premonitory symptoms. The presence of the disease is usually announced by itching, redness, and heat in the skin of the part, succeeded by a vesicle, with some swelling and inflammation. Under the vesicle, which contains a white, thick mucus, the head of the worm may be generally discovered; but sometimes not till several days after the ulceration. Occasionally a small ulcer is the first thing observed; at other times, tumour of the whole limb, with much inflammation. The worm sometimes appears like a hair, several inches long, and becomes thicker as it is extracted; but it generally has a sharp point, and is all of the same thickness. It may often be felt and traced by the fingers, like the string of a violin, under the skin, where it excites no very sensible uneasiness, till the skin is perforated by the animal.

When removed from the body it exhibits no appearance of life, even when extracted at one operation. In length, it varies from 18 inches to six feet. It is elastic, white, transparent, and contains a gelatinous substance.

When the disease is seated in parts that are tender—when there is extensive ulceration—or where the constitution is irritable, there is generally some fever, loss of appetite, debility, and evening exacerbation, especially if the worm happen to be drawn too tight. Swellings of the inguinal glands are sometimes sympathetically induced when the complaint is situated in the lower extremities.

Various have been the opinions respecting the generation of this insect. Both ancients and moderns have attributed its production to the drinking of putrid stagnant waters containing the ova of the worm. Some have regarded the worm as produced from ova deposited in the skin by insects. This last supposition is by far the most probable, notwithstanding the ingenious arguments brought forward by Dr. Chisholm, in favour of the aqueous generation, and for the following reasons:—1st. The disease most frequently attacks those parts of the body that are exposed to wet, as the feet and legs. Thus the Bheesties or water-carriers in India, who carry the water in leather bags on their backs, are observed to be much afflicted with Guinea worm in those parts that come in contact with the mushuk or bag.—2d. It prevails in wet seasons, and damp situations more than in dry. Many causes, however, may contribute to the production of the disease, as confinement, heat, want of cleanliness in person and habitation, &c. and the means of prevention are founded on these premises, viz. cleanliness—avoiding dampness—keeping the feet and legs covered, [which few European soldiers and sailors attend to in tropical climates,] bathing in the sea, in preference to lakes and rivers—and avoiding contact with those infected ; for there is great reason to believe that the disease is propagated by contagion when once produced by other causes.

Methodus Medendi—Mercury, carried to the length of impregnation of the system,[*] has been considered by some as a specific, and so has assafœtida in Guinea worm ; but the local means are those most to be depended on. *Sublata causa, tollitur effectus.*

When an inflammatory tumor ushers in the disease, leeches, cataplasms, fomentations, and other antiphlogistic measures are to be pursued till suppuration occurs, and the head of the worm becomes apparent. It should then be seized by the forceps, and pulled very gently and gradually until there be a little resistance, and the worm becomes moderately tight. The extraction is often facilitated by friction with warm oil, and well adjusted pressure in the line of the worm towards the wound. When as much of the animal has been drawn out as the resistance and pain will admit, the end of it should be secured by a ligature or thread passed round it ; the thread should then be tied to a piece of small bougee, twisted lint or small quill, an inch and a half in length, and with the slack part of the worm, is to be rolled up until it be moderately tight, taking care that it be not on the stretch, as it will occasion fever, or endanger the breaking of the worm. A piece of adhesive plaster is necessary to retain it in its place, and poultices may be continued, especially where there is tumour, to promote a discharge and the expulsion of the worm.

In general, the extraction should only be attempted once in twenty-four hours. Sometimes a foot of worm can be extracted at

* Vide Chisholm in Edin. Journal, vol. 11

once, sometimes not an inch. When the whole is drawn out, the sore may be treated as a common ulcer, making moderate pressure on the original track of the worm.

When by injudicious extraction the animal is broken, then tumour, fever, and tedious suppuration in that or other parts are the frequent consequences. Here recourse must again be had to fomentations and cataplasms, until the ruptured end of the worm can be again discovered, and laid hold of.

When the worm can be distinctly felt by the fingers under the skin, before breaking through, it is advisable to extract it by means of a small incision made over the part where it is most superficial, and, as near as possible, over its middle. A ligature should then be applied, and the worm extracted double, in the manner before mentioned. —*Bruce.*

ELEPHANTIASIS.*

Sec. XIII.—Mr. Robinson conceives that two distinct varieties, if not different diseases, are confounded under one name ; " and what is worse, are treated alike, though they require very different remedies." As elephantiasis, the lepra arabum, is one of the most common, as well as " one of the most gigantic and incurable diseases" of Hindostan, I shall present a full analysis of Mr. Robinson's paper in this place, as it will thereby have a considerable circulation through our oriental and occidental dominions.

Variety 1*st.* Exhibits the following symptoms. One or two circumscribed patches appear upon the skin, (generally the feet or hands, but sometimes the trunk or face,) of a rather lighter colour than the neighbouring parts, neither raised nor depressed, shining and wrinkled, the furrows not coinciding with the lines of the contiguous sound cuticle. The skin of these patches, is insensible even to a hot iron. They spread slowly until the skin of the legs, arms, and whole body is completely involved, and deprived of sensibility. It is in this state, chiefly, that the disease is remediable.

After a period, varying from two months to five or six years, symptoms indicative of internal disease, or functional derangement, are developed. The pulse becomes slow and heavy, the bowels torpid, the toes and fingers numbed, as with frost, appearing glazed, somewhat swelled, and nearly inflexible. The mind exhibits corresponding traits of torpor and inactivity ; the soles of the feet and palms of the hands crack into fissures, dry and hard, as the parched soil of the country, the extremities of the toes and fingers, under the nails, being encrusted with a furfuraceous substance, and the nails themselves raised up until absorption and ulceration occur. Still there is no pain. The legs and arms now swell, the skin is every where cracked and rough, cotemporary with which symptoms, ulcers appear at the inside of the joints of the toes and fingers, di-

* On the Elephantiasis, as it appears in Hindostan. By James Robinson, Esq. Superintendent of the Insane Hospital at Calcutta, Medico-Chirurgical Transactions, Vol. x.

rectly under the last joint of the metatarsal or metacarpal bones ; or they corrode the thick sole, under the joint of the os calcis or os cuboides, without any preceding tumour, suppuration, or pain, but apparently from simple sloughing off of the integuments, in layers of half an inch in diameter. A sanious discharge comes on ; the muscles, in ther turn, are destroyed ; and the joint being penetrated as by an auger, " the extremity droops, and at length falls a victim to this cruel, tardy, but certain poison." The wound then heals, and other joints are attacked in succession, every revolving year bringing with it a trophy of this slow march of death ! The patient, though a spectacle of horror to others, and a burden to himself, still clings to life, and endeavours to cherish its remaining spark, by voraciously devouring all he can procure. " He will often crawl about with little but his trunk remaining, until old age comes on, and at last he is carried of by diarrhœa or dysentery, which the enfeebled consti--tution has no stamina to resist." Although the general health and the digestive functions do not suffer much throughout this long and tedious dismemberment, yet " a sleepy inertness overpowers every faculty, and seems to benumb, almost annihilate, every passion, as well of the soul as of the body, leaving only sufficient sense and activity to crawl through the routine of existence." This our author considers as a distinct variety of elephantiasis, to which, on account of its most prominent trait, he would give the name of elephantiasis anaisthetos. He has never seen the larger joints attacked, (a strange assertion after telling us that the patient creeps about with " little but his trunk remaining,") the nose destroyed, or any bones affected, save those of the hands and feet. The tuberculated species, hereafter to be described, sometimes supervenes, " but is by no means connected with, caused by, or necessarily subsequent to this disease."

Treatment. If we see the patient in the first stage, before described, the prognosis may be favourable. A combination of mercury and anti--mony, with tropical stimulants, will generally succeed. A blister alone kept open for a few days will often restore the sensibility of the skin, and check the disease.

" Whenever the foot or hand alone is affected, I usually apply a strip of blistering plaster one inch and a half wide all round the limb, just upon the line which marks the sound from the affected parts. Where this is inapplicable, from the extent of the disease, I apply a solution of muriate of mercury, made as follows :

R. Hydr. muriat. gr. viij. acid. muriat. ġt. xx. Tere in vit. mort. deinde adde spt. vini rectif. ℥ ſs aq. font. Oij. M. This must be rubbed well on the skin, wherever affected."

Mr. R. at the same time, gives to an adult, half a grain of calomel, three grains of antimonial powder, and from six to ten of rad. asclepiæ giganteæ every eight hours. This last medicine was discovered several years ago by Mr. Playfair, and our author thinks the professional world greatly indebted for the discovery of " the most valuable medicine hitherto derived from the vegetable kingdom." Mr. Playfair emphatically describes it as " a vegetable mercury, specific in the cure of lues venerea, leprosy, and cutaneous eruptions in general, the most powerful alternative hitherto known, and an excellent deobstruent. In all affections of the skin, says he, I have found it very effectual; and in the jugaru or leprosy of the joints, I have never failed to heal up all the ulcers, and often have produced a perfect cure."

In the complaint under consideration, Mr. Robinson agrees with Mr. Playfair, that the asclepias, called in Hindostan "Mudar," is possessed of great virtues. He can also bear witness to its powerful effects as a deobstruent and sudorific in almost all cutaneous eruptions, arising from obstructed perspiration, and an apathy of the extreme vessels. It causes a sense of heat in the stomach, which rapidly pervades every part of the system, and produces a titillating feel upon the skin from the renewed circulation through the minute vessels. It is inadmissible where the affection is inflammatory, or the eruption pustular. Mr. R. tried it freely in lues venerea, but cannot venture to recommend it as a substitute for mercury. "It will enable you to heal a chancre, but does not eradicate the poison." In secondary symptoms, he considers it an admirable ally. Where mercury has been used, but cannot be safely pushed further, the Mudar rapidly recruits the constitution, heals the ulcers, removes the blotches from the skin, and perfects the cure. The bark of the root is the only part of the plant that is useful in medicine, and should be gathered in March, April, or May. The bark, when well dried, is easily beaten into a fine powder, of which the dose is from three to ten grains. It grows in great plenty and wild throughout Hindostan.

Variety 2d. Mr. Robinson would denominate elephantiasis tuberculata, which has been often described, and is now occasionally seen in this country. A very exquisite specimen was lately exhibited at Edinburgh, a plate and case of which is given in the Monthly Series of the Medico-Chirurgical Journal, by Dr. Lee. I shall not, therefore, copy Mr. Robinson's description of the disease, as he draws his delineation principally from the late Dr. Adams, and Dr. Bateman. In the tuberculated variety, the asclepias does harm; and is therefore inadmissible. Arsenic, in small doses, is the most useful medicine our author has found, but it is very far from being generally effectual.

Upon the whole, this is an interesting paper; and Mr. Robinson is entitled to the thanks of the profession for having made known to them a vegetable possessed of such valuable properties as he ascribes to the asclepias gigantea.

Miscellaneous Observations on certain indigenous Customs, Diseases, and Remedies, in India. By Daniel Johnson, Esq formerly Surgeon in Hon. Company's Service, Bengal Establishment.

SEC. XIV.—The climate of India not being salutary to European constitutions, it is highly necessary for those who are doomed to reside there great part of their lives, to do all in their power to coun-

teract its baneful influence ; for which purpose, I recommend them
to pay particular attention to the prevailing customs of the natives,
which have been handed down to them by their forefathers, who
were more enlightened than the present inhabitants, or even, perhaps, than we can have any idea of from their, present state ; and
although Europeans in general look down on them with contempt, I
am persuaded much may be learnt from them, by any one who will
give himself the trouble to observe them narrowly.

When a European first arrives amongst them, he is sensibly struck
with their strange appearance, their dress being so very different
from what he has been accustomed to see in Europe, where fashion
and elegance of appearance are studied in preference to ease and
usefulness.   In India the same method of dress has continued for
centuries, and is, in fact, a part of their religion ;. and I imagine was
first adopted from physical principles, as being the best suited to that
hot climate.   The rich natives have every thing on them loose, except their cumberband, (that is, a cloth bound round the lower part of
their loins,) which is of great use in supporting the belly, and thereby
preventing ruptures.   The poorer classes go almost naked, and be-
smear their bodies with oil, to prevent the direful effects of a burning
sun on their naked skins.   The females dress very like the men, all
loose except their breasts, which are tightly suspended in cloth or
silk, to prevent their falling down from their weight and relaxation.
They ornament their persons in a variety of ways, which, though
considered by them as adding to their charms and beauty, is at first
viewed by Europeans with disgust, and notwithstanding that a residence for some time amongst them may somewhat reconcile such un-
becoming decorations, few ever give themselves the trouble to think
much on the subject, or trace them to their first principle, *physical
utility*, from which, I conceive, they for the most part originated.   I
will now enumerate a few, which I think will be sufficient to elucidate my observations ; and, although I do not approve of all their
customs, many of them I can account for very differently from the
generally received opinion, and can excuse them for adopting them.
The few I shall notice I think will clearly show that we ought not
to condemn them all hastily, for we should recollect that length of
time and experience have established them.

I shall begin with observing the custom which females have of colouring the palms of their hands, soles of their feet, and nails, *red;*
which they do by pounding the leaves of *mindy* or hinnah, (a species
of myrtle,) mixing it with lime, and applying it to those parts, where
it remains some hours.   This is considered an ornament, but I imagine it was first used to check the inordinate perspiration in the hands
and feet, which prevails to a great degree with the natives of India,
giving their hands a very disagreeable cold clammy feel, like the sensation produced by handling a frog, and which the application alluded
to entirely removes.

The next custom I shall remark, is their blacking the eye-lids with
powdered antimony.   It produces a strange contrast to the whites of
their eyes, which are exceedingly clean.   This, also, I conceive not

to have been first used for ornament, but to cure or prevent the oph-
thalmia tarsi, and it is one of the best remedies I know for it.

Again, females, after they attain a certain age, or get married, use
an application to stain their teeth black.   This, I also believe, was,
and is, used to destroy the tartar, and preserve the teeth and gums,
which it certainly does.   The time of life at which they first begin
to use it, is when tartar collects most, and were it used solely for ornament, the young would all have their teeth black, which none of
them ever have.   This application is called " *Miscee*," and what it
is composed of, I cannot say ;—whatever it is, it destroys the tartar,
hardens the gums, and makes the teeth of a jet black, without destroying the enamel.

The next custom I shall notice, is their chewing pawn, in the leaf
of which is enclosed a small quantity of betle nut, cardamon seeds,
a clove, some gum : Rub : Astring : and a small portion of lime.
The poorer people use it without spices.   This is universally chew-
ed both by men and women, and is offered to all strangers, as a compliment.   It is a fine aromatic, acts as a stimulus to the fauces and
stomach, and sweetens the breath.   It causes the saliva to flow,
and reddens the mouth, giving it an appearance not pleasing to Europeans.

Another custom is their sitting always on the ground with their
knees up to their chins, which I know not how to account for, unless
it is that in this position there are very few muscles in action, and
the pendulous parts of the body are then, as it were, hung upon ligaments, in the same manner as a soldier "stands at ease," by suspending the weight of the trunk on the ligaments of the thigh and
hip.   Europeans in India cannot sit long with ease, without using a
morah, (a kind of stool to put their legs on ;) if they have not got
that, they put their legs on the table, and it is not uncommon to see
a whole party after dinner with their legs on the table.   A restless
uneasiness, occasioned by languid circulation, in the feet and legs,
causes this, which I attribute to the heat of the climate causing great
exhaustion, and relaxation ; for Europeans after having resided long
in India, do not feel the same inclination on their return to their native country.

Tattooing and Shampooing, (that is, using percussion and pressure,) have also the effect of assisting the languid circulation, and
the relief experienced from it after fatigue, can only be judged of
by those who have experienced it.   Smoking is another custom in
general throughout India, and I firmly believe, is of salutary effect,
particularly if not indulged in to excess, or poisoned by the introduction of intoxicating ingredients.   Smoking pure tobacco acts as a gentle stimulus to the intestines, and causes regular evacuations ; without the use of which, recourse to medicines would be often found
necessary.   I can vouch from experience that the first pipe of a
morning always causes a desire to go to stool, and such as are in the
habit of smoking, and are deprived of it any morning, seldom have
an inclination to visit Cloacina's temple that day, and are generally
troubled with head-aches in consequence.

The last of their salutary customs that I shall notice, is their daily habit of bathing in cold water, and washing out their mouths after every thing they swallow ; a custom much to be commended in every country, particularly in a hot one, where animal and vegetable matter soon becomes putrid under any circumstance. I shall here digress a little, and remark that Europeans too often accustom themselves to wash their feet many times a-day, in hot water. Although pleasing at the time, and apparently of trifling consequence, it is, I am convinced, a serious evil, by increasing the secretions which were before too copious, and if persevered in for a length of time, will add considerably to other unwholesome practices, which together with the heat of the climate, will soon wear out an English constitution, and bring on premature old age.

I shall now give an account of a few of the diseases of India as they affect the natives, and their method of curing them. Silk winders, who are people employed to wind off the silk from the coocoons, (chiefly women,) from being constantly in a sitting position, and from their relaxed habits, are subject to a prolapsus of the anus, to obviate which, they use a plug, (or pessary,) every time they have an evacuation ; which they make of the clayey sort of earth that surrounds the tanks. Hundreds of those plugs may be seen close to the edges of the water near every silk factory, of a conical figure. A new one is made every time those places are visited.

Elephantiasis.—(The Black Leprosy, or as some call it, Falling Leprosy, by the natives called Judham,) is not general throughout India, but rather local—at all events it is much more prevalent in some parts than others, attacking people of particular habits ; and whether it is hereditary as some think, or not, is, in my opinion very doubtful, for although it attacks the son whose father had it, it should be remembered that the son always follows the same business that his father did, and as this disease attacks chiefly such people as have their feet and hands frequently in cold water or earth, (such as the peasants in the low marshy countries of Bengal and Orissa,) I conclude that this, together with poorness of living, is the first cause. I am induced to think so from the circumstance of its attacking chiefly Dobys. (washermen,) and Mollies, (gardeners,) in the upper provinces of India, and I conceive that cold and poorness of blood cause the circulation in the extreme capillary vessels to become too languid ; the consequence is, a gradual decay or depopulation of those parts, for they have much the appearance of persons who lose their fingers and toes from having been frost-bitten, with this difference, that it does not proceed so rapid, and also, that after a joint has fallen off, it heals again, and remains well for some months, when it breaks out afresh. Thus it continues until all the intercarpal and sometimes carpal joints are destroyed, when in many instances, it heals altogether, and they often live to a tolerable good age, without ever experiencing any return, which I think indicates that it does not proceed from any humour in the constitution, but that it is solely owing to a defect of the circulation in the extreme vessels. It should also be observed, that having lost both the use of their hands and feet, they cannot follow their occupations, but become mendicants. I have had several natives with this complaint under my care, and I have tried a variety of medicines without experiencing much good from them. A native doctor told me of a specific, and I gave it to a (Doby) servant of mine labouring under the complaint ; he took it for some time, and it appeared to arrest its progress, but unfortunately I was obliged to quit India before I could ascertain if it would entirely remove it. The specific consisted of pills made with arsenic, bread, and black pepper, proportions of each I do not recollect, having lost all memoranda on the subject. I have noticed this, deeming it worthy of a further trial by any medical gentleman who may have an opportunity.

Since writing the above I recollect having seen a paper on the same subject in one of your Journals, and I have just been looking at it, and find that in many points my description agrees with Mr. Robinson's, and in others not. As it is my intention to give you my own obsertions unsophisticated, without reference to, or borrowing a single idea from others, I shall make no alteration in this, and only add the following remarks on Mr. Robinson's paper.—I am clearly of opinion that it is a distinct disease from common leprosy, and ought not to be classed with it, or considered as Leprous. The latter I consider to be a disease entirely of the skin.—The Mudar Mr. R speaks of I believe is called by the natives of India Midaur, from Midaun a plant, it being a shrub that is to be found on all the uncultivated plains of India,—the milky juice of which is the only part that I have ever known used, and that externally for herpetic complaints ; however, for ought I know, it may be a good medicine, internally—for I verily believe there are a variety of simples in India possessing virtues unknown to the natives, and far many more whose virtues they are acquainted with, the Europeans know nothing of, although the plants may be familiar to them. Even this Mudar may not be the plant I take it to be.

The next disease that I shall notice is called by the natives Boss, which is a chronical enlargement of the spleen, and prevails throughout Indostan, but is most common in the Jungles and hilly parts (as Ramjhur.) It attacks almost every Indian residing there who is not a native of the hills, (but comes from the low countries,) and sometimes it attacks the native inhabitants. In most instances it follows intermittent fevers, and the spleen often becomes enormously large. In such cases I have never found it to give way to any medicines I used, yet I have seen them considerably reduced by the natives themselves, by using the actual cautery with freedom, and taking half a pint of vinegar every morning. They apply the cautery to the swoln part, and sometimes all over the abdomen, giving them an appearance, like a horse's leg that has been fired for a breaking down, (as the Jockeys term it,) of the large tendon of the leg.

As we have improved in the knowledge of Anatomy of the human body, in operations of Surgery, the knife has gained ground to the total disuse of the actual cautery, an improvement to be highly valued, still I am of opinion that the actual cautery will again get into use, I do not mean generally, God forbid, but for particular cases ; such as require contraction, or union of parts, for which I believe we know of nothing equal to it. An idea has often struck me, that it may be applied with wonderful good effect to prevent the descent of ruptures.

Would not a deep impression of the actual cautery over the ring of the abdominal muscles, (through which an intestine has passed,) so contract them, as to prevent the possibility of the guts falling down again ? If it would have that effect, it would go far to explode the use of trusses, and be of great benefit to mankind. '

Nyctalops, is also very common in India, and when not accompanied with a diseased liver or spleen, may be removed by a few doses of calomel united with some other purgative. I am of opinion that this complaint, as also inflammation of the Eyes, are often caused by eating rice ; not that it is owing to any quality in the nourishment produced from the rice, but solely owing the rice not being cleaned from its husks, which are as sharp as needles, and very capable of irritating the coats of the stomach. The Indian sailors are very subject to such complaints, and they often receive the rice with the husks on, it being cheaper to the owners of the ships; and also keeps better in that state ; the consequence is, that the poor creatures are obliged to pound off the husks, almost every time they prepare their meals, and often they are not half cleaned.

Naukera, (a kind of Ozœna,) is another very common complaint in India. It is an inflammation of the membrana pituitaria, seldom attended with such discharge as is common in England. If neglected, it becomes a complete Ozœna, or foul stinking ulcer. The natives prevent it, by introducing a sharp-edged grass, and scratching the membrane, which being in state of inflammation, bleeds copiously and soon relieves them.

Hydrocele, is also common in India.—A Mr. Glass, Surgeon of Bauglepore, has given an account of natives being often cured of it, by being employed to beat indigo oats. The native doctors cure it with a poultice made with the pounded leaves of the indigo plant, and crude Sal Ammoniac. They also apply tobacco leaves to the Scrotum, (which they also do for the hernia humoralis,) and sometimes perform the operation for a radical cure by incision.

For local swellings of the joints or other parts, and also for partial paralytic affections, they use a caustic application, which I have found very efficacious. It is made and applied in the following manner—equal quantities of quick lime and crude Sal Ammoniac are incorporated together, and then put into a cloth bag and quilted, and then sprinkled slightly with water, and applied to the swollen part : it causes considerable heat and pain, and when it becomes very violent it should be removed, and repeated as often as thought necessary, taking care not to keep it on so long as to cause blistering or sloughing.—Since my return from India I applied it to a horse that had his knee swoln to twice its natural size ; it remained on a whole night, during which time the animal seemed to suffer great pain from his incessant restlessness, and to my astonishment in the morning, the knee was reduced to its natural size, and the horse never after went lame. In swellings of the knee joint in men, from a want of absorption of the Synovia, it is a very powerful medicament, and I conceive well worthy a trial by the profession in this country.

The effect pressure has on the human body from wearing tight apparel, may in some measure be judged of, from the effect it has on our feet from tight shoes, the Indians who never wear tight shoes, use their feet as second hands.—Deformity also is of very rare occurrence in India, and may be accounted for on the same principle —that of never checking nature by any thing tight on their body.

I began with observing that the customs of the natives of India ought to be attended to by Europeans, and I shall leave off, with this observation, that they did follow them in many instances on their first settling there, which they have now foolishly left off. One in particular I shall mention, and that is—their dressing with cool and light apparel, during the hot weather. When I first arrived in India, a broad-cloth coat was scarcely ever seen in the hot months, except on formal visits. At that time the Governor-General, Earl Cornwallis, always set a good example at his own table, by taking off his coat at dinner time, which was generally followed by all the company. When I left India in 1809, broad-cloth coats were worn at dinner in the hot months by almost all the European inhabitants; which I conceive was owing to the examples set them by the heads of the settlement. Also throughout the army, they were worn at all times. In this—etiquette and fashion have prevailed over good sense in not adopting that which contributed both to comfort and health, and I hope *if properly noticed* as adding considerably to the many other causes in that hot climate tending to impair European constitutions, that the heads of Government will take it into consideration, and be induced to set an example to the contrary ; and also that when discipline and duty do not absolutely require it, commanding officers will do the same, and not oblige officers and men to wear warm clothes at those times, when they are panting with heat, and perspiring at every pore, to the great injury of their constitution, and eventually of the Government by whom they are employed.

D. JOHNSON.

TORRINGTON, DEVON, *Jan.* 1821.

MEDITERRANEAN.

General observations on the Climate.

SEC. I.—When we cast an eye along the beautiful shores of this great inland ocean, and survey the classic scenes which present themselves at every step—when we recollect that in peace or in war, the British flag, commercial or belligerent, waves in every port, and off every promontory, from the pillars of Hercules to the shores of the Hellespont, we cannot but acknowledge that the medical topography —the Endemic—and the contagious diseases of this quarter of the globe are not less interesting to Britons than those of either the

Eastern or Western Hemisphère. The more intimately we become acquainted with the various climates of the earth we inhabit, the more we shall be convinced that the " balance of comfort" is not so unequally poised as some querulous philosophers imagine. The Eastern world has its *Hepatitis*—the Western its *causus*—the Northern shores of the Mediterranean have their " *pestilential fevers*"—the Southern and Eastern are annually desolated by the *plague!* If " Happy England" knows not these but by report, or in their se-quelæ, she every year sacrifices nearly *sixty thousand* of her inhabit-ants at the altar of *Phthisis!*

In exploring this interesting track, the labours of many must be united in *analytical* concentration ; and it is upon this plan, hitherto unattempted, that I hope to condense into one focus, a stronger body of light on MEDITERRANEAN DISEASES than has ever yet been collected through a single medium.

Before entering on localities, however, it may not be improper to make a few general observations on this extensive inlet.

Placed between the burning sands of Africa on one side and the Alps and Pyrenees on the other, the Mediterranean skies are alter-nately parched by the South-east—chilled by the North-west, or stifled by the sirocco winds. Thus from Barcelona to Genoa, the iron-bound Coast presents a succession of dreary mountains and craggy rocks, the tops of the *former* being frequently covered with snow, from the beginning of March till the end of May. From these the frigid Euroclydons descend in whirlwinds upon the contiguous ocean ; while at other times, the sirocco breathes fire from the deserts of Sahara and Lybia. During the continuance of this wind, all nature appears to languish ; vegetation withers and dies—the beasts of the field droop ; while those who are strongly susceptible to electrical changes in the air, such as precede and attend a thunder storm, will easily understand the effects of the sirocco on the human frame, as an increased degree of the sensations which they then experience. The animal spirits seem too much exhausted to admit of the least bo-dily exertion, and the spring and elasticity of the air, appear to be lost. The heat exceeds that of the most fervid weather in Spain or Malta. This accession of temperature is rapid—almost instantane-ous ; and the whole atmosphere feels as if inflamed. The pores of the skin seem at once opened, and all the fibres relaxed. It some-times blows for several days together, at a medium heat of 112°, de-pressing the spirits, and so suspending the powers of digestion, that people who venture to eat a hearty supper are generally found dead next morning. Fortunately for animated nature, it is commonly suc-ceeded by the Tramontane or north wind, which, in a short time, re-stores the exhausted powers of animal and vegetable life.

After this description, the Mediterranean climate could hardly be set down as one that was favourable to the lungs of a Northern inva-lid seeking refuge from the atmospherical vicissitudes of England. Yet numerous writers describe this portion of the globe as enjoying a happy medium between intertropical heat and hyperborean cold. But we must not calculate on heat, cold, or evenness of temperature by the parallel of latitude ; on the contrary, as a modern author has justly observed, "storms most tremendous occasionally burst from the mountains, with the most piercing coldness, on many of the boasted retreats along the Northern shores of the Mediterranean." But from words we shall proceed to facts. The following table shows the *comparative* receipt of pulmonic and other diseases into the hospitals of Minorca, Malta, and Gibraltar, from the Mediterranean fleet, during the years 1810—11—12, from official returns :

Diseases.	Malta.	Gibraltar.	Minorca.	Total.
	1810–11–12	1810–11–12	1810–11–12	
Phthisis Pulmonalis	149	187	119	455
Pulmonic Inflammation - - - -	52	51	37	140
Fever - - - -	747	138	357	1242
Dysentery - - -	36	79	60	175
Total—Phthisis and Pneumonia - -	202	238	156	596
Other Complaints	883	217	417	1517

Ratio of Pulmonic to the other great complaints, 1 to 2½.

The foregoing table shows only the comparative receipts into hospital of the grand divisions of disease. The rate of mortality is quite another thing. Out of 455 cases of Phthisis alone, 151 died before the remainder could be shipped off for England, where, in all probability, most of them perished! Whereas out of 1242 cases of fever, only 58 died, and a very small number were invalided. This authentic document will speak volumes on the climate of the Mediterranean. In no other possible way could so fair a calculation be made, as to the *relative* prevalence of complaints, as in a fleet, where the crews of ships are subjected to a similarity of regimen, occupation, clothing, and discipline unknown in civil life, or even in the best regulated army.

That the abrupt vicissitudes of the climate under consideration were extremely productive of pulmonary consumption, the government, and the medical officers of our fleets and hospitals have long been aware ; but in private practice, this is little known ; and many valuable lives are annually sacrificed by the very means designed to prolong their range.

An ingenious little Thesis has lately been written in Latin by Dr. Sinclair, formerly a surgeon in the Royal Navy, on the Mediterranean Phthisis, from which I shall translate and condense a few passages.

Symptoms.—Dr. S. divides the disease into two stages, the inflammatory and suppurative. The first often advances on the patient with insidious pace, and without giving much alarm :*—frequently

* Dr. Burnett, while speaking of pneumonia in the Mediterranean, observes that—" He wishes to caution the practitioner against the *insidious form of the milder attack of this disease,* which is but too often considered of little moment —*as a catarrh*—and the cure entrusted to small doses of antimony and a great coat—often to nature. With pain has he witnessed the effects of this treatment in the *melancholy increase of consumptive cases,* which the summer's heat has brought before him."—*Preface to 1st Edition.*

'with symptoms of catarrh, or slight pleurisy, as rigors, heats and chills alternately—thirst—cough—fever.   By degrees these symptoms become more marked, and attended with lassitude—pains in the back, loins, and limbs.   To these are occasionally added, nausea, vomiting, head-ache, &c.   The pulse is generally from the beginning, quick, hard, and full—sometimes the contrary.   Acute pains, more or less severe, now shoot in between the sixth and seventh ribs near the sternum.   Sometimes this pain is complained of as deep under the breast bone—quite through to the spine—or stretching to the clavicles, or shoulder bones, with difficulty of breathing.   These symptoms will often become suddenly increased, with such oppression about the præcordia, and obstruction of the vital functions as lead to suspicion of inflammation of the heart itself or its coverings. The patient is now harassed with a dry, irritating cough—dyspnœa, and inability to lie down.   These symptoms are somewhat mitigated on the appearance of expectoration, which is rarely free, or tinged with blood.   In some people, who are biliously inclined, the pain in the right hypochondrium will imitate Hepatitis, till purulent expectoration reveals the true nature of the disease.

The termination is either by resolution—suppuration with ulceration of the worst kind—or effusion.

Resolution.—In this case, the graver symptoms subside before the close of the first septenary period—that is, about the seventh day, the pain ceases—the pulse becomes slow—the expectoration free, whitish, and thick—the skin relaxes into a gentle perspiration—the thirst is assuaged—and the appetite returns.   If these salutary events do not take place before the fourteenth day, suppuration is generally the consequence.

Suppuration.—In many cases, although the violence of the disease is mitigated by appropriate remedies ; yet a deep-seated, obtuse pain continues obstinately fixed in one side, with a sense of weight there. The difficulty of breathing remains, and the patient cannot lie down. Debility now increases fast—emaciation takes place—the pulse is easily accelerated—the expectoration from being viscid and frothy, becomes, in a few weeks, opake, yellow, or green.   In short, hectic fever is established, and PHTHISIS carries the victim to his grave in the course of five or six months—generally towards the latter end of August or September.*

Post mortem appearances.—Vomicæ of various dimensions were very often developed.   The larger contained from a few ounces to a pint of fœtid, green, or yellow pus.   In some cases empyema—in others, the lungs were ulcerated—beset with tubercles of different sizes, or entirely destroyed, with only a mass of tubercles remaining —and that too within six weeks after the stage of acute inflammation !

Methodus Medendi.—During the inflammatory period, nothing but the most decisive evacuations from the vascular system will save the structure of the lungs from that dreadful disorganization described above, and which supervenes on inflammation in the lungs in a more rapid manner, here, than in any other climate.   Twenty-four or

* Autumnus tabidis malus. Hippoc.

thirty ounces of blood must be immediately abstracted, and this reiterated according to the violence of the disease. Saline cathartics
—cool air—cool drink—rigid abstinence—antimonials—blisters, &c.
are to be used as secondary means. In these cases, it is not always
easy to limit the extent of ulterior venesection. If we bleed *too* far,
we risk effusion—if *too* little, suppuration.—This is a most critical
and dangerous period of the disease. About the fourth or fifth day
we shall apparently have conquered all the more violent symptoms,
and the patient will be considered convalescent—but all at once, he
is seized with darting pains in the chest—the muscles of respiration
are spasmed—and strangulation is threatened by the convulsive
cough! Blood must again be drawn, but with caution, for the transition from this state to irremediable effusion is awfully sudden and uncertain. Here local evacuations and other local means may be beneficially put in requisition.

When PHTHISIS approaches, nothing but a retreat from the Mediterranean before the autumn sets in, can give a shadow of hope or safety
to the patient—

> Frustra per autumnos nocentem
> Corporibus metuemus Austrum. *Hor.*

as has been proved by the *recovery of many invalids*, when sent home,
in the autumn, from our fleet. " Non alio modo evitari possunt,
" quam Cœlum salubriori mutando ; quod *invalidi plurimi domum* e
" classe nostra, in autumno quotannis remissi, sanescendo, confir-
" mant." *Thesis, p.* 30.

Dr. Sinclair remarks that as in the months of *January and February*, the air is clear, temperate, and steady in the Mediterranean,
they are the only months in which a *physical* invalid can safely sojourn on the shores, or navigate the waters of this inland ocean.

MEDITERRANEAN FEVER.

Analytical Review of Dr. BURNETT's *Work on the Bilious Remittent
Fever of the Mediterranean.*

SEC. II.—If the destructive war, which ravaged the world for more
than twenty years, has consigned millions to an early grave, it has,
like most human events, been productive of good as well as evil.
In a medical point of view it has called forth original genius, in combating the maladies to which we are subjected by our emigration or
military enterprizes ; and we are much mistaken, if it has not thrown
great light on a disease, the nature of which has puzzled the physicians and philosophers of all ages. The awful forms which FEVER assumes in fleets and armies beneath the burning skies of the East and
West Indies, and around the romantic shores of the Mediterranean,
gave rise to bold and energetic measures of cure, which never could
have originated in the retired paths of private practice. A cursory
view of our military and naval medical writings, must clearly evince
the truth of this remark. But these innovations were regarded with

a dubious eye by our medical brethren at home ; and although the host of prejudices engendered in the humoral, spasmodic, and Brunonian Schools are now fast dispersing, it is necessary to give every new *fact*, illustrative of a more rational theory and successful practice, the widest publicity, since the phantoms of " debility and putrescency" continue still to haunt the minds of a very considerable portion of medical practitioners.

The first part of this volume proposes to give " a faithful and practical account of the disease, as it appeared in the ships and hospitals of the Mediterranean fleet."—*Preface.*

Dr. B. states that excepting in one instance, the ships of the fleet enjoyed an exemption from fever during the spring months, and early part of the summer, the disease occuring in its epidemic state, either while the ship was in port refitting, or shortly afterwards. The exception was in H. M. S. *Kent*, where the disease broke out while cruising off Toulon, *three months* after leaving harbour. It is towards the end of June, or beginning of July, that febrile affections present themselves ; and the usual symptoms are head-ache, nausea, prostration of strength, suffused eyes, flushed countenance, tongue white and moist, thirst, skin variable, both as to temperature and perspiration. The same may be said of the pulse : but the bowels, are generally costive, and the appetite impaired. These are the milder symptoms of the disease in summer ; but where the patient has committed excesses, or been exposed to the sun and night dews, it frequently assumes a severer aspect, resembling the autumnal fever of hot countries. At this time, gastric symptoms are seldom formidable, the head being the organ which principally labours ; the relief of which, and intestinal evacuations, are the paramount objects of the practitioner's care.

As the summer advances, the disease is more dangerous. After a sense of lassitude and prostration of strength, a chilliness extending along the spine succeeds ; and this is followed by considerable vascular action, accompanied by head-ache, deep-seated pain in the orbits, with sometimes a prominence of the eye-balls, which appear watery, inflamed, and impatient of the light. A flushing, and even tumefaction of the face, extending down towards the breast, are not unusual, with loaded tongue, and bad taste in the mouth. Amongst the usual symptoms may also be enumerated, uneasiness in the epigastric region, nausea, bilious vomiting. pains in the joints and back, and constipation. The pulse is generally full and hard, sometimes oppressed, but rises under the lancet.—Partial perspirations are sometimes observable ; but generally the skin is dry, and the temperature increased. Severe rigors sometimes, but not very commonly, precede the hot stage of the disease. In many cases, the disease makes a sudden impression, the patient dropping down in a state of insensibility, while at his usual work. In these cases, reaction soon takes place, with violent determination to the brain.

" During the *winter months*," says Dr. B. " the morbid affection of the brain is not, at all times, so prominent a symptom," p. 6.

I have seen *intermittents*, and irregular remittents, the consequence of obstructed viscera, occur at this season ; but if vegeto-animal miasmata be the cause of " the bilious remittent," when aided by atmospherical heat, the winter is an unusual time for such a disease.

Dr. Burnett very justly remarks, that if the fever is not early combated, or if treated as a typhoid affection, the appearances will be very different. The head-ache will be accompanied by stupor, and an indifference to surrounding objects ; the eyes will have a duller look than usual, or have a yellow tinge spreading more or less, rapidly to the neck and body. The tongue will be covered with a thick yellow coat, while it is brown and dry in the middle. The prostration will be considerable ; the anxiety and pain in the limbs great ; the uneasiness in the epigastric region will be urgent, with bilious vomiting and harassing singultus.

" In the severe attacks," says he " about the third day, there is often an appearance of complete remission, but the evening puts an end to the delusion ; an exacerbation takes place, with great increase of all the dangerous symptoms. Unhappily, this deceitful period has often been mistaken for a real remission of the symptoms, and tonics and stimulants have been given, with a view to prevent the recurrence of the paroxysm ; but vain, indeed, are all such efforts, they serve but to increase the malady," p. 8. " As the disease advances, the pain and uneasiness about the *epigastric region* continue to increase ; there is constant vomiting ; considerable pain upon pressure, with restlessness and oppression at the præcordia. The abdomen is likewise painful, with frequently thin, black, fœtid, and sometimes gelatinous stools. The suffusion, at first of a bright yellow, now assumes a darker hue," &c. p. 9.

The symptoms which precede death in this fever, are pretty similar to those observable in the fevers of hotter countries, such as coffee-coloured vomiting, intolerable uneasiness in the epigastric regi on, hæmorrhages, subsultus tendinum, floccitatio, black encrusted tongue and teeth, sinking of the pulse, cold extremities, and finally death, which terminates the scene—" frequently on the third or fourth, but generally from the fifth to the eighth day ; though sometimes, death is protracted beyond that period," p. 10. Dr. Burnett, contrary to the observations of Cleghorn, asserts that " in by far the greater number of cases, though there are even exacerbations, there is but seldom any evident and clear remission in the morning.

Under the head of " probable causes," Dr. Burnett traces the influence of marsh miasmata in the fevers which prevail at Minorca, Malta, &c. with many interesting and sensible remarks on the topography of those places. Dr. B. reiterates the sentiments of former writers on the *exciting* causes of this fever; namely, intemperance, exposure to the sun by day, and the dews by night. The young and plethoric are most subject to the disease, particularly the crews of boats, and ships' companies, who have shared much prize-money, and are permitted to spend it on shore, p. 17.

Our author has not been able to detect the agency of contagion in its production, but rationally, we are sure, allows that " in the latter stages of this fever, where proper attention may not have been paid to personal cleanliness, to the removal of the excretions, and to ventilation, where the sick are crowded, the surrounding atmosphere may be vitiated," *ibid.*

Method of Cure.—Dr. Burnett judiciously enough divides the disease into four stages. 1st. From the beginning till the commencement of gastric symptoms or yellow suffusion, a period of about three days. 2d. From this period till the appearance of nervous symptoms, the duration of which is various. 3d. From the accession of these last symptoms, marked by increased uneasiness in the epigastrium, ischuria, singultus, coffee-coloured vomiting, &c. till death or convalescence. 4th. From the commencement of convalescence till final recovery.

Our author but too truly observes, that in the first stage of the disease, the prostration of strength, watery eyes, axiety, syncope on the abstraction of blood, &c. are well calculated to deceive the inexperienced observer.

" Blood-letting, both general and local, should be had recourse to, and repeated, according to the urgency of the symptoms : the benefit derived will be greatly increased by the use of purgatives and free ventilation. It will often happen, after a few ounces of blood have flowed, that syncope will be induced ; this must not prevent the repetition of the bleeding, while the symptoms require it," p. 20.

Dr. B. in imitation of Dr. Irvine, prefers arteriotomy at the temples.

- " In the course of an hour, the bleeding may generally be repeated, and thirty or forty ounces may be taken away without producing syncope. In bleeding, the patient should be laid in a horizontal position," *ibid.*

The purgatives which Dr. Burnett recommends, are those of Dr. Rush, namely, calomel and jalap. He justly remarks, that the oppressed pulse will rise under the lancet, and that an accession of strength is actually obtained by the loss of blood.

" The great object, says Dr. Burnett, is the removal of the local affection of the brain, or other organ, and the production of a complete remission of the febrile symptoms in the least possible time. In one instance, I ordered blood to be taken from the temporal artery, to the amount of ninety ounces in the course of six hours ; he was convalescent in three days," p. 22.

If, notwithstanding all our efforts, the febrile symptoms should continue, Dr. B. recommends in the evening, after a repetition, if necessary, of the bleeding, a pill composed of calomel and antimonial powder, each two grains, followed by a dose of julep. ammon. acetat. with cool drink, and the most strict antiphlogistic regimen.

In a note at page 34, Dr. B. states, that " it is but justice that I should add, that *some surgeons* thought benefit was derived from the use of calomel in the *first stage*, carried so far as to excite ptyalism."

After recommending decisive evacuations from the vascular system and the bowels, during the whole of the first stage, but condemning emetics, Dr. B. proceeds to the second stage, premising, that much confidence must not be placed in cold and tepid affusions, excepting as auxiliaries to the above measures.

In the second stage, he thinks, that where the symptoms indicate the necessity of venesection, it may still be resorted to, though in smaller quantities, and the blood is best drawn from the temporal artery. Blisters to the head, and daily evacuations from the bowels, are here proper ; but the cathartics should be of the less powerful kind, such as castor oil, assisted by enemas. The irritability of the stomach is to be allayed by the application of leeches, and the exhibition of saline draughts, in a state of effervescence to which may be added, *small* doses of tinct. opii. The application of a large blister to the stomach has been also attended with success. In this stage, Dr. B. speaks highly of the warm bath, and we entirely coincide with him.

In the third stage, " little more can be done than to look on, and endeavour to obviate occasional symptoms as they occur," p. 29. As the pulse sinks, the stimuli must be increased ; and Dr. B. thinks that he has seen much benefit from carbonate of ammonia and aromatic confection, in this dangerous stage of the disease. We must take care, however, while we labour to restore the balance of the circulation, not to induce a state of secondary excitement, and thus exhaust the flame we were endeavouring to keep alive. Even here, constant attention must be paid to the bowels, and daily evacuations procured. Dr. B. asserts, that the disease has seldom terminated in intermittent, under his own treatment ; but frequently under that of others.

" It appeared to be in general, occasioned by some morbid affection of the *brain*, liver, or other viscera," p. 31.

In these cases, he recommends mercurials till the mouth becomes affected. In the fourth or convalescent stage, the only interesting remark relates to the care we should take, in guarding against a relapse from repletion. While noticing the different remedies which have, in their day, been celebrated in this fever, Dr. B. asserts of cinchona, that, " under its use, mortality has been great, relapse frequent, and as in the cases of the Temeraire and Invincible, dysentery attacked nearly all the patients who had had fever in a severe form ; nor was there an instance, that when given during a supposed remission of the symptoms, it prevented a return of the paroxysms," p. 34.

On dissection, the vessels of the brain were generally found distended, and even gorged with blood, while the membranes were inflamed, and the ventricles containing serous effusions. In the thorax, the lungs and other parts were inflamed. In the abdomen, liver generally enlarged, frequently livid towards the lower edge of its concave side. Gall bladder moderately full of inspissated bile. Stomach generally, more or less inflamed, as also the intestines, p. 37. et seq.

The cases and dissections occupy more than eighty pages of the first part of our Author's work. They more than prove the grand object of Dr. Burnett, and of many judicious writers, who have laid the result of their experience before the public ; namely, that the lancet must be boldly used in those fevers, and in those climates, where the dogmas of the schools, and the timidity of practitioners, had nearly proscribed it. In this point of view, the accumulation of facts will firmly support the rising edifice of a more rational and successful mode of treatment than has formerly been employed, and Dr.

Burnett's work therefore, entitles him to the thanks and esteem of the public.

The second part of the work opens with a sketch of the Author's observations and practice in the Mediterranean, while serving on board the Goliath, Diadem, Athenienne, and finally, as physician to the fleet.   In the year 1799, a part of the Goliath's crew, that had been employed in watering the ship at Marsa Scala, in the Island of Malta, suffered an attack of bilious remittent fever, the prominent symptoms of which were, nausea, vomiting, head-ache, flushed face, full and frequent pulse, thirst, white tongue, and in most cases delirium.

" The patients were liberally evacuated on their complaining, and the bleeding repeated according to the urgency of the symptoms ; an open state of the bowels was preserved, and a mild diaphoresis kept up.   Blisters were applied to the nape of the neck and forehead, and a strict antiphlogistic regimen pursued.   This soon produced a cessation of the pyrexia, when tonics and a well-regulated diet completed the cure," p. 132.

In the succeeding year forty of the Diadem's crew were similarly affected at Port Mahon, " and so speedily was a remission procured by the free use of the lancet, that I had only occasion to send two or three to the hospital," p. 133.   Dr. B. here acknowledges that the use of emetics in a few of the first cases was highly prejudicial, a fact that will be experienced in the fevers of most warm climates.   In this fever, small doses of calomel and antimonial powder were given with advantage, after liberal evacuations ; and a simultaneous application of cold water to the head, and warm water to the lower extremities, was productive of beneficial effects, a circumstance that accords with our own experience in fevers of a similar type.   In one case, which proved fatal, Dr. Burnett's assistant gave the patient an emetic of tartarized antimony, the consequence of which was, that " the vomiting increased, and never afterwards for a moment left him ; he passed blood by the nose, mouth, and anus, and finally died in the hospital," p. 134.

, Let this prove a lesson against emetics in fevers of the warmer regions, where gastric irritability is one of the most formidable symptoms we have to encounter.

The Athenienne's ship's company having been much exposed to the ardour of a summer sun at Malta, while the vessel was docking and refitting there, was attacked with fever attended by great local determination, " but," says our Author, " by a proper use of the lancet in the *early stage*, joined to purgatives, they all speedily recovered," p. 135.

Shortly after Dr. Burnett was appointed physician to the fleet, in 1810, a fever broke out in the Achille, of 74 guns, at Cadiz, which was reported to the admiral, " *to be the yellow fever of the West Indies*, and of a very malignant and infectious nature."   This caused great alarm in the squadron ; but Dr. B. found that the symptoms were similar to those he had observed in the fevers at Mahon, &c. and that there was great determination to the thoracic viscera in particular. " Emetics, bark, camphor, wine, and opium were employed in the treatment of these patients," which Dr. B. very properly ordered to be laid aside, since two deaths had already occurred ; and "the lancet was had recourse to and used freely, and also purgatives ; this soon produced a change in the features of this disease, and the whole, except one man, speedily recovered," p. 136.

- Dr. Burnett arrived at Gibraltar in September, at which time the garrison was healthy. The thermometer ranged from 75 to 80, and about the 18th or 19th, a deluge of rain fell, and continued three days, the torrents from the upper parts of the rock sweeping down great quantities of putrefying vegetable and animal substances, which lay stagnant with the water in many places where the outlets were not pervious. After this the weather became very warm with easterly winds. In the last three days of the month 26 men, belonging to the St. Juan guard-ship, were sent to the hospital with the bilious remittent fever, four of whom died, none of which had been bled. The general treatment was purgatives, calomel, blisters to the region of the stomach, and gentle diaphoretics. The cold affusion was also tried, and proved useful.

From Mahon Dr. Burnett proceeded to Sicily, where he found that experience had already pointed out the necessity of evacuations when DEBILITY was the most prominent symptom, as is evinced in the communications from Dr. Ross, of the Warrior, and others. The army practitioners had, indeed adopted the most decisive depletory measures among the troops in Sicily, previously to this period, as our readers know, from the writings of Irvine and Boyle ; but in the navy it was only slowly introduced, and we believe Dr. B. met with some difficulties, which however, his zeal surmounted, in banishing from the minds of the medical gentlemen under his control, the phantom *debility*, and the delusive theories of the schools.

There is one circumstance which I have not yet noticed, though it has made a deep impression on my mind, namely, that throughout the descriptions which are given of this "bilious *remittent* fever," by Dr. Burnett and his numerous correspondents, no mention whatever is made of either diurnal or alternate *remissions;* excepting in the Temeraire and Invincible ; and I cannot help expressing my suspicion, that a great proportion of the cases were fevers occasioned by atmospherical transitions and irregularities, rather than by the application of vegeto-animal miasmata ; and that consequently, they were attended with more marked inflammatory symptoms, and assumed a less remittent type, than the fevers under whose denomination they are classed. Perhaps the term "bilious fever," (gastric irritability being so very general,) would be more proper ; and where the cause can be clearly traced to the operation of marsh miasmata, the epithet "remittent" might be properly added, because it is rare indeed that remissions on alternate day in particular, cannot be distinctly perceived. I have offered these suggestions because I am of opinion that some modification of the practice detailed by the author, is necessary in the more fatal endemics of the warmer climates, where that wonderful and powerful morbific cause—"marsh miasma," attains a state of concentration unknown in Northern latitudes. In the Temeraire and Invincible, where the fever was evidently the bilious remittent of hot climates, the treatment was founded on the directions of Lind, Clarke, and Balfou·, whose works continue still to produce incalculable mischief in the hands of inexperienced practitioners. But the more rational and successful doctrines and practices which have lately been promulgated by judicious medical men, both in the army, and navy, will dissipate, er long, the mists of prejudice, and annually save the lives of thousands of our countrymen. 'We have only to read the melancholy account of the fever in the two ships above-mentioned, to be convinced of these truths.

" On making inquiry, says Dr. B. as to the method of treatment which had been pursued with those men, I found it to have been by the use of *emetics*, calomel, antimony, *bark and wine in large quantities*, with full meals of animal food from the beginning, p. 158.

I hardly know how a surgeon could prescribe, or a patient take, " full meals of animal food," in a violent and acute fever, where all appetite is almost invariably destroyed. But the medicines were quite sufficient to produce the fatal catastrophe which followed. Those who did not fall immediate sacrifices, " were constantly relapsing ; several as frequently as three times, most of them once, and some of them were daily attacked with dysentery," p. 159. This was not all ; for the visceral derangements induced by these protracted and repeated attacks incapaciated them in great numbers for the service of their country, and left them to drag out a miserable existence in indigence and disease ! Such a e the fruits of adhering to Brunonian theories, and the doctrines of debility and putrescency, taught with such complacency and importance " in academic bowers and learned halls."

I have hinted that certain modifications of the treatment pursued by our author, would be necessary in the bilious remittent fevers of warmer climates, and the reason is obvious ; although in the Mediterranean the range of the thermometer equals at certain seasons the scale of tropical temperature, yet there is not that perennial ardor which, in equatorial regions, keeps the functions of the liver in so deranged a state as to render that organ peculiarly predisposed to disease, when the balance of the circulation is violently disturbed, as in remittent and intermittent fevers. On this account, liberal evacuations, in the early stages of Mediterranean fevers, and slight tonics or bitters afterwards, are in general sufficient to conduct to a happy termination : whereas, in other and hotter regions, particularly in India, the use of *mercury*, in addition to the means alluded to, is absolutely requisite to secure the biliary organs from obstruction or abscess.

" In the Repulse," says Dr. B. " Mr. Boyd reports that he had been very successful in combating it, [the fever,] by the early use of the lancet and purgatives ; cold and tepid affusion he likewise found serviceable, as auxiliaries. In some cases, copious and sudden affusion produced a diminution of febrile heat, sweats, and a remission. In *several* of the patients, he mentions *calomel* as having had *very excellent effects*. In one case of *great danger*, benefit appeared to be derived from the inunction of *mercurial ointment* on the epigastric region," p. 149.*

I have already stated my doubts respecting the propriety of classing all Mediterranean fevers under the head of " *bilious remittent*," as our author has done, and my belief that a great many of them occured totally independent of marsh miasmata. The following extracts will support this opinion. Mr. Allen, Surgeon of the hospital at Malta, after describing the general symptoms of a fever which broke out on board the Pomone, and remarking, that " The *head and liver* seemed to be the principal viscera affected in this fever," goes on thus : " The Weazle sloop, refitting at the dock-yard, has also sent us about thirty, with similar symptoms to the Pomone's. Our method of treatment has been, in the first instance, by the abstraction of thirty ounces of blood, the exhibition of a cathartic, and a bolus composed of calomel and antimonial powder, of each two grains, twice a day ; the mist. salin. In the evening, the bleeding, if necessary, was repeated. Next day, if the symptoms required it, recourse was again had to abstraction of blood, a blister applied to the epigastric region, and the febrifuge medicines continued. I consider this fever to have been brought on by *intemperance and exposure to heat*, constituting the bilious or yellow fever of the island. It is not contagious," p. 168.

In a subsequent fever, in the Weazle, Mr. Wardlaw, whom our author highly eulogises for his abilities, and whose statement consequently deserves attention, reports thus : " The state of the weather for these six weeks past has been extremely warm ; the thermometer ranging from 80 to 87 in the shade. The Weazle arrived at Malta in the month of June, and went up to the dock-yard to refit; the ship's company were then perfectly healthy. Liberty being given to go on shore, and they having received a considerable share of prize-money, intemperance was the consequence ; and next day, while very much debilitated, their duty necessarily exposed them to the heat of the sun. On the first attack, I took away from 20 to 30 ounces of blood, with saline draughts and cathartics, a bolus of calomel and antimonial powder, of each two grains twice a-day, *till the mouth was slightly affected*, generally completed the cure. The *liver and brain* seemed to be the only viscera affected ; the liver from obstructed ducts, and the brain from the great determination of blood to it," p. 170.

The remainder of the second part of Dr. Burnett's work is occupied in sketching the fevers of different ships, and stating the reports of their surgeons on the method of treatment, which entirely corresponded with what I have detailed in the foregoing pages. Bleeding, purging, and the exhibition of mercury were the prominent items in the " *Methodus Medendi*," and will, I am convinced, triumph over the boasted list of stimulant, antiseptic, and febrifuge remedies, so long imposed on the credulity of mankind by the fetters of prejudice, and the bigotry of preconceived theories.

* See Dr. Denmark's Paper on the Mediterranean Fever in the Medico-Chirugical Transactions, and Dr. Boyd's Paper on the Minorca Fever in a subsequent section.

- When the gates of Janus shall once more be thrown open, and the scourge of war, (which heaven avert !) be again suspended over the restless nations of the world, the medical officers of our fleets and armies will profit by the labours of the present race ; and the bold energetic measures of modern practitioners in the West, in the East, and in the North, will be remembered and imitated, when the authors who practised and promulgated these tenets shall have mouldered in the dust !

THE MINORCA FEVER ;

Translated and condensed from a Latin Thesis,

WRITTEN BY DR. WILLIAM BOYD,

(Formerly Surgeon of Mahon Hospital,)

Entitled—DE FEBRE MINORCÆ, &c.—1817.

SEC. III.—Although Dr. Boyd did not meet with this fever under the *remitting* type, as described by Dr. Cleghorn, yet he considers it as only differing in *grade*, from the marsh or bilious remittent of that and other authors. It is produced by the same causes—appears in similar places—affects the same organs—proves fatal to the same classes of people ; and only differs in consequence of atmospherical influences, and a greater intensity of force in the remote and predisposing causes.

This fever could be clearly traced to a *local* origin in Port Mahon ; and was therefore not contagious, but a primary and idiopathic disease ; assuming the *epidemic* character only from the state of the air, and the crowding of the sick. In spring, therefore, it appeared in its simple form. But these fevers, in various instances, *acquired* a contagious quality—that is, the power of propagating themselves from one individual to another. "*In casibus variis vim contagiosam haud raro acquirunt : id est, vim gignendi propagandi quoque eundem morbum ab alio ad aliud corpus,*" p. 3.*

Symptomatology—The first symptom was a sensation of cold, which crept along the spine, and over the lumbar region. To this succeeded head-ache, generally confined to the forehead, temples, and orbits. The face became flushed and tumid — the eyes inflamed and suffused with tears—the carotids and temporals pulsated violently. The countenance now became entirely changed, and in a manner not to be described in words ; while the patient betrayed great anxiety, restlessness—dyspnœa, with sometimes pain and sense of tightness in the chest, cough, inappetency—lassitude—thirst, and watching. The tongue is now whitish or yellowish ; but for the

---

* Dr. Denmark, Physician to the Fleet, who was at Mahon during the prevalence of this fever, and who declares that he was a noncontagionist, observes—" These occurences, however, served to stagger our belief ; and a combination of subsequent events has conspired to make me a convert to the opposite side of the question."—*Med. Chir. Trans. vol. vi.*

most part moist, with a bitter taste in the mouth. The heart beats with great strength against the ribs—all the tangible arteries feel hard and full—and a soreness in the flesh is complained of all over the body. The epigastric region is now very tender ; and there is nausea with bilious vomiting. Pains assail the loins—stretch down the thighs, and ultimately affect every joint and member. The bowels are obstinately costive. As the disease advances, the pulse feels less full, and is often weaker than in health ; while the thirst and anxiety are aggravated. At this period, the superior parts of the body will sometimes be covered with a profuse sweat, while the skin underneath shall feel burning and rigid. If the fever proceeds, the hot stages are generally, but not always, preceded by rigors.

When the patient neglects himself for one or two days after the first attack ; or if the treatment have been inefficient or improper, then a very different train of symptoms takes place. Together with stupor, there will also be great pain in the head—a disinclination to answer questions—and an insensibility, or at least inattention to passing occurrences. The eyes will be more turbid—often inflamed. A yellow tinge will cover the adnata, and suddenly spread to the face and neck, and thence over the whole surface of the body, in less than twenty-four hours. The tongue now exhibits a thick yellow crust—brownish and dry towards the middle—red and inflamed at the sides. The strength becomes remarkably diminished—the stomach is harassed with nausea and bilious vomiting—the heart beats less strongly, and more quickly—the countenance is collapsed, and the red tints unequally scattered over it.

After several accessions, and about the third day, these symptoms are suddenly and signally mitigated—the skin comes nearly to its natural temperature—the fever disappears, and nothing but debility apparently remains. But in a short time, an exacerbation supervenes. The disease acquires a renovated force, and shows itself under quite a different aspect. A new train of symptoms assail, with the greatest violence, the epigastric region. The sense of anxiety at the precordia is now changed into acute pain, which is greatly aggravated by pressure—the redness of the eyes changes into yellowness—the countenance is sunk—the tongue is brown, and trembles immoderately when attempted to be thrust out—the pulse is rapid and weak—all desire for food or drink vanishes—there is perpetual vomiting of putrid bile—the precordia are exceedingly oppressed—the patient sighs frequently—the stools are liquid—fœtid—slimy, and often bloody. The whole body is now of an intensely yellow colour, [totum corpus alte flavescit,]—and emits a fœtor resembling that of putrid bile. The patient's mind is now completely collected, and he answers questions with promptness and clearness—sometimes there is a little aberration or negligence of surrounding circumstances. From this time, that is to say, from the 5th till the 7th day, the patient is harassed with a train of nervous symptoms, as subsultus tendinum, tremors of the whole body, &c. which tend to exhaust the strength. ' With pain in the abdomen, there is difficulty of swallowing, and a sense of ulceration in the fauces, with vomiting of a glairy, or black matter resembling the *grounds of coffee.* [Nec non vomitus

materiæ glutinosæ nigræque, *fecibus choavœ* similis.]   Pain about the
pubes, an inability to make water—a dangerous symptom.*

In many cases, we observed swelling and suppuration of the parotid glands, with petechiæ before death.   In others, there were discharges of blood from the nostrils, gums, fauces, &c.   In others still,
instead of gastric irritability, we had diarrhœa, with discharges of
black fluid, which occasioned great tormina, and rapidly prostrated
the patient's strength.   The face, which lately exhibited a yellowish
or livid appearance, now became tumefied—the eyes lost all expression, and became glassy—the pupils dilated—clammy sweats broke
out unequally over the body—the tongue and gums turned quite
black—the breathing became more difficult—the anxiety more distressing.   From this time, coma or delirium, with coldness of the extremities and intermitting pulse took place ; and convulsions terminated the scene, from the 5th till the 8th day, sometimes sooner,
sometimes later than this period.

All the above symptoms were not apparent in the same person,
nor ran an equally rapid course.   In the young, strong and plethoric,
the march was more violent and hurried—in the elderly and enfeebled the disease was infinitely milder.—Turbid urine letting fall a copious sediment—discharge of bilious stools, at first black, afterwards
yellow' and copious, were favourable symptoms.   When the disease
continued beyond the usual time, and especially if the skin kept its
yellow tinge, the liver was almost always affected.   Relapses were
not unfrequent, particularly if great attention was not paid to a restricted diet during convalescence.

Ætiology.—*Intense heat*, which during the summer months prevail
without intermission in Mahon harbour, where a breeze seldom ruf-
fles the surface of the water—violent exercise in the open sun—intemperance of every kind, in which sailors, on getting ashore, so un-
guardedly indulge—exposure to the night, or to dews, wet, or cold,
after the body had been heated ; these were the principal exciting
causes that gave activity to VEGETO-ANIMAL EXHALATIONS which issue
in profusion from the harbour and vicinity of MAHON.

This port, so destructive to the health of belligerent seamen, is
situated low, and the surrounding sea is so tranquil, and the tides so
imperceptible, that whatever is thrown into the water remains almost
always in the same spot.   Now when we consider the quantities of
putrefying animal and vegetable substances that are daily launched
into the harbour, or exposed to a tropical heat on its shores ; and
couple these circumstances with the *stagnant* state of the water itself,
during the summer and autumn months ; and moreover, when we observe a pretty extensive lake in the vicinity of the port, which, in
winter, is filled by rains and springs, but in summer exposes its half-
dried, slimy bottom to the sun, whence pestiferous effluvia incessant-

---

* The above authentic document, drawn up by a gentleman of great talent
and observation, at the bedside of sickness, must remove all doubt relative to the
existence of yellow fever in the Mediterranean ; while the Section on Endemic
of Batavia must have convinced the most sceptical that the same disease appears
in the Eastern world, modified of course by climate, constitution, and cause.
Compare this description with Mr. Amiel's account of the Gibraltar fever.

ly emanate, [prope portum adest lacus, cui hieme ex aquis pulvis ac fontanis, constat ; sed estate fere arescit, et limosam massam putrescentem relinquit, ex qua pestifera effluvia haud cessant emanare,] we cannot be at a loss for the generation of those *morbific miasms*, which, in all hot climates and similar situations, give origin to fevers analogous to the one under consideration.

Prognosis : Favourable.—Little, or only mucous vomiting at the beginning of the second stage—moist skin—slow advance of the yellow suffusion—bowels becoming loose, with bilious stools—integrity of the nervous system and its functions.

Unfavourable.—Early accession of the yellow suffusion—deepness of its tint—early disturbance of the sensorial functions—deep redness of the face—dullness of the eyes—laborious respiration—feeble, creeping, and intermitting pulse—difficulty of swallowing—great tremour of the tongue—involuntary discharge of fœces, especially of a black, liquid quality—incessant vomiting of dark-coloured matters and great in proportion to the fluid swallowed—much anxiety.

Post Mortem Appearances.—The vessels of the brain much distended—coverings not rarely inflamed—depositions of coagulable lymph between the convolutions—adhesions occasionally between the hemispheres—ventricles sometimes distended with lympid or yellow lymph—*lungs* sometimes inflamed, with adhesions or effusions—pericardium inflamed with more than usual water in its cavity. Diaphragm often inflamed, with coats of coagulable lymph. Liver. in most instances, enlarged—often inflamed, with its inferior margin livid—Gall-bladder distended with viscid bile. Stomach and intestines often inflamed, and the villous cost of a dark colour.

These appearances, like the symptoms, were not all found in the same person, or together. In some dissections we found one set of organs, in others another, bearing the marks of disorganizing action. In general, however, the brain and lungs seemed to bear the greatest onus of disease.

Consilia Medendi.—The disease naturally divided itself into two stages—the first of reaction ; the second of collapse. In the first stage the object was to moderate or repress the violence of reaction ; in the second, to obviate symptoms, and support the energies of nature.

1st Stage.—Venesection is here our sheet anchor. No man can lay down a rule of *quantity*. Blood must be drawn till the symptoms are signally mitigated, whether at twice, thrice, or four times in the day. I do not think it of much consequence from what part of the body the blood be drawn. Some prefer the arm, some the jugular vein, others the temporal artery. To alleviate the head-ache, I think I have found arteriotomy at the temples most powerful But the vascular system must be promptly, and well depleted, through whatever outlet the current flows, otherwise some texture or organization will give way, and then the chances of recovery are faint indeed.

Mean time the head is to be shaved, and kept constantly enveloped with cloths wetted with the coldest water. This is an important measure, which should never be neglected. In my own person I experienced its good effects, in soothing the pain—diminishing the heat—and tranquillizing the irritability of the system.*

. *Purgatives.*—Our next step is to open the bowels, which indeed must be done through the whole course of the disease. For this purpose, and also to correct the vitiated secretions of the intestinal canal and liver, I have exbibited eight or ten grains of calomel every four hours, without ever observing any bad consequences from hypercatbarsis. In every case where ptyalism came on, the patient convalesced—the stools became natural, and the tongue clean—" In omni casu in quo (hyd submur) salivam movit, æger plerumque convaluit, naturales fiunt fœces, lingua nitida, ac humida." A cooling regimen is, of course, to be rigidly observed. The cold affusions and spongings are also valuable auxiliaries ; and where the reaction is not in a salutary degree, and the interior organs appear oppressed — tepid affusions will be necessary.

To relieve local symptoms—leeches to the temples, or cupping may be employed when general bleeding dare not be ventured on, Blisters also to the head—neck—spine—or precordial region must be had recourse to. In cases of great collapse and deficiency of the *vis vitæ*, the tepid bath will prove an important measure in drawing the circulation to the surface. The abdomen and extremities may also be fomented often as a substitute, or auxiliary to the bath.

Finally, when all danger of inflammation or congestion is over—and where great irritability of the heart and nervous system prevails, opiates may be administered, and with great solace to the feelings of the patient.

In the *second* stage, the great difficulty is to restrain the vomiting. Fomentations to the epigastric region are here useful, with opium, æther, and camphor internally—to which means must be added blisters. · Effervescing draughts with small doses of tinct. opii. ether, infusion of columba, may be tried, and even hot wine with spices—or brandy and water. Glysters with laudanum will sometimes restrain the gastric irritability ; and I have frequently given, where the strength was much exhausted, 30 or 40 drops of spirit of turpentine every two hours, with great advantage. Where stimulants are necessary at the close of the disease, port wine cautiously administered is the most grateful. Quassia and porter in small quantities during convalescence. But a constant attention should be paid lest the patient take too much food, which will readily induce a relapse.

I shall conclude this section with a few short extracts from Dr. Denmark's paper on the same fever. "A case of this fever will seldom occur wherein the use of the lancet, more or less, will not be applicable. But this powerful remedy is not in all cases infallible. The danger consists in either applying it too late, or too often ; and the abstraction of blood, under my own direction, has accelerated the patient's death, when circumstances seemed to justify the measure."

" I shall now say a few words on Mercury, our " sheet-anchor"

* Dr. Boyd nearly perished under this fever himself, but was saved by profuse bleeding. Dr. Denmark states that Dr. B. caught the fever from one of his patients. *Med. Chir. Trans. Vol. vi.* p. 301.

in affections where the biliary organs are implicated. Viewed in any way, the utility of mercury is incontrovertible. Calomel is beneficial in whatever way it operates. Whether it produce catharsis, when exhibited with a view to salivate ; or salivate, when intended to act as a cathartic, the result, in either case, will be salutary, though perhaps not to the same extent. I have prescribed it in various forms, in order to fulfil both these intentions, and the result has enabled me to speak most favourably of it. I have frequently recommended calomel in three grain doses, with as much pulv. antim. every three or four hours. The antimony seemed to assist the purgative operation of the calomel, and seldom failed to procure copious bilious stools, without creating nausea. In the treatment of this fever, however, I usually gave the calomel *in scruple doses* twice a-day, in many cases from the first invasion of the complaint, with the intention of speedily attacking the disease, through the system. But in this I commonly failed during the first days, in plethoric habits. Before the system was lowered, it evinced no effect through the medium of the circulation—it only kept the bowels clear. But after the lapse of two or three days, and the use of free venesection and purging ; and at an earlier period in debilitated subjects, and in cases of relapse, the mouth often became suddenly sore with profuse ptyalism, and rapid convalescence as certainly ensued. I do not recollect any deaths after the specific action of the mercury showed itself ; nor did the yellow suffusion occur after this symptom appeared." *Med. Chir. Trans. vol. vi. p.* 307.

I trust that this document will prove a standard record and faithful picture of the MINORCA FEVER, as long as that Island offers a commercial port, or belligerent rendezvous to the naval flag of Great Britain.

SICILY.

SEC. IV.—The climate of Sicily is always oppressively hot in summer, and seldom very cold in winter. Between April and August there is little or no rain ; towards the end of the latter month, the rains begin, but the heat continues till the middle of September, when it rapidly declines. From November till May, the heat is moderate, the mercury ranging from 50 up to 65 or 70°. In the summer months, and particularly in July and August, the thermometer *averages* 86 in the day, and is but a very few degrees less in the night. Sudden vicissitudes of temperature, however, are considerable—20 or 30 degrees in the twenty-four hours. Of course, local inflammations and congestions are common, and *phthisis pulmonalis* is frequently fatal.* Here, as in most hot climates, the houses are more calculated for counteracting heat than resisting cold, or preserving an equilibrium of temperature. Stone floors and unfinished casements ill suit the delicate frames of the consumptive in winter ; while in summer, the sensation of heat is so great, that many expose

* Hepatitis, according to the testimony of Irvine, frequently occurs in Sicily.

themselves to dangerous transitions rather than bear excessive warmth within doors. It is in this way, that many refer the origin of their pulmonary complaints to the most fervid season of the year. *Light* rains in autumn are observed to be unhealthy—evidently from their putting the surface of the earth in a state capable of evolving febrific effluvia : whereas, nothing is so salutary as *heavy* rains about the middle of September, which at once mitigate the heat and check the extraction of miasmata.

Sicily is penetrated in several directions by ridges of primitive hills of considerable height : between these are numerous water courses, which are dry in summer, and occasionally filled by torrents in winter. They are designated by the Sicilians, FIUMARI, and are used as roads in the dry seasons. Many of them are extremely unhealthy in the latter part of summer, and in autumn, and infested by what the natives term MALARIA. The state of this *Malaria* varies much according the state of the season. A very wet season will *overwhelm*, as it were, the sources of this febrific ; while a very dry one will so parch up the surface of the earth as to produce a similar effect. At LENTINI, however, around which the country is marshy, with a considerable lake in the vicinity, the ground is *partly* freed from water in hot weather, but is never so dry as to prevent the formation of miasmata. Here then is a Malaria every year. In many of the *fiumares* the stream disappears in the gravel, and percolates under the surface of the ocean. Thus at the bottom of the large *fiumare* which bounds Messina on the northern side, fresh water will be found at a foot depth close to the sea. It is in these kinds of fiumares that a Malaria prevails, according to the opinion of the natives, throughout the year ; and this probably accounts for the extrication of miasmata in many parts of the West Indies as well as Europe, where there are apparently no materials for their production. Thus some places in Sicily, though on very high ground, are sickly ; as Ibesso or Gesso, about eight miles from Messina, situated upon some *secondary* mountains lying on the side of the primitive ridge which runs northward towards the Faro, which has always been found an unhealthy quarter for English troops. It stands very high ; but still there is higher ground at some miles distance. Water is scarce here, and there is nothing like a marsh —At this station, however, sickness seldom occurs " unless after rains falling while the ground is yet hot, which is during the heat of summer; or early in autumn, when all circumstances combine for the production of miasmata." *Irvine, p. 6.* This may apply in elucidation of the Gibraltar fever. " I remember, says Dr. Irvine, a muleteer passing over the hills near Obessa, in the middle of August, during a heavy rain, who remarked that these rains falling on the heated ground would cause a stink, (puzza,) and that many would be poisoned." *Ib.*

In Sicily the north wind is cold—the west rainy—the south-east is the celebrated Sirocco, which seems to derive its noxious qualities from heat combined with dampness.—Here, as in most sultry latitudes, the summer and autumn are the unhealthy seasons.

The fevers of Sicily have been divided into three classes, those of summer, autumn, and winter. Those of summer have appeared to Irvine, Boyle, and others, to be of an inflammatory nature—to be principally owing to excessive heat—intemperance, and inordinate exercise. The head seems to bear the onus of disease. Dr. Irvine bled from the temporal artery, repeating the operation *pro re nata*. Blisters were applied to the head, and purgatives were administered internally. The cold affusion was then applied on the principles of Dr. Currie. " I never, says Dr. Irvine, in any one instance, saw the bleeding fail to remove the pain in the head, and when delirium was present, it lessened also that," p. 24. Encouraged by the alleviations of the symptoms, I persisted in my plan. I bled a third time from the head, and blistered again between the scapulæ, continuing the cold affusion. The number of times that this treatment was repeated was necessarily regulated by the effect produced. I never had occasion, however, to bleed more than four times. But the standard rule of my practice was to continue the bleeding and blistering of the head while any degree of head-ache remained, or any symptom of determination to the head was visible." *Ib.* Dr. Irvine found the bleeding pave the way for, and render more efficacious the cold affusion, which when applied without this preliminary, afforded only transient relief.

" The appearances on dissection were somewhat various. In some cases, nothing very remarkable could be, or was discovered in the brain or its membranes. In others the cerebral veins were turgid with blood. In many there was a red spot on the dura mater, about the middle of the longitudinal sinus, of the size of a dollar. Sometimes a little pus, or rather inflammatory exudation appeared upon this spot." *Irvine, p.* 36.—" I find it difficult, says Dr. Irvine, to reconcile the facts here stated, with the ingenious opinion of Dr. Clutterbuck. I do not think that phrenitis, or any analogous disorder of the brain, often, far less always, exists in fevers," p. 62.

In the autumnal fevers of Sicily, a great many, when the disease was violent " became excessively yellow" without any alleviation of their disorder. The stomach is more irritable—the vomiting is bilious, and of a dark-green colour—the region of the liver sometimes tender. These run out to a much greater length than the summer fevers, but only differ from them in being accompanied with earlier prostration of strength." " I can safely state, says Dr. Irvine, that the same sort of treatment which I have used in the summer fever, also proved successful in these," 45. Purging, however, was more necessary, and calomel and James's powder were found useful in protracted cases. " Touching the mouth with mercury is sometimes useful in cases where the yellowness is great," 47.

The winter fevers, according to Irvine, had nothing remarkable in their phenomena or progress ; but ran a course analogous to the ordinary cases of Synochus in England. " They hardly ever fail to yield to the four grand means of topical bleeding, [arteriotomy,] blistering—cold affusion, and purging," 60.

To the above observations by Dr. Irvine, which appear, on the whole, judicious and correct, I shall add some from the pen of Mr. Boyle, who, in my opinion, has given a more rational explanation of the symptoms, while his *Methodus Medendi* is equally effective as Dr. Irvine's.

When the epidemic first appears, says Mr. Boyle, in the early part of autumn, the fever preserves nearly a continued form, and only remits after the violence of the excitement has been subdued. It bears a strong analogy to the bilious remittents of all warm climates —is closely allied to the fever which visits other points of the Mediterranean shores, and seems to differ only in degree from those great endemics which have repeatedly ravaged the western hemisphere.

" In Sicily, says Mr. Boyle, this fever usually makes its appearance about the same time that cholera morbus and other disorders of the biliary organs are known to prevail, and both diseases seem to arise from causes of nearly a similar nature. It indeed appears to be essential to the production of this fever that a considerable diminution of temperature, accompanied with much humidity of the atmosphere, should *suddenly* succeed to the long-continued heat of summer. By those causes, an important change is effected in the *balance of the circulation*, causing an unusual determination to the abdominal viscera, and producing congestion or inflammation of the hepatic system, in various degrees, followed by an increased and vitiated secretion of bile." *Ed. Jour. vol.* viii. 184 *

The succession and order of the symptoms, marking the different stages and types of this fever, will be readily explained by the appearances on dissection, and seem to depend chiefly on the degree of inflammation, and the sensibility of the part concerned. When the liver is very violently affected, the symptoms sometimes even resemble those of hepatitis, and which more especially appear at the commencement of the fever ; and inflammation of the stomach is sufficiently characterized by the anxiety, restlessness, vomiting, and prostration of strength which immediately follow.

As a common consequence of extensive peritoneal inflammation, we sometimes find a quantity of serum effused into the cavity of the abdomen, and various adhesions formed between its parietes and the contained viscera ; and the omentum at other times so much wasted, as to resemble merely a tissue of red vessels. The liver almost always exceeds its natural size, and is also considerably altered in colour and texture. It is always softer than natural ; and the system of the vena portæ is always turgid with blood. The peritoneal covering of the liver is often thickened and opaque, and is sometimes studded with white spots, or with flakes of coagulable lymph. Sometimes its surface is irregular, and small indurated portions are discovered on its convexity, which, when cut open, are found to proceed from obstruction of some ramification of its excretory ducts, produced by inflammation of its coats, and favouring the accumulation of viscid bile.—The coats of the cyst generally partake of the inflammation. The colour of the bile it contains is various, and it is sometimes so viscid and thick, that it can scarcely be forced out by strong pressure.

A remarkable alteration also takes place in the appearance of the

* The reader will not fail to perceive the coincidence of Mr. Boyle's ideas with my own, though the writers were separated many thousand miles at the time.

spleen. It does not always, however, exceed the natural size, but its softness is often such, that it can only be compared to a mass of coagulated blood ; while, at other times, it has an unusual degree of hardness, with thickening and whiteness of its peritoneal coat.

The stomach is frequently found contracted and empty, or inflated with air, or distended with variously-coloured fluids, and even pure bile . Sometimes inflamed spots are covered on its peritoneal coat ; but the internal surface is the most frequent seat of disease. The texture of the villous coat is often completely destroyed, and it exhibits an uniform red, of the deepest hue, in several places approaching to a livid colour, and is covered with coagulable lymph, or a secretion of puriform matter tinged with blood. In other cases, the inflammation is more limited, and appears in rosy patches over its internal surface or in numerous minute red specks.

This inflammation is never of the phlegmonous kind, but like true erythema, successively invades one part after another, frequently creeping along the whole course of the alimentary canal, attended with thickening and pulpiness of its coats.

The brain and its membranes show no uncommon appearances, or marks of previous inflammation.

The lungs are not affected, but I have often found a large quantity of serum, of a yellowish colour, collected in the pericardium, while the heart seemed to have suffered from inflammation ; and in two or three cases, I observed white patches of coagulable lymph, apparently converted into firm glistening membrane, easily separated from its proper coats, on different parts of its external surface.

Such, indeed, is the rapid progress of the disease, and the great delicacy of the organ principally concerned, that our measures must necessarily be prompt and vigorous ; and under whatever varieties it may appear, with respect to type, the local symptoms always require our first attention, and indicate the necessity of copious evacuation of blood. If the fever be of the continued form, under such treatment it very often becomes intermittent, and when of this latter form, we thereby prevent its being changed into a more dangerous type, in the course of its progress.

From the use of this remedy, we are not always to be deterred by the smallness of the pulse ; and even if deliquium should come on after the abstraction of a few ounces of blood, the operation may be repeated soon afterwards, without the occurrence of the like accident.

This indiscriminate use of the term *debility*, derived from some of the more general phenomena of disease, without regard to its essence or cause, has led into egregious error in the treatment of this, as well as of some other complaints, which are commonly considered as simple idiopathic fevers. The anxiety, languor, restlessness, and prostration of strength which accompany this epidemic, are not symptoms of debility, but of gastritis, and depend on the peculiar structure of the organ, and its extensive sympathy with the whole system. A free use of the lancet is required ; and, in order that this remedy may be productive of beneficial effects, it must be had recourse to at an early period of the disease. Even when the disease was too far advanced for any permanent advantage to be expected from venesection, its effects have been discovered by a temporary increase of fulness of the pulse. What is here said, applies equally to general and local blood-letting ; and this last mode may be employed with considerable advantage.

In the inflammation of all delicate and highly sensible membranes, unless we succeed in the first instance, we in vain attempt to subdue it afterwards, by acting on the arterial system at large, and still further diminishing the *vis à tergo :* for the disease makes rapid progress ; the texture of the organ is speedily destroyed, and its vitality is irrecoverably lost.

Recourse must, therefore, at the same time, be had to such means as possess some control over the vessels of the part suitable to its peculiar functions and organization ; and the effects of local blood-letting, by the application of a number of leeches to the region of the stomach, are to be further assisted by large and repeated blisters.

Nothing so much aggravates all the symptoms, as the presence of acrid bile, and accumulated feculent matter. All irritation, therefore, from such causes, is to be carefully prevented ; and, with this view, the contents of the intestines are to be dislodged on the first approach of the disease, and their accumulation cautiously guarded against during its continuance. For this purpose, small doses of purgative medicines must be frequently administered. It too often happens, however, that the irritability of the stomach is such, that medicines of this class cannot be retained, but are instantly rejected ; and recourse, therefore, must also be had to large emollient and laxtive glysters, which must be frequently injected, and are in all stages of the fever, of the most essential service. As a purgative, no medicine is so well adapted to this complaint as the sub-muriate of mercury ; and its operation may be sometimes advantageously alternated with the use of sulphate of magnesia dissolved in water, and plentifully diluted.

The effects of mercury, however, are not to be estimated solely by its purgative quality ; but it seems to be chiefly useful on account of its specific action on the hepatic system, and its power of affecting, through the medium of the circulation, secreting surfaces endowed with high irritability, and in a state of inflammation. This remedy is, therefore, to be used externally, as well as internally ; and is to be resorted to immediately, as the most powerful remedy we possess in the treatment of this disease. Its effects, however, do not always depend on the quantity introduced ; but on certain conditions of the system, by which the latter is rendered more or less susceptible of its action, and which I do not pretend to explain.

This susceptibility is indicated by the effects produced on the salivary glands ; some degree of ptyalism follows, which affords the surest prognostic of a favourable termination ; and the change produced in all the symptoms is generally quick and rapid. It sometimes, however, happens, that the largest doses will not produce salivation, and in such cases, the event is invariably fatal.

From the rapid manner in which we are frequently induced, on account of the severity of the disease, to introduce this medicine into the system, copious salivation is frequently occasioned, and often appears suddenly, with bleeding from the gums ; but as no advantage is to be expected from the mere secretion from the salivary glands, I have succeeded equally well, after having ascertained its influence over the disease, by continuing its use in small doses, merely sufficient to keep up the mercurial irritation in the system, until the disease was completely overcome. From what has been said, it needs scarcely to be observed, that the practice of besmearing the gums with mercurial ointment, or rubbing them with calomel, for the purpose of encouraging this secretion, is extremely ineffectual.

Sometimes severe diarrhœa comes on during the early stages of recovery, attended with want of sleep ; in which case I have derived the greatest advantage from small doses of opium, combined with calomel.

We are usually advised, in *all* fevers which show a tendency to intermit, to watch this period carefully ; and to avail ourselves of the earliest opportunity such circumstances afford, of exhibiting bark in large doses, with a view to obviate the *debility* which, it is said, predisposes to the formation and return of another paroxysm. That in *some* fevers, and in certain habits and constitutions, this may be highly expedient and advisable, I do not venture to deny, as such practice stands supported by the best authority, and is justified by ample experience.

Without entering, however, into an examination of the above principles, which generally direct its use, I feel myself warranted to affirm, from the result of several cases in which this plan was adopted, in *the fever now under consideration*, that bark served only to exasperate the local disease, and to aggravate every symptom of the succeeding paroxysm.

In many cases which occurred towards the final cessation of the epidemic, at the close of the autumnal season, the local symptoms were much milder, and the fever became intermittent, after a moderate evacuation of blood, and a free use of laxative medicines. In those cases, calomel was the medicine I chiefly employed ; and I almost invariably observed that, when carried to an extent sufficient to manifest its action on the system by the usual criterion, the paroxysm soon after ceased to return."—*Ed. Journal.*

The testimony of such a man as Boyle in favour of the *union* of depletory measures with a mercurial treatment, will have some weight ; and in conjunction with the various documents brought forward in this essay, must remove all doubts on the occasional necessity of such a modification of practice.

EGYPT.

Sec. V.—Independent of those sensations of pride which every Briton must feel at the mention of Cairo, Alexandria, or the Nile, the memorable theatres of British valour, Egypt presents an interesting link in the medical topography of tropical and tropicoid climates. Stretching, in the shape of one of its own pyramids, from Cancer to the Mediterranean, and flanked on both sides by burning sandy deserts, the thermometrical and barometrical qualities of its atmosphere bear little similarity to those of parallel latitudes ; and hence the influence of this anomaly in climate on the health of the human race, is a matter of useful inquiry.

The thermometer at noon, in the shade at Cairo, averages 97° in the months of May, June, July, August, September, and October, with a diurnal vicissitude of 30 or 40 degrees. In the winter months, it averages 70°, and is never seen below 40.   During the hot season, from March till November, the air is inflamed, the sky sparkling, and the heat oppressive to all who are unaccustomed to it.   The body sweats profusely, and the slightest suppression of perspiration is a serious malady.   The departure of the sun tempers, in some degree, these heats.   The vapours from the earth soaked by the Nile, and those brought from the sea by northerly and westerly winds absorb the caloric dispersed through the atmosphere, and produce an agreeable freshness, which causes the susceptible Egyptian to shiver with cold ; excepting in the winter, and near the sea, a shower of rain is rarely seen.   The winds vary in their temperature and dryness or humidity, according to the point from whence they blow, and the season of the year.   From the north and west they are moist and cool, as passing over the ocean ; from all the other points they are hot and dry, as coming over vast tracts of burning sand.   The south wind, in particular, is called the *Kamsin, Simoom, Samiel, &c.* the heat of which is similar to that of a large oven at the moment of drawing out the bread.   The atmosphere now assumes an alarming aspect—the sky becomes dark and lurid—the sun loses his splendour, and appears of a violet colour.   The wind increasing gradually as it continues, affects all animated nature.   Respiration becomes difficult —the skin parched and dry ; and the body is consumed as though by an inward fire, for no quantity of drink can restore the perspiration. In December and January, however, these southerly winds are *cool*, as they then come over the snow-capt mountains of Abyssinia, the sun being at his furthest southern declination.

Now, as, in summer, the most prevalent winds come from the Mediterranean sea, impregnated with aqueous particles, so copious dews are precipitated in the nights of this period, all through the delta in particular, occasioned by, and increasing the diurnal transition.   Thus at Alexandria, after sun-set, in the month of April, the clothes exposed to the air, and the terraces are soaked by the dews, as though there had been a fall of rain.   To this it may be added that a portion of the valley of Egypt is annually overflowed, for two or three months in the summer, by the waters of the Nile, either by natural inundation, artificial canals, or machinery.

If this slight medico-topographical sketch, be compared with what I have said respecting Bengal and the Coast of Coromandel, it will, at once, be perceived that the climate of Egypt combines, in a considerable degree, the peculiarities of both the former.   It has the *inundation* from its central river, as Bengal ;—it has its *samiels* or hot land-winds, with an excessively high range of temperature, as Madras. Now if these two peculiarities equally prevail in Egypt, we may expect to find an equal ratio of the diseases peculiar to the two Asiatic localities above-mentioned ; whereas if we find one of the climates predominate over the other, and also one of the classes of disease obtain a proportional superiority, it will surely go far to elucidate and confirm the origin and nature of those endemics peculiar to the two oriental provinces, described in the early part of this work.

First, the inundations of Bengal and Egypt are very different. Accompanying the *former*, there are constant deluges of rain that keep all parts of the ground in a plash In the *latter*, what is not inundated is dry. In Bengal, the bed of the inundation, when the waters have subsided, remains long in a miry state. In Egypt, such is the power of the sun, the aridity of the atmosphere, and the force of perflation, that the water has no sooner deserted the plains than the *latter* are turned into a solid crust, which soon splits into innumerable segments. "At that time, the soil, in hardness, resembles one continued rock, and is fissured every where with deep chinks. When we encamped in the delta, it was impossible to drive a tent pin into it, except by fixing it in one of the openings ; and the detached clods, lying around, were hard enough to be used as mallets." *Dewar on Dysentery in Egypt*, p. 3—4.

From these circumstances, we are prepared to find that the extrication of *miasmata* in Egypt is on a very confined scale indeed, when compared with Bengal, and consequently that remittent and intermittent fevers are in proportion. "Egypt, says Dr. Dewar, is less ex-
"posed than most other flat countries, in high latitudes, to bilious
"fevers of the intermittent and remittent kind, as it is free from those
"marshy miasmata which serve to generate and to cherish the con-
"tagion of these diseases. Intermittent fevers only prevail during
"the decrease of the Nile, *in houses surrounded with stagnant water.*
"At other seasons they are confined to places in the neighbourhood
"of extensive *rice grounds*, such as the town of Damietta," p. 5.

It is true, indeed, that in particular situations, those natural causes which have happily secured Egypt from the deleterious influence of paludal effluvia, are counteracted by the perverseness and filthiness of the inhabitants. "This advantage, however, is counterbalanced by the dirty mode of living that generally prevails. The people seldom wash their clothes, and never shift them on going to bed. The offals of butchers' stalls are left in the open street, where they perpetually spread putrefaction and poison in the atmosphere. The sun would in some degree, obviate this mischief, by drying them into hardness ; but after they accumulate in the streets, they are thrown into the river or the sea, where they not only pollute the water, but *lying just within water mark.* [there are no tides,] are soaked with that quantity of moisture which is sufficient to keep the putrefactive fermentation in its most active state, and which allows them to disseminate their effluvia in the air." *On Dysentery in Egypt*, p. 6.

Now, having satisfactorily accounted for the *comparative* immunity from miasmal fevers, which the Egyptians enjoy, beyond the Bengalese, let us turn to the parallel between Egypt and the Coromandel coast." But here the disparity of climate is not so great as in the other two instances, and the great prevailing diseases are proportionally analogous. I have traced the *gradual* deterioration of the biliary apparatus on the Coromandel coast to a high range of temperature, and its *sudden* derangements to atmospherical transitions. The very same thing happens in Egypt—from similarity of cause. " Elephantiasis and leprosy, says Dr. Dewar, are frequent diseases in Egypt. *Obstructions in the liver and dropsies are still more frequent*," p. 6. How much our troops suffered from *dysentery*, which I have proved to be connected with *liver* disease, is well known to our army surgeons; and Baron Larrey was so struck with the prevalence of *hepatitis* in Egypt, that he has taken some pains to frame a theory for its explanation. He attributes the cause to a high range of temperature dissolving the fat of the mesentery, which becomes clogged in the liver. I do not quote his theory for its ingenuity, but to show the extent of the disease. And now I trust the idea of Dr. Saunders and many others, that hepatitis in India is owing to a *local indigenous poison* there, unlike any thing in any other country, will no longer be held. —This section has proved an identity of cause and a similarity of effect in India and Egypt, and consequently has solved a mystery that obstructed the path of medical science on an important point in pathological investigation.*

Before leaving the banks of the Nile let us glance at a few *indigenous* customs, from which the medical philosopher may often glean useful hints. The natives, during the hot season, subsist chiefly on vegetables, pulse, and milk. They make frequent use of the bath, and avoid stimulating beverages. Those who live in tents take care to have their coverings constructed double, in order that the nonconducting stratum of air may defend them from the atmospheric heat. Again, as in the East, the various folds of the turban form a powerful non-conductor, when they are exposed to the direct rays of the sun, and preserve them from *Coups de Soleil*, while the sash, like the oriental *cummerband*, encircling the abdomen, preserves the important viscera within from the deleterious impressions of cold, during a sudden vicissitude of temperature, or an exposure to the dews or night air ; thus forming an article of utility as well as ornament.

* I have already hinted that on the Coast of Africa where the heat is excessive, liver complaints are very prevalent. Of this I lately saw a striking example in the Tigress brig after returning from that station. No ship from India ever presented a more distressing picture of hepatitis and dysentery than this vessel did. Captain Beaver in his African memoranda gives the following thermometrical ranges of the six winter months, viz. from August to April. August 74 to 82—Sept. 77 to 85—Oct. 81 to 91—Nov. 84 to 96—Dec. 64 to 92—Jan. 63 to 98 —Feb. 88 to 96—March 86 to 95—April 85 to 94°. Captain Beaver's work shows the prevalence of hepatic diseases on the coast.

LOIMOLOGIA;

OR,

Practical researches on the Plague.

Sec. VI.—Many philosophers have attempted, and with no mean success, to trace a chain of animated beings from man down to the polypus ; and thence through the vegetable creation to the mineral in the bowels of the earth ; so that—

—————————————————" Whatever link we strike,
" Tenth, or ten thousandth, breaks the chain alike."

It would not, perhaps, be very difficult to show a similar catena-tion in the circle of diseases by which we are surrounded. There are scarcely two diseases, however opposite in their phenomena when viewed in an insulated shape, that are not linked together by others partaking in the nature of both. At a first glance the yellow fever and small pox would seem unmeasurably separated and widely dis-tinct in every respect ; yet the *plague* presents as fair a connecting link between them as the polypus does between the animal and vege-table kingdoms. Like Causus, the Plague is under the influence of the *atmosphere*, and limited within certain *thermometrical* ranges :— like small pox, it is propagated by contact, inoculation, or exhala-tion ; and productive, in general, of local eruptions. Nevertheless it is as distinguishable from either, as the polypus is from the Lord of the Creation on one side, or the Cedar of Lebanon on the other.

This destructive and mis-shapen enemy of the humane race has ever been clothed in darkness and mystery, which add not a little to its real and imaginary terrors.—It may justly be characterized as a—

" Monstrum horrendum *informe*, ingens cui *lumen* ademptum !"

Which unites all the bad qualities of the two diseases alluded to. It combines the rapid march and fatal issue of the western causus, with the dire contagious influence of the eastern Variola !*

Such an engine of destruction must, long ere this, have annihilated mankind, had not the omniscient Creator encircled it with various atmospherical barriers which are constantly arresting its progress, or suspending its powers. If " the pen of writers has done little more than record the times and places when and where it proved most fatal —its devastations, and the variety of modes of treatment which had no certain success," be it remembered that this very sentence, so dis-heartening to the medical philosopher, was, not long since, applied to *dysentery*, over which we have now a very strong control. All then may not be lost in respect to the plague. It may yet come under rule, and bow beneath the influence of medicine. At all events, it

* One of the latest writers on the subject of plague, Dr. Calvert, asserts that its poison radiated through the *atmosphere* on the inhabitants of Valletta, from a vessel in the centre of the quarantine harbour, and consequently that all precau-tions against *contact* were useless and delusive.—*Med. Chir. Trans. vol. vi.*

is our duty, as it ought to be our pride, never to succumb without a struggle. Let the Ottoman lie supine under the fetters of fatalism, while the Christian philosopher exerts those faculties bestowed on him by his Creator, in defending that Creator's noblest work from *premature* decay!

Although the venerable and laborious Russel shall form the text or basis of this section; other and more recent writings will not be overlooked. But as *references* and formal *quotations* would swell the work too much; and as I have no particular theory or practice to support on the occasion, the reader will probably give me credit for fidelity and accuracy in the compilation, and absolve me from all suspicion of misrepresentation.

Previously, however, to entering on the symptomatology, &c. of the disease, it is necessary to state that I have derived much assistance from my esteemed and able friend Dr. Dickson of Clifton, in this section of my work. Dr. Dickson, while stationed in the Levant, in the year 1803, had frequent opportunities of collecting interesting information relative to plague, and particularly from Padre Luigi de Trincon who, for a great number of years, had been superintendant of the plague hospital at Smyrna. The history of this venerable and benevolent man, as related by himself, and authenticated by others, is briefly this. Having been most severely attacked by the plague, about thirty-six years previously, and his life being despaired of, he made a vow, in the event of recovery, to dedicate his services to those who should be similarly afflicted. He recovered, and for some time adhered to his resolution; but the desire of revisiting Pavia, his native country, induced him to leave Smyrna. His vow, however, continually recurred to him; and he soon returned again to Smyrna, where he has ever since pursued his original resolution of attending on those afflicted with plague. He administers to his patients with his own hands;—consoles and cheers them;—sits, and even sleeps upon their beds; and in fine has been principally indebted for his success to such attentions, as he knows little of medicine.

Sub-sect. I.—*Symptomatology.* Fever.—This, according to Russel, was, with very few exceptions, a constant attendant at one stage or other, but varying greatly in different subjects. Usually preceded by sense of weariness, shivering, and confusion rather than pain in the head. Cold stage shorter than in tertian; but the symptoms in hot stage more anomalous and alarming. In many cases, however, the pyrexia differed so little from that in other fevers, as to lead to no diagnosis, unless buboes were protruded, which left no doubt. Fever usually declined in the morning of the second day: but varied much in intensity of force, even in the 24 hours; the exacerbations being irregular as to violence and duration. Generally speaking, there were morning remissions and evening exasperations. Still the march of the disease was rapid—the patient, on the second or third day, being reduced, in point of muscular strength and sensorial energy, to the condition of one in the last stage of typhus. Yet to this desperate state would succeed a remission in which his senses and intellectual faculties were restored—the vital functions went on calmly, and all but weakness seemed to have vanished like a dream.

Remissions of this kind, when early in the disease, or unpreceded by a sweat, were often fallacious ; but when on the third day, or later, and induced by a sweat, especially if the pulse kept up, and the head clear, they gave hopes of a favourable issue.*

Delirium.—Not so high as in some other fevers †—seldom commenced before the second day, increasing in the exacerbation, lessening in the remission—sometimes going off for some hours in the day, but returning at night. Padre Luigi corroborates this statement, but has seen delirium and insensibility come on early.

Coma.—Very often alternated with the delirium.—It was always a dangerous symptom ; but more so as it approached early, and failed to abate in the remissions. The patient is roused without difficulty —answers rationally at first, but soon becomes impatient—denies having slept, and as soon as left, relapses again into slumber.‡

Loss of speech, faultering, and tremor of the tongue, were not uncommon symptoms. Impediment of speech sometimes continued for months after recovery. Dr. Dickson, who had frequent opportunities of seeing plague in the Levant, observes that the tremor of the lips is often of a peculiar kind, a sort of biting motion, which is a dangerous symptom.

Deafness was seldom observed ; though the sense of hearing was occasionally impaired. Dr. Dickson informs me that the patients sometimes became deaf.

Muddy Eyes.—This was a remarkable symptom. It sometimes was visible from the first day, but more commonly from the second or third, remaining till some favourable change took place. It is a strange compound of muddiness and lustre—is little affected by the remissions ; but, in the exacerbations, the eyes acquire a redness that adds wildness to the look. The disappearance of this symptom is always favourable. It was almost invariably present in fatal cases. Sir B. Faulkner considers it without doubt one of the most leading and faithful monitors of the presence of plague. He was seldom wrong in his diagnosis, where any unusual whiteness of the tongue accompanied this appearance of the eye—" even though there was no intumescence or redness about the glands, nor any confession of complaint." In the first instance which Dr. Dickson saw of the plague, and where he was unintentionally a visitor, he was particularly struck with the drunken appearance of the eye, and was at a loss what to think of the case, until the patient showed him a bubo in his groin !

White Tongue.—The tongue was often natural ; but when it changed, it generally became white, and remained moist. Sometimes it

* The *initiatory* symptoms, according to Faulkner, the latest writer, were at Malta, besides the foregoing, pain of the back opposite to the kidneys—drunken appearance of the countenance—inability to stand upright—aversion to being thought ill. " I have neither drunk wine nor spirits," said General Menou, " and yet I feel as a drunken man."

† Sir B. Faulkner found it rise to *maniacal fury* in some instances, at Malta.

‡ The comatose symptoms strongly resemble those of the Mariegalante fever, so well described by Dr. Dickson in a subsequent section.

was parched, with a yellowish streak on the sides, and a reddish in the middle ; but its condition rarely corresponded with the febrile symptoms.

Pulse, is generally low, quick, and equal ; in some bad cases, fluttering or intermittent, or low and nearly natural.—In the more advanced stages of the disease, instead of rising in the exacerbations, the pulse was apt to quicken and become so small as scarcely to be felt.   At Malta, in the last plague, the pulsations in ulterior periods, seemed to succeed each other in a continued stream, and defied calculation.   But this function varied so much as to be *res fallacissima.*

Respiration was seldom affected, except in the exacerbations of advanced stages, when it became laborious.   No pain felt on a full inspiration.   Yet the patients frequently sigh, as if from oppression on the lungs.

Anxiety, that is, a sense of oppression about the præcordia, is a constant attendant on the plague ; and its early appearance was unfavourable. " The sick," says Russel, " showed how severely they suffered, by their perpetually changing posture, in hopes of relief ; but when asked where their pain lay, they either answered hastily, ' they could not tell,' or with a fixed, wild look, exclaimed—' *Kulbi ! Kulbi !*' (my heart ! my heart !)   This anxiety encreasing as the disease advanced, terminated at length in mortal inquietude," p. 88.

Pain at the Heart.—Though this was often conjoined with, it was often distinct from the anxiety above-mentioned.   The patients often exclaimed, as in the other case, my heart ! my heart ! pointing to the *Scrobic. Cordis ;* but then they would add *eujani Kulbi,* my heart pains me ! or *naar fi Kulbi ;* my heart is on fire !   They could not bear the slightest pressure at the precordia.

Debility.—The sudden prostration of muscular strength and nervous energy appertains in a particular manner to the plague, beyond that observed in any other disease.   By its higher degree the more fatal forms of plague were distinguished. " In the most destructive forms of the plague, the vital principle seems to be suddenly, as it were, extinguished, or else enfeebled to a degree capable only for a short time to resist the violence of the disease.   In the subordinate forms, the vital and animal functions, variously affected, are carried on in a defective, disorderly manner, and denote more or less danger accordingly."—*Russel,* p. 89.

Fainting, in different degrees, was a very common symptom, and sometimes, though rarely, terminated in syncope.   It was not so much aggravated by the perpendicular, nor relieved by the horizontal posture, as in other fevers.

Convulsions sometimes mark the access of the fever ; and convulsive motions of the limbs frequently attend the course of the disease, especially where there is a numerous eruption of carbuncles.   *Subsultus tendinum* is not a very common symptom ; but a continual trembling of the hands is generally observed.   Luigi informed Dr. Dickson that singultus was not an uncommon symptom, and that sneezing was a very favourable phenomenon.

Urine.—Nothing decisive can be learnt from this excretion.   Luigi, however, frequently observed it of a very high colour, and depositing a lateritious sediment.—*Dickson.*

Perspiration.—Where the skin remains torpid and dry continually; or where short and precipitate sweats are attended with no favourable symptoms, danger is to be apprehended, On the other hand, the spontaneous supervention of an early perspiration is a flattering omen.

Vomiting.—This symptom, according to Russel, is "absent in a large proportion of the sick." Where it began early, and continued obstinate, it was a fatal symptom.—Bile was sometimes thrown up, accompanied with bitter taste in the mouth —" a yellowness in eyes," and "a blackish liquor sometimes came off the stomach in the last stage of the disease, in the production of which, blood may, perhaps, have had some share."—*Russel.* Faulkner makes no mention of *vomiting* in the late plague at Malta; but says, that in the worst species the " stomach was extremely irritable." Russel admits that *nausea* was more common. Is not "stomach extremely irritable" equivalent to the mention of vomiting?

Diarrhœa,—sometimes comes on the first day, but more usually supervenes in the advanced stages of the diseases, and in either case, unless other things were favourable, may be set down as a *signum funestissimum.* Russel, and Faulkner. The latter observes that, in the plague at Malta, the alvine evacuations were commonly of a darker appearance than natural—sometimes of a greenish tinge mixed with scybala, particularly where voracity of appetite attended. . Dr. Russel sometimes saw dark-coloured blood discharged by stool, unmixed with feces, and without griping. " *Costiveness was attended with no harm, and often with little inconvenience.*" Russel. Luigi confirms this remark.

Hœmorrhages were, in general, unfavourable symptoms.

Thirst, the never-failing attendant on febrile diseases, is by no means invariably present, even in the worst forms of the plague. "The like remark holds of want of appetite. Throughout the disease, this function is not only *not* impaired but augmented to a degree bordering on voracity." *Faulkner.*

We shall not follow Dr. Russel through his six classes of the disease, but rather adopt the concise and less complicated divisions of Sir Brooke Faulkner, in his recent description of the plague at Malta.

Species I.—That in which, at the first attack, the energy of the brain and nervous system is greatly impaired, indicated by coma, slow drawling or interrupted utterance. In this description of the disease, the tongue is white, but little loaded with sordes, and usually clean, more or less, towards the centre and extremity; the anxiety is great; cast of countenance pale; stomach extremely irritable, and the strength much impaired. Rigors and pain in the lower part of the back are among the early precursors of the other symptoms. This was observed to be the most fatal species of plague, and prevailed chiefly at the commencement of the late disasters. Those who were thus affected died sometimes in the course of a few hours, and with petechiæ.

Species II.—The next species I would describe is, that in which the state of the brain is the very reverse of what takes place in the former, the symptoms generally denoting a high degree of excitement : the pain of the head is intense ; thirst frequently considerable, though sometimes wanting ; countenance flushed ; and utterance hurried. The attack is ushered in by the same rigors and pain of back as the foregoing. Epistaxis not unfrequently occurs in this class of the disorder. The glandular swellings come out very tardily, and after appearing, recede again. without any remission of the general symptoms. Carbuncles arise over different parts of the body or extremities, which are rapidly disposed to gangrenous inflammation. The delirium continues extremely high and uninterrupted, and the patient perishes in the course of two or three days. Sometimes he lingers so far as the seventh. yet rarely beyond this period, without some signs of amendment. Of this second description. the examples have been very numerous, and were nearly as fatal as the preceding. In the countenances of some, just previous to the accession of the more violent symptoms, there is an appearance of despair and horror which baffles all description, and can never be well mistaken by those who have seen it once.

Species III.—The third species which I would enumerate, is nearly a kin to the last. only the symptoms are much milder. and the brain comparatively little affected. The buboes and other tumours go on more readily and kindly to suppuration, and by a prompt and early employment of remedies, to assist the salutary operations of nature, the patient has a tolerable chance of surviving. Cases of this kind are often so mild, that persons have been known to walk about in seeming good health, and without any evident inconvenience from the buboes. Of this last species, the instances have, thank God, not been unfrequent, chiefly occurring towards the declension of the malady.".

Buboes and Carbuncles.—The presence of these, separately or in conjunction, is diagnostic of true plague ; and removes all doubt as to its nature ; " but fatal has been the error of rashly, *from their absence*, pronouncing a distemper not to be the plague, which, in the sequel, has desolated regions, and which early precaution might probably have prevented from spreading."—*Russel.*

Although in some of the worst forms of the disease, [for instance in Russel's and Faulkner's *first* classes, where the patients frequently perished in twenty-four or thirty-six hours,]—buboes and carbuncles are rare, yet. generally speaking, they may be considered as constantly concomitant phenomena :—not so carbuncles, which were observed in about one-third of the infected only. The inguinal, axillary, parotid, maxillary and cervical glands were the seats of buboes in the order they are set down ; but the *first* was by far the most frequent. The inguinal pestilential bubo was, for the most part, situated lower in the thigh than that of the venereal. A burning. shooting pain, is often felt in the part, anterior to the appearance of swelling ; and, when the tumour is once formed, there is always pain on pressure. In the incipient state of the bubo, a small, hard, round tumour is felt by the finger, more or less deeply. seated, but generally moveable under the skin, which is yet colourless and non-protuberant. As the gland enlarges, it commonly takes an oblong form—becomes more moveable,—and the integuments thickening, protrude into a visible, circumscribed tumour, without external inflammation. The progress to maturity is more or less rapid ; but not apparently influenced by strength of constitution or the contrary—hence the prognosis from the bubo is very uncertain.

In Dr. Russel's experience, the bubo seldom began to inflame *externally*, or show symptoms of maturation till the fever had abated, and was manifestly on the decline. This happened at various periods, but rarely sooner than the 8th or 9th day, the inflammation then advancing, the tumour, by degrees softened, and opened of itself between the 15th and 22nd day. The buboes that did not suppurate, dispersed gradually in one or two months.

In a very large proportion of Dr. Russel's patients the buboes made their appearance in the course of the first day. In the slightest cases, they were often the first sympto n of infection.

Carbuncles were seldom observed by Dr. Russel before the month of May—they grew rife in the summer, and became gradually less common in autumn. The carbuncles that fell under the observation of Sir Brooke Faulkner in the late plague in Malta were of that kind described by authors as the *wet carbuncle*, sloughing into very deep sores, and attended during the progress of inflammation, with an extremely painful burning sensation. At first, they arose like a phlegmon, gradually acquiring a diffused and highly inflamed base, and having, not far from the apex, a concentric areola of a deep livid, and more internally of a cineritious colour, and a glossy appearance. These carbuncles were not confined to any particular part of the body or limbs, though most commonly they are situated upon some part of the extremities. Of the *dry* carbuncles, as they occurred in a few cases, the description corresponds with that of authors—being of a dark, gangrenous colour, without much pain, with little or no inflamtion, or elevation above the surface. *These* were always unfavourable symptoms.

Petechiæ in the plague at Malta were various in point of size and colour—in some, of a dark, or dusky brown—in others livid—in some, so small as to be almost imperceptible—in others, as large as flea bites. *Situation*, over the breast, arms, wrist—sometimes over the back, or lower extremities.

Pathology.—As scarce a ray of light beams upon this subject from *Post Mortem* researches,* and probably never will, we are left to ground our pathological *opinions* on the phenomena of the disease, in its course to recovery or death. Upon a careful review of these, it is but too plain that *remedial measures* have had, as yet, scarcely any control over plague. In the *graver* forms, medicine has been

* Baron Larrey opened a few bodies dead of the plague in Egypt, and found the liver engorged and disorganized—the stomach and intestines gangrened—the heart soft and flabby. The brain was not examined. One of the assistants who helped to open the bodies caught the plague and died. The above phenomena are little different from those presented as the effects of other fatal congestive fevers.

confessedly useless—in the *milder,* it was probably unnecessary—in the intermediate shades it may have had some influence. From this, and various other considerations, we may most safely conclude that plague, though influenced by the atmosphere, is propagated by a poison or contagion, strictly *sui generis,*—equally as much so indeed, as that of variola. Now, over any one of these *eruptive* contagions, excepting the syphilitic by *mercury,* and the variolous by inoculation, we have not one particle of power, *after* it is received into the system.* In what way they produce their baneful influence on the living machine we are nearly, if not totally ignorant ; but their effects are expressed by three great features or phenomena—depression and reaction, with a local determination. In the *first,* when excessive, and consequently dangerous, the powers of the system seem paralyzed or *stifled,* and are not unfrequently annihilated ;—In the *second,* when excessive, and consequently dangerous, Nature appears in her frantic efforts, to commit suicide on herself, by destroying some organ essential to life, or exhausting, beyond recruit, the whole fabric ; —In the *third,* or local eruption, some *sanative* process is effected, of which we *only* know that it *is* sanative—

> ————————————Sive illis omne per ignem
> Excoquitur vitium, atque exudat inutilis humor :—
> Seu plures calor ille vias, et cæca relaxat
> Spiramenta.   *Georgicorum, lib.* 1—*p.* 87.

Now till we find out *specifics* for the other contagious poisons, as mercury proves in syphilis, the sum total of our knowledge leads but to this ; that in the *first* instance, we are to endeavour to rouse or animate—in the *second,* to curb or restrain, and in the *third,* to leave alone, the EFFORTS OF NATURE.

This reasoning, indeed, will very nearly apply to the whole range of fevers ; but unfortunately there is something more mysterious and intractible in those accompanied by *eruptions,* than in any of the others. This is particularly the case, in those forms of plague where nature appears to lie prostrate under the influence of the poison, without the power of resistance, much less of reaction ! Here we may apply the warm bath to the external surface of the body, and cordials or stimulants to the internal ; but alas ! the nervous and vascular systems are so entirely deranged, that nature, unable to avail herself of our assistance, sinks in the struggle, without the means of extricating herself from the mortal grasp of the enemy, or the power of accelerating her own destruction !

Plague, as an eruptive fever, differs so essentially from endemic or miasmal fevers, not only in respect to its contagious origin, but its critical determinations, and also the mode of treatment, that one would hardly expect to find an amalgamation attempted in the present day. Yet such a doctrine has been recently maintained by two medical gentlemen, Dr. Robertson, and Mr. Torrie.† The latter asserted that the plague was *not* contagious, and fell, of course, a victim to his own infatuation ; the former endeavours to show that the

---

* I mean we have no power in arresting the progress of the *poison;* though we have much in mitigating the violence of reaction in the *system* itself.
† London Medical Repository, Dec. 1817.

causes of plague and remittent fever are the same, that the symptoms, and *post mortem* appearances differ only *in degree*. He acknowledges, however, that he never saw the plague, and independently of this, his arguments are not of that weight that require a serious refutation.

Therapeutics.—The following is an abstract of Dr. Russel's *Methodus Medendi.* One early *bleeding*; which was very seldom repeated, excepting where circumstances unequivocally demanded it. Where vomiting was a concomitant symptom, it was encouraged by draughts of warm chamomile tea, till the stomach was well cleared of bile or other colluvies. Where this was not sufficient, an emetic of ipecacuan, was exhibited, after which an opiate. *Purgatives* were rarely given.

As soon as the stomach was settled, mild sudorifics were administered in small doses, as the acetate of ammonia and citrate of potash. If a diarrhœa prevailed, as it was never observed to prove critical, it was restrained by diascordium and opiates. Dilution—cool air in the beginning; but towards the height of the exacerbations, upon the first appearance of moisture on the skin, the sick were kept moderately covered up from the chin downwards. The diet was the lightest possible. For the coma and delirium, sinapisms and pediluvia were employed. For the oppression at the præcordia, mild cordials, accidulated drinks, and cool air were serviceable. After the height, and through the decline of the disease, bark in powder or tincture was exhibited. In the decline of the disease purging was employed by the European, but seldom by the native practitioners. Relapses, though exceedingly rare, do sometimes take place.

Treatment of the Plague at Malta.—Sir Brooke Faulkner's indications are, 1st. when inflammatory symptoms are violent at the *beginning*, to moderate them cautiously. 2nd. to restrain all inordinate efforts of nature; or support her when exhausted. 3d. to counteract putrescency. 4th. to evacuate the morbific matter. These indications are proposed to be fulfilled by evacuants, tonics, antiseptics, blisters, sudorifics.

Evacuants.—Purgatives are rarely ventured on by the Maltese, except in very strong, plethoric habits, when sulphate of magnesia is given. At other times, supertartrite of potash, manna, almond oil, &c. are most esteemed. *Bleeding*, even locally, was a precarious remedy, and no decisive benefit was obtained from its use. *Blisters* to the temples, nape of the neck, head, and shoulders were applied, in high delirium, or very low coma. Sinapisms to the soles of the feet. Mild emetics of ipecacuan, at the very beginning.

The Maltese prescribe bark, colombo, gentian, and serpentaria, as soon as the state of the head allows. As a *sudorific*, the acetate of ammonia was preferred. Opium in some cases was useful; but required caution in the administration. Wine was given in the advanced stages, and often with benefit; but required great limitation. The same of cordials. The surgeon of the 3d Garrison Battalion, Mr. Stafford, has published several cases in the 12th vol. *Ed. Journal*, where mercurial frictions, externally, and calomel internally, proved very successful. The warm bath also proved useful. The cold af-

fusion was tried in a few cases, and Sir B. Faulkner is inclined to
augur favourably of it, when guided by the principles laid down by
Currie.

Such is nearly the sum of the information Dr. F. has been enabled
to collect upon this disheartening subject.   It only verifies the words
of the Poet—

> Dum visum mortale malum tantoque latebat
> Causa nocens cladis, pugnatum est arte medendi,
> Exitium superabat opem, quæ victa jacebat.

Prophylaxis.—Since we have made so few advances in the *cure*,
we must be the more vigilant in regard to *prevention*.   Of all the
means which have been recommended by ancients or moderns, none
are equal to personal cleanliness—temperance—avoiding *contact*, or
using immediate ablutions afterwards—shunning the breath, or vapour exhaling from the bodies of the sick—ventilation—moderate
exercise—attention to the great functions of digestion, perspiration,
biliary secretion, &c.—Confidence.   But a most important measure
is the use of *oiled dresses*, the texture of which is so completely close
as to prevent the passage of the most minute particles of any matter
from without.   By these means every attendant on the military pest
hospitals in Malta escaped the contagion.   As to oil frictions, they
are precarious preventives, though highly recommended by some,
particularly Baldwin and Luigi.

The oil dress over every part of the body, while a sponge moistened with vinegar is held to the face, seems the most certain prophylactic.   Might not a mask be annexed to the oil dress, with a tube
of leather fitted to the mouth, and leading out of a door or window,
through which the medical attendant might breathe while visiting the
infected in Pest Hospitals and Lazarettos ?

Since writing the above, a mask has actually been constructed by a
foreigner, composed of pieces of light fine spouge, which are to be
soaked in different kinds of fluids, according to the nature of the de-
leterous gas or febrific miasm against which we are to guard.   This,
upon the whole, seems better than the mask and tube.

Since the second Edition of this work was printed, one or two Members of the House of Commons were deluded by Dr. M'Lean's writings into a persuasion that Plague was not contagious.   Accordingly
a committee was appointed, and the Author of this work, among
others, was examined.   But nearly the whole of the evidence went
so completely against the wild speculations of the learned Doctor,
that the Plague question has dropped to the ground !

COAST OF AFRICA.

Some Account of the Climate and Medical Topography of the West Coast of Africa. From the Quarterly Journal of Foreign Medicine and Surgery for January, 1821.*

In the view we shall endeavour to present of the topography of the coast of Africa as influencing the human system, our observations, although confined to that part, commonly known under the appellation of the coast of Guinea, will, nevertheless, from the general aspect and nature of the soil and seasons, be applicable to a considerable portion of country extending in both a northerly and southerly direction from that embraced in the following Memoir. That part of the African coast to which we shall limit our description, (and which was presented to our personal observation,) commences at Cape de Verde in lat. 15° north, and 16½° west longitude, and extends first in a southeast direction, and afterwards direct east to Cape Formosa, in 4° north lat. and 5° east longitude, comprehending upwards of two thousand miles of the African shore within its range.

This part of the coast becomes interesting in many points of view. Towards each of its extremities are situated all the African settlements possessed not only by this country, but also those belonging to the Dutch and Danes. Its centre is the least known to the Europeans. To the medical philosopher, the nature of its soil and climate renders it a fertile field for speculation, and its diseases a subject deserving of closer inquiry. To every one interested in the mental and moral elevation of our species it affords prospects the most humiliating and degrading. Tribes of negroes, different in the degree of savage existence, inhabit the coast, and extend towards the interior ; and although the difference of their customs and superstitions modify, in some respects, the extent of their social and moral perceptions, still they are not many degrees removed above the feræ naturæ. Tribes of Anthropophagi inhabit various places on the sea coast, and in the interior ; one was seen by ourselves on the western boundary of the Ivory coast, all of them most likely descendants of the Ethiopes Anthropophagi of Ptolemy, or the savage Ethiopians described by Herodotus. A race of almost amphibious Ichthyophagi exist on the Grain coast in a state of migration, plundering the inhabitants, who are not more than a degree removed above themselves in the scale of civilization ; and human sacrifice is performed by all, with the most wanton indulgence and exultation, even in those districts that have enjoyed an intercourse with Europeans for nearly three hundred years.

No account of the discoveries made by the expedition sent out by Necho king of Egypt, nor in the subsequent one undertaken by Hanno, has reached our times, sufficient for us to form an opinion of the aspect of the country, during the remote periods of antiquity. The

* The reader will readily perceive that there are some *doctrines* in this article a little at variance with what I have maintained in other parts of the work. They do not, however, require discussion here.—J. J.

very limited and superficial description given of the west coast of
Africa by the less ancient philosophers, Ptolemy and Pliny, merely
shows that the north-west extremity of this part was not unknown to
them.   If we may be allowed to speculate on the subject, the nature
of the soil and climate, and general aspect of the country, are perhaps nearly the same at the present day, as they were at that period.
If, however, they have undergone any material change, it cannot be
supposed to have been towards a state of amelioration.   The decomposition of the superior and more exposed strata of rocks, and the
continued production and decay in the vegetable kingdom, that must
have been going on during the intervening ages, render it more probable that an opposite change has been the result.   We are induced
to conclude that an accumulation of soil has thus taken place, which
every successive age would render more rich and absorbent, and consequently more exuberant in its productions.   With this increase of
luxuriance upon its surface, this country would necessarily become
more fertile in disease.
                                                                    1

> —————————Macies, et nova febrium
> Terris incubuit cohors.   HOR. Book I. Ode 3.

   The Portuguese navigators were the first of the nations of modern
civilization to visit this coast, and to erect settlements.   They began
towards the middle of the fifteenth century to extend their voyages
beyond Cape de Verde, and every successive adventurer proceeded
further than his predecessor, until, before the end of that century,
the whole of this coast was visited.

   We shall commence our description of this coast, with the part
first visited, and proceed along its shores to the southern limit, which
we assigned ourselves in the proemium.

   The first novelty that strikes the visitor of the African coast is its
extreme lowness.   The earliest indication of its approach will be afforded him by the temperature of the sea diminishing considerably,
even before the seaman's plummet has declared the depth of water.
Its depth begins gradually to lessen, and at length the soundings are
reduced to ten or twelve fathoms ; the land at last appears ; the tops
of trees appear to emerge out of the water, towards the eastern horizon ; and in a few hours the appearance of a dense and nearly level
forest indicates its near approach.   While advancing towards the
coast, or sailing in its parallel, the nights are enlivened by the constant flashes of lightning upon the land, or when at too great a distance to descry it, they are seen gleaming in constant succession towards that quarter of the horizon in which it lies.

   The River Gambia flows into the Atlantic Ocean in lat. $13\frac{1}{2}$° north,
and 16° west long. about half way between Cape de Verde and Cape
Roxo.

   The general appearance of this river, from the account given by
Ptolemy, seems to have been nearly the same in his time as at present.   The country adjoining is low, and in most places thickly
wooded.   The soil is generally sandy ; in low situations it approaches
to a black mould, while, in the lagoons, and near the banks of the river, the constant inundations during the rainy season, and the accumulation of mud and ooze which takes place, render it extremely

rich and absorbent. The banks of the Gambia swarm with musquitos, the different species of termites, formicæ, and with all the other insects and reptiles that are generally natives of similar climates. They are particularly numerous after the termination of the rains. At that season the earth may indeed be said to teem with them, marking a soil extremely fertile in the elements requisite to the production and growth of that class of the animal creation ; as well as in those principles which are productive of disease.

The settlement of St. Mary is placed near the entrance of this river, and although not so thickly wooded as most of our African settlements, yet, from the sources of disease supplied from its banks and adjoining swamps, it has been found as fatal to European constitutions. The nature of the soil and its less dense vegetation, render at some seasons the degree of heat frequently greater than in most of the other settlements on this part of the coast ; and when the sun has considerably passed the equator, towards his greatest northern declination, the thermometer in the shade has frequently indicated upwards of 100°. The rainy season commences in July, and continues about four months. During this season, but more especially about its commencement and termination, fevers of the intermittent and remittent types are very general, and frequently prove malignant. The diseases that are most prevalent are continued, remittent, and intermittent fevers, dysentery, and cholera morbus.—These are endemic at all seasons among recent visitors, if they remain sufficiently long ; and also very frequently attack seasoned residenters. The fever alters its type here, as in all other places on the coast, according to the period of residence in the country, and individual circumstances of the patients.

The quantity of rain which falls throughout the year may be considered from ninety to a hundred and fifteen inches. The prevailing winds during the dry season, are the usual sea and land-breezes. Tornadoes are frequent about the setting in of the rains, and at their conclusion. During their continuance the winds prevail from the W. S. W. fraught with the accumulated moisture exhaled from the equatorial Atlantic. The harmattan wind is more feeble in its effects towards this part of the country. That part of the coast which extends from $12\frac{1}{2}°$ to 10° north lat. is particularly shelving, and in many places is elevated into dangerous shoals and sand banks. These shoals, in consequence of greater elevation in some places, assume the appearance of small islands, and lie detached at a considerable distance from the continent.

The *Rio Grande* falls into the sea in $12\frac{1}{2}$ degrees—in the place where the coast is prominently marked by a shelving character. Its mouth is almost concealed in the approach from the sea, by several considerable islands. They appear from the assimilation of their surface and degree of elevation, as if separated from the continent by the course of the river ; while the aspect of their shores, and the character of the soil, render it as probable that they have been formed from the accumulating debris, washed down by the rivers during the rainy seasons from the adjoining country, as well as from the extremity of the Kong mountains, which, crossing Africa, terminate at

no great distance from this part of the coast.   From among this immense range of mountains, the more considerable streams, which afterwards by their increase form the majestic rivers of the Gambia, Rio
Grande, Sierra Leone, and others that present themselves along this
part of the coast, derive their origin.   Of the islands scattered before the mouth of this river, the most considerable and most adjacent
to the continent is the island of Bulama—a name become notorious in
medical controversy, from its having been the source from which many of those who espouse the doctrine of the contagious nature of the
yellow fever suppose the epidemic to have been derived, which ravaged the West Indies during 1793 and following years.   We shall
endeavour to present our readers with a view of its topography.
- Its situation, in the very entrance of the Rio Grande, gives the appearance of two distinct mouths to that river.   In length it is about
fifteen miles, and about ten in breadth.—It presents in every direction
an almost level superficies thickly wooded, and the stems of the more
considerable trees surrounded by a dense underwood.

Places more devoid of the bulky vegetable productions are covered by a thick and deep grass.   The soil varies from a loamy earth to
a heavy clay; and the shores assume either a sandy or muddy appearance, according as they are washed on one side, by the currents
of the sea, and on the other, by the stream of the river.   On the
sides which in fact form part of the banks of the river, every retiring
tide leaves it in some degree covered by the ooze and mud borne on
its current, and there left to rapid decay in a moist and hot atmosphere.   No situation could be chosen more fertile in the causes of
endemic fever : both from its peculiar position, and also from the nature of the soil and exuberant vegetation.

· The situation, in the mouth of the river, renders it obnoxious to
the effects of the land-wind, which may naturally be expected to be
fraught with the noxious exhalations produced from its banks, the
adjoining lagoons, and rice grounds ; while towards the sea it is in a
considerable degree sheltered from the salutary effects of the sea-
breeze, by the numerous and even large islands that lay without it.
No one acquainted with a tropical climate, but would conclude *á priori*, from such a position, and from such a soil and climate as we have
described, that the most severe cases of endemic fever must be the
result.   We cannot be surprised that the wretched individuals who
attempted to settle upon this island were so deeply afflicted ; we
would have been much more astonished had any escaped.   That the
disease did not make its appearance among them until a considerable
time after they had deserted this miasmal hot-bed, was to be expected by every one experienced in its causes.   Even when most concentrated, they never, we believe, affect the system before the seventh day ; and in many cases a considerable number of weeks elapse
before the febrile action commences.

The time which was subsequently spent by them at Sierra Leone,
where many of them died, and others sickened, afforded those who
escaped at Bulama, and whose minds were under the sedative effects
arising from disappointment, a fresh exposure to causes not a whit
less potent in producing malignant effects.   Many of our enlighten-

ed brethren, who are conversant with the great length of time the miasmal poison will lay dormant in the system, operating changes in it, preparatory to bursting into actual disease, will join us in the belief, that those who sickened during their passage across the Atlantic, and by that means gave rise to the fallacious appearance of contagion, derived their disease on the African shores, by the direct operation of the endemic causes of yellow fever upon their individual systems. If there were any who had no decided symptoms of disease until they reached the West Indies, and then were seized, we consider it very likely that the state of the atmosphere, so faithfully described by Dr. Clarke, as most prevalent throughout these islands at that time, might have brought into full action, as soon as they came within its influence, those seeds of disease which were sown in the system in Africa, and which otherwise might have never appeared, but by this super-addition of epidemic causes. If, however, this should be rejected as not being sufficiently probable, we can assign another cause, one by no means unlikely to have had effect after the mental and physical privations of such an attempt, followed by such a voyage. It is highly probable that states of the system might have been possessed by those individuals, which resisted the even highly concentrated causes of endemic fever to which they were presented in Africa ; yet subsequently, when both the mind and body must have undergone some change, from the scenes in which both suffered, they surely could not be supposed proof against the more energetic causes, which are necessary to the generation of an epidemic form of the disease, and which was then commencing in the West Indies. It is by no means a fair conclusion, because several of the inhabitants of Grenada, who visited the vessel that conveyed the settlers from Bulama, were afterwards seized with this epidemic at the time of its making its appearance in the island, that therefore they were infected from that vessel. It is well known that the epidemic was then commencing, not only in the West Indies, but also throughout the United States of America ; therefore it becomes infinitely more likely, that the disease in those individuals was produced by causes quite unconnected with the Bulama settlers ; and would have appeared under exactly the same circumstances if they had never visited the island. The epidemic state of the atmosphere so sensibly felt, so far as this fever extended, giving rise to a malignant modification of the disease, was materially different in character from the usual endemic of the African coast.

The fever, which proved so fatal to the Bulama settlers was the seasoning, or endemic produced by causes strictly confined to the place from which it was derived, acting upon the susceptibility of new comers, and assuming either the continued, or remittent type, according to the peculiar circumstances of the patient, but with no peculiar malignity in the disease ; whereas, the West Indian epidemic put on a much more violent aspect, affecting not only those lately arrived in that island, but also seasoned individuals and long residenters, evidently the result of causes more multiplied and intense than those by which they had been previously affected.

34

If the origin of both diseases be closely looked into, the former will be found derived from the products of vegetable decay, floating in a warm and moist atmosphere ; the latter combined those causes, with the extrication from an exposed surface of the more subtile elements, necessary to the constitution of a rich soil, and both were joined to a peculiar condition of the air, particularly favouring their production, as well as disposing the human system to their direct operation.

To the state of the electric fluid contained in the atmosphere, this peculiar alteration may have been owing in no inconsiderable degree ; and that such was actually the case, not only in this, but also in other epidemics, we could adduce the most convincing proofs, did we not consider ourselves as having strayed sufficiently long from the subject under consideration. From our knowledge of the African endemic we must conclude, that no proof has been ever adduced of its being capable of propagation by means of contagion, and we believe it impossible.* We therefore consider the ingenious attempt of Dr. Chisholm and his followers to convey a contagious yellow fever from Africa, and propagate it at once not only throughout the West Indies, but also through America, like the fabled flight of Dædalus—one to which the solar beams are inimical.

————Dædaleis
Nititur pennis.———   HORACE.

After leaving the entrance of this river and passing along the coast, which takes a south-east direction, a low and swampy country every where presents itself, exhibiting the same unvaried aspect of luxuriant vegetation. The whole distance, (upwards of 200 miles,) until we approach the colony of Sierra Leone, does not exhibit a single hill, or even prominence, that can serve as a land-mark to the mariner.

Within this extent many large rivers, deriving their origin from the high land forming the base of the Kong mountains, flow into the sea. The most considerable are the Rio Nunez, the Rio Pongas, and the Dembia. These rivers, during the rainy season, inundate a great part of the surrounding country.

Sierra Leone.—As we approach this river the country assumes rather a more varied aspect. The mountains of Sierra Leone, the first that have presented themselves along this extensive range of coast, overlook the river from its southern banks, while their western base is washed by the waters of the Atlantic. When viewed from the sea, the uniformly low and marshy country, seen extending in every direction, give them a more majestic appearance than their actual elevation would otherwise entitle them to. These mountains run in an easterly direction, and nearly parallel with the course of the river, for about twelve miles, without diminishing in altitude ; they then terminate abruptly in low swamps, through which the Bunch river flows in a slow and muddy stream. On the side toward the sea a chain of hills extends along the coast for several miles. These mountains are covered on every side to their summits by immense forests and luxuriant vegetation.

* I consider this expression of the writer as far too strong.—J. J.

Free Town, the British colony upon this river, is situated about six miles from its entrance, upon its south side, and is elevated from forty to seventy feet above the general rise of the river, which at this place is about ten miles across.   The soil is an argillaceous earth of a red colour, covering iron clay stone, which apparently rests on syentic rock.   Unless where built upon, it is covered by majestic trees, and a vast profusion of shrubs and grass.   Among these, the wild cotton tree, (bomax ceiba,) the palm tree, (carica papaya,) the cocoa tree, (cocos nucifera,) &c. hold a conspicuous place.   The swamps, so abundant at the foot of the mountains, and along the banks of the Bunch, which falls into it about seven miles from the colony, are covered by an impenetrable vegetation, chiefly consisting of mangrove bushes, (rhizophera mangle ;) which, by the very extensive manner they propagate themselves in all wet situations, (by shoots thrown off from their upper branches,) form impervious tracts ; and are so intricately wove together as to defy eradication by the most powerful means.   They cover the banks of these, and indeed all the African rivers ; and by furnishing a natural barrier, preserve them in the same channels.   They also contribute most powerfully in rendering such situations the certain source of disease, by retaining the mud and ooze, and other matters conveyed by the river, among their entangled branches.   The country to the north and east of Sierra Leone is inhabited by the extensive native States of Timmances and Benna Soosoos, and on the north by the Bulams.

No situation on the African coast could have been more unfavourably chosen for European constitutions than the one now under consideration : an abundant supply of good water is the only circumstance we can adduce in its favour.   On the south and south-west, the colony is overhung by the mountains already mentioned, the only range that arrests the eye of the voyager for upwards of 1,000 miles in either direction along the coast.   These with undivided attraction, arrest and condense at all seasons of the year the moisture exhaled, not only from the Atlantic Ocean, but at the same time from the very absorbent soil, and the numerous marshes and rivers that surround them in every direction.   Hence in opposition to a well known law in the science of climate, " that the number of days of rain diminish as we approach the equator, while the quantity of rain that annually falls increases."   The actual number of days in which rain falls is greater than in most northern climates.   By a register kept at this colony, the number of rainy days amounted to 204 ; and of the remaining dry days, although the moisture in the atmosphere was not actually condensed into rain, yet the greater proportion of them exhibited its progress towards that state ; not only the adjoining mountains, but the river and its banks being covered by fogs and haze.   Indeed few days occur throughout the year, which afforded a clear view of the mountain tops : clouds are seen generally either covering their heads, or resting upon their sides, at different degrees of altitude.

The rainy season commences in June, and terminates with October, and is both introduced and closed by tornadoes.   Their number, by an account kept, during one whole year amounted to fifty-four ; no part being more obnoxious to them than this and the grain coasts.

The quantity of rain during the year may vary from one hundred to one hundred and twenty inches. We cannot suppose it often to fall short of the former. Thunder and lightning are of frequent occurrence here, as they also are along the whole coast; the former by the loud reverberation from the sides of the mountains, becomes doubly tremendous. The winds during the rains generally blow from the S. W. or W. S. W. About their commencement, and after their conclusion, the atmosphere is generally tranquil. At other seasons the sea and land-winds occur, but not in regular succession. The sea-breeze seldom appears, and when it does, it generally dies away in a few hours, leaving the air sultry and stagnant. The land-winds come on about sun-set, and only amount to very light breezes ; and from blowing over the adjoining rivers and swamps, are generally a source of disease, especially to such vessels as may lie in the river within their noxious influence. The harmattan is less frequently and more feebly felt here than on the Gold coast.

The temperature of the air at Sierra Leone is generally not greater than 95°, but its tranquil state, in regard to its horizontal motion, favours the concentration and multiplication of the foreign ingredients, derived from the soil and decaying vegetation ; consequently, the atmosphere in this state feels very sultry and oppressive. The mean temperature obtained from the degree of heat observed at different periods of the day throughout the year, was from 83° to 83½°. The hypothetical scale laid down by Professor Lesslie,* from the empirical law discovered by Professor Mayer of Gottingen, gives for the same latitude 83-2°. The harmony here observable in conclusions from data so different, is not a little surprizing.

The diseases which the medical philosopher would be led to expect, resulting from the operation of this climate upon European constitutions, are exactly those which are constantly presenting themselves. They are, however, considerably modified in many of their phenomena by the period of residence, and circumstances peculiar to the patient. Accordingly, continued and remittent fevers, (commonly called yellow fever,) intermittents, dysentery, cholera morbus, enlargements of the spleen, and chronic inflammation of the liver,—are the diseases of most frequent occurrence, and generally prove annually fatal to about one-third of the white population. Of those who die, about eight-tenths are carried off by fever, the type of which varies according to the period of residence and the constitution of the individual ; but whatever aspect it may assume, it derives its origin from the same causes. An occurrence took place, here, which affords the most convincing proof of the correctness of our position :—Nine sailors direct from England, and belonging to the vessel in which we were, all of them having previously been either on this coast or in the West Indies, were put into a boat to convey our party to the colony, the vessel being becalmed at a considerable distance from the entrance of the river. Of those nine individuals, five had had yellow fever on either the African or American coast. The season of our arrival was in the end of June : the periodical rains had just commenced. The day was far advanced

* Article, climate.—Supplement to Encyclo. Britan.

before we landed at Free Town, and the overcast sky that had succeeded a cloudless morning, was pouring down its rain in torrents. The men were detained under shelter till the evening, when the weather appearing more favourable, they were allowed to return to the vessel. On their way they were overtaken by a tornado, which drove them upon the north and more swampy bank of the river. There they remained in their drenched clothes, inhaling the miasmata disengaged from this productive source until next morning, when they reached the vessel. These were the only individuals composing the ship's crew that had any intercourse with the land, and in them the effects of this exposure were soon expected to follow. About ten days after this occurrence the first man sickened, and within three weeks eight out of the nine had fever, under various forms. The vessel only remained nine days at Sierra Leone, and consequently was beyond the influence of the common causes of disease in that climate, before any one was taken ill. Of the four who had never before been in a warm climate, three had the disease in the continued and most concentrated type, the other in the remittent form. Of the five who, at a former period of their lives, had suffered from the same disease, three had it now in the remittent form, one a regular tertian, and the fifth, had no disease at the end of two months.* These eight men were treated according to the type of fever, and prominent symptoms which were developed in the course of the disease. They all recovered; but they were, during the treatment, completely removed from the causes from which the disease originated.

After passing Sierra Leone, the country appears studded by hills, covered with wood to their summits. As we approach the bay of Sherbro', they gradually diminish in elevation, and soon entirely disappear. From Sierra Leone to Sherbro', the distance is about eighty miles; within this extent four considerable rivers fall into the sea. This bay is formed by a range of low islands, whose southeast extremity touches the continent, and leaves it in an oblique direction, thus presenting a capacious opening towards the north-west. The country, so far as it can be viewed in either direction, is low and swampy; and although a fine sandy beach is seen edging the land, yet the soil is of a deep and heavy clay. Upon passing the large, but low island of Sherbro', (one of the range just mentioned,) and for upwards of seventy miles, the country is uniformly low and swampy, and much intersected with rivers, until we arrive at Cape Mount. This nearly conical mountain is situated on the south side of a spacious river, bearing the same name. As we advance along the coast, the elevation so abruptly assumed on the south bank of this river gradually diminishes; and within the space of a few miles the characteristic feature of lowness is again presented to our view. The country is every where thickly wooded. Proceeding from Cape Mount, along nearly a straight shore, Cape Mezurado, an elevated head-land, appears. The latter is about fifty miles distant from the

* We afterwards understood from the captain of the vessel—that, at a period of between three and four weeks subsequently, this man died after five days illness; but they were then lying within the influence of the usual causes of the disease.

former, and like it forms the southern barrier to a large river, which bears the same name usually given to the Cape. These rivers inundate. most of the country during the rainy season.-

The *Grain Coast* commences at this river, (Mezurado,) which is situated in 6. 30° north lat. and 10° west long. and terminates at Cape Palmas, in 4° north lat. and 7. 20° west. This coast runs between these limits in an even direction, without affording the least variety of appearance. Not a prominence is seen throughout. A dense forest covers an uniformly low land, through which a great number of small stremes flow with a sluggish course. None. of them are large enough to be dignified by the name of a river ; nor can they admit of navigation, but by the small canoes of the natives. The coast is every where shelving, and the immense swell, especially during the rainy season, that rolls in from the Atlantic, renders this unsheltered shore generally impracticable to all, but the almost amphibious negroes.

Their villages are built upon the sea side, near the swampy mouths of those rivulets ; affording them a greater facility of obtaining sub sistence from both elements. The soil is a deep, rich, and heavy earth, no where leaving a stone or rock exposed. This immense plain, during the rainy season, is almost one entire morass ; hence rice is generally cultivated, and forms the chief food of the inhabitants. While viewing the land at a distance of two or three miles, the slow and successive billows are heard breaking, with a continued roar, upon the extended and narrow beach ; and the continued line of foaming surf separates like a zone that tumultuous element from the compact and variously-shaded productions of the soil, which form one immense forest as far as the view can extend. Occasionally, one or more trees are seen greatly elevated above the rest, forming the most striking land-mark, by which seamen may recognize the different parts of this coast. Places designed for the growth of any of the farinaceous grasses or roots, usually cultivated in this country, have, towards the end of the dry season, their exuberant, but now withered productions, set on fire ; and with little further preparation the seeds are put into the ground. The quantity of rain during the year is nearly the same as on that part of the coast already described. This season commences with June, and continues about four months, attended with almost continued thunder and lightning. The wind during this time generally blows from the south-west. To this season succeeds about a month of continued fogs, with an almost tranquil state of the atmosphere. arising from the exhalation of the moisture from the absorbent soil. Although during these fogs the actual rise of temperature is inconsiderable, yet this is constantly the most noxious season of the year ; and were it not, that the almost daily occurrence of tornadoes carry before them the rapidly disengaged malaria in their tumultuous sweep, this part of the coast would be uninhabitable to the nobler class of animals. As it is—they exhibit in all their species, the lowest varieties of formation. ·

Ivory Coast.—At Cape Palmas we enter upon the Ivory coast, which runs E. N. E. to Cape Lahou, in 5° north lat. and 4° west long., where it terminates. This part, like the Grain coast, is throughout its greater extent low and swampy ; where it approaches the Gold

coast, the country in many places assumes the appearance of a low
table land. The quantity of rain and prevailing winds, and degrees of
temperature, are nearly the same in this district of the country as in
the last described. Indeed the whole extent of coast from the Bay
of Sherbro' to Cape Lahou, embracing about 700 miles, possesses an
uniform character in the soil and seasons, and in the luxuriance of the
vegetable kingdom. An everlasting sameness in the face of the country reigns throughout; and with a single exception, not a mountain,
or hill, presents itself as far as the sight can reach towards the interior. The uniformly low surface is frequently intersected by small
rivulets, but it no where presents any considerable or navigable rivers. Places devoid of the more majestic vegetable production are
completely covered by mangroves and brambles, through which, paths
between the native towns, and from them to their cultivated fields,
are with difficulty formed ; or even kept open. Those luxuriant natives of the soil extend to the very edge of the sandy beach, scarcely a rock being exposed. Where, however, the violence of the surf
has succeeded in removing the deep clay soil, rocks of the primary
formation are met with. Granite, micaceous schistus, and clay-slate,
have been thus in various places exposed.

The Gold Coast.—After passing Cape Lahou, we enter upon the
Gold Coast. It derives this appellation from the gold obtained by
washing the alluvial soil. It extends in almost the same direction
with the former, running nearly east, in the lat. of 5° north, until it
reaches the Rio Volta in 2° east longitude, where it terminates ; thus
embracing an extent of 300 miles.

This district of country assumes a more favourable aspect, than
any other upon the western side of Africa. The natural wealth of
the country, the more varied soil, and the situation it enjoys in respect of proximity to the interior kingdoms of this extensive quarter
of the globe, render it better calculated, than any other we have visited, for European trade and colonization. To the voyager accustomed to view the dull uniformity displayed by the Grain and Ivory
coasts, this exhibits more attractions. The great variety of scenery
and the regular succession of low hills, that present themselves as
we advance, with occasional rocky prominences, running into the
sea, afford more striking prospects than before presented. This is
also enlivened by the appearance at distant intervals, of the seats of
small but civilized societies, forming the different European settlements, that are met with on the African coast. There are, however,
many striking disadvantages under which it labours, and indeed in
common, with the greater part previously described.

The want of navigable rivers, and the unprotected nature of the
shore, from the deficiency of creeks and harbours, are alone great
detriments to mercantile intercourse. In many situations in this particular district, the scarcity of good water during the dry season, is a
matter of serious inconvenience, and even a source of disease.

The native inhabitants are more numerous, and their circumstances considerably superior to the other Negro tribes, who had hitherto fallen under our observation.

Apollonia is the first European settlement we meet with upon this coast.   It belongs to the British African Company, and is situated in an extensive plain, in $2\frac{1}{2}°$ west lat.   In most places it is thickly wooded, but in others subjected to the cultivation of rice.   It is intersected by small rivers, that inundate the greater part of the country during the rainy season.   The soil is a deep loamy clay.   The plain terminates in low hills as we advance towards the interior of the country.   Between these and the settlement is situated a fine lake of about seven or eight miles circumference, its banks are marshy, and even during the dry season cannot fail of loading the land-winds with miasms ; with which, indeed, the surrounding country, from its low and wet soil, and exuberant vegetation, must abound, through the greater part of the year.   As we proceed up the country, large open prairies, or meadows of long rank grass, are frequently met with, in which elephants are found browsing even within a very few miles of the sea shore.   This place is fruitful in the usual endemic diseases of tropical climates.

After leaving Apollonia, the coast is more hilly and varied in its appearance, and generally densely wooded, excepting the small patches of cultivated ground required to raise sustenance for the inhabitants. *Axim*, a small fort belonging to the Dutch, standing upon one of the promontories, forming Cape Three Points, next presents itself.   The soil here is a deep and fine red earth, in the lower strata ; towards the surface it is more loose and sandy.   The surrounding country is every where covered by a thick vegetation.   After quitting this place we arrive at. *Hollandia*, once a considerable fort belonging to the Dutch, but now deserted.   It is situated upon the sea side, as are all the European settlements on this coast.   The appearance of the country is nearly the same with the part already mentioned.

Dixcove, a British fort, is built upon an elevated prominence, forming the boundary of a large creek, in 1. 30° west long.   The country adjoining is hilly, and nearly impenetrably covered by large trees and bushes.   The soil is generally a deep tenaceous fine clay, leaving no where a rock in sight, unless upon the sea side.   The limited view afforded, led us to suppose them entirely of the primitive formation ; quartoze and syenitic blocks being thrown upon the beach by the immense surf.   The mouth of this creek is greatly obstructed by coral reefs.

This small fort is picturesquely situated, overlooking the small bay and Negro Town on the one side, and on the other the extended ocean, while the adjoining country exhibits a mass of verdure in various tints ; and from the abrupt elevation of immense trees, amidst the other comparatively dwarfish productions of the soil, a diversified light and shade are produced, new to those recently arrived in a tropical country.

Succondee is the next place deserving of observation.   Here the British and Dutch have settlements.   The Dutch fort is erected upon a prominence of micaceous rock of considerable elevation, forming the eastern boundary of a spacious bay.—The British settlement stands at a short distance from the head of this bay in a low and marshy situation.   The soil in most parts is a deep and fine absorbent clay ; in others, a dark and rich earth ; and with the exception of cultivated patches, that are uncommonly fertile, the country is quite uncleared of its luxuriant productions. Insects and reptiles, usually found in hot climates in all very moist soils, are very abundant. The very absorbent nature of the soil along the whole of this part of the country, and its moist state during a great portion of the year, render this place productive of fevers and diseases of the secreting organs. In our progress towards the eastern part of this coast, we arrive at Commenda, an English fort. It is placed in a low marshy situation, but the country towards the interior is more elevated. The soil is either wet and swampy, or of a deep and loamy clay.

St. George del Mina is the chief settlement belonging to Holland, and the seat of their African Government. It is the best fortress upon the coast, and is situated on a small peninsula, formed by an inconsiderable river running obliquely into the sea. The immediate vicinity of this fortification and adjoining town is better cultivated than any part upon the coast ; even here the Dutch have in some degree pursued their favourite recreation of horticulture. The surrounding country is level, and profusely covered by the usual vegetable productions. The soil is in some places of a light earth, covering a deep, heavy, and tenacious clay ; in other places it is a deep clay throughout, of nearly the same kind as is usually met with on this coast. The adjoining native town is populous, and its inhabitants even wealthy.

Cape Coast Castle, the principal settlement belonging to this country, stands upon a very low and insignificant prominence of granite and quartz rocks. The native town is placed near the walls of the castle, between it and the adjoining country. This town is built of the tenacious and heavy clay which forms the soil on which it stands, and the houses are so closely placed to each other, as scarcely to allow a passage between them ; during the rainy season every house appears placed in a mire of clay and mud.

In every considerable vacancy, and on the grounds immediately surrounding the town, accumulations of every species of filth would soon take place, did not the moist and warm atmosphere promote its decomposition and carry off the volatilized products, while insects, reptiles, and birds, assist in furthering the same effect. The soil is rather various, in some places it is a rich black earth, in others a brown heavy clay, interspersed by small fragments of mica and quartz ; but in all places it is uncommonly deep, and exuberant in its wild productions ; from which, with exception of the patches of corn or rice fields under cultivation, it is completely uncleared. There is no river in the vicinity, and consequently the supply of good water is very deficient during the dry season. It then abounds with animalculæ and the noxious gases, disengaged in the low and marshy ravines, from which it is generally obtained.

In our eastern progress along the coast, the next place of importance to which we will turn our attention, is *Anamaboo*, a fort belonging to this country. It stands upon the sea side, in a very low situation, with a large native town between it and the neighbouring country, which is hilly and covered with clumps of majestic trees, every where surrounded by a dense underwood. The soil does not differ from that we have already mentioned. In travelling along this part of the coast several other forts and settlements, belonging both to this country, to the Danes, and the Dutch, present themselves ; some have been relinquished since the abolition of the slave trade, but all of them are similarly situated with those we have already mentioned, and the soil and aspect of the country continue the same until we arrive at Accrah, in 1° east longitude.

The Accrah Country, in which the English, Dutch, and Danes have settlements, is one most extensive and beautiful plain. As far as the sight can reach, not a hill can be seen, unless in days of unusual clearness, very distant mountains may be descried in the interior of the country. This very extensive plain may be considered as one immense meadow of long grass, with occasional picturesque clumps of trees. The unincumbered state of the soil, as well as its peculiar nature, are favourable to cultivation, and the health of both natives and Europeans. The alluvial earth, through the whole of this country, and for nearly 100 miles eastward, varies from almost a pure sand, to a sandy mould, resting upon horizontal strata of primary sandstone, and allowing the rains to percolate and flow along the inferior layers. Owing to this, and the open state of the country, agriculture is more attended to ; and endemic diseases, that abound in all the countries we have hitherto described, more seldom occur here. This comparative salubrity of climate induces convalescents from the neighbouring settlements to resort to this place ; and the advantages they obtain are most striking. Nor is the different effects of these climates confined to the human species ; many of the more perfect animals, such as horses, dogs, &c. which either cannot live for a short time, or enjoy a sickly existence on most parts of this coast, are abundant in this district of country. From the nature of the soil permitting the moisture to find a ready passage through its strata, the sun's rays produce a higher degree of temperature on its surface, and consequently the sea and land-breezes blow in more regular succession. The former is more refreshing, while the latter is infinitely less fraught with the noxious gases.

The greater extent of the Gold coast, with the exception of the beautiful county of Accrah, is of a deep and rich clay soil, covered by an exuberant vegetation and lofty forests. The different European settlements scattered along its margin, are generally erected and retained without regard to salubrity. This is particularly the case with those belonging to this country ; most of them being placed in low situations, and either surrounded by, or in the immediate vicinity of, the most fertile sources of malaria. Every breeze must waft it into the apartments of the susceptible tenant. The great depth of the absorbent soil, and its dense verdure and impenetrable underwood, absorb the greater part of the periodical rains ; little of it finds its way to the sea, hence the paucity of rivers along this part of the coast. The rains commence in May, and terminate about the beginning of August. They are afterwards quickly evaporated by a vertical sun from the retentive soil, conveying the gases generated from it and the decaying vegetables. This is very sensibly evinced by a month's continuance of fogs and haze, which always follows this season. The moisture and gases thus produced from the soil, in conjunction with that obtained from the neighbouring ocean, are again precipitated, and constitute what is called the after rains, which fall about the end of September and in October. The quantity of rain during the year is from 80 to 100 inches. The wind during the first rains always blows from the sea. During the foggy season the air is generaly tranquil, owing to the copious evaporation from the earth's surface, after its almost deluged state. This condition of the atmosphere favours the concentration of the noxious elements given off by the soil, &c. and renders it more sultry and oppressive, than is indicated by the actual rise of temperature. Its mean through the whole year does not exceed $83\frac{1}{2}°$, generally ranging from 72 to 96". The barometer does not vary above one-eighth of an inch on either side of 30°.

During the dry season the sea and land-breezes are regular; and on this part of the coast the harmattan, or dry east wind is of frequent occurrence in this season. Its beneficial influence in promoting recovery from all the diseases experienced in this country is always remarkable; nor are its effects confined to promoting recovery, or invigorating the debilitated; epidemics are arrested in the midst of their progress, and even the virus of small-pox will not begin to act upon the system, during its continuance, and if already commenced, the progress will always be favourable.

Throughout the greater part of this district of the African coast, vegetable productions form the chief source of subsistence. But animal food, although not abundantly supplied them, is still within the reach of the more wealthy, especially in the northern countries embraced by this sketch, and in the richer kingdoms of Akim, Dahomey, and Ayo, that are situated inland, from the eastern extremity of the Gold coast.—The surface of the soil may be considered, generally speaking, as entirely uncultivated. The preparation it receives can scarcely deserve the name of cultivation, nevertheless it seldom fails in producing abundantly from the seeds committed to it; as, however, they only subject to culture what they consider sufficient for their sustenance until the return of the season, a scarcity occasionally happens. This is always the effect of a shorter or longer duration of the rains, and consequently gives rise only to a partial failure in their crops —According to the soil and situation, they cultivate rice, millet, maize, (zea mays,) yams, (dioscorea bulbifera,) plantains, (musa sapientum,) sweet potatoes, (convolvulus batatas,) sweet or innocuous cassada, (jatropha janipha;) the poisonous species, (I. manibot,) is also cultivated, and is employed in sauces with the capsicum annuum, or C. frutescens, or also with the amomum grana paradisii; during the boiling it undergoes in the process, it loses its noxious qualities. Ground-nuts, (arachis hypogea,) form another considerable article of food; these grow near the extremity of the root of the plant. In addition to those, we may enumerate the following fruits that are abundant:—Ananas, (bromelia bananas,) bananas, (musa paradisaica,) cocoa-nuts, (cocoa nucifera,) guayavos, (guayava psidium,) papaws, (carica papaya,) water-melons, (anguria tri-lobata,) limes, (citrus medica,) and several species of the tamarind.

After passing along the champaign and open country of Accrah, we arrive at the similarly situated settlements of Prampram and Ningo. The soil on this part of the coast is light and sandy, and generally open and well cultivated.—Game may be had in tolerable abundance; deer, hares, patridges, guinea-fowls being seen in great numbers, Domestic animals are also much more abundant in this part of the coast. From Ningo a few miles brings us to the Rio Volta, a large river, at the entrance of which the Danes have a fort. Although ca-pacious at the entrance, and so far as it has been navigated, apparent-ly of considerable magnitude, yet the numerous sand banks and rocks at its mouth render it of dangerous navigation. This, as the rest of the large rivers on this part of the coast, abounds with crocodiles and hippopotami. The coast to the eastward of this river (frequent-ly received the appellation of the Slave coast,) for many miles retains nearly the same species of soil with that just mentioned. This coun-try formerly possessed two settlements on this part of the coast, in the dominions of the King of Dahomey; they were relinquished af-ter the abolition of the slave trade.

The Slave Coast commences at Rio Volta, and extends to the Bay of Biafra, in lat. 3° north and $7\frac{1}{2}$° east longitude.—The whole of this coast is remarkably low and swampy, and deeply indented by creeks, and the capacious but often shoaly mouths of the large rivers that flow into this part of the Gulf of Guinea. The most remarkable of these are the Formosa, old and new Calabar, and the Cross and del Rey rivers. According to Reichard, these are different mouths of the Niger, by which it disembogues itself into the Atlantic. These rivers flow through the extensive kingdoms of Benin, Warree, and Biafra, and are navigable to a considerable distance from their en-trance. Owing to the extensive traffic carried on with the different States in their vicinity, in palm oil, ivory, and ebony, &c. given in exchange for British manufactures; and to the facilities which they afford to the native traders from the more inland States, for the transport of their commodities, these rivers are more frequented than any on this coast. Their banks, however, are so swampy, and the soil in general so richly wooded, as to render commercial specula-tion an undertaking of surprising enterprise on the part of Eu-ropeans, constituting the crews of vessels proceeding to this country. We believe half of those who proceed on such a voyage never return; and we have known instances of one-forth only surviv-ing their short stay in this climate. The necessity for vessels pro-ceeding some distance up these rivers, in order to enter upon the field of traffic, necessarily brings them within the sphere of action of the malaria generated from the mud, ooze, and decaying vegetables, which continually cover their banks. These sources of disease are greatly multiplied, both during and after the rainy season, from the nearly inundated state of the country, and by the sultry and stagnant state of the atmosphere. The diseases which prove so fatal to the crews of vessels, (who are the only visitors of this country,) are con-tinued and remittent fevers, dysentery, and cholera morbus. The unhappy victim of disease may consider himself so far fortunate, if he escape with an attack of one of these only ; not unfrequently dysentery carries off the individual whom fever had spared. The soil in this part of the coast is generally a muddy clay. The district that adjoins the Gold Coast, and forms a part of the kingdom of Dahomey, is more open ; and the soil is generally sandy, or varying from that to a gravelly clay. The quantity of rain, and the rise of temperature, may be considered the same here as in the countries previously described. The sea-breezes are neither so strong nor so regular in succession on this part of the coast as in most of its divisions already mentioned.

From the account we have attempted to give of this part of the African coast, our readers must be struck by the sameness of aspect, which the whole of it affords. This, as may naturally be supposed, gives rise to a similar uniformity in the character of the diseases to which Europeans, either lately arrived, or for a considerable time resident in it, are subject. These, as may be expected, vary according to the time of residence, the intensity of the causes, and individual circumstances of the patient.

We shall conclude this article with a few brief observations on the more fatal diseases of the country—fevers and dysentery. Those who arrive in this country are subject, within the first nine months, and more frequently within as many weeks, to the endemic yellow fever, to bilious diarrhœa, to cholera morbus, and dysentery. If a bilious diarrhœa or cholera precede an attack of fever in the new comer, (or what is usually called the seasoning,) of a tolerably sound constitution, both diseases may be comparatively mild.

Fever is the disease which produces the greatest degree of mortality, and may attack new comers at all periods of the year. Nor do residenters remain long without suffering from its visits, although under a different type. When unacclimates, of a phlegmatic or melancholic temperament, are subjected to the causes of the disease in considerable concentration, the vital energy may be so completely overwhelmed as to be incapable of reaction, and none of the symptoms of that stage of the disease can be discernible. In such cases the frame of the subject, in the space of from one to five days, sinks into dissolution, exhibiting a liquescent form of fever ; the body being semiputrescent, even before vitality has entirely relinquished her seat. In those of a full habit, of a strong muscular formation, or of the sanguine or irritable temperaments, violent symptoms of reaction rapidly supervene to those which indicated the stage of invasion ; these, if not arrested by judicious treatment, exhaust the vital energy in a period proportionately to their degree of intensity, and the resistance made by the constitution. This consequent exhaustion may be so great as to be incompatible with the continuance of life ; or some important organ may, during the height of the excitement, suffer in such a manner as to put a speedy stop to the vital relations of the system. Either of these effects may individually operate in producing death, or they may combine in being its more immediate cause. In long residenters the fevers that terminate fatally are generally of a remittent type ; in them, the changes wrought upon the system, previous to the last and grand change, are seldom so simple ; along with considerable exhaustion of the vital energy, there is always present considerable visceral disease.   Intermittents are common among the acclimatés, and often induce visceral disease.

Dysentery is more frequent upon the Gold coast than on any other part.   This may be owing to the scarcity of good water.   The mode of living has also a considerable share in giving rise to this disease. In new comers it is chiefly confined to the mucous membrane of the colon and rectum, with increased action of the muscular fibres, especially the longitudinal fasciculi ; these contract the colon into cells, and from being considerably shorter than the intestines, even in the healthy state, this viscus is drawn into folds that meet those of the opposite side ; thus forming complete valves against the further progress of the contents, or of the matters thrown into this by the small intestines.*

In unacclimatés this disease is more acute, and generally requires depletion, with medicines calculated to allay the irritation and spasms, constituting some of the leading symptoms of the disease.   Irritating purgatives, &c. only tend to prolong the disease.   In long residenters it is generally combined with considerable disease in the liver and spleen, and then not unfrequently assumes the chronic form ; such a complication will consequently point out the treatment. - Our limits prevent us from taking a view of the other but less prevalent diseases.

Among the natives fever seldom appears ; they are not however, exempt from its attack.   It generally assumes an ephemeral form, and is frequently complained of according to the organ chiefly affected, as when the head, stomach, or bowels become considerably deranged through the course of the febrile action.   Fever, however, sometimes commences, and runs through the regular stages, without any particular organ suffering the onus of disease ; but the different stages are always of shorter duration in them than in Europeans ; and the action of the heart becomes more rapidly increased.   During the course of the excitement, it more frequently is the case that some particular organ or tissue suffers in such a manner as to arrest the attention of both patient and physician to that alone.   Dysentery is of frequent occurrence among them, and often assumes an epidemic character.

* We have met with the pure idiopathic cases of this disease, in which no derangement was visible in the liver.   We consider the exclusive manner of treating dysentery with mercury, recommended by many, as evincing narrow views of pathology, inasmuch as it attributes its origin to diseased secretion of the liver. We do not doubt, that both diseases may take place stimultaneously, or the one supervene on the other ; and thus both may be prolonged or exalted, either individually or conjunctly.   Of this we have seen proofs, established by post mortem inspection.   We also disagree with those, especially our continental brethren, who consider dysentery as a colonitis.   That there is inflammation of the mucus membrane of this intestine, frequently extending along the rectum on one side, and to the small intestines on the other, we grant ; but there are also an irritable state and spasmodic action existing in the muscular fibres, and were inflammation also existing in them, these in our opinion, could not take place.   The inflammation no doubt extends to the cellular tissue connecting both coats, and in its progress in this connecting membrane detaches the mucous tissue.—*Reviewer.*

During the course of this hasty sketch, our readers cannot fail of perceiving from the nature of the soil and its productions, from the topography and climate of the country, that it must be productive of the sources of these endemic diseases.

To trace the effects of those causes upon the frame—to inquire by experiment and observation into the series of causes and effects, as they are sensibly developed in the system, as well as into their primary mode of action—were the objects that chiefly led us to encounter a climate, in which no one could be placed a night without danger. These inquiries will be soon laid before our brethren : we have only to regret that no facilities were afforded us for extending them as we could have wished ; but, notwithstanding, we have some reason to be satisfied with the result."—*Foreign Journal.*

I have introduced the foregoing.

WESTERN HEMISPHERE.

ON YELLOW FEVER.

The disease which I am now to consider has no common claims to the attention of the Medical Philosopher.—The extent and frequency of its epidemical visitations ;—its fatal tendency and rapid career ;—and the merciless selection of the more robust and healthy as its legitimate prey,—are circumstances in the history of Yellow Fever, which cannot fail to command a deep feeling of interest in the investigation of its origin and nature.

Much light has, of late years, been thrown on this subject by the contributions of various practitioners in the public service, who have meritoriously employed a portion of their retirement subsequent to the war, in giving to the world the sum of their observation and experience. It is to be regretted, however, that an increased familiarity with the scenes of woe, has not produced a corresponding unison of sentiment in regard to the ætiology of the disease from which those events have sprung ;—It may even be said, that no question in medical science has been more keenly agitated than that of the contagious or non-contagious origin of Yellow Fever. The discussion of this point will be brought forward hereafter. Omitting the names of the older writers, I shall here confine myself to a brief enumeration of the principal of those who have subsequently published their opinions in favour of, or in opposition to the doctrine of contagion, without, however, aiming at giving a complete list, or of being scrupulously exact as to the priority of their respective publications. In favour of the contagious nature of Yellow Fever, we have the authority of Lind, Blane, William Wright, Chisholm, W. Currie, Thomas, Pugnet, Bally, Gonzales, Pym, and Fellowes. On the other hand, in the list of authorities who consider it as not contagious, are included the names of Hunter, Jackson, Moseley, Rush, Miller, Bancroft, Lempriere, Devèze, Saverésy, Valentin, Dickson, Mc Arthur, Burnett, Doughty, Veitch, Ferguson, Dickinson, Mortimer, Sheppard, Robertson, &c. It will be seen that, numerically, the advantage is greatly on the side of the latter ; and it is but candid to admit that, in opportunities, also, the preponderance is still more in favour of the non-contagionists, many of whom, for a series of years, held official situations in the West Indies which afforded them ample means of observing this fatal disease, in various places, and in all its forms.

I shall first lay before my readers copious reviews of the essay and sequel of Dr. Bancroft on Yellow Fever, which will be found to include a full discussion of the controverted points ; to these will succeed two philosophical papers by Drs. Dickson and Ferguson ; and the subject will be concluded by the correct and valuable histories and methods of treatment of this formidable endemic by Dr. Mc Arthur and Mr. Dickinson. The department will thus, I trust, be found to present a comprehensive exposé of the opinions of the most recent writers on Yellow Fever ; of whom it is but justice to add, that their acknowledged abilities and ample experience in this disease, are sure pledges of the importance and accuracy of whatever proceeds from their pens.

———

An Essay on the Disease called YELLOW FEVER, *with observations concerning Febrile Contagion, Typhus Fever, Dysentery, and the Plague ; partly delivered as the Gulstonian Lectures, before the College of Physicians, in the Years* 1806 *and* 1807. By EDWARD NATHANIEL BANCROFT, *M. D.* Fellow of the Royal College of Physicians, Physician to the Army, and late Physician to St. George's Hospital. London, 1811, pp. 811.

SEC. I.—Dr. Bancroft having, in the year 1806, been appointed to deliver the Gulstonian Lectures before the College of Physicians, made choice of the Yellow Fever as the subject for that occasion ; and certainly no subject can be more interesting than fever, the nature and causes of which are still involved in so much obscurity, and in the medical treatment of which disease we are still so far from being universally successful, that every attempt to add to our knowledge, and improve our treatment of so dreadful a scourge to mankind, deserves to be received with thankfulness and examined with candour.

The Essay on Yellow Fever is divided into four parts ; the first of which contains observations on the Symptoms and Mode of Treatment. Previous, however, to giving a detail of the history and progress of the disease, the author enters into a discussion respecting the propriety of its present name. This is derived from one particular symptom, the colour of the skin ; pretty general, indeed, but not universal, nor even essential to the existence of the disease, nor proportioned to the magnitude of its violence and danger. Were the name of the disease to be derived from a single symptom only, the author thinks *Causus* would be a more appropriate title ; not only as a burning heat of the skin occurs more generally than yellowness of it, but because also the degree of heat existing, affords some indication for the successful treatment of the disease. A great objection that may be urged against both these names is, that these symptoms occur in various degrees in most other fevers, and are not characteristic of the nature and properties of any one. The fever in question has been called by Sauvages *Typhus icterodes*, but it is not generally connected with any morbid state of the liver or the bile ; by Cullen, *Typhus cum flavedine cutis ;* by the French, *Maladie de Siam*, and *Fievre Matelotte ;* by the Spaniards, *Chapetonada*, and *Vomito prieto ;* the latter of which names the author thinks equally objectionable with Yellow Fever, since neither the black vomit nor yellowness is universally present, nor peculiar to this disease. Sporadic fevers, occurring in very warm climates from any accidental cause, are, the author observes, liable to be accompanied with the same severe and fatal symptoms which occur in the epidemic yellow fever, and have accordingly been confounded with this latter. They are to be distinguished, first, by the causes of the former being generally some excess, over-fatigue, taking cold, or affections of the mind, operating therefore on a few individuals only ; while the causes of the latter are of a more general nature, and operate on a considerable number of persons at the same time : Secondly, by their progress ; the first being always of a continued type, the latter almost always manifesting a disposition to remit. It is of the epidemic disease the author principally treats, although his observations are equally applicable to both diseases.

There is reason, however, to apprehend, as frequently happens in nosological arrangements, that the above distinction of type is rather artificial than founded in nature. In the plethoric stranger, and in arid situations, the Fever is usually ardent and continued ; while in those who have resided some time in the climate, whose systems are reduced from a state of high health and European vigour, and in uncleared woody places, it frequently assumes the remittent form : in other words, the type will much depend on the habit of the patient, season, locality, and the nature and intensity of the peculiarly exciting cause.

Symptoms. As the attack and progress of these are well described by the author, I shall give them in his own words.

" The progress and violence of the yellow fever differ greatly, according to the force of its cause, the vigour and excitability of the patient, and season of the year. When it prevails epidemically in hot climates, and attacks young and robust men, lately arrived from temperate regions, the disorder commonly appears in its most aggravated form. In this, the patient first complains of lassitude, restlessness, slight sensations of cold and nausea, which symptoms are soon succeeded by strong arterial action, intense heat, flushing of the face, redness of the eyes, great pain and throbbing in the head and in the eye-balls, uneasiness and pain in the stomach, oppression of the præcordia, a

36

white fur on the tongue, and a dry parched skin, with a quick, full, tense, and generally strong pulse, though it is sometimes oppress-ed and irregular.   These symptoms are speedily accompanied by frequent efforts to vomit, especially after swallowing food or drink, with discharges, first of such matters as the stomach happens to con-tain, and afterwards of considerable quantities of bile, appearing first yellow and then green, sometimes tinged with blood, but in the pro-gress of the disorder with matters of darker colours ; an increase of pain, heat, and soreness at the præcordia, also occurs, with constant wakefulness, and frequently with delirium, more or less violent. This paroxysm, or exacerbation, which has been called the inflam-matory, or the febrile stage, generally lasts thirty six hours, but is sometimes protracted for seventy-two hours, and even longer, proba-bly in consequence of either general or local inflammation, (particu-larly in the brain or stomach,) or of irregularity in the circulation, which are known to prolong the paroxysms in fevers of type.

" A remission then occurs, in which many of the symptoms sub-side, so often as to induce a belief that the fever is at an end, and recovery about to take place. Frequently, however, the foundations of irreparable injury to the brain or stomach have already been laid in the former paroxysm ; and in such cases the remission is short and imperfect.   During these remissions, the pulse often returns appa-rently to the condition of health, the skin feels cool and moist, and the intellect, if previously disturbed, sometimes becomes clear ; sometimes, however, the patient remains in a quiet and stupid state, a symptom generally denoting great danger.—Another sign of danger, as denoting a very morbid condition of the stomach, is the renewal of the efforts to vomit, when pressure is made on that organ, or food is swallowed.   After a certain interval, this remitting stage is suc-ceeded by another, which may be called a second paroxysm,- and which, probably, would appear as a renewed exacerbation, if the violent effects of the first had not almost exhausted the patient's ex-citability, and in conjunction with the extreme depression of strength which usually attends inflammation of the brain or stomach, rendered him nearly unsusceptible of those morbid actions which are neces-sary for that purpose.—In this latter stage, then, instead of great fe-brile heat, and strong arterial action, the wamth of the body, and the frequency and strength of the pulse, are often less than when the patient was in health ; but frequently the pain and heat in the sto-mach become excruciating, with incessant strainings to vomit, which in most of the fatal cases, are followed by hiccough, and repeated discharges of matters resembling turbid coffee, more or less diluted, or the grounds of coffee, and also by evacuations of similar dark matters from the bowels.   Here it is to be observed, that when these symptoms occur, (indicating a violent affection of the stomach and bowels,) the patient is, in general, sufficiently in possession of his intellects to know those about him, and to give distinct answers to questions made to him, although his excessive weakness often renders him incapable of mental exertion, and his inability even to raise his head, may induce the appearance of coma.   In those cases, however, in which the brain has suffered greater injury than the stomach, the retching and black vomit, just described, do not so commonly occur, but, instead of them, low muttering, or coma, with convulsions of the muscles of the face, and other parts of the body, supervene. About this time, also the tongue and teeth are covered with a dark brown fur ; yellowness of the skin and petechiæ make their appearance ; the urine, when passed, has a putrid smell and dark colour ; the fæces likewise become most offensively putrid ; hæmorrhages sometimes take place from the nostrils, gums, and various other internal surfaces ; there is in some patients, a suppression of urine ; in others an involuntary discharge of it, and of the fæces : the pulse becomes feeble and intermits ; the breathing is laborious ; portions of the skin assume a livid colour ; the extremities grow cold ; and life is gradually extinguished."

The above description of the disease accords with the distinction which the author has attempted to establish ; but as he is here delineating the most severe and fatal form of yellow fever, the propriety of characterizing the subsidence of great heat and vascular action at the close of the first stage as " a remission," is very questionable. It is, in fact, the transition from inordinate action to exhaustion—to that almost hopeless state which, (the foundation of almost irreparable mischief having been already laid in the most important viscera,) is speedily to terminate in disorganization and death, and has nothing in it of the salutary tendency of a remission. As Dr. Gillespie observes, " it is proper to caution young practitioners against a mistake very common with regard to the yellow, or ardent fever ; that is, of taking the fatal stage which follows the cessation of ardent heat and great excitement, and which accompanies a sphacelus of the viscera, for a salutary crisis of the disease."—*Diseases of Seamen.* " Cette diminution des symptômes en impose quelquefois au malade, et meme aux médecins in expérimentés."—*Dict. des Sciences Medicules—tome* xv. p. 336.

This declension of fever at the close of the first stage excited early attention, and is often so marked as to have been frequently mistaken for a proof of returning health. It is noticed by Dr. Hume, who had the charge of the naval hospital at Jamaica between the years 1739 and 1749, and was afterwards a Commissioner of the Sick and Hurt Board, in the following terms : " The pulse is at first full, quick, and strong, but in forty-eight hours after seizure, or thereabouts, it sometimes becomes calm and regular, scarce to be distinguished from the pulse of a person in health."—See *Dr. Hume's Account of the Yellow Fever,* published by Dr. Donald Munro.

The preceding, (says Dr. Bancroft,) is a description of the disease in its most violent form, and it sometimes proceeds with such rapidity as to destroy the patient on the third or fourth day, or even sooner. It seldom happens that in the most severe cases the head and the stomach are both equally affected ; one of those organs however generally suffers such derangement as to destroy the patient. Those who die early in the disease appear to perish from an affection of the head, with less vomiting, whereas those who have the stomach more violently affected, are usually found to have their mental faculties clear though much weakened ; and they seldom expire before the end of the fourth, or the beginning of the fifth day, p. 17.

The *dissections* of patients dying of this fever have discovered appearances correspondent to the affection of the part most violently attacked by the disease.—Where the affection of the head has formed the principal feature of the disorder, the integuments of the brain have generally been found more or less inflamed, especially near the temporal bones ; the vessels of the dura mater and of the pia mater were not unfrequently observed to be very turgid with blood, which was also sometimes extravasated. Effusions of watery fluid have likewise been seen over the surface of the brain, or in vesicles between the pia mater and the tunica arachnoidea. In some cases the integuments have been so firmly attached to each other, and to the brain, that in attempting to raise, or separate them, a part of the substance of the brain has been torn up. The volume of the brain is often increased, and the substance of it is, in some instances, more firm than usual ; when cut, the vessels distributed through it have been so distended with blood, that the medullary part has immediately become thickly spotted with red points, owing to the oozing of blood from the divided vessels ; and it was not rare to find that some of those vessels had been ruptured, and that blood had escaped into the substance of the brain. The ventricles usually contained water, of a yellow colour, and were in some cases quite filled with it. The plexus choroides has often been loaded with blood.

In those cases of the disease where the symptoms indicating a severe affection of the stomach have been predominant, inflammation of that viscus has been discovered upon dissection. In some cases, almost the whole inner surface was inflamed ; very often portions of the villous coat were abraded, nor unfrequently observed floating among the contents of that viscus. Marks of inflammation, but less violent than these, have also been often seen in the smaller intestines, especially near the pylorus. The inflammation seems to be of the kind denominated erythematic ; this kind of inflammation is apt to spread, the author observes, wherever there is a continuity of membrane or of structure ; and as such continuity exits through the whole alimentary canal, the viscera nearest to the stomach must be liable to participate in the inflammatory affection of the latter.

The *Black Vomit* is so universal a symptom in severe cases of yellow fever, that it becomes an important object to ascertain its source and origin. Many writers have attributed it to a superabundant and altered secretion of bile, but certainly without foundation, as is evident from the facts stated by our author, both from his own observation and that of several other physicians. In the greater number of dissections the liver has been found in a healthy state, and where it has differed from its natural appearance, it has frequently been of a paler colour ; the gall-bladder has also at the same time been found in a healthy state, containing its usual quantity of bile, not at all altered in its appearance or properties.

At a time when the stomach has been distended with black vomit, the passage from the duodenum into the stomach has been completely obstructed by the pylorus valve, so that no portion of the matter could have deen derived from the hepatic system, in every part of which system the bile was quite natural in colour, taste, and consistence. The matter of black vomit, compared with bile, differs materially from it in all its physical qualities ; " it differs from it in colour ; for however dark the bile may appear in its most concentrated state, it always displays a yellowish, or greenish yellow tinge, when spread on a white surface, or when diluted ; and this is never observed with the matter of black vomit. It has also been found that an addition of bile to the latter, altered its nature so much as to give it an appearance different from what it had before ; nor could the black vomit be imitated by any mixture of various proportions of dark-coloured bile with the fluids found in the stomach. It differs most decidedly in taste ; the black vomit being always insipid, when freed from other foreign matters, whereas the bile can never, by any means, be deprived of intense bitterness."

If then the black vomit is not bile in a morbid state, nor contains any portion of that fluid, whence is it derived ? It must proceed from the stomach itself, and appears to be in most cases, a consequence of inflammation of that viscus. Some physicians have entertained an opinion that the black vomit is a particular morbid secretion by the inflamed vessels or glands of the stomach ; Dr. Bancroft thinks, that " it is merely blood which has been effused from some of the small arteries, ruptured in consequence of the separation of certain portions of the villous coat, and has coagulated within the general cavity of the stomach, or on the surface over which it was effused ; and having been afterwards detached and triturated by the violent and frequent contractions of that organ in the efforts to vomit, has had its appearance as a coagulum of blood altered, and its colour darkened by the gastric juice, or by some chemical decomposition, either spontaneous, or produced by the action of the air, or other matters contained in the stomach." In confirmation of this opinion it is stated that in many cases, portions of the inner surface of the stomach have been covered with a coat of thick blackish matter, and upon removing this coat, the parts beneath it, and no other, were found inflamed. The substance thus obtained was exactly similar to black vomit, and there is reason to believe that it must have been derived from the vessels of the inflamed part. At those spots' moreover, where the villous coat had been abraded, the extremities of arteries have been frequently seen filled with this dark coloured matter ; and collections of the same matter have even been discovered immediately under the villous coat. A relaxation of the vessels of the stomach may give rise to hæmorrhage from that viscus, as we find happens in some cases of extreme debility, and, probably, this may take place in some very few instances of yellow fever, where the coats of the stomach remain entire ; but the author concludes, with great reason, " that the black vomit is much less frequently the consequence of a relaxation of vessels, than of a separation of some portions of the internal coats of the stomach."

The *Affections of the Skin* in this disease are in some respects similar to those which take places in other fevers ; during the strong arterial action which succeeds the first attack, the skin becomes excessively dry and parched, with an intensely burning or pungent heat. Sweats are in this stage a very rare occurrence ; and when they do appear, no relief is afforded by them.   A feeling of general soreness of the skin also takes place in many patients.   Of the yellow suffu- sion, which has given name to the disease, we have the following des- cription :

" The yellowness beings in a few cases, within the first forty-eight hours ; sometimes on the third day, and frequently not until the fourth or fifth.   It is, indeed, sometimes observed but a few minutes before, or a little after death.   I believe, that in many instances it might, with attention, be discovered on the eyes ; but it is commonly first observ- ed on the cheeks, extending towards the temples, and about the angles of the nose and mouth ; about the lower jaw and on the neck, along the course of the jugular veins, whence it afterwards spreads in stripes and patches along the breast and back, downwards, so as at last to be- come universal in some patients, though in others it remains partial. The yellowness is sometimes of a dingy or brownish hue, sometimes of a pale lemon, and at others, of a full orange colour.   When the yellowness appears only in patches or spots, and of a dingy or brown- ish hue, these are frequently intermixed with other spots of a florid red, or a purple, or livid colour."

This yellowness of the skin is, with one partial exception, deriv- ed from the bile ; and the manner of its entrance into the blood-ves- sels is thus accounted for by the author.   " When there has been very frequent and violent vomiting for some length of time, the sto- mach, diaphragm, and abdominal muscles, are apt to become irritable to an extreme degree, so that at each effort of the former to discharge its contents, the latter will frequently be thrown instantaneously into strong spasmodic contractions, and the liver, together with the gall- bladder, will be as it were, suddenly caught, and tightly squeezed in a powerful press ; the necessary consequence of which pressure seems to be, that all the fluids contained in that viscus will be driven towards both extremities, backwards as well as forwards, in those vessels which are not provided with valves to prevent their retro- grade motion. Under such circumstances it can scarcely be doubted, that the bile will be forced to regurgitate in this manner, and pass from those ducts into the vena cava at each violent compression of the liver ; and that by continued and strong spasmodic contractions of the before-mentioned muscles in vomiting, a considerable quan- tity of bile may be carried into the circulation, and a yellow suffusion resembling jaundice be very speedily produced."

In this manner also is the yellowness of the skin accounted for which succeeds from the bite of venomous reptiles, and the poisoning by some species of mushrooms, and certain poisonous fishes ; in all which cases, violent convulsive vomiting is a usual symptom.   The exception to the yellow suffusion being derived from the bile, refers to those cases in which the yellowness of the skin occurs partially, or *in patches* or spots ; in these instances it is thought to be produced by a cause similar to that which produces the yellowness that follows ecchymosis, and to be connected with that particular state of the blood and of the vessels which gives rise to hæmorrhages from various parts of the body, external and internal. It is accordingly in these last cases that extreme danger is more certainly indicated, than in the general suffusion arising from compression of the liver.

Having given Dr. Bancroft's account of the Black Vomit and the Yellow Suffusion, I may remark that his explanation of the nature and origin of the former, (though somewhat different from the view of Dr. Jackson in his sketch of the history and cure of febrile diseases, p 63 —4,) nearly coincides with that of other accurate observers of the phenomena of the disease and the appearances on dissection.*

With respect to the yellowness of the skin, Dr. Bancroft's explanation is not quite so satisfactory. Drs. Dickson and Mr. Arthur both inform me, that they have occasionally seen this symptom, previous to the occurrence of vomiting ; as well as in cases, where from great attention to allay the gastric irritability, or other causes, as when the head is greatly or chiefly affected, but little vomiting comparatively, had occurred in the course of the disease ; and Mr. Dickinson, in his work, also remarks, " that vomiting does not always precede, nor does it always occur when the bilious suffusion takes place," p. 171.

That of Broussais appears the more correct exposition. He is of opinion that the yellow colour depends solely on the violent irritation of the duodenum, which is propagated to the secretory organ of the bile ; that all the other symptoms of this fever are those of inflammation of the stomach and small intestines; and that the researches of Pugnet, Tommasini, Dubrieul, and many others, have no doubt of the correctness of this determination respecting the seat of the disease.

The yellow dingy patches in the advanced stage, which our author considers an exception, produced by a cause similar to the yellowness following ecchymosis, and probably connected with that peculiar state of the blood and loss of power in the smaller vessels which gives rise to passive hæmorrhage, is indicative of the worst stage of the disorder ; and is probably dependent on the peculiarly unfavourable habit, or deleterious nature of the exciting cause, and sometimes on the previous treatment of the patient.

The yellow fever has, by several authors and practitioners, been confounded with the Plague as well as with Typhus, from both of which it essentially differs. Reserving for discussion in another part of the volume the question, whether yellow fever, like the others, can be propagated by contagion ; the author next lays down several *diagnostic signs* by which these diseases are to be distinguished from each other : the yellow fever differs from the plague, in that it prevails only in those countries, and in those seasons, in which the heat is, or has recently been, so great as would destroy or stop the progress of the plague; in the intertropical climates, therefore, so favourable to the existence of the yellow fever, the plague is not at all known. The glandular and cutaneous affections, called buboes and carbuncles, so constantly accompanying the plague, are not found to exist in

* See Dr. Bancroft's appendix, No. I, containing " Observations on the Black Vomit," by Dr. Physic, and Dr. Ffirth, extracted from the New-York Medical Repository, vol. 5th, p. 129, and Dr. Cox's Medical Museum, vol. 1st. p. 116-118, also Dr. Mc.Arthur's account in the subsequent pages.

the yellow fever. 'A violent febrile paroxysm is essential to the character of yellow fever, whilst, according to the best authority, persons have been attacked with the plague without having the least febrile affection, as sometimes happens in small- pox, scarlet fever, and measles. Blacks are very rarely seized with the yellow fever ; and when seized are much less violently affected by it than Whites, living under the same circumstances ; whereas they are not less susceptible than Whites of the plague, and die of it in a far greater proportion.

" Yellow fever differs from typhus in the following circumstances, viz. it prevails, as I have already mentioned, only during, or immediately after, very hot seasons, in which typhus is soon extinguished ; and it is, in its turn, completely extinguished upon the accession of cold weather, in which typhus is commonly most prevalent ; it attacks most readily and most violently the young and robust, over whom typhus is allowed to have the least power ; it begins with much greater exertions of the living power than typhus ; is attended with many different symptoms, and terminates much sooner ; it is, besides, disposed to remit, and it frequently changes into a regular remittent, and sometimes even into an intermittent fever, which true typhus is never observed to do."

Having thus given a general outline of the symptoms and progress of the disease, the author proceeds to a consideration of the various remedies proposed for its cure, and offers some observations on the propriety and utility of each.

Bleeding.——A great contrariety of opinion, the author observes, has subsisted on the subject of *bleeding* in yellow fever ; some considering it as an indispensable remedy, and others alleging, that nearly all who were bled had died. Independently of actual experience, several circumstances attending this disease appear to render it probable, that the evacuation of blood would be serviceable to the patients labouring under it. This fever, especially the violent forms of it, seldom occur among any other persons than strangers recently arrived from temperate climates ; the greater part of whom will commonly be found to be young, robust and vigorous. In its first stage it is frequently accompanied with a very considerable degree of general inflammation, (which is, the author thinks, perhaps greater than in any other kind of fever,) indicated by a hard, full and strong pulse ; the distressing sense of universal distension, the red, starting, watery eye, and the parched skin. Those who have fallen victims to the disease have generally exhibited, on dissection, signs of considerable inflammation in various organs, and especially in the head and stomach. That the duration of a paroxysm of fever is lengthened, and its distressing consequences augmented by general inflammation, is well ascertained by experience, and no method is so likely to obviate these as bleeding. To render it beneficial it should be resorted to very early, (as within 24 hours, or even twelve, if possible, from the attack ;) and to prove effectual, it should be performed copiously, from a large orifice, soon after general inflammatory action is perceived ; more benefit arising from taking away a large quantity of blood at once, than by a larger evacuation at two or more bleedings. The propriety of the evacuation being made at all, however, and the quantity of blood to be taken, must be determined by the circumstances of each patient.

The above recommendation of blood-letting, is feeble when compared with that of several other modern authors, but I am not disposed to cavil with the writer on this account, or to place my faith too exclusively in any remedy ; for in different epidemics and states of the constitution, the same measure will be followed with very different results.—There can be no doubt, however, that in so powerful a disease, our hopes must chiefly rest on powerful means ; and that in the class of subjects generally selected by this fever, the young and robust, the lancet should be used with a bold hand. But it should be ever kept in mind, that the chance of success will almost entirely depend upon its being used within a few hours after the commencement of the attack. When employed too late, it will certainly hasten, though it may smooth, the passage to the grave,—for it has often been observed that patients who had been blooded died with much less suffering than those who had not undergone this operation.

Cold Water is, our author thinks, a very efficacious remedy in the yellow fever ; and when applied externally, affords very great relief to the feelings of the patient, who is frequently distressed with a sensation of burning heat ; the temperature of the skin, at the same time, being actually raised so much as four degrees of Fahrenheit's thermometer above the natural standard. It is only when the heat of the body is above the natural standard that cold water should be applied externally ; and the period of its application, and the frequency of its repetition, must generally be determined by the feelings of the patient ; for, should he become chilled by it, much mischief might ensue. To avoid the fatigue to the patient, which the usual mode of applying this remedy is apt to induce, the author recommends, as a useful substitute, that he should be covered, as he lies in bed, with a single sheet wetted with cold water, which, by evaporation, will gradually reduce the temperature of his body to a proper standard.

Notwithstanding this caution, the affusion of cold water in the first stage is by much the best and most efficacious mode of proceeding ; but as the disease advances, aspersion, or ablution, may be substituted with advantage, for then the shock might be injurious, and the object is to allay morbid heat and febrile irritation.

The author is of opinion that much benefit also arises from cold water taken internally as drink ; small quantities of which, frequently repeated, he has observed to moderate the excessive heat of body, as well as the violence of general febrile action ; it is efficacious likewise in disposing the skin to perspire gently, and in preventing inflammation of the stomach, or diminishing and removing it after it had been excited. The author's experience is confirmed by that of several other practitioners ; and the general utility of cold drinks in fevers has been acknowledged by all physicians, ancient as well as modern, while the author thinks it has been too seldom employed by British and American physicians in their treatment of yellow fever.

Purgatives are proper, to obviate that state of costiveness which frequently precedes, and generally accompanies, yellow fever ; they should be such as will not offend or irritate the stomach by their bulk or quality ; the author appears rather to employ them for the purpose of preventing an accumulation of fæcal matters, which might produce morbid irritability in the whole intestinal canal, and aggravate other symptoms, than as means of carrying off the fever, as has been proposed by Dr. Hamilton in the fevers of this country.

Here, also, the author is too sparing in his approbation of so valuable an auxiliary as purgatives ; though he very properly recommends such as will not offend the stomach by their bulk or quality. Full doses of calomel combined with jalap, compound extract of Colocynth, &c. assisted by enemas, if necessary, should be given so as to insure early free evacuations—nor should we rest until this object be obtained ; and such quantities of medicines of this class should be repeated during the course of the disease as will obtain two or more motions daily.

Emetics are very properly reprobrated by Dr. Bancroft in the yellow fever, on the grounds that gastric irritability is usually a very early symptom—one of the most difficult to allay—and of the most dangerous tendency. So far from being removed it is too invariably aggravated by the use of emetics ; as indeed must be expected when the irritability of this organ, instead of being caused by bile, undigested aliment, or other offending matter, originates from sympathy with the morbid condition of the brain or of the surface, or, as is too often the case, from rising inflammation in the coats of the stomach itself. Neither, observes our author, are their pernicious effects confined to this viscus, for the violent efforts to vomit exhaust the strength and propel a larger quantity of blood to the brain, already suffering from undue excitation. Instead of increasing, therefore, the object is to calm and allay the irritation of the stomach as much as possible ; and the most likely method of effecting this indication is by an active and judicious employment of such means as lessen the general fever and local inflammatory action—by keeping the bowels freely open, by abstracting morbid heat from the surface, by avoiding the irritation of distension from drink or medicine, and by the counter irritation of a large blister over the epigastrium. With the same view Dr. B. has tried small doses of opium, as half a grain, at intervals, but though it might succeed in allaying a slight degree of gastric irritability, the utility of opium is not only very questionable, but in the early stage, or in a high state of vascular or cerebral excitement it must prove decidedly injurious.

Sudorifics are also justly disapproved of by Dr. Bancroft, as tending to increase that disposition to vomit, from which the greatest danger is to be apprehended. The preparations of antimony, especially, too often leave behind them a degree of gastric irritability which resists all our endeavours to appease it, and there can be no doubt that by aiding this formidable symptom, they have been too frequently employed to the irreparable injury of the patient, while the intention with which they are exhibited cannot be effected by such means. For this purpose saline draughts in a state of effervescence, and other mild febrifuges, may be used ; but the most effectual mode of restoring the natural functions of the surface, is by cold or tepid affusion, or ablution, and such other measures as lessen morbid heat, and febrile action.

The Peruvian Bark, Dr. B. thinks, may be exhibited as soon as the febrile commotion subsides ; but, like opium, the early use of cinchona is of very questionable propriety : there will be a risk of its reproducing vomiting if it has subsided, and if it continues, any attempt to make bark remain upon the stomach is equally hopeless and objectionable. Indeed, Dr. B.'s caution not to give it " when there is a parched skin, a hard pulse, a dry tongue, great heat and pain at the stomach, or delirium," is tantamount to a prohibition in a vast majority of instances ; for too often are some of those or other dangerous symptoms, where it is equally inadmissible, the very difficulties with which we have to contend.

These observations, however, chiefly apply to the ardent continued form of yellow fever. For in cases where decided remissions are observed, in marshy situations, and in habits reduced by long residence or otherwise ; in fine, where the febrile movements are neither of the same rapidity, nor inflammatory tendency, the bark is often of the greatest service, and is chiefly depended upon in the French, and some of the other Islands, most fruitful in vegetable life and decay. When the violence of the first stage is passed, and the patient is rapidly merging in a state of great exhaustion and depression of the nervous energy and vital power, cordials and stimulants, as wine, or even spirit diluted, ammonia, capsicum, &c. are to be resorted to ; and small quantities of some bland nutritious matter should be cautiously but assiduously administered. But instead of attempting to do too much in the advanced period, we should carefully remember, that it is only in the first and inflammatory stage, and soon after its onset, that we can hope by active measures either to subdue the disease, or to disarm it of its dangerous tendency to rapid disorganization and death.

It is not to be wondered at, that in a disease so frequently fatal in its event, and so unmanageable by mild and ordinary methods, recourse should have been had to *Mercury*, whose effects upon the animal œconomy, whether salutary or deleterious, are generally very powerful. It certainly has been employed to a considerable extent in yellow fever, but whether advantageously or not, is a matter of some doubt. No inconsiderable authorities may be adduced on each side of the question, and their decision of the point in dispute, is said equally to rest on the basis of experience. The most common operation of this metal, when exhibited internally, is either to produce copious evacuations by stool, or to act upon the salivary glands, so as to excite considerable salivation ; and in both cases, benefit has been said to be derived from its exhibition. In those cases of recovery which have followed the employment of mercury, some evident effects of its operation have been commonly manifested, while in cases which have terminated fatally under its use, no perceptible action has arisen from it ; whence the recovery in the former case has been attributed to the action thus produced, while the fatal event has been sup-

posed to be owing to the want of such action. Such reasoning, however, there is ground to think is too often fallacious. Supposing that
the patients labouring under yellow fever, in whom a salivation can
be excited, generally recover, it is not necessarily to be inferred, that
their recovery was effected by the salivation ; or that when patients
died, to whom mercury had been given, and no salivation had been
produced, such patients died, because mercury had not been taken
in sufficient quantity to produce that excretion. It is far more reasonable to conclude, Dr. B. thinks, that where persons had recovered
from the yellow fever, after having been salivated, their recovery
was not occasioned by the salivation, but was the consequence of such
a condition of the powers of life, and of the functions connected
therewith, as induced a mitigation of the disorder ; for the same reason, and, perhaps, in the same degree as it favoured the operation of
the mercury upon such persons ; and, therefore, that although recovery
very has not unfrequently followed or accompanied salivation, the
latter was not the cause of the former.   In like manner, there is
reason to conclude, he thinks, that when patients die of yellow fever,
after all attempts to excite salivation in them have failed, their deaths
have resulted, not from the want of any good effect which salivation
may be thought capable of producing, but because the condition of
their living or sensorial power, and of the functions depending thereon, had already become so morbid, as to render their recovery impossible.   We shall here give the summary of our author's reasoning upon this important subject, the exhibition of mercury.

   " In order, however, to attain the truth upon this important subject, it is not sufficient for us to discover, that recovery generally
follows salivation in yellow fever, though even this is contradicted by
many very respectable authorities ; but we must ascertain whether
those practitioners who excite salivation in as many of their patients
as may be susceptible of it, under that disorder, do in fact lose a
smaller proportion of them than those who purposely abstain from
all endeavours to produce that discharge ; and on this point, I must
declare, that after some experience, assisted by no ordinary portion
of inquiry and information, I have not been able to discover that the
salivators were more successful than the others.   And, if not more
successful, their practice has certainly been hurtful ; because in
most of the persons who have recovered, the (perhaps useless) salivation had retarded the convalescence, and produced very troublesome affections of the tongue, mouth, and throat, with other ill consequences, as is well known and acknowledged, even by its advocates.   Dr. Chisholm, (at page 357, of vol. i. of his Essay,) warmly
acknowledges his " obligations to Dr. Rush, for supporting in a mas-
terly manner," and " pursuing the mercurial mode of treatment,"
and expresses both " admiration and respect" for his " fortitude" in
doing so.

   But Dr. Rush, notwithstanding this support and this fortitude, has
candidly stated, that ' in the City Hospital,' (of Philadelphia,) where
bleeding was sparingly used, and where the Physician depended chiefly
upon salivation *more than one-half died*, of all the patients who were
admitted.'

" To one who is sincerely desirous of discovering and adhering to the truth, it is extremely difficult to reconcile, or account for, the very opposite testimonies given on this subject ; and the doing it would moreover be too invidious for me to attempt it. This, however, appears certain, that the good effects of the mercurial treatment have been greatly exaggerated by persons, who either were deceived, or were willing to deceive others ; that many persons have died of the fever in question, although mercury administered externally or internally, had produced a copious salivary discharge ; and that in very many others who have recovered, this discharge did not begin until after a solution, or a great mitigation of the disease had evidently taken place ; which solution or mitigation, therefore, could not have been the effect of salivation."*

After having thus gone through the account of the symptoms and treatment of the Yellow Fever, we come to a consideration of its causes. A belief has prevailed of the contagious nature of this disease ; and the origin of it, in different places, has been ascribed to the action of contagion. Our author strongly controverts this opinion ; and while he denies that any instances of the fever have ever been clearly shown to arise from contagion, he enters into an elaborate discussion, to show the impossibility of its doing so. It has been asserted by some authors of eminence, that *all* fevers are naturally contagious, and capable of exciting fever in other persons.† Among those who have so asserted, Dr. George Fordyce is to be found, and he has expressed himself very strongly on this subject ; his opinion is, that a peculiar matter is *generated* in the body of a man in fever, which being carried by the atmosphere, and applied to some part of the body of a person in health, causes a fever to take place in him ; and he adds, that this infectious matter is produced by *all fevers whatever.* In confirmation of this opinion, he adds, that " by repeated experience it is now known that, although it very frequently happens that a man coming near another afflicted with fever, is not afterwards affected with the disease, yet, of any number of men, one-half of whom go near a person ill of this disease, and the other half do not go near a person so diseased, a greater number of the former will be affected with fever than of the latter, in a short period afterwards." Again, he says, " the author has known seven out of nine, who went near a person afflicted with fever, seized with the disease in the space of three weeks afterwards ; there is, therefore, a perfect ground from experience, for believing, that coming near a person afflicted with fever is a cause of the disease."

Dr. Bancroft's objections to this opinion of Dr. Fordyce are thus stated. " This general indiscriminating assertion, if it were true, could only prove that some fevers are contagious ; not that all are so. But the assertion is manifestly founded upon a supposed probability, or presumption, that such effects would result from the causes here described ; for no one can believe, that an actual experiment was

* Mr. Sheppard in a very able Paper in the 13th Volume of the Edinburgh Medical and Surgical Journal has adduced the opinions of various modern Practitioners in corroboration of the inutility of attempting to affect the system with Mercury, during the active stage of Yellow Fever.

† Drs. Cleghorn, Robert Hamilton, John Clark, Fordyce, &c.

ever made by selecting a certain number of persons, and sending one-half of them into close communication with a febrile patient, and after-wards contrasting what happened to those who were not allowed to approach any person labouring under fever.   Nor would a single experiment afford any conviction on this subject, for reasons too obvious to require explanation.   Much also would depend on the species of fever to which the individuals in question are supposed to have been exposed, which is not mentioned by Dr. Fordyce.   Few persons, if any, doubt of the contagious quality of what is called Jail Fever, and few believe that intermittent fevers possess that quality."

Before we go further, I must reply, in answer to these objections, that we can scarcely allow Dr. Fordyce's assertion to be founded upon a *supposed probability or presumption*, when he affirms that by *repeated experience* it is now *known*, &c. ; and although we cannot prove that Dr. Fordyce actually made the experiment of selecting a certain number of persons, and sending one-half of them into close communication with a febrile patient, and afterwards contrasting what happened to these with the condition of those who were not allowed to approach any person labouring under fever ; we may be convinced from the well known character of the Doctor, that he would not neglect any *practicable* method of ascertaining the truth of an opinion he was about to publish to the world.   Would he not have been warranted in his conclusion, if he had ascertained, that out of a given number (sufficiently large) of patients coming under his care with fever, *more than one half* had, within a short period, been near persons affected with fever ?   I do not think the validity of the argument at all depends on the *species* of fever, since it is evident that Dr. Fordyce was not now speaking of fevers propagating themselves by *specific* contagions, but of the *generation* of infectious matter in fevers, which might produce in other persons fever, either similar to themselves or different from them, depending on circumstances peculiar to the persons exposed to its action ; and that he did not deny to intermittents the power of thus generating infectious matter we are assured, by his saying that intermittent fevers produce this matter, or, in other words, are infectious ; and that, " he *knows this from his own observation*, as well as that of others."   So far as argument goes, grounded on facts, I think we have another in favour of Dr. Fordyce's opinion.   Do we not sometimes see an individual in a family seized with fever, when no intercourse with other febrile persons could be traced, where indeed it was almost impossible any should have taken place ?   and do we not see afterwards several members of the same family affected with fever, communicated as far as we can judge by the person first affected ?   In this case, one of two things must be true ; either the action of contagion cannot be so limited in extent, as has been contended, if the first person took the fever from infection ;   or a matter must have been *generated* in the person first affected capable of producing fever in others.   We must choose between the unlimited diffusion of febrile infection, or the generation of it in fevers arising from other causes.

Of *Negative proofs*, I confess, Dr. Bancroft has produced sufficient to show that fever may sometimes exist to a considerable extent, without producing fever in other persons communicating with those originally attacked ;· some of these proofs I shall lay before my readers, only remarking first, that they are all instances of marsh remittent fever, and that Dr. Fordyce says intermitting fevers are not nearly so apt to produce contagious matter, at least to propagate it, as continued fevers ; and secondly, that most of these instances occurred in climates very different from that of this country, and it is to this country Dr. Fordyce's observations are perhaps chiefly intended to apply.

The first instance mentioned by Dr. Bancroft, is that recorded by Dr. Trotter, in his Medicina Nautica, occurring at the Island of St. Thomas's, 1762, where *all* the people who were lodged ashore during night, died afterwards on the passage, while the rest of the ship's company remained remarkably healthy. A similar instance also occurred in the crews of the Ponsborne and Nottingham East Indiamen, at the Comora Islands, in the years 1765 and 1766. Of this fever, Dr. Badenock, then surgeon of the Nottingham, observes, it infected *only those who slept on shore*, and having gone through them the fever ceased ; this he says, was also the case with those on board the Ponsborne, of whom, it appears, no less than seventy died. A· similar occurrence is related by Dr. John Clark, in the first volume of his Observations on the Diseases which prevail in Long Voyages to Hot Countries, page 124 ; after describing the low place, " covered with impenetrable mangroves, at North Island, near the Streights of Sunda, where most of the East India ships take in wood and water for their homeward voyage ;" he adds, that " a Danish ship, in 1768, anchored at this island, and sent twelve of her people on shore to fill water, where they only remained two nights. *Every one* of them were seized with a fever, of which *none recovered ;* but, although the ship went out to *sea, none,* except the twelve who slept on shore, were attacked with the complaint. Here again was a fever so violent as to kill every one in whom it was excited, and from a cause so powerful as to effect every one who was exposed to it ; which, notwithstanding, did not reproduce itself in a single instance."

One of the most decisive instances of the non-contagious quality of the marsh remittent fever is, the author thinks, to be found in the late unfortunate Walcheren expedition, wherein nearly thirty thousand men and officers were attacked by fever, which proved fatal to nearly one-sixth of the whole number of sick ; and yet not a single case could be discovered in which there was reason to suppose that any one person caught the fever from another, either upon the island of Walcheren, or among the sick removed to this country ; so that we may fairly conclude, if fevers of this description are ever contagious, and communicated to those not previously exposed to marsh miasmata, the instances are rare and solitary, and that, in general, they must be ranked as non-contagious ; we shall see, hereafter, the author's reasons for classing the yellow fever among the species of marsh remittents, and his proofs of its non-contagious quality.*

* In enumerating the chief writers for, and against contagion, at the commencement of this section, I have omitted Drs. Palloni, Arejula, Hossack, and several others, because they consider this disease as contagious, or infectious, in some situations, and in others not contagious ; and therefore cannot, with propriety, be classed with either party.

Another question, amply discussed by our author previous to his enumeration of the causes of yellow fever, is, whether a fever, strictly contagious, can be generated by an accumulation of filth, or of putrefying or putrid matters, or by the crowding of healthy persons into confined, or ill-ventilated, and unclean places ? With respect to the first part of the proposition; the generation of contagious fever by the accumulation of putrefying or putrid *dead* animal matter, I believe the general opinion of the medical world is against putrefaction being a source of febrile contagion, and therefore it is unnecessary to repeat the various instances related by the author, of large masses of these matters existing in different places, and no fever having been traced to arise from them ; but physicians are not so unanimous in their belief concerning the power of emanations from the healthy *living* body, to generate, when accumulated and concentrated, fever of a contagious nature, and therefore it may be worth while to state some of the arguments and facts adduced by Dr. Bancroft, in favour of the innoxious qualities of human effluvia, so far as regards the production of fever. That crowding, filth, and deficient ventilation, may take place in a variety of situations without producing contagious fever, the author has shown in instancing the mode of life led by the inhabitants of the more northern climates, who are shut up for a long severe winter in jourts, or subterraneous dwellings, each common to many families, in which they live in horrible filthiness, among whom fever is not known to arise ; the wretched confined situation of the slaves on the middle passage of the slave ships, in a sultry climate, without any production of contagious fever among them ; and the memorable occurrence of the confinement of British subjects in the Black hole, at Calcutta, in June, 1756, where, out of 146 persons shut up a whole night in a dungeon, about a cube of 18 feet, only 23 remained alive in the morning ; none of whom were afterwards affected with fever. All these instances, however, having occurred in climates where the extremes of temperature might be supposed to counteract and destroy the tendency to contagion arising from these circumstances, it becomes of great importance to examine Dr. Bancroft's explanation of the supposed production of contagious fevers from similar circumstances in this country.

The first memorable instance of mortality from the apparent effects of morbid contagion noticed by our author, is that occurring at the Black Assize; at Oxford, in the month of July, 1577. The circumstances of this event are well known; and the opinion has been generally prevalent, that the disease was communicated by infection. The author, at great length, and with much ingenuity, endeavours to controvert this opinion ; I must refer our readers to the work itself for the arguments he makes use of for this purpose, and content myself with giving the conclusion he draws as the result of his investigation.

" The most probable *meaning* of all these accounts would seem to be, that, about the time when sentence was passed on the prisoners, a noxious vapour, in some degree perceptible to the senses, and

proceeding either from the prisoners or the earth,* had been suddenly diffused through the hall, and that, in consequence thereof, a
great part of those who were present had been almost immediately
attacked, and that many died within a few hours.

" There is, however, no cause of disease with which I am acquainted, whose effects would have been such as are here described. Pestilential contagion cannot be suspected, because that would have required *contact*, and because the symptoms of the disease were not like
those of the plague, nor was it contagious. And there is as little reason to suspect the contagion of typhus, or jail fever, (especially at
that season of the year) there being no instance recorded, or known,
of its producing disease so suddenly, nor of that disease, when produced, terminating so speedily in death. Nor were the symptoms
such as occur in jail fevers : nor does the contagion of that fever
spare women, children, and *poor people*, as the cause of this disease
is stated to have done, (but on the contrary :) nor do the stoutest and
most robust sooner perish by it, as the Register of Merton College
declares to have happened in this disease. (' Et ut quisque fortissi-
mus, ita citissime moritur.') " Whether the facts connected with
the production, and nature of this disease have been misrepresented,
or, whether it proceeded from a cause which has ceased to operate
in later times, I leave for the decision of others."

Passing over the accounts of sickness and mortality occurring at
Exeter, in 1586; at Taunton, in 1730; and at Launceston, in 1742,
since Dr. Bancroft does not seem to deny there being instances of
jail infection, we come to the remarkable occurrence which took
place at London in May, 1750, at the Sessions of the Old Bailey,
which proved fatal to the Lord Mayor and two of the Judges, with

---

* Camden makes use of the words *venenoso et pestilenti halitu sive foedore incar-
ceratorum, sive ex solo* ita correpti sunt plerique omnes qui aderant, &c. and Sir
Richard Baker says, " suddenly they were surprised with a pestilential savour;
whether arising from the noisome smell of the prisoners, or from the *damp ground*,
is uncertain." Dr. Bancroft in a note, observes, " the expressions seem to point
at marsh effluvia, which, at that season of the year, would be more likely to occasion disease than typhus contagion, and in a shorter space of time, and chiefly
upon vigorous men; probably, also, the situation of the place was suitable for
their production. The old Shire Hall, in which sentence was passed on Rowland
Jencks, was placed in the *yard* of Oxford Castle, (once deemed impregnable,)
which stood on the west side of the town, at a small distance from the river *Isis*,
whose banks, especially at that time, were low. The prison was also within the
Castle, at about 200 yards distance from the Hall, and consisted of a multangular
tower, called St. George's, (on the west side of the Castle,) together with an ad-
joing church, which also bore the name of St. George, and two square rooms, all
connected one with the other, and made the common jail for the county, by a sta-
tute in the reign of Henry the Third. See Grose's Antiquities of England, vol.
iv. p. 182–3; also, King's Vestiges of Oxford Castle, p. 28. In the Appendix to
Thomas Hearne's Preface to Gulielmi Neubrigensis Historia, &c. p. 88, is a print
representing the Castle of Oxford, and on the other side of the river is a mount,
at the foot of which are the ruins of an old building, which are thus described in
a note to the plate, viz. Reliquiæ domûs in quâ *assizæ* olim tenebantur, donec
ob pestem subitaneam ad alium civitatis locum regnante *Elizabethâ* transferre pla-
cuit." But though I think marsh miasmata a more probable cause of the disease
in question than typhus contagion, I am far from believing that they would have
produced effects, such as are said to have occurred at this Black Assize."

several eminent and other persons. These were supposed to have been infected by the contagion of jail fever, brought into the court from Newgate. Such was the opinion of Sir John Pringle, Dr. Hales, and other eminent men. Our author, however, is of a far different opinion ; and having given in the Appendix a copious statement of the whole transaction, and pointed out an important fact, acknowledged by those who have recorded the occurrence, viz. *the opening of a large window* in front, and on the *left* hand of the court, proves that the mischief done, or sickness produced, was confined to* those who were placed in the direction of this stream of *cold air*, which, *therefore, contained and conveyed the morbid influence, whatever it was, that occasioned the fever ;* and endeavours to show that this stream of air did not direct the *putrid streams* to that part of the court where the Judges were seated, as asserted by Sir John Pringle ; but that the disease which took place in the different individuals, was in consequence of *the morbid affection from the application of cold.* Whatever objection may be urged against the opinion of this fever being produced by cold, on account of the *great mortality* which took place, will apply, the author thinks, with equal force, against its having been produced by contagion, since the most concentrated and virulent jail infection ever known in this country, has never produced a fourth part so many deaths among an equal number of sick ; and he adds, " though the mortality in question was greater than I should have expected from a fever produced by the sudden application of cold, yet, so many things are capable of increasing and aggravating the morbid effects of that cause, particularly by inducing local and mortal inflammation in some important organ, or viscus, that it is much less surprising that a fever so produced should occasion an unprecedented mortality, than it would have been, if so many deaths had resulted from a jail or typhus fever." See Appendix No. iv. p. 653.

I have been thus full in stating our author's view of the question respecting the generation of contagion, because it is one of serious importance, and one on which much uncertainty still prevails. Little doubt has been entertained by many men of respectable talents and extensive observation, of the generation of contagion in close and ill-ventilated apartments ; I shall instance two only, the late Dr. Murray, of London, who took so active a part in the establishment of a fever-house of recovery in the metropolis, and Dr. Ferriar, who directed his attention to a similar establishment in Manchester, because they may be supposed to have inquired into the subject with the greatest care. The latter says, " It is a fact, equally alarming and true, that many persons in indigent circumstances are exposed in our great towns, to such evils as I have shown to be *productive* of febrile contagion."

" One of the most satisfactory instances of this sort was observed by Dr. Heysham, at Carlisle, in 1778 or 1779. A fever of the nervous kind raged in that city, which did not seem to have been introduced from any neighbouring place. Dr. Heysham, with great in-

---

* Dr. Bancroft has given an engraved plan of the Old Bailey, describing the precise situation of the Judges, Jurors, &c.

dustry, traced its *origin* to a house near one of the gates, which was tenanted by five or six very poor families ; these unhappy creatures had blocked up every avenue of light with which even wretchedness could dispense, and thus contaminated the air of their cells to such a degree, as to *produce* the poison of fever among them " " The plague itself appears to *originate* with the crowded inhabitants of the miserable villages in the East."*

No doubt, however, can exist of the propagation of the febrile infection being facilitated by want of cleanliness and ventilation ; and this knowledge will be a sufficient inducement to obviate this source of its diffusion when practicable.

The most frequent, or rather, according to our author, the only exciting cause of yellow fever, is the application of marsh miasmata to the human body, and the disease, therefore, is really a marsh remittent fever. The opinion held by some eminent men, that fevers of this description might be produced by simple moisture alone, is, I think, successfully controverted by Dr. Bancroft ; and he accordingly looks for the specific cause of the fever arising into the air in something from the decomposition of animal or vegetable matters. Sufficient has been stated in the former part of the volume to show that the most extensive decomposition of animal matters may be going on, without any disease taking place in those exposed to the exhalations therefrom ; it follows then, that the noxious particles, whatever they be, in marsh exhalations, arise from the decomposition of vegetable substances ; and this opinion is strengthened by the fact, that fevers are sometimes produced in persons employed in the preparation of flax and hemp, and in those who continue near the heaps of indigo plant, laid together after the colouring matter is extracted. Whether any one particular gas, known to be produced by vegetable decomposition, or a combination of several of these gasses, or some matter not yet detected, is the efficient cause of the disease, can, in the present state of science, be no more than matter of conjecture. We know, however, that the *action* of this cause is facilitated and increased by the concurrence of certain circumstances, and that its operation is more powerful in hot climates and hot seasons, than in the contrary ; but our author points out a difference of *susceptibility* in persons exposed to marsh miasmata, which renders their influence on the system more or less powerful ; his observations on this subject are so important, that I cannot refrain from laying them before my readers.

" There is, however, *another condition of the body*, which is of great importance, in regard to the production of yellow fever, and which, therefore, requires a particular investigation ; I mean, the *cause* of that remarkable *susceptibility* to this *disease*, which is commonly found in persons who have just arrived at places where it occurs, from cold or temperate climates ; and of the equally remarkable exemption from it, which is commonly experienced by the *old* inhabitants of hot countries ; and which in the latter, is universally ascribed to their having become seasoned, as it is called ; but, however familiar this term may be, and of whatever importance its pro-

* Ferriar, Vol. 1. pp. 240 and 245.

per signification really is,*(since it involves the means of preservation from one of the most dreadful maladies which afflict the human
race,) it has been long employed either without any precise meaning, or with meanings which are inadmissible. Thus it is often said,
that a person is seasoned who has once had the yellow fever ; but
very improperly, because the same individual may have the disorder
several times ; besides which, many persons become exempt from the
fever, and ought, therefore, to be considered as being truly seasoned,
without having ever suffered an attack of the disease. It is also frequently believed, that one may become seasoned by residing long in
those towns in which the yellow fever is apt to recur ; but the very
great numbers of the inhabitants of Philadelphia, New-York, Malaga,
Cadiz, Seville, &c. who have been swept off by the distemper, within
a few years, are melancholy proofs that an efficacious seasoning is
not to be acquired merely by such residence. Nor can it be said,
that those who live near marshes are peculiarly seasoned, because,
in hot countries. numbers of persons, who live at a distance from
marshes, are proof against the yellow fever, although they are sometimes attacked with slight remittents or intermittents.

" After some reflection on this interesting subject, the various degrees of susceptibility which are observed in different individuals or
in different places, seem to me capable of explanation on a very simple principle ; I mean the effects of temperature on the human frame,
which does not appear to have been sufficiently noticed.

" The body, whilst in health, is found always to be, with very
slight variation, at the temperature of 98 degrees of Fahrenheit's
thermometer, and there is good reason to think that any considerable
variation from this point, would necessarily produce morbid effects.
It seems, therefore, to be of high importance, that the body should
be preserved from such deviations ; and the Author of Nature has,
accordingly, provided efficacious means for that end. Different opinions are indeed entertained concerning these means ; and since the
later chemical discoveries have been made, it has been generally believed, that, in an atmosphere, the temperature of which is less than
98 degrees, the heat of the human body is maintained at that point,
by a process similar to that of combustion, and depending upon a
combination of oxygen gas, (taken into the lungs by respiration,)
with carbon and hydrogen ; and that, in an atmosphere heated above
98 degrees, the temperature of the body is kept down at that point
by the effect of an evaporation of matters perspired from the skin.
There are, however, insurmountable difficulties opposed to this doctrine, but a full statement of them would, in some degree, be foreign
to the subject under our consideration ; I will, therefore, at present,
only remark, that it is *utterly incredible* that these *opposite processes*
should ever be carried on so *accurately in reference to each other*, and
be so exactly. *balanced*, as invariably to keep the body at the heat of
98 degrees, in all the diversities of temperature that occur in different climates and situations, and therefore, that this important *conser-
vatory* function must depend on a power more *exalted* in its nature,
and more *certain* in its operations, which can be no other than the

power of life; a power which, in proportion as it is more vigorous in robust individuals at the prime of life, notoriously enables them to resist the *opposite extremes* of heat and cold, and preserve their bodies at the proper standard more perfectly, and for a greater length of time, than at a more advanced age. I will not venture to assert that no addition to the heat of the body can be made, either directly or indirectly, by the combination of oxygen with the blood, and I readily admit that its temperature may be diminished by a copious evaporation from its surface; but if either of these causes should cooperate with the living power to a small extent, the one in raising and the other in lowering what is called animal heat, it must always be in complete *subordination* to the higher principle of which I have been speaking, and to which nature has committed the important charge of preserving the temperature of the body at the standard of health, amidst all the varieties of climate, and of external circumstances. This is a charge which cannot be fulfilled in an atmosphere like that of England, the mean temperature of which may be estimated at 50°, without a considerable expenditure of the living power, in order to generate constantly at the mean rate of 48° of animal heat; and after the body has been, for a length of time, accustomed to make this exertion, it is easy to perceive that, upon removing into a warm climate, such as that of the West Indies, the general mean temperature of which may be taken at 79° or 80°, very material changes in the functions of the system become absolutely necessary for the preservation of health.—But these changes are not to be suddenly effected; and, until the body becomes perfectly accommodated to the heat of this new climate, the whole animal economy must be considered as almost in a state of morbid excitement. It is not this state, (of excitement,) however, which alone is productive of fever; since we know that innumerable persons have gone from Europe to the hottest regions of the globe, and have continued there for years, without being attacked by fever, when other causes did not assist in producing that disease. The inhabitants of South Carolina, as I have lately mentioned, were exposed to this kind of excitement, in an extreme degree, during a great part of the summer of 1752, and yet had never been more healthy; and other instances of the same import might, if necessary, be adduced."

" But, although the simple operation of the warmth of hot climates upon the human body be not the cause of this disease, yet it is chiefly, if not entirely, to the various degrees of that derangement which it occasions in persons not accustomed to warm climates, that I attribute all those varieties of liability to the epidemic yellow fever, which are observable in different individuals, from the extreme susceptibility of northern strangers to the almost complete immunity of Creoles, and more especially of African negroes. It may be very difficult to point out the particular means by which heat occasions this extreme susceptibility; and yet it is not difficult to understand, that a morbid cause may be able to produce a much more violent disease, when it is assisted by the co-operation of so powerful an agent as heat, than it could produce when acting by its own single influence; and it is upon this principle that I shall endeavour to explain the general law, by which the susceptibility to the yellow fever is *cæteris paribus*, regulated," p. 254.

The author then takes a concise view of the climates in which the yellow fever has principally raged, and applies the principle just mentioned, to the results which the experience of several years in each of them has afforded. It appears, that negroes are far less liable to be affected with yellow fever than white persons ; and it was observed at Cadiz in 1800, that persons lately arrived in that city from the West Indies, did not suffer an attack of the epidemic, while those persons who had come from *Canada* and other *northern* countries, were very liable to the disease. The security from the attacks of this fever derived from the " *ability to endure great heat*," continues only so long as this ability continues ; for if the inhabitants of warm climates remove for a few years into cold countries, and afterwards return, they are then found liable to the fever. From all the facts stated, and from the repeated observations made by the author, he thinks himself justified in his opinion, that the joint influence of marsh miasmata, and of an atmosphere unusually and sufficiently heated, upon persons habituated to a cold or temperate climate, is of itself, fully capable of causing an epidemic yellow fever, exactly resembling that which has committed such ravages in the West Indies, the United States of America, and the South of Europe.

Upon the preceding theory, that those varieties of liability to the epidemic yellow fever which are observable in different individuals are to be attributed " chiefly, if not entirely, to the various degrees of that derangement which heat occasions in persons not accustomed to warm climates," it may be necessary to offer some observations ; for there is reason to fear that this view of the subject is much too limited. · The ability to endure great heat is undoubtedly a considerable, but it is not the only, or perhaps even the chief source of immunity ; otherwise those who have been inured to other tropical regions, where the temperature is as high, or higher than it is in the West Indies, would be protected from the yellow fever, which is far from being the case. The leading features of Dr. Bancroft's writings are, great industry in research, and acuteness in argument. Admiring these talents, it is not from a disposition to criticise, but from the momentous importance of this part of the subject, that I am induced to reconsider his discussion of the question—in what does this seasoning consist ? He contends, that it is not from having previously undergone the fever, because the same individual may have it several times ; and because many persons become exempt without ever having suffered an attack of it. To this it may be answered—it is true that a person is not secured by having had the fever once, as some writers of limited experience have discovered, but it is also true that he will be less liable after having sustained an attack of this, or any disease which reduces the tone and vigour of the system ; and that those who escape altogether do not acquire their security by mere length of residence, and consequent habituation to the predisponent, tropical heat, but also because they have been *gradually*

exposed, and inured to the other remote causes of the disease.*
Again, Dr. B. observes, it is not from residing long in *any* place in
which the yellow fever is apt to occur, as the multitudes who were
swept off at Philadelphia, New-York, Malaga, Cadiz, &c. abundantly
demonstrate ; but these are places in the temperate zone, whose variations of climate must ever prevent the inhabitants from acquiring
unsusceptibility, as will appear more clearly hereafter ; and if seasoning cannot be induced by intertropical residence alone, with how
much less reason, *a fortiori* can such effect be expected from the
ultra-tropical situations above specified. The last argument of Dr.
Bancroft is—that it is not from residing habitually near marshes, because numbers of persons who live at a distance from marshes in hot
climates are proof against the yellow fever, although they are sometimes attacked with slight remittents or intermittents, (p 246.) Now,
in the first place, the living at a distance from marshes proves little
or nothing, because the whole bearing of Dr. B.'s researches is to
show that febrific exhalations "are often emitted from soils and situations which have no resemblance to a marsh," (Sequel, p. 254 ;)
and secondly, as these people do suffer attacks of the milder recurrent type, they certainly would be liable, at particular seasons, to the
more aggravated form of fever, if they had recently arrived, instead
of having been gradually inured to these miasms ; or if, though favoured by longer residence, they were exposed to more concentrated
miasmata. Upon the whole, then, it is not upon any simple principle—as the being accustomed to great heat, that we can explain the
grounds of exemption from yellow fever.

If this disease were simply a calenture as Moseley and some later
writers seem to consider it, then indeed we need look for no further
source of exemption than the power of resisting the effects of high
temperature ; but as the novelty and consequently the force of the
impression of insolation must be greatly diminished by habit, and as
notwithstanding individuals have too frequently fallen victims to yellow fever who have been exposed for years together to a tropical
heat, when brought fully under the operation of noxious causes, the
conclusion is inevitable, that habituation to the local febrific effluvia,
be they from the soil or other source,—and to other agency, beyond
that of solar heat, is indispensable to security. In proof of this, medical men who have resided for a length of time in the Antilles, have
repeatedly observed individuals fall victims to the yellow fever, after
having been two, three, four, or more years in that country ; evincing that the being inured to a high temperature is but one disqualify-
ing property, and of itself unable to confer immunity, (though I am
far from questioning its relative importance in greatly contributing to
this result,) when other powerful exciting causes are applied.

The Fourth Part of this Essay contains a history of the yellow
fever in the various places in which it has often prevailed as an epidemic ; the intervals of its appearing epidemically are sometimes
considerable, while at other times the fever rages more frequently.

* Mr. Sheppard has further illustrated this subject in a paper inserted in the
47th No. of the Edinburgh Medical and Surgical Journal.

In no instance, however, can its origin be traced to contagion, but it seems always to have been produced by local causes, aided by the increased temperature of the season. Our author therefore next endeavours to establish the *identity* or *near affinity* and *connexion* of the yellow fever with the fevers which are indisputably and notoriously produced by marsh miasmata. . These latter have certain *characteristic peculiarities*, which are pointed out by the author, and afterwards compared with those phenomena which accompany the yellow fever, to show the very great similarity and near resemblance be-between the two diseases.—These characteristic peculiarities of marsh fevers, as stated by Dr. Bancroft, are, 1st. That of occurring in their simple and mild form of intermittents during the spring. 2nd. That of being exasperated, converted to *remittent*, and apparently to *continued* fevers, by excessive summer heat ; and this, generally, with a great increase of malignity, (especially in low and moist situations,) when this excessive heat is long continued, and accompanied with *a total, or very unusual, deprivation of rain*. 3d. That of their being re-converted and brought back to their mild intermittent form, at the approach or commencement of winter, and afterwards extinguished, or suspended, by a continued frost. 4th. That of most frequently and violently attacking strangers from colder climates and more salubrious situations. And, 5th. That of never being communicated from person to person by a contagious property.

In addition to the facts and authorities already mentioned in the former part of the volume, as tending to prove these peculiarities in marsh remittent fevers, the author brings a great number of additional proofs to the same point, and afterwards shows the existence of similar phenomena in the yellow fever, in his account of the history of its origin and progress in almost all the West India Islands, and at several places in North America. To follow Dr. Bancroft through the whole of this diffuse statement is impracticable, but I shall subjoin his inferences on the subject of the identity of the two diseases, which naturally arise from the history and statement he had previously given.

" Those of my readers who, by a love of truth, may have been induced to follow me attentively in the *view* which I have now taken of the yellow fever in different parts of America, and whose minds are unbiassed, will, I am confident, clearly recognize in that disease, *all the peculiar features and characteristic marks* by which *marsh* fevers are distinguished in all parts of the world. And they will naturally conclude, that though it be the most aggravated and virulent of the fevers arising from miasmata, this aggravation and violence are produced only by a greater concentration or virulence in the latter, joined to a greater intensity of atmospherical heat, acting on persons but little accustomed to bear it, whilst they retain the excitability of cold or temperate climates, together with an habitual disposition to generate that portion of animal heat which such climates require. They will have seen that the yellow, like other marsh fevers, is always exasperated by great heat, and extinguished or mitigated by cold ; that between the tropics it prevails *simultaneously* with the milder forms of marsh fevers, violently attacking *strangers* from cold climates, whilst the natives or long residents are at most only subject to intermittents or mild remittents. , They will have also seen, that in temperate situations this disease, in the early part of summer, before the atmosphere has become intensely hot, is commonly preceded by, *or rather shows itself in*, the forms of intermitting or remittent fever ; and that when being exasperated by excess of heat, it has assumed, and for some time prevailed under, the appearance of an epidemic yellow fever, the accession of cool weather speedily reduces it again to its milder forms, and that a freezing temperature soon puts an end to its appearance, even in those forms, as it commonly does to other fevers occasioned by exhalations from marshes, *and to no others.* And they will also have seen, that the common bilious remittent of hot climates, which is universally admitted to be the effect of miasmata, differs from the yellow fever only by being a little less violent ; that, at the utmost, their symptoms vary only *in degree ;* and that, in truth, even this difference is often so imperceptible, that the College of Physicians in Philadelphia, when anxious to assign a distinction between the *yellow* and the *bilious remittent* fevers, thought it necessary to allege *one*, which is not only *invisible*, but without *existence*, i. e. contagion. In fact, there is no difference between these fevers, excepting the greater violence, and consequently, greater danger attending the former than the latter ; for the yellow colour appears in both : and supposing the fatal *black vomit*, with profuse hæmorrhages and petechiæ, to occur only in what is called *yellow* fever, (though they are sometimes seen in fevers known and admitted to arise solely from marsh effluvia,) they cannot be included among its essential or distinguishing symptoms, unless *death* be also considered as essential to the disease. Nor can any exasperation of symptoms, which has been preceded by a great degree of heat, give any reason to suspect that a fever, whose symptoms are thus exasperated, did not originate from miasmata, because such an exasperation is invariably produced by th.it *cause* in marsh fevers ; and by it they are susceptible of the most dangerous and malignant appearances.

" With so many proofs of identity in their cause, and of the nearest affinity in their symptoms and reciprocal conversions into each other, as well as in their effects on the human body, and their changes by heat and cold, &c. it would be highly unreasonable not to consider them as being only *varieties of one disease.* And I think with Dr. Rush, that we might as well ' distinguish the rain which falls *in gentle showers* in Great Britain, from that which is *poured in torrents from the clouds in the West Indies,* by different names and qualities, as impose *specific* names and *characters* upon the different *states* of bilious, (or marsh,) fever."*

* That the fatal Endemic of the West Indies is the highest grade, or most aggravated form of Tropical Fever, is now, with some exceptions, the general conclusion of the best informed practitioners. Besides many authorities, incidentally cited on this point, in the course of this discussion, it is also the opinion of the following able Physicians, whose. opportunities of witnessing Fever in various Climates, have, from their official situations, been very extensive, viz.—Drs. Pinckard, Cole, Gray, Muttlebury, Denmark, Veitch, Mortimer, Macmullin,

The Fifth Part commences with a Chapter on Typhus or Contagious Fever; a term vaguely applied at present to designate generally all low or slow fevers arising from great fatigue, cold and damp habitations, unwholesome or insufficient food, anxiety, grief, fear, and other depressing passions and debilitating causes, having no connection with contagion, nor any power of producing a contagious disease, but which should, the author thinks, be restricted to a fever *sui generis*, strictly contagious, and derived exclusively from its own specific cause, or contagion. I have before stated Dr. Bancroft's opinions on the origin and propagation of febrile contagion, and pointed out wherein he differs from the generally received notions on this subject. The difficulty of determining whether any individual case of typhus has originated from some of the causes which have usually been considered adequate to its production, or whether common low fever may have degenerated into typhus, as has been sometimes supposed, must be very great, if, as the author is inclined to believe, an interval of five or six months may sometimes elapse before the actual production of fever by typhus contagion received into the system, especially if the summer should intervene previous to an attack; in which case the occurrence of fever would, the author thinks, almost always be postponed until the following winter. Under such circumstances, I do not see how the question is to be determined satisfactorily, since it is nearly impossible to demonstrate that any person has not been unconsciously exposed to typhus contagion many months before, whilst his fever has apparently been produced by fatigue, cold, &c.

The history of contagious fever is involved in great obscurity; nor is it until lately that it has been observed and distinguished with any tolerable accuracy. Typhus differs in almost every particular from yellow fever; it is properly a disease of cold climates: the heat which is favourable to yellow fever, soon puts an end to the ty-

Vance, Forbes, &c. See Bancroft's Sequel, and also a very good Paper by Dr. Musgrave, Medical and Chirurgical Transactions, Vol. ix.

Some highly respectable observers are also of opinion, that the modifications impressed on the endemic febrile cause by the influence of locality and of season, are manifested not only by variety of type, but also by the production of the dysenteric and ulcerative forms of fever. Dr. Jackson remarks, " In the interior of most of the Islands, at an elevation of five or six hundred feet above the level of the sea, among a series of mountainous ridges, not exposed directly to currents of exhalation from swampy and low grounds, the form of disease is sometimes intermittent, sometimes remittent, or continued, but more generally dysenteric, for the most part slight and manageable, sometimes violent and dangerous. The eruptive and ulcerative, or sore leg belongs also to the elevated situation, especially in the dry season." Sketch of Febrile Diseases, p. 8.—On the conversions of the febrile cause, Dr. Lempriere thus expresses himself—" In low flat situations, where during the rainy season the water did not readily pass off, I found active continued and remittent fevers, and obstinate and fatal intermittents to prevail In the vicinity of Lagoons, where water was always present, dysentery and common intermittents were observable. In the first elevation of mountains, mild intermittents, in the second elevation obstinate ulcers, and in the third and still higher elevation neither fevers, dysenteries, nor ulcers were common."—On the difference of situation and elevation, as favouring a tendency to fevers, dysentery, or ulcer, Dr. Porter, who served in the West Indies at the same period, holds an opinion very similar to that of Dr. Lempriere.

phus contagion ; whilst the cold seasons and climates, which stop the ravages of yellow fever, are the most prolific in fevers of contagion. The susceptibility to typhus is also in direct opposition to that for the yellow fever. We have seen that persons going from cooler into hot climates, are more obnoxious to the yellow fever than the natives or long residents in those climates ; whereas, " those who by birth and residence have been long habituated to intertropical climates, are, when they remove into the cold, particularly susceptible of the action of typhus contagion, if exposed to it. The accession and progress of the symptoms also are very different in the two diseases ; typhus is generally accompanied with less mortality, and the derangement which it occasions in the system is much less permanent and mischievous, than that which accompanies or results from even the remittent fever of Europe." As a proof of this, the author compares the events produced by typhus in the British army, subsequently to the return of the troops from Corunna in 1809, with those which attended or followed the expedition to Zealand in the same year, when our soldiers had been exposed to the causes producing the remittent fever. It appears, that in the former instance the deaths did not exceed one in ten of the sick, notwithstanding some disadvantages of accommodation and treatment under which they laboured ; whereas, on the Zealand expedition, the deaths were but a small fraction less than one in eight, although no such disadvantages existed ; and " the recoveries much more tedious, relapses perhaps one hundred times more frequent, and very often followed by permanent obstructions or morbid alterations of the viscera, ending in dropsy, or other chronical affections."

Dr. Bancroft having been employed with the troops from Spain, labouring under typhus, availed himself of the opportunity of ascertaining the time which the contagion may remain latent after its application to the human body. For this purpose he procured returns of the orderlies and nurses who had attended the sick in question, and had been afterwards attacked with the same fever ; and also an account of the time when the attendance of each began, and of the interval which succeeded previous to the attack. The sum of his observations is thus stated.

" It results, therefore, from this statement, that among the ninety-nine orderlies and nurses, who had probably *not* been exposed to the contagion before their attendance on the sick commenced, the *earliest* attack was on the 13th day, and the *latest* on the 68th ; but these returns were made up about the 20th of April, and it appears that some who had escaped till that time, were afterwards attacked."

The second Chapter contains observations on Dysentery, wherein the author contends against this being a disease of contagion, except when it exists together with typhus fever, (a connection, however, he seems much inclined to doubt ever taking place ;) but he asserts, that for the most part it is produced by the same causes which give rise to remittent fever, viz. heat and marsh miasmata. The circumstances which determine the morbid influence of marsh effluvia towards the intestines, so as to excite the disease in question, rather than intermitting or remitting fevers, do not, he thinks, seem to be yet well understood. Various facts are stated by Dr. Bancroft, proving the non-contagious property of dysentery, and showing that it is frequently epidemic at the same periods and in the same places with marsh remittent fever,and the probability of their acknowledging the same cause is increased by the alternate *succession* of one disease to another, which so often takes place. The author's treatment of the disease is accordingly founded upon this view of its nature and cause ; and as his directions on this head are comprised in few words, I shall here give them.

" As in this disease there is manifestly a morbid determination of febrile or inflammatory action upon the intestines, I think, and have always found it beneficial, speedily to counteract this disposition, and produce an opposite determination, so far at least as to create a salutary distribution of the blood, and of the living power, throughout the body, and especially upon its surface, by suitable diaphoretics, combined with opium, in small doses ; by the application of flannels immediately to the skin, and more especially round the abdomen ; and in urgent cases by the warm bath, (continued for the space of an hour, if the patient can bear it so long,) warm fomentations, and especially blisters upon the belly, taking care at the same time to promote sufficient evacuations by stool, to relieve the intestines as much as possible from all irritation and uneasiness, which they might suffer by a retention of hardened fæces or scybala, and other matters. For this last purpose the neutral purging salts with manna are proper, or a mixture of the oleum Ricini, with the juice of a ripe orange, and a little mucilage of gum arabic, which will agree better with most stomachs, and prove equally efficacious ; emollient purgative clysters may also be employed. Should the disease be attended with considerable fever, care must be taken not to increase it by too frequent use of diaphoretics and opium. When the disease, by long protraction, has occasioned ulcerations of the intestines, and more especially when it is complicated with an affection of the liver, calomel should be preferred as a purgative, and it should also be employed with opium, so as to excite a soreness of the mouth." In addition to this, the food should be light and easy of digestion ; when the patient has any particular craving, it may almost always, the author says, be safely indulged. The last Chapter is on the Plague.

Here I shall conclude the present section, and introduce an able analysis of Dr. Bancroft's subsequent Work, entitled " A Sequel to an Essay on Yellow Fever," drawn up for the *Medico-Chirurgical Journal* for Feb. 1818, by my esteemed friend Mr. Sheppard, of Witney, a gentleman of much experience and of sound judgment. It stands in the plural number as originally written.

—————

A Sequel to an Essay on the Yellow Fever, principally intended to prove, by incontestible facts, and important documents, that the Fever, called Bulam, or Pestilential, has no Existence as a distinct, or a contagious Disease. By EDWARD NATHANIEL BANCROFT, M. D. Fellow of the Royal College of Physicians, Physician to the Army, and late Physician to St. George's Hospital. London, 1817. 8vo. pp. '487. [*Medico-Chirurgical Journal.*]

Sec. II.—The Medical History of our West India possessions presents a melancholy detail of a vast destruction of human life from the ravages of the disease which forms the subject of the volume before us ; and the painful feelings which the retrospect is calculated to produce, are certainly not lessened by the reflection, that the state of active and protracted warfare in which we have been involved, has, in addition to the other miseries which have flowed from that source, principally contributed to swell the catalogue of victims to this scourge ; —that many thousands of our brave countrymen have escaped the fury of battle, and all the varied dangers "*per mare, per saxa, per ignes,*" incidental to the life of the soldier and sailor, only to fall an inglorious sacrifice to this insatiate foe ! Nor have its visitations been limited to the transatlantic shores alone ; the inhabitants of many of the southern parts of Europe have, on various occasions, felt severely the pressure of affliction and mortality from this widely extended cause. While in common with every feeling mind, we regret the discrepancy of opinion respecting its origin and nature, which has prevailed among the only legitimate judges of the question, and condemn the asperity and intemperateness in which the contending parties have too frequently indulged, we cannot but rejoice in the prospect which now opens on us, of the discussion being at length brought to a speedy termination. The overwhelming mass of evidence which Dr. Bancroft has now brought forward, in disproof of the existence of contagion in yellow fever, will, we confidently anticipate, put to flight a chimera, which has in too many instances seduced the attention from the true sources of the disease. The periodical publications, it is true, have lately teemed with refutations of the doctrine of contagion ; but in the fleeting and insulated form of those communications, much of their weight and authority is necessarily lost. We therefore hail with real satisfaction the appearance of a work containing an invaluable store of original and highly respectable documents, collected and arranged with no ordinary research and ability, and supported by argumentative talents of the first order. Since the appearance of the Author's former volume, two publications have issued from the press in support of 'the distinct nature and contagious quality of the " Bulam," or yellow fever ; and by one of the writers a claim has been preferred to the discovery of the alleged peculiarity of its attacking the human frame only *once*. With the view of effecting the subversion of these doctrines, Dr. Bancroft has again entered the Arena ; and on all the principal bearings of the question, we conceive that his triumph is complete. The quantity of matter accumulated in the present volume, almost defies an adequate analysis ; but as from the analogy of our opinions on the subject with those of the author, we find very little to oppugn, or to criticize, we shall endeavour to lay before our readers a condensed view of the most important topics under discussion.

We are informed in the Introduction, that the Lords of the Privy Council deemed the opinions of Dr. Pym of sufficient importance to induce them to make application to the College of Physicians for information on the two chief points which he has endeavoured to establish ;—the contagious nature of yellow fever, and the peculiarity of its attacking only once. The reply of the College, although on the whole favourable to Dr. Pym's pretensions, was undecided, as they properly alleged, for want of experience in the disease. Application was then made by the Council to the Army and Naval Medical Boards. Concerning the communication from the former Board, Dr. Bancroft has not been authorized to give any information. The latter, having collected the opinions of those naval medical officers whose experience enabled them to adduce facts and observations in support, or in refutation of Dr. Pym's propositions, transmitted a concise analysis thereof to the Lords of the Council, together with the original Reports. To these their Lordships have been pleased to allow Dr. Bancroft free access, and from that source a large portion of the evidence contained in this volume is derived.

The author begins his Inquiry by controverting the diagnostics by which Dr. Pym distinguishes his Bulam from the bilious continued, and bilious remittent Fevers ; and we are of opinion, that he has undeniably proved that no *specific* difference exists between these forms of fever ; that the points on which Dr. Pym has attempted to found a diagnosis, are merely differences of degree, and, that, (excepting the last, the black vomit,) they are not peculiar, uniform, nor essential to the fever in question. Indeed, it appears to us, that they obtain more or less in most dangerous fevers, as, we conceive, must be evident not only to all personally and extensively conversant with yellow fever, but even with fever in general : and, further, that Dr. Pym has himself proved the futility, and destroyed the foundation of such diagnosis, (if we were to grant his assumption, of which, however, an *ipse dixit* is the substitute for proof,) by asserting, that even Dr. Rush himself mistook the bilious remittent for the Bulam Fever. —*Pym's Obs.* p. 209.

Of these alleged diagnostics, the two first, the appearance of the eyes, and the nature and seat of the head-ache, the author satisfactorily shows from various authorities, to be vague and indeterminate, and, therefore, perfectly useless in diagnosis. With regard to the absence of remissions, constituting the third diagnostic of the Bulam, Dr. Bancroft adduces a mass of evidence to prove " the simultaneous appearance of both forms of the fever, and their reciprocal *conversions* into each other at particular places and seasons ; together with the invariable appearance of remittents at the same places, both *before* the high atmospheric temperature has operated sufficiently to give them the continued form, and also *after* the effects of this high temperature have ceased to exist." Further, Dr. Pym has derived the epidemics of Gibraltar by importation from those of Cadiz, Malaga, and Carthagena, and has thereby identified them with the fevers of those places ; and Sir James Fellowes states, that Arejula, Gonzales, and Flores are " the three most eminent physicians in Cadiz, and he believes in Spain." Now, unfortunately for this principal diagnostic, all those writers distinctly mention remissions in their descriptions of the Spanish epidemics ; and as regards the fever in Gibraltar, remissions are proved by evidence of seven medical officers of that garrison in the epidemic of 1814. The fourth, or the infrequency and paleness of the yellow colour of the skin, cannot be viewed otherwise than a relative expression ; and it will be sufficient to state, that, from the accounts of Sir James Fellowes, Sir Joseph Gilpin, Mr. Donnet, and others, the suffusion of the skin is observed in every intermediate shade between a lively yellowness, and a dingy, or dark hue. The author also rejects the fifth diagnostic, the duration of the disease, on the principle of the want of uniformity. Dr. Pym says, it runs its course in from one to five days ; it is admitted, that it commonly does so in its most aggravated form ; but it is proved from Arejula, Sir James Fellowes, Dr. Burnett, Labat, and Dr. Chisholm, that it often continues much longer : further, Dr. Pym states, that " the *remittent* sometimes proves fatal on the second or third day ;" and according to Dr. Hunter it even runs its course in twenty-four hours. We have ourselves witnessed death on the third day, in a violent remittent imbibed in the month of September, in one of the most *northern* rivers of the United States. Lastly, respecting the sixth alleged diagnostic, the gangrenous state of the stomach, and the appearance of black vomit, Dr. Bancroft exposes the futility of such criteria, the first of which can only be known after death ; and the latter " is the almost unerring harbinger of death." The chief value of a diagnostic is to enable us to ascertain the true nature of a disease ; but this refers to its consequences only. Neither is the black vomit peculiar to the continued form ; for the authorities of Pringle, Cleghorn, Hunter, Rush, and Burnett, prove its occurrence in the remittent.

" I shall only add, concerning this black vomiting, that as it is a mortal symptom, never occurring, it may be said, *in those who recover*, and one which is often wanting among those who die, its appearance in this disease must be much rarer even than death ; and this circumstance, joined to that of its *not* being ' peculiar' to the fever in question, render it very unfit to be produced as a diagnostic thereof," p. 30.

Adverting to the inconsistencies contained in Dr. Pym's account of the condition of the pulse and skin, " for which," he says, " the Bulam Fever is remarkable," the Author thus expresses himself :—

" Descriptions of symptoms being simply records of natural events in disease, which stand unalterable, however opinions about them may change, will the confusion, the inconsistencies, and errors, every where apparent in Dr. Pym's attempt to frame a diagnosis for the Bulam Fever, be deemed very excusable in one who claims merit for discovering peculiarities therein, which had escaped the sagacity and penetration of all other observers."

We apprehend that sufficient has been said to show, that the question of the continued form of fever, or the Bulam, is merely one of degree ; that the peculiarities which are said to distinguish the Bulam from all other fevers, do not exist ; and that, therefore, the supposed distinct fever must be as imaginary as the peculiarities themselves.*

* Dr. Musgrave, of Antigua, who also has successfully controverted all Dr.

The second chapter is devoted to the consideration of other alleged peculiarities, more especially the non-liability to a second attack ; which it is stated was brought under the notice of the Privy Council, in consequence of an application from Dr. Pym.

The merit of originality in this supposed discovery is disputed ; Sir James Fellowes awards it to the Spanish practitioners generally ; Dr. Pym claims it as exclusively his own, and fixes on the 20th day of October, 1804, as the period when that event took place in the garrison of Gibraltar.—The security, he represents, to be similar to that which an individual acquires by having undergone the small-pox. Now, Professor Berthe, in his " Précis Historique," &c. published in 1802, gives an extract of a printed letter, dated at Cadiz, May 6th, 1802, in which the writer plainly states, that, like small-pox, after one attack, a future seizure rarely occurs. This opinion, however, the Professor designates as fallacious and dangerous. In the epidemic of Cadiz also in 1800, towards the decline of the fever, the civil authorities of that place grounded their police measures on this opinion :

" Guards where stationed at the gates, to exclude all persons from entering the city, who did not produce certificates of having already had the fever."

Arejula had likewise pointed out the security afforded by an attack of the fever, in the epidemics of Medina, Sidonia, Malaga, and other places in Spain ; and states in page 319, that

" At these places, and almost every other, he selected as assistants to the sick, those who had previously undergone the epidemics."

So much for the originality of the alledged discovery, to the credit of which, even had it been confirmed by experience, we apprehend, on the principle of " *suum cuique*," Dr. Pym had no claim. As to the reality of this supposed " peculiarity," we consider the evidence adduced by Dr. Bancroft from the Reports of the naval medical officers, before adverted to, as well as the result of the examination of the different Journals of naval surgeons employed in the West Indies, to be perfectly conclusive in the negative. This opinion is corroborated by the answers of five army surgeons, and three assistant surgeons of the garrison of Gibraltar during the epidemic of 1814, to the questions proposed to them by Deputy Inspector Fraser ; they all bear distinct testimony to second attacks.

We can only briefly notice the author's exposition of the frailty of Dr. Pym's alleged proofs of absolute immunity after one attack. In the instance of the epidemic of Gibraltar in 1804, (on which the sup-

Pym's principal positions, remarks :—" Had Drs. Pym or Gilpin, or any one holding their opinions, practised in Antigua during the late Epidemic, still prepossessed with the idea of Black Vomit being distinctive of Yellow Fever, I venture to assert, without fear of contradiction, that he or they, (spite of every preconceived notion,) must in candour have admitted, that a disease at least answering in every respect the description given by themselves, could ostensibly be produced by miasmata alone ; and that in comparing a mass of cases occurring in town and country, with Creoles and Europeans, a continued chain could be traced, link by link, from the most concentrated form as it invades new comers, to the simple intermittent, which we so frequently meet with among the slaves," p. 123.—*Medical and Chirurgical Transactions*, vol ix.

posed discovery seems to have been founded,) it is stated, that one hundred and twenty-two men who had escaped the fever, were found on inquiry to have been in the West Indies at some former period, which is inferred to have been the cause of their exemption ; and that the 57th regiment, which had recently served in Trinidad, was introduced into the garrison during the prevalence of. the epidemic, with impunity.   These are alleged to be proofs of the Bulam Fever not attacking a second time ; but both instances obviously involve the assumption, that all who have visited the West Indies, have necessarily undergone an attack of Yellow Fever ;—a fallacy we need not stop to refute.   The instance of the men of the 10th regiment, which acquired their security by service in the *East* Indies, is still more palpably defective ; because, Dr. Pym having laboured to prove that the Bulam has never appeared in the East Indies, the men of the 10th regiment could not, on his own principles, have obtained their immunity by previous attacks.

Indeed, it appears to us, that Dr. Pym has not steadily contemplated the security, constituting his alleged discovery, in a determinate point of view. In general, he compares it to the almost absolute immunity which an attack of the small-pox confers ; but at other times he plainly speaks of it as, (what in truth it amounts to,) merely a relative security ; for instance, in his account of the epidemic Yellow Fever of the 70th regiment in Martinique, in 1794, he says, every individual in the regiment was attacked ; and, that three officers who had been several years in the West Indies, some time before, had it in so mild a form, as to make it unnecessary for them to be confined to bed :— again, the regiments in Martinique that had been some years in the West Indies, he says, were attacked, (in 1794,) equally with the corps lately arrived from England ; but *with this difference*, that the former " *suffered a comparatively small mortality :*"   And further, in the above-mentioned case of the 10th regiment at Gibraltar, he states, that " eight officers who had been in India, were attacked with the fever, and all recovered.—Seven officers who had not been in India, had the disease in so different a form, that five of them died." These we take to be fair illustrations of relative security, acquired by habituation to, or seasoning in, a tropical climate ; and prove, that in order to obtain such comparative security, it is not necessary that the individuals should have passed through an attack of Yellow Fever ; while on the other hand, we may safely trust to the evidence adduced by Dr. Bancroft, to establish that one, or even a repetition of attacks, does not confer *absolute* non-liability.

We have been somewhat diffuse on this point, from a sense of its importance ; and because we are anxious to exhibit the merits of the case in as distinct a form as our observation of the subject permits ; and we refer to the evidence itself in support of our opinion, that the supposed non-liability to a second attack, so far from resembling the immunity after small pox, is strictly a relative security, to be acquired as certainly, though more gradually, by tropical residence, (which involves habituation to the remote cause,) as by having passed through an attack of the disease ;—a condition of the habit which confers se-

40

curity only when the concentration and force of the endemic causes do not exceed the degree to which the individual may have been previously habituated ;—and, lastly, a mean of exemption which is liable to be destroyed by (e converso,) the regenerated susceptibility which a return to, and residence in a northern climate effectuate. That the exemption is absolute after one or more attacks, we consider to be perfectly, and most satisfactorily disproved ; and we cannot well abstain from expressing our astonishment how Dr Pym could ever have entertained such an idea, much less have vaunted it as a *discovery* ; for very little reflection might have shown him, that it *could not* have escaped the observation, but *must* have been evident to, and eagerly caught at by those who had passed a series of years amidst Yellow Fever, had such absolute immunity any existence. The facts included in the documents now brought forward by Dr. Bancroft, will, we cannot doubt, be deemed decisive ; and consign to oblivion the premature notion of a discovery in a supposed " peculiarity," which he has proved, does not exist ; and which, even for a moment supposing its existence to be any thing more than relative, had been pointed out, and acted on by the Spaniards many years previous to the 20th of October, 1804.

Dr. Fergusson, Inspector of Military Hospitals in the Windward Islands, in his Communication to the Army Medical Board, observes on this point,

" Another piece of doctrine has been promulgated from the writings of the authors above alluded to, (Drs. Pym and Fellowes ;) that the Yellow Fever cannot be received by the same subject more than once. Of this we again, who live amongst Yellow Fever, not only know nothing, but we see it contradicted by the daily experience of our lives." Page 87.

We have always protested with Dr. Bancroft against the subtilty of making the black vomit a criterion of the Bulam Fever, and regulating the admissibility of the proofs of future attacks by that assumed standard. By acknowledging the legitimacy of such a criterion, as few or none recover after that symptom has appeared, a difficulty, nearly tantamount to impossibility, is incurred, of ever adducing in the course of even a long life, an unobjectionable instance of a second attack. When black vomit, and its usual immediate sequel, death, take place, the patient is relieved from future attacks of any kind ; but in less aggravated forms of Yellow Fever, where there has been no black vomit, and the patient has recovered, then in the event of a second attack, say the advocates for the Nova Pestis, the original one was not a case of Bulam, for one of our diagnostics was wanting ; there was no black vomit !—and vice versa. Accordingly, we find this subterfuge incessantly resorted to. Against such sophistry, arguments are vain ; and facts, for the reasons we have assigned, difficult to be applied. The Report of Inspector Fergusson from Barbadoes, amongst other cases of second attacks, contains, however, one decisive instance of even black vomit occurring twice in the same individual.—A patient of Dr. Caddel, a physician of the greatest experience in Barbadoes, miraculously recovered from yellow fever with distinct black vomit, " and died some years afterwards of the same disease, and with the *same symptom.*"—Against a fact of such decisive import, we know not what reply can be opposed, unless it be, " *Non persuadebis, etiamsi persuaseris.*"

In a rejoinder of considerable extent, Dr. Bancroft adverts to Dr. Pym's examination of the authorities he has adduced in his Essay against the doctrine of contagion. He complains of a disingenuous and partial selection of those authorities for that purpose ; and expresses his conviction, that they have passed the ordeal without injury.

"Here Dr. Pym closes the account of what he terms my authorities ; and he manifestly intends to have it believed, that he has noticed and refuted *all* those which I had adduced ; when in fact, he has completely shunned even the mentioning of nine tenths of them. The few whom he notices were obviously selected only because they had said or admitted something capable of being distorted contrary to the real and sincere meaning of each ; and in effecting this distortion he exults, as ' having by cross-questioning my witnesses, brought out *the truth,*' and ' convicted me upon my own evidence :' although in regard to the great body of those who are more properly my witnesses, he is so far from having cross-examined them, that he has not even looked them in the face ; and my readers, I firmly believe, will be convinced that he has not been able to invalidate or weaken any *one* testimony or opinion which I had alleged to prove the fever in question to be void of contagion," page 110—111.

A similar complaint is preferred of an equally uncandid and partial selection of some of his evidences against contagion, for the purpose of examination ; and the irrefragable character of the remainder is thence very justly inferred. We think it but an act of common justice to Dr. Bancroft, to insert in his own words, the recapitulation of the evidences against contagion, contained in his former volume, which Dr. Pym has not thought proper to oppugn, or even to notice ; leaving our readers to draw their own inferences as to the probable motives for such cautious proceeding.

"I have now examined all that in any way merited notice of what Dr. Pym has advanced against my authorities and arguments, with the exception of some circumstances relative to Cadiz and Gibraltar, which are reserved for future consideration ; and I cannot but believe that my readers will have been convinced of the fallacy of those principles upon which he has endeavoured to explain, or rather to evade, my inferences, and of the abortiveness of his endeavours to invalidate, in a single instance, either my testimonies or my reasonings. There remains besides a great mass of evidence of which he has studiously avoided even the smallest notice ; and this must of course be considered not only as subsisting in full strength, but as having been deemed by him unquestionable and invulnerable : for otherwise, with his dispositions, and the latitude of every kind in which he has indulged, it may be presumed, that it would not have been left without some hostile attempt. To this evidence, therefore, I refer my readers with confidence, and more especially to the very accurate and respectable one of Dr. James Clarke, at pages 332, 333, 334, and 760, 761 of my Essay ; and that of Mr. Young, Inspector-General of Hospitals, and of all the superior medical officers of the army under Sir Ralph Abercromby in the Windward Islands, p. 334, 335 ; those of M. M. Desportes and Valentin at St. Domingo, p. 338—341 ; that of Doctor Hector M'Lean, with the opinions of Drs. Jackson, S ott, Wright, and Gordon, and nearly, if not all, the other medical officers of the British army at St. Domingo, p. 341, 342 ; and that of Dr. Hume, p. 346, 347 ; those of Dr. Walker and of Dr. Grant of Jamaica; p. 350, 351 ; that of Dr. Ramsay, and of all the medical practitioners of the State of South Carolina, declared unanimously at a General Meeting in Charleston, p. 355, 359 ; that of Dr. de Rosset of Wilmington, in North Carolina, p. 359 ; the opinions of Drs. Valentin, Taylor, Hansford, Selden, and Whitehead, in Virginia, p. 360, 362 ; that of Dr. Davidge at Baltimore, p. 363, 366 ; that of Dr. Vaughan, in the State of Delaware, p. 367, 369 ; the opinions of many Physicians at Philadelphia, between pages 372 and 386 ; and at New-York, p. 387, 389 ; and those of Dr. Coit of New London, Dr. Wheaton, of Providence, and Drs. Warren and Brown of Boston, p. 401, 406.   I request also the attention of my readers to the facts partly stated, and partly recapitulated between pages 406 and 430 ; and, finally, to the very important Official Message from the President of the United States on this subject to the two houses of Congress, p. 430, containing such an uncontradicted and incontrovertible statement of facts, as ought, in every unprejudiced mind, to remove every suspicion of the existence of contagion in the Yellow Fever, at least, in that part of the world," pages 120—122.*

Although Dr Bancroft considers this quantity of uncontracted evidence to be " more than sufficient to overthrow Dr. Pym's superstructure, more especially as the foundation of it has been removed in the first chapter of the present publication," he adduces a multiplicity of additional facts and authorities in proof of the local origin of Yellow Fever, and of its being destitute of the quality of contagion.   Among other documents, one from New-York is not the least curious, which proves from the Contagionists themselves, *that a Fever in every respect resembling the Bulam, prevailed in that city, nearly two years before the arrival of the Hankey at Grenada!* page 124—126.

In illustration of the identity of cause of the continued Yellow Fever, and of the recurrent forms, the following Extract from the Official Report of Dr. Dickson, the late able physican to the Leeward Island Fleet, will be duly appreciated.

" At Barbadoes and Antigua, I had generally seen the disease of an

---

* The above references include the opinions of Drs. Caldwell, Miller, and other eminent Physicians. Several other very recent authorities might be adduced who consider the Yellow Fever of Endemic origin, and concur in ascribing it to local causes and atmospherical influence—but to these a brief allusion only can here be made: see the Treatises of Doctors Girardin, Irvine, Reese, Le Fort, &c. and the accounts of Doctors Watts, Revere, and other Writers, in the different Periodical Works lately published in the United States. Dr. Watts, speaking of America, observes, " from one end of the Continent to the other, it has been officially announced during the last season, that the Yellow Fever was not communicated from one person to another, and not even in Hospitals where the sick have been admitted in great numbers."—*New-York Med. and Sur. Register, Part. ii.—Vol.* 1, 1820. See also, lately republished, the work of the experienced M. Devèze.—Paris, 1820.

ardent *continued* form, and did not fully understand why authors talk-
ed of a Bilious *Remittent* Yellow Fever, until after the capture of the
French and Danish Islands.   But the anomalies of fever, the shades
and changes which it assumes according to the intensity of the exciting causes, (which *there* were *purely* and *wholly local*,) the state of
predisposition, or the spot of residence, could no where be more
strongly pourtrayed than in the destructive epidemic of Mariegalante
in the autumn of 1808, from the most concentrated marsh miasmata ;
when the different types of fever were *converted* into each other, of
the *worst* and *most aggravated species* I have ever witnessed.   Some
were affected with the *highly concentrated* Yellow Fever in the continued form ; others with *comatose remittents* or *intermittents*, the exacerbations of which were so violent as to carry off a patient in two
or three paroxysms ; while others sunk into a low protracted character of fever resembling typhus," p. 143—144.
    After stating the opinions of the Naval Medical Officers who re-
ported on the question of contagion, Dr. Bancroft gives the following
summary of them ; from which it will be seen that the evidence
against contagion is as great and uniform, as perhaps can ever be expected on any disputed point.
    " Having stated the opinions delivered in the Reports transmitted
to the Privy Council, it may be proper to give a summary of them ;
and, I will therefore mention that, of the twenty-four Gentlemen from
whom these Reports were obtained, *three*, (Mr. Gregory, No. 12,
Dr. Kein, No. 15, and Dr. Magrath, No. 17,) have omited the statement of any opinion on the subject of contagion, as connected with
the fever in question : *three* others, (Dr. Weir, No. 1. Dr. Blair,
No. 2, and Mr. Tobin, No. 21,) have expressed their opinions that
it is contagious : one of them, (Mr. Brien, No. 20,) declares his belief that, in individual or solitary cases, it is ' incapable of communicating itself to those who are contiguous,' but ' that, when several
were labouring under the disease at the same time, he believes it to
be highly contagious.'   And, *another* Gentleman, (Dr. Gardiner, No.
9,) appears to think, that *local* causes contributed at least as much to
the production of the fever in Gibraltar in 1813, as contagion.   Of
the remaining *sixteen*, the majority have *absolutely* and *positively denied* the existence of any contagious property in this fever ; and the
rest have declared their belief, that it is not *naturally* or *properly* a
contagious disease, although several of them are inclined to believe
that it may, (as they suppose to happen with most other diseases,) acquire a contagious property by crowding, filth, &c.   Most of the sixteen gentlemen, who declare that the fever under consideration is
not contagious, have alleged decisive facts to support their declara-
tions, some of which I have already quoted ; and, I shall hereafter
have occasion to notice some of the others," p. 178—179.
    When we reflect that this evidence in great part proceeds from
physicians to fleets, and surgeons of hospitals who have lived among
yellow fever for a series of years ; and, that the reports here adduced
are few indeed, when compared to the great body of medical officers,
who, with very few exceptions, we have had occasion to know, are
uniformly opposed to contagion ; when to these are added the opi-

nions of Drs. Fergusson, Muttlebury, and Adolphus, who have long
held official situations of the highest responsibility in the West Indies;
when the number and length of service of those who have given
their opinion so decidedly against contagion are considered,—the
preponderance is immense; especially as far as the yellow fever of
the West Indies is concerned.

It would appear from the Report of the College of Physicians to
the Lords of the Privy Council, that they entertain the opinion that
Yellow Fever *may* prevail in the British Islands. They express
their belief that " the cold of our climate would not prove a preservative against the contagion," (of Yellow Fever,) because " it appears that during the months of October and November, when the
fever raged at Gibraltar, Malaga, and Leghorn, the temperature was
greatly below the average heat of our summer." This inference
we beg leave to dissent from; and in extenuation observe, that the
College in deducing such conclusion does not appear to have been
aware of the necessity of a certain *preceding duration of high temperature*, which experience proves to be indispensable to the developement of epidemic Yellow Fever. Within the tropics the requisite
degree of heat is never absent: and in those places without the tropics which have been occasionally visited by the disease, as North
America, and the Spanish Peninsula, the meteorological observations
of the various years in which it has prevailed concur in the pre-ex-
istence of high atmospheric temperature, for many weeks before the
appearance of the epidemics. Temperature to this requisite extent
seldom obtains in this climate; and when it does occur, is very tran-
sitory. Such evanescent influence is totally inadequate to the production of the disease; and while from insularity, or other causes,
our climate retains its *mutable* character, we may, without temerity,
discard all apprehensions of the existence of Yellow Fever among
us. In corroboration of the steady pre-duration of high atmospheric temperature, as the " *sine qua non*" of the developement of epidemic Yellow Fever, the following extract from a provincial news-
paper is not inapplicable.

" It has been ascertained from tables and records for the last twenty-four years, that in Philadelphia, the Yellow Fever does not prevail when the months of June and July do not exceed 70 degrees; but
that in every summer since 1795, when the average heat of these
months has exceeded 79 degrees, then the fever has raged; and that it
has been most fatal in those years, in which the thermometer has indicated the greatest altitude.—*Hampshire Telegraph, Nov.* 1, 1817.

In several of the Reports transmitted to the Privy Council, a belief is expressed that the Yellow Fever, although it does not originate in contagion, or legitimately possess such quality, *might* acquire
it under accumulation of the sick, and deficient ventilation. The author admits, that the disease may be aggravated by such circumstances; but unconditionally denies the possibility of its acquiring
such fortuitous contagious power. On this point, (as far as the *tropical* endemic is concerned,) we concur with Dr. Bancroft; because on
reference to our experience of many years in the West Indies, we
cannot charge our recollection with any instance of Yellow Fever

having manifested such contingent property of contagion, *under any circumstances*. One source of fallacious deduction on this point, seems to have been the too narrow limitation of the range of predisposition ; for example, a ship enters an unhealthy port ; her men imbibe the local noxious exhalations, and are exposed to the other remote causes of fever ; she sails with a long list of fevers ; the attacks continue at sea, in the order of predisposition, while the local source of the fever has been left behind some hundreds of miles, and is, perhaps forgotten ; the sick are unavoidably crowded, and at length, in the absence of the original cause, the seizures are ascribed to a contagious property acquired by accumulation ; when in fact, the various periods of attack should have been referred to the varied degrees of predisposition. In offering this explanation in favour of the ultra opinion, we merely state the result of our observation. Neither can we admit the justice of the inference, that such alleged contingent property is favourable to the doctrine of a peculiar and distinct disease, the Bulam ; which its advocates contend is contagious *ab origine*, independent of those fortuitous circumstances, under which only, some have supposed, (not proved,) the Yellow Fever to become contagious. Moreover, we imagine, that those most inclined to this opinion, will not agree with Dr. Pym, that it can be conveyed and re-conveyed across the Atlantic, and from one place to another ; because we conceive that such a property, *if ever possessed*, is not of that permanent and imperishable nature to admit of transportation whenever the Contagionists wave their wand ; but is dependent upon a casual, local, and transient coincidence of agency ; we therefore agree with Dr. Bancroft, that it proves nothing in favour of Dr. Pym's view of the subject, its nature or origin. ,

We are glad to find, that the author has now bestowed due attention on a prolific source of fever under high temperature, the noxious exhalations from the foul hold of a ship. By disregarding this common cause of fever, a contagious origin has been erroneously assigned to fevers, which, making their appearance without exposure to land influence, could not be supposed to have sprung from an endemic source. Of the frequency of such a cause of even the most aggravated Yellow Fevers, no one can doubt after perusing the facts contained in the fourth chapter ; to which we are the more desirous of directing the attention of our readers, because we are of opinion that they will satisfactorily reconcile several seeming instances of contagious fever, with their true origin, an impure atmosphere from the exhalations from a foul hold. It is needless to dwell on the importance of the distinction ; the history of the transports from Carthagena, in which the epidemic of Gibraltar in 1810, was reported to have been imported, will hereafter be shown to be a strong case in point. The accounts of the Regalia transport, by Drs. Fergusson and Mortimer, and of the Antelope and Childers ships of war, in which Yellow Fevers of a destructive order recently prevailed from this cause, as attested by Dr. Crichton and Mr. Niell, will be read with the greatest interest. The observations of Dr. Fergusson will show, that had the Regalia arrived *a year later* in Barbadoes, she would probably have enjoyed equal notoriety with the much calumniated Hankey ; the late sickness in that island would have been referred to a second African importation in the Regalia, and error thus confirmed. Dr. Fergusson concludes his observations on this subject with the following important Remarks.

" I am aware how much I have been favoured by circumstances, and what a different interpretation the facts I have collected would have borne, had the present epidemic that now afflicts the islands, (1816,) broken out in the ordinary course of seasons, *a year earlier*, at the time the Regalia was here ; my task would then have been a much more difficult one, for these, (facts,) instead of assisting me to elicit the truth in the manner I have done, would in that case have been turned to the confirmation of error, and the perpetuation of the delusions, in regard to imported contagions," p. 239.

From abundant experience of the danger, we fully coincide with the author in deprecating the practice of heaving down vessels of war, in the West Indies, in the ordinary routine of service at least ; as well as from the excessive fatigue and exertion it demands, as because it is a process which requires for its execution, local security ; or, in other words, a landlocked, and therefore, generally an unhealthy harbour. The instances of sickness and mortality from the effects of clearing a foul hold, in an unhealthy harbour, are numberless ; Dr. Bancroft relates a remarkable one, amongst several others, in the " highly interesting" Report of Doctor Dickson.

" Of the production of Yellow Fever, accompanied, in twenty-two cases with *black vomit*, and consequent *death*, on board the Circe frigate, principally from the duties of *clearing the hold* and *heaving down ;* by which so many of the ship's company were soon after attacked with this fever, that a hundred and forty-six men were sent to the hospital at Antigua," p. 210.

The fifth chapter refers to the origin of the Spanish epidemics. In speaking of the Peninsula Fever, we wish distinctly to state, that our conclusions are drawn from the analogy of the laws of the Yellow Fever of the West Indies, with which our acquaintance has been sufficiently extensive ; and as the Contagionists have themselves identified those diseases, we presume the propriety of reasoning by such analogy will not be disputed. By employing the term " marsh miasmata" to designate the exhalations from the soil, to which Dr. Bancroft in his former work, ascribed the origin of Yellow Fever, he has given his opponents an opportunity of apparently convicting him on his own evidence, by adducing the obvious inference, that where there is no marsh, the Yellow Fever could not have been caused by such miasmata. The topography of some places, where the epidemic has prevailed, as Cadiz and Gibraltar, but where there are no ostensible marshes, has been accordingly exhibited with exultation, as a positive refutation of his doctrine. The error arises wholly from the inadequacy of the term employed to express the origin of such miasmata ; and to show that it is incorrect to ascribe to the author the opinion, that Yellow Fever is always the product of a distinct and ostensible marsh ; we subjoin an explanatory quotation.

" In treating of the Ardent or Yellow Fever, as it has occurred at Gibraltar, Cadiz, and other southern parts of Spain, I ascribed its production to the action of those vapours, or exhalations which result from the decomposition of vegetable, or vegetable and animal matters, in a temperature of not less than 80° of Fahrenheit's thermometer, and which are commonly called marsh or paludal miasmata ; an appellation which, in compliance with custom, I had occasionally adopted, though I well knew, and had repeatedly declared, that such exhalations or vapours are often emitted from soils and situations which had no resemblance to a *marsh*," p. 253—264.

Again, in a Note, at page 91 of his Essay, he says,

" I beg to state in this place, that, in joining the epithet *marsh* or *marshy*, to the terms miasmata, exhalations, effluvia, &c. and in considering these as a cause of fever, *I do not mean to intimate that such miasmata, &c. are emitted solely from marshes; (it being certain that they frequently arise from soils in a different state ;)* but only to designate *the quality of those vapours*, which are eminently the product of *marshy* grounds."

This ought to have been a sufficient security against the misconstructions which his opinions on this point have suffered. With respect to the existence of paludal effluvia at Cadiz and Gibraltar, he adduces the prevalence during the summer and autumn of remittent fevers at those places, the acknowledged offspring of such exhalations, as indisputably demonstrating their presence and influence, however they may be produced, or from whatever source derived ; and as further proof of the universality of this cause of fever throughout the Peninsula, the statement of Sir James M'Grigor is not irrelevant, which shows, that 22,914 cases of ague were altogether admitted into the British military hospitals in that country.

In the investigation of the alleged proofs of the importation of the various epidemics into Spain, the author has displayed his usual ability and research ; and we must observe, that his exposures of the frailties, inconsistencies, and anachronisms, with which those statements abound, refer equally to the proofs of Sir James Fellowes, and of Dr. Pym. Of the first epidemic of Cadiz in 1800, he naturally asks, if the disease is *sui generis*, and has not appeared for thirty-six years previous to 1800 ; from whence was it imported on that occasion ?

" There must have been somewhere on our globe, a spot on which this disease had existed not long before the time of its supposed importation, and where it was found to possess a contagious power. That they have either proved this, or that there is in fact any such place on earth, I must confidently deny."

We cannot accompany him through his scrutiny of the pretended importation into Cadiz, in 1800. and into Malaga in 1803 and 1804 ; for these we must refer to the volume itself. The meteorological statements of Sir James Fellowes afford to our minds, an adequate explanation of the aggravation and epidemical extension of the usual endemic at Cadiz in 1800 ; while the gradual progress of the disease, and the imperceptible conversion of the ordinary and milder, into the more rare and exalted form, constituting yellow fever, as manifested by the difficulties and dissentions which the Spanish physicians experienced in their attempts to fix the date, when the usual autumnal fever could be said to have ceased, and the epidemic yellow fever to have begun, confirm us in our opinion, that the question of Bulam, or continued Yellow Fever, is truly one of degree, and not of specific difference.

The author's former remarks on the defective signification of the term " marsh miasmata," to express the miasm of decomposition, are more especially applicable to the medical topography of Gibraltar, not unfrequently styled " *par excellence*" the Rock. The idea of the developement of paludal effluvia from a surface ostensibly so dissimilar to a marsh, has not merely been denied ; it has been assailed by ridicule. The rarity of agues in Gibraltar has also been adduced in proof of the non-generation of those exhalations at that place. This, however, as the author shows, betrays a very limited acquaintance with the modifications which are impressed on endemic fever by the influence of locality ; and while remittents are acknowledged to be the usual form of the autumnal fever in Gibraltar, (as well as in Cadiz,) we need take very little pains to prove the existence and influence of febrile exhalations from the soil, however ingeniously the speculators on the locality of an elevated rock, and on the absence of agues, may argue to the contrary. The examination of the importation account of the epidemic into Gibraltar in 1804, is prefaced by this observation.

" At present, therefore, it will be sufficient for me to suggest as *obvious* and *prominent causes* of the epidemic in question, the accumulation of decomposable matters within the town *and the long prevalence of a dry and scorching east wind*, which produced a very high atmospheric temperature, without any salutary ventilation of the place, as it was completely obstructed in its course by the high mountain behind the town, *in* and *over* which the air was for many weeks nearly stagnant. A similar dry and scorching east wind, blowing with too little force to change and purify the atmosphere, has invariably preceded, and accompanied every recurrence of the yellow fever at Cadiz, and other cities of Spain. And its effects, in the year 1804, were very extensive and remarkable, p. 342—343.

We learn from the result of the inquiry into the alleged importation of that year, that Santos, the person who is accused of having imported the contagion into Gibraltar, from Cadiz, according to one account on the 28th of August, but according to another, on the 25th, left Cadiz several days *before* the time which Dr. Arejula, the chief official superintendant of all things belonging to the Andalusian epidemic, has declared to be the day on which the existence of the yellow fever was first discovered at Cadiz. He could not therefore have imported a disease from Cadiz which had no existence there. The importation by Santos, has been attempted to be corroborated by the evidence of a Mr. Pratt, who was also in Cadiz, and from whom Santos is alleged to have derived his contagion, while they resided in the same tavern. But the author says, that a very cursory view of his examination is sufficient to make any one " sensible of the obvious and irreconcileable contradictions which it contains, and of the absolute impossibility of its being true." 'The affidavit of this person states, that he was taken ill while living in a tavern in Cadiz, about the 18th or 20th of August; that eight days afterwards, he had symptoms of black or bloody vomiting; that then, fearful of being sent to an hospital, he removed to another part of the town, and ultimately recovered; and that *after* his recovery he applied for a passage to Gibraltar in the same vessel in which Santos returned to that place, but was refused on account of his very yellow look. The primâ facie improbability of a person who laboured under black vomit, being able to shift his quarters from the apprehension of any contingency, needs not to be insisted on; but the conclusion of the story is fatal to its credibility, and destroys all relation between the deponent's and Santos's illness; for the vessel in which Santos returned to Gibraltar, and in which Mr. Pratt says, he was refused a passage *after* his recovery, left Cadiz, *at the latest,* on the 24th of August, (as Santos and Sir James Fellowes assert, and public records prove,) *several days before* the occurrence of the alleged *black vomit* in the course of Mr. Pratt's illness.

From such a tissue of contradictions, we know not what points can be selected as entitled to belief. The statements intended to establish the fact of importation, reciprocally destroy their respective foundations. We, therefore, recur with unshaken confidence to the domestic origin of the epidemics; and proceed to show, that the bases of the subsequent attempts to fix the mode of importation are equally deficient in solidity.

A coincidence of local and atmospherical causes, similar to those which produced the epidemic of 1804, again aggravated the usual remittent of Gibraltar, (which had regularly prevailed there in every intermediate year,) towards the close of the autumn of 1810, to the degree of concentrated yellow fever. The epidemic of that year has also been alleged to have been imported by some transports from Carthagena, crowded with French deserters. The substantiability of this allegation may be in some degree appreciated by stating, that it rests wholly on the gratuitous assumption of a breach of quarantine. Some cases of fever had appeared among the soldiers in the transports, previous to their arrival at Gibraltar, of which one man had died. Sickness ceased shortly after their removal into hulks provided for their reception, and it does not appear that the fever was there communicated to any person; but the contagious nature of the disease was inferred from the subsequent attacks of the seamen, who remained in the transports, and of Mr. Arthur, who was sent on board them from the garrison to treat the sick. The cause of fever in those vessels, the author justly ascribes to the noxious emanations from their holds, which, in a former chapter, he has shown to be capable of producing the worst yellow fevers. The attacks of Mr. Arthur and the seamen, are not proofs that the disease was contagious: the cause being local, every person exposed to its influence, might be expected to suffer, without the assumption of contagious agency. Dr. Bancroft refers to Dr. Burnett's previous statement in support of his rejection of the opinion of an imported contagion by these transports; but, it is necessary to repeat, that these vessels having been placed in strict quarantine immediately on their arrival at Gibraltar, the contagionists, in order to explain the origin of the epidemic by importation, are driven to the extremity of assuming a breach of quarantine. We would ask, if assumptions so perfectly gratuitous, be expected to be received as bonâ fide proofs of an affirmation, what fable, however preposterous, could be rejected on the score of want of evidence?

In the next epidemic in 1813, Sir Joseph Gilpin was at the head of the medical department in Gibraltar. In a letter to Dr. Chisholm, published in the Edinburgh Medical and Surgical Journal, in speaking of the contagious nature of yellow fever, and of its importation in 1793 from Africa in Grenada, he states, " of the infected state of the Hankey, 1 never did, nor ever shall, entertain the least doubt." This is certainly sufficiently declaratory of the tendency of his antecedent opinions. He says, that the first cases of the epidemic of 1813, occurred in two strangers, who imported it into Gibraltar on the 11th of August, in a vessel called the Fortune, from Cadiz, where he states, (very erroneously, as will be shown,) the epidemic in question prevailed at the period of their departure. Now, Lieutenant General Campbell, the Lieutenant Governor of Gibraltar, writes to Sir James Duff, the British Consul at Cadiz, on the 13th of September, 1813, stating, that some cases of fever had lately occurred in the garrison, " but that there was not one of a contagious nature, as they were peculiar to the season only." Here we have the highest authority that no contagious disease prevailed in Gibraltar for more than a month after the arrival of the strangers from Cadiz ; and the non-existence of the epidemic at Cadiz, not merely at the time of their departure from thence, but for a considerable time afterwards, is proved by the testimony of Sir James Fellowes, who in speaking of Cadiz, states, at page 256, "in fact, until the end of August, the people collectively were, according to all the reports at the time, in a healthy state, and at page 261, he remarks, that it was only on the 14th of September that he observed any case in the British hospitals that excited his suspicions." These statements prove, (as in the instance of 1804,) that no disease prevailed at Cadiz, at the time of the departure of the Fortune from that port ; she could not therefore, have imported a nonentity. Further, it has been seen, that more than a month elapsed after the arrival of the Fortune at Gibraltar, before the epidemic was observed in that garrison ; on which point Dr. Bancroft observes,

" As Dr. Pym confidently asserts that the contagion of the Bulam produces disease *in four days*, at least in Gibraltar, its existence must have been made manifest by the occurrence of very many attacks within that interval ; while, if it had been known to have produced *even one*, Sir Joseph Gilpin must have been highly culpable, had he not informed the Lieutenant Governor thereof," p. 375—376.

It is not a little curious, that " the garrison of Gibraltar was in strict quarantine *for several months before* the malady made its appearance, and a Board of Health was sitting *almost daily* on account of the plague which had broken out at Malta,"   *t*   *

This circumstance, added to the *assumed* breach of quarantine in

1810, inevitably involves the dilemma, of either acknowledging the futility of quarantine regulations for the prevention of the Bulam ; or otherwise, that the disease was not in either case imported. The advocates for quarantines are at liberty to choose their difficulty—the impossibility of supporting both positions is palpable.

The origin of the epidemic of 1814, the last which has occurred in Gibraltar, has not been attempted to be referred to importation, except by one individual, who advances no facts in support of his opinion. By the replies to the questions proposed by Deputy Inspector Fraser to the medical officers of the garrison, seventeen in number, we learn, that twelve declared it to be their belief, that the disease originated in domestic or local causes, unconnected with importation. Three were neutral ; one declined offering an opinion ; and one only derived it from importation. The original documents adduced in proof of the domestic origin of the epidemic of that year, are too numerous for us even to glance at. We, therefore, take our leave of the subject of yellow fever at Gibraltar, by repeating our perfect concurrence with the author, after a deliberate consideration of the question, that the fever which has prevailed there epidemically several times within the present century, originated from local or domestic causes, and was destitute of any contagious property.

The seventh and last chapter contains an inquiry into the causes of the epidemics of Cadiz, and other places in Spain in 1810, and in some subsequent years ; but, as the disease was avowedly the same with that of former periods, it will not be incumbent on us to notice all the particular subjects, which, in order to leave nothing relating to these epidemics without investigation, Dr. Bancroft has deemed it his duty to examine. With respect to the fever of Carthagena in 1810, which caused the deaths of 3000 persons in six or eight weeks, he observes,

" We are told by Dr. Burnett, (p. 274.) that Dr. Riseuno, Physician to the Spanish Royal Hospital there, ' positively asserts, that the fever was brought from Cadiz and Gibraltar, in 1810 ;' while Dr. Pym as positively asserted it to have been carried from Carthagena to Gibraltar. This last assertion has already been proved to be erroneous, (see page 359, &c.) and the former must be so, because the ardent yellow fever, or Bulam, did not appear at Gibraltar, (except in the transports,) until near the middle of October, a month after the disease had been prevalent in Carthagena ; and this observation is also applicable to Cadiz, which continued healthy till the middle of September, ' before which time many deaths had occurred at Carthagena ;' and these contradictory assertions serve only to manifest the readiness with which the contagionists, who believe that an epidemic yellow fever must always proceed from imported contagion, hazard tales to account for it," p. 415.

The history of an epidemic yellow fever, which prevailed in the 54th regiment at Stony Hill in Jamaica, has been brought forward by Dr. Pym, as a proof of the contagious origin of that disease. This opinion rests on the circumstance, that a detachment of the 54th regiment, which was sent from Stony Hill to Fort Augusta, and there quartered with a negro regiment and some European troops, became sickly ;

and that after their return to Stony Hill, fever passed through the whole regiment. It is not said from *whence* the contagion was derived ; certainly not from the Negroes at Fort Augusta, who know nothing of yellow fever ; nor yet from the European troops in those quarters ; nor is it stated, that the other regiments in the same quarters with the detachment of the 54th, were not affected by the fever. " If therefore no contagion existed in Fort Augusta, none could have been carried to Stony Hill."

This statement had already been controverted by Mr. Doughty in his valuable publication on Yellow Fever.

" That the 54th Regiment was 'attacked with the aggravated form of yellow fever, as described in these letters, (published by Dr. Pym,) I readily admit ; and, that the other corps in the same quarters did not suffer, as stated by Mr. Rocket, I also most firmly believe. Now, as Mr. Redmond and Mr. Pym agree that the fever which prevailed in the 54th regiment was highly contagious, and Mr. Rocket asserts the other corps remained unaffected with it, I ask from what source did the 54th imbibe its contagion ? The fever developed itself at the season when the endemic cause prevailed, and which might that year be more powerful, and exert its influence to a wider extent, than it had done the preceding years. The soldiers of the 54th were susceptible of its influence, whilst those of the other corps were not in the same degree ; because one of those latter regiments had been in the island, to my knowledge, not less than *three*, and the other *six* years, and a great part of the time in quarters, annually visited with yellow fever." *Observations on Yellow Fever*, p. 54.

There remains the history of another epidemic yellow fever, recorded by Dr. Pym as owing its origin to contagion, which we are somewhat surprised to find that Dr. Bancroft has omitted to notice ; more especially as his local knowledge of the scene of the transaction, (with which we also have some acquaintance,) would, we apprehend, have rendered the task of its refutation void of difficulty. We allude to the fever of the 70th regiment in Fort Edward, Martinique, in 1794 ; and refer to Dr. Fergusson's excellent topographical remarks on Fort Royal ; (Med. Chir. Trans. Vol. viii. p. 119 to 122,) and also to Mr. Mortimer's introductory letter to his valuable report on Yellow Fever, published in the Medico-Chirurgical Journal, in proof, that the sickness of that regiment, attributed by Dr. Pym to contagion, (Obs. on the Bulam Fever, p. 10—14,) depended wholly upon local and indigenous causes.

We conclude this subject with the author's exhortation respecting the preconceived opinions of contagion, which strangers usually carry with them into tropical climates ; but which, in by far the majority of instances, ultimately yield to a more intimate acquaintance with the habitudes of the disease in question.

" I earnestly request my readers attentively to reflect upon the facts stated in this chapter ; and especially upon the readiness with which numerous medical men, respectable by their characters, their conduct, and their professional ranks, have come forward to make confessions which are generally felt as in some degree humiliating, by acknowledging that they had, when they first arrived in the regions of yellow fever, entertained opinions, deeply fixed in their minds by the ordinary course of medical education, which however, after more extensive observation and better means of information, they had found reason to abandon as erroneous, and been forced to adopt conclusions directly the reverse, in regard to the alleged contagious nature of the yellow fever. This is stated to have been done by Dr. M'Lean, Dr. Fergusson, and all their colleagues on the hospital staff at St. Domingo; it was done also by myself, and almost all on the hospital staff in the Windward Islands, (see the letter of Mr. Young, Inspector General, on this subject, at page 335 of my Essay ;) it was done by Dr. Dickson, and as he declares, generally by others in the circle of his acquaintance ; and, beside many others, it will soon appear to have been done by Dr. Erly at Sierra Leone, on the very coast where Dr. Pym and Dr. Chisholm pretend to derive their Bulam fever. In all these cases, the change of opinion has been made spontaneously and disinterestedly, by the silent and gradual, but certain operation of truth ; and without any desire to gain credit by a supposed preservation of many lives from a danger which had no existence, and without any of those views to promotion and reward, which may have produced some of the exertions and erroneous statements lately made, in regard to the fever under consideration," p. 189—191.

On the subject of typhus within the tropics, we think Dr. Bancroft has somewhat, and with advantage, modified his former opinions ; for his admission, page 174, seems to sanction a greater latitude of inference, than could be deduced from his former volume, respecting its being carried as far as Barbadoes. We also are of opinion, that typhus may, and does exist occasionally within the tropics ; and we have seen what we consider to be the unequivocal cases of that disease on the Atlantic Equator ; but we coincide with the author, that the climate is extremely unfavourable to the existence and perpetuation of typhus contagion, and that it ultimately exhausts itself.

Upon the occasional occurrence of a hybrid disease, which Dr. Bancroft simply alludes to as having noticed in his Essay "without either approbation or disapprobation," we do not profess to offer any decided opinion. It is known, that Sir John Pringle, Sir Gilbert Blane, Dr. Lempriere, and others, have spoken of a mixed or hybrid fever ; and we have understood, that Dr. Dickson is of opinion, that he has seen some instances which favour the existence of such character of disease ; where the appearance and duration of the symptoms were so indeterminate between typhus and yellow fever, that it was difficult to say, to which order of fever they most belonged. But we believe, at the same time, that he considers such occurrences as extremely rare ; that he has not detected any satisfactory evidence of their possessing an infectious quality ; and that under the influence of climate, they soon disappear, and are succeeded by the legitimate endemic of the West Indies. Such questions can only, we conceive, be ultimately decided by those who may enjoy similarly extensive opportunities of witnessing the disease under all varieties of circumstances and character.

We conclude by expressing our sense of the ingenuity, acuteness, and research, which the author, has exerted with equal facility and effect in the present elaborate production ; and we are satisfied, that the voluminous mass of irrefragable evidence which he has been en-abled to adduce, will impress conviction on every unprejudiced mind, of the perfect triumph he has achieved by the complete refutation of the opposite opinion, of the existence of the Bulam as a distinct con-tagious fever, attacking but once. In the preceding analysis, we have aimed at the inclusion of the most prominent parts of the dis-cussion ; for its length we plead the importance of the inquiry, and the desire to diffuse a portion, at least, of the information with which the pages of this " Sequel" are enriched, as well as to contribute our mite to the advancement of what we consider to be the cause of truth, and to the correction of a popular error ; for as the author justly ob-serves in his conclusions, the supposition of the existence of conta-gion " accords with the prejudices and apprehensions of the greater part of mankind, who are prone to believe that all diseases are con-tagious when they become generally prevalent." To those whose lot and duty it has been to alleviate the sufferings inflicted by yellow fever, and who, therefore, with us, naturally feel a peculiar interest in the discussion, we need not say more to induce them to avail them-selves of the information and experience accumulated in this volume.

Topographical Remarks, illustrating the causes and prevention of the Tropical Endemic or Yellow Fever, by Dr. DICKSON, F. R. S. Ed. F. L S. Fellow of the Royal College of Physicians of Edinburgh, and late Physician to the Fleet, and Inspector of Hospitals in the West Indies.

————Quod sol atque imbres dederant, quod terra creârat
Sponte sua.   LUCRET. Lib. v.

SEC. III.—As the knowledge of a disease is of interest in propor-tion to its danger or frequency, and as the means of prevention de-pend upon a correct appreciation of its causes, the investigation of the laws which govern the Tropical Endemic is confessedly of the highest importance.—With this view I offered some topographical re-marks on the Etiology, and Prevention of the Yellow Fever, in the 13th Vol. of the Edinburgh Medical and Surgical Journal ; and, on the present occasion, I have endeavoured, by the addition of several observations and illustrations, still further to elucidate the subject.

Marsh Miasma has been very generally, and justly considered as a grand source of the fevers of warm climates ; and it is a very fre-quent though not the only source of the destructive form of the Tro-pical Endemic. While its operation has been too exclusively insisted upon by some authors, it has been admitted under great limitations only by others. The term, indeed, is not free from objection, since it has caused the latter to receive it in a sense far too strict and lite-ral, and to question the existence of such exhalations, except in the vicinity of a complete swamp or marsh.

I am at present to consider the miasmata of decomposition, with reference to their effect, and not to their intimate nature, in whatever situation they may occur ; and, in this general sense, it appears to me, that, in a temperature so uniformly high as that of the West Indies, and where decomposition is so rapidly promoted by the agency of heat and moisture, there can be very few places where the occasional production of noxious effluvia may not be calculated upon on shore; and sometimes, also, on ship-board. Of fever arising in particular ships, from impure exhalations emanating from a foul state of the hold, continuing notwithstanding every attention to preventive measures, and ceasing only upon the hold being cleared, I have seen many well-marked instances. As the most unseasoned part of a ship's company, and especially strangers, will be most liable to suffer ; in this case, it is easy to perceive that such attacks might sometimes be construed in favour of infectious fever ; but that they proceeded solely from the source above mentioned, appears to me clearly demonstrated by the previous inefficacy of ventilation and cleanliness, —by the impunity with which promiscuous intercourse, elsewhere, is maintained with other ships,—by the extinction of the disease upon the hold being cleared, and not till then,—and by its not being propagated or communicated by the sick, when removed from its original source. I shall adduce one example, where, from the peculiar construction of the vessel, the source of the febrific exhalations could be more clearly ascertained than when they arise from a foul state of the ballast in general. In April, 1807, a fever prevailed in the Dart, lying guard-ship at Barbadoes, which, at first, was attributed to land influence, and irregularities committed by the men employed on shore ; but as it continued from time to time, to attack new comers, especially after sleeping two or three nights on board, an internal cause became suspected. The ship was divided into compartments below, so as to allow of the water being carried into large tanks or cisterns, instead of the usual manner ; and these, having been disused in harbour, their bottoms were found to be covered with an offensive deposition of slimy mud. On the 17th of May, cases of fever still supervening, I find by my notes that this evil had been detected, and remedied ; and communications between the divisions had been opened, so as to allow a free circulation of air below ; and on the 24th I find it stated, " for the last week no fresh attacks of fever had occurred on board the Dart." The fatal cases terminated at the hospital with the usual symptoms of yellow fever. As such fevers may occur at various periods after exposure, consequently, after the cause has been removed, the early cessation of the disease, in the present instance, is more material, where the ship was constantly receiving new men ; because their not being affected subsequently, showed that the cause which had existed previously, existed no longer.

Impure effluvia will be most apt to be generated in a new ship, particularly if built of green wood ; or where the shingle ballast has not been restowed for a length of time, or had not been, originally, carefully selected. If such exhalations, (between which and animal

effluvia, confined or produced by the human body under disease, a
wide distinction obtains, though their effects have been often confounded,) be admitted to occur, occasionally in a man of war, where
cleanliness is proverbial, it is easy to perceive, that, by the agency
of heat and moisture, they may, under particular circumstances, in a
transport or merchantship, become so abundant and concentrated,
that the hold, without the expression being very figurative, might be
denominated a ship marsh.*

  But a grand source of obscurity and of contradictory opinions appears to me to originate from a want of attention to those, different
states of the system, involving a great diversity of liability to the
Yellow Fever, from the lowest grade of European susceptibility to
the highest degree of disposition to the disease, short of actual Fever. Consistently with this diversity, it follows that a quantum of
cause altogether innoxious and insignificant in the former, would be
fully competent to induce the disease in the latter state of the system ; hence it is easy to understand, that according to the gradations
in the scale of susceptibility will be the power of the noxious impression ; and moreover that, what in one subject would constitute a predisponent, in another, possessing a higher degree of disposition,
would prove an exciting cause of the Yellow Fever. I have here
used the word Disposition instead of Predisposition, (though I should
have preferred the more familiar term,) because it might be contended that the latter ought to imply an original, or, at least, a previous. rather than an acquired tendency.

  The degree of such disposition may fluctuate considerably during
the earlier period of an European's residence in the West Indies,
according to his age, habits, locality, the season of the year, and as
various stimuli have a greater or less influence upon the system ; or,
in other words, in proportion as it has been freely and suddenly, or
cautiously and gradually exposed to their operation. In such a climate, where the youthful, sanguine temperament is, at any rate,
goaded by the stimulus of unnatural heat, into a degree of febricu-
lar excitement, it is not extraordinary that, from free living, intemperance, or undue exposure or exertion, there should be much danger of this artificial excitation terminating in real fever, until the
system becomes gradually inured, and less sensible of such influence
by the effect of habit, or assimilated by the supervention of, what
have been called, seasoning, or milder attacks of sickness.

  The dangerous increase of susceptibility may be often observed in
ships recently arrived from Europe, continuing healthy, while refitting in harbour, for ten days, a fortnight, or longer, according to the
season, and becoming very sickly afterwards. Its variation, and decline, are sufficiently exemplified in the disparity of health enjoyed by
the crews of ships under repair, at the same time, and in the same har-

* A very apposite and striking illustration of this remark has subsequently appeared in the account of the sickness in the Regalia transport, by Drs. Fergusson and Mortimer.—*Vide* Medico-Chirurgical Transactions, vol. viii. p. 108 ; and
Bancroft's " Sequel," p. 217, et sig. In the latter able Work, several other instances of Fever, arising from an impure state of the hold, are extracted from my
official Report to the Naval Medical Board, and other sources.

bour, and exposed to precisely similar exciting causes, but differing in the length of their residence in a tropical climate, or the degree of exposure or sickness to which they had been previously subjected. The variation in these respects will cause such dissimilar results, that a fatal fever will become general, in a short time in one ship; in another the sickness will be partial, and less dangerous; while a third will be altogether exempt, or experience only mild and occasional attacks. This gradation will be sufficiently obvious, although its uniformity may be somewhat affected by peculiarities in season, modes of discipline, and various minuter causes, while the chief circumstances are apparently the same.

The danger of a West India climate, or, in other words, the tendency to yellow fever, I conceive, then, to be in the compound ratio of the disposition, and the force of the exciting cause; a weaker exciting cause being sufficient when the system is strongly disposed, and vice versa; for, fortunately these often obtain in an inverse proportion; and the constitution has been more or less habituated, previously to any considerable exposure. How greatly the preservation of health must depend upon the inurement being gradual, is too obvious to require any comment. The degree of security, however, that may be acquired, will be relative; for the susceptibility will be less after an attack of this fever,—or from being habituated to miasmata, or other remote causes, than from mere length of residence.

Marshy effluvia, or similar impure emanations in other situations, I have already stated to be, in my opinion, a great source of yellow fever, either as a predisposing or exciting cause; but, if the above premises be correct, it further follows, that the causes of yellow fever may be the same as the remote causes of fever in general; that they may act in various degrees of intensity, or combination; that the weaker require the aid of disposition, to become efficient; but when the system is highly excited, or prepared to fall into fever, that any additional agency, though of itself inoperative and insignificant, may become the occasional cause; and consequently, that this disease may be called into action, in some cases, by such as are feeble, dissimilar, and so obscure as to elude investigation.

In speaking of causation, then, I do not mean to express individual agency, but any concurrence of circumstances which constitutes a cause; for I imagine we can seldom, in pathological physics at least, calculate upon either singleness of cause, or simplicity of effect. If the preceding principles are well-founded, it will not be necessary here to enter into any length of illustration to show, that sporadic cases may arise, in this way, at all seasons of the year, from insolation or undue exposure, intemperance, fatigue, or other irregularities, as well as from circumstances so minute, as often to escape detection; that a number of men, such as a regiment, or a ship's company, or any part of them, from similarity of temperament, employment, or situation, will often suffer simultaneously, particularly during the hurricane season, and all the latter half of the year; and that in particular years, from previous unseasonable weather, or an epidemic constitution of the atmosphere, and in all years, during the sickly months, when a considerable number of unassimilated men have been recently introduced into the West Indies, the yellow fever may be expected to become general among them, and to be attended with great mortality, particularly after much exposure and exertion, often inseparable from active warfare. As the constitution will suffer less excitement from the heat, the coming from another part of the torrid zone, or a southern climate, will confer a certain degree of protection, but this will be only sufficient to guard against the weaker, or ordinary causes of yellow fever. The gradation which I have above attempted to explain, is well illustrated by the following unstudied, but impressive extract of a letter from Mr. Sheppard, now lying before me :—" While we were all ill, and dying in the Alligator, in English Harbour, shortly after our arrival in the West Indies, the Emerald, which had been two or three years in the climate, remained near us healthy, though under precisely the same circumstances of duty and exposure. The Emerald was succeeded in her situation by the Carysfort, fresh from Europe, which ship, in a few weeks, buried almost all hands."

From regarding the habits, as well as the ætiology of tropical endemic, the laws which govern its appearance seem to me to be entirely different from those of the plague and typhus fever, with which it has been sometimes compared. To those disorders, strangers, and the natives of the countries in which they prevail, are cæteris paribus, obnoxious in the same degree ; and all such as are equally exposed, may be said to be equally endangered. But it is totally different in the legitimate yellow fever in the West Indies. It is the disease of manhood, of the excited, unassimilated, full habit. It more rarely attacks an earlier or later period of life ; and seldom females, or only in proportion, as from intemperance or other causes, they approach to the habit of the male sex ; while old residents, whether native or assimilated, and people of colour, though subject to remittent and other milder forms, may be said to be almost entirely exempted from this severe form of disease,—for they are so, with as rare exceptions as we witness in the application of any other general rule.

" But whatever may be the peculiar coincidence of circumstances, or modification of cause, most fertile in the generation of yellow fever, an uniformly high temperature is the causa sine qua non. This is literally and eminently entitled to be so denominated, because it indispensably precedes the effect. In the Carribean Archipelago, the temperature is not only high, but equably and durably so ; and from its little variation in this respect, I consider the yellow fever as the legitimate product of the climate ; for in the more southern colonies on the Continent, where, from the vicinity of woods, mountains, &c. the temperature, though often as high, is not uniformly so, and where the winds are more variable, and the nights cooler, the disease is much less prevalent, and oftener assumes a remittent type.

To the importance which I attach to an equably high atmospheric temperature, it may be objected by some persons, that, in countries which should be still more favourable to this disease, because the heat is more intense, and also in places lying in the same latitude, the yellow fever is not known. But, in the first place, it becomes incumbent on such persons to show, why a temperature above a certain height ought to be more favourable; for, on the contrary, I should expect that great heat would dissipate and destroy, if not prevent, the formation of the miasmata of decomposition; and, secondly, it by no means follows that the climate of two places is alike, because they lie at the same distance from the equator.

Mr. Humboldt remarks, that the salubrity of tropical climates depends more on the dryness of the air, than on any of its other sensible qualities : " The burning province of Cumana, the coast of Cora, and the plains of Caraccas, prove that excessive heat, alone, is not unfavourable to human life."

All historians concur in admitting the different laws to which the corresponding degrees of the two hemispheres are subject, with respect to the distribution of heat and cold ; for the exceptions, from local causes, stated by Calvigero, cannot affect the general principles. The difference in the same latitude has been estimated at 12 or more degrees ; but according to relative situation, it must be often much greater.

The dissimilarity of climate, between the eastern and western sides of the New Continent. from this cause, and from the greater variableness of the wind, is also noticed by various writers, and particularly in the voyages of Ullon, Anson, and others.

At Lima, which is but a little further on one side of the equator than Carthagena is on the other, the heat is far more moderate ; and the observations made by the academicians at Quito show, that, from its elevated situation, although close to the line, the thermometer does not rise there so high in summer as it does in Paris ; nor does it fall so low as in the temperate climates of Europe in winter, so uniform are the seasons. See Rees, Pinkerton, Walton, &c.

This disparity of Old and New Continent. and of places lying in the same parallel, is sufficiently accounted for upon philosophical principles, and depends on the elevation, depression, extent, or configuration of country, direction of the winds, nature and cultivation of the soil, proximity and height of mountains, vicinity of the sea, and many circumstances which modify the temperature of a climate, besides its distance from the equator, and the consequent more vertical, or more oblique incidence of the solar rays.

Dr. Robertson observes, " while the negro on the coast of Africa is scorched with unremitting heat, the inhabitant of Peru breathes an air equally mild and temperate, and is perpetually shaded under a canopy of grey clouds, which intercepts the fierce beams of the sun without obstructing his friendly influence. Along the eastern coast of America, the climate, though more similar to that of the torrid zone, in other parts of the earth, is nevertheless considerably milder, than in these countries of Asia and Africa, which lie in the same latitude."

He afterwards shows, that the trade wind is still further cooled in its passage from the Atlantic to the Pacific shore of the New Continent. " As this wind advances across America, it meets with immense plains covered with impenetrable forests, or occupied by large rivers, marshes, and stagnating waters, where it can recover no considerable degree of heat ; at length it arrives at the Andes, which run from north to south through the whole Continent. In passing over their elevated and frozen summits, it is so thoroughly cooled, that the greater part of the countries beyond them hardly feel the ardour to which they seem exposed by their situation. In the other provinces of America, from Tierra Firmè, westward to the Mexican empire, the heat of the climate is tempered in some places by the elevation of the land above the sea, in others by the extraordinary humidity, and also by' the enormous mountains scattered over this tract."—History of America, vol. II. p. 9, *et seq.* 9th edit. Hence the great salubrity of the table-land, in the centre of New Spain, compared with the low marshy lands upon the coast.

-᷾On the opposite side of Mexico, where the distance is so much less than across the other parts of the Continent, the influence upon disease is yet considerable. Thus we learn that although bilious fevers and cholera morbus prevail, the black vomit has never yet been observed on the west coast of New Spain, while Vera Cruz is considered as the chief seat of that terrible distemper.

The disastrous results of the expeditions to Carthagena, Porto Bello, Vera Cruz, &c. which have been the theme of the historian, and of the poet, have, indeed, fatally proved the peculiar noxiousness of the extremely hot, alluvial, and marshy soil of the eastern shore.

Even in the short distance of 60 miles, between Panama and Porto Bello, the difference is sufficiently perceptible, although, from improvements, it may be less so of late years. Ulloa remarks, that the garrison detachments sent from the former to the latter, " though coming from a place so near, are affected to such a degree, that, in less than a month, they are so attenuated, as to be unable to do any duty, till custom again restores them to their strength ;" and that " the inhabitants of Panama are not so meagre and pale as those who live at Carthagena, and Porto Bello."—Translation by Adams, vol. i. p. 98, and 123, 4th edit.

I am the more anxious to advert to these points, because they assist in explaining the influence of locality and susceptibility in the production of yellow fever.

For, besides the lower and more variable temperature and winds on the extensive coast washed by the Pacific Ocean, the introduction of Europeans is more gradual and limited, and their constitutions may be supposed to have lost that freshness, (if I may use the expression,) so favourable to this disease, by the length of the voyage and climates through which they must pass ; or by the seasoning attacks, to which they are liable before they reach their destination, if they land at an eastern port.

There are two powerful reasons, then, why Europeans, on the other side, are so much less subject to yellow fever : They have not only lost a considerable share of their original susceptibility by pre-assimilation, but their equatorial parallelism is so far counteracted by the difference of climate, that they may be considered, though *actually* living in the same, as *virtually* living in a more northern latitude.

The converse of this proposition appears to me well adapted to explain the occasional appearance of the fever which has excited so much controversy in America and in the south of Europe. *During the unusual and long continued height of the thermometer, by which these epidemics have been preceded, the inhabitants are virtually placed in a new or tropical climate; and the same general effect follows which would result from the sudden transition of a body of men to the West Indies, with a considerable share of northern susceptibility. In both cases the constitution, being unassimilated to the change, will be liable to be affected by the unusually heated and peculiar state of the atmosphere, whether its influence may be admitted to consist in producing the dispositional tendency of which I have spoken, or the developement of those miasmal products most favourable to this form of fever, or in both.*

Hence the natives of the torrid, and of the temperate zone, are upon a very different footing in respect to susceptibility. For while the former may be considered as exempt from yellow fever, the inhabitants of the United States, and of Spain, (though probably somewhat less liable than more northern strangers,) cannot be seasoned against it by any length of residence in their native country. For, from the variations of temperature to which they are exposed, they may be expected to lose during the winter any degree of assimilation they may have acquired during the almost tropical heat of the preceding summer; and, (like the natives of the Antilles, after residing a certain time in Europe,) they become liable to be attacked by the yellow fever, when the thermometer has maintained, for a certain period, the degree of heat necessary to produce the requisite disposition, or the evolution of sufficiently concentrated miasmata.

As illustrating the grounds upon which the occasional appearance of the yellow fever may be anticipated in ultra-tropical situations, and at the same time pointing out some of the sources by the remedying of which the chance of its occurrence may be diminished, I shall here introduce the remarks of M. Devèze, on the locality of Philadelphia, quoted from the second volume of the Quarterly Journal of Foreign Medicine and Surgery, p. 434—5.—" M. Devèze enters upon the first chapter with a topographical description of Philadelphia; and from its situation upon a plain on the banks of the Delaware, intersected by large ditches, from which the winter's rain can only escape by evaporation, carrying along with it the detritus of the clay soil, and the vapours and gasses arising from the decomposition of the vegetable and animal substances which cover their banks; from the sudden transitions of temperature and humidity of the atmosphere, not only in regard to its annual or monthly variations, but in respect to what usually takes place within the twenty-four hours; concludes that Philadelphia from these combined causes, must frequently not only be the seat of sporadic cases of fever, but also of the more destructive epidemic forms of this disease. That the character of the fever which appears in the southern parts of the United States, should put on the same form with the fevers of tropical climates is indeed almost to be expected, from the excessively rich, deep, and absorbent nature of the soil; combined with the other adventitious circumstances of stagnant pools and ditches, filth of various descriptions, gasses arising from decomposed organized remains, floating in an atmosphere, whose temperature, during the summer months, almost exceeds that within the tropics, and which, according to M. Devèze, was found by the French emigrants at Philadelphia more debilitating than they experienced at St. Domingo."—Traite de la Fièvre, Jaune ; Par Jean Devèze, 1820. See also the grafical remarks of Dr. Robertson ; and those of Dr. Girardin on the topography of Louisiana.

M. Devèze, moreover, found that the quantity of electric fluid existing in the atmosphere was there extremely variable ; and that the number of insects was unusually great, during the hot months, when the epidemic raged in that city,—a strong indication of insalubrity. It may be proper in this place to remark that, in such climates, results drawn from the greatest and smallest elevations of the thermometer at certain periods, give no information respecting the mean temperature ; for, from inattention to this point, in discussing the question whether the heats might be considered as extraordinary in epidemical seasons, it has been affirmed that the heat was greater in some healthy, than in unhealthy years, because the thermometer rose a few degrees higher in the former than in the latter.

- Upon ultra-tropical yellow fever I do not propose to offer any observations at present ; but I am inclined to believe, that the discrepancy of opinion is much to be attributed to partial and incomplete views of disease in limited and detached situations ; and that the more we see of fevers in the various quarters of the world, the more we shall be induced to refer to general but determinate principles their phenomena, as well as their mode of action or effects upon the body; though the latter, of course, will be susceptible of great diversity, according to the nature or concentration of cause, individuality of constitution and structure, and relative importance of the organs particularly affected.

In his celebrated work on the political state of New Spain, to which I have already alluded, M. de Humboldt seems to have justly appreciated the influence of uniformity of temperature, situation and, individual susceptibility, in the production of yellow fever. I shall quote from my notes, as I have not the book before me. He is of opinion that the yellow fever has occurred sporadically whenever persons born in a cold climate have been exposed in the torrid zone to air loaded with miasmata ; and he very properly cautions us against confounding the period when a disease was first described, with the date of its first appearance.

The yellow fever, he informs us, is still unknown at Acapulco, though, from the uniformity of the heat, he is apprehensive that, if ever developed, it will continue the whole year, as in other situations where the temperature varies only two or three degrees during the year ; and he most judiciously remarks, that, if this port, instead of being frequented by ships from Manilla, Guayaquil, and other places of the torrid zone, received ships from Chili, or the north west coast of America, if it were visited at the same time by a great number of Europeans, or of Highland Mexicans, the bilious would probably soon degenerate into the yellow fever, and the germ of this last disease would develope itself in a still more fatal manner than at Vera

Cruz.; M. Humboldt afterwards gives a still more satisfactory reason why it is not brought from Chili, viz. that it does not exist there ;—which I imagine to be not a little applicable to the Bulama, and some other instances of imputed importation, like that from Siam, characterised by Dr. Lind as "truly chimerical." For, after stating that the yellow fever has not appeared upon the coast of the Pacific Ocean during the last fifty years, except at Panama, and that there, as at Callao, the commencement of a great epidemic is often marked by the arrival of some ships from Chili, he adds, not that they imported the disease from a country where it never existed, but because the inhabitants coming from the healthiest country in the world, experienced the same fatal effects of a sultry air vitiated with putrid emanations, as the inhabitants of the north. See the 4th Volume, by Black, and the 29th Number of the Edinburgh Medical and Surgical Journal.

The same reasoning, I may observe, particularly applies to the error which has been so often committed, of mistaking epidemic for contagious diseases, and supposing them to be imported by new comers, because, from unassimilation to the new atmosphere, they are generally the first and greatest sufferers from local causes. Thus, Ulloa states, though he does not seem to believe it, that, when the black vomit first appeared at Guayaquil in 1740, the galleons of the South Sea having touched there, it was the general opinion that they had brought that distemper, and that great numbers died on board the ships, together with many foreigners, but very few of the natives.—Adams, vol. i. p. 161. I need hardly remark how infinitely more probable it is, that the sailors, coming from a pure air, suffered from the unhealthy marsh in the vicinity, which Estalla describes as infecting the city, at particular seasons, with pestilential vapours ; but which to the natives, from habituation, were comparatively inoxious. Even in ordinary seasons, in the West Indies, it is not unfrequently observed, that men, though partially seasoned in one place, are, nevertheless, liable to be again attacked by fever upon their removal to another, or even to a different part of the same island ; and this sometimes happens, although the latter may be esteemed as healthy, or even a healthier situation ; proving the influence of a new, or in some respect differently modified atmosphere, or of other circumstances which the apparent locality, though it may in some degree, is insufficient wholly to explain.

It is therefore probable, that in different places and seasons there is not only a difference in the power or intensity, but in the nature and combination of febrific miasmata, upon which the increased liability to sickness, on a change of residence, may, in a great measure depend.

Indeed, we not only observe striking peculiarities in the features of disease, in different climates, but often a considerable change in the state of health from a seemingly inconsiderable change of situation ; and if such effects happen from modifications of climate, soil, or other circumstances, for which we are so often unable to account, it is necessarily much more to be expected that strangers arriving at

the commencement of a sickly or epidemic season, should be the earliest victims ; and thus, erroneously, they have been sometimes
thought to have brought a disease, merely because they were the
first affected by new miasmata, or other local causes, increasing the
susceptibility of a habit probably already prone to febrile or inflammatory action.

As for the reasons already given, and from personal observation of
the tropical endemic in almost every variety of situation—proving it
to arise in hot, low, moist, close places, when new men are exposed
to miasmata, intemperance, insolation, or fatigue—I must consider
the yellow fever, not as an imported or contagious disease, but as a
strictly local and indigenous evil, " quod sol atque imbres dederant,
quod terra creârat sponte sua," to use the words of Lucretius in a
different application. I shall only remark here, that if it possessed
any contagious property, it is to me altogether unaccountable, that
conviction thereof should not have been coerced, almost with the
force of mathematical demonstration, long before the present day,
considering the continual and unrestricted intercourse generally carried on between the ships, as well as between the opposite sides of the
Isthmus of Darien. But, on the contrary, examples of individual disease, or of a limited number only, are constantly occurring in the same
ship, again and again, without extending further ; and it becomes epidemic. as I have endeavoured to explain, only when a generally operating
cause produces a general effect. Hence it is legitimately endemic in the
West Indies, and becomes often epidemic there at particular seasons,
and occasionally, in other countries, after exposure to the influence of
tropical heat. If the fever of Gibraltar and other parts of Spain be
the same disease, and if it possess any such property, which I consider as still remaining to be proved. I must therefore contend that it
is not a native, but an adventitious character, and that, like other diseases attended with febrile action in temperate climates especially,
it is susceptible of being modified by the occasional coincidence of peculiar circumstances, such modification placing it in a class which, in
my official report on the subject to the Naval Medical Board, (perhaps inaccurately, but for the sake of distinction merely,) I called
Diffusible Disorders, the power of dissemination in such not being,
as in other communicable diseases, native and inherent, but contingent and acquired.* Although I do not mean here to enter further

---

* Although decidedly of opinion that the yellow fever of the West Indies is
not a contagious disorder, and that the climate is highly inimical to the very existence of contagion, Dr. Dickson does not mean to deny the abstract *possibility*
of *any* fever becoming so, under particular circumstances, at least in temperate
climates ; but he contends, that a distinction ought to be made between an inherent, and an adventitious property. In a former communication to the author he
observes, that he uses the term Diffusible Disorders to express not a native and
permanent, but an acquired and temporary power of dissemination ; and he proposes indicating the degree of such power by a change of termination. Thus using the same epithet, [for the propriety of which he does not contend, but only
for the sake of illustration,] a diffus*ive* disease might signify that which can or
may diffuse itself ; and a diffus*ible* one, that which can or may *be* diffused ; the
latter requiring for this purpose the co-operation of a peculiar, but transitive
coincidence of circumstances. For such purposes, he remarks, we have the potential *active*, and potential *passive* adjectives as they are called by Horne Tooke.

upon the question of the Peninsula fever, yet, as its progress has been considered by some to be satisfactorily traced, and its prevalence to be unaccounted for by any supposition of an epidemic change of the air, or endemic origin, without a reference to contagion,. I may be permitted to remark, in passing, without dwelling upon the inference, that, in the latest work upon the subject, and in which this opinion is temperately supported, the concurrence of a certain height of tempe-. rature, and of a combination of circumstances difficult to define, but connected with the climate and individual predisposition,—is never-theless admitted to be necessary to the existence of the disorder.

Indeed, stronger evidence of a highly deleterious state of the at-mosphere, as exemplified by its pernicious influence upon animal life, in these instances at least, cannot well be adduced, than that furnished by the author of the reports himself ; for, in the fever at Cadiz in 1800, Sir James Fellowes, I believe in page 45, speaking of the air, says, " its noxious qualities affected even animals ; canary birds died with blood issuing from their bills ;" and he quotes the authority of Arejula in further proof of similar fatal effects upon domestic animals, particularly dogs, cats, horses, poultry, and birds.

In equinoctial regions the effect of elevation, (as indeed was con-jectured by some of the ancients,) is equivalent to that of latitude. We are informed, that the farm of *L'Encero*, beyond Vera Cruz, which is 3043 feet above the level of the Ocean, is the superior limit of the *Vomito ;* and that the Mexican Oaks descend no further than this place, being unable to vegetate in a heat sufficient to develope the germ of the yellow fever. The situation of Vera Cruz, indeed. is peculiarly adapted to establish the nature and indigenous origin of this disease. The traveller by the ascent of a few hours is carried beyond its reach, from the rapidity with which the ground rises to the westward, for it is not felt beyond ten leagues from the coast ; while, converse-ly, the Creoles who inhabit the elevated table-land of New Spain, where the mean temperature is about 60°, and where the thermome-ter sometimes falls below the freezing point, when they descend the eastern declivity of the Cordillera, are plunged as it were at once " unanointed, unannealed" into the extremely hot and deleterious atmosphere of Vera Cruz, and suffer even in a greater proportion than European strangers who approach it gradually by sea. In fact, these Mexican Mountaineers in descending from Perote to the coast, in sixteen hours are transported from the temperate to the torrid zone, and by this sudden change are exposed to all the dangers of a new and fatal endemical disease. This concentrated variety of cli-mate, and its influence on the vegetable, as well as the animal crea-

Belonging to the *former* we have the termination *ive*, borrowed from the La-tin, and *ic* from the Greek :—belonging to the *latter* we have, (from the Latin *bi-lis*,) the terminations *able* and *ible ;* and also the contraction *ile* having one com-mon signification.—Scaliger distinctly points out the force of the two terminations *ilis* and *ivus*, ' duas habuere apud latinos, totidem apud græcos, terminationes— in *ivus* activam in *ilis* passivam, &c.' Dr. Dickson further suggests whether, in speaking of absolutely contagious or infectious diseases we might not, by the noun substantive or adjective, indicate a *greater* or *less* degree of such power : as in the *latter* by the terminations *osus* and *ivus*, &c. ex infectio*sus* and infect*ivus*. " Hæc omnia infectiva appellantur."—Vitr.

tion, is depicted with such force and beauty by Baron Humboldt, that I cannot resist laying before the reader a description which, in a few lines, carries him from the burning plains in the vicinity of the sea, to the regions of perpetual snow : " The admirable order with which different tribes of vegetables rise above one another by strata, as it were, is no where more perceptible than in ascending from the port of Vera Cruz to the table-land of Perote. We see there the physiognomy of the country, the aspect of the sky, the form of plants, the figures of animals, the manners of the inhabitants, and the kind of cultivation followed by them, assume a different appearance at every step of our progress.

As we ascend, nature appears gradually less animated, the beauty of the vegetable forms diminishes, the shoots become less succulent, and the flowers less coloured. The sight of the Mexican oak quiets the alarms of travellers newly landed at Vera Cruz. Its presence demonstrates to him that he has left behind him the zone so justly dreaded by the people of the North, under which the yellow fever exercises its ravages in New Spain.

This inferior limit of oaks warns the colonist who inhabits the central table-land how far he may descend towards the coast without dread of the mortal disease of the vomito. Forests of liquidamber near Xalapa, announce, by the freshness of their verdure, that this is the elevation at which the clouds suspended over the ocean, come in contact with the basaltic summits of the Cordillera. A little higher, near La Banderilla, the nutritive fruit of the banana tree comes no longer to maturity. In this foggy and cold region, therefore, want spurs on the Indian to labour, and excites his industry. At the height of San Miguel pines begin to mingle with the oaks, which are found by the traveller as high as the elevated plains of Perote, where he beholds the delightful aspect of fields sown with wheat. Eight hundred metres higher, the coldness of the climate will no longer admit of the vegetation of the oaks ; and pines alone there cover the rocks, whose summits enter the zone of eternal snow. Thus in a few hours. the naturalist, in this miraculous country, ascends the whole scale of vegetation, from the heliconia, and the banana plant, whose glossy leaves swell out into extraordinary dimensions, to the stunted parenchyma of the resinous trees."
—Political Essay on the kingdom of New Spain, translated by Black, vol. ii. p. 251—2.

In accounting for the tropical endemic becoming epidemic at particular seasons, the eminent traveller just referred to, further shows the intimate connection on the coast of Mexico, between the progress of the disease, and the temperature and state of the seasons ; and, accordingly, that, at Vera Cruz, the vomito prieto does not commence generally, till the medium heat is 75° Fahr. It is, therefore, seldom seen in December, January, and February, unless it has been very violent in the summer, when it continues more or less through the winter ; but, as he observes, although it is hotter in May, its ravages are more dreadful in September and October, because a certain duration seems necessary to develope its full force ; which must, moreover, be augmented after the rains have ceased, which last from June to September, as well as be influenced by the direction of the winds. The same increase of disease, I may remark, is observed in the islands, during the hurricane months; and this is also in proportion as the previous weather has been unseasonable; but the medical heat at which the disease begins to be prevalent, may be calculated at, at least, from 5° to 10° higher; from which it may be deduced, that, in proportion as the air is more loaded with miasmata, as on the Atlantic shores of New Spain, the disease may become active at a lower temperature, than when these effluvia are less abundant and concentrated; and it may further account for its appearance beyond the tropics, during the summer heat.

In proof of the effect of seasons, I have now before me a letter from Doctor Macarthur, who ably conducted the Naval Hospital at Barbadoes for several years, corresponding with his report to the Medical Board in September, 1809, in which he says :—" I remarked, while at Barbadoes, that the fever was more frequent, and more violent when the rains were partial, than when continued and general. The heat of the sun produced the decomposition of animal and vegetable substances more rapidly when the earth was slightly moistened by rain, than when perfectly drenched. In these years, when the rain fell abundantly during the months of June, July, and August, the fever did not appear until September, October, and November. On the contrary, when June, July, and August, were comparatively dry months, the fever invaded us earlier.—We know in Europe that the effluvia from marshes are more deleterious a week or two after the beginning of dry hot weather, than immediately after the rains are over; the first evaporation from the surface of the marsh being inoxious, compared with that which afterwards follows." Upon the same principle, as has been well explained by Dr. Bancroft and others, it is not during excessively wet or dry seasons, but sometime after the rains, or after partial showers, that marshy effluvia are most abundant and concentrated, as I saw dreadfully exemplified in the garrison epidemic at Mariegalante, in the autumn of 1808. At certain seasons, therefore, in hot countries, wherever there are vegetable and animal life and decay, even though no water be stagnating on the earth, the whole flat surface may be considered as a marsh; and, consequently, there can be very few situations, as I mentioned at the commencement, exempt from the occasional influence of such miasmata.

It is only by tracing its connection with the seasons, then, that we can rationally expect to unfold the laws of the tropical endemic, and such topographical hints as I have here offered, if followed up, I should hope would materially contribute to this end, although the peculiar and intimate combination of circumstances, as well as its sporadical occurrence, must often depend upon causes so minute as to elude all investigation.

The degree of exemption from the disease will be, generally, conditional, and contingent upon various circumstances; for though indemnity to a considerable extent may be purchased by a previous attack, or by mere length of residence, yet such protection is but relative, and, though a sufficient security against ordinary causes, is not proof against such as are of great intensity.

The Circe frigate, after having been several times at Antigua, and escaping with a limited number. or only individual instances of yel-low fever, by putting to sea before it became general, entered English harbour, which was then healthy, on the 4th of January, 1808, no man requiring medicine. In five days afterwards the fever appeared, and, from being engaged in the unwholesome duty of clearing the hold, and heaving down, between that period and the 2nd of February, 146 men were sent to the hospital, of which number 22 died with black vomit, although it was then the healthiest season of the year, and the ship had been nearly two years and ten months in the West Indies..

Still, though the immunity was far from amounting to insusceptibility, the danger here was much lessened by partial assimilation ; for it may be fairly inferred, that the mortality would have been much greater if the ship had been recently from England.

A great proportion of these men had suffered previous attac ks of fever ; and I think there can be as little doubt, that some of them, at least, would have terminated in the same way, if they had not been controlled.

As the degree of immunity will be modified by various circumstances, so will the success in the treatment of the yellow fever be modified by season, situation, severity of the attack, habit of the patient, &c. But, without entering into any detail upon the mode of cure, which I have treated of elsewhere,* and which is ably laid down in the following pages by others, I shall content myself with observing shortly, that though success will be greatly influenced by locality and constitution, and though the symptoms of this malady do not always permit, nor can they, where they do authorize, be always arrested by the copious abstraction of blood ; yet I feel justified in saying, that it is only from this remedy, employed while the fever is forming, or within a short time after it is formed, aided, of course, by purgatives, and by the cold affusion, if indicated, that we can entertain any plausible expectation of arresting a disease where the morbid motions are of such inordinate power and rapidity. In making this remark, I more particularly allude to that which I have most frequently witnessed, the ardent continued form of this disease, where the deceitful pause, during the transition from one stage to the other, has been so often mistaken for a remission. To admit the effects of the morbid action upon the stomach, contiguous intestine, and brain, often in the course of a few hours, would appear to me equivalent to admitting that we could only rationally hope to counteract them by such powerful means, provided we put aside preconceived opinions and theory.

The ability with which men bear the loss of blood, I have already allowed very much to depend upon habit and locality ; and its efficacy entirely on the early stage of the disease.

In situations peculiarly pestilential, or where, from concentration of cause, the animal energy is so far depressed, as early to incapacitate the functions for the performance of those duties by which life

* Edinburgh Medical and Surgical Journal, vol. 9th.

is supported,—or after sufficient time has elapsed to have allowed the establishment of fatal congestions,—I do not pretend that there is any hope of these being removed, but, on the contrary, death will be accelerated by the use of the lancet. All I mean to say is, that, during the first stage, at least in the shape in which I have most frequently seen the disease, and while the progress of inflammation in the most vital parts is rapidly proceeding, yet still remediable, I am acquainted with no other remedy which has either time or power to save them from disorganization.

Having had but too many opportunities of being convinced of the want of commensurate efficacy in those inerter means by which the fevers of temperate climates are often conducted to a safe termination, I feel perfectly satisfied when I hear of great success in the treatment of this disease, either that results so fortunate have been the reward of a prompt and decisive plan of treatment at the very commencement, or that the disorder was of a far milder, and more remediable nature than that which I have been accustomed to, under the name of yellow fever. Would to God I could say, that the most prompt and decisive measures will be generally attended with success; but I may say, that this will almost entirely depend upon the earliness of their application; or upon the judgment to determine when the disease has so far advanced, that they are no longer applicable, and must be succeeded by an immediate, and entirely opposite mode of treatment.

The mediocrity of remedies often causes them to retain that reputation which they have previously, and sometimes unjustly acquired; but the power of a remedy so active as venesection, yet whose utility is so entirely dependant, not only on time and quantity, but on the varying state of the system, is in continual danger of being rated too high or too low. I am sorry, therefore, to observe, that it is spoken of with too much confidence by some writers; because this tends on failure to bring its character into disrepute with others, though it oftener suffers from the opposite extreme of unfounded apprehension.

Upon the now undisputed and general utility of purgatives, it is quite unnecessary to say any thing here: they have not only the great advantage of being eminently serviceable where blood-letting is proper, but where it cannot be resorted to, and in a vast variety of milder cases of fever, where it is not required.

The general healthiness of the West Indies, as well as of particular Islands, varies considerably in different years, and at different periods. It is liable to be affected by certain states of the air, as unusually wet, or dry and close, or otherwise unseasonable weather for the time of the year, by calms, by variations, (especially to the southward,) from the usual trade winds, and in the quantity of the Electric Fluid, and in certain years, by what has been termed "an Epidemic Constitution of the Atmosphere."

Individual safety in the Western Hemisphere will be best consulted by attending to the comprehensive maxim of Celsus—viz. by avoiding various predisposing and exciting causes, until the physical sensibility of the system is reduced by habit; and in proportion as this advice is adhered to, the Naval Practitioner may be assured that not only the chance of sickness will be greatly diminished in his own person, but that in a well regulated ship, aided by the earnest and judicious co-operation of the officers, the lives of the men under his charge may be preserved to an extent beyond his expectations, in ordinary seasons and circumstances.

During war, indeed, when the influx of unassimilated Constitutions is considerable, and especially after much exertion and active service, great sickness and mortality are, I fear, unavoidable ; but, generally speaking, the result will depend upon the number of Europeans introduced, the time and situation chosen, and the exposure being limited at first, and gradually increased, or otherwise. It is, therefore, of the utmost consequence that bodies of men, whether soldiers or sailors, should arrive in that country at the coolest season of the year, (and if such can be selected as have previously served in a warm climate, they should invariably be preferred ;) that the former should be sent to the healthiest Islands, or positions at first ; gradually exposed to duty under a vertical sun, and, instead of being quartered in the low, hot, alluvial ground, in the vicinity of the towns skirting the leeward bays, that their barracks should be built on hills of moderate elevation, sufficiently distant from marshy, damp ground, infested with insects, and from thickly wooded ravines, where the rank and luxuriant vegetation bespeaks the existence of exhalations unfriendly to health.

. The importance of such selection was eminently exemplified by the saving of health and of life that accrued from the erection of new barracks for the troops, in a more interior and elevated situation, after the capture of Guadaloupe, in 1810, by Admiral the Hon. Sir Alexander Cochrane, then Governor of the Island. The humanity of this measure, and the judgment previously displayed by the Commander in Chief in the scite and construction of the Naval Hospital at Barbadoes, &c. have been warmly and deservedly eulogized by the most experienced men in both services ; suffice it to mention the names of Drs. Jackson* and Mc.Arthur :—to me it may be permitted to pay a not less just and earnest tribute of respect to that unwearied benevolence which prompted his immediate attention to every proposal for the welfare of the seamen, and insured not only his concurrence, but active co-operation in whatever could add to their comfort in health, or alleviate their misery in sickness.

۱ The healthiness of the ships stationed in the Caribbean Sea, will very much depend upon the state of discipline, and degree of attention paid to the crews It will be especially preserved by staying in harbour as little as possible ; and by cruizing to the northward, or resorting to Halifax, or elsewhere, during the hurricane season, or when repairs which will require detention for any length of time in port are necessary. In fine, it will chiefly depend upon avoiding all undue exposure to the sun, rain, night air, fatigue, intemperance, and unwholesome shore duties ; and upon attention to different regulations, and preventive measures, of which I have had ample oppor-

* Vide Jackson's Sketch of the History and Cure of Febrile Diseases, 1817—
pp. 386—and 392-3.

tunities of appreciating and stating the value, from the inspection, and the medical reports, of generally between sixty and seventy vessels of war.

Many of these being of a local and temporary nature, it would be needless to specify here ; but I may shortly notice that the intermission of labour during the hottest hours of the day, working as much as possible under cover, giving a portion of cocoa before going to duty after sunrise, wearing flannel, injoining a soluble state of the bowels, serving spruce beer or sound wine instead of rum, and when this could not be done, issuing the latter of a certain age and quality, and finally, (for of the victualling, in the improved state of the navy, it is unnecessary to speak,) the adoption of every means to diminish the frequency of intoxication, were the chief of those measures from which the most beneficial effects were observed.

But of all occupations the most desirable to avoid is that of clearing a foul hold in the West Indies ; and, therefore, whenever it is possible, ships requiring this to be done should be sent out of the country : for not only is it highly dangerous in itself, on account of the noxious gasses disengaged, but because it is generally necessary to perform it in a secure, or land-locked, and consequently unhealthy harbour, such as that of Antigua.

Where the subject is of such importance, though at the risk of tautology, I request leave, in conclusion, to repeat, that the bad effects of staying in port too long at one time, and of harbour duties, particularly early in the morning and after the setting of the sun, as well as during his meridian power, cannot be too strongly adverted to ; and, therefore, a measure of paramount importance is the employment of negroes, natives of the country, or at least of men accustomed to the torrid zone, in wooding, watering, transporting stores, rigging clearing, careening ships, &c. and in fine, in all such occupations as must subject men to excessive heat, or deleterious exhalations, which cannot fail of being highly dangerous to the health of the unassimilated European.

But the great object, I conceive, is to relieve the ships on that station, (the prospect of which, alone, has a wonderful effect on the health and spirits of the men,) so often that a foul state of the hold, and the necessity of cleaning it in that country, shall as seldom as possible arise. During the most active period of nearly eight years of the war, considerable sickness and mortality must necessarily have occurred ; but in that time, I have likewise had the great satisfaction of witnessing, in various ships, and on various occasions, that a degree of health was maintained in that climate beyond my most sanguine expectations,—particularly latterly, when the season of active warfare being past, the necessity was precluded, and consequently the unwholesome duties of clearing the hold, heaving down, or undergoing lengthened repairs in the close harbours of the West Indies, were interdicted ; and I am therefore led to conclude, that to avoid the stronger exciting causes of yellow fever, is, to a great extent, to escape the disease.

Observations on the locale of Yellow Fever, by Dr. FERGUSSON, *F. R. S. Ed. Inspector of Military Hospitals.*

Sec. IV.—The principal West India towns and garrisons for the troops are situated on the leeward shores of the country, at the bottom of the deepest bays that can be found, as a protection to their trade against the winds from the sea. The soil must consequently be alluvial, and is often marshy. Nine-tenths of the towns are inclosed by high hills rising immediately behind them, which exclude the sea-breeze that, in its natural course, ought to reach them from the windward side of the country. As their elevation is generally little above the level of the sea, we have abundant reason to conclude, that if the highest degrees of reflected tropical heat, defective perflation, and the miasmata that reside in marshy soils, or may be formed in the drier alluvial ones by heavy rains, can produce aggravated remittent fever, it must happen under such circumstances, especially where police and cleanliness are entirely disregarded.

The settlements of the planter, in like manner are formed, not on the elevated mountain ridge from which the periodical rains have washed away the soil, but in the alluvial ground beneath, where his labour can with more certainty be turned to profit. Nor is it to be wondered at, under such circumstances, that a body of raw troops or young civilians, come to settle in town or country, should be swept away by tropical fevers. The wonder is why it does not happen with more unerring certainty; for there are seasons, and even courses of seasons under apparently similar circumstances of heat and moisture, when even the declared swamp is comparatively innoxious to the newly arrived European, and still more so to the seasoned inhabitant. This begets in the young adventurer or hardened votary of wealth, a fatal delusion of confidence which, though so often exposed by the melancholy recurrence of fatal fevers is never cured.

The pestiferous quality of miasmata does not appear to depend *necessarily* either upon aqueous or vegetable putrefaction, however frequently it may be found combined with both. Every one knows that the miasmata are not generated from the body of the lake or pool, but from its drying, or half-dried margins. The swamp is no more than this margin rolled up under another shape. Water, without being absorbed by the subjacent soil, gives out no febrific effluvia. One of the healthiest quarters in the West Indies, is that of the field officers on Berkshire hill, the bed-room of which is placed over a deep stone reservoir of water. But this said febrific miasma is very certainly generated from the *paucity* of water where it has previously abounded, provided that paucity be short of actual dryness. To the production of this a high atmospherical temperature is indispensable;—and in proportion to the intensity of temperature is the intensity of power in the miasma produced, varying its effects on the human frame, from the ordinary ague of Europe, and the West India Mountain fever, to the highest degree of remittent, and yellow fever, which is never found remote from the level of the sea. It is comparatively innoxious to those who have had the good fortune to

become habituated to its influence ; and attacks with singular peculiarity of selection the robust, the young, and the healthy, in their
fi st approach to its abode. If these be granted, I think we may be
able to explain from the various compositions of soil, its elevation,
aspect, and texture, as affording capacity to retain moisture, why
every dry one can be brought, during an uncommonly wet season,
through the influence of tropical heat, into the state of a marsh that
gives out noxious vapours ; while a marshy one approaching to dryness through previous drought may be made perfectly healthy from
the same abundant rains. Thus Barbadoes, which from its cleared
calcareous soil, is far more salubrious, in general, than Trinidad, has
been lately afflicted severely with the worst forms of yellow fever ;
while the latter island remained perfectly healthy. In both places it
has rained abundantly—particularly in Trinidad, whose extensive
marshes have been overflown ; while the alluvial soil on the shelves
of table-land at Barbadoes has been converted into a temporary
swamp. So at St. Lucia, when the garrison on the lofty position of
Morné Fortuné is healthy during the fine dry weather, the inhabitants
of the town of Castrus, at the base of the same hill immediately below, and within half cannon shot, are visited by the worst fevers, and
vice versa :—The dry weather gives activity to the miasmata which
the rains dilute, refresh, or condense, at the same time that they are
forming pools, and temporary swamps on the shoulders of the hill;
immediately beneath the barracks, on the summit of Morné Fortuné.

So a deep ravine, impervious to the rays of the sun, and free current of air, that has been a water course, may still, after its surface
appears dried by the summer heat, retain sufficient underground
moisture to give out the most dangerous miasmata—the more dangerous because the more concentrated for want of perflation ;—and so,
in fine, salubrious and insalubrious soils may, under such circumstances, change places, in regard to health ; and localities in the
neighbourhood of each, under the same modifications of climate, be
very differently affected.*

It has been inferred that yellow fever belongs to a different family
from that of intermittent, because it seldom occurs at the same time
with, or breaks off, in convalescence, into ague. Ague indeed is not
a common production in the hot low-land on or near the level of the
sea—where alone the yellow fever is found. It is very rare, for instance, to hear of an ague originating in the leeward sea-port town
of Basseterre, Guadaloupe, either amongst the troops or inhabitants ;
but in the barracks on the cool marshy hills above the town, at an
elevation of less than a thousand feet, it is a very common disease,
among officers and soldiers, while their comrades in the town are devoured by concentrated remittents. The same may be said of nearly the whole of the West India towns. They are all so marshy that

---

* The reader is probably aware that some Authors, as Dr. Jackson and Mr.
Doughty, consider an excess of the principle of Vegetation as the cause of Fever:
" It would appear that the materials of vegetation abounding in excess, acted
upon by a powerful cause, give out a principle, which not being expended in the
growth and nourishment of Plants, is diffused to a certain extent in the atmosphere, occasioning a derangement of such bodies as come within the sphere of its
action."—Jackson's Outline of the History and Cure of Fever.

in colder latitudes, they could not possibly escape agues, which however, very seldom originate, and are nearly unknown amongst them.. The inhabitants of Barbadoes boast that they are exempt from agues,' though the island has several marshes. Thus the reason is plain :— There are very few ridges there of sufficient elevation to belong to the region of intermittents, even supposing their sides to be marshy, which they never are. The swamps are all in the lowest levels of the land ; and when their morbific miasmata act upon the human body, they produce the greater or less concentrated forms of remittent fever, according as their powers are regulated by the temperature and climate of the season, or as the subject is presented under more or less favourable circumstances of seasoning, excitement, &c.

I am far from presuming to deny, says Dr. Fergusson, that there are fevers from pure excitement ; "*for soldiers and others have been attacked and died of yellow fever before they landed in the West Indies, or could be exposed to the influence of land . miasmata in any shape.*" From this it would appear that a calenture, [the synocha of Cullen,] the pure offspring of heat, as pneumonia is of cold, runs a course similar to the yellow fever.

" To the argument that the highest degree of concentrated remit-
" tent or yellow fever, should neither remit nor break off into ague,
" it seems sufficient to reply, that for any disease to observe regular
" laws, it is necessary that the vital organs principally affected should
" continue in a certain degree of integrity ; that their functions
" should only be disturbed and preverted to a given point ; that they
" should still be, discernible as functions, and not be utterly over-
" whelmed and extinguished by the violent cerebral action and
" speedy gangrene of the stomach that take place in aggravated yel-
" low fever. As the ulcer of a specific poison that would run a regu-
" lated course according to acknowledged laws, if it be driven to a
" high inflammation or sphacelus, no longer belongs to the original
" stock, and is emancipated from those laws ; so the violent actions
" of the above fever impair and destroy the animal functions by which
" its crisis and remissions are regulated, or speedily engender a new
" disease ; as new as the conversion of an ordinary venereal chancre
" into a phagedenic slough, through the application of a potential
" cautery."

I may refer to the section on *Bilious Fever*, in the first edition of my work, for a similarity of doctrine.

By *Malaria*, Dr. F. means to express something that is more decidedly than miasmata the product of underground moisture, which can only be sublimated, so as to produce its specific effects, by long-continued solar heat — a more subtle miasm, in fact, of which the surface gives no warning, but of which the existence is proved from its effects on habitations that are placed in the draught of the dry ditches of forts, no matter how rocky or dry, if they are deep, and also of deep ravines. At Fort Matilda, in Basseterre, Guadaloupe, a well-raised artillery store-house and guard-room, placed in Bouchure, at the confluence of two of the ditches, was found to be utterly uninhabitable. , The same malign influence affected the houses that were placed opposite the deep ravines of rivers, no matter how pure and pebbly the channel, as also all the dwellings situated on the leeward base of the mountains.*

It would also appear that these effluvia, during certain states of stagnation of atmosphere, as during the sultry calms of the hurricane months in the West Indies, *accumulate* in the dirty ill-ventilated streets of West India towns, to the danger of all who are unseasoned to their influence. Here *strangers* will have the highest degree of ardent fever.

It is probable, too, that the healthiness of seasons in unhealthy climates, depends less on the *amount* of heat and moisture, than on the *ventilation* of the climates by powerful, regular trade winds, like the trade winds between the tropics ; for whenever these have been withheld for a time, the accumulated morbific emanations from underground moisture will act upon the human body, like the accumulated typhoid principles in crowded hospitals, when undiluted with a due proportion of atmospheric air.†

I shall conclude this section with some observations on the Fever of Mariegalante, in the West Indies, communicated to the Author by Dr. Dickson.

The history of the fevers at Mariegalante, from July to December, 1808, is not only well calculated to show the destructive powers of concentrated marsh miasmata, in tropical climates, at certain seasons ; but also the modifications of fever which arise according to intensity of cause, locality, atmospherical vicissitudes, epidemic influence, or degree of constitutional predisposition. The difference of effect, however, as marked by difference of type, or anomalous appearances, is here particularly worthy of attention, because the men were limited to a small space, insulated and exposed to the same causes which were strictly local and indigenous, but affected by differences of temperament or habits, degree of habituation or exposure, and other relative circumstances. I can, however, only propose here to give a hasty and imperfect sketch of the sickly period in question, owing to deficiencies in the reports during the illness of the successive medical officers, and the space and time it would occupy, minutely to analyse those in my possession. For some months after the capture of the Island, the marines composing the garrisons enjoyed a very fair degree of health ; but from the beginning of July, (the usual commencement of the sickly season there,) after heavy rains succeeded by intense heat, fever became daily more frequent in occurrence, and aggravated in character. Upon my arrival on the 29th of the same month, I found the disease had made such progress as caused me to entertain the most painful apprehensions for the fate of the garrison. It originally consisted of only 350 men, and there were then 150 on the medical list, 40 of whom were affected with fever, 15 with dysentery, and 75 with ulcers, many of which owing to the sickess of the surgeon, and the accumulation of cases, had attained a considerable degree of malignancy. Of the first disease, many had the yellow or endemic fever of the

* See the section on Scily.

† See Dr Fergusson's paper in the *8th vol. Med. Chir. Transactions,* from which the above has been abstracted and condensed.

West Indies, in its most aggravated form, with black vomit ; in'
others, it was of a more protracted character, and with symptoms
more resembling those of typhus ; while the remainder had remittent or intermittent fevers.. On my first view of the sick, and of
the low swampy situation of the town of GRAND BOURG, together
with the season of the year, I was impressed with the most unfavourable anticipations, and represented to the Commander in Chief,
that although I had expected to find much sickness at Mariegalante,
I had not been prepared for the conclusion I was then obliged to
form — viz. the total reduction of the strength of the garrison in the
course of the hurricane months, unless the sickness could be arrested.   That my prognostic was but too accurate, will appear in the
sequel.   The closest inspection, on the following day, tended but to
confirm and extend this conclusion : my report expressed the grief
with which I offered my opinion that the garrison would be shortly
incapacitated for any duty ; and that the only chance of averting this
depended on the adoption of measures of the greatest promptitude
and energy.

The first object was to remove, as far as it was possible both the
sick and well from their unhealthy habitations ; rendered still more
noxious by the accumulation of disease ; and where this could not
be effected, to cleanse and purify the apartments, and to arrange, and
to separate the sick. &c.   The next considerations were the clearing away of whatever was filthy and offensive around them ; the employment of negroes for this, and various other fatiguing and dangerous duties ; the avoiding of exposure to the sun and rain ; a more
regular supply of fresh diet, and of wine and spruce beer to the
troops, instead of rum ; and lastly, the adoption of every measure
which could prevent the facility of intemperance, and excess with
noxious new spirit.   A more elevated situation was procured for the
convalescents, on the hill ; and a large house on the sea-shore to the
eastward, and consequently generally to the windward of the swampy
grounds, was selected for an hospital ; but the latter, owing to reports of its insalubrity and other difficulties, was never occupied ;
though I was decidedly of opinion that the removal of the men, any-
where, was preferable to their remaining in their former situation,
which had been replete with disease and death.   After making those
arrangements, Dr. Mortimer, then surgeon of the flag-ship, who had
handsomely volunteered his services, was left in charge of the sick ;
and according to his official report, published in the Nineteenth
Number of the Medico-Chirurgical Journal, for the first two or three
days, such was the amendment produced by the measures concerted,
that a considerable diminution of disease was calculated upon.   But
alas ! the remission was but temporary : the men could not be removed beyond the reach of noxious exhalations, emanating in all directions from the low swampy ground covered with rank vegetation ; the concentration of the marsh miasma ; and the predisposition favoured by apprehension and irregularities, increased daily,
and the fever proceeded with augmented power and rapidity, until
it had swept off half the garrison.   The aspect of the country, Dr.
Mortimer observes, " seems particularly favourable to such exhala-

tions. On viewing it, you almost constantly find hills of easy ascent, intersected by lesser declivities, and these on both sides encompassed by swamps ; so that whether in the interior, or the town, sickness nearly equally obtains." The enemy taking advantage of the disabled state of the garrison, attacked the island on the 23rd August, and although in a short time it was re-captured, and reinforced by fresh detachments, the sickness was necessarily much increased by the fatigue, exposure, and irregularities incidental to warfare. Many of the old as well as the new troops were seized with the fatal fever : indeed the worst cases were second attacks, brought on by exposure and excesses, and by the end of September, this ill-fated little garrison had lost by disease 234 men. As a most faithful description of the yellow fever by Dr. Mc. Arthur appears elsewhere, and, as Dr. Mortimer's report on the endemic in question has been inserted in the Medico-Chirurgical Journal, as above noticed, I do not propose giving any further account of it here.

The only treatment which appears to have had any effect was that of blood-letting and purgatives, if resorted to sufficiently early ; but even these measures were inefficacious unless employed at the very commencement ; and after what has been said, it is hardly necessary to add that the power and rapidity of the disease were too often such as to set medical control at defiance ; indeed, in its highest grade, there is so little chance and time for the interposition of our art, that it may almost be considered irremediable ; and, in some instances, men who complained of head-ache and giddiness in the afternoon, were dead by the next morning.

Dr. Mortimer was taken ill before he had finished his report, and was received on board the flag-ship in a state of extreme danger, from which he with difficulty recovered.—He was succeeded by Mr. Waller, (who like his predecessors suffered much from the unhealthiness of the situation,) and from whose communications chiefly I have extracted the remaining account of disease at Mariegalante. The yellow fever declined towards, and indeed altogether ceased by the end of September, when the season become rainy ; and it was succeeded by cases of a protracted description, extending to the period of twenty days or longer ; and though characterized by some peculiar and anomalous appearances, with symptoms much resembling those of typhus. During the months of October and November, the weather was wet and squally ; and there was comparatively but little fever, with the exception of quotidian intermittents, which were by no means severe, and yielded readily to the moderate use of bark. In December, the tertian became the prevalent type, but early in this month intermittent paroxysms occurred of an alarming character; and of such an intensity, that in some cases, after one or more attacks the patient was carried off by coma and convulsions. In this way seven men died within twenty-four hours ; and some even in a much shorter period, so as at first to induce a suspicion of poison. The symptoms may in some have been partly attributable to their having taken a large quantity of rum, with the view of preventing the ague ; but they also occurred in others who had not tried this pernicious experiment. In one man who died in about two hours, a green sediment, supposed at first to be some poisonous vegetable, was found in the stomach. In others who were opened, however, no such matter was discovered; but only a bilious looking fluid, similar to what was ejected by many, but not by all, before death. In almost every dissection a large quantity of this fluid was found in the stomach, dying every thing it touched of a very deep yellow colour—very turbid, saponaceous, adhering to the sides of the vessel, with an odour of ammonia so strong and pungent, as to excite the olfactory nerves, and appearing to be particularly acrid; but not at all resembling the matter with the green sediment abovementioned, nor the black vomit of yellow fever, nor even the yellow fluid which is first thrown up in that disease. The action of this fluid on the nerves of the stomach seemed to be the cause of the comatose symptoms which came on, soon after the invasion of the paroxysm, or at the commencement of the hot stage; as, whenever an emetic was previously given, a considerable quantity of it was brought up; but the remedy seemed also to increase the secretion of it; for as much would be ejected in the course of the succeeding day as had been discharged by the emetic.—In the greater number, the comatose symptoms did not appear till after the patient had sustained two or three paroxysms: many, however, died in the first paroxysm, when the coma did appear, but more in the second paroxysm. To this account of the severity of the disease, I can well give credit, from the cases which fell under my own observation, while at Mariegalante. In one instance I recollect to have seen a man in whom, not only, as mentioned by Senac, the hot and sweating stages occurred together, but all the three stages seemed to be concentrated at once; for while his teeth were chattering and his body shivering from the sensation of extreme cold, his skin felt excessively hot to the touch, and large drops of perspiration were standing on his face and breast.* . When the disease was of the tertian type, Mr. Waller observes that the symptoms lasted about thirty-six hours, or until about two o'clock in the morning of the day after the attack; when of the quotidian type the duration was about eighteen . hours, and somewhat milder, but the intermissions being only six hours were less complete than in the tertian paroxysms. In the latter part of the paroxysm the pulse and skin sunk remarkably low, as in the fever about to be described; but they rose again during the apyrexia, nearly to the natural standard, and the patient then complained chiefly of debility. In every instance where the patient survived the second shock, he recovered ultimately, but seldom without having had six or seven paroxysms. In this disease, denominated by Mr. Waller, " *the comatose intermittent,*" his practice was to give an emetic, an hour before the accession of the attack, which appeared of considerable service in mitigating it : a blister was applied to the head, and sometimes between the shoulders, and the bowels were kept very open with calomel. His principal reliance, however, was on mercurial frictions repeated every hour;

* Besides Senac, Cleghorn, Stork, Pringle, Frank, Burserius, and various other authors adduce instances where the order of the paroxysm was deranged, or some of the stages wanting, and of various anomalous appearances in intermittents.

and by this remedy he thinks many lives were saved, though in one instance only was ptyalism the consequence of it: When the paroxysms ceased, it was discontinued ; and the bark was substituted. The patients continued long in a state of convalescence ; and frequently showed symptoms of diseased spleen. Towards the end of November the northerly winds set in ; vast quantities of rain fell during the night ; and soon afterwards, that is, early in December, fever became prevalent. This fever occurred at the same period, and in some respects bore a strong similitude to the aggravated intermittent above described ; but it was of a different type, and appeared in duration and symptoms to be intermediate between yellow fever and typhus. As this fever was characterized by the supervention of extraordinary symptoms, viz. coma, reduction of temperature, and periodical vomiting, I shall give a more particular account of it, as it is described, though more summarily than in the minute, and I have every reason to suppose, faithful report of Mr. Waller.

Description of the Fever.—The patient complains of being taken ill in the evening ; but, upon more· minute inquiry, it is generally found that a slight head-ache was felt in the morning, with a sense of lassitude and pain in the limbs ; which symptoms were relieved at dinner, but returned, in an increased degree; about sun-set. Slight rigours then occur, and are often felt for some time after the heat has accumulated on the surface of the body ; they generally continue about an hour, when the temperature becomes steady ; though at a lower point than is usual in the commencement of yellow fever, and considerable thirst and anxiety suceed, while the face and general surface become flushed ; and the blood-vessels of the eye turgid. The pulse is now full, firm, and frequent ; but the skin, though hot, is seldom without some degree of moisture and softness. Perspiration usually comes on early, and continues free and general, during the remainder of the paroxysm, which ceases about two or three hours before daylight. The patient then falls asleep for some hours, and awakes refreshed, and with a considerable remission of all the febrile symptoms ; the pulse is now less full ; but still frequent, and often irregular ; and the tongue, which was nearly white before, is found thickly coated with mucus, whitish round the edges, but very foul and brown in the middle. The patient complains now only of debility, and a dull heavy sensation of the head increased on motion, and shows a propensity to sleep. The apyrexia continues till about noon, when the same febrile symptoms recur, but increased in violence and duration. The remission next morning is less complete, and the exacerbation comes on earlier. In general there is no third remission ; the fever becomes continued, and is early accompanied by great irritability of stomach beginning with vomiting of bilious matter, and afterwards of every thing that is taken, with very distressing retching, uneasiness and pain when it is empty. The dull heavy pain in the forehead, with vertigo on motion, is always complained of, which, with the pains of the limbs, generally continues through the disease. The bowels are for the most part relaxed, sometimes very loose, and the stools watery. The patient most frequently continues in this state four or five days,

.when a new train of symptoms appears, which give the distinguishing character to this fever ; sometimes, however, they appear earlier, at others not until signs of convalescence have occurred.   The
first symptom is a remarkable degree of stupor ; the patient displays
the greatest indifference to every thing around him ; is with difficulty
aroused to answer questions, or to take any thing ; and seems much
disconcerted at having been disturbed.   The pulse, which was before
tolerably full and firm, sinks rapidly, and throbs with a quick unequal
motion under the finger ; sometimes it is scarcely perceptible, and
not unfrequently it cannot be felt at the wrist at all.   The heat of the
surface too, generally subsides, but in this stage it is very variable,
though there is reason to believe that if the patient were left to himself he would become quite cold ; indeed this coldness of the skin is
very remarkable in a great number of cases ; and in some appears
to be beyond what is felt in the living body under any circumstances ;
yet the patient does not appear to feel any uneasiness from it.   With
this extraordinary reduction of temperature, the skin is not anserat-
ed, but cold and clammy ; and it sometimes continues for several
days.   The tongue is now found to be dry and hard, and the teeth
and lips become covered with a dark-coloured fur.   The patient appears to sleep much during the day, or rather he lies in a kind of stupor without sleeping, but at night is, for the most part, delirious.
He now seldom complains of pain, or only in the region of the
stomach, where it is sometimes very severe.   The vomiting, at this
period, often subsides ; but frequently also it comes on every day
about the same time, and is attended with very painful spasmodic
contractions of the stomach.   This periodical vomiting observes its
periods with great regularity : is a very untractable symptom, and
little susceptible of alleviation, by any remedy that has been tried.
The vertigo is also exceedingly distressing, and increases so much, in
an erect posture, that the patient immediately falls down ; and even
when recumbent he complains of the giddiness or a very unpleasant
sensation in the head.   It sometimes continues after the other symptoms have disappeared, and is always extremely tenacious.   The
symptoms just enumerated continue three, four, or five days ; and
then gradually subside.   But this, though the most favourable, is not
the most frequent termination ; it oftener happens that the stupor
increases to a state of complete coma, or accompanied by muttering
delirium, subsultus tendinum, and involuntary discharges.   The pulse
sinks until it can be no longer felt any where ; the whole body becomes cold and cadaverous ; and, in some cases, of a deep yellow
colour, with no other signs of life than a feeble respiration.   Sometimes, at uncertain intervals, the pulse and heat rise, and the patient
becomes anxious and restless for two or three hours ; then falls again
into the former state.   But these changes may be effected by the remedies employed, as it is more than probable that they would not so
often appear if the patient were left to himself.   In this stage, death
very frequently happens ; but however bad the patient may be, when
the formidable symptoms continue above forty-eight hours, it affords
a strong presumption that he will recover ; and this sometimes has
taken place after he has lain in this state for four days.   In such in-

stances, when the system emerges from torpidity, the coma first disappears by degrees, and the pulse gradually rises; but the patients continue for a long time in a state of excessive debility, and not unfrequently fall victims to second attacks or to dysentery. This disease first attacked many of those who had suffered from concentrated fever in July and August; its average duration is twelve days, when it terminates in a quotidian intermittent, convalescence, or death.

It may appear but little in favour of the plan of treatment, to state that out of sixty-one seized with this fever, in December, half of them died; yet when those very formidable symptoms are taken into consideration, it is but fair to infer that remedial measures were not only employed with much advantage in the early, but also in the ulterior stages of the disease, from there being time to put them in practice, according to the existing indications. In the early period of the disease, Mr. Waller observes, it was always considered necessary to lessen the excitement by bleeding, purgatives, and the other parts of the antiphlogistic regimen. But as this stage of excessive excitement was in some cases of much shorter duration than in others, it frequently happened that the patient did not complain sufficiently early to receive much benefit from depletion, or even to bear any abduction of blood. Indeed symptoms of exhaustion sometimes appeared even in the first paroxysm, and in a number of cases, no remission supervened; but whenever it was authorized, the lancet was invariably and freely used in the first stage, and always with advantage; in every instance, the bowels were well evacuated by purgatives, and by large and frequent doses of calomel. Emetics, he says, were frequently tried, at first, but not with so good an effect as was expected from them; and but a very short relief from the nausea was experienced after their use, when this symptom existed, in a considerable degree, in the first stage. Upon this point I shall wave any remarks, as occasionally they may have been useful in the modified disease under consideration; but in the inflammatory and rapid yellow fever, I am of opinion that the exhibition of emetics, or of antimonial or other nauseating medicines, cannot be too strongly deprecated. In the present case, it was only in the first attack, or during the exacerbation, that the patient could bear any evacuation, except by the bowels, which were always kept very open, so long as the pulse was at all full, or retained any firmness; but, when the stupor supervened, he could no longer bear any debilitating process. To allay the gastric irritability, blisters, mercurial frictions, effervescing draughts, small pods of capsicum, &c. were employed, but generally with very little effect. The best remedy seemed to be a grain of opium in a pill, repeated according to the vomiting; but even this was often rejected. So soon as stupor or coma appeared, stimulants were resorted to; blisters to the head, wine, camphor, ammonia, and mercurial frictions; and, in the low state above described, there is no doubt that the friction itself, as well as the remedy, was of service. The delirium was generally immediately relieved by blistering the head. The formidable degree of coma, Mr. Waller observes, mostly came on in the morning early; but he was unable to ascertain whether it was preceded by any peculiar sensation, by which its approach could be certainly known. The prognosis was unfavourable in proportion to the intensity of coma, reduction of heat, and gastric irritability ; little dependence could be placed on the circulation. The danger was great when the patient lay in a state of reverie: much greater when there was delirium in the day time, than when in the night. In the comatose affection, he speaks in the most favourable terms of mercurial frictions, and adduces their success in some cases considered desperate, when the patient had been lying in this lethargic state for four, five, or more days, with the pulse, for many hours, imperceptible, and the remarkable coldness of skin above described. These frictions required to be frequently and perseveringly repeated ; and latterly he was in the habit of rubbing in a drachm or two drachms of the strong ointment every hour ; which method seemed preferable to any other. To his opinion of the value of mercury in protracted or congestive cases, after the active stages of fever are past, and particularly to its efficacy in visceral obstructions and derangements which are the sequel of certain fevers, I perfectly subscribe. In many such cases, it is not only a most valuable resource, at a period when we have no other indication to pursue, but also, perhaps, where no other remedy would be successful ; but of its inutility, except as a purgative, where there is *high febrile and inflammatory action*, as in the early stage of concentrated yellow fever, I am fully convinced ; and trust I need not here deprecate the wasting of those precious moments, when only the disease can be controlled, in fruitless attempts to institute the mercurial action. With respect to the combination of this with the depletory plan of treatment, I am inclined to think that the mercury has often enjoyed a larger share of the credit than it has been entitled to ; because in many such cases, it has been indebted for the power of exerting its specific action, to the depletion, which, at the same time, has been employed. When we can command a warm bath, in cases like those above, I need not say how much it would contribute to the object in view : it is to be regretted that there does not appear to have been an opportunity of ascertaining the actual temperature of the skin by the thermometer. With respect to the causes of this fever, Mr. Waller does not offer any decided opinion. It was, at first, attributed to the northerly wind wafting a very offensive odour from the burying-ground ; owing to the hasty and imperfect inhumation of the bodies, which was accordingly remedied. The disease certainly began to prevail after the northerly winds set in ; but it is unnecessary to add any ætiological observations after what has been said of the abundant sources of deleterious exhalations at Mariegalante.

Account of the Causus ; or, Yellow Fever of the West Indies. By Dr. Mc. ARTHUR, *F. L. S. Licentiate of the Royal College of Physicians of London, and late Physician to the Naval Hospital at Deal.*

SEC. V.—The following concise, but animated description of the fatal Western Endemic was written in 1809, by Dr. Mc. Arthur, late physician to the Royal Hospital, Deal ; and as he had the superintendence of a public hospital nearly six years, at Barbadoes, in the West Indies, with the most extensive field for observation, this document will be found highly interesting and valuable.

The endemic fever, commonly called the yellow fever, certainly excites the first interest, both on account of the mortality which attends it, and the discrepancy among professional men respecting its nature and treatment. The inhabitants of the West India Islands are subject to various fevers of the simple continued, catarrhal, and remittent kind. These attack indiscriminately the native, or the seasoned European, and are as mild as fevers of a similar type in Europe. But the fatal fever, of which I am about to give some account, for the most part attacks persons from Europe, within the first *year and a half* after their arrival in the country, and more particularly seamen and soldiers.

It generally appears at a certain period of the year, earlier or later, milder or more aggravated, according to the state of the weather during that season. Solitary instances, however, occur at all seasons of the year, when favoured by predisposition, assisted by strong exciting causes. The natives are not entirely exempt, but to them it rarely proves fatal.

It is certain that all the West India islands have their healthy and unhealthy seasons, varied by the condition of the surface, by being mountainous or flat, woody or cleared, dry or intersected with swamps, &c. Barbadoes is clear of wood, the land is moderately raised above the level of the sea, and every spot is cultivated ; there are but few swamps and those are inconsiderable—and some rivulets only occasionally swelled by the rains.

From the middle of January to the beginning of May, the air is temperate and dry. In May the rainy season begins and continues till the end of September. October and November are generally dry, if much rain has fallen in the preceding months. Rain again falls towards the latter end of December, and till the middle of January. Bridgetown and its vicinity are extremely hot from June to November, the thermometer at noon varying from 84 to 90° in the shade.

The parallel of health between the Army and Navy is worthy of notice. The fever for some preceding years has appeared in both about the same time, and attacked men of similar habits ; but has in general been more aggravated on shore than at sea, or even on board the ships lying in Carlisle Bay.

This fever is usually ushered in by the sensations which precedes other fevers ; such as lassitude, stiffness, and pain of the back, loins, and extremities ; generally accompanied by some degree of coldness. These are soon succeeded by a severe pain of the head ; a sense of fullness of the eye-balls ; intolerance of light ; skin dry, and imparting a burning heat to the hand ; pulse full and quick ; tongue covered with a whitish mucus, but often not materially altered from the state of health ; bowels bound. I may here remark, that the actual degree of heat, as indicated by the thermometer, is not proportionate to the intensity communicated to the touch. It generally varied between 99 and 102°, very seldom exceeding 103° ; yet the skin imparted a burning caustic sensation to the hand at these times..

- If the patient has been attacked in the night, he awakes with oppressive heat, head ache, and the other symptoms of fever, the sensation of cold having passed unnoticed. At other times, after fatigueing exercise in the sun, and sometimes after a hearty meal, the violent head-ache, and other symptoms of the fever, are ushered in by an instant loss of muscular power, and immediate depression of nervous energy. The patient, as if he were stunned by a blow, falls down, his eyes swimming in tears. In those cases, delirium is an early symptom. In a few hours, the pain of the loins increases, and, in aggravated cases, stretches forward towards the umbilicus ; the countenance is flushed ; the white of the eye as if finely injected by blood-vessels, the albuginea appearing through the interstices of the net-work of vessels, of a peculiar blue, shining, cartilaginous whiteness.

During the first twelve hours, the patient is not particularly restless, enjoys some sleep, and, when covered with the bed-clothes, has partial perspirations on his face, neck, and breast. ◄

About the end of this period, there is a great exacerbation of the fever ; he becomes restless ; the heat and dryness of the skin increase ; there is much pain of the eyes and frontal sinuses ; the pain of the thighs and legs is augmented ; thirst is increased, with a sensation of pressure about the region of the stomach. Nausea and vomiting occur towards the end of the first twenty-four hours. If the fever has not been arrested within thirty-six hours from its commencement, the patient is in imminent danger, and all the symptoms are aggravated ; the pulse is strong and full, and pulsation of the carotids appear distinct on each side of the neck. The skin continues hot and dry ; the thirst is increased ; there is much anxiety, the patient continually shifting his posture ; the urine becomes high-coloured ; all his uneasiness is referred to his head and loins. A sensation of pain is felt about the umbilicus, when pressed upon ; the white of the eye now appears of a dirty concentrated yellow colour, and apparently thickened, so as to form a ring round the margin of the cornea. The blood-vessels of the eye appear more enlarged and tortuous ; knees drawn upwards to the abdomen ; frequent vomiting, with much strainings ; mucus, and his common drink only, being ejected. Delirium comes on about the end of the second day. There is now a dryness, or slight sensation of soreness of the throat when swallowing ; and about this time, an urgent sensation of hunger frequently comes on, and a remarkable want of power in the lower extremities, resembling partial paralysis of the limbs. About this time, also, the pain of the loins is so severe, that the patient expresses himself as if his " back was broken."

The third day, or stage, begins by apparent amelioration of all the bad symptoms, the vomiting and thirst excepted. The matter ejected has small, membranaceous looking flocculi floating in it, resembling the crust washed from a port-wine bottle. The thirst is now urgent, and there is an incessant demand for cold water, which is almost immediately rejected by the stomach. The heat of the skin is reduced ; the pulse sinks to, or below its natural standard ; the patient, for an hour or two, expresses himself to be greatly relieved, and at this time, a person unacquainted with the nature of the disease would have hopes of his recovery. This state, however, is of short duration, amd the delusion soon vanishes.—The delirium increases ; the matter ejected from the stomach becomes black as coffee-grounds, and is somewhat viscid. Diarrhœa comes on ; first green, then black, like the matter vomited. The patient often complains of being unable to pass his stools, from a want of power in the abdominal muscles. There is an acrid, burning sensation of the stomach, and soreness of the throat, extending along the whole course of the œsophagus, in attempting to swallow ; eyes, as if suffused with blood ; skin a dirty yellow ; parts round the neck, and places pressed upon in bed, of a livid colour. More hæmorrhage or less takes place from the nose, mouth, and anus, and a deposition of blood from the urine. The delirium becomes violent ; the body as if it were writhed with pain, the knees incessantly drawn up to the belly. The patient seizes, with convulsive grasp, his cradle, or any thing within his reach, and prefers the hard floor to his bed. The pulse now sinks ; respiration becomes laborious ; the countenance collapsed—the lustre of the eye gone.—For some hours he lies in a state of insensibility before death ; at other times, expires after some convulsive exertion, or ineffectual effort to vomit. The tongue is sometimes but little altered during the course of the fever ; and if loaded in the early stages, it often becomes clean, and of a vivid red before death.

Such is the regular succession of symptoms which characterize this fever, but of longer or shorter duration, according to the violence of the disease, or strength of the powers of life to resist it.

In weakly habits, the vascular action at the beginning is less marked ; and in these cases, the fever is generally more protracted, and the patient expires unaffected by the laborious respiration, and convulsive motions, which attend the last struggles of life, in the more violent degrees of this endemic. Very often the patient retains his senses till within a few minutes of his death ; and sometimes will predict, with considerable precision, the hour of his dissolution.

In the early stages of the worst cases of this fever, there is much anxiety in the countenance of the patient, who expresses a despair of recovery. This fear does not appear to proceed from any *natural* timidity, but seems rather a symptom of the disease. In the last stage, there is as much *resignation* to his fate, as there was apprehension at the beginning. The fever of the Amelia in 1804, and of the Northumberland and Atlas in 1805, terminated fatally from the second day to the fourth day. The fevers of 1807 and 1808, extended from the third day to the fifth. I have never noticed a remission during the whole course of the fever. Several cases of remittent fever under my care terminated in the endemic fever.

A certain number of those attacked by this fever, if prompt measures to subdue it had been employed, recovered from its first stage.

They exhibited evident signs of amendment within the first twenty-four, or at furthest thirty-six hours, from its first attack. ' Also a considerable proportion recovered from the second stage ; that is to say, previously to black vomiting unequivocally appearing. But I have only known thirteen cases, in above five years, to have recovered from the last stage. Some of these were afterwards invalided, in consequence of dyspeptic complaints, and generally disordered state of the stomach, and other abdominal viscera.

In these cases, the stomach gradually became retentive ; the eyes and skin became of a more vivid yellow : they had refreshing sleep, but continued extremely weak and languid for a long time. The oozing of blood from the fauces and gums also continued for some days : and the deposition of blood in the urine remained longest ; this excretion being always the last to return to its natural healthy condition.

Pain of the back, early stretching round to the navel—soreness in the throat and œsophagus—heat and acrid sensation in the stomach—urgent thirst—hunger—want of power, resembling paralysis of the limbs—violent delirium—despondency—enlargement of the blood-vessels, and a red-yellow colour of the white of the eye, either singly or collectively, indicate extreme danger ; and when the black vomit has appeared, scarcely a hope remains !

The following were the appearances after death, [four cases excepted,] in above an hundred bodies which I have inspected.

Omentum little altered.—Peritoneal coat of the stomach occasionally marked, in a slight degree, by inflammation.—The stomach contained more or less of a viscid, black fluid, such as was ejected by vomiting.—Irregular spots, patches, and streaks of the internal surface of the stomach, in a state of inflammation, gangrene, or sphacelus.—Sometimes large portions of the villous coat destroyed, as if corroded by some acrid matter.—The small intestines and coccum inflated with air, and often containing lumbrici, and a small quantity of dark-coloured fœces, were inflamed, and in many places approaching to the state of gangrene. No marks of inflammation in the colon, but it was singularly contracted.—Lower part of the rectum frequently excoriated—Concave surface of the liver occasionally inflamed.—Gall-bladder turgid with ropy bile ; and, in some instances, its coats were one-fourth of an inch in thickness.—Other viscera of the abdomen little changed.—In the thorax, the posterior part of the superior lobules of the lungs, generally were very turgid with blood. Internal surface of the œsophagus, throughout its whole extent inflamed.

In ten cases of a peculiarly aggravated degree of fever. where much delirium' had been present, I opened the head. The blood-vessels, in some instances, seemed more turgid with blood than usual. In two cases, there were about two ounces of serum effused into the lateral ventricles ; but in five cases the brain did not exhibit any marked appearance of disease.

The black matter found in the stomach did not resemble bile ; but evidently was blood poured into the stomach from the relaxed vessels, or excoriated and gangrenous surfaces, altered by the vitiated secretion of the gastric fluids.*

Europeans, within the first eighteen months after their arrival in the country, being almost exclusively obnoxious to the yellow fever, it is natural to suppose, that there is something in the European constitution, favourable to the morbid motions which constitute this fever ; and that this peculiar habit consists in a disposition to take on inflammatory action. Persons seasoned to the climate, and even natives, by sudden alterations in their mode of life, sometimes acquire this predisposition. Young people born in the West Indies, and educated in England, and persons having resided some years in England, after they had passed the greatest part of their lives between the tropics, are liable to this fever on their return to the West Indies.

This disposition is excited into action by a variety of causes ; the chief of which are—intemperance ; excessive fatigue in the sun ; perspiration checked, by being exposed to a current of air, or sleeping exposed to the dews ; costiveness, &c.—In fact, whatever becomes an exciting cause of fever in any country, is equally so in this ; but unfortunately it is not the same fever that is induced.

It has been observed, and very frequently urged by the *bon vivant,* as an excuse for his mode of life, that men who live in the most temperate manner, are as liable to fever, if not more so, than those who follow the opposite extreme.—There is an appearance of truth in this remark. Often the temperate and sober are seized with this fever, under circumstances where the drunkard escapes.

A stranger, on his arrival in this country, unless possessed of more than ordinary resolution, is assailed by so many temptations, that he has not the power to follow the plan he may have laid down for his own regulations. He commits an *occasional* excess, and next morning awakes in a high fever ; while the man accustomed to his " *mosquito dose,*" probably feels no uneasiness, or if he has a slight headache from his last night's debauch, flies for relief to his hot punch or sangaree. The more temperate and regular a man has lived, any deviation will become, in a proportionate degree, a stronger exciting cause of fever. But if the drunkard and the sober man should be attacked with fever, the former has by no means an equal chance of recovery with the latter.

Contagion as a source of this fever is entirely rejected by those professional men who have the greatest opportunity of information, now resident in the West Indies. No case occurred where the fever could be traced to a contagious source. No place could be better adapted to spread contagion than the building appropriated to the sick in Bridgetown, before the occupation of the excellent new hospital, in May, 1807. The patients and their bedding were carried to it through the town by any hired labourers : they were often obliged to take shelter in houses by the way ; and this to the credit of the poor inhabitants, was never refused them. From want of

* This was written two years previous to Dr. Bancroft's publication. It very nearly agrees with his opinion, and those of the American practitioners, noticed in the first section.

means of separation, fevers and other complaints were huddled together in the same ward.' The officers and nurses lodged and visited
in every part of the town ; and lodgings were procured for sick officers wherever there was room in the town, when they were required, without hesitation. Yet, notwithstanding all this unrestricted
communication, no instance occurred where fever could be traced to
a contagious source : and surely, if it were contagious, it would not
be so generally confined to men recently arrived in the country.

In the very first stage of this fever, it would probably be difficult
to distinguish it from the other continued fevers of the country. Its
violence is one criterion by which we might form a judgment. We
must also look to the particular circumstances of the person attacked.—If he has been but a short time from Europe ;—if he has been
taken ill after a debauch—fatigue—or unusual exposure to the sun,
or to a partial current of air, or after sleeping in the night air, there
is much reason to apprehend yellow fever ; more particularly if the
eyes be inflamed, and the pain of the loins stretched forward to the
navel, with soreness of the throat—heat and acrid sensation in the
stomach, a feeling of pressure there, and urgent desire for cold
drink. These, and the other symptoms already described, will indicate the nature and the danger of the disease.

In the early part of my superintendance, I gave the fairest trial to
every mode of practice recommended by eminent practitioners, including the mercurial plan of treatment.—But in no instance in the
worst cases that terminated in death, however protracted the fever
might have been, could the mouth be affected ; while in the milder
cases, where the fever subsided in 36 or 48 hours, the mercurial action became manifest within that period. In some protracted cases,
ptyalism did not appear for several days after the mercury had been
discontinued—and in others, after the gums were affected, where the
patients had a relapse, the mercurial immediately ceased, or was suspended. But the submuriate of mercury I continued to employ with
much advantage, as a purgative but in smaller doses of course, than
when I attempted to excite salivation.

Bleeding largely, in the early stage of the fever has been found
of the most eminent service. When employed after the first stage of
the fever had passed by, it did injury, and certainly hurried on dissolution. The following plan is that which has been pursued at this
hospital, for several years ; it is that which has been practiced on this
station, and has been attended, (would I could say with uniformly the
happiest effect !) with at least superior success to any other.

From twelve to twenty-four ounces of blood and upwards are
drawn from the arm, as soon after the accession of the fever as possible. The blood should be drawn until derangement of the vascular action has taken place, by the quantity of blood extracted ; indicated by approaching syncope, nausea, and vomiting. Should fainting
come on, from mental emotion, such as the dread of the lancet, sight
of the blood, &c. the bleeding is to be continued after the patient has
revived, until a quantity proportioned to the strength is drawn off.
Six grains of calomel, and double that quantity of cathartic extract,
are to be immediately given ; and if this medicine does not operate

in three hours, it is to be repeated. At the end of six hours, if the purgative has not yet had effect, it is to be assisted by an enema ; and either an ounce and a half of sulphate of magnesia or soda, or half a drachm of jalap, with an equal quantity of supertartrate of potass, is to be given.

In eight hours after the patient has been blooded, six or eight full copious evacuations should be procured.

During this time, if the skin be hot and dry, the cold affusion is to be employed every two hours. Partial perspiration, in the early stage of the fever, should deter from its use. The greater the force with which the water is applied, the more benefit is to be derived from it. When there is much pain of the head, the hair is to be shaved off. Thus the treatment, during the first twenty-four or thirty-six hours, consists in one full, large bleeding—purgatives, so as to procure several copious alvine evacuations—the cold affusion*— shaving the head ; and the liberal use of barley water, or any other weak drink.

Under this plan, fifty patients out of one hundred, attacked by the genuine endemic fever, will show evident signs of amendment within the above-mentioned period. A general perspiration, not profuse, will break out ; the heat of the skin will be reduced ; head-ache and pain of the thighs and legs will be abated ; the red vessels in the white of the eye will disappear ; the thirst will be lessened ; and in short, all the feelings of the patient will become more agreeable. From this state they recover with extraordinary rapidity. In one week they are restored to perfect health.

If this favourable change does not take place within the period alluded to, there is much danger. The patient becomes restless ; the sensation of pain is more acute ; delirium, vomiting, and other bad symptoms succeed. In this stage, the bowels are to be kept loose—two or three stools are to be procured every twenty-four hours, by calomel, given in four grain doses, three or four times a-day, as the state of the bowels may indicate. The cold affusion is to be continued, lessening the force with which the water is applied, as the vascular action and heat diminish. The warm bath will also be advisable in certain cases, and removing the irritation of heat by frequently sponging the palms of the hands, arms, and other parts with lime juice, spirit, &c. where a cold affusion cannot be employed. If delirium and vomiting are present, blisters are to be applied to the head and nape of the neck. Before the heat is reduced, and the vascular action brought down to its natural standard, stimulants are employed ; such as wine, at first in small quantities, gradually increasing it ; capsicum, in the form of pills. If the patient has been much addicted to spirits, toddy in lieu of wine is to be allowed ; but the stimulant from which I have observed the greatest benefit, is the carbonate of ammonia, in doses of six or eight grains every two hours, with doses of nitrous æther, diluted with water. When vomiting is urgent, the patients are to be restrained from drinking much ; and

* The vapour bath, now coming into use at the naval hospitals abroad, bids fair to prove a powerful auxiliary in soliciting the blood to the surface, and thus relieving the internal organs from the effects of CONGESTION.

when the stomach is empty, more benefit is derived from two table-spoonsful of arrow-root every half hour, than from any medicine I have known. Sulphuric æther, and even ardent spirits, to restrain vomiting, as the heat and vascular motion subside, have been taken with partial relief.

This state may continue for two days, or even longer, before there is any relief. The first favourable symptom is usually a refreshing sleep, and the absence of delirium. A warm and moderate perspiration covers the surface ; and if the skin and eyes have been yellow, the colour becomes more bright.

Convalescence from this stage of fever is much more slow than from the first. Much attention to the state of the bowels, and the liberal use of the decoction of bark, with vitriolic acid, if there be much oozing of blood from the gums and fauces, are necessary. From that stage in which the black vomit is the prominent symptom, few—very few recover.—Dark-coloured fluids, however, have been often taken for black vomit, where the latter did not exist, and thus nurses, and even medical men, have been deceived. All the cases that recovered at this hospital were certainly unexpected.—This dreadful symptom had continued in all of them about twelve hours ; oozings of blood from various parts, stools as black as ink, &c. were present. The first sign of amendment was the stomach becoming retentive, and the enjoyment of a few hours sleep. The yellow colour of the eyes and skin became daily brighter, till at last the patient had the most perfect jaundiced look ; the colour of the stools keeping pace with that of the eyes and skin. The stimulating plan of treatment, after full and copious evacuations in the earliest stage of the disease, was gradually begun with these patients long before the vascular action had been reduced to its natural standard. Wine frequently, and in small quantities—the carbonate of ammonia—capsicum, with arrow-root, were assiduously administered ; and whenever the appetite of the patient craved for brisk porter, spruce beer, &c. they were never denied ; but these and other drinks were given in small quantities at a time, as larger caused instant vomiting.

Relapses from this fever frequently terminate fatally.—Want of appetite, and sensation of fulness at the stomach, usually precede the common train of symptoms. In these cases, I found an emetic give instantaneous relief. The patient generally vomits a large quantity of æruginous-coloured matter, and the evacuation is attended by immediate ease : two or three drachms of the tartarised antimonial wine, (Edin. Phar.) are generally sufficient for the purpose. In the usual practice of the hospital, emetics are omitted : they delay the exhibition of brisk purgatives, which are required to move the bowels in this fever. But there is one form of the endemic commencing with diarrhœa, and sometimes dysenteric symptoms, in which emetics are employed with advantage. When the fever, however, commences in this way, it is less dangerous, though more protracted, than where costiveness and torpidity of the bowels attend.*

* " The most favourable cases of the yellow fever, are those in which a bilious " diarrhœa comes on; while the most fatal are those in which the bowels are so " torpid as to be insensible to any stimulus, either from their own contents or " from medicine."—Blane, 3d ed. p. 450.

It has been said, that persons who have once had the yellow fever are not again liable to be attacked. This is not the fact : I have more than once had a man under my care with yellow fever, who afterwards died of another attack of the same disease,

In this, as in other diseases, anomalous symptoms will occasionally occur, requiring slight modifications of treatment ; but these can be only learnt at the bedside. On this account, I forbear to enumerate laudanum, æther, ginger tea, effervescing draughts, champaigne, &c. which in high practice are sometimes prescribed.

On the Inflammatory Endemic of New Comers to the West Indies from temperate Climates. By NODES DICKINSON, *Esq. Member of the Royal College of Surgeons, &c.**

SEC. VI.—*Introduction.*—This disease is the effect of sudden change of climate upon new comers of a sanguine temperament ; and is commonly designated the *yellow* Fever, from the occurrence of an incidental symptom.

In a few weeks the stranger is brought from a climate in which the atmospheric temperature, at the time of his departure is, perhaps, under 30° to 90° of Fahrenheit in the shade ; and 130° when exposed to the direct action of the solar rays.

The inflammatory endemic being, exclusively, incidental- to strangers from the temperate regions, will be found to occur with a prevalency proportioned to their numbers : sporadically when these are few, and, in appearance, epidemically when many are introduced at the same time.

When it happens in a mild degree it is appropriately called a " *seasoning.*" The reduction of the system by the evacuations employed for its removal is very frequently preventive of a future seizure.

The probability of an attack of the inflammatory endemic very much depends upon the degree of inflammatory diathesis. The causes which produce a severe affection in young and plethoric strangers, seldom affect the older residents. Natives of the country and Africans escape its seizure. Women and children, the aged and weakly, are less liable than the robust and strong.

The inflammatory endemic, which, in its mildest form, has been regarded a " *sporadic febricula*" is under a severer aspect, when attended by a yellowness of the skin and black vomiting, often erroneously considered an infectious epidemic of malignant character.

It is a disease in which there is from the beginning a state of universally increased excitement, with a direct tendency to general inflammation, soon accompanied by the actual inflammation of certain organs. Very much of the mischief ensues from a want of moderat-

* The following valuable observations have been kindly drawn up by my able and esteemed friend, Mr. Dickinson of this Metropolis, whose ample experience, as a Staff Surgeon in the West Indies, enabled him to present to the public an important work on the inflammatory Endemic in question, of which the present paper may be considered a very concentrated Analysis. It will be observed that Mr. D. confines himself to that form of the fever which attacks new comers, and is produced by Insolation.

ing the first excitement.   If this be subdued there is little to apprehend from consequent debility.   The patient will recover, and with
the advantage of a system prepared for the climate in future, in so
far as the inflammatory endemic is concerned.

Producing Causes and Prevention.—The causes of the inflammatory endemic are predisponent and exciting.   The *predisposition* consists in an inflammatory diathesis—an aptitude to diseases of general
increased excitement : this appears sufficiently manifest by a consideration of the subjects already stated as exclusively liable to its attacks.
The exciting cause is an exposure to solar radiation while unaccustomed to its influence, and unprepared to resist the force of its impression by the adoption of preventive measures.   The effect of heat
is liable to augmentation if accompanied by violent exercise, by full
living, and intoxication.

Whatever tends to diminish the predisposition forms the ground-
work of prevention : it is founded in reason and proved by experience.   The detail consists in bleeding, purging, cold bathing, abstinence from fermented liquors, and a spare diet of animal food.   These
should be employed, agreeable to the state of individual predisposition, until the inflammatory diathesis is reduced.   If the immediate
exciting cause be diminished in its power, by the new comer repairing
at his arrival in the West Indies to an elevated situation, where the
temperature is low, compared with the heat of the maritime towns,
his safety will be greatly inured.   To avoid, as much as possible, exposure to the direct and powerful radiation of the sun : to use exercise, in moderation only, and to observe an undeviating rule of temperance and sobriety, are to obviate the action of the exciting causes
and prevent the disease.   Diurnal vicissitudes of temperature should
be carefully guarded against by the unseasoned stranger.   A dangerous state of excitement is liable to result from the increased susceptibility induced by the sudden application of cold to the surface, when
this, although trifling in degree, is immediately succeeded by the stimulation of inordinate heat.

Symptoms and Treatment.—The history of the inflammatory endemic and its general character are such as the nature of its causes
must obviously suggest.

It occurs with different degrees of severity in the ratio of the impression of its exciting causes and individual predisposition.   Two
cases are seldom precisely alike in this particular.   It varies from a
" seasoning" or mild synocha to the most formidable seizure.

A slight attack has seldom been recognised to bear strict affinity
with the much dreaded " yellow fever."   Considered merely a
" seasoning," it has rarely been regarded of the same kind, produced
by the same causes, and prevented, or removed by the same general
means, which are applicable to the more violent disease.

The inflammatory endemic in its severe aspect, and when neglected
at the attack, consists of two stages.   In the first, there is increased
excitement, resulting from an unusual stimulus applied in an excessive degree to a system peculiarly sensible to its impression : it produces a derangement in the functions of some or many viscera.   If
this goes on, the second stage appears, in which the structure of

these viscera is altered to a degree incompatible with the living state.—Thus the disease proceeds from high excitement to irreparable exhaustion, as we shall perceive by attending to the history of its symptoms. In the less severe example there is chilliness at the onset, soon followed by a permanent and universal sense of heat—flushed face—inflamed eyes—head-ache—increased susceptibility to the impressions of light and sound—vertigo—drowsiness—sighing——white tongue—arid fauces—thirst—wandering pains—loss of appetite—costiveness—high-coloured urine—dry skin—nausea—full and frequent pulse ;—should these symptoms in a severe degree remain without control, the disease is soon increased to its most aggravated form. The patient is extremely restless, with a continual desire to alter his position, but without relief. The heat and head-ache are intense—the carotids throb with unusual violence. There is sometimes a furious delirium—tinnitus aurium and even loss of sight. There is, occasionally, a dry cough with pain in the side, and almost invariably a sense of heat, oppression, and pain on pressure at the præcordia, accompanied by constant sighing. Vomiting sometimes comes on very early in the attack. There is often great drowsiness but no refreshing sleep. In some cases an acute pain is felt in the right side : and a yellow colour of the skin often supervenes. This yellowness is occasioned by the presence of bile, which is also detected in the urine and serum discharged from blisters. Should the passage of the bile into the intestines spontaneously take place or be procured by the action of purgatives, this jaundiced appearance, will, generally, be prevented : nevertheless, in some cases it may possibly arise from a redundant secretion, even when the bilious canals are free : and a bilious vomiting and purging may occur with the yellowness of the skin and carry off the attack. These symptoms proceed with various degrees of violence, and they occupy an uncertain period. Within 12—24—or 36 hours ; or, perhaps, after a longer, but indefinite time, an important change takes place. It marks the commencement of the second stage. Many of the most urgent symptoms decline. The pain and heat of surface subside. There is a sense of cold with dampness of the skin. This change at first so much assumes the appearance of febrile remission as to give great hope to the inexperienced practitioner ; but it speaks a state of the utmost danger. In some cases the patient sinks, at once, after the subsidence of excitement, apparently destroyed by the general affection, without any previously severe determination of blood to particular organs ; and he dies at the moment of hope in his amendment. But more commonly the catastrophe is not so sudden. With the diminution of heat and pain, the pulse falls—the countenance exhibits great distress—the eye is sunk—the pupil dilated, sometimes delirium continues—at others, there is great insensibility with tendency to coma. Vomiting, occasionally, continues without intermission :—at times, however, the stomach remains tranquil : and this, when there is much cerebral disturbance.

As the disease advances a discolouration of the skin often takes place. It appears in yellow, brown, and livid patches. This discolouration never comes on until the subsidence of the symptoms of

excitement, however early in point of time.   It occurs with the passive hæmorrhagy from various parts : from the nose, corners of the
eyes, ears, &c. ; and at the same time with the black vomiting.
This change of colour appears to arise from e :chymosis proceeding
from exhaustion of the vis vitæ in the ˚capillary vessels of the surface in consequence of previous inordinate excitement.   It is very
dissimilar from the bilious yellowness already noticed as an incidental symptom of the first stage of the disease.

The first discharges from the stomach are merely the ingesta ; afterwards a large quantity of serous fluid is ejected when little has
been drunk.   In a more advanced stage of the complaint the material thrown up is ropy and mixed with numerous small shreds, flocculi, or membranaceous films which float in the ejected liquid.
These soon acquire a dark brown, purple, or black colour, but do
not, at first, communicate much general tint to the fluid in which
they are suspended.   Afterwards, the matters vomited are more intimately mixed together ; and with the addition of dark-coloured
blood which is effused into the stomach, vitiated bile, and other morbid secretions, give an appearance in the aggregate of coffee-grounds.
There is at this period, usually, a purging of dark-coloured matter
resembling tar mixed with black blood.

Sometimes within the first forty hours, at others after a more protracted period, the scene draws toward a close with the ordinary
phenomena of approaching dissolution, which accompany the last
stages of acute disease in general.   There are dilated pupil—strabismus—singultus—subsultus tendinum—coma – deliquium—hæmorrhage from various channels—suppression of urine—low muttering
delirium— total insensibility—occasionally violent raving, and an incessant disposition to rise in bed.   These are among the last symptoms of an unsubdued attack, and they mark the near approach of
death.

An examination *post mortem* exhibits unequivocal vestiges of previous inflammation.   In the brain, increased vascularity and a deep
redness of the membranes—rupture of the vessels—adhesion of the
hemispheres and membranes—coagulable lymph—extravasated blood
—serous effusion.   In the stomach, a lymphatic film adheres to the
surface of the villous coat in different parts ; but is easily detached.
During the last remains of life it is ejected with the fluid contents of
this organ.   Numerous dark-coloured spots are interspersed upon
the villous coat which present the mouths of vessels from whence
there oozes black blood.   The same appearances are seen throughout the track of the intestines—the liver is occasionally much diseased : it is livid and overspread with dark-coloured patches—frequently of a deep purple colour throughout its structure—greatly
enlarged, and filled with blood.

These are the usual symptoms of the inflammatory endemic, and
of its destructive inroads, upon the healthy fabric of the body, supposing it to pursue an uninterrupted course in an example of great
severity.   These symptoms are, nevertheless, very irregular both
in their general appearance, their degrees of violence, their precise
order of succession and duration.   Thus we find that after a period of

violent and uncontrolled excitement, exhaustion succeeds. The increased action of the heart and augmented heat of the surface subside, healthy secretion is not performed—the blood passes into the capillaries, without undergoing the necessary change in the secreting organs, giving rise to congestions and effusion, and passive hæmorrhage from every outlet.

The consideration of these stages of increased excitement and exhaustion determines the rationale of the treatment ; as an attention to the nature of the producing causes afforded the ground of prevention. The curative indication is established upon the inflammatory character of the disease at the attack ; and, therefore, comprehends the means of subduing general excitement, and of preventing thereby the determination of blood upon particular organs. The treatment is simple at the commencement of the disease, and is fully announced by the symptoms of that stage. In the first place, every cause of irritation should be removed. These will be obvious to the practitioner as they may present themselves on particular occasions. Their removal is to be effected by the " antiphlogistic regimen," which should be strictly enjoined.

If, at the moment of attack, the stomach is loaded with food, or over stimulated by strong drink, an emetic should obviate the impression of this exciting cause. After which, we must resort to general bleeding—the warm bath—cold lotions to the head—cool air—cold drink—active purging—blisters—cold ablution when the heat returns—injections of cold sea-water. These measures must be used to reduce excitement and prevent the debility liable to result from over-exertion generally, and from over-distention of particular vessels, causing congestion ; while, in the occurrence of determination of blood to the head, stomach, lungs, or to the hepatic region, topical bleeding and blisters must be employed to remove congestions already formed and allow the weakened vessels to recover their tone. If, however, the exhaustion of the second stage has supervened, the practitioner can administer but feeble aid. Quietude, a cool atmosphere, gentle laxatives, nourishment, and sleep, present the only means of restoration.

In this disease the restorative powers of nature must not be waited for. It does not possess any salutary reaction—any adequate means of curing itself. The chance of recovery is always diminished in a ratio proportioned to the length of time which is suffered to elapse without the employment of decided antiphlogistic measures.

———

TETANUS.

Sec. VII.—This *opprobrium medicorum*, though an occasional sojourner in all climates, has its principal seat and throne between the tropics. The disease, however, is equally fatal, though not near so frequent in a cold, as in a warm climate. According to my own experience, and that of most of my naval and military friends, the

47

traumatic is greatly more dangerous than the idiopathic species, though this sentiment does not accord with that of Dr. Morrison, the latest writer on the subject.

The *Symptomatology* of Tetanus is by no means necessary in this place, since it is impossible for the variest tyro to mistake the disease. Some pathological and therapeutical observations only will here be introduced.

Pathology.—Dr. Morrison, in his recent treatise on Tetanus, asserts that dissection has thrown little if any light on the seat or nature of the disease. But some late papers and investigations would seem to diffuse a ray of light on the obscurity of this pathological track, and induce us to believe that we have too long neglected the morbid anatomy of the spinal cord, and of the medulla oblongata, in diseases attended with violent spasmodic affections. Dr. Sanders, of Edinburgh, has long laboured in the developement of this dark subject, and not without some success. The harmonious balance, not only of the circulation in itself, but in its relation with the nervous system, has too long been overlooked ; but new light is now breaking in upon our minds from the tomb. The *inequilibrium* in the balance of the *excitement*, which exists in almost all diseases, is here evinced, in characters that can hardly fail to be understood. While the class of voluntary muscles is in complete spasm, various organs —more especially the chylo-poetic viscera, are utterly torpid.— This inequilibrium in the balance of the excitement shows itself, even before the developement of spasm, in the torpor and costiveness of the alimentary canal *precursory* of, and contemporaneous with Tetanus, as was sagaciously remarked by that accurate observer of nature, Dr. Dickson, in the 7th volume of the Medico-Chirurgical Transactions.

We must therefore look to the origins of those nerves which supply spasmed muscles, for the immediate seat of the mischief ; and there it will be found, without a doubt. Dissections of the base of the brain, medulla oblongata, and medulla spinalis, have not, till lately, been prosecuted with any thing like accuracy.

Dr. Reid has now forcibly drawn the attention of the medical world to this subject, and it will, no doubt, be well investigated. It has long been remarked, indeed, that in Tetanus the natural functions are little affected, and the same may be said of the intellectual functions, and those muscles and organs supplied by the nerves of sense. These considerations naturally lead to the conclusion that the thoracic and abdominal viscera are not primarily affected, and that the origin of the disease is not in the nervous substance supplying those organs— in short, that the cerebral and ganglionic systems are only drawn in *subsequen ly*, and that the spinal cord is the original and principal seat of Tetanus.

Case in elucidation, [from Dr. Reid.] – A boy 14 years of age, after receiving a severe bruise in the toes of the right foot, was exposed to the vicissitudes of the weather in the month of February. He was seized four or five days afterwards, with tetanus, and died in thirty-six hours. *Dissection.*—Viscera of the abdomen and thorax perfectly sound, as were all the muscular parts. On opening the spine, *from the back part,* and on raising the nervous mass, (with its dura mater entire,) from the spine, "there appeared a considerable effusion of blood in the cellular tissue, connecting it to the upper lumbar, and lower dorsal vertebræ. A similar effusion occurred also along the bodies of the upper dorsal and two lower cervical vertebræ. On slitting up the dura mater on the anterior surface, the nervous mass appeared highly vascular, and the vessels of every description remarkably tortuous. The only appearance in the nervous substance itself, was a deeper tinge than natural in its cortical and medullary parts."

From these appearances, corresponding with the investigations of Dr. Sanders, it follows that tetanus is radically an inflammatory disease. But general blood-letting here will not be near so efficacious as local abstractions of blood from the spine—blisters—purgatives—and finally, mercury and opium to equalize the balance of the circulation and excitement. The following observations from Dr. Morrison, the latest writer on tropical tetanus, may be appropriately introduced here.

Dr. Morrison was led to compose his present Treatise on Tetanus, from having had considerable experience in that disease, during an eight years practice in the Colony of Demerara, where it is of frequent occurrence. The land of this part of the South American Continent is low, flat, and marshy, abounding with swamps, and, with the exception of a strip along the banks of the Demerari, is covered with trees of various dimensions, whose roots, for a great part of the year, lie bedded in water The prevalent diseases are intermittents, fevers, hepatitis, enteritis, rheumatism, dysentery, and, among children, hydrocephalus.

Dr. M. does not look upon Tetanus, even the traumatic form, as so very dangerous a disease, in tropical climates, as authors have represented it. He has witnessed many instances of recovery both from traumatic and idiopathic tetanus, and, strange as it may appear, the instances of cure in the *former* have been nearly as numerous as in the *latter.* In upwards of twenty cases of this disease which he witnessed among negroes, the pulse was, in no instance, accelerated in the manner related by Dr. Parry. He has never known it above 98, whether the termination was favourable or fatal.—The following prognostic passage we shall transcribe.

" When the disease comes on gradually ; when for the first three or four days the muscles of the jaws are solely affected, and that perhaps not in any alarming degree ; when the abdomen is not preternaturally hard, or the bowels obstinately costive ; when the skin is moist and moderately warm, and above all, when the patient enjoys sleep, we may, (by the means hereafter to be spoken of,) entertain strong hopes of an eventual recovery. An increased flow of saliva where mercury has, or has not been used, is always to be regarded as favourable ; the less the general air of the countenance is changed, the better. On the other hand, when the attack is violent and sudden : when the muscles of the neck, back, and abdomen are rigidly contracted ; when the patient complains of a shooting pain from the sternum towards the spine ; when the belly feels hard like a board, and the least pressure thereon produces spasmodic twitch-ing or contractions of the muscles of the neck, jaws, &c. ; or when the same effect is brought about by the presentation of any sub-stance, (solid or fluid,) near the mouth, we have much reason to fear a fatal termination. Spasmodic startings of the muscles set in some-times early in the disease, and recurring every eight or ten minutes, are to be regarded as very unfavourable," p. 29.

The only disease which tetanus can be confounded with, is rabies contagiosa. In the latter, however, there is generally fever ; fre-quently increased heat of the body. In rabies contagiosa, vomiting is common at the commencement ; not so in tetanus. The delirium too, of hydrophobia is absent in tetanus. The shooting pain from the sternum to the spine is seldom wanting in tetanus, or present in the other.

Treatment of Tetanus.—Dr. M. believes, that spontaneous cures do occasionally take place in tropical climates. One decided instance of traumatic tetanus giving way to the efforts of nature fell under his own observation. The treatment of idiopathic and symptomatic te-tanus is considered the same. For although it is common and pro-per in the West Indies to apply some stimulating substances, as ol. terebinth. or the like, to recent wounds, together with emollient ca-taplasms, so as to induce free suppuration, yet when constitutional tetanic symptoms have once commenced, there is little or no depend-ence on local treatment. By way of prevention, Dr. Clarke advises a slight mercurial ptyalism to be brought on after wounds in hot cli-mates, or under suspicious circumstances. For the same purpose, the complete division of half divided nerves, tendons, &c. might be proper. The Spanish physicians bathe the wound, for an hour or more, in warm oil, while some subsequently apply lunar caustic, su-peracetate of lead, &c. The principal general remedies that have been recommended are, the cold affusion, mercury, opiates, wine and bark, the warm bath, cathartics, blisters, antispasmodics. We shall not stop to notice the history of each of these remedies, but give the substance of Dr. M.'s own remarks and experience. During the doctor's first three years residence in Demerara, and in the first eight or ten cases, the *cold affusion* was invariably used, but with so little success that it was ultimately left entirely off, and the warm bath substituted.

Mercury.—Spontaneous salivation has often been observed in teta-nic patients whose cases terminated favourably, hence probably the first idea of using mercury. In hot countries tetanus is seldom so rapid as to prevent the introduction of mercury in quantity sufficient to salivate, before the disease runs its course, whether favourably or fatally ; and, as in all climates mercury interferes not with other re-medies, Dr. M. thinks its administration ought never to be omitted.

" I undoubtedly have had many examples of the good effects from mercury in the cure of this disease. Four grains of calomel given two or three times a-day, with three or four drachms of the ointment well rubbed on the neck and spine night and morning, I believe to be excellent practice. A much larger quantity of the ointment may be used on different parts of the body : indeed, the more continued the friction, the better. The constitution labouring under this disease, will mostly appear as proof against the usual effects of this medicine ; but when salivation can be brought about, it will, in a great majority of cases be found to be attended with the happiest consequences. Allowing the spontaneous salivation, which sometimes occurs, to be more the effect than the cause of the cure, still we should be inclined to throw in large quantities of mercury, merely with a view of bringing on any different action in the system."

The submuriate of mercury with scammony or jalap as a purge is also recommended by our author.

Opium.—This appears the sheet-anchor of our author in this disease. He has met with more than a dozen cases where the cure of tetanus could be fairly attributed to this medicine ; and he has met with no instance of recovery in which he did not conceive that it bore a principal part. It must be given, however, in very large doses, the system under tetanus being little affected by doses of opium that in other circumstances would produce striking effects.

" A practitioner," says Dr. M. " for whose acuteness and discernment I have great respect, gave to an old man, in my presence, who was in an incipient stage of this disease, about *half an ounce* of tincture of opium in four ounces of rum, as a *first dose*, directing, at the same time, the spirit to be frequently repeated, and the man got perfectly over the complaint in a few days," 57.

Dr. M. directs that an adult should commence with one hundred drops of the tincture, (bowels being opened,) increasing each succeeding dose one-third every two hours; unless sleep or stertor in the breathing ensue ; ordering at the same time, wine or ardent spirits, in as large quantities as the patient can be induced to swallow. A pint of spirits, or double that quantity of wine in the twenty-four hours will not be too much. Tincture of opium is also to be rubbed on the spine.

The Warm Bath is regarded by our author in a favourable point of view. It has afforded much present relief on several occasions under his own eye, where the spasmodic twitchings were frequent and troublesome. He depends very little on it, however, and justly observes, that the exertion or movement which the patients must undergo, in order to get into the bath, will often more than counterbalance any good effects that can be expected from it. Patients are so alive to all external impressions, that the least exertion is often sufficient to excite violent spasms. On this account the patient should be kept as quiet as possible, and very few questions asked him. The chamber should be kept darkened, and every thing tending to excite mental exertion avoided.

Blisters, though recommended in high terms by a few medical practitioners, can only be looked upon in the light of adjuvants. The course of the spine appears the best site of their application.

Bark and Wine.—Dr. M. recommends, that during the exhibition of opium, large quantities of wine or diluted alkohol be administered, in order to second its effects.

Recapitulation.—" The bowels should be kept as free as possible. We must endeavour to bring about an operation every twelve hours.

This, even by the aid of strong cathartics, or purgative injections, will be found very difficult to be obtained ; the sphincter ani sometimes scarcely admitting the introduction of a clyster-pipe, and the exhibition of the strongest purgatives may often be attended with little or no effect.   Sulphate of soda, jalap and calomel, scammony, pil. aloes cum colocynthide, &c. are as proper for this purpose as any other, aided by stimulating clysters, such as solution of muriate or sulphate of soda, with olive oil ; the resin of turpentine, suspended by the yolk of an egg ; solutions of soap, &c. I have found it, on two or three occasions, impossible to open the bowels freely, till after large quantities of opium had been taken, which seemed to bring about a general relaxation ; or until the system had been evidently under the influence of mercury ; and, indeed, these are the two medicines on which we are to place the greatest confidence, in the treatment of this disease : they must be given, however, as before remarked, in large doses, and frequently repeated.   I once gave a patient, who is, I believe, still living, ten grains of opium and twenty of calomel, in pills, and five ounces of tincture of opium, in wine, all in the space of twelve hours.

" Next to opium, I certainly look on the preparations of quicksilver as the most valuable.   Large quantities of the ointment may be rubbed in on the spine, neck, legs, &c. with repeated doses of submuriate internally.   Wine and ardent spirits should be given freely ; indeed, the constitution here appears as insensible to their usual effects, as to those of opium ; and quantities, which in a state of health, would produce stupid intoxication, now neither exhilarate the spirits, nor disturb that serenity of mind so conspicuous throughout the disease.

" The *warm bath* will often be found a useful auxiliary ; when we expect to derive advantages from it, the vessel used should be so capacious, as to allow the patient to be as little confined as possible, and the water should be sufficient to cover the shoulders completely. I have found a common rum puncheon sawed across at the centre, very convenient for the purpose.

" I have generally used blistering plasters, but confess I have never experienced much benefit from their application.

" When the disease is conquered, the patient should take wine and bark for many weeks," p. 70.

On the above passage I would remark that the local abstractions of blood by leeches and cupping from the neighbourhood of the spine, with subsequent blisters there, are not inconsistent with the plan of treatment recommended by Dr. Morrison.   For it must be remembered that such is the unequal distribution of the blood and excitability in the system, under this disease, that one part is completely torpid while another is on the point of extravasation from turgescence or inflammation.   It is evident from this view of the affair, that we must stimulate the torpid organs at the very moment we are employing sedatives, and counter-irritants, or abstracting blood from the congested parts.—Hence too the great value of purgatives and mercury.   The former bring back the excitement to the abdominal viscera, and powerfully determinate from the spine ; the latter sets all the secretory and excretory apparatus to work, while it equalizes the circulation in every part of the system.

Observations on the Dysentery of New Orleans. By ARCHIBALD ROBERTSON, M. D. Resident Physician at Northampton.*

SEC. VIII.—About the middle of November, 1814, the expeditionary force destined to act against New Orleans arrived at Jamaica, under the command of Vice-Admiral the Hon. Sir Alexander Cochrane ; and the whole fleet of ships of war and transports, having rendezvoused there, took their departure from Negril Bay, at the west end of that island, about the end of November, full of health and hope.

Before the middle of December, the fleet arrived on the coast of Louisiana, and took steps for disembarking the troops without delay —a measure against which nature seemed to have opposed ample and almost insurmountable obstacles. Moreover, the passage of those lakes which formed the only practicable approach, was obstructed by five large American smacks or gun vessels, mounting several heavy guns each, and admirably adapted, from their build, for operating in those shallow waters.

The latter vexatious impediment, however, was soon conquered by our sailors, who showed, on this occasion, all that "æs triplex,"— that hardy, careless, characteristic valour for which they are so illustrious. The boats of the fleet, manned and armed, were sent away, and, after a tiresome row of thirty-six hours, succeeded in penning the enemy up in a creek, where they attacked them against the superior odds of their position and their force, and after a furious engagement, captured every one of them. This achievement was decidedly gallant, and would have stood amidst the most brilliant feats of naval warfare, had not the subsequent failure of the main object of the expedition thrown a bleak shade over its lustre.

About the beginning of January, (1815,) bowel complaints, which had previously appeared amongst the boats' crews and the fatigue parties of the army, began to be very rife.—They varied in degree of severity, from the milder symptoms of dysentery to its most aggravated forms. I may enumerate in a few words the symptoms of the disease. The patients, for the most part, complained of severe tormina, tenesmus, scanty blood dejections, want of appetite and strength, general pains and soreness, and strong disposition to vomit on taking either food or drink. The tongue was white or yellow ; the eye languid ; the pulse above 100, small and easily compressed ; the skin often dry, or covered with clammy sweat, but always considerably increased in temperature.

The causes were, generally speaking, obvious enough.—The men had been rowing all day, and sleeping all night in the open boats. They had incautiously drank the brackish water of the lakes, and

* I have been obliged, for want of space, to greatly curtail Dr. Robertson's valuable paper, by omitting the part of it which treats on fever—a subject which has occupied a great portion of this work.—J. JOHNSON.

had sometimes been obliged to eat their beef or pork raw, when, on · an emergency, they were deprived of an opportunity of cooking it. They were often drenched with rain, or dripping with spray, without being able to put on dry clothes. Added to all this the weather was extremely cold, particularly in the night, the thermometer before sun-rise being often as low as 25 or 26 degrees, rising no higher during the day than 30 or 38 degrees, and seldom above 50.*

The locality of the general rendezvous for the boats was very bad, (though the best that could be found,) being a miry place, covered with reeds, and abounding in miasmal exhalations.

The encampment of the army, too, was on a swampy spot on the left bank of the Mississippi, about six miles from New Orleans. Indeed, the whole vicinity is a swamp, which, after the rains so frequent at that season of the year, became a perfect puddle. Having the Mississippi on their left, they drank its discoloured and polluted water, and were exposed to the effluvium of its slimy mud, as well as to the paludal exhalations of an impracticable wooded morass on their right. The huts, also, in which the troops were sheltered, were far from being impervious either to rain or cold : so that, upon the whole, the army and navy, in point of privations, were much upon a par.

On the first appearance of Dysentery, its treatment was commenced by a flannel roller bound tight round the abdomen, and ordering flannel clothing next the skin, if the patients had it not already. Saline cathartics, and particularly oleum ricini, with now and then a few grains of calomel were repeatedly given, until the stools were increased in quantity and more freely rendered. At the same time, plentiful dilution with tepid gruel, warm tea, rice, or barley-water, (with a tinge of port-wine and a little sugar, so as to remove its nauseous insipidity, and allure the patient to drink it in such quantities as would prove useful,) as also decoctions of linseed or of gum arabic, I always considered of primary importance as well in promoting the cure, as in alleviating symptoms. Demulcent drinks I hold to be of much moment in this complaint, as they, no doubt, in some measure, defend the irritable or semi-inflamed coats of the bowels from the stimulus of the ingesta, besides sheathing the acrimonious secretions which, during this disease, are unquestionably poured out from the intestinal glands, and supplying the want of excretion from the mu-

* The Physiologist might have contemplated with interest, on this occasion, the marked difference in the effect of cold on the European and the African constitutions. While the former were, comparatively, only incommoded, the latter were severely injured by it. Many soldiers of the Negro regiments had their feet frost-bitten, and lost their toes by the consequent gangrene and sphacelus. Some of them even died in the camp or in the boats, from excessive cold. Of our own people, many of the boat's crews, and even of the officers, on their return from boat service, were incapacitated for six or ten days, by pain, numbness, shooting, and tingling of the lower extremities. They expressed their distress to be as great as if their feet and legs, from the knees downwards, had been *one immense chilblain !* Various remedies were tried for this teasing affection ; but nothing I could devise gave any relief. Temporary ease was derived from frequently bathing the feet in cold salt water. This peculiar affection I no where find mentioned by writers on the effects of cold.

cous follicles.—I have had occasion to see even olive oil given with this view, in doses of an ounce or two, and the relief that always followed it, even though it had no laxative effect, was very conspicuous.

When the primæ viæ had been fully evacuated, an attempt was made to restore the natural secretions, and the balance of the circulation, by opening the pores of the skin. Antimonial powder, with opium was employed for this purpose ; but more generally the pulvis ipecacuanhæ compositus, which certainly seemed to succeed best.

Whenever tormina and straining returned in a worse degree than ordinary, a cathartic was given in the morning, followed by a large dose of opium, or an anodyne diaphoretic at night.

Believing, as I firmly do, that wherever there is morbid activity of the vascular, and increased mobility or excitability of the nervous system, (the former evinced by undue velocity and force of motion of the heart and great vessels, and the latter by morbid evolvement of. animal heat, general pains, lassitude, &c.) there blood-letting is very seldom inadmissible, whatever be the name or nature of the disease, —it is almost unnecessary to say that, in the complaint I am now describing, the lancet formed a leading agent in the methodus medendi. Whenever the stools resembled the "lotura carnium," I practised depletion with as much freedom as if there had been active hæmorrhage from the intestines from any other cause ;—the amended appearance of the alvine discharges, and the diminution of the pyrexial symptoms not only justified but sanctioned the apparent boldness of a measure, which, I have reason to know, has succeeded equally well in other hands besides my own. Many of our primary cases, however, were not so severe as to require venesection.

By these means, aided by perfect quietude, repose, and low diet, the febrile state soon disappeared, and nothing remained but debility and irregularity of the bowels, which were to be removed by the mistura cretæ cum opio, the infusum quassiæ excelsæ, or the mistura cinchonæ, given thrice or four times a-day, and a gentle laxative once in three or four days.

Many of our earlier and milder cases yielded to this treatment ; but those of a severer sort required measures less inert. In these malignant forms of the disease, I began by giving a strong saline or lubricating cathartic. Here, too, blood-letting was very freely practised, when the patients were young and robust, or indeed, whenever the force of the pulse and pyrexia seemed on general principles, to justify it. I never once saw cause to repent of this evacuation, though I have more than once carried it to a great extent. It often moderated local pain of the abdomen, diminished the severity of the griping, and, when practised with prudence, did not perceptibly increase the subsequent debility.—These preliminary steps being taken, I immediately commenced the use of calomel, and pushed on undeviatingly to salivation, from the belief, which seems to be wellfounded, of an occult connection betwixt dysentery and a morbid condition of the liver.

The doses I gave were regulated by the constitution of the patients, and the actual state of the symptoms ; but one scruple night and

48

morning, was the most usual prescription,—seldom less than ten grains thrice a-day! I gave a scruple night and morning so often, and in such great variety of habits, that I soon ceased to be at all fearful of hypercatharsis, or, indeed, of any other unpleasant effect. It certainly seldom, in any case increased tormina and tenesmus, but generally lessened both very materially, and produced five or six large motions, voided with less straining, and less tinged with blood. I have in this way given 16, 24, or 32 scruples of calomel in the course of half as many days, before the mouth became affected. When the gums were fairly sore, with some ptyalism, the calomel was omitted, the tormina, tenesmus, and general fever disappeared *as a matter of course*, and the bowels gradually returned to their natural state, the stools often changing, in one night's time, from a dark brown or *spinage* colour, to a bright healthy yellow, with the odour of natural fæces. Some tonic or stomachic was prescribed during the days of convalescence; and generally, as soon as the mouth was well, the patients were fit for duty.

Calomel was often thus given alone and uncombined; but often I thought it preferable, on account of occasional symptoms, to conjoin with it two grains of opium, or to give at noon, (in the interval between the doses of calomel,) twelve or fifteen grains of the pulvis ipecacuanhæ compositus.—This was done in order to lessen the irritability of the bowels, and to support the cuticular discharge. Under such management, every case recovered where no visceral obstructions existed, or where the co-existent disease of the liver was not irretrievable from having passed into disorganization.

As to the fact of visceral obstructions, I believe they are a more frequent occurrence, even in our own climate, than is generally supposed; but I am persuaded that, of those who have lived for any length of time within the tropics, scarcely fewer than *four-fifths* have one viscus or other in the abdomen, more or less altered by morbid action. This opinion is deduced from a very considerable number of dissections of such subjects.

Opium is one of those remedies of doubtful utility in dysentery, which has been by some violently decried, and by most rather sparingly used, from its alleged tendency to suspend the natural secretions, lock up the excretory ducts, and check the transpiration by the skin. Candour obliges me to say that I have used it largely, particularly in the chronic forms of the disease, and that I have never noticed any of the unfavourable effects urged against it; but on the contrary, can bear witness with the illustrious Sydenham, Dr. John Hunter, and several living authors, to its beneficial power. Given after purgatives, it can seldom be unsafe,—and, if it does no more, it procures a temporary truce from the disease. How important a cessation from suffering is, in every illness, but more especially in so endless and harassing a complaint as dysentery, I need not say—prejudices, probably illusory and theoretical, ought to give way to an advantage so substantial.

Nevertheless it must be admitted, that in the early or acute stage of dysentery, this remedy must be administered with a very cautious and discriminating hand,—inasmuch as, at that period of the disease,

inflammation either exists overtly, or disguised under some of its peculiar modifications. Under such circumstances, therefore, it becomes necessary not only to premise the opium with blood-letting and
purgatives, but also to combine it with some unirritating diaphoretic,
such as pulvis ipecac. aqua acetetis ammoniæ, &c. in order to prevent it from increasing vascular action, and suppressing cutaneous
excretion.

Almost the whole body of the profession have concurred in prais-
ing injections in this disease. I, of course, defer to the experience
of others, while I detail my own. Having found them almost uniformly hurtful, I entirely laid them aside. The irritation produced
by the introduction of the pipe, more than counterbalances the soothing effects of the injection. Besides the disagreeableness of this
species of remedy, when often repeated, to the good old English habits of delicacy, I have always seen that, were the enema ever so
bland, or ever so small in volume, it could not be retained beyond a
very few minutes, and always occasioned more straining and tenesmus
in the sequel. As a commodious substitute for injections, I have directed patients to insinuate into the anus a *small* crumb or two of
opium, softened betwixt their fingers for the purpose ; —or have
caused warm fomentations to be used to the parts, and bladders of
hot water to be applied to the hypogastric region. These are wont
to succeed so well, that the patients themselves speak in the strongest terms of the relief afforded by them.

The diet of the sick is of the utmost consequence in this complaint. It should be so regulated that nothing *cold* either in the
shape of food or drink, be taken into the stomach. Sago, arrow-root,
weak soups, &c. may be used during the pressure of the disease ;
and animal jellies, and other articles, easy of digestion, during convalescence. When the disease has yielded, it is of the first consequence that we do not prematurely indulge the patient with animal
food, even though his appetite strongly crave it ; for it must be obvious that such food will be received into an alimentary canal, as yet
by far too weak to digest or assimilate any but a very small portion
of it. Hence springs a dreadful source of irritation to the weak
and irregular bowels ; and I am satisfied that I have seen some fatal
relapses of dysentery brought on by the injudicious kindness of the
patient's friends, who have clandestinely indulged him with animal
diet, under the erroneous impression of thereby strengthening him.
In many other instances, I have seen apparently very venial excesses
either in the quantity or quality of the food during convalescence,
induce true lienteria : in truth, the latter complaint is too apt to be
the consequence of long-protracted attacks of dysentery, do what we
will, and be our dietetic restrictions what they may. I need scarcely add that vegetables and fruit, unless well boiled, and used in very
sparing quantity, are quite inadmissible, — owing to their proneness
to run into the acetous fermentation, in all instances where the chylo-
poetic organs are debilitated.

Blisters to the abdomen I have occasionally used, and that with
some apparent advantage, in this disease. But I believe, most practical men will agree with me when I say, that if due use has been

made of the lancet at the outset of the complaint, the subsequent and subordinate aid of vesicatories will very rarely be any way essential, or necessary.   Besides, they labour under the objection of causing often difficult micturition from the absorption of the cantharides ; and it must be recollected that, in most cases of dysentery, strangury is already existing, from sympathy betwixt the bladder and the rectum, while the latter is in a state of constant and almost inconceivable irritation from tenesmus.   It might be well to try whether the interposition of a bit of muslin betwixt the blister and the skin, would have the effect, as it is said to have, of preventing the absorption of cantharides.

The advanced-guard of the army was disembarked on the 24th of December, and took up a position on the only road to New Orleans, and there awaited the landing of the remainder.   After several minor skirmishes, the troops, (with whom the marines of the fleet and sailors trained to small arms, had previously been incorporated,) were formed into columns, and on the morning of the 8th of January, before day-light, advanced to storm the American lines. These works were defended by a broad ditch filled with water, as also by a palisade, and a wall mounted with numerous pieces of cannon.   The enemy, apprised of our intended invasion, had drawn these lines quite across the only route to New Orleans.   They were absolutely inaccessible at their flanks, as their right touched the Mississippi, and their left rested on an impassable wooded morass.   This was the spot which the laws of nature as well as the rules of art had concurred to strengthen ; this was the strait which the Americans would fain compare to the immortal pass of Thermopylæ ; but entrenched, as they were, to the teeth, and fighting, in effect, completely under cover, there was no call for the self-denying devotedness of a Leonidas, and no exercise for either the active or passive valour of Sparta.

The attempt to storm failed : our columns were beat back at every point, with a loss, I believe, of more than five hundred killed, and upwards of twelve hundred wounded.   -

The expedition being thus foiled in its object, the troops were once more collected on board the fleet, and proceeded off Mobile river, to attack the town of that name.   Fort Bowyer, which defends the harbour's mouth, being quickly and regularly invested, was captured on the 11th of February : but the ulterior operations were suspended by the arrival, from England, of the news of the peace of Ghent.   The troops were disembarked on a sandy uninhabited spot, called *Dauphin Island*, there to await the ratification of the treaty, and the arrival of such supplies of provisions as would enable them to prosecute the voyage homeward.

It is worthy of remark, that, notwithstanding the almost unexampled fatigues and privations of all sorts to which the army and navy had been exposed while before New Orleans, sickness of any kind, up to the 8th of January, had made comparatively little progress amongst them.   The bowel complaints, though numerous, were for the most part, easily removed ; and no other disease of any consequence prevailed. It is not a little remarkable in the medical history of fleets and armies, that, during the fatigues and sufferings of a hot campaign, or the active progress of warlike operations, the men are very little subject to illness of any sort ; as if the elation of hope, and the other great passions with which they are agitated, had the virtue to steel the constitution against the most powerful causes of disease. This circumstance no less curious than true—proudly proves the ætherial origin of our nature, and goes far to assert the almost omnipotency of mind over matter !—No sooner, however, does a great failure, and the dejection it draws after it,—a cessation of operations and a return to the " vita mollis" allow the spirit of enterprize to flag, than the previous fatigues, and exposures begin to tell upon the constitution by their usual results—disease. Like a machine wound up beyond its pitch—the excitement of accumulated motives once withdrawn,—the human frame rapidly runs down, and yields with a facility almost as unexpected as its former resistance. Hence, after a campaign, diseases of every kind are prone to a type of debility and aggravation, and the proportion of deaths is unusually numerous.

Accordingly, in the instance before us, the pressure of ill success began to be severely felt after the failure of the 8th, and the consequent re-embarkation of the army. By this time unremitted fatigue, poor living—and that at short allowance, with the total want of fresh beef and succulent vegetables, not only altered for the worse the character of the bowel complaints, and produced a fatal relapse in some recently cured, but also introduced scurvy, with its multiplied series of perplexing symptoms. Exposure to marsh miasmata, also, produced many cases of fever, which were at first intermittent, but as the weather grew hot, put on the violent remittent, or, more generally, the ardent continued form. The great increase of atmospheric heat which now took place evidently exasperated the type of the prevailing dysentery, as well as that of the fever : this, along with some other facts, which I shall state hereafter, induced me to believe that one common miasm gives rise to these two forms of disease, and that the former is essentially different from the dysentery of cold climates, which, being merely a vicarious discharge from the intestines, owing generally to suppressed perspiration, is, for the most part, rendered milder, if not altogether extinguished by the genial warmth of the season.

Dysentery now put on that aggravated form in which it has so often scourged our camps and fleets ; and never shall I forget the terrible force of this invisible enemy. In all cases it was a very baffling untractable disease, but in those who had previously served long in warm climates, and whose livers were thereby affected, it was almost uniformly mortal.—When the disease attacked such persons, it was a subject of melancholy but curious speculation to witness the headlong course of the malady, and how unavailing any species of treatment invariably proved. It knew neither pause nor hindrance. but like the fabled vulture of ancient mythology, pursued its cruel task from day to day. Dissection always brought to light extensive visceral obstructions, particularly chronic inflammation or abscess of the liver, with or without enlargement of that viscus.

Nothing but experience can convey adequate ideas of the ungovernable nature of this disease, or of the insidious masked approaches of its attack.   Days of an indisposition, apparently trivial, sometimes occur, ere the peculiar symptoms of dysentery show themselves, and would induce a practitioner unacquainted with tropical diseases, and unaware of the peculiar character of the prevailing epidemic, to pronounce the complaint trifling, or as being nothing more than slight fever, symptomatic of gastric disorder ;—at other times, smarter pyrexia, and occasionally a pain in the right side, obtuse or acute, followed by frequent copious dark-green stools, (like *boiled spinage*,) slightly tinged with blood, are the form of the disease.

In most of the cases, griping was little complained of.   There was merely a sense of weight in the hypogastric region, and a copious *flux* of green or dark brown colluvies, voided without straining. The tongue was covered with a yellow fur, which, in the advanced stage of the disease, became thick, dark, and immoveable as a slab of black marble.   The pulse was sharp, frequent and weak : frequent retching and hiccup attended, and a sensation as if all the drink swallowed hot or cool, ran speedily through the intestines.   Oftener the complaint would make its attack with the common introductory symptoms, and no pain in the right hypochondrium was felt throughout the disease, either on inspiration, or strong pressure under the false ribs. In whatever garb of disguise it made its appearance, disease of the liver, (as I have before stated,) and consequently a vitiated state of its secretions, were undoubtedly the primary cause of the mischief. Dissection of the fatal cases showed structural derangement,—a soft friable condition, and general suppuration of that gland.   I have often found two separate abscesses in the parenchyma of its large lobe, the one generally less deep-seated than the other, and containing, in some instances, a quart of pus, similar in colour and consistence to what is usually found in psoas abscesses.   How such extensive disorganization, and formation of matter could take place without any preceding palpable indication of local mischief, is to me still a mystery. But such was the fact.*

* Since these observations were first published in the Edinburgh Journal, almost every one has expressed his surprise at the co-existence of such extensive hepatic disease with tropical dysentery : nay, the thing is so striking in itself, and is so contrary to established opinion, that not a few have gone so far as to deny it altogether, or to assert that it must be a very rare occurence indeed , and that the affection of the liver is merely contingent, and not necessarily connected with dysentery.   I think I am warranted by facts in maintaining the contrary,—viz. That the co-existence is very frequent, if not uniform; and that the connexion is no less strict than that of cause and effect.

I can, however, well excuse a degree of scepticism on this point, knowing that what happened to myself may equally happen to others,—namely, that many cases of dysentery may be examined after death, without the concomitant disease of the liver being discovered :—for who would dream of cutting minutely into that viscus, in a disease generally supposed to bear no relation to it ? ,

It was by accident I first discovered the fact, and I shall relate it concisely, just as it happened : a Naval Officer, for whose talents and virtues I shall ever entertain the highest respect, whose memory I shall ever affectionately cherish, and

On the villous coat of the colon and rectum, there were numerous excoriated points, with small superficial ulcers here and there ; but no morbid alterations were found *there* sufficient to account for death : —no gangrene—no ravages in short, like those related by Sir John Pringle, Harty, and others, in their accounts of this malady.

In fact, (to give a condensed view of the whole matter,) the phenomena of the cases that recovered, as well as the morbid appearances of those that died, impressed upon my mind a conviction that, the diseased condition of the liver was the soil from which dysentery drew its malignant growth, strength, and nurture. This was the

whose death I shall ever regret as the loss of a valued friend, was the first on board H. M. S. Cydnus that fell a martyr to dysentery off New Orleans.—He happened to die at sea, and it became desirable to preserve his body until we should reach some port, where the funeral honours due to his rank might be decorously paid. In order to effect this, it became necessary to remove the intestines. While doing so, I ascertained that the liver was much enlarged, and therefore thought that it also had better be removed. Having separated it from its lateral connections, I passed my hand up under the ribs in order to detach it from the diaphragm. While making a slight pressure for the latter purpose, I was astonished to find the points of my fingers pass through the thin parites of a large abscess in the upper and central part of the right lobe, from which upwards of a quart of pus forthwith flowed. After the liver had been removed and laid out for minute inspection, I found the abscess of such extent, and so lined in its inner surface with a thick, fretted, and irregular exudation of coagulable lymph, that it resembled a familiar and homely object,—namely, a large winter glove lined with worsted!—On accurate examination, a second abscess was found, lower down in the large lobe, containing a pint of pus.

This officer had never at any period of the disease felt any pain in his side :— from his general intelligence, and from the accurate descriptions he gave me daily of his minutest sensations, I am convinced he would have mentioned that pain, had it existed even to the extent of a " sensus molestiæ." Besides, he was one of the last men in the world that one would have suspected of hepatic affection, being florid in complexion, and having previously enjoyed the best health all his life.

Instructed by this insidious case, I had my eye to the liver ever afterwards; but pain of side, or pain on pressure under the ribs, was by no means often felt, though dissection after death brought to light hepatic disorganization equally extensive as in the above case. In many, the liver to appearance, had the colour and size of health, and it was not till on cutting into its parenchymatous substance that the extensive abscesses were discovered.

These facts are of such high importance in the pathology of dysentery, and so much depends upon the degree of credit that may be attached to them, that I am sincerely glad in being *now* able to say, that they do not rest upon my solitary or isolated observation. Within these few days I have been favoured with an excellent and most interesting communication from James Simpson, Esq. Surgeon, R. N. in which he details to me the cases and appearances on dissection of several dysenterics that were treated by him in the East Indies. At the time he made the observation, he was not aware that similar ones had been made by myself in the Western Hemisphere ; therefore his remarks must carry with them the force of unbiassed and independent observation. The symptoms before, and the morbid changes, after, death, were substantially—nay, exactly—the same as I have detailed in this paper, and in my Inaugural Dissertation : and Mr. Simpson, speaking from the facts he has so often witnessed, expresses his conviction that " future experience will unfold to us that liver disease is an inseparable attendant of dysentery in warm climates."—I am sorry that want of space prevents me from copying more amply his able and satisfactory details. I have reason to know that the observations of some other practitioners exactly concur with those of Mr. Simpson and myself.

" fons et origo mali ;" by it the dysentery was excited, and, only by
its removal could it be removed ! This view of the disease I conceive
to be of great consequence, and trust it will meet with due consideration from the profession, inasmuch as it is a view not taken up hastily, or out of complaisance to a favourite hypothesis, but deduced
from nearly two hundred cases, and built upon the corner-stone of
morbid dissections.   I hope the time is not far distant when more
accurate observation will teach medical men at large, to regard this
disease merely as secondary to, and symptomatic of hepatic affection,
and to seek its more immediate cause in a morbid condition of that
important organ, the liver.   Whatever may be the *mode* of connection* between hepatic derangement and dysentery, I am convinced
from analyzing my own sensations, as well as from having counted in
others the links of the pathological chain, that, at least in tropical climates these two diseases are connected like cause and effect.   The
practice which most readily removes the disease, too, tends much to
confirm me in this conviction ; for the " mercurial method" I have
pushed to a great extent, and its results have been such as to give it
a very decided preference in my estimation.   Calomel, (that great
specific in obstructions of the liver, and justly styled by Dr. Curry,
of London, a *cholagogue*,) given in large doses—say one scruple twice
a-day—combined with opium, to cause it to be retained in the system,
corrects the condition of the liver by emulging its ducts, unloading
its congested or over-gorged vessels, removing undue determinations
of blood to its yielding texture, prompting the healthy secretion of
its peculiar fluid, and thereby resolves Pyrexia.—As soon as ptyalism
takes place, the dysenteric symptoms disappear, and the appetite
gradually returns.   Upon the whole, my own experience, as well as
that of some others who served on this expedition, warrants a far

* About the mode of that connection I have indeed speculated pretty freely and
pretty largely elsewhere, having employed a good many pages of my Thesis in
the discussion of the ratio symptomatum as well as of the ratio causarum—yet I
must confess, that the opinions are purely, or at least in a great measure speculative ; and that they are not satisfactory, even to my own mind.

I shall not further detain the reader in this place, but pass the matter over entirely, resigning to writers of greater native talent, and better inured to habits of
difficult investigation, the task of establishing a theory of the disease which shall
at once be rational, and shall satisfactorily explain all the phenomena.

I may, however, be permitted to hint that no hypothesis which has simplicity
for its basis will ever explain this disease : unquestionably Dr Johnson's leading
idea is a most valuable one, viz. that in our investigations of this malady we must
seek its source not in one morbid cause, but in a series of morbid causes.

I wish it to be distinctly understood that it is my inability alone that induces me
not to attempt the theory of this disease ; for I shall never fall in with that tone
of affected contempt for all theories, in which presumptuous dulness so often shel-
ters its imbecility, and vapid indolence so often masks its habitual and insuperable
torpor.   Such ill-bestowed contempt may be sufficiently reproved by simply stating the undeniable fact, that not only in medical, but in every other branch of natural and experimental science, few brilliant discoveries have been made except
by those acute and industrious men who were labouring to establish some darling
hypothesis.   Though they were often disappointed of the results they had in view,
still they were generally compensated by the discovery of something equally or
more valuable ;—just as the peasant who was told to dig for hidden treasure,
though disappointed of the prize he expected, derived a more rich and permanent treasure, from the digging and fertilizing of the land during his vain search.

more certain expectation from this mode of treatment than from the alternation of purgatives with astringents, or any other heretofore in use.—I must here observe, however, that I by no means go the length of saying that dysentery in our own climate always requires the excitement of ptyalism by mercury for its cure ; because with us it is almost always a slight disease, and compared with the fell and fatal form of tropical flux, might be termed the " spurious dysentery." In ordinary cases, therefore, to push mercury the whole length of salivation, would be merely substituting one ailment, and that perhaps a more troublesome one, for another less so : (for let it ever be remembered that ptyalism is not without its inconveniencies, and sometimes not without its dangers, as I myself have seen :) consequently in such instances, if we equalize the circulation by the warm bath, a purgative, and a sudorific or two, we shall generally find the disease yield. Frequent discharges of slimy mucus, attended with tormina, tenesmus, and feverishness, though designated by the general name of dysentery, are, in this country, often dependent merely on aërial vicissitudes and consequent suppression of the cuticular discharge, and differ widely both in their cause and character from the *true* dysentery of warmer, but less salubrious regions. But even* in this climate, I contend, the principles of cure here laid down will apply with utility, and that in cases which resist the more ordinary treatment, calomel given in larger or smaller doses, (according to circumstances,) will be equally beneficial as within the tropics, provided the patient be always kept in a room whose temperature is between 60 and 70.

I have no hesitation in affirming that at New Orleans the success of the treatment by calomel was far greater than that by the usual mode, and I shall here relate a fact which may be regarded as decisive of the rival merits of the two methods of cure. The *Cydnus* frigate, in which I served, remained in the Gulf of Mexico, after all the rest of our force had retired. From the large expenditure of calomel, I at last had none left, and there was not a grain to be procured.—At this time I had several cases of dysentery, which, from necessity, I was obliged to treat, for several days, on the *old* plan, by neutral salts or oleum ricini alternated with anodyne sudorifics, rhubarb, diluents, mistura cretacea, &c. One case was, indeed, of so bad a type that I had made up my mind for its ending fatally. Luckily, however, our arrival at the Havanna enabled me to procure a supply of good calomel ; and I immediately commenced with ten-grain doses thrice a-day. *Next morning* the patient was better ; had passed a more tolerable night ; had less tormina and tenesmus, and a cleaner tongue. I increased the dose to one scruple night and morning, and thenceforth his improvement was perceptible from day to day. The pyrexia soon abated, and, in ten days, his dejections from being green and fœtid, had recovered the natural yellow colour or nearly so. No complaint remained but a sore mouth. This patient, like most of the others, had been very liberally bled at the onset of the disorder. He is now living, (so far as I know,) and is an example of the superior efficacy of this mode of treatment.—The above

49

is merely one of many instances where I have seen calomel work rapidly, and like a *charm.*

To prove with how little apprehension calomel may be given to persons of all ages, I may state that to a boy of 14, *one hundred and fifty-two* grains were given during the acute stage of a most dangerous attack of dysentery, before his mouth became fairly sore ! ! He fully recovered.

Though mercury had, in this manner, such commanding influence over the disease, still experience here was not always uniform, for there were several vexatious instances where it failed. I do not speak of the fatal cases, of which, unhappily we had fifteen, (for in them neither, laxatives, astringents, fomentations, blisters, opiates, mercurial frictions on the abdomen, nor calomel pushed to salivation, ever were able to keep off the unhappy event,) but expressly of those few instances where the patients, after being apparently cured, relapsed without any assignable cause, or where ptyalism mitigated the symptoms somewhat—perhaps even suspended the disease entirely until the mouth was well, and then it returned with much of its original violence. The disease thus ran into the chronic form, and harassed the patient for weeks, or even months—with the various symptoms arising from a weak, irritable condition of the primæ viæ, irregular hepatic secretion, and imperfect formation of the chyme.—The chief of these symptoms were vomiting after meals, night sweats, febriculæ, watching, arid skin, pains in the lower belly, occasional tenesmus, frequent costiveness, followed by spontaneous diarrhœa and discharges of blood, attended also with frequent prolapsus ani and difficult micturition.

In conducting the cure, very delicate·management was requisite ; —in fact the disease required rather to be led than driven. A strictly regulated diet, and the use of flannel next the skin, were of the highest consequence. At the same 'time the patient was put under a gentle and gradual course of calomel, taking three or four grains morning and evening, and rubbing in a portion of mercurial ointment on the belly and right side. Laxatives and astringents were employed occasionally, but, above all, the greatest use was made of opium both internally, and locally per anum, and it really effected most conspicuous benefit. Sulphate of zinc I now and then tried ; but from the nausea which it excited, even in three grain pills morning and evening, and from its apparent inefficacy in the disease, I should scarcely, in future, be tempted to give it further trials. The tonic power of Peruvian bark was very useful both as an astringent to the bowels, and as a restorative to the whole system. When the mouth was recovered from the first gentle course of mercury, if the complaint had not yielded, I did not hesitate to use calomel again and again in the same gradual manner, till the gums were repeatedly somewhat affected, and then gave tonics as before. This assiduous perseverance, and the patient attention which it implied, I am happy to say, were well rewarded—many patients were thus recovered from a state—not hopeless indeed—but very precarious, and were re-established in firm health.

It is worthy of remark that relapses in this disease are, more than in any other I know, peculiarly frequent and fatal. Most of the deaths occurred in relapsed cases. In one instance a patient relapsed thrice, and the third was more untractable than the preceding ; in him a large abscess sprang up in the epigastric region towards the close of the disease, and burst—discharging profusely bloody and bilious sordes, evincing that the abscess had its radicle in the liver, as dissection afterwards more clearly proved. In two or three instances, the belly, during convalescence, became tumid and tense —and remained thus for a considerable time after their recovery from dysentery. This tumefaction the patients attributed to the state of their liver, and believed themselves to be " Liver-grown," as they expressed it ; but from the spontaneous and ofter sudden disappearance of this peculiar symptom, I am rather induced to ascribe the distension to the secretion and extrication of flatus, from the weakened villous coat of the intestines, and from its accumulation in their convolutions and in the cells of the colon.

I never had any reason to suspect this disease, or the pyrexia which ushered it in, and attended it, to be in any measure contagious ; inasmuch as it did not appear indiscriminately, or spread from man to man by communication ; but was entirely confined, both primarily and ultimately, to that portion of the crew whom duty led on shore, or who were employed in the boats on the river *Apalachicola*. Every boat's crew that returned from such service was sure to bring a reinforcement to the sick list ; and out of six new patients thus added, three would be found labouring under ardent fever—(for the weather was by this time hot,) and the remaining three under dysentery of the above-described type. From this fact, repeatedly and constantly observed, I am induced to draw the conclusion that both these complaints are excited by one and the same special miasma ; for, of a given number of men taken ill in consequence of exposure to the predisposing and exciting causes, it seemed as uncertain as the toss-up of a half-penny whether the one or the other of these diseases would develope itself in an individual or individuals so exposed. This, however, I advance rather as an opinion countenanced by facts, than as being in itself a fact ; for I am well aware of the weight of authority that is against me on this point, and must confess that my means of observation have not been sufficiently extensive to warrant a *positive* induction.

PART III.

TROPICAL HYGIENE;

OR,

HINTS FOR THE PRESERVATION OF HEALTH IN ALL HOT CLIMATES.

———

Prestat argento, superatque f ulvum
Sanitas aurum, superatque censum
Quamvis ingentem, validæque vires
Omnia prestant.

As prevention is better than cure, it might seem more natural to have detailed the means of preserving health, before entering on the treatment of diseases themselves. This plan has accordingly been adopted by Dr. Moseley; but I think it an injudicious one. In describing *effects*, I have traced pretty minutely their *causes*; and in that way must have obviated a vast tautology in this part of the work. Besides, by exhibiting both causes and effects in one view, I am convinced that the salutary impression is always stronger. For example; could the gravest anathema, denounced with all due solemnity, against sleeping ashore on insalubrious coasts, excite half so much interest in the mind of an European, as the fatal catastrophe at Edam Island? —But another great point is gained by this plan. The various reasonings and remarks which accompanied the treatment and description of diseases, will enable even the general reader to comprehend, with infinitely more ease, the *rationale* of those prophylactic measures, which I am now to delineate; and which, at every step, will recall to his memory the deplorable effects, resulting from a contempt of them. This is no inconsiderable object; for we all know the gratification which springs from understanding what we read. And, in truth, it is a pleasure—nay, it is a positive advantage, to be able to explain, even, on a *false theory*, the principles of a *useful practice*. But as theory, in this instance at least, is the legitimate offspring of experience, so, I trust, the superstructure is as firm as the foundation.

It has been remarked, by a very competent judge, " that by taking the general outline of indigenous customs for our guide, if we err, it will be on the safe side." This is a good rule; but unfortunately it is impracticable—by those, at least, who stand most in need of one. For, before we can become acquainted with these indigenous customs, it will be too late for many of us to adopt them; and could we see them at one *coup d'œil*, when we first enter a tropical climate, how are we to avail ourselves of them, unless they happen to be in unison with the habits of our countrymen already resident there, who would not fail to sneer at the adoption of any plan which had not the sanction of their superior experience. But independently of this, it would be strange if the progress which has been made in the knowledge of the animal economy, as well as in other sciences, did not enable us to correct many "indigenous customs," which, in reality, have ignorance, superstition, or even vice for their foundation. This applies particularly to the Eastern World, where the natives are neither in a state of nature, nor yet refinement ; but where we see a strange medley of ludicrous and ridiculous customs—of Hindoo and Mahommedan manners, from which the European philosopher may glean much useful local knowledge, while he exercises his reason and discrimination, in separating the grain from the chaff.

Another advice has been given us ; namely, to observe and imitate the conduct of our own countrymen long resident in the climate. This is certainly the most practicable ; but, in my opinion, it is not the safest plan. And for this plain reason, that *residence* alone confers on them immunities and privileges, of which it would be death for us, in many instances, to claim a participation, before the period of our probation has expired. I think I shall be able to show, hereafter, that the unseasoned European may apply, with safety, certain preventive checks to the influence of climate, which would be inconvenient, if not hazardous, to those on whom the said influence had long operated.• The stranger, then, must go with the general stream of society, especially at the beginning ; but there is no situation even here, where he may not obviate, in a great measure, the first and most dangerous effects of the new climate, by a strict observance of two fundamental rules — TEMPERANCE and COOLNESS. The latter, indeed, includes the former ; and, simple as it may appear, it is, in reality, the grand principle of Inter-tropical Hygiene, which must ever be kept in view, and regulate all our measures for the preservation of health.

Common sense, independently of all observation or reasoning on the subject, might, *a priori*, come to this conclusion. From *heat* spring all those effects which originally *predispose* to the reception or operation of other moribific causes. And how can we obviate these effects of heat but by calling in the aid of its antagonist, *cold*.* To the *sudden* application of the *latter*, after the *former* has effected its baneful influence on the human frame, I have traced most of those diseases attributable to climate ; nothing, therefore, can be more reasonable, than that our great object is to moderate, by all possible means, the *heat*, and habituate ourselves from the beginning to the impressions of cold. The result will be, that we shall thereby bid defiance to the alternations or *vicissitudes* of both these powerful agents. This is, in truth, the grand secret of counteracting the influence of tropical climates on European constitutions ; and its practical application to the common purposes of life, as well as to particular exigencies, it shall now be my task to render as easy and intelligible as I can. For the sake of perspicuity, I shall here, as hitherto, class my observations under separate heads ; though, from the nature of the subject, I shall consider myself much less tied down to forms, than in the two preceding parts of the essay ; and consequently shall

* I overlook the useless litigation respecting cold being the absence of heat.

not be over nice in confining myself to a dry, didactic rehearsal of medical rules and precautions. The scope and purport of any digression, however, shall always point to my principal design—the preservation of health.

DRESS.

Sec. I.—I shall not stop here, to inquire whether this be an unnecessary luxury of our own invention, or originally designed for us by our Creator. The force of habit is no doubt, great ; and the Canadian who, in reply to the European's inquiry, respecting his ability to bear cold applied to his naked body, observed, that " he was all face," gave no bad elucidation of the affair. Passing over the great African peninsula, where man enjoys that happy state of nudity and nature, mental as well as corporeal, on which our learned philosophers have lavished such *merited* encomiums, we come to the ancient and civilized race of Hindoos ; and here, too, we shall be constrained to admire the almost omnipotent power of custom, as exemplified in the persons of some of the first objects that arrest our attention.

The habiliment of the Bengal *dandy* or waterman, who rows or drags our *budjrow* up the Ganges, consists in a small, narrow piece of cloth [doty] passed between the thighs, and fastened before and behind to a piece of stout packthread, that encircles the waist. In this dress, or undress, corresponding pretty nearly to the *fig-leaf* of our great progenitor, he exposes his skin to the action of a tropical sun,— a deluge of rain, or a piercing *north-wester*, with equal indifference ! After " tugging at the oar," for hours together, in the scorching noontide heat, till perspiration issues from every pore, he darts overboard, when necessary, with the track-rope on his shoulder, and wades through puddles and marshes—this moment up to the middle, or the shoulders in water—the next, in the open air, with a rapid evaporation from the whole surface of his body ! All this, too, on a scanty meal of rice, being seldom paid more than—*three pence per day board wages !*

Here is one of those indigenous customs, which we shall not find it very safe to imitate ; though many of our keen European sportsmen have undergone for pleasure, or in search of a snipe, what the poor *dandy* is forced to perform for a livelihood. It is hardly necessary to remark, that such pursuits are at the risk of life, and are highly destructive of health.

But, independent of habit, Nature has previously done a great deal towards the security of the *dandy*, by forming the *colour*, and in some respects the *texture*, of his skin, in such a manner, that the extreme vessels on the surface are neither so violently stimulated by the heat, nor so easily struck torpid by sudden transitions to cold. Certain it is, that the action of the perspiratory vessels, too, is different from that of the same vessels in Europeans—at least, they secrete a very different kind of fluid ; being more of an oily and tenacious nature than the sweat of the latter. This, in conjunction with the oil so assiduously and regularly rubbed over the surface every day by all ranks and casts of both sexes, must greatly tend to preserve a softness and pliability of the skin, and a moderate, equable flow of perspiration.*

But if we look beyond the hardy and labouring casts of natives, we observe both Hindoo and Mahommedan guarding most cautiously against solar heat, as well as cold. The *turban* and *cummerband* meet our eye at every step :—the former, to defend the head from the direct rays of a powerful sun ; the latter, apparently, for the purpose of preserving the important viscera of the abdomen from the deleterious impressions of cold. This [cummerband] is certainly a most valuable part of their dress ; and one that is highly deserving of imitation.

Such are the *essential* articles of native dress ; the light, flowing robes of cotton, silk, calico, &c. varying according to the taste or circumstances of the wearer, and being more for ornament than use. A very good substitute for the *turban* is a large cotton handkerchief, folded up in the hat ; and were we are exposed to the direct influence of solar heat, it may, with much advantage, be kept moistened with water. In situations where atmospherical vicissitudes are sudden, a fine shawl round the waist forms an excellent *cummerband*, and should never be neglected, especially by those who have been some time in the country, or whose bowels are in any degree tender.

When we enter the tropics, we must bid adieu to the luxury of linen—if what is both uncomfortable and unsafe, in those climates, can be styled a luxury. There are many substantial reasons for so doing. Cotton, from it slowness as a conductor of heat is admirably adapted for the tropics. It must be recollected, that the temperature of the atmosphere, *sub dio*, in the hot seasons, exceeds that of the blood by many degrees ; and even in the shade, it too often equals, or rises above, the heat of the body's *surface*, which is always, during health, some degrees below 97°. Here, then, we have a covering which is *cooler* than linen ; inasmuch as it conducts more slowly the *excess* of external heat *to* our bodies. But this is not the only advantage, though a great one. When a *vicissitude* takes place, and the atmospherical temperature sinks suddenly far below that of the body, the cotton, still faithful to its trust, abstracts more slowly the heat *from* our bodies, and thus preserves a more steady equilibrium there. To all these must be added the facility with which it absorbs the perspiration ; while linen would feel quite wet, and during the exposure to a breeze under such circumstances, would often occasion a shiver, and be followed by dangerous consequences.

That woollen and cotton should be *warmer* than linen in low temperatures, will be readily granted ; but that it should be *cooler* in high temperatures, will probably be much doubted. If the following easy experiment be tried, the result will decide the point in question. Let two beds be placed in the same room, at Madras, we will say,

* It is curious, that the upper classes of native ladies, especially Mahommedan, as if determined that nothing of European complexion should appertain to them, are in the habit of staining red, with the *mindy* or hinna plant, the palms of their hands and soles of their feet, the only parts of the external surface where the *rete mucosum*, or seat of colour among them, cannot maintain its deep tint, on account of the friction.

when the thermometer stands at 90° ; and let one be covered with a pair of blankets, the other with a pair of linen sheets, during the day. On removing both coverings in the evening, the bed on which were placed the blankets, will be found cool and pleasant ; the other uncomfortably warm. The reason is obvious. The linen readily transmitted the heat of the atmosphere to all parts of the subjacent bed ; the woollen, on the contrary, as a non-conductor, prevented the bed from acquiring the atmospherical range of temperature, simply by obstructing the transmission of heat from without. This experiment not only proves the position, but furnishes us with a grateful and salutary luxury, free of trouble or expense.—The musical ladies of India are not unacquainted with this secret, since they take care to keep their pianos well covered with blankets in the hot season, to defend them from the heat, and prevent their warping.

' From this view of the subject, flannel might be supposed superior to cotton ; and indeed, at certain seasons, in particular places—for instance, Ceylon, Bombay, and Canton, where the mercury often takes a wide range, in a very short space of time, the former is a safer covering than the latter, and is adopted by many experienced and seasoned Europeans. But, in general, flannel is inconvenient, for three reasons. First, it is too heavy ; an insuperable objection. Secondly, where the temperature of the atmosphere ranges pretty steadily a little below that of the skin, the flannel is much too slow a conductor of heat from the body. Thirdly, the spicul of flannel prove too irritating, and increase the action of the perspiratory vessels on the surface, where our great object is to moderate that process. From the second and third objections, indeed, even cotton or calico is not quite free, unless of a fine fabric, when its good qualities far counterbalance any inconvenience in the above respects.

In some of the upper provinces of Bengal, where the summer is intensely hot, and the winter sharp, the dress of native shepherds, who are exposed to all weather, consists in a blanket gathered in at one end, which goes over the head, the rest hanging down on all sides like a cloak. This answers the triple purpose of a chattah in the summer, to keep out the heat—of a tent in the rainy season to throw off the wet—and of a coat in the winter, to defend the body from the piercing cold. Hence our ridicule of the Portuguese and Spaniards, in various parts of the world, for wearing their long black cloaks in summer, " to keep them cool," is founded on prejudice rather than considerate observation.   ♥

The necessity which tyrant custom—perhaps policy, has imposed on us, of continuing to appear in European dress—particularly in uniforms, on almost all public occasions, and in all formal parties, under a burning sky, is not one of the least miseries of a tropical life ! It is true, that this ceremony is often waved, in the more social circles that gather round the supper-table, where the light, cool, and elegant vestures of the East, supersede the cumbrous garb of Northern climates. It is certainly laughable, or rather pitiable enough, to behold, for some time after each fresh importation from Europe, a number of griffinish sticklers for decorum, whom no persuasions can induce to cast their exuviæ, even in the most affable company, pinioned, as it were, in their stiff habiliments, while the streams of perspiration that issue from every pore, and ooze through various angles of their dress, might almost induce us to fear that they were on the point of realizing Hamlet's wish; and that, in good earnest, their

        " Solid flesh would melt—
    " Thaw, and resolve itself in a dew !"

It too often happens, however, that a spice of ceremony attaches to the kind host—or perhaps hostess, in which case, as no encouragement will be given to derobe, the poor griffin must fret and fume, with prickly heat and perspiration, till the *regalement* is concluded. By this time he is, doubtless, in an excellent condition for encountering the raw, chilling vapours of the night, on his way home !

It were " a consummation devoutly to be wished,"—though, I fear, little to be expected, that the European badges of distinction, in exterior decoration, could be dispensed with, at all festivals, public and private—formal, social, or domestic, within the torrid zone. It requires but the most superficial glance to perceive, that coolness during our repasts is salutary, as well as comfortable ; and that, from the extensive sympathies existing between the skin and several important organs, particularly the stomach and liver, the converse of the position is equally true ; especially as, in the *latter* case, we are led a little too much to the use of " gently stimulating liquids," to support the discharge ; the bad consequences of which are pointed out at page 16 of this essay, and will be again considered in the section on Drink.*

There is an injurious practice, into which almost every European is led, on first visiting a tropical climate, but particularly the Eastern world, which has never been noticed, I believe, by medical writers, though well entitled to consideration. In the country last mentioned, body linen, or rather cotton is remarkably cheap, and washing is performed on such moderate terms, that one hundred shirts may be even *bleached* for about 10s. sterling, on an average. A large stock of these useful articles is, then, the first object of northern strangers, which " *Blackey*," indeed, knows full well, and takes especial care to turn to his own advantage. But this is a trifling consideration.—The European, contemplating, with great satisfaction the multitude of changes he has thus cheaply amassed, and calculating the very reasonable terms of ablution, determines to enjoy in its fullest extent a luxury, which he deems both salutary and grateful, independently of all considerations respecting appearance. It is therefore very common to see him shift his linen three or four times a-day, during the period of his novitiate, when perspiration is indeed superabundant. But, let me assure him, that he is pursuing an injudicious,—nay, an injurious system ; that the fluid alluded to, already in excess, is thus powerfully solicited ; and the action of the perspiratory vessels, with

* I am sorry to learn that European Habiliments and *Regimentals* are still *more* in use on all occasions of festivity now, than in my time, in India. Nothing can be *worse* policy, with all due submission to their High Mightinesses the Nabobs of the East.

all their associations, morbidly increased, instead of being restrained. But what is to be done? The newly arrived European justly observes, that he finds himself drenched with sweat three or four times a-day, in which state he cannot remain with either safety or comfort. Certainly it would be useless to point out the evil, without suggesting the remedy ; and happily it may be obviated to a considerable extent, in a very simple and easy manner. In those climates, when linen becomes wet in a few hours with perspiration, it by no means follows that it is soiled thereby, in any material degree. It should not, therefore, be consigned to the wash, but carefully dried, and *worn again*, once, or even twice ; and that, too, without the smallest infringement on the laws of personal cleanliness, but with the most salutary effect on the health. It is astonishing how much less exhausting is the linen, which has been once or twice impregnated with the fluid of perspiration, than that which is fresh from the mangle. By this plan, no more than one shirt is rendered unfit for use every day ; and in cool weather, or at sea, not more, perhaps, than four shirts a week. Necessity, the mother of invention, first taught me this piece of knowledge, in consequence of having lost my stock once, by sailing suddenly from Trincomalee ; but I know that, however trivial the circumstance may *appear*, an attention to what I have related, will, in reality, prove more beneficial than precautions of seemingly greater magnitude. Its rationale is in direct unison with the grand and fundamental object in tropical prophylactics — TO MODERATE, WITHOUT CHECKING THE CUTICULAR DISCHARGE.

The property which *frequent* change of linen has, in exciting cuticular secretion, and the effects resulting from the sympathy of the skin with the stomach, liver, and lungs, may account, in a great measure, for the superior health which accompanies cleanliness, in our own climate ; and, on the contrary, for the diseases of the indigent and slovenly, which are almost invariably connected with, or dependent on, irregularity or suppression of the cuticular discharge. Intelligent females well know the *peculiar effect* of clean linen on themselves, at particular periods.

To the above observations on dress, I may add, that no European should, where he can avoid it, expose himself to the sun between the hours of ten and four in the day. If forced, during that period, to be out of doors, the *chattah* should never be neglected, if he wish to guard against *coup de soleil*, or some other dangerous consequence of imprudent exposure.

FOOD.

SEC. II.—Although I entirely agree with Celsus, that—" *sanis omnia sana ;*" and with a late eminent physician, that an attention to *quantity* is of infinitely more consequence than *quality* in our repasts ; and although I also believe, that an over fastidious regard to *either* will render us unfit for society, and not more healthy after all ; yet, when we change our native and temperate skies of Europe for the torrid zone, many of us may find, when it is too late, that we can hardly attend too strictly to the quantity and quality of our food, during the period of assimilation, at least, to the new climate ; and that a due regulation of this important non-natural will turn out a powerful engine in the preservation of health.

It is now pretty generally known, from dire experience, indeed, that instead of a disposition to *debility and putrescency*, an inflammatory diathesis, or tendency to plethora, characterises the European and his diseases, for a year or two, at least, after his arrival between the tropics ; and hence provident Nature endeavours to guard against the evil, by diminishing our relish for food. But alas ! how prone are we to spur the jaded appetite, not only " by dishes tortured from their native taste," but by the more dangerous stimulants of wine or other liquors, as well as condiments and spices, which should be reserved for that general relaxation and debility which unavoidably supervene during a *protracted residence* in sultry climates. Here is an instance where we cannot *safely* imitate the seasoned European. Indeed, there are no points of Hygiene, to which the attention of a new comer should be more particularly directed, than to the *quantity and simplicity* of his viands ; especially as they are practical points entirely within his own superintendence, and a due regulation of which, is not at all calculated to draw on him the observation of others—a very great advantage.

Every valetudinarian, particularly the hectic, knows full well the *febrile paroxysm* which follows a full meal : the same takes place in every individual, more or less, whatever may be the state of health at the time. How cautious, then, should we be, of exacerbating these natural paroxysms, when placed in situations where various *other* febrific causes are constantly impending over, or even assailing us ! The febrile stricture which obtains on the surface of our bodies, and in the secreting vessels of the liver, during the *gastric digestion* of our food, as evinced by a diminution of the cutaneous and hepatic secretions, (vide page 134;) will, of course, be proportioned to the duration and difficulty of that process in the stomach, and to the quantity of ingesta ; and as a corresponding *increase* of the two secretions succeeds, when the chyme passes into the intestines, we see clearly the propriety of moderating them by abstemiousness, since they are already in *excess* from the heat of the climate alone, and this excess is one of the first links, in the chain of causes and effects, that leads ultimately to various derangements of function and structure in important organs, as exemplified in hepatitis, dysentery, and in many parts of this essay.

That vegetable food, generally speaking, is better adapted to a tropical climate than animal, I think we may admit, and particularly among unseasoned Europeans :—not that it is quicker or easier of digestion, (it certainly is slower in this respect,) but it excites less commotion in the system during that process, and is not so apt to induce plethora afterwards. It is very questionable whether the ancient Hindoo legislators had not an eye rather to policy than health, when they introduced the prohibition of animal food as a divine mandate.—They probably thought, and in my opinion with good reason, that the injunction would tend to diffuse a more humane disposition among the people, by strongly reprobating the effusion of blood, or depriving any being of existence ; and these prejudices were admirably sustained by the doctrine of transmigration.

But, whatever might have been the medical objections of BRAMHA to carnivorous banquets, certain it is, that a race of what now may come under the denomination of " *natives*," (the Mahommedans,) amounting to, perhaps, a seventh or eighth of the whole population, make no scruple of indulging freely in most kinds of animal food : who, in the face of the shuddering Hindoo, will sacrilegiously slay and eat that great Indian deity, the *cow* ; and who, in their turn, look with perfect abhorrence on the polluted Englishman, who regales himself—not, indeed, on four-footed deity, but in the Mussulman's opinion, with worse than cannibalism, on devil incarnate—PORK ! Yet Hindoo, Mahommedan, and European—at least, the two first, while *moderation* is observed in their respective meals, enjoy equal health, and attain equal longevity.

If, however, we critically examine the different casts, or rather classes of society, in India, we shall find that their physical powers and appearances are considerably modified by their manner of living. Nothing strikes the stranger with greater astonishment, than the personal contrast between the rich and the poor ! Almost the whole of the upper classes are absolutely FALSTAFFS ; and often have I been puzzled to know how some of them cold stow themselves away in a palankeen, and still more so, how their bearers could trot along under the pressure of such human porpoises ! The truth is, that the Hindostanee fops, (and most of the superior orders are such,) pride themselves above all things, on rotundity of corporation, and particularly on the *magnitude of their heads*.

To acquire such elegant distinctions, one would be tempted to suspect, that they occasionally broke the vegetable *regime*, and indulged in better fare than BRAMHA thought proper to prescribe. But no ; all is accomplished by *ghee* and indolence ! Of the former, which is a kind of semi-liquid butter, made by evaporating the aqueous part from the rich milk of the buffalo, they swill immense quantities ; and whatever we may hear, from the *fireside* travellers, of Hindoo temperance and abstemiousness, these gentry contrive to become as *bilious*, occasionally, as their European neighbours, and manage to curtail the natural period of their existence full as efficaciously as their brother " *gourmands*" on this side of the water—making their exits, too, by the same short routes of apoplexy, and other fashionable near cuts to heaven.

The lower or industrious classes, on the other hand, who live almost exclusively on vegetables, certainly bear a striking resemblance to " Pharaoh's lean-fleshed kine." But although they have not the physical strength of a European, they make up for this, in what may be termed " *bottom* ;" for it is well known, that a native will go through three times as much fatigue, under a burning sky, as would kill an Englishman outright—witness the palankeen bearers, coolies, dandies, hircarrahs, &c.. Nor is temperance always a prominent feature in the character of these gentry ; for what with bang, toddy, arrack, opium, and other inebriating materials, which all countries produce in some shape or other, and which all nations have shown their ingenuity in manufacturing, they not seldom "muddle their brains," with as much glee as the same description of people in our own latitudes. Those, on the other hand, who, from local situation, poverty, or principle, adhere to the dictates of their religion and cast with great pertinacity, and seldom admit animal food within the circle of their repast, (milk excepted,) are certainly exempted from numerous ills that await our and their countrymen, who transgress the rules of temperance. Yet, when they are overtaken by disease, they have not *stamina*, and debility characterises the symptoms. Upon the whole, I am inclined to think that, taking the average longevity of all ranks and classes throughout the vast oriental peninsula, the period of human life falls a full *eighth* short of its European range. —But as this does not quadrate with the opinions of speculative philosophers at home, who *will* equalize the age of man all over the world, I shall cite the authority of a very intelligent Officer, whom I have so often quoted before, and who had some twenty year's acquaintance with the country in question. " Longevity," says he, " certainly is not characteristic of India. Whether this is owing to the excessive heat, or the indolence of the upper, and drudgery of the lower classes, it may be difficult to decide; but certain it is, that we rarely see an instance of *any one* arriving at sixty years of age."[*]

From indigenous customs, then, in respect to animal and vegetable food, we can draw no inference that absolutely prohibits the *former*, but enough to convince us, that during the first years of our sojourn between the tropics, we should lean towards the Hindoo model ; and as the tone of the constitution becomes lowered, or assimilated, we may safely adopt the Mahommedan manners.

The period of our meals, in hot climates, indeed in all climates, is worthy of notice. Both Hindoo and Mahommedan breakfast early— generally about sunrise. Their early hours cannot be too closely imitated by Europeans. This is a very substantial meal, particularly with the Hindoo ; for rarely does he take any thing else till the evening : a custom, in my opinion, that would be very prejudicial to Europeans.—Breakfasts, among the latter, are often productive of more injury than dinners, especially where fish, eggs, ham, &c. are devoured without mercy, as not unfrequently happens. Many a nauseous dose of medicine have I been obliged to swallow, from indulging too freely in these articles ; but I saw my error before it was too late. Most people suppose, that as a good appetite in the morning is a sign of health, so they cannot do sufficient honour to the breakfast table ; but the stomach, though it may relish, is seldom equal to the digestion of such alimentary substances as those alluded to, where a sound night's rest has hardly ever been procured. I have seen the most unequivocal bad effects from heavy breakfasts, in others, as well as in my own person ; and I shall relate one instance that may well serve as a drawback upon the pleasures of a luxurious *déjeunée* in the East. Mr. B—— Purser of a frigate, a gentleman well known on the station, was as determined a *bon vivant* as ever I had the honour of being acquainted with.—" *De mortuis nil nisi verum.*"—He certainly had possessed a most excellent con-

[*] Oriental Field Sports, vol. 1, p. 236.

stitution ; for I have seen it perform prodigies, and falsify the most confident medical prognostications! He had served many years in the West Indies, where he passed through the usual ordeals of yellow fever, dysentery, &c. with *eclat ;* and he came to the East with the most sovereign contempt for every maxim of the Hygeian goddess! Although he never neglected, even by accident, his daily and nightly libations to the rosy god, yet no sportsman on the Caledonian mountains could do more justice to a Highland breakfast than he. Indeed, he rarely went to sea without an ample private stock of epicurian provender ; and I have seen him thrown into a violent paroxysm of rage, on finding that two nice-looking hams, which he had purchased in China, resisted all attacks of the knife, in consequence of a certain *ligneous* principle, which " Fukki" had contrived to substitute, with admirable dexterity, for the more savoury fibres of the porker! The items of the *last* breakfast which he made, minuted on the spot by a *German* surgeon who attended him, are now before me. The prominent articles were, four hard-boiled eggs, two dried fishes, two plates of rice, with chillies, condiments, and a proportionate allowance of bread, butter, coffee, &c. Many a time had I seen him indulge in this kind of fare with perfect impunity ; but all things have an end, and this proved his final breakfast! He was almost immediately taken ill, and continued several days in the greatest agony imaginable! Notwithstanding all the efforts of the surgeon, no passage downwards could ever be procured till a few hours before his death, when mortification relaxed all strictures. Let the fate of the dead prove a warning to the living!

The newly arrived European should content himself with plain breakfasts of bread and butter, with tea or coffee ; and avoid indulging in meat, fish, eggs, or buttered toast. The latter often occasions rancidity, with nausea at the stomach, and increases the secretion of bile, already in excess. Indeed, a glance at master *Babachee*, buttering our toast with the greasy wing of a fowl, or an old, dirty piece of rag, will have more effect in restraining the consumption of this article, than any didactic precept which I can lay down ; and a *picturesque* sight of this kind may be procured any morning, by taking a stroll in the purlieus of the kitchen.

In regard to dinner, Europeans appear of late to study convenience rather than health, by deferring that meal till sunset. This was not the case some forty or fifty years ago ; and many families, even now, dine at a much earlier hour, except when tyrant custom and ceremony prevent them. In truth, the modern dinner in India is perfectly superfluous, and too generally hurtful. The *tiffin,* at one o'clock, consisting of light curries, or the like, with a glass or two of wine, and some fruit, is a natural, a necessary, and a salutary repast. —But the gorgeous table—the savoury viands—the stimulating wines of the evening feast, prolonged by the fascination of social converse, greatly exacerbate the nocturnal paroxysm of fever imposed on us by the hand of nature, and break with feverish dreams, the hours which should be dedicated to repose! The consequences resulting from this are quite obvious. It may be observed, that the natives themselves make their principal meal at sunset, when the heat is less distressing, and insects neither so numerous nor teazing ; but it must be recollected, that they, in general, eat nothing between breakfast and dinner ; and that among the Hindoos and lower classes of Mahommedans, &c. the evening meal is by no means of a stimulating quality, while no provocative variety, or other adventitious circumstances, can have much effect in goading the appetite beyond its natural level. Add to this, that in the upper provinces, among Mahommedans of distinction, who can afford more substantial, and animal food, the dinner hour is *one or two o'clock*, and after that, little or nothing, except coffee, sweetmeats, or fruit, is taken during the evening.

He, then, who consults his health in the Eastern world, or in any tropical climate, will beware of indulging in this *second* and *unnecessary* dinner, particularly during the period of his probation ; but will rather be satisfied with the meridian repast, as the *principal* meal, when tea or coffee, at six or seven o'clock in the evening, will be found a grateful refreshment. After this, his rest will be as natural and refreshing, as can be expected in such a climate ; and he will rise next morning with infinitely more vigour, than if he had crowned a sumptuous dinner with a bottle of wine the preceding evening. Let but a trial of one week put these directions to the test, and they will be found to have a more substantial foundation than *theory*.

Of supper it is not necessary to speak, as it is a mere matter of ceremony in hot climates, excepting after assemblies, or on some public occasions, which indeed are badly suited to the torrid zone.

A limited indulgence in fruits, during the first year, is prudent. Although I myself never had any reason to believe that they actually occasioned dysentery, yet, where the intestines are *already* in an irritable state, from irregular or vitiated secretions of bile, they certainly tend to increase that irritability, and consequently *predispose* to the complaint in question. Particular kinds of fruit, too, have peculiar effects on certain constitutions. Thus, *mangoes* have something stimulating and heating in them, of a terebinthinate nature, which not seldom brings out a plentiful crop of pustules, or even boils, on the unseasoned European. A patient of mine, who died from the irritation of an eruption of this kind, had been much addicted to an unrestrained indulgence in fruit, particularly mangoes ;— indeed their effect in this way is familiarly known in India. Neither is pine apple, (though very delicious,) the safest fruit to make too free with at first. Good ripe shaddocks are very grateful in hot weather, from their subacid and cooling juice, so well adapted to allay the unpleasant sensation of thirst. Plantains and bananas are wholesome and nutritious, especially when frittered. The spices and condiments of the country, as I before hinted, should be reserved for those ulterior periods of our residence in hot climates, when the tone of the constitution is lowered, and the stomach participates in the general relaxation. They are then safe and salutary.

DRINK.

SEC. III.—I shall not here attempt to prove, that WATER is the simple and salutary beverage designed by Nature for Man, as well as other Animals. 'In every nation, even the most refined and modern, a great majority appear, by their practice at least, to entertain no such belief. They have, with no small ingenuity, contrived so to medicate the native fountain, that they are always either outstripping, or lagging behind, the placid stream of life ! The same magic bowl which, this moment, can raise its votaries into heroes and demi-gods, will, in a few hours, sink them beneath the level of the brute creation !

The moralist and philosopher have long descanted on this theme, with little success ; for, until people begin to feel the corporeal effects of intemperance, a deaf ear is turned to the most impressive harangues against that deplorable propensity ; and even then, but very few have resolution and fortitude to stem the evil habit ! Let us do our duty, however, in conscientiously pourtraying the effects of drink in a tropical climate.

I have already observed, that the grand secret, or fundamental rule, for preserving health in hot countries, is, " TO KEEP THE BODY COOL." I have also alluded to the strong sympathy that subsists between the skin and several internal organs, as the stomach, liver, and intestinal canal. On this principle, common sense alone would point out the propriety of avoiding heating and stimulating drink, for the same reasons that we endeavour to guard against the high temper of the climate. But no ; a wretched, sensual theory has spread from the vulgar to many in the profession, (who ought to know better,) that since the heat of the climate occasions a profuse perspiration, and consequently renders that discharge the more liable to a sudden check, we are to aid and assist these natural causes by the use of " gently stimulating liquids," and, of course, increase those very effects which we pretend to obviate ! " A little shrub and water," says Mr. Curtis, (Diseases of India,) " or Madeira and water, between meals, is useful, and in some measure necessary, to keep up the tone of the digestive organs, and to supply, [i. e. augment,] the waste occasioned by an excessive perspiration," p. 281. I can assure Mr. Curtis that, however necessary this practice might have been thought in his time, (forty years ago,) it is now considered not only unnecessary, but disgraceful ; and that in no respectable circle in the Eastern world, beyond the confines of the " Punch-house," where no European of character will ever be seen, [especially in Bengal,] is any sangaree, porter-cup, or other " gently stimulating liquid," made use of " between meals." And I take this opportunity of informing and warning every new-comer, that the very call of " brandy-shrub-pauny !" will endanger his being marked as a " vitandus est," and that a perseverance in such habit will inevitably, and very quickly too, exclude him from every estimable circle of his own countrymen, who will not fail to note him as in the road to ruin !

Nor did these most excellent habits of temperance originate in any medical precepts or admonitions—far from it ! The professional adviser was by no means solicitous to inculcate a *doctrine*, which it might not suit his taste to *practise*. But in a vast empire, held by the frail tenure of opinion, and especially where the current of religious prejudices, Brahmin as well as Moslem, ran strong against intoxication, it was soon found necessary, from imperious motives of policy, rather than of health, to discourage every *tendency* towards the acquisition of such dangerous habits. Hence the inebriate was justly considered as not merely culpable in destroying his own health, *individually*, but as deteriorating the European character in the eyes of those natives, whom it was desirable at all times to impress with a deep sense of our superiority. Happily, what was promotive of our *interest*, was preservative of our health, as well as conducive to our happiness ; and the general temperance in this respect, which now characterises the Anglo-Asiatic circles of society, as contrasted with Anglo-West-Indian manners, must utterly confound those fine-spun theories, which the votaries of porter-cup, sangaree, and other " gently stimulating liquids," have invented about—" supporting perspiration," " keeping up the tone of the digestive organs," &c. all which *experience* has proved to be not only *ideal* but *pernicious !* " On the meeting together of a company of this class," [planters,] says a modern writer on the West Indies, " they were accustomed *invariably*, to sit and continue swilling strong punch, (sometimes half rum,) and smoking segars, till they could neither see nor stand ; and he who could swallow the greatest quantity of this *liquid fire*, or infuse in it the greatest quantity of ardent spirits, was considered the cleverest fellow." *Account of Jamaica and its Inhabitants*, 1808.— p. 189. And again ; " The inferior orders, in the towns, are by no means exempt from the reproach of intemperance ; nor are the more *opulent classes*, generally speaking, *behind hand* in this respect. Sangaree, arrack-punch, and other potations, are pretty *freely drank, early in the day*, in the taverns," p. 199.

I can conceive only one plausible argument which the trans-atlantic Brunonian can adduce, in support of his doctrine after the unwelcome *denouément* which I have brought forward respecting oriental customs ; namely, that as the range of atmospheric heat, in the West Indies, is several degrees *below* that of the East, it may be necessary to counterbalance this deficit of *external* heat, by the more assiduous application of *internal* stimulus ! For this hint he will no doubt, be much obliged to me, as he must consider the argument irresistible.

I may here remark, that too much praise cannot be given to the Captains of East Indiamen, for the lessons of temperance and decorum that are generally taught on board their ships, (whatever may be the motives,) during the outward bound passage. The very best effects result from this early initiatory discipline, in a thousand different ways. Rarely, indeed, in the vessels alluded to, does the decanter make more than half a dozen tours, (often not so many,) after the cloth is removed at dinner, before the company disperse,- by a delicate, but well-known signal, either to take the air upon deck, or amuse themselves with books—chess—music, or the like, till the evening.   After a very frugal supper, the bottle makes a tour or two; when the significant toast of—" *good night, ladies and gentlemen !*" sends every one at an early hour to repose.

It may readily be conceived, of what incalculable utility five or six months' *regimen* of this kind must prove to Europeans, approaching a tropical climate ; especially when policy and imperious custom will enforce its continuance there ! It is true, that at each of the presidencies, there may be found several individuals of the old bacchanalian school, whose wit, humour, or vocal powers, are sometimes courted, on particular occasions, to—" set the table in a roar." , But let not such expect to mingle in the *domestic* circles of respectable society, (where alone true enjoyment is to be found,) either in the civil or military departments.   No such thing as a regimental mess exists in India ; and as convivial association thus becomes perfectly optional, the least tendency to inebriety will assuredly *insulate* the individual who, from solitary indulgence and reflection, soon falls a martyr to the baneful effects of INTEMPERANCE !

The navy presents a different aspect.   Fewer of these have an opportunity of becoming acquainted with the domestic manners either of the natives or Europeans on shore ; and therefore, they more frequently pursue their usual course of living, both in food and drink, for a considerable time after arriving on the station ; verifying the observation, that—

" Cœlum non animum mutant qui transmare currunt."

And although they are fortunately less exposed, in general, to many of those causes which aggravate the effects of inebriety ashore, yet much injury is produced before they see their error.

A very common opinion prevails, even in the profession,—and I am not prepared to deny its validity, that during the operation of wine or spirits on the human frame, we are better able to resist the agency of certain morbid causes, as contagion, marsh effluvium, cold, &c.   But let it be remembered, that it is only while *the excitement* lasts, that we can hope for any superior degree of immunity from the said noxious agents ; after which, we become doubly disposed towards their reception and operation ! Nor am I fully convinced, by all the stories I have heard or read, that *inebriety* has, in any case or emergency, even a *momentary* superiority over *habitual* temperance.

The delusion in respect to vinous and spirituous potations, in hot climates, is kept up chiefly by this circumstance, that their bad effects are, in reality, not so conspicuous as one would expect ; and they rather predispose to, and aggravate the various causes of disease resulting from climate, than produce direct indisposition themselves ; consequently, superficial observation places their effects to the account of other agents.   But the truth is, that as *drunkenness*, in a moral point of view, leads to every vice ; so, in a medical point of view, it accelerates the attack, and renders more difficult the cure of every disease, more particularly the diseases of hot climates ; because it has a *specific* effect, I may say, on those organs to which the deleterious influence of climate is peculiarly directed.   If the Northern inebriate is proverbially subject to hepatic derangement, where the coldness of the atmosphere powerfully counterpoises, by its action on the surface, the internal injury induced by strong drink, how can the Anglo-East or West Indian expect to escape, when the external and internal causes run in perfect unison, and promote each other's effects by a wonderful sympathy.

It has been considered wise, as I before hinted, to take the seasoned European for our model, in every thing that respects our *regime* of the non-naturals. "Strangers," says Mr. Curtis, "arriving in India, if they regard the preservation of health, cannot too soon adopt the modes of living followed by the experienced European residents there." I do not conceive this to be a good medical maxim, even in India, where temperance is scarcely a virtue; and certain I am, that it is a most dangerous precept in the West, for reasons which I have lately rendered sufficiently obvious. It confounds all discrimination between the very different habits of body, which the seasoned and unseasoned possess. It is consonant with experience, as well as theory, that the *former* class may indulge in the luxuries of the table with infinitely less risk than the *latter ;* and this should ever be held in view. In short, the nearer we approach to a perfectly *aqueous* regimen in drink, during the first year at least, so much the better chance have we of avoiding sickness ; and the more slowly and gradually we deviate from this afterwards, so much the more retentive will we be of that invaluable blessing—HEALTH !

It might appear very reasonable, that in a climate where *ennui* reigns triumphant, and an unaccountable languor pervades both mind and body, we should cheer our drooping spirits with the mirth-inspiring bowl ;—a precept which Hafiz has repeatedly enjoined. But Hafiz, though an excellent poet, and like his predecessor, Homer, a votary of Bacchus, was not much of a physician ; and without doubt, his " *liquid ruby*," as calls it, is one of the worst of all prescriptions for a " pensive heart." I remember a gentleman at Prince of Wales's Island, [Mr. S.] some years ago, who was remarkable for his convivial talents and flow of spirits. The first time I happened to be in a large company with him, I attributed his animation and hilarity to the wine, and expected to see them flag, as is usual, when the first effects of the bottle were past off ; but I was surprised to find them maintain a uniform level, after many younger heroes had bowed to the rosy god. I now contrived to get near him, and enter into conversation, when he disclosed the secret, by assuring me he had drunk nothing but water for many years in India ; that in consequence his health was excellent—his spirits free—his mental faculties unclouded, although far advanced on time's list : in short, that he could conscientiously recommend the " *antediluvian*" beverage, as he termed it, to every one that sojourned in a tropical climate.

But I am not so *utopian*, as to expect that this salutary example will be generally followed ; though it may lead a few to imitate it, till the constitution is naturalized, when the *pleasures of temperance* may probably induce them to persevere. At all events, the new comer should never exceed three or four glasses of wine after dinner, or on any account, admit it to his lips between meals, unless excessive fatigue

and thirst render drink indispensable, when cold water might be injurious. Spirits, of course, should be utterly prescribed.

One circumstance, however, should always be kept in mind, to wit,
that when a course of temperance is fully entered on, no consideration should induce us to commit an occasional debauch, especially
during our seasoning ; for we are at those times in infinitely greater
danger of endemic attacks, than the habitual bacchanal.

It has been remarked, by many sensible observers; that *acids* are
injurious to the stomach and bowels between the tropics. I will not
contradict, though I cannot confirm this observation. I never saw
any bad effects myself from their use ; and I know some medical gentlemen, long resident in India, who drank very freely of sherbet, at
all times when thirst was troublesome. Nature seems to point out
the vegetable acids, in hot climates, as grateful in allaying drought,
and diffusing a coolness from the stomach all over the body. It is
very probable, however, that where the alimentary canal is in an irritable state, they may excite diarrhœa ; and this last frequently
leads to more serious disturbance in the functions of the digestive organs. Where the tone of the stomach, too, is weak, (as is often the
case,) and that organ is disposed to generate acidity, the acids in question may readily prove injurious.

It has also been said, that a too free use of cocoa-nut water, or
milk, as it is sometimes called, has produced bowel complaints. My
own observations are not in unison with this remark. It was my favourite beverage, and never did I feel in my own person or perceive
in others, the slightest inconvenience from indulging in this most delicious liquid. It ought, however, to be fresh-drawn, limpid, sweet,
and never drunk after the deposit on the inside of the shell begins to
assume the form of a consistent crust.

I have alluded to the danger of drinking cold fluids when the body
is heated, and particularly where perspiration has continued profuse
for any time. I could furnish many instances, illustrative of this position, but shall only adduce the following :—

Lieutenant Britton, of the Royal Marines, (at that time belonging
to his Majesty's ship Grampus.) a very fine young gentleman, had
heated and fatigued himself, by driving about the streets and bazars
of Calcutta, in the autumn of 1803, in which state, he had the im-
prudence to swallow an ice-cream, for the purpose of allaying his
thirst. Of the effects of this he died, a few weeks afterwards, on
his passage to Madras, under my own care. It brought on inflammation about the fauces, which subsequently spread down along the
membrane lining the trachea, to the lungs, producing symptoms exactly resembling croup. He died in dreadful agonies, flying from one
part of the ship to another, for relief from the dyspnœa and oppression on his chest. Various remedies were tried, but all in vain. Let
this prove a caution to the living ! " The danger, says Dr. Dewar,
" of drinking cold water in that state of the system, was most strik-
" ing when a copious draught was quickly taken after extraordinary
" heat and fatigue. An acute pain was instantly produced in the
" stomach, and rapidly extended through the rest of the body which
" threatened to overpower the whole vigour of the frame." *On Dy-*

sentery, p. 50. A navy surgeon died at Marmorice in Asia Minor, after a very short illness contracted by taking a draught of cold water in a hot state of body. For numerous examples of a similar nature, see Currie's *Medical Reports.*

EXERCISE, &c.

SEC. IV.—This is one of the luxuries of a northern climate, to which we must, in a great measure, bid adieu, between the tropics. The principal object and effect of exercise in the *former* situation, appear to consist in keeping up a proper balance in the circulation —in supporting the functions of the skin, and promoting the various secretions. But perspiration and certain secretions, (the biliary, for instance,) being already in excess, in equatorial regions, *a perseverance* in our customary European exercises, would prove highly injurious, and often does so, by greatly aggravating the natural effects of climate. Nevertheless, as this *excess* very soon leads to debility and *diminished action*, in the functions alluded to, with a corresponding *inequilibrium* of the blood, so it is necessary to counteract these, by such active or passive exercise as the climate will admit, *at particular periods of the day, or year;* a discrimination imperiously demanded, if we mean to preserve our health. Thus, when the sun is near the meridian, for several hours in the day, on the plains of India, not a leaf is seen to move—every animated being retreats under cover— and even the "*adjutant*," [gigantic crane,] of Bengal, whose stomach will bear an ounce of emetic tartar without complaining, soars out of the reach of the earth's reflected heat, and either perches on the highest pinnacles of lofty buildings, or hovers in the upper regions of the air a scarcely discernible speck. At this time the Hindoo retires, as it were instinctively, to the innermost apartment of his humble shed, where both light and heat are excluded. There he sits quietly, in the midst of his family, regaling himself with cold water or sherbet, while a mild but pretty copious perspiration, flows from every pore, and contributes powerfully to his refrigeration.*

As soon as the cool of the evening, however, commences, all nature becomes suddenly renovated, and both men and animals swarm in myriads from their respective haunts! Then it is, that the esplanade at Calcutta, and the Mount road near Madras, pour on the astonished eye of the stranger a vast assemblage of all nations, casts, and complexions, comprehending an endless and unequalled variety of costume and character, hurrying to and fro, in all kinds of vehicles as well as on foot, enjoying the refreshing air of the evening! The same scene is witnessed early in the morning, particularly during the cool season, in Bengal ; but in the rainy season there, and while the hot lands-winds prevail on the Coromandel coast, the life of a European is irksome to the last degree! Perspiration being then profuse, the most trifling exertion is followed by languor and lassi-

* What with the smoke of the house, [for there is no chimney,] and the oil on his skin, a native is hardly ever annoyed by mosquitoes, as foreigners are.

tude. Cooped up behind a *tatty*, or lolling about under a *punka*, he can neither amuse his mind, nor exercise his body, and *tœdium vitœ* reigns uncontrolled during these gloomy periods ! It need hardly be urged, how injurious active exercises would be to Europeans, at such times ; or indeed, during the heat of the day, at any time Yet hundreds annually perish from this very cause ; particularly in the West Indies, after each influx of Europeans during war !

Who would expect to find *dancing* a prominent amusement in a tropical climate ? The natives of the West Indies are excessively fond of this exercise ; but in the east there are *wise wen* still, for instead of dancing themselves, they employ the *nautch-girls* to dance for them.

It might seem ill-natured if I animadverted on the custom of my fair countrywomen, who *show off* with such eclat, at the *Pantheon* in Madras, regardless of all thermometrical indications.   The practice is not *salutary*, however *politic* it may be found—and it certainly does not *appear* to agree so well with *married* ladies as with *virgins*, whatever may be the reason.

I have shown that the range of atmospherical heat is considerably higher in the East than in the West, and that in the latter part of the world they are exempted from hot land-winds, and more favoured with cool sea-breezes, than the inhabitants of the former.   Still, Europeans, although they may not enjoy better health, experience infinitely less mortality in the peninsula of India, than in the West Indian Archipelago.   If a thousand European troops, for instance, are debarked at Kingston, Jamaica, and an equal number at Madras, at the same time, we shall find the former lose, in all probability, one-third—perhaps one-half their number, during the first eighteen months : while the other corps will not lose more than a thirtieth or a fortieth part of their total, in the same period. But if we examine the two bodies of men at the end of five or six years, we shall not find the same disproportion. Hepatic and dysenteric complaints, by that time, will have brought the Eastern corps somewhat nearer a *par* with their Western countrymen.   The great *onus* of disease bears on the *first year* of a European's residence in the West Indies, because that is the period within which the endemic or yellow fever makes its attack ; after which, he feels the effects of climate in a more moderate degree.— In the East, fever, (excepting in Bengal,) is by no means general ; and the first year is not distinguished by mortality. But the climate being much hotter, and the atmospherical vicissitudes more sudden and extensive, each subsequent year produces great mischief in important organs ; and the wonder is, why he does not suffer infinitely more than the Anglo-West-Indian !

I have already adduced several causes for this disparity ; (vide pages 70 and 71,) one, the greater length of an East India voyage, with its concomitant abstemious regimen, the reverse of which so much predisposes to the violent assaults of the Western endemic.   Another, is the laudable temperance and decorum, prescribed by general custom in the Eastern world, obviating, in no slight degree, the deleterious influence of climate.   I shall now proceed to make some observations on other differences in the modes of life, and means of preserving health in the two countries, as elucidatory of this subject, hoping that the interest and utility of the discussion will sufficiently excuse its informal position in this section.

First, then, the HOUSES of the East, whether permanent mansions or temporary *bungalows*, are better calculated for counteracting the heat of the atmosphere than those of the West. As there is no dread of earthquakes or hurricanes, in the former place, the dwellings are *solid*—the apartments lofty—the windows large, and the floors, in general, composed of *tarras*, which being often sprinkled with water, is cool to the feet, and diffuses an agreeable refrigeration through the room. Add to this, that the spacious *verendahs* ward off the glare of the sun, and *reflected* heat, (an important consideration,) by day, and afford a most pleasant retreat in the evening, for enjoying the cool air. The *tatties*, which are affixed to the doors and other apertures, in the hot season, and kept constantly wet by *bheesties*, or water-carriers, whereby the breeze is cooled by evaporation, in its passage through the humid grass, of which the tatty is constructed, prove a very salutary and grateful defence against the hot land-winds ; since this simple expedient makes a difference of twenty or thirty degrees, between the *bheesty's* and the *European's* side of the *tatty!* It appears, however, that in the East we have not been sufficiently attentive to the prevention of *reflected heat and glare ;* a circumstance of infinitely greater consequence than the freest ventilation. Let us learn from the native. His habitation has very few apertures, and those high up. His floor, and the inside of the walls, are moistened two or three times a-day, with *a solution of cow-dung in water*, which, however disagreeable to the olfactories of a European, keeps the interior of the dwelling as cool as it is dark. Here he sits on his mat, enjoying his aqueous, but salutary beverage ; and with such simple means and materials, counteracts the heat of the climate more effectually than the European, in his superb and costly edifice. " Those who live in houses," says Dr. Winterbottom, " the walls of which are plastered with mud, frequently, during the continuance of hot weather, wet the walls and floor, to cool the air ; this is a very *hurtful* practice, as it renders the air *moist*, and brings it nearly into the state it is in during the rainy seasons."—On Hot climates, p. 16. This, like many other observations founded on *contracted* views, and favourite theories, is completely contradicted by the broad basis of facts. It reminds us of a passage in Dr. Robertson's third volume on the Diseases of Seamen, where he undertakes to prove, that it is the *moisture* of the air over marshes that causes disease ; and, in short, questions whether *miasmata* ever produced fever —— *except on board the* WEAZLE *sloop of war, when he was surgeon of her on the coast of Africa !!*

The upper classes of natives, also, have not been inattentive to the prevention of reflected heat. The houses of Benares, for instance, are of solid stone, and generally six stories high, with small windows. The streets are so extremely narrow, that the sun has very little access to them ; obviating thereby the disagreeable effects of glare. The windows are small, because, from the height of the houses it would be impracticable to apply tatties during the hot winds; whereas, in low country-houses, or bungalows, they are large, in order to extend the refrigerating influence of the tatties.

The dazzling whiteness of European houses in India is not only inconvenient, but in some degree injurious, to the eyes, at least; and a verendah, entirely encompassing the mansion, would contribute greatly to the refrigeration of the interior apartments; the most comfortable of which, by the by, on the ground floor, used to be appropriated to the use of palankeens, and lumber, but are now wisely converted into offices, &c.

The *punka*, suspended from the lofty ceilings of the Eastern rooms, and kept waving overhead, especially during our repasts, is a very *necessary* piece of what may be fastidiously styled "Asiatic luxury." Indeed, were it not for this and the *tatty*, some parts of India would be scarcely habitable by Europeans, at certain seasons.

It is observed, in a recent "Account of Jamaica," by a gentleman long resident there, that the "*Asiatic effemindcy* of being carried about in a palankeen, has not yet reached the West Indies." It would be well if several other Asiatic effeminacies, [temperance for example,] were more generally adopted in the transatlantic islands. But that the Anglo-West-Indian rejects this luxurious vehicle, *merely* through any scruple respecting its *effeminacy*, is rather too much for credence. If a dozen of sturdy *balasore-bearers* could be hired in Jamaica for the trifling sum of four or five shillings a day, including all expenses, the Western Nabob and Nabobees would soon condescend to recline in the palankeens, with as much state as their "*effeminate*," brethren of the East. But the plain reason is, that neither the country itself nor its *imported* population will admit of a conveyance, which is cheap, elegant, and convenient, on the sultry plains of India.*

Gestation in a palankeen, however, is a species of passive exercise exceedingly well adapted to a tropical climate. The languid circulation of the blood in those who have been long resident there, is pointedly evinced by the inclination which every one feels for raising the lower extremities on a parallel with the body, when at rest; and this object is completely attained in the palankeen, which indeed renders it a peculiarly agreeable vehicle. On the same principle we may explain the pleasure and the utility of *sham-pooing*, where the gentle pressure and friction of a soft hand, over the surface of the body, but particularly the limbs, invigorate the circulation after fatigue, and excite the insensible cuticular secretion. I much wonder that the *swing* is not more used between the tropics. In chronic derangements of the viscera it must be salutary, by its tendency to determine to the surface, and relax the sub-cutaneous vessels, which are generally torpid in those diseases. It might be practised in the evenings and mornings—and within doors, when the state of the wea-

* Cheeks of kuss-kuss, a sort of grass, of which the *tatties* are made, being affixed to the doors of palankeens, and kept moist, enable Europeans to travel during the hottest weather. A wet *palampore*, or covering of calico, is a tolerable substitute.

ther, or other circumstances, did not permit gestation, or active exercise in the open air.

A propensity towards *smoaking* would not be expected, *a priori*, in a tropical climate. Yet the practice is very general among Europeans and Natives, and seems to spring from that listlessness and want of mental energy, so predominant in the character both of sojourners and permanent inhabitants of sultry latitudes. As the custom may not be insalutary at certain seasons of the year, in particular places, where marshy or other deleterious exhalations abound ; and as it is often a succedaneum for more dangerous indulgences, it is best, perhaps, to pass it over with little comment. Yet it has ever appeared to me a degrading habit, for a gentleman to become a *slave* to his hookah ; and it is beyond endurance, to see a great, lusty *hookah-burdaar*, insinuate the pipe of his long *snake* into the delicate hand of a European lady, after dinner, who plies the machine with as much glee, as the sable and subordinate nymph of the country does her *nereaul!* For the honour and delicacy of the sex, this practice is by no means common ; and the wonder is, that it ever should have existed.

In the article of *dress*, the Anglo-East Indians have a manifest advantage over those of the West. The delicious and salutary beverage of *cool drink*, too, is more in use among the former than the latter ; partly owing to custom, and partly to opulence, which enables all ranks of Europeans to have their wine, water, &c. refrigerated with saltpetre, by a particular servant, set apart for that sole purpose, and called in Bengal—*Aub-daar*. The effect of these gelid potations on the stomach is diffused from thence, by sympathy, over the whole frame, but especially over the external surface of the body, counteracting in no mean degree, the natural influence of the climate. It is true, the bottles are brought on table in the West Indies, enveloped in wetted napkins ; but the effect is far inferior to that produced by the nitrous solution ; and as the aub-daar's art is extended to all kinds of drink, this grateful luxury is ever at hand.

BATHING.

Sec. V.—" I dare not," says Dr. Moseley, " recommend cold bathing, [in the West Indies ;] it is death with intemperance, and dangerous where there is any fault in the viscera. It is a luxury denied to *almost all*, except the sober and abstemious females, who well know the delight and advantage of it,"—3d ed. p. 90. In respect to its being " death with intemperance," I believe that numerous inebriates could tell the doctor a different story ; but, as it is presumed he never deigns to look into a modern author, he is unacquainted with various facts that militate against his dogma. The well-known instance of Mr. Weeks, of Jamaica, who always went to sleep in cold water, when intoxicated, is sufficiently in point. Many a time have I seen it bring the drunken sailor to his senses at once ; and *invariably* have

I observed it to moderate the excitement of spirituous potations. I knew a getleman who always went to sleep with his head on a *wet* *swab*, whenever he had taken a good " *mosquito dose ;*" and the consequence was, that he very seldom complained of head-ache next day. It is true, that if the cold bath be injudiciously used, during the indirect debility *succeeding* a debauch, there may not be sufficient energy in the constitution to bring on re-action ; and then, of course, it would be injurious. But this is a discrimination to which the genius of a Moseley could not stoop. Granting, however, what is certainly true, that the cold bath is dangerous, where visceral obstructions obtained, I cannot conceive why it should be denied to *almost all*, except females, in hot climates ; unless we take those visceral derangments with us from Europe. Surely we might be allowed " the delight and advantage" of it till these disordered states occur !

But whatever *theory* may have discouraged bathing, and recommended the use of " gently stimulating liquids," in the West ; wide *experience* has completely settled these points, long ago, in the East. There, the Native and European—the old and the young—the male and the female, resort to the BATH, as the greatest luxury, and the best preservative of health. In truth, it is one of the most powerful engines we possess, for counteracting the destructive influence of a hot climate, because it connects the most grateful sensations with the most salutary effects—it is indeed both *utile et dulce*.

Nature, or instinct itself, points out the external application of cold water to the body, to moderate the action of atmospheric heat. The buffalo is a familiar example. In the middle or hot period of the day, these animals repair to pools or marshes, and wading in, either stand or lie down there, with every part except the nose immersed in water ; or, where there is not water, in the mud. At these times, by the by, it is very dangerous for Europeans to approach their haunts. They generally start up all at once, on being disturbed ; and if one or two begin to snort and advance, the European is in imminent peril : nothing but the most rapid retreat to a place of safety, can secure his life. A red coat is a very unfortunate dress at such critical rencontres, as the animals in question have a decided antipathy to that colour.

It requires but little penetration to see, that the Brahminical injunctions, relating to ablutions, were founded on the preservation of *present* health to the body ; though the *future* happiness of the soul was artfully held out as a superior inducement to the performance of these ceremonies, so necessary beneath a burning sky. The superstitious Hindoo rarely omits bathing, once or oftener, every day, in the sacred stream of the Ganges, [or other consecrated river,] from which he is not deterred even by the voracious alligator, who frequently carries him off in the religious act ! He generally wades out to a moderate depth—then, shutting his eyes, and putting his fingers in his ears, he squats himself under water two or three times—washes his *doty*—and returns, cool and contented, to his humble cot.

The Europeans and upper classes of Mahommedans, however, feeling no great desire for risking *tete-a-tetes* with sharks or alligators, are, in general, satisfied with a few pots of cold water thrown over their heads, at home, once, twice, or oftener every day, according to the season of the year, and the person's own inclinations. This, being unattended either with fatigue or expense, is well adapted to all circumstances and situations, and answers the end in view effectually enough.

I have shown, in various parts of this essay, that most of the diseases of tropical climates are attributable to *atmospherical vicissitudes*. Now, there is nothing that steels the human frame, with more certainty, against the effects of these, than the cold bath. We are the very creatures of habit ; and, consequently, *habituation* is the surest prophylactic. The cold bath not only counteracts the influence of heat, by suspending its operation for the time, but it safely inures us to the sudden application of cold, the fruitful source of so many disorders. By keeping the skin clean, cool, and soft, it moderates excessive, and supports a natural and equable cuticular discharge ; and from the " *cutaneo-hepatic sympathy*," so often noticed, the functions of the liver partake of this salutary equilibrium—a circumstance hitherto overlooked.—The use of the *cold bath*, then, should be regularly and daily persevered in, from the moment we enter the tropics ; and when, from long residence there, the functions above alluded to begin to be irregular and defective, instead of in excess, we may prudently veer round, by degrees, to the *tepid bath*, which will be found a most valuable part of Tropical Hygiene among the *seasoned* Europeans.

As the cold bath is passive, (for it is seldom that the exhausting exertion of swimming accompanies it,) so it may be used at any period of the day ; though the mornings and evenings are generally selected by Europeans in the East ; immediately after leaving their couch and before dinner. The bath is very refreshing, when we rise unrecruited from a bad night's rest ; and powerfully obviates that train of nervous symptoms, so universally complained of by our countrymen between the tropics. Before dinner it is salutary, apparently from that connexion which subsists between the external surface and the stomach, in consequence of which the tone of the latter is increased, and the disagreeable sensation of thirst removed, that might otherwise induce to too much potation during the repast. —It is, however, imprudent to bathe while the process of digestion is going on in the stomach, as it disturbs that important operation. Where visceral derangements of any extent, particularly in the liver, have taken place, the cold bath must be hazardous, from the sudden afflux of blood directed from the surface to the interior, and also on account of the subsequent vascular reaction. The tepid bath, taking care to avoid a chill afterwards, will in these cases, be substituted with great advantage.

SLEEP.

SEC. VI.—When we bid adieu to the temperate skies of Europe, with all its "long nights of revelry," and enter the tropics, particularly in the Eastern hemisphere, we may calculate in a great falling off in this "solace of our woes." The disturbed repose, which we almost always experience there, has a greater influence on our constitutions than is generally imagined, notwithstanding the silence of authors on this subject. Nature will not be cozened with impunity. Whatever we detract from the period of our natural sleep, will assuredly be deducted in the end, from the natural range of our existence, independently of the predisposition to disease, which is thus perpetually generated. This is a melancholy reflection; but it is truth, and it should induce us to exert our rational faculties in obviating the evil.

When the sun withdraws his beams, and the intense heat of the atmosphere is mitigated, we might expect a comfortable interval of repose—but this would be a vain hope. A new host of foes instantly appear in arms to annoy us! mosquitoes, ants, and cock-roaches, lead on the insect tribes—the bat wheels in aerial circuits over our heads, on which he sometimes condescends to alight, without ceremony—while the snake patroles about, in the purlieus of our apartment: coils himself up under our beds, or even deigns to become our *bedfellow* without waiting the formality of an invitation !*

The great object of a European is to *sleep cool*. This enables him to procure more rest than he otherwise could do; and by giving his frame a respite, as it were, from the great stimulus of heat, imparts to it a tone and vigour—or as Dr. Darwin would say, "an accumulation of excitability," so necessary to meet the exhaustion of the ensuing day, as well as to repair that of the preceding.

A great waste of strength—indeed, of life, arises from our inability, on many accounts, to obtain this *cool* repose at night. Thus rains, heavy dews, or exhalations from contiguous marshes, woods, or jungles, often render it unsafe or impossible to *sleep in the open air*; a practice fraught with the most beneficial consequences, where the above-mentioned obstacles do not prevent its execution. But, pending the hot and dry season in Bengal, and almost always on the Coromandel coast, except during the hot land-winds, or at the change of the monsoons, we may indulge, not only with safety, but with infinite advantage, in the seemingly dangerous luxury of sleeping abroad in the oper air.

I am well aware of the prejudices entertained against this custom, by great numbers, both in and out of the profession; but I am con-

---

* Many instances have occurred of snakes being found coiled away between children in bed. It is said, that if a chaffing-dish, filled with clear, live embers, be quietly placed on the floor of a room, in such emergency, the reptiles will repair to it; especially if some new milk be also left near the chaffing-dish—Great presence of mind is here necessary, in order not to disturb those dangerous creatures suddenly in their retreat.

vinced, from personal experience and observation, that the practice, under the specified restrictions, is highly salutary, and I know it is sanctioned by some of the best-informed veterans, who have spent most part of their lives between the tropics. Speaking on this subject, the judicious Captain Wiliamson remarks that—"few, very few instances could be adduced, of any serious indisposition having attended it ; while, on the other hand, it is confessed by all who have adopted it, that the greatest refreshment has ever resulted ; enabling them to rise early, divested of that most distressing lassitude, attendant upon sleeping in an apartment absolutely communicating a febrile sensation, and peculiarly oppressive to the lungs."—*East India Vade-Mecum.*

If it be observed, that I have all along held up to view the danger of atmospherical vicissitudes, to which this practice would *apparently* expose us ; I answer, that I have also maintained, that *early habituation* to these was the surest preservative against their injurious effects, as exemplified in the use of the bath. The truth is, however, that while the custom of sleeping in the open air steels the human frame against these same effects, it is, in reality, attended with less exposure to *sudden atmospherical transitions* than the opposite plan. Nature is ever indulgent when we observe her ways, and obey her dictates. Excepting the periods and places alluded to, the *transition in the open air*, from the scorching heat of the day to the cool serenity of night, is gradual and easy. To this the human frame bends with safety, and we sink into a grateful and sound sleep, that renovates every corporeal and mental faculty. Whereas, those who exclude themselves from the breath of heaven, whether from necessity or inclination, become languid, from the *continued* operation of heat, and the want of repose ; in consequence of which, the slightest aerial vicissitude, (either from leaving their couch, or admitting a partial current of cool air, which they are often compelled to do,) unhinges the tenor of their health, and deranges the functions of important organs ! These are they, who require the afternoon *siesta*, and to whom, indeed, it is necessary, on account of the abridged refreshment and sleep of the night ; while the others are able to go through the avocations of the day, without any such substitute—a great and manifest advantage.

Indigenous custom is, generally speaking, in favour of sleeping in the open air, during the hot seasons, in most Eastern countries. The practice, indeed, is less adopted in Bengal, for very obvious reasons, than on the Coromandel coast ; but the Native sleeps much cooler, at all times, than the European, from this circumstance—that his bed seldom consists of more than a *mat*, while a piece of *calico* wrapped round him, supplies the place of bed clothes. The more closely we imitate these the better will it be for us. Indeed, a thin hair matress, with a sheet and palampore, are the only requisites, independently of the thin gauze or mosquito curtains, which defend us from insects, and, when we sleep out on the *chabootah*, arrest any particles of moisture that may be floating in the atmosphere. Early hours are here indispensable. The fashionable nocturnal dissipation of Europe would soon cut the thread of our existence between the tropics. The order of nature is never inverted with impunity, in the most temperate climates ; beneath the torrid zone, it is certain destruction. The hour of retirement to repose should never be protracted beyond ten o'clock ; and at day-light we should start from our couch, to enjoy the cool, the fragrant, and salubrious breath of morn.

We shall conclude this section with a few remarks on Incubus, or Night-mare—a very troublesome visitor to a tropical couch.

The *proximate cause* of Incubus has given rise to various speculations. A very general opinion prevails that this affection is produced by mechanical obstruction to the blood's circulation, from particular position of the body. It is a certain fact, however, that no posture is a security from night-mare among the predisposed ; neither is a full stomach to be accused as the cause, nor an empty one to be expected as the antidote of this disorder. There is, however, an almost universal opinion, that incubus attacks persons *only* while on their backs ! and this opinion *seems* to have some foundation in fact, from the following circumstances. One of the symptoms almost inseparable from the disease is this, that the patient *appears to himself* to be kept down upon the back by some external force ; and as, at the moment of recovering the power of volition, a great confusion of ideas prevails, a person may easily imagine that he has recovered himself by some effort of his own, by turning from his back to his side. But these things are extremely fallacious, as there is no trusting to the senses during a paroxysm of incubus.

It appears, however, from the mode of treatment to which this disease gives way, that the primary cause, in whatever manner it may act, has its seat in the digestive organs, and that night-mare originates in defective digestion, whereby the food which should be converted into good chyle, is transformed into a half-digested mass of *acid* matter, which is productive of heart-burn, eructations, flatulence, gripes, with the whole train of dyspeptic and hypocondriacal complaints.

There are many stomachs which convert every thing they receive instantly into an acid ; and such will be generally found to be the case with persons subject to habitual night-mare, or frightful dreams and disturbed sleep. Such stomachs are too frequently distended with some acid gas, which alone gives rise, in many cases, to paroxysms of incubus ; and may often be instantly removed by any warm cordial, as peppermint, gin, brandy, carbonate of ammonia, &c. Whytt used generally to take a small wine-glassful of brandy going to bed, in order to keep off night-mare and terrific dreams to which he was very subject.

Of all medicines, however, the carbonate of soda, taken in a little ale or porter, as recommended by Mr. Waller, will be found the most efficacious. About a scruple, going to bed, is a sufficient dose : and where acidities prevail in the stomach, the same quantity, twice in the day will be useful. This medicine not only neutralizes any acid in the first passages, but likewise brings away by stool, vast quantities of viscid slimy matter, so acrid as to burn and excoriate the parts it touches. The appetite now generally improves; but the propensity to acidify remains for a long time in the stomach, and requires great attention to diet and regimen. There are few people with whom particular kinds of food do not disagree, and these being known should be avoided. Thus chesnuts or sour wine will almost always produce incubus among those predisposed to it, as was observed by Hildanus. " *Qui scire cupit quid sit Incubus ? Is ante somnum comedat castaneas, et superbibat vinum fæculentum.*" In this country, cucumbers, nuts, apples, and flatulent kinds of food, are the articles most likely to bring on night mare.

The following draught I have found very efficacious in preventing attacks of incubus, viz. carbonate of ammonia, ten grains, compound tincture of cardamoms, three drachms, cinnamon water, two ounces, to be taken going to bed.

Intemperance of any kind is hurtful. Most vegetables disagree; and pastry, fat, greasy, and salted meat, are to be avoided. Moderate exercise is as beneficial, as sedentary employments, intense study, and late hours are prejudicial.

THE PASSIONS.

SEC. VII.—I have not yet alluded to the conduct of the Passions, because most of the precepts that apply to the regulation of them in cold climates, will be equally applicable here. But I may be permitted to correct an erroneous, (I think,) though very general opinion, that there is something peculiar in a tropical climate, which excites certain passions in a higher degree than in temperate regions. "There is," says Dr. Moseley, "in the inhabitants of hot climates, unless present sickness has an absolute control over the body, *a promptitude and bias to pleasure,* and an alienation from serious thought and deep reflection. The brilliancy of the skies, and the beauty of the atmosphere, conspire to influence the nerves against philosophy and her frigid tenets, and forbid their practice among the children of the sun,"—p. 87. This is a very superficial, and a very false view of the affair. It is likewise a very immoral one; for it furnishes the dissolute libertine with a *physical* excuse for his debaucheries, when the real source may be traced to relaxation of religious and moral principles! I would ask Dr. Moseley to explain the reason why, if the "*promptitude* to pleasure" be increased in a hot climate, the *ability* to pursue or practice it should be lessened?—a truth well known to every debauchee.

If the prevalence of polygamy in warm climates be adduced, I answer, that in countries where plurality of women is allowed, a minute and accurate investigation will show, that among the lower orders of people the licence of the prophet is an empty compliment, for *they* find one wife quite enough. And as for the *higher ranks* of society, there is not *one in twenty* who has more than one wife, nor one in five hundred who has more than two. If we compare this last part of the statement with the picture of life in the *beau monde* at home, we shall not have much reason to congratulate ourselves on the great *physical continence* resulting from our gloomy skies, as contrasted with the " bias to pleasure" which springs from levity of atmosphere between the tropics.

May we not attribute the premature decay of Native women in hot climates, to the long-established custom of early marriages in that sex, originally introduced by the despotism of man, but which has now effected an actual degeneracy in the female part of the creation. " It is a disgrace to a woman not to be married before twenty years of age ; and we often see wives, with children at their breasts as soon as they enter their teens." I have no doubt that, to the continued operation of this cause, through a long series of centuries, is owing the deterioration in question ; for it is not conformable to the known wisdom of the Creator, that such an inequality should *naturally* exist between the sexes.

But to return. The removal of religious and moral restraint— the temptations to vice—the facility of the means, and the force of example, are the real causes of this " bias to pleasure ;" and in respect to the *effects* of licentious indulgencies between the tropics, I can assure my reader, that he will find, probably when it is too late, how much more dangerous and destructive they are than in Europe.

He now has explained to him the nature of this " propensity ;" and as the principal cause resides neither in the air, nor the " brilliancy of the skies," but in his own breast, he has no excuse for permitting it to sprout into the wild luxuriance of unbridled excess.

The monotony of life, and the apathy of mind, so conspicuous among Europeans in hot climates, together with the obstacles to matrimony, too often lead to vicious and immoral connexions with Native females, which speedily sap the foundation of principles imbibed in early youth, and involve a train of consequences, not seldom embarrassing, if not embittering every subsequent period of life! It is here that a taste for some of the more refined and elegant species of literature, will prove an invaluable acquisition for dispelling *ennui,* the moth of mind and body.

THE END.

ImTheStory.com

Personalized Classic Books in many genre's

Unique gift for kids, partners, friends, colleagues

Customize:

- Character Names

- Upload your own front/back cover images (optional)

- Inscribe a personal message/dedication on the

  inside page (optional)

Customize many titles Including
- Alice in Wonderland
- Romeo and Juliet
- The Wizard of Oz
- A Christmas Carol
- Dracula
- Dr. Jekyll & Mr. Hyde
- And more...

Lightning Source UK Ltd.
Milton Keynes UK
UKHW02f2012060218

317475UK00016B/373/P